The Birth of a
New Europe

The Birth of a
New Europe

STATE AND SOCIETY IN THE

NINETEENTH CENTURY

THEODORE S. HAMEROW

The University of North Carolina Press

Chapel Hill and London

Library of Congress Cataloging in Publication Data

Hamerow, Theodore S.
   The birth of a new Europe.

   Includes index.
    1. Europe—Economic conditions—1789–1900.
2. Europe—Social conditions—1789–1900. 3. Europe—
Politics and government—1789–1900. 4. Europe—Foreign
relations. I. Title.
HC240.H314 1983   940.2′8   82-20162
ISBN 0-8078-1548-9

Part of chapter 2 appeared in a somewhat different
form in the *Proceedings* for 1978 of the Consortium on
Revolutionary Europe, 1750–1850, ed. Robert Holtman
(Athens, Ga., 1980), pp. 3–19.

To Judy and Helena

CONTENTS

TABLES AND FIGURES

FIGURES

PREFACE

The idea for this book came to me while I was teaching for more than twenty years courses in the history of Europe during the nineteenth century. The experience persuaded me that the era extending roughly from Waterloo to the Marne is a distinct period in the development of the West, characterized by a complex of attitudes, beliefs, insights, and perceptions uniquely its own. It is, to use Arnold J. Toynbee's phrase, "an intelligible field of historical study." Yet most of the books written on the nineteenth century are basically compilations of thumbnail national histories, beginning with England and France in the west and proceeding eastward through Germany, Italy, and Austria-Hungary to Russia and the Balkans. They generally have a few chapters that cross territorial boundaries, chapters dealing with economic, cultural, and diplomatic questions, for example. But their approach is to a large extent determined by the historical experience of the countries making up Europe rather than of Europe as such. I concluded therefore that there was need for a study emphasizing those revolutionary changes that, in a variety of ways and degrees, affected all the nations of the Continent, whatever their political system or geographical location. Some eighty years ago, Lord Acton declared that "General History naturally depends on the action of forces that are not national but proceed from wider causes." I have tried to follow that principle.

It was not my intention, then, to publish a systematic account embracing all the major developments in politics, economics, society, culture, and diplomacy. That would have been much too ambitious. I sought rather to write a series of interrelated essays dealing with certain aspects of the European experience that, though of crucial importance, have not been sufficiently studied in the context of the period and the area as a whole. In doing so, I was forced to include some material that is already familiar. I have tried to keep it as brief as possible, however, without destroying the thrust of the narrative. My criterion for the use of the well-known has been the extent to which it could help illuminate the less well-known. I have relied in my research, moreover, on secondary works as well as primary sources, whichever seemed most appropriate. The only test was the relevance of the evidence to the problem I was examining or the question I was asking. The underlying hypothesis of this work is that the fundamental changes in the methods of producing goods known as the industrial revolution profoundly altered the structure of society, the

nature of politics, and the system of relations among states. The emphasis
of many historians in the past on national history has tended to obscure a
process of transformation that was international in scope. My purpose
has been to draw new attention to that process.

I knew from the outset that such a venture was foolhardy. To begin
with, the scholarly literature on the history of Europe in the nineteenth
century is so vast that merely to enumerate it would require several
volumes. In every country there are countless monographs and articles
dealing with its special problems, not to mention those works that are of
broader range and interest. If I had waited with the writing of my book,
however, until I had mastered all of this material, it would never have
been written. The task was further complicated, but also simplified, by
the fact that I can read only English, French, German, and a little Italian.
For all parts of the Continent, therefore, I was forced to rely on what has
been written about them in these languages. Nevertheless, my admitted
shortcomings have not kept me from forming opinions or passing judgments. While I may have been rash in some of them, I decided early in
the game to take my chances and face the consequences. "Gefährlich
leben!" Nietzsche enjoins us. In any case, I believe now, as I did when I
began, that a book such as this should have been written, and I am glad
that I tried to write it. But it is clearly not a task for the timid or cautious.

In the course of my work I received the assistance of a number of
people and institutions, and it is a very pleasant obligation now to thank
them. There are, first of all, various units of the University of Wisconsin
in Madison that treated me with great generosity. The Research Committee of the Graduate School provided a semester's leave in 1976–77, and
the Institute for Research in the Humanities another semester's leave in
1979–80. Free of the normal academic duties, I could devote myself
entirely to writing. The staff of the Memorial Library gave unstintingly
of its time, effort, and budget to obtain for me materials from its own
collections and those of other libraries. Herbert C. Van Deventer, Jr., was
of great help in preparing the tables and figures. Five of my friends, all of
them experts in the field—James S. Donnelly, Jr., Raymond Grew, Vernon L. Lidtke, Charles S. Maier, and Stanley G. Payne—read the manu-
script and offered suggestions for revision. Their advice was sound and
discerning, although I must confess that in my willfulness I did not always follow it. That may well have been a mistake. Finally, there is the
debt I owe my family for putting up with a moody and temperamental
author. I can only acknowledge that debt; I cannot repay it.

Theodore S. Hamerow
Madison, Wisconsin
September 1982

Part One

THE ECONOMIC FRAMEWORK

La filosofia attuale non vuole de' Locke
e de' Kant, ma uomini industriosi che
applichino lo spirito alle più elevate
questioni, che in ogni tempo abbiano
interessato l'uomo. I Cockerill sono i
grandi del secolo nostro!

Rivista Europea (1838)

I

THE RISE OF INDUSTRIALISM

Between the conclusion of the Napoleonic Wars and the outbreak of the First World War, Europe underwent a transformation unparalleled in its history. In the course of a century the system of production in industry and agriculture was profoundly altered, the population increased at an unprecedented rate, rapid urbanization shaped a new human environment, the standard of living began to improve dramatically, the relationship between classes and occupations suddenly shifted, learning became accessible to the propertyless, the function of the state expanded from security to welfare, the masses entered political life, economic and social reforms grew and multiplied, the Great Powers rushed into a last spree of imperialist expansion, and the methods of warfare were revolutionized by technological improvements. No comparable change in the way of life had occurred since the prehistoric era, when Neolithic man first mastered the techniques of husbandry, ceasing to be a nomad and becoming a farmer. At the time of the Battle of Waterloo, the prevailing technologies, institutions, and attitudes on the Continent were still those of the preindustrial environment of enlightened despotism in which most men had been born. When the guns of August began to boom some hundred years later, European society had already entered the age of industrialism and individualism, of finance capitalism and mass democracy. A world of new ideals, aspirations, and achievements had emerged.

The key to this transformation was a rationalization of production that came to be known as the industrial revolution. Its essential character was understood almost from the beginning by those who were living through it. In 1835 the Scottish chemist and economist Andrew Ure described the nature of the change in manufacture taking place about him:

> The term *Factory*, in technology, designates the combined operation of many orders of work-people, adult and young, in tending with assiduous skill a system of productive machines continuously impelled by a central power. . . . The principle of the factory system then is, to substitute mechanical science for hand skill, and the partition of a process into its essential constituents, for the division or graduation of labour among artisans. On the handicraft plan, labour more or less skilled, was usually the most expensive element of production . . . but on the automatic plan, skilled labour gets

progressively superseded, and will, eventually, be replaced by mere overlookers of machines.[1]

Ure touched on the two basic elements of the industrial revolution: the mechanization of manufacture and the concentration of labor. They represented an extraordinary breakthrough in the method of production that for the first time made it possible for society to escape the constrictions of a marginal economy. To be sure, the substitution of inanimate for human energy had not been entirely unknown. The windmill and the water mill, the cannon and the sailing ship prove that. But the large-scale employment of machinery in such basic industries as textiles, mining, smelting, and steel making represented a decisive departure from traditional techniques. The introduction of complicated and costly equipment meant in turn that the distribution of labor had to be altered. The division of output among many small manufacturing establishments was possible only as long as tools remained simple and inexpensive. Once the necessary investment in the instruments of production began to exceed the financial capacity of the skilled craftsman, a concentration of the work force in factories occurred that drastically altered the system of manufacture. Thereafter, the master artisan and the handicraft shop were forced into a long retreat before the march of industrialism.

The process of mechanization can be measured in several ways. The number of patents issued in England in the early period of the industrial revolution provides one index of the increasing use of machinery in production (see figure 1.1). In the first half of the eighteenth century, the figures were modest, ranging from twenty-two in 1700–1709 to eighty-two in 1740–49. In the second half, the tempo increased noticeably, although economic rationalization was still in its initial stage. Then, in the nineteenth century, came a flood of technological innovations that dwarfed all previous achievements, reaching 4,581 in 1840–49. In a hundred years the number of discoveries and inventions had multiplied almost fifty times.

Another rough but useful measure of the degree of mechanization is the capacity of the steam engines employed in production and transportation. Although the figures are only approximate, they unmistakably reflect the growing use of machinery (see table 1.1). In fifty-six years mechanically generated energy increased forty-seven times, a remarkable rate of growth. Every industry felt the effects of mechanization, although its intensity varied considerably. In 1840 Great Britain had 72 percent of the total, but by 1896 only 34. France's share during the same period

1. Andrew Ure, *The Philosophy of Manufactures: or, an Exposition of the Scientific, Moral, and Commercial Economy of the Factory System of Great Britain* (London, 1835), pp. 13, 20.

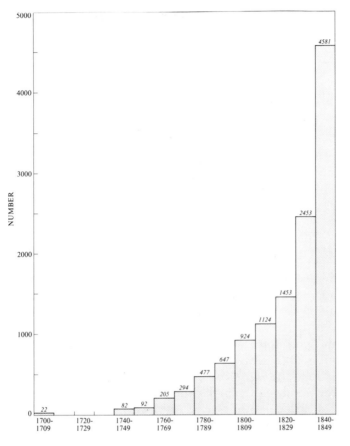

Figure 1.1. Patents Issued in England, 1700–1849

SOURCE: B. R. Mitchell, *Abstract of British Historical Statistics* (Cambridge, 1962), p. 268.

increased from 10 to 15 percent. Still more impressive were the gains of Germany, whose horsepower went from 5 to 20 percent of the total. Even small or backward nations experienced a substantial growth. The steady advance of economic rationalization transcended political boundaries and ideological differences dividing the states of the Continent.[2]

The concentration of labor was the inevitable accompaniment of the mechanization of production, the two processes providing mutual reinforcement and stimulation. There are no figures for Europe as a whole, but numerous regional studies suggest that a fundamental change in the

2. B. R. Mitchell, *Abstract of British Historical Statistics* (Cambridge, 1962), p. 268; David S. Landes, *The Unbound Prometheus: Technological Change and Industrial Development in Western Europe from 1750 to the Present* (Cambridge, 1969), p. 221.

Table 1.1. Capacity of Steam Engines in Europe, 1840–96

| | Thousands of Horsepower | | | |
	1840	1860	1880	1896
Great Britain	620	2,450	7,600	13,700
Germany	40	850	5,120	8,080
France	90	1,120	3,070	5,920
Russia	20	200	1,740	3,100
Austria	20	330	1,560	2,520
Belgium	40	160	610	1,180
Italy	10	50	500	1,520
Spain	10	100	470	1,180
Netherlands		30	250	600
Sweden		20	220	510
Europe	860	5,540	22,000	40,300

SOURCE: David S. Landes, *The Unbound Prometheus: Technological Change and Industrial Development in Western Europe from 1750 to the Present* (Cambridge, 1969), p. 221.

organization of the work force was taking place. Consider the situation in the Swiss canton of Zürich. In 1827 there were 106 mechanized spinning mills; by 1836 the figure had dropped to 87, and in 1842 there were only 69. The number of spindles, on the other hand, rose from between 180,000 and 200,000 to 293,000 and then to 330,000. In the southeast highland district of the canton, the average number of spindles per spinnery increased from 3,410 in 1836 to 5,499 in 1853 and 8,358 in 1870. Even more pertinent are the data from the Ruhr region of Germany, where, during the early phase of industrialization, the number of collieries grew from 190 in 1850–54 to 241 in 1870–74. By 1880–84, however, there were only 188 collieries, and by 1890–94 there had been a further decrease to 168. The process of concentration then seemed to abate, for in 1900 the figure was 169. Yet the number of workers per colliery was increasing steadily, going from 81 in 1850–54 to 128 in 1860–64, 281 in 1870–74, 470 in 1880–84, 834 in 1890–94, and 1,337 in 1900.

Statistics for all of Germany reveal that between 1882 and 1895 the percentage of the industrial labor force employed in establishments with five or fewer workers declined from 55.1 to 39.9, and by 1907 it had dropped to 29.5. Those working in establishments with between six and fifty employees increased during the same years from 18.6 percent to

23.8 and 25.0. The largest growth occurred in establishments employing more than fifty workers. Their share rose from 26.3 percent to 36.3 and then 45.5. Even in Russia there was a remarkable concentration of manpower beginning in the 1890s, although it was the result less of natural economic development than of a policy of hothouse industrialization pursued by the government at the urging of the Minister of Finance S. Y. Witte. By 1910 more than half of the factory operatives were in enterprises employing over five hundred workers; in Germany only 8 percent of the industrial labor force was in plants with more than one thousand workers, but in Russia the percentage was 24.[3]

The direct effect of economic rationalization was a striking increase in the efficiency of manufacture. Between 1870 and 1913 output per man-hour in all sectors of the economy grew at an average annual rate of 1.5 percent in the United Kingdom, 1.8 in France, 2.0 in Belgium, and 2.1 in Germany. These figures reflect only in part the rising productivity of industrial manpower, but more specialized data suggest that factories and mines deserve major credit for the improved performance of the work force as a whole. In the German iron industry, for instance, the average number of workers per blast furnace rose between 1880 and 1910 by 303 percent, from 151 to 458. The average annual production of pig iron per blast furnace, on the other hand, climbed 768 percent, from 19,500 tons to 149,800. In the Russian cotton industry handlooms represented 83 percent of the total number in operation in 1866, but power looms accounted for 62 percent of the output. In England the average daily production of cotton yarn per worker increased from two skeins in 1820 to four in 1840 and eight in 1870, and the average blast furnace, which cast 2 to 3 tons of pig iron a day in 1815, cast 30 to 35 in 1865 and 120 in 1878.

The mining of coal displayed the same tendency toward more efficient production, as the data in figure 1.2 show. Another way of measuring the growing efficiency of industry is the declining cost of labor per unit of production. Thus, the price of a pound of cotton yarn in England included 7.8 pence for wages in 1820, 2.1 in 1860, and only 1.4 in 1880,

3. Rudolf Braun, *Sozialer und kultureller Wandel in einem ländlichen Industriegebiet (Zürcher Oberland) unter Einwirkung des Maschinen- und Fabrikwesens im 19. und 20. Jahrhundert* (Erlenbach-Zürich and Stuttgart, 1965), p. 19; Jürgen Kuczynski, *Die Geschichte der Lage der Arbeiter unter dem Kapitalismus*, 38 vols. (Berlin, 1960–71), 14:16; Werner Sombart, *Die deutsche Volkswirtschaft im neunzehnten Jahrhundert und im Anfang des 20. Jahrhunderts*, 4th ed. (Berlin, 1923), p. 505; Peter I. Lyashchenko, *History of the National Economy of Russia to the 1917 Revolution* (New York, 1949), p. 669; Jonathan Hughes, *Industrialization and Economic History: Theses and Conjectures* (New York, 1970), p. 95.

although the real earnings of an average worker during those years rose about 70 percent.[4]

Here lies the ultimate significance of the industrial revolution: the ability to expand output without a corresponding increase in the expenditure of human energy. During the nineteenth century the volume of production in all the countries of Europe grew at an unprecedented rate, making possible for the first time a humane balance between supply and demand. Poverty had traditionally been accepted as an inescapable reality of life, because there appeared to be no way in which the economy could satisfy all the material needs of the community. Then, in the decades following the defeat of Napoleon, techniques and technologies began to emerge that made a society of mass consumption attainable. Not that privation as a common experience of mankind disappeared, but a basic transformation in the method of manufacture became apparent that promised to cope with it effectively. The available statistical data trace in detail a dramatic growth throughout the Continent of the output of the basic commodities of industrialization: coal, nonferrous metal ores, nonmetallic minerals, iron ore, pig iron, crude steel, and cotton textiles. Between 1815 and 1913 the volume of industrial production in the United Kingdom multiplied 11 times and in France 5 times. There are no reliable statistics for other European countries in the early decades, but in Germany the volume of industrial production multiplied 10 times during the period 1850–1913, in Russia 11 times during 1860–1913, in Italy 3 times during 1861–1913, in Sweden 7 times during 1862–1913, and in Austria 3.5 times during 1880–1913.[5]

Economic rationalization became a cornucopia, pouring out an inexhaustible abundance before an astounded Europe. Marc Séguin, a French engineer, reflected in 1839 the sense of exhilaration with which many men regarded the new world being created before their eyes by industrial progress:

> The dominant idea of civilized nations today is to increase well-being and the enjoyment of material life. All efforts have turned

4. Landes, *Unbound Prometheus*, p. 420; A. R. L. Gurland, "Wirtschaft und Gesellschaft im Übergang zum Zeitalter der Industrie," in *Propyläen Weltgeschichte*, ed. Golo Mann, Alfred Heuss, and August Nitschke, 12 vols. (Berlin, Frankfurt, and Vienna, 1960–65), 8:331; Pierre Léon, "L'évolution démographique, économique et sociale," in *L'Europe du XIXᵉ et du XXᵉ siècle*, ed. Max Beloff, Pierre Renouvin, Franz Schnabel, and Franco Valsecchi, 6 vols. (Milan, 1959–64), 1:343; E. A. Wrigley, *Industrial Growth and Population Change: A Regional Study of the Coalfield Areas of North-West Europe in the Later Nineteenth Century* (Cambridge, 1961), pp. 38–39; Kuczynski, *Geschichte der Lage der Arbeiter*, 24:198.

5. B. R. Mitchell, *European Historical Statistics, 1750–1970* (London and Basingstoke, 1975), pp. 355–57, 360–64, 378–81, 385, 387–88, 391–94, 399–401, 427–31, 434–35.

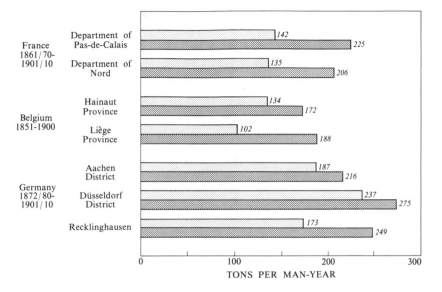

Figure 1.2. Efficiency of Coal Production, 1851–1910

SOURCE: E. A. Wrigley, *Industrial Growth and Population Change: A Regional Study of the Coalfield Areas of North-West Europe in the Later Nineteenth Century* (Cambridge, 1961), pp. 38–39.

toward industry, because it is from industry alone that we can expect progress. It is industry which gives birth to and develops new needs in men, and which at the same time gives them the means to satisfy them. Industry has become the life of the peoples [of Europe]. All our wishes, all our talents, all our intelligence should lead toward its development. Superior minds which aspire to the honor of contributing to our social regeneration should rally around this powerful lever.

What are the limits at which human power will stop? Commonplace minds never imagine them to lie beyond their own narrow horizon, and yet every day that horizon broadens, every day those limits are extended. Let us look around us. In the last twenty years the elements of our old civilization have everywhere been modified, perfected, renewed. Everywhere miracles have taken place. The pleasures and conveniences of life which had been reserved for wealth only are now at the disposal of the artisan. A few more steps and they will also be distributed among all classes. A thousand industries, a thousand inventions have been born simultaneously which have brought other discoveries, and these in turn have become or will become the point of departure for new progress. All

> these changes work to the profit of the public at large, and they tend
> to make well-being common property. This is a new era, based on
> love of the good and the beautiful, which is rising on the ruins of
> class prejudices and the monopolies of wealth.[6]

There was seemingly no problem that technology could not solve, no
obstacle that the machine could not surmount. Mankind appeared to be
witnessing the dawn of a new golden age.

The industrial revolution had effects that were felt in every corner of
Europe, although its scope and intensity varied from region to region.
Generally speaking, it tended to radiate from a center of origin in the
British Isles toward the east and the south. For example, by 1816 the
amount of coal produced in the United Kingdom already exceeded 15
million tons, but Germany reached that figure only in 1857, France and
Belgium in 1872, Austria-Hungary in 1880, Russia in 1900, Spain in
1957, and Italy never reached it. The United Kingdom consumed one
hundred thousand tons of raw cotton for the first time in 1830, France in
1860, Germany in 1871, Russia in 1878, Austria-Hungary and Italy in
1890, Belgium in 1911, and Spain in 1915. The United Kingdom first
produced 1 million tons of pig iron in 1835, France in 1862, Germany in
1867, Russia in 1891, Austria-Hungary in 1894, Belgium in 1897, Italy
in 1939, and Spain in 1958. In the output of crude steel, the United
Kingdom passed the million-ton mark in 1879, Germany in 1882, France
and Russia in 1896, Austria-Hungary in 1898, Belgium in 1904, Italy in
1915, and Spain in 1929. Each successive measure of the degree of industrialization shows that England was a pioneer, although her lead over her
Continental competitors diminished steadily with the growing sophistication of manufacturing technology.

During the 1840s, the well-known German economist Friedrich List
portrayed Great Britain as a modern Rome, enjoying a supremacy that
"the world has never seen before." He described as "vain" the efforts of
those "who sought to establish their universal domination on armed
might alone, in contrast to the great attempt of England to transform her
entire territory into one immense manufacturing, commercial, and maritime city." Some sixty years later, another distinguished economist, the
Englishman Alfred Marshall, was complaining that "a part of England's
leadership was destroyed rapidly." In the future, he warned, Britons
must regard business as seriously as their American and German competitors were doing. "The time had passed at which they could afford
merely to teach foreigners and not learn from them in return."

6. Marc Séguin, *De l'influence des chemins de fer et de l'art de les tracer et de les construire* (Paris, 1839), pp. i–iii. This and all subsequent translations into English are by the
author.

There is ample statistical illustration of England's decline as economic leader in the face of a challenge from rivals in both the Old World and the New. By the beginning of the twentieth century, the relative intensity of industrialization in other countries was beginning to approach her level. As early as 1801, industry accounted for 23 percent of the national product of the United Kingdom; in 1901 it accounted for 40. France, where the percentage was 25 in 1825–35, reached 37 in 1908–10. More significant was the increase in Germany, from 24 percent in 1860–69 to 39 in 1905–14. Even in Sweden industry, which represented only 17 percent of the national product in 1861–65, rose to 38 percent by 1901–5. Changes in relative industrialization, moreover, led logically to changes in relative production. The figures in Table 1.2 clearly reflect the long-term shift of economic power from the British Isles toward Central Europe and across the Atlantic. All the leading nations were experiencing rapid industrial growth, but their respective positions changed substantially in the course of a generation.[7]

A word of caution regarding the extent of industrialization is in order, however. Although large-scale output altered the economy of Europe, it did not completely eliminate the many small manufacturing establishments that continued to employ the tools and techniques of the skilled artisan. Industrial and preindustrial modes of production coexisted in an uneasy balance that shifted more and more in favor of the machine and the factory. According to the English census of 1851, one-third of the 130,000 shop proprietors who responded had no hired workers, and only some 10,000 had ten or more employees. In 1914 about 80 percent of the 62,762 active joint-stock companies in Great Britain were still essentially private enterprises, family firms, or old-fashioned partnerships in disguise. In France in 1852 there were 6,500 industrial establishments with steam engines totaling 76,000 horsepower, an average of 11.7, whereas in 1912 there were 63,000 establishments and 3,235,000 horsepower, an average of 51.3. Since these figures include the giants of mining and metallurgy, it becomes apparent that the typical manufacturing unit on the eve of the First World War was an atelier with a machine of between five and ten horsepower, not much different from what it had been fifty years earlier. This conclusion is reinforced by data showing that between 1896 and 1906 the percentage of French establishments employ-

7. Mitchell, *European Historical Statistics*, pp. 360–68, 391–96, 399–402, 427–32; Friedrich List, *Schriften, Reden, Briefe*, 10 vols. (Berlin, 1927–35), 6:369; Great Britain, *Parliamentary Papers*, 107 (*Accounts and Papers*, 46, 1908), no. 321, "Memorandum by Mr. Alfred Marshall on the Fiscal Policy of International Trade," pp. 21–22; Simon Kuznets, *Modern Economic Growth: Rate, Structure, and Spread* (New Haven and London, 1966), pp. 88–90; League of Nations, *Industrialization and Foreign Trade* ([Geneva], 1945), p. 13.

Table 1.2. Shares of World Manufacturing Output, 1870–1913

	1870	1896–1900	1913
	(percentage)		
United Kingdom	31.8	19.5	14.0
Germany	13.2	16.6	15.7
France	10.3	7.1	6.4
Russia	3.7	5.0	5.5
United States	23.3	30.1	35.8

SOURCE: League of Nations, *Industrialization and Foreign Trade* ([Geneva], 1945), p. 13.

ing 5 workers or less actually increased slightly from 93.2 to 93.4, while those employing between 51 and 100 workers remained unchanged with 0.2 and those employing between 101 and 500 workers rose from 0.1 to 0.2. Even in Germany, skilled craftsmen continued to resist the most powerful current of industrial concentration on the Continent. As late as 1907, there were 1,094,921 manufacturing establishments, out of a total of 10,852,873, with only one worker, usually the owner himself, and another 2,105,361 had between two and five workers.[8]

Some of the small shops managed to adjust to industrialization, adopting its technology and spirit. They became miniature factories, differing from large enterprises only in the scope of their operation. Others accepted the position of auxiliaries of large-scale manufacture, concentrating in those branches of the economy that were not yet mechanized. There was always room for a good tailor who could sew custom clothes for a well-to-do clientele. Shoemakers and carpenters were still able to make a decent living catering to those wealthy enough to afford hand-crafted wares. But there were also countless artisans whose livelihood had been destroyed by the advance of machinery. Throughout the nineteenth century, a literature of popular protest, portraying the enslavement of the little man by heartless industrialism, mourned the passing of a traditional way of life. The address of an English journeyman cotton spinner in 1818 expressed the anguish of those millions throughout Europe who were being uprooted by the industrial revolution:

8. Llewellyn Woodward, *The Age of Reform, 1815–1870*, 2d ed. (Oxford, 1962), pp. 603–4; F. H. Hinsley, "Introduction," in *The New Cambridge Modern History*, 12 vols. (Cambridge, 1960–70), 11:13; J. H. Clapham, *The Economic Development of France and Germany, 1815–1914*, 4th ed. (Cambridge, 1966), p. 259; "La concentration des établissements en France de 1896 à 1936," *Études et conjoncture* 9 (1954):848; Sombart, *Die deutsche Volkswirtschaft*, p. 505.

> When the spinning of cotton was in its infancy, and before those
> terrible machines for superseding the necessity of human labour,
> called steam engines came into use, there were a great number of
> what were then called *little masters*; men who with a small capital,
> could procure a few machines, and employ a few hands men and
> boys (say to twenty or thirty). . . . A few years however changed the
> face of things. Steam engines came into use, to purchase which, and
> to erect buildings sufficient to contain them and six or seven
> hundred hands, required a great capital. The engine power produced
> a more marketable (though not a better) article than the little
> masters could at the same price. The consequence was their ruin in a
> short time; and the overgrown capitalists triumphed in their fall.[9]

A profound dislocation in the established pattern of society was the price
of the blessings that economic rationalization, the unbound Prometheus,
bestowed on mankind.

The most serious obstacles in the path of the industrial revolution,
however, were technical rather than social. The skilled artisan and small
businessman who could not compete with the factory were left to sink or
swim, to adjust to new methods of manufacture or lose their livelihood.
But serious problems of distribution arising out of basic changes in production had to be solved in order to provide free scope for mechanization. The promise of industrialism could not be fully realized until new
ways had been found to convey goods from producer to consumer. The
earliest attempts to meet this challenge involved the adaptation of preindustrial modes of transportation to the requirements of large-scale
output, specifically, the improvement of roads and the construction of
canals. But this was only the beginning. The situation called for something more fundamental than the refinement of existing techniques. The
solution was a transformation of distribution comparable in magnitude
to the transformation of production. Only the application of mechanical
energy to the movement of commodities made possible the creation of a
market for their vastly increased volume.

The keystone of the revolution in transportation was the railway. Once
the business community recognized the crucial role that the locomotive
could play in the economy, the construction of railroad lines became a
major area of investment. "The extent to which the passion for Railway Gambling had penetrated the upper and middle classes is scarcely
credible," commented a well-known work on economics around the mid-
century. "In every street of every town persons were to be found who
were holders of Railway Shares. Elderly men and women of small realised

9. *Black Dwarf*, 30 September 1818, pp. 623–24.

fortunes, tradesmen of every order, pensioners, public functionaries, professional men, merchants, country gentlemen—the mania had affected all." In 1840 Europe had a total of only 3,805 kilometers of track. Then came a period of striking growth, as one country after another decided, for strategic as well as economic reasons, to modernize its system of transportation. The trackage rose to 23,024 kilometers in 1850, 49,548 in 1860, 73,261 in 1870, 157,071 in 1880, 208,227 in 1890, 265,583 in 1900, and 307,535 in 1910. In seventy years the rail network multiplied eighty times. Even the most backward states sought to stimulate their economies with ambitious programs of railroad construction. Between 1870 and 1913 the length of track in Bulgaria rose from 224 kilometers to 2,109, in Greece from 12 to 1,584, in Portugal from 714 to 2,958, in Rumania from 248 to 3,549. As for the cost of this new method of moving freight, the German scholar Werner Sombart has calculated that the average annual investment in the European railroads was 762 million marks in 1841–50, 941 million in 1851–60, 1,181 million in 1861–70, 2,150 million in 1871–80, 1,855 million in 1881–90, about 2,200 million in 1891–1900, and more than 1,800 million in 1901–13. The expenditure required for the rationalization of distribution was comparable to that going into the rationalization of production.[10]

The other major innovation in transportation was the steamship. Although less far-reaching in its consequences than the locomotive, it affected the delivery of goods by water as profoundly as the railroad affected their delivery by land. Its rate of growth, however, appears at first glance to have been much slower. During the period 1840–1910 the number of sailing vessels in Europe declined 18 percent, while the number of steamships increased 1,595 percent. But these figures tell only part of the story, and not the most important part. Of greater significance than the number of ships using sail or steam was the change in their relative and absolute capacities. Statistics on the British merchant marine illustrate this point. Table 1.3 shows that in 1850 sailing vessels accounted for 95 percent of the total number of ships and of the total tonnage in the United Kingdom. In 1883 steam tonnage exceeded sail tonnage for the first time, although there were almost three times as many sailing vessels as steamships. By 1913 sailing vessels still accounted for 40 percent of the merchant ships but only 7 percent of their capacity. In sixty-three years the tonnage of merchant vessels driven by steam had multiplied sixty-seven times.

10. Thomas Tooke and William Newmarch, *A History of Prices, and of the State of the Circulation*, 6 vols. (London, 1838–57), 5:234; Mitchell, *European Historical Statistics*, pp. 581–84; Werner Sombart, *Der moderne Kapitalismus: Historisch-systematische Darstellung des gesamteuropäischen Wirtschaftslebens von seinen Anfängen bis zur Gegenwart*, 2d ed., 3 vols. (Munich and Leipzig, 1924–28), 3:289–90.

Table 1.3. Conversion of Shipping from Sail to Steam, 1840–1913

	Europe				
	1840	1860	1880	1900	1910
Total Vessels (thousands)	74	92	91	80	84
Percentage steam-powered	1	3	10	22	29

	United Kingdom		
	1850	1883	1913
Sailing Vessels			
Number (thousands)	25	18	8
Percentage	95	75	40
Tonnage (thousands)	3,397	3,514	847
Percentage	95	49	7
Steam Vessels			
Number (thousands)	1	6	13
Percentage	5	25	60
Tonnage (thousands)	168	3,728	11,273
Percentage	5	51	93
Total Vessels			
Number (thousands)	26	25	21
Tonnage (thousands)	3,565	7,242	12,120

SOURCE: B. R. Mitchell, *European Historical Statistics, 1750–1970* (London and Basingstoke, 1975), pp. 614–23.

In other words, a process of consolidation was taking place in distribution as well as production, and for the same reason. Mechanization meant that while the aggregate of units performing a given economic function did not keep pace with the growing availability of goods and services, the efficiency of each unit increased substantially. The number of ships in the French merchant marine, for example, rose by 19 percent between 1860 and 1913, from 14,922 to 17,719. The average tonnage per vessel, however, rose 33 percent, from 67 to 89. Steamships alone were responsible for this development, for their average tonnage rose 138 percent, from 217 to 517, while that of sailing vessels actually declined 41 percent, from 64 to 38. In both transportation and manufacture, preindustrial methods and techniques were thus in retreat before mechanization. What the factory did to the artisan shop, the railroad did to the horse-drawn vehicle and the steamship to the sailing vessel. Those who could not adjust to the new technology were forced into the backwaters of the economy, into functions and occupations not profitable enough to warrant large-scale mechanized operation.[11]

What made the social cost of the revolution in transportation acceptable was its material achievement. It led to a new system of distribution capable of absorbing the increase in production arising out of industrialization. To give two examples, the railroads of Austria-Hungary carried 118,000 metric tons of freight in 1840, 22,898,000 in 1870, and 161,529,000 in 1900. The Italian railroads carried 4,757,000 metric tons of freight in 1870 and 41,422,000 in 1913. Such a rapid growth was the result not only of expanded trackage but also of increased efficiency. Consider Germany, whose railroads carried 1,630 million ton-kilometers of freight in 1860 and 37,000 million in 1900, an increase of almost twenty-three times in forty years. Yet the length of the German rail network rose from 11,089 kilometers in 1860 to 51,678 in 1900, an increase of not quite five times. Similarly, between 1880 and 1913 the length of railroads in Belgium grew 14 percent, from 4,112 kilometers to 4,676, but the volume of freight they carried grew 170 percent, from 32,770,000 metric tons to 88,427,000. The system of distribution was obviously undergoing a process of intensive rationalization in which an improvement of operation proved even more important than the enlargement of scale.

The capacity of the railroad was in part at least a function of its speed. By carrying goods and passengers in only a fraction of the time required by a horse-drawn vehicle, it was able to expand its total volume accordingly. A train journey from Liverpool to London in 1845 took little more than a third of what it had taken ten years earlier by stagecoach. In 1841, on the eve of the railroad age, a freight wagon leaving Friedrichshafen on the Lake of Constance needed four days to reach Zürich, six days to arrive in Mannheim or Mainz, fifteen days to get to Genoa, sixteen to Hamburg, and twenty-four to Leghorn. The locomotive delivered the same load in less than half the time.

The cost of transportation declined sharply, moreover, making it possible for people and commodities to travel farther and more frequently. Freight wagons in Great Britain had charged twelve to fifteen pence per ton-mile, and canal barges six to twelve pence. The railroad carried coal in 1849 for one penny per ton-mile, and general merchandise for from two to four pence. In 1825 the cheapest passage from Europe to America was about one hundred dollars, but by the 1880s the price had dropped to between twenty and thirty. Steerage from Liverpool, so important to many emigrants, cost only eight dollars. Wheat rates from New York to

11. Mitchell, *European Historical Statistics*, pp. 614–23.

England, which had reached a high of over twenty-one cents a bushel in 1873, dropped to less than three by 1901. Australian wool rates declined by about half between 1873 and 1896. In 1905 jute rates from India were only a fourth of what they had been in 1873.

As the cost of transportation diminished, the market began to broaden, crossing regional and national frontiers. In 1817 a bushel of wheat in the Rhine Province of Prussia sold for 16.63 marks and a bushel of rye for 13.25, yet less than four hundred miles to the east, in the province of Posen, a bushel of wheat sold for 9.68 marks and a bushel of rye for 5.68. The price differential was 6.95 and 7.57 marks respectively. By 1855 the differential between the highest and the lowest price of grain in the Prussian provinces had dropped to 1.70 marks for wheat and 2.30 for rye, a decline of more than 70 percent. The danger of famine, a frightening specter throughout history, began to recede as the large-scale exchange of foodstuffs between nations and hemispheres became technologically feasible. The material needs of society, which a preindustrial system of production and distribution had been unable to satisfy, could now be met. The methods and objectives of a localized economy emphasizing self-sufficiency gave way to those of a continental and world market based on extensive specialization. This new balance between supply and demand meant in turn a rising standard of living.[12]

Not all results of the revolution in transportation, however, could be weighed and measured. For example, how was the way of life altered by the fact that in the nineteenth century the movement of large masses of people became commonplace? According to official statistics, about 300 million passengers traveled on the railroads of Europe in 1860; in 1880 the figure was 1,355 million, in 1900 it was 3,169 million, and in 1913, 5,234 million. Such a vast flow of humanity dwarfed the great migrations of the nomadic peoples of the past. Neither the infiltration of the Roman world by the Germanic tribes nor the conquest of the south shore of the Mediterranean by the Arabs nor the establishment by the Mongols of a vast empire in the Eurasian heartland could compare with it. To what extent did this new availability of the means of travel affect the practices and habits of those who experienced it?

A redistribution of population was clearly one major effect of the

12. Ibid., pp. 581, 583, 589, 591–93; Herbert Heaton, *Economic History of Europe* (New York and London, 1936), p. 547; Sombart, *Die deutsche Volkswirtschaft*, p. 245; William Woodruff, "The Emergence of an International Economy, 1700–1914," in *The Fontana Economic History of Europe: The Emergence of Industrial Societies*, ed. Carlo M. Cipolla (London and Glasgow, 1973), p. 697 (n. 38); Douglass North, "Ocean Freight Rates and Economic Development, 1750–1913," *Journal of Economic History* 18 (1958):544–45; Ludwig Pohle, *Die Entwicklung des deutschen Wirtschaftslebens im 19. Jahrhundert* (Leipzig, 1904), p. 10.

revolution in transportation. It could be seen in its most dramatic form in the millions who left Europe to build new homes on distant continents. But there were also many more millions who traveled for shorter distances and reached more modest destinations: a neighboring city, a county fair, a place of employment, the home of a relative, the residence of a friend. "Thanks to the modern Genius of Speed and the Science of the Rail," wrote a British architect in 1860, "a wholesome future is in store for us. . . . They will best appreciate the improved intercourse between London and its environs who recollect the *stage coaches* to Paddington, Hammersmith, or Hackney—the stopping and horn-blowing at every turn—the time consumed on the journey, and the money charged for it. Our bankers from Lombard Street now reach the sea-coast by the time they used to arrive at Clapham." The provincialisms of the village and the small town with their deadening monotony were encountering new experiences and attitudes engendered by mass mobility.[13]

Greater freedom of movement had still another effect, psychological yet tangible, which should be noted. It was a leveler of distinctions and privileges rooted in a preindustrial economy. The ability to travel had traditionally been a prerogative of the well-to-do, helping to differentiate their position from that of the lower classes. The means of transportation had been so costly that most men were of necessity forced to spend their lives in their native communities, practicing traditional village occupations. The railroad changed all that. It enabled the peasant and the artisan to leave their ancestral homes, to seek greater opportunities, to find a new way of life. More than that, it established an unprecedented equality in the mode of travel. Rich and poor alike had to submit to the discipline of a schedule that governed departures, arrivals, connections, and layovers. The passengers in a first-class compartment might still enjoy the plush seats and tasseled curtains denied to the occupants of the third class. Such differences were negligible, however, compared to the barriers that a generation or two earlier had separated those who could afford to travel by stagecoach from those whom poverty had confined to their place of birth with little hope of escape. The use of steam in transportation thus had subtle but unmistakable democratic implications.

That was why, from the earliest days of the railroad, there were highborn observers who expressed uneasiness at the prospect of mass mobility. They recognized that a diminution of class differences in travel might prepare the way for their diminution in social and political relationships as well. "All barriers, classes, enjoyments, and needs are then also being leveled," complained the German countess Ida Hahn-Hahn

13. Mitchell, *European Historical Statistics*, pp. 601–6; Thomas Morris, *A House for the Suburbs; Socially and Architecturally Sketched* (London, 1860), pp. 1–2.

during the 1840s. "Old and young, great and small, rich and poor, man and beast glide about in steam coaches for a pittance." Czar Nicholas I of Russia expressed himself with greater forcefulness. He admitted that the construction of railway lines was a "necessity of the times." How else could a nation maintain its economic and military strength? But the easy availability of the new means of travel would change everything, a French diplomat reported him as saying. "The filth which stayed quietly on the bottom will rise to the surface." Here was a consequence of the revolution in transportation as significant as the miles of track built or the tons of freight carried. A change in the way men saw themselves within the established pattern of social classes and economic interests was of basic importance in the transformation of European society in the nineteenth century.[14]

It is easier, however, to determine the material than the psychological effects of the new system of distribution. The railroad and the steamship produced a revolution in commerce, creating a market far exceeding in volume and scope the international trade of the preindustrial era. In 1887 an Austrian scholar, Franz Xaver von Neumann-Spallart, described the emergence of a world economy made possible by mechanized means of transportation:

> In order to understand the future correctly, we must today no longer overlook the fact that the economic conditions of all the countries on earth have been consolidated. . . . It is becoming ever more apparent that the economic condition of individual nations is determined by their dependence on all other nations, to which they are connected by countless ties. With the advance of big industry and international commerce, that community of interests which formerly existed only between neighboring states or European countries has been extended over all parts of the earth. Today the course of trade in general is being decided outside the continental boundaries of Europe; it is being decided on one side in the far west, beyond the Atlantic Ocean, and on the other side in the far east, in the British East Indian colonial empire, in China, and in the other parts of the Oriental world.[15]

In this new global economy the states of Europe controlled the lion's share, although by the beginning of the twentieth century their ascendancy was beginning to weaken. The head start provided by industrial-

14. Ida Hahn-Hahn, *Reisebriefe*, 2 vols. (Berlin, 1841), 1:7; Alfred Stern, *Geschichte Europas seit den Verträgen von 1815 bis zum Frankfurter Frieden von 1871*, 10 vols. (Berlin and Stuttgart, 1894–1924), 6:19–20.

15. Franz Xaver von Neumann-Spallart, *Uebersichten der Weltwirtschaft: Jahrgang 1883–84* (Stuttgart, 1887), p. 83.

ization enabled them to remain in the lead for more than a hundred years, and at the outbreak of the First World War they were still occupying the dominant position in which the world had become accustomed to see them.

The revolution in commerce, like the revolution in production and distribution, had its roots in the eighteenth century, when the more intensive application of preindustrial techniques made possible an increase in the volume of goods flowing across national frontiers. Caution should be used in describing this process, for the data are spotty and often imprecise. But E. J. Hobsbawm has estimated that international commerce "for all the countries within the purview of European economic statistics at this period" more than doubled in value between 1720 and 1780. In the next sixty years, it increased again more than three times. By 1870 the per capita value of foreign trade in the United Kingdom, France, Germany, Austria, and Scandinavia was four to five times what it had been in 1830, and in Belgium and the Netherlands the increase was about three times. Jonathan Hughes, though conceding that "strict accuracy would be a laughable pretense," has calculated that the index of value of world exports rose from 100 in 1800 to 173 in 1840, 453 in 1860, 907 in 1873, 1,247 in 1895, and 2,703 in 1913. A rate of growth of this magnitude was unprecedented in historical experience.

Even if the details of such estimates are open to question, quite apart from the complication created by the shifting relationship between the value and the volume of commerce, the generalization that the expansion of international trade was roughly comparable to the expansion of manufacture and transportation remains valid. It is supported by statistical information covering the last prewar decades, when the data reached a high level of accuracy and completeness. The average annual increase in the volume of exports of several European countries in the period 1890–1913 suggests continued vigorous growth. The percentages were 5.1 for Germany, 4.6 for the Netherlands, 3.8 for Sweden, 3.5 for Belgium, 2.8 for France, and 2.1 for the United Kingdom. For Western Europe as a whole the rate was 3.2, but for the United States it was 3.8 and for the entire world 3.5. The most complete and reliable figures on foreign trade, moreover, show that between 1890 and 1913 the value of the international commerce of all European states rose 137 percent.[16]

There is still another way to illustrate the tenacity with which Europeans held on to their lead in the exchange of goods. Throughout the nineteenth century, the real value of foreign trade in the world increased

16. E. J. Hobsbawm, *The Age of Capital, 1848–1875* (New York, 1975), p. 50; Hughes, *Industrialization and Economic History*, p. 144; Angus Maddison, *Economic Growth in the West: Comparative Experience in Europe and North America* (New York, 1964), p. 166; Mitchell, *European Historical Statistics*, pp. 489–97.

at a rapid rate ranging from 10.1 percent in the period 1820–30 to 61.5 in 1840–50. The average per decade was 42.2. Europe's share of the total remained by and large unchanged until the 1880s, when a slow but steady decline set in. During the eighteenth century, European nations had accounted for more than 70 percent of world commerce, and they still controlled 70.2 as late as 1840–50. There was a slight drop to 69.0 in 1850–60, but then the percentage exceeded 70 again in the next two decades. In the 1880s a slowdown of business activity occurred, reflected in a smaller share of international trade amounting to either 69.4 or 65.6 percent, depending on which of two methods of computation is employed. Thereafter the trend became unmistakable. The percentages were 64.6 in 1891–95, 65.3 in 1896–1900, 62.8 in 1901–5, 58.5 in 1906–10, and 60.0 in 1911–13. The end of the supremacy of Europe in world commerce could now be seen in the distance, yet a relative decline of 11 percent in thirty-three years does not suggest an economic breakdown.

The diminishing role of the Old World in foreign trade was a direct result of the growing role of the New. The increased importance of the Western Hemisphere, especially America, largely accounted for the slow ebb of European domination. The share of the United States in international commerce rose from 8.8 percent in 1870–80 to 10.1 in 1911–13; Canada's percentage increased from 1.4 in 1881–85 to 2.9 in 1913; Latin America climbed from 5.1 in 1880–89 to 7.5 in 1913. At the other end of the globe, India, Japan, and Australia were making their economic influence felt with growing urgency. To many Europeans these were alarming developments. They saw dark portents that power would soon slip from their grasp. Neumann-Spallart warned that "the economic climate of Europe is no longer being created in Europe alone, but also in America and Asia." Traditional commercial relationships among the nations bordering the Atlantic were being altered by the fact that "the United States has itself created big industries," and "it has, moreover, for the most part paid off its debts." East Asia was increasingly exchanging "the exuberant abundance of its natural products for the achievements of European labor and European capital." The result of these developments would be a gradual "shift in the center of gravity of the world economy." Indeed, there was reason to fear that "first Great Britain and then the entire European continent are approaching a process of aging and cooling." The future looked dark and menacing.[17]

There were many other Europeans in the closing decades of the nineteenth century who feared that their economic domination was coming to an end, a feeling especially pronounced in England. Her lead in world commerce, which had at one time appeared beyond challenge, was now

17. Kuznets, *Modern Economic Growth*, pp. 306–8; Neumann-Spallart, *Uebersichten: Jahrgang 1883–84*, pp. 83–85.

dwindling in the face of competition from younger and more vigorous rivals. Germany in particular posed a threat alarming millions of Britons. They felt that their economy, more dependent on international trade than any other, was being undermined by ruthless and unscrupulous opponents. In 1886 a "Royal Commission Appointed to Inquire into the Depression of Trade and Industry" concluded: "The increasing severity of this competition both in our home and in neutral markets is especially noticeable in the case of Germany. A reference to the reports from abroad will show that in every quarter of the world the perseverance and enterprise of the Germans are making themselves felt. In the actual production of commodities we have now few, if any, advantages over them; and in a knowledge of the markets of the world, a desire to accommodate themselves to local tastes or idiosyncrasies, a determination to obtain a footing wherever they can, and a tenacity in maintaining it, they appear to be gaining ground upon us." The cries of warning became louder and more frequent, reaching a climax ten years later in Ernest E. Williams's book *"Made in Germany,"* which asserted point-blank that "on all hands England's industrial supremacy is tottering to its fall, and this result is largely German work." The mood engendered by the loss of mastery was a gloomy foreboding that at times bordered on hysteria.

Yet the growing chorus of doom reflected fears of what might be rather than what actually was. By 1914 Europe's control of world commerce was no longer as complete as a century earlier, but with about 60 percent of the total, it was solid enough to last a long time. The future was likely to bring a gradual adjustment to more modest economic circumstances, not a disastrous decline and collapse. During the 1890s an English writer reminded his countrymen that even "if we exported nothing, the services of our ships (our 'invisible exports') would pay for imports to the amount of £70,000,000, and rank us at once as a second-rate trading power, with only France, Germany, United States (America), Holland, Belgium, and Austria ahead." As for the Anglo-German trade rivalry, in 1910 the value of the United Kingdom's commerce with the German Empire was 99 million pounds, greater than that with India and second only to the United States. The value of Germany's commerce with the United Kingdom in the same year exceeded that with any other nation except Russia. Material interests were simply ignoring political differences, diplomatic tensions, and mass fears. Europe remained a vigorous economic organism that was approaching middle age but was still far from senescence and decrepitude.[18]

18. Great Britain, *Parliamentary Papers*, 23 (*Reports from Commissioners, Inspectors, and Others*, 11, 1886), C. 4893, "Final Report of the Royal Commission Appointed to Inquire into the Depression of Trade and Industry; with Minutes of Evidence and Appen-

Its ability to oppose the challenge from other continents depended in large measure on control of a world-wide system of finance that had developed during the nineteenth century in response to needs created by economic rationalization. The industrial revolution was in fact a series of simultaneous and interdependent revolutions in production, distribution, commerce, and credit. The function of the new financial structure was to regulate and coordinate the flow of investments into the economy, raising efficiency and maximizing profit. The volume of capital required by factories, mines, foundries, railroads, and steamships was so vast that the primitive credit system of preindustrial society, with its private moneylenders and family banks, could not begin to provide it. What was needed was a form of business organization capable of channeling the savings of millions of small investors into large-scale enterprise without the risk of unlimited liability. The answer was the joint-stock company, which combined a far-flung source of capital with a restricted level of accountability in the event of failure. Yet although it had been known in Europe long before industrialization, conservative bureaucrats continued to regard it with suspicion. It evoked memories of the South Sea Bubble and John Law's Mississippi Scheme; it suggested speculation and fraud. Those whose economic attitudes had been shaped in a precapitalistic milieu saw in the joint-stock principle the machinations of unscrupulous financiers more interested in lining their pockets than in serving the general welfare. The authorities therefore insisted on examining and approving individually every application for incorporation, thereby restricting a form of business organization adapted to an industrialized economy.

It took years of agitation by publicists and promoters to persuade the governments of Europe to permit the free establishment of joint-stock companies. As late as 1869, the Congress of German Economists was still trying to convince the politicians in Berlin that "the requirement of a state concession for the formation of a joint-stock company should be rejected, because the state is unable to examine in adequate fashion either the question of need or the question of confidence. The redirection of the founding of joint-stock companies to a level which is economically permissible should be entrusted entirely to growing economic insight." But by then freedom of incorporation was finally beginning to win the acceptance that business circles had been advocating with such persistence. Great Britain, the pioneer of industrialism, took the lead with a partial liberalization during the late 1850s, culminating in 1862 in a compre-

dices," p. xx; Ernest Edwin Williams, *"Made in Germany"* (London, 1896), p. 44; Arthur L. Bowley, *A Short Account of England's Foreign Trade in the Nineteenth Century: Its Economic and Social Results* (London, 1893), pp. 116–17; Mitchell, *European Historical Statistics*, pp. 526, 573.

hensive law making limited liability generally available. A few years later, France granted free incorporation and limited liability to companies with a capital stock of not more than 20 million francs, and in 1867 even this restriction was removed. Spain followed in 1869, the North German Confederation in 1870, and Belgium in 1873. The financial crash of that year had the effect of delaying further decontrol for a decade, but then came Italy in 1883, Portugal in 1888, Sweden in 1895, and Austria in 1899. By the opening of the twentieth century, only Russia and Turkey among the major countries still required specific authorization for incorporation.[19]

The effect of the new form of business organization on the economy of Europe was profound. As early as the 1850s, the Cologne banker and politician Gustav Mevissen had correctly analyzed the transformation which the financial system was undergoing:

> The alliance within the field of industry of capital and intellectual forces in the form of the joint-stock company has increasingly become a striking feature of the present time. . . . On the basis of what has already occurred, it seems clear today after the passage of a few decades that the joint-stock company has developed in modern society with the energy and speed of a force of nature. As a result of conditions in Europe and America, it has arisen simultaneously in all states which have assumed the great task of material progress. . . . The energies united within its form have in the course of a few decades created works of material civilization before which even the great works of antiquity and the Middle Ages must bow. . . . The resistance which develops against all new creations bearing the seeds of a great future has not been and is not absent. But so far the young giant has overcome all his opponents, and every day enlarges his power. . . . The newest achievements of modern times, the railway and the steamship companies, allied with the banks and insurance companies belonging to an earlier period, were the first to be molded in the form of the joint-stock company. Based on these fields, the form has gradually gained control of a number of branches of industry in which capital plays the leading role, and individual activity and talent a secondary one. It seeks to penetrate deeper and deeper into the domain of industry.[20]

19. *Bericht über die Verhandlungen des eilften Kongresses deutscher Volkswirthe in Mainz am 1., 2., 3. und 4. September 1869* (Berlin, 1870), pp. 45–46; Rondo E. Cameron, *France and the Economic Development of Europe, 1800–1914: Conquests of Peace and Seeds of War* (Princeton, 1961), p. 35.

20. Joseph Hansen, *Gustav von Mevissen: Ein rheinisches Lebensbild, 1815–1899*, 2 vols. (Berlin, 1906), 2:532–33.

The introduction of freedom of incorporation intensified this process of penetration. In England 902 new companies with a nominal capital of 307 million dollars were founded during the period 1856–58, as the government began to relax its control over business expansion. In the period 1863–65, on the other hand, after the last restrictions were lifted, the number rose to 2,749 million dollars and the nominal capital to 2,798 million. In all the years before 1850, only 123 firms capitalized at 161 million dollars had been formed in Prussia, and no more than 295 capitalized at 573 million in the next two decades. Yet during the four years following the establishment of freedom of incorporation in 1870, 833 firms capitalized at 595 million dollars were organized. On the eve of the First World War, there were 60,754 joint-stock companies in Great Britain with a capital of 11,806 million dollars, 5,400 in Germany with a capital of 4,171 million, 9,431 in the Netherlands with a capital of 864 million, and 812 in Austria with a capital of 844 million. In the case of France, no data are available for any single year after 1898, but there are figures showing that during the period 1889–1913 over 25,000 joint-stock companies capitalized at 3,916 million dollars had been founded. A more sensitive measure of the accessibility of credit is the ratio of gross national capital formation to gross national product. In the United Kingdom it rose from 12.5 percent in 1860–79 to 14.0 in 1900–1914. But this was not as impressive as the increase in Germany, where it rose from 14.4 percent in 1851–70 to 24.1 in 1891–1913, or in Italy, from 8.5 in 1861–80 to 17.3 in 1901–10. Even in the Scandinavian countries the average percentage during the opening years of the twentieth century was about 10 or 11. Such a volume of credit could not only satisfy domestic demand but also finance investments overseas or in the underdeveloped regions of Europe.[21]

The end of close government supervision of the financial system led at first to a wave of speculation, as small investors rushed to the stock market to enjoy a new freedom that would surely make them all wealthy. George Joachim Goschen, the British statesman and businessman, was delighted with the willingness of the public to lend money to promoters promising quick profits. "Never before has there been so keen a desire on the part of the whole community to invest every reserve shilling they may have, in some remunerative manner," he declared in 1885 before the Manchester Chamber of Commerce. "There is competition between men who have a few tens of pounds and a few hundreds of pounds to put

21. Leland Hamilton Jenks, *The Migration of British Capital to 1875* (New York and London, 1927), p. 238; Landes, *Unbound Prometheus*, p. 198; Sombart, *Der moderne Kapitalismus*, 3:213; Clapham, *Economic Development of France and Germany*, pp. 399–400; Kuznets, *Modern Economic Growth*, pp. 236–37.

them into business, and into business they are put. Joint-stock enterprise has swept up all these available resources. Like a gigantic system of irrigation it first collects together all the reserved savings of the community and then pours them through innumerable conduit pipes right over the face of the country, making capital accessible in every form at every point." The Viennese satirist Daniel Spitzer was less enthusiastic in his assessment of the consequences of free incorporation. He spoke bitterly about "joint-stock companies . . . founded to ship the aurora borealis in underground pipes to St. Stephen's Square, and to win new market outlets for our boot polish among the South Sea Islanders." His tone reflected the disillusionment of those countless thousands whose hopes of easy riches had turned sour.

For the combination of great expectations and great risks proved too much for most business ventures during the early chaotic years of the financial revolution. About a third of the 20,500 British companies registered between 1856 and 1883 were small or abortive. Of the other two-thirds, 17 percent were eventually sold, amalgamated, or reconstructed; 28 percent were forced into insolvency; 32 percent closed their doors voluntarily; and 11 percent simply disappeared. Some 33 percent of the companies lasted less than five years, and 50 percent less than ten. But the initial phase of boom-and-bust speculation gradually gave way to a more regular flow of credit controlled by large corporations and by investment banks organized on the joint-stock principle. The gambling promoters willing to take big chances in order to make big profits were replaced by calculating financiers to whom stability meant more than opportunity. Entrepreneurship became formalized and institutionalized, leaving less room for the small independent businessman operating on a hunch and a shoestring. About 10 percent of the German joint-stock companies early in the twentieth century were financial institutions, another 10 percent were engineering concerns, almost 10 percent were in transportation, 6 percent in coal and iron, and 18 percent in the food and drink trades, mainly breweries. Their average capitalization was nearly 3.3 million marks. Large business enterprises, in alliance with banks, which were providing more than half the capital for net domestic investment, helped to stabilize and regularize the availability of credit.[22]

Whenever the opportunity for profitable lending at home diminished, the money markets of Europe would seek outlets abroad. Throughout

22. George Joachim Goschen, *Essays and Addresses on Economic Questions (1865–1893)* (London, 1905), pp. 199–200; Daniel Spitzer, *Wiener Spaziergänge: Dritte Sammlung* (Vienna, 1877), p. 25; Heaton, *Economic History*, pp. 593–94; Clapham, *Economic Development of France and Germany*, p. 399; Walther G. Hoffmann, Franz Grumbach, and Helmut Hesse, *Das Wachstum der deutschen Wirtschaft seit der Mitte des 19. Jahrhunderts* (Berlin, Heidelberg, and New York, 1965), p. 813.

the nineteenth century, the leaders in the race for economic development, especially the United Kingdom, extended loans to laggard countries on the Continent and overseas. As early as the 1830s, Nathan Mayer Rothschild declared that England "is, in general, the Bank for the whole world —I mean, that all the transactions in India,—in China,—in Germany,— in Russia,—and in the whole world,--are all guided here and settled through this country." Between 1815 and 1830 the British invested at least 243 million dollars in the securities of various European governments, 97 million in one form or another in Latin America, and around 25 million in the United States. In France net cumulative capital exports amounted to 10 million dollars in 1830, 371 million in 1847, and 468 million in 1851.

But this flow of credit abroad had to compete with a strong domestic demand for capital. Around the mid-century an English financial periodical maintained that "so long as there is a bog to drain, a fertile mountain side to cultivate, a shoal of fish to gather at home . . . the Government of England ought not to suffer a pound of British capital to be lent to foreign states for the want of a market in London." The economist John Francis rejoiced that money that formerly "had been thrown into war loans" or "wasted on South American mines" was now "forming roads, employing labour, and increasing business" in Great Britain. Capital invested at home "was at least an absorption, [even] if unsuccessful, in the country which had produced it," and English railroads, "unlike foreign mines and foreign loans . . . could not be exhausted with the one or be utterly valueless with the other." During the heroic years of industrialization, the domestic appetite for credit remained large enough to consume the surplus wealth that the economy was generating.[23]

The export of capital began to mount rapidly, however, in the last decades of the nineteenth century, as the capacity of the financial system outstripped the growth of production and transportation. In England in particular foreign loans exerted a growing influence on the national economy. Investments abroad of a long-term or permanent nature, which had amounted to 116.3 million dollars annually in the period 1880–84, rose to 900.3 million annually in 1910–13. By 1914 the total foreign ownership of the British was about 19 billion dollars, more than a fourth of the national wealth. Money invested outside the country accounted for about 50 percent of net capital formation and for nearly 10 percent of the national income. It enabled Great Britain to retain a leading eco-

23. *Penny Magazine of the Society for the Diffusion of Useful Knowledge*, 20 May 1837, p. 185; Jenks, *Migration of British Capital*, p. 64; Cameron, *France and the Economic Development of Europe*, p. 79; *Circular to Bankers*, 22 November 1844, p. 173; John Francis, *A History of the English Railway; Its Social Relations and Revelations, 1820–1845*, 2 vols. (London, 1851), 2:136–37.

nomic position in the world despite a declining rate of industrial growth. But it also made her financial stability dependent on circumstances in distant parts of the globe over which she exercised a diminishing control.

Conditions across the English Channel were in most respects comparable. Even in the early decades of the nineteenth century, France had been an exporter of capital, but the sluggish domestic economy of the Third Republic transformed a brook into a torrent. Memories of the Crédit Mobilier and the Panama Company made the French investor suspicious of risky undertakings in industry or transportation. The longing of the petty bourgeoisie for the safe and predictable income of a rentier inhibited the formation of venture capital. Why sink money in dubious projects at home, when there were handsome profits to be made in foreign loans? "The same capital which will produce 3 or 4 percent in agricultural improvements on the soil of France," wrote the economist Paul Leroy-Beaulieu in 1882, "will bring 10, 15, 20 percent in an agricultural enterprise in the United States, Canada, La Plata, Australia, or New Zealand." Investors therefore sought their opportunities abroad, especially in the government bonds of other nations. By 1914 some 9 billion dollars had been exported, representing 15 percent of the national wealth and providing almost 6 percent of the national income. There was tragic irony in the fact that their obsession with security led the French to put so much of their money into the least secure investments of all, long-term loans to Russia, Austria, Turkey, and the Balkan states.

Germany, on the other hand, demonstrated that vigorous industrial expansion at home was the best defense against an excessive reliance on investments abroad. The average annual increase in exported capital during the twenty years preceding the First World War was about 143 million dollars, a rate of growth no larger than that of the economy as a whole. German foreign ownership totaled 1 billion dollars in 1883, 2 to 3 billion in 1893, about 4 billion in 1905, and 5 to 6 billion in 1914. During the last prewar decade, less than 6 percent of net capital formation was leaving the country, and only 3 percent of the national income was derived from foreign investments. Since such investments represented at most some 7 percent of the total wealth, the economy remained largely immune to the financial vicissitudes of borrowers abroad. Equally fortunate were the secondary exporters of capital: Switzerland with a total of around 1.5 billion dollars in 1914, the Netherlands with 1.0 billion, and Belgium with 0.5 billion. The limited volume of their surplus capital protected them against the dangers to which England and France were becoming exposed.[24]

24. Herbert Feis, *Europe, the World's Banker, 1870–1914: An Account of European Foreign Investment and the Connection of World Finance with Diplomacy before the War*

All in all, foreign investments at the outbreak of the First World War amounted to 45.5 billion dollars, of which the United Kingdom owned 44 percent, France 20, Germany 13, the United States 8, Switzerland, Belgium, and the Netherlands together 11, and other countries, primarily Russia, Japan, Portugal, and Sweden, 4. The destination of capital exports varied from lender to lender (see table 1.4). The British directed almost half of their loans to their dominions and colonies, with Canada, Australia and New Zealand, South Africa, and India and Ceylon far in the lead, followed by Latin America and the United States. The countries of Europe received only 6 percent, and the rest of the world 7. The French, on the other hand, for political as well as economic reasons, invested most of their capital exports in Europe, with Russia getting the lion's share. As for the Germans, they also favored Europe in their lending, allocating 53 percent of their loans to neighbors on the Continent and across the North Sea.

The results of European control over the financial system of the world were mixed. Motivated primarily by a quest for profit, it was unable to respond to humanitarian considerations. For most of mankind, therefore, loans from London, Paris, or Berlin had little direct impact. Asia and Africa, with 65 percent of the world's population, received only 25 percent of total foreign investments. But Europe with 26 percent of the world's population, North America with 5, and Latin America with 4 received 26, 24, and 20 percent respectively. Even the nations fortunate enough to obtain substantial capital from abroad often found the strain of modernization almost as great as the burden of backwardness. As an illustration, the average per capita tax in Greece more than doubled between 1875 and 1893, yet the national debt more than tripled, consuming a third of the government's budgetary receipts.

The risks were especially great for countries with political or military ambitions out of proportion to their material resources and potentialities. There were others, however, like Canada, New Zealand, Sweden, and Denmark, where imported capital made an important contribution to economic development. The rapid industrialization of Russia after 1890, to give another example, would have been impossible without the steady influx of loans. Even regions receiving the smallest share of European investments or paying the highest price for them were exposed to new concepts of technology and entrepreneurship. Borrowed money often stimulated the expansion of production or financed essential public works.

(New Haven, 1930), pp. 11, 14–16, 47–48, 71–72; Landes, *Unbound Prometheus*, p. 331; Paul Leroy-Beaulieu, *De la colonisation chez les peuples modernes*, 2d ed. (Paris, 1882), p. 537; Oron J. Hale, *The Great Illusion, 1900–1914* (New York, Evanston, and London, 1971), pp. 75–76.

Table 1.4. Foreign Investments of Great Britain, France, and
Germany, 1914

Recipients	Great Britain	France	Germany
	(percentage)		
Europe			
Great Britain			{6}
France	.2		
Germany	.2		
Russia	2.9	25	8
Austria-Hungary	.2	5	13
Italy	.3	3	
Spain and Portugal	.7	9	7
Balkan Countries	.5	6	7
Turkey	.6	7	8
Rest of Europe	.8	7	5
Total Europe	6	61	53
British Empire	34		
Canada	14	{4}	{16}
United States	20		
Latin America	20	13	16
French Empire		9	
Africa	{6}	7	9
Asia		5	4
Other			2

SOURCE: Herbert Feis, *Europe, the World's Banker, 1870–1914: An Account of European Foreign Investment and the Connection of World Finance with Diplomacy before the War* (New Haven, 1930), pp. 23, 51, 74.
NOTE: Asian and African figures reported for Great Britain and France exclude their colonies, but those for Germany include them. The French figure for Canada and the United States also includes Australia.

Only 10 percent of British capital exports, for instance, were used for the exploitation of mineral resources and raw materials, a form of investing least beneficial to the recipient country, whereas 40 percent went into railroads, 30 into state or municipal securities, 15 into industry, finance, and commerce, and 5 into utilities. The effect of foreign investment by Europeans on the rest of the world was thus neither clear-cut nor one-sided.[25]

25. William Woodruff, *Impact of Western Man: A Study of Europe's Role in the World Economy, 1750–1960* (New York, 1967), pp. 103, 154–55; Feis, *Europe, the World's*

There could be little doubt, however, about its effect on the Europeans themselves. It enabled them to retain a position of economic supremacy even after their lead in the production of goods began to diminish. The steady inflow of returns on capital sent abroad helped to counterbalance a declining share of total output among the pioneers of the industrial revolution. By 1914 the nations of Europe no longer regarded the future with the same serene confidence as they had a generation or two earlier, but they could still find reassurance and satisfaction in the enormous material accomplishments of the nineteenth century. In the course of only a lifetime, they had seen the economy grow from the artisan shop to the mechanized factory; from the dray horse, the stagecoach, and the sailing vessel to the railroad, the automobile, and the steamship; from the semaphore and the carrier pigeon to the telegraph, the telephone, and the wireless; from the family firm to the joint-stock company; from the private moneylender to the giant investment bank. Contemplating this extraordinary transformation, they could share the wonderment of the Italian publicist who had exclaimed, upon beholding a new factory in 1842: "Our age does not [lack] either poetry or monuments. . . . What could signify better that God has chosen [man] as the first and most beloved among his creatures? What could signify better that his origins are divine?" The achievements of economic rationalization still appeared miraculous, inspiring religious awe in an age of growing materialism.[26]

Banker, pp. 22–24, 27, 50–51, 74; L. S. Stavrianos, "The Influence of the West on the Balkans," in *The Balkans in Transition: Essays on the Development of Balkan Life and Politics since the Eighteenth Century*, ed. Charles and Barbara Jelavich (Berkeley and Los Angeles, 1963), p. 203; John H. Dunning, "Capital Movements in the 20th Century," *Lloyds Bank Review*, no. 72 (1964), pp. 18–19.

26. A. Sagredo, "Fabbrica di panni a feltro della ragione Reali, Bonfil e Comp., in Venezia; fondamenta San Girolamo," *Annali universali di statistica, economia pubblica, storia, viaggi e commercio*, 71 (1842):211–12.

2

THE TRANSFORMATION OF AGRICULTURE

The vast increase in the output of manufactured products during the nineteenth century would have been impossible without a parallel increase in the output of farm commodities. How else could a growing proportion of the European population find employment in mines, factories, railroads, shops, and banks, without creating a disastrous shortage of food? The peasant masses had traditionally practiced subsistence farming, growing only enough to feed themselves, to satisfy their manorial obligations, and to pay for those few essentials that they could not produce themselves. Their emphasis was on self-reliance and self-sufficiency. There was a national and even international trade in agricultural goods, but its volume was limited by the fact that the rural labor force consumed the great bulk of what it raised. Such subsistence farming left little surplus for other groups in society: the landed aristocracy; the court, bureaucracy, army, and clergy; and the small urban population of artisans, shopkeepers, merchants, little businessmen, and petty financiers. The transformation of this primitive system of husbandry into a rationalized agrarian economy represented a revolution as profound as that in industry, commerce, or banking.

The first step in this revolution was a change not in the utilization of the land but in the form of its ownership. The concept of agrarian property, which Europe had inherited from the Middle Ages, was appropriate to a society of hereditary castes resting on a static rural economy. Both nobleman and peasant had rights to the soil from which they derived their livelihood, rights that generally also involved obligations. Although a great disparity existed in the benefits that they derived from their respective social and legal positions, each had claims to ownership legitimized by law or tradition. There was a complex of manorial dues, payable in money, kind, or service, that the rustic owed the lord. But the lord in turn could not as a rule withhold from the rustic his heritable tenure or deny him use of the village meadowlands and woodlands, wastes and commons.

Jerome Blum has estimated that "in 1770 about two-thirds of the population of Europe, or about 100 million people, lived in lands in which [society denied the peasants] certain freedoms and privileges enjoyed by those who belonged to higher orders, and compelled them to be dependent upon and subservient to persons of the higher estates. The degree of their subservience and the extent of their dependence formed a spectrum that ranged from light but often bitterly resented restrictions and impositions in western European lands to a serfdom that was scarcely distinguishable from slavery in some of the lands of eastern Europe." This servile status of the rural population and the intricate structure of joint property rights associated with it had to be replaced by a free labor force and an unencumbered ownership, before economic rationalization could produce the same results in farming as in manufacturing. A basic change in the control and distribution of land was thus an essential element in the revolution that European agriculture underwent during the nineteenth century.[1]

In some countries, to be sure, the rural economy emerged from manorialism much earlier. Wherever husbandry ceased to be the major source of wealth, landowners generally proved willing to transform their seigneurial dues into redeemable quitrents, making possible a free and propertied peasantry. This was the result, for instance, of the growing importance of manufacture in Belgium, commerce in Holland, or fishing and shipping in Norway. Switzerland, on the other hand, originated in the resistance of independent farmers against an alien feudal aristocracy. Thus the development of a vigorous city or village patriciate led to a diminution in the political and economic authority exercised by the nobility.

The teachings of the Enlightenment, with their emphasis on a just social order and the betterment of mankind, further strengthened the movement for a reform of agriculture. Benevolent rulers began to recognize the need to end the servile status of the rural population, thereby making possible a more efficient form of husbandry. The duke of Savoy ordered the emancipation of the peasants in 1771, as did the margrave of Baden in 1783 and the king of Denmark in 1788. But it was the French Revolution that demonstrated most dramatically that the only alternative to a voluntary transformation of landholding was rebellion. The overthrow of manorialism in 1789 set an example that was followed during the next twenty-five years in many states of Europe allied with or subjugated by France. The defeat of Napoleon reduced the pressure for reform, but it could not preserve the old agrarian order. Philanthropy, expediency, and self-interest combined to complete the process of peasant emancipation in the 1860s with the promulgation of important rural legislation in Russia and Rumania.

Although the transformation of a collective into an individualized form of landed property occurred everywhere in Europe, the resultant distribution of holdings varied considerably from country to country. Two

1. Jerome Blum, "The Condition of the European Peasantry on the Eve of Emancipation," *Journal of Modern History* 46 (1974):395.

distinct forms of agrarian ownership emerged, separated roughly by a huge semicircle extending from the North Sea along the Elbe and the Alps to the Pyrenees. To the west and north of this line the small peasant farm predominated, the major exception being the United Kingdom. On the other side, the decisive role in agriculture belonged to large estates owned by noblemen whose position was sometimes that of absentee landlords, sometimes that of gentlemen-farmers. In the states of south Germany, for example, the Restoration witnessed the gradual commutation of manorial obligations to rents redeemable by a lump payment, while the aristocracy withdrew to the court, the bureaucracy, and the army, or to the spa and the casino. The northeast, on the other hand, remained the country of Junker estates that were cultivated by a free labor force but were owned by a nobility whose political and economic control of the village had not been diminished by peasant emancipation. Indeed, throughout the region of the latifundia, primarily Prussia, Russia, Austria-Hungary, southern Italy, and many parts of Spain, the modernization of agriculture failed to end the traditional dominance of the aristocratic landowner over the countryside.

It was here also that rural reform encountered the most bitter resistance. The proprietors of large estates not only objected to the loss of dues and services but feared the hopes and expectations that even minor concessions would arouse among the peasant masses. They distrusted the rustic, however loyal, subservient, or meek he might appear. In 1813 the authorities of Austrian Silesia, reflecting the views of the nobility, declared that "it does not seem desirable, and indeed it might have the most serious consequences for the public welfare, to make the lowest class of the population independent of the educated class of people through the redemption of [labor services], especially since the cultivation of the mind of the peasants neither can nor will reach that level which is required so that they will not make wrong use of complete independence, once they get it." Nicholas I of Russia was informed in 1845 by one of his advisers that most aristocrats "dread [the changes likely to result from peasant emancipation] which every sensible person, knowing the common people and their inclinations, ought to dread." The attitude of the great landowners, whether the Junkers in Prussia, the magnates in Hungary, or the *dvoriane* in Russia, was everywhere the same. They were afraid that the peasantry, once freed from personal servitude and manorial obligation, would reject the entire system of political and social authority in the countryside.[2]

2. Ibid., pp. 395–96; Alfred Stern, *Geschichte Europas seit den Verträgen von 1815 bis zum Frankfurter Frieden von 1871*, 10 vols. (Berlin and Stuttgart, 1894–1924), 1:270; Jerome Blum, *Lord and Peasant in Russia from the Ninth to the Nineteenth Century* (Princeton, 1961), p. 574.

Yet despite its distrust of the rural masses, the nobility gradually became reconciled to the abolition of serfdom and manorialism. There were two primary considerations that helped overcome its fear of peasant emancipation. The first was the recognition that a servile labor force and a collective form of landholding were incompatible with an efficient system of specialized farming. The old order had been appropriate to a static rural economy in which sufficiency was more important than efficiency. But the growing demand for agricultural commodities generated by the spread of industrialism exerted heavy pressure for the modernization of food production. In Russia, Minister of the Interior L. A. Perovsky reported around the mid-century that many noblemen "are beginning to understand that the peasants are a burden to them, and that it would be desirable to change relationships which are disadvantageous to both sides." Since they were now convinced, he explained, that free hired labor would prove more profitable than the system of manorial obligations, they "no longer fear that the abolition of serfdom will ruin them." The economic advantages of agricultural reform thus helped persuade most landed aristocrats to accept peasant emancipation, provided it did not threaten their political and social domination of rural society.

The other reason for their acquiescence was the fear that the only choice before them was reform or rebellion, that what they did not concede voluntarily would be taken from them by force. They were haunted by visions of the "great fear" of 1789 in France and of the March days of 1848 in Germany. There were constant reminders, moreover, that what had happened once could happen again. Outbreaks of peasant unrest in Russia totaled 148 in 1826–34, 216 in 1835–44, 348 in 1845–54, and 474 in 1855–61. Many conservative bureaucrats, therefore, began to support a revolution from above to forestall one from below. Especially in times of crisis, after losses on the battlefield had shaken public confidence in the state, there were urgent warnings that the alternatives now were peaceful change or mass violence. In 1807, soon after the Treaty of Tilsit, for example, Karl August von Hardenberg, who had just resigned as prime minister of Prussia, tried to persuade Frederick William III that "a revolution in the good sense, leading directly to the great purpose of ennobling mankind through the wisdom of government and not through violent impulses from within or without, that is our goal and our guiding principle." At the same time, Karl vom Stein zum Altenstein, Prussian councillor for financial affairs, was arguing that "the state itself should bring about a domestic revolution. Then all the salutary effects of such a revolution would follow without the painful convulsions which are connected with one occurring arbitrarily." A sense of necessity finally led the government to emancipate the peasantry a few weeks later.

In Russia the road to rural reform was similar. As early as 1839, A. K.

Benckendorff, chief of the secret police, had reported to the czar: "The entire soul of the people turns to one goal, to liberation. . . . Serfdom is a powder barrel under the state, and is all the more to be feared because the army is made up of peasants." His conclusion was that "it is necessary to start somehow, and it is better to start gradually and cautiously rather than wait until things should be set in motion from below, that is, from the people." But the government failed to act on this advice, weighing the pros and cons, pondering, agonizing, and procrastinating. Only after the Crimean War did Alexander II decide at last to liberate the peasants, sounding a familiar note in his famous speech of 11 April 1856 to the representatives of the Moscow nobility: "All of you understand that the existing conditions of owning souls cannot remain unchanged. It is better to begin to destroy serfdom from above, than to wait until that time when it begins to destroy itself from below." Abolition of the personal servitude of the village population followed in the next decade, a direct result of military defeat, for the effect of Sevastopol on rural reform in Russia was the same as that of Jena in Prussia.[3]

The men responsible for peasant emancipation in the region of the latifundia, however, were themselves members of the landed nobility whose economic position depended on the form that the modernization of agriculture assumed. They saw to it that the elimination of serfdom and manorialism changed only the appearance, not the substance, of aristocratic domination of village life. As long as the large estates remained intact, they had little to fear from the freedom acquired by the rural masses. Indeed, the new system of unencumbered proprietorship made it possible for a well-to-do landowner to enlarge his holdings at the expense of the independent farmer. In the period after emancipation, for example, the latifundia of eastern Prussia acquired about 420,000 hectares of peasant land in compensation for the loss of manorial rights, 200,000 more through purchase, and 300,000 to 500,000 by the absorption of abandoned farms and plots. All in all, close to 1 million hectares or 10 percent of the total area owned by small proprietors passed into the hands of owners of large estates as a result of rural reform. The peasants of Russia were more fortunate. In the course of the fifty years following the abolition of serfdom, they managed through purchase to increase the land in their possession by some 15 percent. Yet at the outbreak of the First World War, about thirty thousand landlords still owned nearly 77

3. Georges Weill, *L'éveil des nationalités et le mouvement libéral (1815–1848)* (Paris, 1930), p. 396; Blum, *Lord and Peasant in Russia*, pp. 547, 557–58, 574, 578; *Denkwürdigkeiten des Staatskanzlers Fürsten von Hardenberg*, ed. Leopold von Ranke, 5 vols. (Leipzig, 1877), 4:116–17, 8*; Alexander Gerschenkron, "Agrarian Policies and Industrialization: Russia, 1861–1917," in *The Cambridge Economic History of Europe*, 7 vols. (Cambridge, 1941–78), 6:709.

million hectares, while 10.5 million small proprietors owned only 82 million, and a third of the peasantry was completely landless. By and large, wherever the latifundia survived the period of peasant emancipation, they continued to dominate agriculture under the new order as completely as they had under the old.[4]

The boundary between the region of large estates and small farms separated not only two distinct landowning systems but two distinct political systems as well. For there was a close connection between the form of agriculture and the form of government, the structure of one helping to shape the ideology of the other. The prevalence of small peasant proprietors generally meant an emphasis in politics on individualism, competitiveness, and the equality of opportunity. The ideal instrument of authority for the independent farmer was a constitutional monarchy, although he could also learn to accept a middle-of-the-road republic, as happened in France after 1870. To him the important thing was a regime that resisted the radical demands of the urban petty bourgeoisie or working class but that also rejected the claims and the pretensions of the aristocracy.

Where the great landowners retained their estates, on the other hand, they were able, except in the case of the United Kingdom, to insure the preservation of an authoritarian system of government. Not only was this true of Russia, where the nobility successfully opposed the introduction of a constitution until 1905, but also of Prussia and Austria-Hungary, where the landed aristocracy continued to dominate the countryside, although national legislatures had been established much earlier. The conservative strongholds on election day were always the villages, in which noble landowners exerted a powerful influence over school, church, police, and administration. The peasants learned early that submission was the best way to survive, so that the acceptance of established authority became a tradition with them. They bowed, cap in hand, to the wishes of the grand seigneur; they professed the loyalties he extolled; they accepted the values he preached; and they voted as he told them to. They became in body and spirit obedient tools of the status quo.

The important role that the peasantry played in the maintenance of authoritarian government accounts for the idealization in conservative circles of the attitudes and values of village life. What the force of circumstances extorted from the rural masses came to be portrayed as the spontaneous expression of a peasant psychology shaped by close com-

4. Friedrich Lütge, *Deutsche Sozial- und Wirtschaftsgeschichte*, 3d ed. (Berlin, Heidelberg, and New York, 1966), pp. 443–44; Gerschenkron, "Agrarian Policies and Industrialization," p. 776; Isaac Deutscher, "The Russian Revolution," in *The New Cambridge Modern History*, 12 vols. (Cambridge, 1960–70), 12:387.

munion with the land. The German sociologist Wilhelm Heinrich Riehl wrote around the mid-century: "The man of education may be inclined toward conservatism by his understanding, but the peasant is conservative as a matter of habit," forming "a natural barrier against the growth of French revolutionary doctrines among the lower classes of society." He expressed faith in "the essential character of the German countryman," maintaining that "in our fatherland the peasant exercises a political influence which he enjoys in no other country of Europe." His analysis concluded on a note of homage to the spirit of the village: "The peasant is the future of the German nation. The life of our people can be inwardly refreshed and rejuvenated only through the peasantry."

Other observers writing at the same time presented a less idyllic picture of rural life amid the latifundia. To the American agriculturist Henry Colman, the position of the landless farm laborers was hopeless and tragic:

> It is obvious that no great improvement can take place in the character and condition of the [agricultural] labouring population while they remain a distinct and servile class without any power of rising above their condition. At present the most imaginative and sanguine see no probability of their rising above their condition, of being anything but labourers, or of belonging to any other than a servile and dependant class. The low state of their wages absolutely forbids the accumulation of any property. They cannot own any of the soil which they cultivate. The houses which they occupy belong not to themselves, and they may at any time be turned out of them. They must ask leave to live, or they must take it by violence or plunder when they will not be suffered to live. Their only home is the grave, and even their repose here is not always secure. . . . They are not slaves; but they are not free. Liberty and independence, to them, are words without meaning. They have no chains upon their hands, but the iron enters into their souls. Their limbs may be unshackled, but their spirits are bound. . . . The large establishments have lost that patriarchal character which used to belong to them; men are employed much more by the day, and the week, than by the year, as formerly; and are used, and thrown aside, as occasion may require, like mere implements upon the farm.[5]

Not all peasants in eastern and southern Europe were propertyless agricultural workers. Many had plots and patches of land, and some even

5. W. H. Riehl, *Die bürgerliche Gesellschaft* (Stuttgart and Tübingen, 1851), pp. 33–34; Henry Colman, *European Agriculture and Rural Economy, From Personal Observation*, 2 vols. (London and Boston, 1844–46), 1:63–64, 66, 140.

owned farms large enough to support them in modest comfort. But the prevailing form of landownership left the rural population exposed to the political, economic, and social domination of the latifundia.

In the region of the small farms, on the other hand, a different distribution of landed property sustained a different system of government. In France, the classic country of peasant proprietorship, the man who tilled the soil was also likely to be its owner. Although there was a large class of sharecroppers, their importance was slowly declining. At the time of the Second Empire, they were still cultivating more than half of the land, but on the eve of the First World War, farmers working on their own property accounted for about 60 percent of the area and 75 percent of the labor force in agriculture. Although detailed statistics for most of the nineteenth century are unavailable, very small and very large holdings diminished between 1892 and 1908, whereas middle-sized and large holdings rose (see table 2.1). Between 1862 and 1908, moreover, the number of properties between one and ten hectares increased 4 percent, those in the ten to forty range increased 17, and those over forty decreased 5. The figures are not altogether reliable, so that generalizations should be made with caution. They do suggest, however, a highly stable pattern of landownership in which the proprietors of medium farms were not only holding their own but were expanding slowly at the expense of their less fortunate neighbors. It was this independent peasantry that provided the main support for the politics of prudent moderation characteristic of the Third Republic.

The situation in Belgium was similar, although the higher density of

Table 2.1. Distribution of Landed Property in France, 1892–1908

Size of Holding (hectares)	1892		1908	
	Number (thousands)	Percentage	Number (thousands)	Percentage
Less than 1	2,235	39	2,088	38
1 to 10	2,618	46	2,524	46
10 to 40	711	12	746	14
40 to 100	105	1.8	118	2.1
More than 100	33	0.6	29	0.5
Total	5,702	100	5,505	100

SOURCE: J. H. Clapham, *The Economic Development of France and Germany, 1815–1914*, 4th ed. (Cambridge, 1966), p. 165.

population meant that the average farm was considerably smaller than in France. The total number of agricultural holdings increased by 45 percent in the period 1846–95, from 572,500 to 829,625, with most of the growth occurring in the category of small properties of less than two hectares. They rose from 400,514 or 70 percent of the total to 634,353 or 76 percent. The next category of properties, those between two and ten hectares, grew in number from 126,120 to 150,586 but declined in percentage from 22 to 18. Middle-sized farms between ten and fifty hectares remained almost stationary during the entire period, with 41,583 at the beginning and 41,102 at the end, although their share of all properties dropped from 7 to 5 percent. The only substantial decline occurred in the category of large holdings of over fifty hectares, which went from 4,333 or 0.8 percent to 3,584 or 0.4 percent. It is clear that small independent proprietors played the leading role in Belgian agriculture, and their economic preponderance meant in turn political backing for the middle-of-the-road constitutional monarchism personified by the two Leopolds.

The weakness of the system of peasant landownership, however, was its inefficiency. In France the average holding during the early 1880s was 8.7 hectares divided among twenty-two separate parcels of land. In Belgium at the same time, 95 percent of all properties were under ten hectares, so that a highly intensive system of cultivation was needed to provide more than subsistence farming. In general, immobility of ownership combined with smallness of operation to inhibit innovation and venturesomeness among the peasantry of Western and Northern Europe.[6]

In Germany the two forms of rural proprietorship, large estate and small farm, met face to face, each helping to mold the political and social traditions of the region in which it predominated. The Elbe River formed a rough boundary between them, although each had exclaves on the other side. The pattern of landownership on the left bank was similar to that prevailing among the French and Belgians (see figure 2.1). The connection between the structure of agriculture and the structure of politics was clearly discernible in this country of independent peasant proprietors. In Baden 88 percent of all holdings were under twenty hectares, in Hesse-Darmstadt the percentage was 85, in Württemberg 80, in the Rhineland 77, and in Alsace-Lorraine 74. Those were precisely the parts of the German Empire in which liberal ideals and institutions found the most receptive environment.

6. Robert C. Binkley, *Realism and Nationalism, 1852–1871* (New York and London, 1935), p. 78; Oron J. Hale, *The Great Illusion, 1900–1914* (New York, Evanston, and London, 1971), p. 37; J. H. Clapham, *The Economic Development of France and Germany, 1815–1914*, 4th ed. (Cambridge, 1966), pp. 165–66; Norman Scott Brien Gras, *A History of Agriculture in Europe and America*, 2d ed. (New York, 1946), pp. 194, 206; Robert Trow-Smith, *Life from the Land: The Growth of Farming in Western Europe* (London, 1967), p. 159.

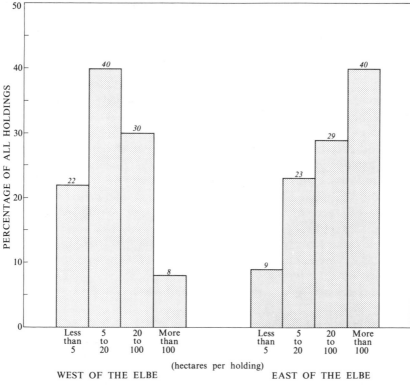

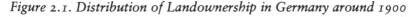

Figure 2.1. Distribution of Landownership in Germany around 1900

SOURCE: Herbert Heaton, *Economic History of Europe* (New York and London, 1936), p. 460.

The situation on the right bank was quite different. This was the classic land of Junker estates. The concentration of landownership, moreover, was highest in those regions where the Junkers exercised the strongest political influence and where the rustics cast the largest number of conservative ballots on election day. In the province of East Prussia 76 percent of all holdings were over twenty hectares, in Pomerania the percentage was 75, in West Prussia 69, in Brandenburg 68, in Posen 66, in the province of Saxony 60, and in Silesia 53. But the most extreme example of aristocratic control of agriculture and politics could be found in the semifeudal Mecklenburgs, where 26 percent of all holdings were between twenty and one hundred hectares and 60 percent were over one hundred. Here the Junker was king.

Large estates could afford the cost of economic rationalization that was beyond the capacity of the small farm. They pioneered in the adoption of improved methods of tillage, the more efficient use of farm labor, the diversification of output through the manufacture of alcohol or sugar, and the adjustment of production to an international market. But the emergence of a capitalistic form of farming also exposed them to the vicissitudes of a business economy. Noble landowners became agricultural entrepreneurs, facing the same risks as industrialists and financiers. Sometimes they were successful, but many succumbed in the unrelenting struggle of competitive farming. Growing indebtedness was a measure of their effort to survive under a system of free enterprise in which land was just another commodity to be bought and sold in the open marketplace. Loans extended by the mortgage banks that the government had established in Prussia rose from 188 million marks in 1815 to 303 million in 1835 and 355 million in 1855. Between 1835 and 1864 there was a turnover of 134 percent in the ownership of 11,771 Prussian latifundia: 14,404 sales and 1,347 foreclosures. By 1885 only 154 or 13 percent of the large estates in the province of East Prussia had been in the possession of the same family for more than fifty years. The price of economic rationalization in farming, as in manufacturing, was an unrestrained competitiveness in which the strong could batten on the weak and unsuccessful.[7]

In Russia the establishment of a system of free agriculture gave rise to even greater social and economic tension. As a result of emancipation, the peasant obtained a share of the land which, when compared with other countries where latifundia predominated, was not inconsiderable. The average family allotment on the lower Volga was thirty-four to thirty-six hectares, in the black-soil region sixteen, and west of the Dnieper between nine and ten. About half of the liberated serfs who were given property received over three hectares. There were two factors, however, that made it difficult for the Russian peasant to eke out a living on a small holding that would have been adequate in Western or Central Europe. First of all, the rural population increased between 1867 and 1898 from some 56 million to more than 80 million, an annual rate of 1.2 percent that added up to an overall growth of 43 percent. Second, agricultural methods were so backward that productivity remained disappointingly low in comparison with other countries on the Continent. According to the census of 1910, about 10 million wooden ploughs and

7. Herbert Heaton, *Economic History of Europe* (New York and London, 1936), p. 460; Werner Sombart, *Die deutsche Volkswirtschaft im neunzehnten Jahrhundert und im Anfang des 20. Jahrhunderts*, 4th ed. (Berlin, 1923), pp. 514–15, 520; Theodore S. Hamerow, *Restoration, Revolution, Reaction: Economics and Politics in Germany, 1815–1871* (Princeton, 1958), pp. 225–26; David S. Landes, *The Unbound Prometheus: Technological Change and Industrial Development in Western Europe from 1750 to the Present* (Cambridge, 1969), pp. 155–56.

hoes and 25 million wooden harrows were still in use, as opposed to 4.2 million iron plows and less than 0.5 million iron harrows. Agricultural machinery was virtually unknown, at least 33 percent of the farmsteads had no implements, and 30 percent owned no cattle. The average yield of grain per hectare was half of that in France and only a third of that in Germany. That was why during the 1870s a rural household in the black-soil region needed about five hectares per member to produce bread for the family and fodder for the animals, while on less fertile land nine hectares were required for mere subsistence. The villagers sought to compensate for overpopulation and technological backwardness by purchasing or leasing land from the aristocracy, but they never succeeded in raising the average size of their holdings to the level of the years immediately following emancipation.

For the noblemen of Russia, the emergence of a system of free agriculture created almost as many problems as for the peasants. Deprived of a servile labor force and confronted by the complexities of capitalistic farming, many lapsed into a bewildered helplessness. "Formerly we kept no accounts and drank champagne," a British observer heard one of them say. "Now we keep accounts and content ourselves with beer." But they could not even keep accounts very well. By 1877 they had to sell about 13 percent of their land, by 1887 close to 24, by 1897 some 35, and by 1905 almost 50. The property that they lost went partly to peasants but partly also to speculators who saw a chance of quick profit in buying up mortgaged estates and then leasing them in small lots to land-hungry villagers. Mme Ranevskaya in Chekhov's *Cherry Orchard* and her brother Leonid Andreevich represent the feckless Russian gentry at the opening of the twentieth century—charming, prodigal, and doomed. On the other hand, the successful real-estate operator Lopahin, the son of a serf, speaks for the rising class of agricultural capitalists who know how to seize the opportunities created by free enterprise in landownership. He is a nemesis that has come to exact retribution from the aristocracy for its exploitation of countless generations of peasants.[8]

Only in the British Isles did the prevalence of large estates fail to coincide with an authoritarian form of government. Yet there was little difference between the system of landownership in Russia and the United Kingdom. If anything, the estates of Great Britain made the transition from manorial to capitalistic agriculture more easily than those of the

8. Hale, *Great Illusion*, p. 47; Gerschenkron, "Agrarian Policies and Industrialization," pp. 742, 776–77; Deutscher, "Russian Revolution," p. 387; D. Mackenzie Wallace, *Russia* (New York, 1877), p. 517; Witt Bowden, Michael Karpovich, and Abbott Payson Usher, *An Economic History of Europe since 1750* (New York, 1937), p. 602; Folke Dovring, *Land and Labor in Europe in the Twentieth Century: A Comparative Survey of Recent Agrarian History*, 3d ed. (The Hague, 1965), p. 259.

Continent. It has been estimated that in 1700 there were 573,000 day laborers and 330,000 farmers in England, so that nearly two out of three rural families were landless. In 1831 there were 686,000 day laborers and 275,100 farmers, with almost three out of four rural families landless. About 400 peers and peeresses owned 17 percent of the total acreage, while some 1,300 other large landowners and 12,000 squires and greater yeomen held most of what was left. Early in the nineteenth century, the reformer William Cobbett portrayed the social consequences of this growing concentration of landownership:

> The taxing and funding . . . system has . . . drawn the real property of the nation into fewer hands; it has made land and agriculture objects of speculation; it has, in every part of the kingdom, moulded many farms into one; it has almost entirely extinguished the race of small farms; from one end of England to the other, the houses which formerly contained little farms and their happy families, are now sinking into ruins, all the windows except one or two stopped up, leaving just light enough for some labourer, whose father was, perhaps, the small farmer, to look back upon his half-naked and half-famished children, while, from his door, he surveys all around him the land teeming with the means of luxury to his opulent and overgrown master. . . . We are daily advancing to the state in which there are but two classes of men, *masters*, and *abject dependents*.[9]

Yet neither warnings nor appeals could halt the expansion of the latifundia. By the 1870s 13 percent of the total area of the English counties, excluding wasteland, belonged to holdings between 40 and 120 hectares, 14 percent to those between 120 and 400, 30 percent to those between 400 and 4,000, and 24 percent to those over 4,000. On the eve of the First World War, no more than 13 percent of the farms in England and Wales were the property of those who tilled them. Not even Russia, Prussia, or Austria-Hungary had a lower rate of peasant landownership.

The British patriciate, however, did not become a bulwark of authoritarianism. Although it dominated agriculture as completely as the grands seigneurs of eastern and southern Europe, land had ceased to be the major source of wealth in the United Kingdom long before the decline of its economic importance on the Continent. English noblemen had to reach an accommodation with commercial and industrial interests, an accommodation by which they agreed to share their civic and material hegemony. The result was that by the nineteenth century a coalition of

9. Trow-Smith, *Life from the Land*, p. 126; John Bateman, *The Great Landowners of Great Britain and Ireland*, 4th ed. (London, 1883), p. 515; *Cobbett's Weekly Political Register*, 15 March 1806, pp. 361–62.

aristocracy and bourgeoisie had emerged that favored an oligarchical government and a capitalistic economy, with rural and urban wealth having a joint predominance in the state. This process of class adaptation could also be seen elsewhere in the region of the latifundia, in Prussia, for example. But there it was only in its beginnings, whereas in the British Isles it had already become a fundamental reality of political and economic life.[10]

Changes in the European pattern of landownership were in part at least a result of changes in the system of farm production. The same techniques of economic rationalization that transformed the artisan shop into a factory could be applied to the soil, transforming a manorial into a capitalistic form of husbandry. An agricultural revolution took place comparable to the industrial revolution in procedure and objective. Its first achievement was the reorganization of landed property in such a way as to make possible a more efficient method of exploitation. This meant partly the utilization of soil that had hitherto lain fallow or untilled. The growth of manufacture and the improvement of transportation generated a new demand for foodstuffs and raw materials that encouraged the expansion of the area under cultivation. Studies of five large estates in Central Europe, three in the Harz region and two in Saxony, have shown that in the middle of the eighteenth century the percentage of arable land left fallow ranged from 5.7 to 71.0, the average being 28.2, whereas by the middle of the nineteenth century one estate had 2.8 percent fallow, another 0.8, and three had none. Between 1800 and 1900 the agricultural acreage of Germany increased from 55.5 percent of the total area to 64.8. The percentage of arable land, moreover, rose from 34.3 to 48.8, while pasturage declined from 10.2 to 5.0 and wasteland from 19.6 to 9.3. Many other countries, adopting the techniques of a rationalized agriculture, enlarged the acreage under cultivation. In France the area allotted to the main cereal and potato crops grew 12 percent during 1817–35, in the Netherlands 16 during 1852–72, in Sweden 32 during 1865–85, and in Hungary 19 during 1869–89.[11]

Even more important than the increase in arable land was its consolidation, that is, the transformation of a mosaic of plots, patches, com-

10. F. M. L. Thompson, *English Landed Society in the Nineteenth Century* (London and Toronto, 1963), pp. 32, 113, 117; Dovring, *Land and Labor in Europe*, p. 169; Bowden, Karpovich, and Usher, *Economic History of Europe*, p. 282.

11. B. H. Slicher van Bath, *The Agrarian History of Western Europe*, A.D. 500–1850 (London, 1963), p. 251; Walther G. Hoffmann, "The Take-off in Germany," in *The Economics of Take-off into Sustained Growth: Proceedings of a Conference Held by the International Economic Association*, ed. W. W. Rostow (London and New York, 1963), p. 102; B. R. Mitchell, *European Historical Statistics, 1750–1970* (London and Basingstoke, 1975), pp. 199, 205, 207, 209.

mons, pastures, woods, and wastes into compact farms or estates adapted to a system of capitalistic farming. In Prussia close to 16 million hectares were removed from common use between 1821 and 1870, mostly in the eastern provinces, thus helping to strengthen the economic position of the latifundia. An equally drastic process of land concentration occurred in England, where the enclosure movement had the effect of ending common rights, dividing open fields, and partitioning the wastes. In the period 1727–60, Parliament passed 56 acts enclosing 29,807 hectares of collectively held land, not including the open fields. In 1761–92 there were 339 acts involving 191,304 hectares; in 1793–1801, 182 acts involving 109,556 hectares; in 1802–15, 564 acts involving 295,897 hectares; and in 1816–45, 244 acts involving 79,720 hectares. Within the space of little more than a century, 1,385 legislative measures were adopted that consolidated a total of 706,284 hectares. The land enclosed by parliamentary enactment amounted to about 20 percent of the total area of England. The end of the manorial form of land tenure, however, was also accomplished in large part by informal procedures resulting in unrecorded enclosures. The upshot was that the common fields were divided among large holdings cultivated with farm machines or improved implements and were planted with new crops in new rotations.[12]

A second element in the agricultural revolution was the application of scientific knowledge, especially organic chemistry, to the raising of crops. The most important development in the science of farming came in 1840 with the publication by Justus Liebig of his *Chemistry in Its Application to Agriculture and Physiology*, which identified the mineral nutrients that plants require for growth. The new understanding of the natural process by which crops develop made it possible for agriculture to improve its methods of fertilization, raising the productivity of the soil without manures, fallows, leguminous plants, or rotating crops. The Germans in particular favored the intensive use of chemicals in farming. Between 1890 and 1911 they increased the consumption of lime and its mixtures from 50,000 to 70,000 tons, of phosphatic fertilizers from 999,000 to 3,128,000, of nitrogenous fertilizers from 354,000 to 884,000, and of potassium salts from 220,000 to 2,533,000. The growth of science helped to reduce the element of uncertainty in agriculture, making possible a more predictable level of production.

Those responsible for the new achievements in soil chemistry often

12. Herbert Heaton, "Economic Change and Growth," in *New Cambridge Modern History*, 10:24; Slicher van Bath, *Agrarian History of Western Europe*, p. 319; Bowden, Karpovich, and Usher, *Economic History of Europe*, pp. 149, 152; G. E. Fussell, "The Agricultural Revolution, 1600–1850," in *Technology in Western Civilization*, ed. Melvin Kranzberg and Carroll W. Pursell, Jr., 2 vols. (New York, London, and Toronto, 1967), 1:132.

recognized the social and political implications of what they were doing. Liebig himself was convinced that agriculture had greater importance for the welfare of mankind than culture or scholarship: "Everything which we do and accomplish, create and discover seems to me insignificant compared with what the farmer can produce. Our progress in art and science does not add to the conditions of human existence," he argued, "and even if a small fraction of human society gains in the spiritual and material enjoyment of life, the sum of misery among the broad masses remains the same. A hungry man does not go to church, and no child goes to school if he does not have a piece of bread. The progress of the farmer, on the other hand, alleviates the needs and cares of people, and makes them sensitive and receptive to the good and the beautiful."

The improvement of agriculture, however, could do more than elevate the lower classes esthetically and spiritually. It could also reduce social conflict and mitigate international strife. For "he who no longer finds a place at the table of society does not simply yield to starvation. As an individual he becomes a thief and murderer, or he emigrates in large masses, or he becomes a conqueror. Every page of world history shows the dreadful effect of this horrible law in the streams of blood with which man has had to water the soil he did not know how to keep fruitful." The improvement of husbandry would thus serve the moral purposes of society by satisfying its material needs.[13]

The final element in the agricultural revolution was the mechanization of farming, a process that most closely resembled what was happening in manufacture. In the second half of the eighteenth century, designs and patents to improve farmers' tools began to multiply. There were ploughs for drainage and trenching, threshing machines to replace the flail, chaff cutters to prepare straw for fodder, and a dynamometer to measure the movement of the share and moldboard through the soil. Early in the nineteenth century, engineers turned to the problem of mechanizing the harvest, their efforts culminating in Patrick Bell's reaper of 1828 in Great Britain and the more famous one designed by Cyrus McCormick in the United States in 1834. In 1841 the Royal Agricultural Society of England held a competitive trial for threshing machines, which had already reached a high level of technical efficiency. At a second trial in 1848, the threshing drums were driven by steam, and the following year the steam plough made its appearance. In the 1870s came the automatic twine binder, representing a considerable saving of labor, and the combination

13. Wayne D. Rasmussen, "Scientific Agriculture," in *Technology in Western Civilization*, ed. Kranzberg and Pursell, 2:348; Ashok V. Desai, *Real Wages in Germany, 1871–1913* (Oxford, 1968), p. 66; *Aus Justus Liebig's und Friedrich Wöhler's Briefwechsel in den Jahren 1829–1873*, ed. A. W. Hofmann, 2 vols. (Brunswick, 1888), 2:110; Theodor Heuss, *Justus von Liebig: Vom Genius der Forschung* (Hamburg, 1949), p. 65.

harvester, which in a single operation cut a swath of grain, threshed, cleaned, and sacked. Finally, at the beginning of the twentieth century, the internal-combustion tractor entered the market, making possible another major increase in the scale of production.

By then America had become the leader in mechanized agriculture, for the lands brought under cultivation west of the Mississippi were too vast to be farmed effectively by hand labor even with the aid of draft animals. The predominance of the New World in the production of agricultural implements can be measured by the rise of American exports of mowers and reapers, which amounted to 66,000 dollars in 1870, 654,000 in 1881, 2,093,000 in 1890, 11,244,000 in 1900, and 11,282,000 in 1910. It was an extraordinary rate of growth, the value multiplying 171 times in forty years.[14]

Germany led the Continent in the adoption of farm machinery as well as the consumption of chemical fertilizers. The use of laborsaving devices was most common on large estates and farms, which could afford the cost of agricultural machines. Of the holdings between twenty and one hundred hectares, 78.8 percent were mechanized in 1895 and 92.7 percent in 1907. But even in the case of middle-sized properties between five and twenty hectares, 45.8 percent employed machinery in 1895 and 72.8 percent in 1907. In France, on the other hand, the prevalence of small farms and a policy of agricultural protectionism inhibited the mechanization of husbandry. Although the country was using increasing quantities of artificial manure, especially after the discovery of the North African phosphates at the time of the French occupation of Tunisia, in 1892 only 1 holding in 14 had a horse hoe, 1 in 15 a threshing machine, 1 in 140 a drilling machine, and 1 in 150 a reaper.

This was a slow rate of technological development in agriculture, typical of countries with small peasant holdings. Between 1880 and 1910 the number of threshers in Belgium increased from 6,900 to 23,000, that of reapers from 1,500 to 19,000, and that of sowing machines from 1,800 to 12,000. In Norway there were 12,100 reapers in 1890, 31,500 in 1900, and 49,200 in 1907, while the figures for sowing machines in those same years were 2,350, 5,600, and 7,000. Increases on such a scale were substantial but not remarkable. Although all of Europe was gradually converted to the use of farm machinery, its growth was most rapid in countries that combined a high level of industrialization with an agricultural system based on large estates.[15]

14. Trow-Smith, *Life from the Land*, p. 148; Fussell, "Agricultural Revolution," pp. 135–36; William Woodruff, *Impact of Western Man: A Study of Europe's Role in the World Economy, 1750–1960* (New York, 1967), p. 202; Gras, *History of Agriculture*, p. 401, n. 29.

15. Sombart, *Die deutsche Volkswirtschaft*, p. 353; T. K. Derry and Trevor I. Williams,

A direct result of the agricultural revolution was a marked increase in the efficiency of the labor force engaged in husbandry. According to the estimates of Paul Bairoch, production per farm worker in England rose about 100 percent between 1700 and 1800. In France the final product per male farm worker increased 24 percent between 1751–60 and 1803–12, and another 38 percent between 1803–12 and 1855–64. In the period 1840–1900, agricultural productivity grew 30 percent in Russia, 45 in Austria, 50 in Belgium and Italy, 75 in Sweden, 90 in Switzerland, and 190 in Germany, an average of 75 percent and a combined annual rate of 0.9.

Werner Sombart has compiled statistics expressing this increase of farming efficiency in terms of the rising yield of husbandry. In France the average production of wheat per hectare amounted to 10.2 hectoliters in 1816–20, 11.9 in 1821–30, 13.9 in 1851–60, 14.6 in 1871–80, and 15.6 in 1891–95. In Belgium the rye crop per hectare rose from 14.75 hundredweight in 1871–80 to 21.31 in 1901–5; in Sweden there was a more modest growth from 13.62 to 14.48 hundredweight. The German potato harvest climbed from 86.3 hundredweight per hectare in 1884–93 to 135.0 in 1904–13. For Western Europe as a whole, the average yield per hectare for all cereals went from 11.52 hundredweight in 1871–80 to 12.37 in 1891–1900 and 13.47 in 1901–5. E. A. Wrigley, however, has provided an even simpler illustration of the effect of the agricultural revolution on farming efficiency, pointing out that at the beginning of the nineteenth century a work force of 1.7 million engaged in husbandry supplied the needs of a British population of 10.5 million, whereas in the middle of the twentieth century about 0.8 million people produced half the food requirements of 55 million.

There is an index of the level of development of agriculture in various European countries, based on highly intricate computations, in which 100 represents the net annual production of 10 million vegetable-based calories per male worker in husbandry. It shows that in 1900 the most efficient system of farm labor was to be found in the United Kingdom with 225 and in Germany with 220. The combination of a highly developed industrial economy and a system of large-scale landholding enabled them to exploit fully the benefits of agricultural rationalization. Then came countries with a pattern of small peasant proprietorship but also moderate technological progress: France with 155, Belgium and Switzerland with 150 each, and Sweden with 130. In last place were the unwieldy giants of the latifundia region, whose advantage of size was

---

A Short History of Technology from the Earliest Times to A.D. *1900* (Oxford, 1960), pp. 685–86; Folke Dovring, "The Transformation of European Agriculture," in *Cambridge Economic History of Europe*, 6:644.

more than offset by economic backwardness, unskilled labor, and timid management: Austria with 110, Russia with 90, Spain with 75, and Italy with 60. Even more important than the ranking of the European nations was the position of the United States, which far surpassed the best performance of the Old World with 310. The data suggest that the farmers of the Continent were facing serious competition from overseas, in which cheap land and intensive mechanization were on the side of the challengers.[16]

The increased efficiency of agriculture was reflected in its increased output. In most countries of Europe the volume of farm production rose steadily throughout the nineteenth century, despite the flow of population from the land to industrial and commercial centers. The statistics for the early decades are incomplete and not always reliable, but after the mid-century the pattern of growth, shown in figure 2.2, becomes much clearer. The techniques of a rationalized agriculture, moreover, could be applied to the raising of livestock as well as the growing of crops. The number of cattle in the Netherlands increased from 1,252,000 in 1860 to 2,027,000 in 1910; there were 442,000 pigs in Denmark in 1870 and 1,168,000 in 1900; Italy had 6,975,000 sheep in 1870 and 11,841,000 in 1910. All in all, between 1855–64 and 1905–14 the value of total farm output, measured in constant currencies, rose 27 percent in France, 122 in Germany, and 77 in Italy. The growth of production was thus slower in agriculture than in industry, but by the same token the increase in the demand for foodstuffs was smaller than that for manufactured goods.[17]

Economic rationalization, which made possible the growing efficiency of agriculture in Europe, also accounted for the increasing severity of foreign competition after the middle of the nineteenth century. Despite a recession during the 1820s, the decades from 1750 to 1850 had on the whole been a period of boom in farming, with handsome profits to be made from the cultivation of cereals and only a little less from the grazing of animals. Then came the lean years, as agricultural exports from distant continents began to penetrate the European market. Around 1850 world production of wheat amounted to 30.0 million metric tons, of which 3.1 million or 10 percent came from overseas countries peopled by white

16. Paul Bairoch, "Agriculture and the Industrial Revolution, 1700–1914," in *The Fontana Economic History of Europe: The Industrial Revolution*, ed. Carlo M. Cipolla (London and Glasgow, 1973), pp. 472, 484; Werner Sombart, *Der moderne Kapitalismus: Historisch-systematische Darstellung des gesamteuropäischen Wirtschaftslebens von seinen Anfängen bis zur Gegenwart*, 2d ed., 3 vols. (Munich and Leipzig, 1924–28), 3:246–47; E. A. Wrigley, *Population and History* (New York and Toronto, 1969), p. 178.

17. B. R. Mitchell, "Statistical Appendix, 1700–1914," in *The Fontana Economic His-*

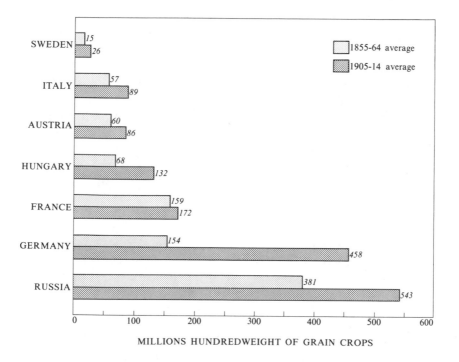

Figure 2.2. European Agricultural Output, 1855–1914

SOURCE: B. R. Mitchell, "Statistical Appendix, 1700–1914," in *The Fontana Economic History: The Emergence of Industrial Societies*, ed. Carlo M. Cipolla (London and Glasgow, 1973), p. 752.

settlers. The United States raised 2.7 million, Canada 0.2, and Australia 0.1; the Argentinean share was too small to be specified in the statistics. By 1878–82 world production had risen to 62.0 million, but the wheat crop of the leading transoceanic farming nations had expanded even more rapidly to 14.3 million or 23 percent of the total. The American harvest was now 12.3 million, the Canadian 0.9, the Australian 0.6, and the Argentinean 0.5. Finally, in 1909–13 world production amounted to 102.9 million, of which 30.2 million or 29 percent was accounted for by the four large overseas exporters of agricultural commodities: the United States with 18.3, Canada with 5.4, Argentina with 4.0, and Australia with 2.5. The global output of wheat had climbed 243 percent in about

tory: The Emergence of Industrial Societies, ed. Carlo. M. Cipolla (London and Glasgow, 1973), pp. 752–53, 764–67.

sixty years, but the output of the New World and Australia combined had climbed 1,007 percent.[18]

The production of foodstuffs in the transoceanic continents was stimulated by a decline in transportation costs, which made it possible to ship cereal crops and meat products to Europe cheaply. The index of American export freight rates dropped from 94 in 1875 to 36 in 1905. The lowest charge for sending a ton of grain from the Paraná River to the United Kingdom fell from 18 shillings in 1889 to 10.5 shillings in 1913. During the period 1866–70 it had cost on an average 23.40 cents to transport a bushel of wheat from Chicago to New York, and another 12.01 cents to ship it from New York to Liverpool. By 1901–5 the Chicago–New York rate was 5.21 and the New York–Liverpool rate only 2.80. All told, while wholesale prices declined about 20 percent between 1869 and 1910, tramp shipping freights declined as much as 50 percent. The growing volume of farm exports from the New World was a measure of the impact of cheaper transportation on European agriculture. During the 1830s average annual shipments of wheat from North America were only 0.24 million bushels; they rose to 5.5 million during the 1850s and reached 22 million during the 1860s. In 1875, on the other hand, wheat exports amounted to 55 million bushels, and in 1880 they totaled an extraordinary 150.5 million. The rise in the value of meat and meat products shipped from the United States, though not as rapid, was still impressive: 14 million dollars in 1860, 21 million in 1870, 114 million in 1880, 124 million in 1890, and 175 million in 1900.

To most Europeans the flood of agricultural goods from overseas was a blessing. It meant that the cost of food would decline despite the fact that a growing proportion of the labor force was employed in industry and commerce. The toil of agriculture could be left increasingly to the farmers of the Western Hemisphere, whose vast fertile plains were cultivated with greater efficiency than the overcrowded fields of the Old World. In Great Britain the price index for cereal foodstuffs declined from 100 in 1871–75 to 63 in 1901–5, while for meat products it went from 104 to 85. The cost of wheat bread, which in 1873–80 stood at 136 on the price index, dropped to 109 by 1906–10. Beef fell from 156 to 109, butter from 135 to 107, and potatoes from 169 to 93. The Hamburg price of 100 kilograms of imported wheat was 24.46 marks in 1871–75 and 13.30 in 1901–5. During the same period, there was a decline in the cost of imported rye from 16.27 to 10.62 marks, of barley from 16.44 to 9.78, and of oats from 15.79 to 12.04. The miracle of the agricultural revolution was that a rapidly expanding population, moving in increasing num-

18. Trow-Smith, *Life from the Land*, p. 152; Bairoch, "Agriculture and the Industrial Revolution," p. 479, n. 10.

bers from country to city, could be provided with a more abundant supply of food than in previous centuries, when a smaller population devoting a greater share of its labor to farming was barely able to keep body and soul together.[19]

Yet rationalized husbandry also exacted a heavy price: the economic decline of those who had to face the unrestrained competition of a more efficient system of agriculture. British farmers were especially hard-hit by the deluge of imported foodstuffs. Although they frequently ascribed their misfortune to the bad harvest of 1879, in fact the prices that they received began to drop a few years earlier because of growing shipments of agricultural commodities from the New World. In 1868 the United Kingdom still produced 80 percent in value of the grain, meat, wool, and dairy products that its population consumed. A decade later the percentage had fallen to barely 50. "In the past ten years," warned a British work on agricultural economics in 1878, "there has been a gradual reduction of the acreage and produce of wheat in this country, and a more than corresponding increase in the foreign supply; the result of which is that we now receive our bread in equal proportions from our own fields and those of the stranger. In regard to meat, and other animal products, ten years ago the proportion of foreign was one-tenth of the whole. It has now risen to nearly one-fourth."

To be sure, the distress of agriculture was not as intense as it often appeared. Although arable farming suffered a permanent decline, owners of livestock managed to limit their losses, partly by increasing the output of milk and partly by taking advantage of the reduced cost of feed. They might not have been able to hold their own against foreign beef and mutton or even against foreign butter, cheese, eggs, and wool. But milk is not an importable commodity, and statistics show that the output of grain crops in Great Britain fell from 70 million hundredweight in 1865–74 to 51.7 million in 1905–14, whereas the number of cattle rose from 5.4 million in 1870 to 7.0 million in 1910. Still, between 1871 and 1901 the farmers of the United Kingdom took more than a quarter of the arable land out of cultivation, and on the eve of the First World War only 8 percent of the British working population was engaged in agriculture, compared with 22 in Belgium, 35 in Germany, and 43 in France. Such a drastic shift in the distribution of the labor force was bound to have a profound effect on the national economy as a whole.[20]

19. Douglass North, "Ocean Freight Rates and Economic Development, 1750–1913," *Journal of Economic History* 18 (1958):549; Woodruff, *Impact of Western Man*, pp. 257, 259; Sombart, *Der moderne Kapitalismus*, 3:280–82; Bowden, Karpovich, and Usher, *Economic History of Europe*, p. 583; Gras, *History of Agriculture*, p. 336, n. 39.

20. Elie Halevy, *A History of the English People in the Nineteenth Century*, 2d ed., 6 vols. (London, 1949–52), 5:294–95, 298; Leland Hamilton Jenks, *Migration of British*

The countries of the Continent made a more determined effort to reconcile the advantage of industrialization with the survival of agriculture. In the United Kingdom the consumer's standard of living was improved by the sacrifice of domestic farming, but the rest of Europe was generally willing to forgo some of the benefits of a rationalized husbandry in order to preserve the economy of the countryside. Sometimes, as was the case in France, the government would adopt a policy of agricultural protectionism in response to pressure from peasant proprietors who wielded considerable political influence. At other times it was the result of agitation by landed aristocrats whose central role in the army and bureaucracy reinforced the defense of their economic position. This is what happened in Germany, for example. The support of farming, however, was everywhere justified by arguments that transcended class interest, like the maintenance of military preparedness. Chancellor Leo von Caprivi declared before the German Reichstag in 1891:

> I am convinced that we simply cannot dispense with a production of grain which would be sufficient, if need be, to feed our increasing population in the event of war from our own resources, though with some limitations. . . . The existence of the state is at stake, when it is not in a position to live on its own sources of supply. . . . I consider it better that Germany should depend on her own agriculture and should support it, even if that can be done only through sacrifice, than that she should rely on uncertain calculations concerning help from a third party in the event of war. . . . It is my unshakable conviction that in a future war the feeding of the army and the country can play an absolutely decisive role.[21]

Most governments in Europe agreed that the national interest, real or imagined, should take precedence over the wishes of the consumer and the principles of free trade.

The result was that at the beginning of the twentieth century only about 12 percent of the grain consumption of the Continent, excluding Russia, was imported, most of it in fact from Russia. There was considerable trade in farm commodities within Europe, however, with the Danube basin in particular providing the industrial nations with cereal foodstuffs. Nowhere was the rural economy so completely overpowered by

Capital to 1875 (New York and London, 1927), p. 329; James Caird, *The Landed Interest and the Supply of Food* (London, Paris, and New York, 1878), pp. 5–6; Mitchell, "Statistical Appendix," pp. 752–53, 764; G. C. Allen, "The Economic Map of the World: Population, Commerce and Industries," in *New Cambridge Modern History*, 12:26–27.

21. Germany, *Stenographische Berichte über die Verhandlungen des Reichstags: VIII. Legislaturperiode, I. Session 1890/92*, 7 vols. (Berlin, 1890–92), 5:3305.

foreign competition as in the United Kingdom. Some states managed to save their agriculture by a planned adjustment to special market conditions. Denmark is the prime example. A country that at the end of the eighteenth century still had a manorial system of landownership with open fields and villein tenures became, with the aid of the government, a stronghold of family farms raising livestock rather than growing grain. By the time of the transatlantic flood of agricultural commodities, it was in a position to benefit from the low prices of imported cereals, instead of being overwhelmed by them. In Holland and Switzerland a similar process of accommodation to the changing economics of husbandry took place, assisted by technical education, cooperative buying and selling, and easy credit provided through rural banks. Most countries, however, relied simply on protective tariffs to save their farmers from foreign competition. It was a crude but effective strategy. By 1912 Germany was spending about twelve dollars per capita annually on imported food, while the figure for France was close to nine dollars. The United Kingdom, on the other hand, spent thirty-five dollars. This difference in expenditure reflected a more fundamental difference in the willingness to accept the economic and social consequences of the agricultural revolution.[22]

The increased efficiency of husbandry led to the emergence of a new society in which for the first time the bulk of the population did not have to engage in the primal task of raising food. Industrialization and urbanization became possible because, to put it simply, far fewer people in the rural economy were producing far more grain, meat, butter, cheese, and eggs. The steady diminution in the economic role of European husbandry could be seen most clearly in the countries of the west and north (see figure 2.3). Yet even more drastic than the decline in the proportion of the labor force engaged in agriculture was the decline in its proportion of the national product (see figure 2.4). The value of farm production was still growing, but more slowly than that of industry or the services.

Changes in agriculture's share of the national wealth, on the other hand, were not as clear-cut. Where farm management was competent and farm technology advanced, it accounted for a higher proportion of the national wealth than of the work force. This was the case in Great Britain during the 1890s, with percentages of 15 and 10 respectively, in Holland with 33 and 22, and in Belgium with 36 and 25. In France, however, the ratio was reversed, with agriculture representing 32 percent of the national wealth though employing 42 percent of the work force,

22. Allen, "Economic Map of the World," p. 26; Trow-Smith, *Life From the Land*, pp. 162–65; Clapham, *Economic Development of France and Germany*, p. 361; Mitchell, *European Historical Statistics* pp. 20, 24.

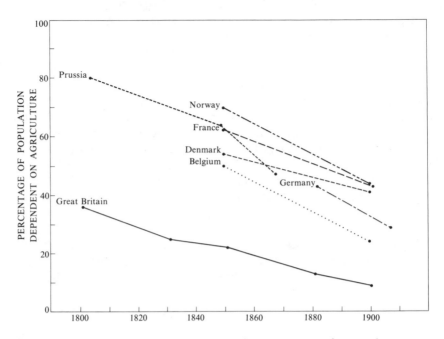

Figure 2.3. Decline of the Occupational Importance of Agriculture in Europe, 1801–1907

SOURCES: Folke Dovring, *Land and Labor in Europe in the Twentieth Century: A Comparative Study of Recent Agrarian History*, 3d ed. (The Hague, 1965), p. 84; A. R. L. Gurland, "Wirtschaft und Gesellschaft im Übergang zum Zeitalter der Industrie," in *Propyläen Weltgeschichte*, ed. Golo Mann, Alfred Heuss, and August Nitschke, 12 vols. (Berlin, Frankfurt, and Vienna, 1960–1965), 8:311–12; Nathan Rosenberg, "The Economic Consequences of Technological Change, 1830–1880," in *Technology in Western Civilization*, ed. Melvin Kranzberg and Carroll W. Pursell, Jr., 2 vols. (New York, London, and Toronto, 1967), 1:530.

NOTE: The figures for Great Britain and France are percentages of the labor force engaged in agriculture.

while in Italy the percentages were 45 and 52. Even in Germany those dependent on farming, 39 percent of the population, controlled only 31 percent of the national wealth, a reflection of the inefficient cultivation of many of the small holdings in the south and west. But the discrepancy between agriculture's share of national employment and national wealth was greatest in Russia, where the percentages were 70 and 43, and in Austria, where they were 62 and 39. Throughout Europe, moreover, the proportion of the national income attributable to farming was consistently smaller than its proportion of either the national wealth or the work force. In some countries the difference between agriculture's share

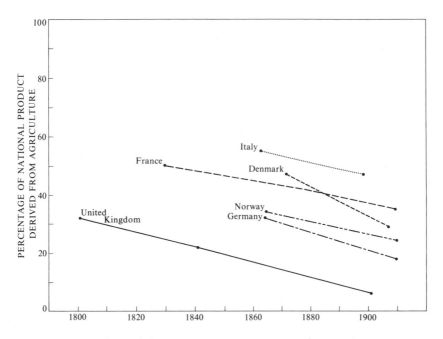

Figure 2.4. Decline of the Economic Importance of Agriculture in Europe, 1801–1914

SOURCE: Simon Kuznets, *Modern Economic Growth: Rate, Structure, and Spread* (New Haven and London, 1966), pp. 88–90.

of labor and income was minor, only 2 percent in Great Britain and 4 in Holland. In others it was quite substantial, 38 percent in Russia and 35 in Austria. Its significance, however, was everywhere the same. The profits and wages to be earned in farming were less than those in other sectors of the economy.[23]

The decline in the position of agriculture represented more than a change in the scale of economic importance. Landownership had historically been the source not only of wealth but of political influence and social prominence as well. An entire complex of class relationships and civic attitudes had developed around the assumption that farming was

23. Nathan Rosenberg, "The Economic Consequences of Technological Change, 1830–1880," in *Technology in Western Civilization*, ed. Kranzberg and Pursell, 1:530–31; A. R. L. Gurland, "Wirtschaft und Gesellschaft im Übergang zum Zeitalter der Industrie," in *Propyläen Weltgeschichte*, ed. Golo Mann, Alfred Heuss, and August Nitschke, 12 vols. (Berlin, Frankfurt, and Vienna, 1960–65), 8:311–12; Dovring, *Land and Labor in Europe*, p. 84; Simon Kuznets, *Modern Economic Growth: Rate, Structure, and Spread* (New Haven and London, 1966), pp. 88–90; Landes, *Unbound Prometheus*, p. 330, n. 3.

the ultimate source of prosperity. But the nineteenth century saw predominance in the economy shifting more and more to those engaged in industry, finance, or commerce. Such a far-reaching redistribution of affluence was bound to lead to demands for a comparable redistribution of power in politics and authority in society. The landed nobility, traditionally the dominant class, found its hegemony threatened by the flow of population from villages to cities and by the movement of wealth from fields to factories. The consequences of this change in the demographic and economic structure underlie the political and social history of Europe in the nineteenth century.

"A large clear landed property is the foundation of dignity and respect in the country," Lord Sefton had been advised in 1791, "for the populace . . . look more to a rich esquire with a large clear estate than a person with a title with a small one." Above all, it was important to avoid "the degrading and indignity that selling townships and lordships, etc. (and such number) brings to a noble family in the eyes and minds of the public." Two generations later, in 1851, another British aristocrat, Lord Monson, was complaining about the decline of land as a measure of economic and social worth: "What an infernal bore is landed property. No certain income can be reckoned upon. I hope your future wife will have Consols or some such ballast, I think it is worth half as much again as what land is reckoned at." It was a grudging admission that the age of agricultural supremacy in Europe, which had lasted more than a thousand years, was finally coming to an end.[24]

24. Thompson, *English Landed Society*, pp. 212, 290.

3

THE DEMOGRAPHIC REVOLUTION

The rationalization of the economy of Europe began at a time when its population was expanding with unprecedented rapidity. To be sure, the total number of inhabitants had been gradually increasing ever since the end of the Middle Ages. There had been 60 million people in 1450, 69 million in 1500, 78 million in 1550, 89 million in 1600, 100 million in 1650, 115 million in 1700, and 140 million in 1750. The rate of growth was thus 15 percent in 1450–1500, 13 in 1500–1550, 14 in 1550–1600, 12 in 1600–1650, 15 in 1650–1700, and 22 in 1700–1750. But then came a steep rise in the curve, as the population climbed to 188 million during 1750–1800, an annual rate of 0.6 percent and an overall increase of 34. It grew even more swiftly during 1800–1850 to 266 million, an annual rate of 0.7 percent and an overall increase of 42. Finally, it reached 401 million at the end of the nineteenth century, an annual rate of 0.8 percent during 1850–1900 and an overall increase of 51. All these figures represent only rough approximations for the early period, and even after 1800 they are subject to a considerable margin of error. Yet the general conclusion to which they point is beyond dispute. Europe began to experience a massive increase of population after the middle of the eighteenth century.

This increase was proportionately larger than the growth in the number of people in the world as a whole. Since here the statistical data are even less reliable than the data for Europe, the element of conjecture becomes correspondingly greater. The best estimates, given in table 3.1, suggest that the European rate of growth was consistently and progressively larger than the global rate. Since the annual increase of the world population between 1750 and 1900 was 0.2 percent less on an average than the European rate, Europe's share of the total number of people rose from 19.2 percent in 1750 to 24.9 in 1900. The growth would have been even greater if it had not been for the increasing flow of emigrants across the Atlantic to the New World. This becomes apparent from an examination of the changing proportion of the world's inhabitants living in the four major continents outside Europe. Asia's share was 65.8 percent in 1750 and 58.3 in 1900. The relative decline of the African population was still more striking: 13.1 and 7.4. The favorite destinations of European emigrants, on the other hand, experienced a rapid increase. North America's percentage rose from 0.1 in 1750 to 5.1 in 1900, while for Central and South America the figures were 1.5 and 3.9. Although such calculations are often no more than informed guesswork, they at least establish the point that at no time in history had the number of inhabitants of Europe grown as swiftly as in the nineteenth century.[1]

The cause of this sudden demographic expansion is more difficult to ascertain. The problem is complicated by its seeming simplicity, by the deceptively obvious relationship between growth of the population and rationalization of the economy. Could there be only a fortuitous connection between two processes coinciding so closely in time and logic? Ever since the latter decades of the eighteenth century, writers have maintained that the progress of industry and agriculture was responsible for the increase of people. In his *Tour through the North of England*, which appeared in 1770, Arthur Young advanced this argument forcefully:

> It is employment that creates population. . . . Marriages are early and numerous, in proportion to the amount of employment. . . . In a great kingdom there must always be hands that are either idle, backward in the age of work, unmarried for fear of having families, or industrious only to a certain degree. Now an increase of employment raises wages, and high wages changes the case with all these hands; the idle are converted to industry; the young come early to work; the unmarried are no longer fearful of families; and the formerly industrious become so in a much greater degree. It is an absolute impossibility that, in such circumstances, the people should not increase. . . . Provide new employment, and new hands will inevitably follow.[2]

The classical economists were equally convinced that the rationalization of manufacture and farming must lead to an enlargement of population by providing greater opportunities for employment, thereby increasing fecundity and longevity. Adam Smith maintained in the *Wealth of Nations* that "the real recompense of labour . . . has, during the course of the present century, increased perhaps in a still greater proportion than its money price." But since "in civilized society it is only among the inferior ranks of people that the scantiness of subsistence can set limits to the further multiplication of the human species, . . . the liberal reward of

1. B. H. Slicher van Bath, *Agrarian History of Western Europe*, A.D. *500–1850* (London, 1963), p. 78; A. M. Carr-Saunders, *World Population: Past Growth and Present Trends* (Oxford, 1936), p. 42; Walter F. Willcox, "Increase in the Population of the Earth and of the Continents," in *International Migrations*, ed. Walter F. Willcox, 2 vols. (New York, 1929–31), 2:78; John D. Durand, "The Modern Expansion of World Population," *Proceedings of the American Philosophical Society* 111 (1967):137.

2. Arthur Young, *A Six Months Tour through the North of England: Containing, an Account of the Present State of Agriculture, Manufactures and Population, in Several Counties of This Kingdom*, 4 vols. (London, 1770), 4:561–62, 565.

Table 3.1. World Population Growth, 1750–1900

European and World Increases	1750	1800	1850	1900
Europe				
Total population (millions)	140	188	266	401
Percentage increase in previous 50 years:				
Total	22	34	42	51
Annual Rate	0.4	0.6	0.7	0.8
World				
Total population (millions)	791	978	1,262	1,650
Percentage increase in previous 50 years:				
Total		24	29	31
Annual Rate		0.4	0.5	0.5

Percentage of World Total				
Europe	19.2	20.7	22.7	24.9
Asia	65.8	66.4	63.9	58.3
Africa	13.1	9.9	8.1	7.4
North America	0.1	0.7	2.3	5.1
South America and Central America	1.5	2.1	2.8	3.9

SOURCES: B. H. Slicher van Bath, *The Agrarian History of Western Europe, A.D. 500–1850* (London, 1963), pp. 78–79; John D. Durand, "The Modern Expansion of World Population," *Proceedings of the American Philosophical Society*, 111 (1967):137; A. M. Carr-Saunders, *World Population: Past Growth and Present Trends* (Oxford, 1936), p. 42.

labour, by enabling them to provide better for their children, and consequently to bring up a greater number, naturally tends to widen and extend those limits." A generation later Malthus explained in the fifth edition of the *Essay on the Principle of Population* that the demographic expansion of recent times "has been occasioned by the stimulus of a greatly-increased demand for labour, combined with a greatly-increased power of production, both in agriculture and manufactures. . . . If the resources of a country will admit of a rapid increase, and if these resources are so advantageously distributed as to occasion a constantly-increasing demand for labour, the population will not fail to keep pace with them."

These early analysts of the rise in the number of inhabitants often differed concerning its social consequences. To some it was a sign of growing prosperity, a manifestation of the benefits that mankind could derive from the application of reason to the processes of production. To others it was only a prelude to certain misery, reflecting the stubborn refusal of the masses to accept the inherent hopelessness of the human condition. Most of them were in agreement, however, that there was a causal connection between economic progress and population increase.[3]

Yet a close examination of the pattern of demographic growth is bound to cast doubt on this plausible hypothesis. For it reveals that the rise in population was largely independent of the level of economic development. The countries that pioneered in the mechanization of industry and modernization of agriculture grew at a rapid pace, to be sure, but so did many regions whose manufacture had not advanced beyond the handicraft stage and whose farming was still in the grip of manorialism or even serfdom. The annual rate of population growth for England was 0.80 percent in the period 1751–1801, and for France 0.45 percent in the period 1740–89. But for Italy it was also 0.45 in 1700–1800, for Württemberg 0.56 in 1740–1800, and for Sweden 0.59 in 1749–1800. More surprising still was the demographic expansion farther to the east along the borderlands of the Holy Roman Empire, where industrial machinery was a rare novelty and agricultural reform was only in its initial phase. The annual rate of population growth was 0.80 for Pomerania in 1740–1800, 0.84 for East Prussia in 1700–1800, 0.94 for Silesia in 1740–1804, 0.94 for Austria in 1754–89, and 1.18 for Bohemia in 1754–89. The data simply do not support the contention of those writers who, familiar only with conditions in Western Europe, had concluded that economic improvement was the cause of demographic increase.

Even in the first half of the nineteenth century, the rise of population in countries with a highly developed economy was on an average no greater than in countries where the rationalization of industrial and agricultural production was just beginning. The number of inhabitants of France grew 31 percent in 1800–1850, but this rate was equaled by Portugal and exceeded by Spain with 48. While the population of Belgium rose 39 percent during the same period, that of the Netherlands increased 48, that of Sweden 52, and that of Denmark 56. Even Great Britain, with an extraordinary 98 percent, was approached by Russia, whose growth has been variously estimated at between 71 and 93, and matched by Finland, whose population actually doubled. Why, then, was there so little corre-

3. Adam Smith, *An Inquiry into the Nature and Causes of the Wealth of Nations*, 2 vols. (London, 1776), 1:95, 97–98; T. R. Malthus, *An Essay on the Principle of Population; or, a View of Its Past and Present Effects on Human Happiness; with an Inquiry into Our Prospects respecting the Future Removal or Mitigation of the Evils Which It Occasions*, 5th ed., 3 vols. (London, 1817), 2:103–4.

lation between economic and demographic expansion? The answer is still not entirely clear, but it has at least been established that before the middle of the nineteenth century the rationalization of production had little effect on the size of population.[4]

Nor does the evidence support another venerable explanation of demographic growth in the early industrial and agricultural revolution, that advances in medicine and hygiene helped bring about a substantial decline in the death rate. It is a superficially reasonable theory that has appeared and reappeared in the scholarly literature for a century and a half. In 1781 John Howlett, in his day a leading authority on demography, maintained that "the arts of medicine and surgery have made no inconsiderable advances . . . to alleviate the miseries of life and not uncommonly prolong its duration." In 1835 the Belgian statistician and astronomer Lambert Adolphe Jacques Quetelet concluded that "medical knowledge and public hygiene have also found valuable means to combat mortality," thereby managing "to prolong . . . the existence of man." And in 1893 Lucien Schöne wrote in his study of the population of France that demographic expansion under the ancien régime was partly at least the result of "a better understanding of hygiene and the daily efforts of medical science."

As late as the 1920s, some scholars were still arguing that the progress of medicine was responsible for the growth of population. M. C. Buer contended that "eighteenth century medicine . . . made a definite and by no means unsuccessful effort to prevent disease, especially epidemic disease, as opposed merely to curing it," while G. Talbot Griffith remained convinced that "the increase of medical skill . . . led to a decline in the death rate and to a prolongation of life." The persistence of this hypothesis can be explained not only by its inherent plausibility but also by the substantial data that seem to support it. While medicine was making swift progress in the years between 1750 and 1850, population was growing at a rapid rate. What could be more logical than to connect two processes that on the surface appear so clearly to have a cause-and-effect relationship?[5]

Yet the thesis that scientific advance led to demographic expansion has been effectively demolished by two British scholars in social medicine,

4. E. A. Wrigley, *Population and History* (New York and Toronto, 1969), p. 153; B. R. Mitchell, "Statistical Appendix, 1700–1914," in *The Fontana Economic History: The Emergence of Industrial Societies*, ed. Carlo M. Cipolla (London and Glasgow, 1973), pp. 747–48; B. R. Mitchell, *European Historical Statistics, 1750–1970* (London and Basingstoke, 1975), p. 23.

5. John Howlett, *An Examination of Dr. Price's Essay on the Population of England and Wales; and the Doctrine of an Increased Population in This Kingdom, Established by Facts* (Maidstone, [1781]), pp. x–xi; Adolphe Quetelet, *Sur l'homme et le développement de ses*

Thomas McKeown and R. G. Brown, who spent some twenty years studying the question. Their conclusion, first published in 1955, was unequivocal: "The fall in the death rate during the eighteenth and nineteenth centuries was not the result of medical treatment. . . . Only in the case of vaccination against smallpox is there any clear evidence that specific therapy had a substantial effect on the prevention or cure of disease earlier than the twentieth century. The decline in mortality from diseases other than smallpox was due to improvement in living conditions, and to changes in virulence and resistance upon which human effort had no influence." An alteration in the condition of life rather than in the severity of illness, they went on, was the probable cause of demographic growth: "It seems most unlikely that the decline of mortality which resulted in a marked and consistent rise in population can be attributed to a modification in the character of the infectious diseases, and we conclude that it was mainly due to changes in the environment."

In 1972 McKeown and Brown, this time in collaboration with R. G. Record, restated their position with still greater precision. There was "an unprecedented expansion" of population beginning in the eighteenth century, and "since the event was unique, so too it seems reasonable to believe must be the explanation for it." That explanation cannot lie in the rise of the factory system, for "it must also be remembered that in Ireland and Sweden . . . as well as in other parts of Europe . . . the . . . expansion of population occurred long in advance of industrialization. This strongly suggests that, in the initial phase at least, agricultural advances leading to better food supplies were the primary influences on population growth." The conclusion rests on three major considerations: "There was undoubtedly a great increase of home-grown food, enough, at times more than enough, to feed the enlarged population; in the circumstances which existed prior to the Agricultural Revolution, an improvement in food supplies was a necessary condition for a substantial and prolonged expansion of population (this interpretation rests on the belief that population growth was previously restricted mainly by lack of food); and alternative explanations which can be suggested for the growth of population in the eighteenth and early nineteenth centuries are not credible." The argument, constructed with great care, is persuasive.[6]

But which "agricultural advances leading to better food supplies" had

---

facultés, ou Essai de physique sociale, 2 vols. (Paris, 1835), 1:240–41; Lucien Schöne, Histoire de la population française (Paris, 1893), p. 216; M. C. Buer, Health, Wealth, and Population in the Early Days of the Industrial Revolution (London, 1926), p. 137; G. Talbot Griffith, Population Problems of the Age of Malthus (Cambridge, 1926), p. 258.

6. Thomas McKeown and R. G. Brown, "Medical Evidence Related to English Popula-

such a profound effect on the growth of population after 1750? Some involved the more effective application of such traditional methods as increased land use, manuring, winter feeding, and rotation of crops. But, in addition, William L. Langer came up with a persuasive hypothesis that the growing consumption of potatoes and maize by the lower classes made possible a significant decline in mortality. At first glance, it is hard to believe that such a humble cause could have had such a profound effect, but the evidence in support of his argument is substantial. The potato in particular was a "miracle vegetable," cultivated with nothing more complicated than a spade, surviving in poor soil, thriving on small parcels of land, and providing four times as much food value as wheat. A peasant could raise enough potatoes on one acre to feed not only a family of eight for an entire year but a cow and a pig as well. Many rustics were at first reluctant to abandon their reliance on wheat and rye bread, but by 1800 millions of them were living primarily on potatoes or maize. A generation later, the latter had become staples in the diet of the poor throughout most of the Continent. A young man with only a plot of land could now marry, so that his bride would have a longer period of child-bearing. And even more important, his children would enjoy a better chance of surviving infancy and reaching adulthood.

Some of the early demographers recognized the connection between the potato and population growth. Patrick Colquhoun commented in 1814 on the "regularly increasing culture and use of potatoes," concluding that "but for potatoes there must have been many famines not only in Scotland and Ireland, but in the more sterile districts of England and Wales, where potatoes have constituted a large portion of the food of the people. . . . Perhaps to this cause alone, (*the abundance of potatoes*) is to be ascribed the rapid and growing population of Ireland." Gilbert Blane in 1831 also noted the effect that cultivation of the potato had on demographic change: "A valuable accession has been made to our stock of farinaceous food in the last hundred years by the introduction of potatoes. In the degree in which they have been cultivated in Great Britain, there can be no doubt of their having added to the substantial comfort of the people, and even to their numbers." Some 150 years later, Langer, piecing together hints and clues scattered in a variety of sources, arrived at the hypothesis that "these American foods [potatoes and maize] would seem to provide the missing link in the story of the population explosion." Writing in 1976, McKeown concluded that they were at least one

tion Changes in the Eighteenth Century," *Population Studies* 9 (1955–56):139–40; Thomas McKeown, R. G. Brown, and R. G. Record, "An Interpretation of the Modern Rise of Population in Europe," *Population Studies* 26 (1972):357, 380–81.

of the missing links, the other being the more efficient use of traditional methods of cultivation. This remains the best explanation of the demographic increase that began in the middle of the eighteenth century.[7]

This is not to deny that secondary causes may have helped to raise natality or lower mortality. The decline of manorialism had perhaps the effect of encouraging a higher marriage rate in the Habsburg empire. The relaxation of guild control in the states of the German Confederation, by enabling a journeyman to become a master at an earlier age, could have added to the number of urban families. It appears likely that advances in obstetrics as well as the founding of lying-in hospitals in the United Kingdom reduced the incidence of stillbirths and childbed deaths. The promulgation of "Improvement Acts" dealing with hygienic conditions in English cities eliminated some of the unsanitary conditions in streams, streets, and sewers. The progress of vaccination against smallpox gradually freed all of Europe from what had long been a major plague. Even the abatement of brutality in warfare during the eighteenth century, which meant less destruction of civilian life and property, might have had significant demographic consequences.

Yet all of these contributory factors were overshadowed by the decline in mortality among the lower classes resulting from the increasing availability of food. This was the major cause of population growth until around 1850. Only thereafter did other influences become dominant: first of all, an improvement in the standard of living of the masses originating in the rationalization of production, and second, the progress of medical science and public sanitation to the point where a substantial reduction in the incidence or severity of disease became possible. The demographic effect of the industrial and the agricultural revolution, in other words, was to intensify and prolong a process of population growth that had already begun.[8]

Statistics measuring the increase of people, however, do not reflect this

7. William L. Langer, *Political and Social Upheaval, 1832–1852* (New York, Evanston, and London, 1969), p. 16; idem, "American Foods and Europe's Population Growth, 1750–1850," *Journal of Social History* (Winter 1975):61; Patrick Colquhoun, *A Treatise on the Wealth, Power, and Resources, of the British Empire, in Every Quarter of the World, Including the East Indies* (London, 1814), pp. 10–12; Gilbert Blane, *Reflections on the Present Crisis of Publick Affairs, with an Enquiry into the Causes and Remedies of the Existing Clamours, and Alleged Grievances of the Country, as Connected with Population, Subsistence, Wages of Labourers, Education, &c.* (London, 1831), pp. 38–39; Thomas McKeown, *The Modern Rise of Population* (London, 1976), pp. 128–31, 142, 153–54, 158–59, 162–63.

8. Langer, *Political and Social Upheaval*, p. 16; Theodore S. Hamerow, *Restoration, Revolution, Reaction: Economics and Politics in Germany, 1815–1871* (Princeton, 1958), pp. 22–30; Richard Harrison Shryock, *The Development of Modern Medicine: An Interpretation of the Social and Scientific Factors Involved* (New York, 1947), pp. 92–93, 319–20;

change in its causation directly. They simply show that the population of almost every country was steadily rising. The most striking growth occurred in Great Britain and Russia. In the former the number of inhabitants more than tripled, from 10.9 million in 1800 to 36.9 million in 1900, an increase of 239 percent. The latter kept pace, with 35.5 to 40 million people at the beginning and 132.9 million at the end of the nineteenth century, a rise of between 232 and 274 percent. Central Europe was in the middle range of population increase, with a percentage of 107 in the case of Germany, a rise from 24.5 million to 50.6 million, and 102 for Austria-Hungary, a rise from 23.3 million to 47.0 million. But Italy's growth of 87 percent, from 18.1 million to 33.9 million, was less than average, a result of mounting emigration from a poor and overpopulated country.

France stood near the bottom of the list. In the eighteenth century, she had been the most populous nation in Europe excepting Russia, with about 25 million inhabitants on the eve of the Revolution. The first official census in 1801 gave a figure of 27 million, which rose to 38 million by the time of the Franco-Prussian War. But then came an unexpected slowdown, so that in 1900 the total was still below 41 million. The French share in the population of Europe declined from 14.1 percent in 1800 to 13.1 in 1850 and 9.2 in 1900. The most drastic departure from the general pattern of demographic growth, however, occurred in Ireland, where the national disaster of the Hungry Forties initiated a mass emigration that reduced the number of inhabitants from 5.0 million in 1800 and 8.2 million in 1841 to 4.5 million in 1900.[9]

For Europe as a whole, the increase of population between 1800 and 1900 was 114 percent, from 187 million to 401 million. The pace of demographic development, however, was not constant. There were two periods of particularly rapid expansion separated by several decades in which the curve continued to climb, but more slowly. The first was in 1821–30, when a number of countries reached the peak of their increase: Norway with an annual rate of 1.47 percent, the United Kingdom with 1.37, Sweden with 1.12, Austria-Hungary with 0.98, and Switzerland

---

Charles Singer and E. Ashworth Underwood, *A Short History of Medicine*, 2d ed. (New York and Oxford, 1962), p. 193; McKeown and Brown, "Evidence Related to English Population Changes," p. 139.

9. André Armengaud, "Population in Europe, 1700–1914," in *The Fontana Economic History: The Industrial Revolution*, ed. Carlo M. Cipolla (London and Glasgow, 1973), p. 29; Mitchell, "Statistical Appendix," pp. 747–48; Claude Fohlen, "The Industrial Revolution in France, 1700–1914," in *Fontana Economic History: Emergence of Industrial Societies*, ed. Cipolla, p. 25; William Woodruff, *Impact of Western Man: A Study of Europe's Role in the World Economy, 1750–1960* (New York, 1967), p. 104; Mitchell, *European Historical Statistics*, p. 21.

with 0.90. The percentage for all of Europe was 0.94, the second highest rate of the century. Then came a slowdown in the population increase, coinciding with the epidemics, famines, and wars of the years between 1831 and 1871. The ensuing period saw a new surge of demographic expansion that culminated in 1891–1900 in an average annual rate of 0.99, the highest Europe had ever experienced. Finland reached 1.54 percent in 1871–80, surpassing its previous high of 1.32 in 1821–30. Russia's largest increase came in 1881–90 with 1.39 percent, while the Balkans attained their maximum in the same decade with 1.10. Germany and the Netherlands peaked in 1891–1900 with 1.32 and 1.27 percent, as did Switzerland and Belgium with 1.14 and 0.99. Indeed, the growth of population accelerated in most countries at the end of the nineteenth century, and the pace became even more rapid as the twentieth opened.

This curve of demographic expansion suggests that there were two distinct causes for the increase in population that began around 1750. It reinforces the view that at first the rise was due to an improvement in the diet of the lower classes resulting primarily from better methods of farming and the spreading cultivation of potatoes and maize. This factor, having produced its maximum effect during the 1820s, gradually declined in importance, so that by the middle decades of the century it could no longer support an accelerating demographic growth in the face of relative overpopulation and recurrent warfare. After 1870, however, the increase in the number of people resumed at an even greater tempo, supported this time by economic rationalization and medical progress. The new wave of expansion continued at a mounting pace until it was suddenly halted by the outbreak of the First World War. The basic cause of population growth was thus an improvement in the standard of living of the masses. But in the beginning that improvement was the effect of a change in diet, whereas in the later period it derived from an enlargement of industrial and agricultural output. The net result of the demographic increase was that the number of inhabitants of Europe almost tripled between 1750 and 1900, and in the nineteenth century alone it more than doubled.[10]

This view is supported by vital statistics showing that the growth of population was due more to a decline in the death rate than a rise in the birth rate. Although the data are spotty and not always reliable, they point to the inference that the number of children in an average family did not increase substantially during the initial period of demographic expansion. According to the best estimates, there were 35.6 births annu-

10. Carr-Saunders, *World Population*, pp. 21, 42; D. V. Glass and E. Grebenik, "World Population, 1800–1950," in *The Cambridge Economic History of Europe*, 7 vols. (Cambridge, 1971–78), 6:62.

ally per thousand inhabitants of England in 1731–40 and 36.9 in 1741–50. The rate rose slowly in succeeding decades, reaching its high point in 1781–90 with 37.7. Then came an equally gradual decrease, until in 1841–50 the figure was 33.9, the same as in 1721–30. In Sweden the highest rate was recorded in 1751–60 with 35.7, but a long period of decline followed, so that by 1791–1800 it was 33.3. There was a brief upturn during the 1820s to 34.6; then the figure dropped again to 31.5 in the 1830s and 31.1 in the 1840s. The total population of the country increased by 28 percent between 1761–65 and 1806–10 and by 54 percent between 1811–15 and 1856–60. Yet the average birth rate during the two periods remained virtually unchanged: 32.60 and 32.58.

Of the Italian states, only Lombardy and Tuscany have vital statistics going back farther than the middle decades of the nineteenth century. In the former, the annual rate was 39.4 births per thousand inhabitants in the 1770s, 41.0 in the 1780s, and 41.6 in the 1790s. There are no figures covering the next decade, but in the 1810s it was 40.2, in the 1820s 41.6, in the 1830s 41.5, and in the 1840s 40.9. Although the data for Tuscany are less extensive, they lead to the same conclusion. The birth rate was 35.1 in the 1810s, 42.9 in the 1820s, 37.8 in the 1830s, and 34.9 in the 1840s. The demography of France is the familiar story of one long uninterrupted decline in natality, which began under the ancien régime. The birth rate fell from 38.4 in 1771–80 to 37.0 in 1781–90, 35.4 in 1791–1800, 31.8 in 1801–10, 31.3 in 1811–20, 30.3 in 1821–30, 28.8 in 1831–40, and 27.3 in 1841–50. Only in European Russia, where the statistical data rest on conjecture to an even greater extent than elsewhere, is there evidence of a substantial rise in the birth rate. The figures were 43.7 in 1801–10, 40.0 in 1811–20, a decade that included years of bitter warfare, 42.7 in 1821–30, 45.6 in 1831–40, and 49.7 in 1841–50. Yet these statistics, even if entirely sound, do not invalidate the generalization that though there may have been a modest increase of natality in Europe before 1850, it cannot account for the unprecedented demographic expansion of the period.[11]

The evidence on this point becomes irrefutable in the second half of the nineteenth century. While population continued to grow more rapidly than ever, the birth rate in every country was starting to decline. Between 1851–60 and 1906–10 the relative frequency of births dropped throughout Europe (table 3.2). Although for some nations the statistical data did

11. D. V. Glass, "Population and Population Movements in England and Wales, 1700 to 1850," in *Population in History: Essays in Historical Demography*, ed. D. V. Glass and D. E. C. Eversley (London, 1965), p. 241; Glass and Grebenik, "World Population," 6:97, 99, 101; McKeown and Brown, "Evidence Related to English Population Changes," pp. 137–38; Carlo M. Cipolla, "Four Centuries of Italian Demographic Development," in *Population in History*, ed. Glass and Eversley, pp. 576–77.

Table 3.2. European Birth Rates, 1851–1910

| | Births per 1,000 Inhabitants | | | | | |
	1851– 1860	1861– 1870	1876– 1880	1886– 1890	1896– 1900	1906– 1910
England	34.1	35.2	35.3	31.4	29.3	26.3
France	26.1	26.1	25.3	23.0	21.9	20.2
Germany	35.3	37.2	39.2	36.5	36.0	31.6
Sweden	32.8	31.4	30.3	28.8	26.9	25.4
Russia	52.4	49.7	50.4	50.5	49.2	46.8
Belgium	30.4	32.2	32.0	29.4	29.0	24.7
Denmark	32.5	30.8	32.1	31.4	29.9	28.2
Netherlands	33.3	35.7	36.4	33.6	32.2	29.6
Austria		39.6	41.0	40.0	38.2	34.0
Italy		37.9	37.0	37.3	33.9	32.6
Rumania		41.8	40.9	39.9	39.3	40.3
Spain		37.8		36.1	34.5	33.2
Portugal			33.3	32.6	31.6	30.9

SOURCE: D. V. Glass and E. Grebenik, "World Population, 1800–1950," in *The Cambridge Economic History of Europe,* 7 vols. (Cambridge, 1941–78), 6:68–69, 97.
NOTE: These figures include Austria and Hungary until 1906–10; thereafter only Austria is included. All figures for Russia cover decades.

not begin to appear until a decade or two later, whenever they became available, they told the same story. Germany appears at first glance to deviate from the pattern, but that is only because her birth rate peaked later than in most countries. Even European Russia conformed to the general downward curve of natality, though more slowly than the other states of the Continent.

The distribution of the birth rate on the eve of the First World War shows that the highest natality was to be found in the east and south, then in the countries between the Vistula and the Rhine, and finally in the northwestern region, with France in last place by a considerable margin. European Russia led the Continent with an annual rate of 45.6 births per thousand inhabitants, followed by the Balkan states (Rumania with 43.1, Bulgaria with 41.0, and Serbia with 38.2) and by Hungary with 36.0. Not far behind was the tier of poor agricultural nations in the south: Portugal with 34.6, Italy with 32.4, and Spain with 32.1. The Teutonic empires, Austria with 31.9 and Germany with 29.5, came next. At the bottom were the Scandinavian and Atlantic countries. The figure for the Netherlands was 29.5, for Denmark 27.1, for Norway 26.0, for England

24.9, for Sweden 24.4, for Belgium 23.4, and for France 19.5. The pattern suggests an inverse correlation between birth rate and economic development. To put it another way, the level of natality was as a rule lower in countries with a higher standard of living, whether their primary source of livelihood was industry as in England, agriculture as in Denmark, commerce as in the Netherlands, or fishing and shipping as in Norway.[12]

The falling birth rate after 1850, at least in some areas of Western and Central Europe, was partly a result of the increasing age and decreasing frequency of marriage. According to genealogical records covering close to four hundred members of a family in Württemberg, the average age at first marriage rose between the eighteenth and nineteenth centuries from 28.9 to 31.1 years for men and from 24.0 to 25.3 for women. The percentage of women in Great Britain who were ever married, moreover, dropped in the period 1851–1911 from 30.4 to 24.0 for ages twenty to twenty-four, from 81.1 to 78.0 for ages thirty-five to thirty-nine, from 84.4 to 81.6 for ages forty to forty-four, and from 86.3 to 83.0 for ages forty-five to forty-nine. Yet these were only contributory factors that could not be principally responsible for the sharp decline in natality. In Sweden, for example, the average number of live births per woman living to the age of fifty fell from 4.6 in 1860 to 4.5 in 1870, 4.3 in 1880, 4.1 in 1890, 3.9 in 1900, and 3.3 in 1910. The basic cause of a decline of such magnitude, 28 percent in fifty years, has to lie elsewhere.

The difference in natality between classes is more illuminating on this point than the difference between countries, although both point in the same direction. There was a close inverse relationship between affluence and procreation: the higher the social position, the lower the birth rate was likely to be. A study of the marriage fertility of various classes in England during the second half of the nineteenth century, expressed as a percentage of the birth rate for all classes, shows (table 3.3) that the "upper and middle class" had the lowest figures, the "higher intermediate class" was also below average, and skilled workers were almost exactly in the center. On the other hand, the groups farther down the social scale —unskilled workers, agricultural laborers, and miners—were consistently above average in fertility.

Another study of the decline in family size in Great Britain, based on occupational categories only, shows a similar pattern for the decade 1900–1909. Professionals had the smallest number of live births per completed marriage in which the wife was under forty-five at the time of

12. Glass and Grebenik, "World Population," 6:68–69, 97; Walther G. Hoffmann, Franz Grumbach, and Helmut Hesse, *Das Wachstum der deutschen Wirtschaft seit der Mitte des 19. Jahrhunderts* (Berlin, Heidelberg, and New York, 1965), pp. 172–73; Armengaud, "Population in Europe," pp. 56–57.

Table 3.3. Marriage Fertility in England by Social Categories, 1851–1901

| | Percentage of the Birth Rate for All Categories | | | | |
	1851–1861	1886–1891	1891–1896	1896–1901	Change, 1851–1901
"Upper and middle class"	89	74	74	76	−13
"Higher intermediate class"	99	87	88	89	−10
Skilled workers	101	100	99	99	− 2
Unskilled workers	103	112	113	114	+11
Agricultural laborers	105	114	115	114	+ 9
Miners	108	126	127	125	+17

SOURCE: R. C. K. Ensor, *England, 1870–1914* (Oxford, 1936), p. 271.

wedlock: 2.33. Then came salaried employees with 2.37, employers with 2.64, nonmanual wage earners wtih 2.89, and those working on their own account with 2.96. Since the mean for all occupations was 3.53, these figures were well below average. Family size rose, however, as occupational status fell. The number of live births for farmers and farm managers was 3.50, for agricultural workers 3.88, for manual wage earners 3.96, and for laborers 4.45. It becomes apparent that social rank and economic position exerted a powerful influence on fertility.

Here lies the key to the sharp decline in birth rate that began during the nineteenth century. Procreation, hitherto considered instinctive and autonomous, came to be regarded as a controllable process subject to calculations of status and affluence. In the marginal economy of a pre-industrial society, the begetting of children appeared as the manifestation of an elemental force of nature, not much different from the cyclical recurrence of seasons, crops, and epidemics. The high rate of infant mortality made conscious control of fertility seem all the more pointless. According to the prevailing view, an attempt to restrict the number of children was bound to prove as ineffectual as a scheme to regulate rainfall. Besides, feeding a few mouths more or less would not change the hopeless poverty accepted as the lot of the great mass of the population.

But then a rise in the standard of living and a concomitant rise in the level of expectation led to a deliberate effort to reduce the birth rate. The parents who had more food and more clothing, who could find more remunerative employment and more comfortable housing, ceased to feel that their children were predestined to eternal and inalterable want. Now they began to make plans for their future. They wanted them to have a better upbringing, a better education, a better livelihood. That is why a widespread attempt to restrict family size became apparent after 1850, especially in those countries and occupations that benefited most from the general spread of affluence. Economic progress led to a break with the pattern of natality that had prevailed throughout history, initiating new attitudes and practices in human fertility.[13]

Since the rapid increase of population in Europe was not primarily the result of a rising birth rate, it must have been due to a falling death rate. The logic of this reasoning seems unassailable, and yet there were writers in the nineteenth century who refused to accept it. The young German economist Gustav Schmoller, dismayed by the disruptive social effects of industrialization and urbanization, maintained in 1870 that "mortality has grown. The assertion that there has been an extension of the mean span of life has long ago been consigned by science to the realm of fairy tales. . . . Life has on the average become a shorter phenomenon. Work and pleasure are destroying it. The struggles and fortunes befalling the lives of most people are more variable and make this result seem natural." But nothing could have been farther from the truth. The decline of the death rate had not been a wishful fancy in the realm of fairy tales but an undeniable reality for more than a hundred years.

Consider the statistical data for England, which may be open to question in some of their details but whose general validity has been established. While the birth rate fluctuated narrowly between 1731–40 and 1841–50, reaching its high point in 1781–90 with 37.7 per thousand and its low point in 1841–50 with 33.9, a difference of 3.8, the death rate was dropping rapidly and steadily. The figures were 35.8 for 1731–40, 33.0 for 1741–50, 30.3 for 1751–60, 30.0 for 1761–70, 31.1 for 1771–80, 28.6 for 1781–90, 26.9 for 1791–1800, 23.9 for 1801–10, 21.1 for 1811–20, 22.6 for 1821–30, 23.4 for 1831–40, and 22.4 for 1841–50, a difference of 14.7 between the high and the low points. By the end of the entire span between 1731–40 and 1841–50, the death rate had declined 37 percent, while the birth rate had declined 5 percent.

The information for most other countries is less complete, but it suggests a similar pattern. The French death rate of 26 per thousand during the opening years of the nineteenth century represented a drop from the levels of the ancien régime. The German figures were 27.9 in 1819, 27.8 in 1829, 27.2 in 1839, and 27.0 in 1849. In Sweden the average birth

13. J. Hajnal, "European Marriage Patterns in Perspective," in *Population in History*, ed. Glass and Eversley, p. 115; Glass and Grebenik, "World Population," 6:104, 107; R. C. K. Ensor, *England, 1870–1914* (Oxford, 1936), pp. 271–72; E. A. Wrigley, *Population and History*, pp. 186–87.

rate between 1811–15 and 1856–60 was 0.02 less than that between 1761–65 and 1806–12. The average death rate, on the other hand, was 4.87 less, declining from 27.56 to 22.69. In Lombardy the death rate was 36.2 in the 1770s, 39.3 in the 1780s, and 38.0 in the 1790s. The statistics for 1800–1809 are missing, but in the 1810s the figure was 38.8, in the 1820s 33.0, in the 1830s 36.8, and in the 1840s 33.3. The fall in the death rate of 2.9 between the opening and the closing decade of the period 1770–1849 was thus a more important factor in the growth of population than the rise in the birth rate of 1.5. In Tuscany, where the data cover a shorter period, there was also a significant decline in mortality: 32.9 in 1810–19, 27.8 in 1820–29, 26.5 in 1830–39, and 26.7 in 1840–49. On the whole, though the case would be more persuasive if the evidence were less meager, what there is strongly suggests that even during the initial phase of the demographic revolution a diminishing death rate rather than an expanding birth rate was primarily responsible for the increase in the number of inhabitants of Europe.[14]

The remaining doubts on this point vanish after 1850, with the growing volume and dependability of the statistical information. Natality was now beginning to decrease throughout the Continent, but mortality was decreasing even faster. For Europe as a whole, the death rate was 30.6 per thousand in 1851–60, 29.7 in 1861–70, 29.6 in 1871–80, 27.5 in 1881–90, and 25.9 in 1891–1900 (see table 3.4). The Scandinavian countries first reached a figure of less than 20 during the 1860s, England around 1880, the Netherlands around 1890, and Italy and Austria around 1910. The states of Eastern Europe and the Balkans could not match this achievement until the 1920s or even the 1930s. At the outbreak of the First World War, therefore, the highest mortality in Europe was to the east and south, Russia being in first place with a rate of approximately 29, followed by Rumania, Hungary, Serbia, and Spain with an average of 22.8; Austria, Portugal, and Italy with 20.4; and France with 18.6. The lowest figures were in the north and west: Germany with 16.5, England with 14.1, and Denmark with 13.2. Here the incidence of death was only about half of what it was at the other end of the Continent.[15]

14. Gustav Schmoller, *Zur Geschichte der deutschen Kleingewerbe im 19. Jahrhundert* (Halle, 1870), p. 692; Glass, "Population and Population Movements," p. 241; Glass and Grebenik, "World Population," 6:69; Félix Ponteil, *L'éveil des nationalités et le mouvement libéral (1815–1848)*, new ed. (Paris, 1960), p. 658; Hoffmann, Grumbach, and Hesse, *Wachstum der deutschen Wirtschaft*, p. 172; McKeown and Brown, "Evidence Related to English Population Changes," pp. 137–38; Cipolla, "Italian Demographic Development," pp. 576–77.

15. Glass and Grebenik, "World Population," 6:68–70; Werner Sombart, *Der moderne Kapitalismus: Historisch-systematische Darstellung des gesamteuropäischen Wirtschaftsle-*

Table 3.4. European Death Rates, 1851–1910

	Deaths per 1,000 Inhabitants					
	1851– 1860	1861– 1870	1876– 1880	1886– 1890	1896– 1900	1906– 1910
England	22.2	22.5	20.8	18.9	17.7	14.7
France	23.7	23.6	22.5	22.0	20.6	19.1
Germany	26.4	26.9	26.1	24.4	21.3	17.5
Sweden	21.7	20.2	18.3	16.4	16.1	14.3
Belgium	22.6	23.8	21.8	20.3	18.2	15.9
Denmark	20.5	19.9	19.4	18.7	16.4	13.7
Netherlands	25.6	25.4	22.9	20.5	17.2	14.3
Austria		31.5	33.2	30.0	26.6	22.5
Italy		30.9	29.5	27.0	22.9	21.1
Rumania		26.6	28.7	30.2	26.8	26.0
Spain		30.6		31.1	29.0	24.0
Portugal			23.2	22.4	22.2	20.0

SOURCE: D. V. Glass and E. Grebenik, "World Population, 1800–1950," in *The Cambridge Economic History of Europe*, 7 vols. (Cambridge, 1941–78), 6:68–69.
NOTE: These figures include Austria and Hungary until 1906–10; thereafter only Austria is included.

The pattern of mortality coincided closely with the pattern of natality, because both were under the influence of the same demographic forces. The rise in the standard of living that tended to inhibit the birth rate also helped to reduce the death rate. Economic progress meant greater resistance to disease; scientific discovery led to better medical care. In England a series of cholera epidemics and sanitary inquiries around the middle of the nineteenth century persuaded the authorities to order the cleaning of streets, the chlorination of water supplies, and the improvement of sewage systems. While population in Germany was increasing 14 percent between 1887 and 1898, the number of physicians was increasing 52 percent. In Austria hospital beds per ten thousand inhabitants rose from 7.1 in 1848 to 17.94 in 1900. There were parts of Eastern Europe, on the other hand, where hygienic practices remained almost unchanged and where the frequency and severity of disease hardly diminished.

Social position and class differences, however, had a greater effect on mortality than geographic location and national differences did. The

bens von seinen Anfängen bis zur Gegenwart, 2d ed., 3 vols. (Munich and Leipzig, 1924–28), 3:359; Armengaud, "Population in Europe," p. 46.

death rate in Glasgow late in the nineteenth century was about 150 percent higher for families living in one or two rooms than for those in five
or more. During the 1880s the 6 percent of the inhabitants of Berlin who
belonged to families having only one room accounted for close to 50 percent of all deaths. The average life expectancy in England around 1850
was forty, but in the worst slums of cities like Liverpool and Manchester,
it was less than twenty. In the country at large, the figure was twenty-
four for the unemployed, thirty-one for tradesmen, forty-nine for the
gentry, and fifty-eight for the sons of ducal families.[16]

The increasing survival of infants and children was the crucial factor in
the decline of the death rate. In the past the highest incidence of mortality
had occurred at the two extremes of the normal life span, the earliest
years and advanced age. The historian Edward Gibbon, born into a
family of well-to-do merchants, the son of a member of Parliament,
commented at the end of the eighteenth century on the frequency of
death among the very young:

> The death of a new-born child before that of its parents may seem an
> unnatural, but it is strictly a probable, event: since of any given
> number the greater part are extinguished before their ninth year,
> before they possess the faculties of mind or body. Without accusing
> the profuse waste or imperfect workmanship of Nature, I shall only
> observe, that this unfavourable chance was multiplied against my in-
> fant existence. So feeble was my constitution, so precarious my life,
> that, in the baptism of each of my brothers, my father's prudence
> successively repeated my christian name of Edward, that, in case of
> the departure of the eldest son, this patronymick appellation might
> be still perpetuated in the family.[17]

The precaution proved unnecessary, since the future author of the *Decline and Fall of the Roman Empire* reached adulthood, but his five
younger brothers did not. Could the chances of survival have been much
brighter for those born without the economic advantages of his background?

Comprehensive statistical information on this point is unavailable, but
calculations of infant and child mortality have been made for royalty and
nobility, whose genealogical records were preserved because of their emi-

16. Phyllis Deane, *The First Industrial Revolution* (Cambridge, 1965), p. 243; Shryock,
Development of Modern Medicine, p. 387; Sombart, *Der moderne Kapitalismus*, 3:614;
Wrigley, *Population and History*, p. 173; Ponteil, *L'éveil des nationalités*, p. 659; T. H.
Hollingsworth, "A Demographic Study of the British Ducal Families," *Population Studies*
11 (1957–58):11.

17. *Miscellaneous Works of Edward Gibbon, Esquire: With Memoirs of His Life and
Writings, Composed by Himself*, ed. John Lord Sheffield, 2 vols. (London, 1796), 1:19.

nence in society. Of 1,000 children born alive to members of the ruling families of Europe who married in the sixteenth century, 193 had died by the age of one, 255 by the age of five, and 288 by the age of fifteen. For marriages concluded in the seventeenth century, the figures were 246, 339, and 372, and for the eighteenth century, 153, 277, and 336. In British ducal families, 31.1 percent of all children during the period 1480–1679 died before reaching sixteen, whereas 21.1 percent died during the period 1680–1779.

Scattered data on early mortality in the population as a whole suggest an even higher rate. A study of a group of parishes in Worcestershire reveals that in 1675–99 the ratio of infant burials to baptisms was 12.3 percent and the ratio of child burials 28.5 percent. The percentages were 11.4 and 26.5 in 1700–1725, 11.5 and 35.7 in 1725–49, 9.2 and 24.7 in 1750–74, and 7.1 and 24.7 in 1775–99. Meager statistics on conditions on the Continent indicate the same pattern. Of 1,000 live births in the Norman town of Sotteville-lès-Rouen during the period 1760–90, there were only 572 survivors ten years later; for the region around Paris, the figure in 1740–49 was 508; and for the Dutch village of Broek-in-Waterland in 1654–1732, it was 474 for boys and 563 for girls. The average mortality among infants and children must thus have been between 40 and 50 percent, although at certain times and in some regions it was substantially higher.[18]

A significant decline in the death rate of the young did not take place in most of Europe until well into the nineteenth century. In 1836 a British medical journal announced triumphantly that "the very great diminution of the mortality of infants in England is one of the most remarkable phenomena of modern times. . . . The *London Bills of Mortality*, for the 100 years ending with 1829, supply one of the best proofs of the diminished mortality of infants. Taking five successive periods of twenty years each, the rate of diminution has proceeded with extreme regularity. In the twenty years, 1730–49, out of 100 born 74.5 died under the age of five years. During the twenty years 1810–29, only 31.8 died out of the same number." Such calculations, however, were overoptimistic. To be sure, the number of deaths under the age of one per thousand births in England was 154 in 1851–60 compared to an estimate of about 360 in 1751–60. It continued to fall, moreover, to 145 in 1876–80 and 139 in 1881–85. But then it rose again to 151 in 1891–95 and 156 in 1896–1900. Only after the beginning of the twentieth century was there an-

18. Sigismund Peller, "Births and Deaths among Europe's Ruling Families since 1500," in *Population in History*, ed. Glass and Eversley, p. 94; Hollingsworth, "British Ducal Families," p. 12; D. E. C. Eversley, "A Survey of Population in an Area of Worcestershire from 1660 to 1850 on the Basis of Parish Registers," *Population Studies* 10 (1956–57):269; D. V. Glass, "Introduction," in *Population in History*, ed. Glass and Eversley, p. 22.

other marked drop to 138 in 1901–5, 117 in 1906–10, and 110 in 1911–15. On the Continent infant mortality was also decreasing, though the pace varied considerably from country to country (see table 3.5). Yet even Russia, with the highest rate in Europe, showed some signs of improvement after 1900.

Although statistics on the death rate of those who had survived infancy but not reached adulthood are less detailed, they suggest an even sharper decrease. In France, for example, the figure for those under age four fell from 129 per thousand in 1867–70 to 55 in 1901–4, for those between ages five and nine from 11 to 5, and for those between ages ten and fourteen from 5 to 3. The data indicate that in most countries there was a gradual reduction in the incidence of death among the young, although intermittent increases, reflecting a deterioration of economic conditions or the onset of epidemic diseases, produced frequent irregularities in the descending curve. The decline was most rapid around 1800, the result of an improvement in diet, and around 1900, in response to better health care. By the time of the First World War, infant and child mortality had dropped to less than half of what they had been 150 years before.[19]

The increase in survival was distributed unevenly, however, benefiting most those who already had the best chance of reaching adulthood. The incidence of death among infants in the ruling families of Europe fell from 15.3 percent in 1700–1799 to 9.6 in 1800–1849 and 4.0 in 1850–99. The percentage of sons of ducal families in Great Britain dying before the age of five was 20 in 1730–79, 18 in 1780–1829, and 14 in 1830–79; for daughters the drop was even sharper: 15, 9, and 6. On the other hand, the death rate in foundling hospitals, where abandoned children of the poor were usually brought, was so high that one writer suggested bitterly that they post a sign reading "children killed at government expense." During the 1770s about a third of all babies born in Paris ended up in the *asile* of Saint Vincent de Paul, but far fewer ever left, for the incidence of mortality within a year of entry into such institutions varied from 33 to 90 percent. Deaths among infants in workhouses in fourteen London parishes during the 1760s have been estimated at between 65 and 88 percent. Even these grim statistics pale beside the record of the Dublin Foundling Hospital, where in the twenty-one years ending with 1796 only forty-five infants survived out of more than ten thousand admitted.

Nor did conditions improve substantially after the opening of the nine-

19. T. R. Edmonds, "On the Mortality of Infants in England," *Lancet*, 30 January 1836, pp. 690, 692; Armengaud, "Population in Europe," p. 47; Shryock, *Development of Modern Medicine*, p. 102; Singer and Underwood, *Short History of Medicine*, p. 720; Mitchell, *European Historical Statistics*, pp. 127–31; Sombart, *Der moderne Kapitalismus*, 3:361.

Table 3.5. European Infant Mortality, 1751–1913

	Annual Deaths under Age 1 per 1,000 Births					
	Period	Number	Period	Number	Period	Number
England	1751–60	360	1851–60	154	1906–10	117
France	1801–10	191	1851–60	173	1901–10	132
Sweden	1801–10	179	1851–60	146	1901–10	85
Germany	1840–49	298	1870–79	267	1900–1909	193
Austria	1850–59	250	1880–89	249	1904–13	203
Italy	1870–79	216	1890–99	179	1904–13	151
Russia	1870–79	270	1890–99	272	1900–1909	250

SOURCES: Richard Harrison Shryock, *The Development of Modern Medicine: An Interpretation of the Social and Scientific Factors Involved* (New York, 1947), p. 102; André Armengaud, "Population in Europe, 1700–1914," in *The Fontana Economic History: The Industrial Revolution*, ed. Carlo M. Cipolla (London and Glasgow, 1973), p. 47; B. R. Mitchell, *European Historical Statistics, 1750–1970* (London and Basingstoke, 1975), pp. 127–31.

teenth century. Between 20 and 30 percent of all children born in France were abandoned by their parents, almost 128,000 of them in 1833 alone. The percentage for Paris was even higher, 36 in 1817–20. The Maison de la Couche in that city reported that, of 4,779 babies admitted in 1818, 2,370 died in the first three months and another 956 in the first year. Yet this rate of about 70 percent was easily exceeded by some Italian foundling hospitals, where infant mortality reached 80 or even 90 percent.

The situation became better with time, but social differences continued to play an important role in the incidence of death among the young. Although the rate gradually declined for all occupational groups, it remained much higher for children of the propertyless than for those of the propertied classes. As late as 1911, the German socialist Otto Rühle was arguing heatedly: "It is a thoughtless phrase to say that the grim reaper is no respecter of persons. Facts prove that he is harder and more ruthless toward poverty than toward property. He spares the rich child, while he mows down the poor in swaths."

His contention was buttressed by an impressive array of statistics. The average infant mortality in Berlin was 18.1 percent, but the fashionable Tiergarten district had a figure of only 5.2, whereas the poor working-class quarter of Wedding had 42. In Bremen the number of deaths per ten thousand persons in each age category was 1,676 for those less than one, 156 for those between one and five, and 29 for those between five and fifteen. Among the well-to-do, however, the figures were 489, 28, and 17, and among the poorer classes 2,558, 262, and 40. Infant mortality in Graz was 0 percent for the wealthy, 4.2 for people of middle rank, 35.9 for the propertyless, and 59.9 for the very poor. Even more enlightening are the statistics from Halle showing that the death rate of infants in families of high government officials, army officers, and those with a higher education was 4.3 percent; business clerks and office workers 11.3; merchants, manufacturers, and independent farmers 13; master artisans and small shopkeepers 13; government officials of middle rank 13.5; government officials of lower rank and noncommissioned officers 14.2; skilled workers 18.9; and unskilled workers 24.1. The connection between economic position and infant mortality was obvious.[20]

Yet the increase in life expectancy in Europe was greater during the nineteenth century than during the preceding two thousand years. All regions and classes, moreover, shared in varying degrees in this sudden spurt of human longevity. Progress may have been halting at first, but after 1850 life expectancy in the economically advanced countries grew more than a year each decade (see table 3.6). The combined average for Denmark, England, France, Massachusetts, the Netherlands, Norway, and Sweden rose for men from 39.6 years in 1840 to 40.3 in 1850, 41.1 in 1860, and 42.3 in 1870; for women the figures were 42.5, 42.8, 43.4, and 44.7. The curve then began to climb even more sharply. By the opening of the twentieth century, most countries in Europe could boast of a significant increase in longevity, although its size varied widely, depending on economic, hygienic, and environmental conditions. Denmark and Sweden had the best record, and Russia and Spain had the worst. The average life expectancy was 46.4 years for men and 49.0 for women, a growth of about nine years since 1850.[21]

Class, however, had a greater effect on survival than geography did. In the country with the highest life expectancy, the figure was not even twice that of the country with the lowest. The longevity of those in the most advantageous economic position, on the other hand, was several times that at the bottom of the scale. As early as 1828, Louis-René Villermé, a Paris physician-turned-sociologist, had investigated the relationship between income and life expectancy in different parts of the capital and in

20. Peller, "Europe's Ruling Families," p. 94; Hollingsworth, "British Ducal Families," p. 9; William L. Langer, "Europe's Initial Population Explosion," *American Historical Review* 69 (1963):9; Wrigley, *Population and History*, pp. 125–26; Singer and Underwood, *Short History of Medicine*, p. 225; Otto Rühle, *Das proletarische Kind* (Munich, 1911), pp. 55–57.

21. Glass and Grebenik, "World Population," 6:72, 79, 82; David Thomson, "The Transformation of Social Life," in *The New Cambridge Modern History*, 12 vols. (Cambridge, 1960–70), 12:48; Glass, "Introduction," p. 21; Wrigley, *Population and History*, pp. 171, 175; Armengaud, "Population in Europe," p. 48.

Table 3.6. European Life Expectancy, 1840–1913

Men and Women

	1840		1860		1875		1895		1900–13	
	M	W	M	W	M	W	M	W	M	W
England	39.5	42.7	42.8	46.5					51.5	55.4
France	38.2	41.3	40.4	42.7					45.4	48.9
Netherlands	38.0	39.9	40.1	42.9						
Sweden	44.3	47.9	46.6	49.5					54.5	56.9
Germany					36	38	41	44	45	48
Austria					31	34	37	39	39	41
Italy					35	36	43	43	44	45
Russia							31.4	33.3		
Denmark	42.6	44.7							56.2	59.2
Spain									40.9	42.5

SOURCES: D. V. Glass, "Population and Population Movements in England and Wales, 1700 to 1850," in *Population in History: Essays in Historical Demography*, ed. D. V. Glass and D. E. C. Eversley (London, 1965), p. 21; D. V. Glass and E. Grebenik, "World Population, 1800–1950," in *The Cambridge Economic History of Europe*, 7 vols. (Cambridge, 1941–78), 6:72, 82; André Armengaud, "Population in Europe, 1700–1914," in *The Fontana Economic History: The Industrial Revolution*, ed. Carlo M. Cipolla (London and Glasgow, 1973), p. 48; E. A. Wrigley, *Population and History* (New York and Toronto, 1969), p. 175.

the provinces of France. His conclusion, disturbing to the complacent social conscience of the Restoration, was that "mortality . . . and therefore the average span of life are very different under affluence and under poverty, [for] affluence preserves our life, while privation shortens it through the possession or the lack of the things necessary for life, through well-being or distress, in a word, through all the circumstances in which they place us." It was an unwitting diagnosis of the revolutionary discontent that was about to overthrow the Bourbons.

In 1842 the British social reformer Edwin Chadwick again pointed out the connection between class and survival. According to his report on "the sanitary condition of the labouring population," life expectancy in Leeds was 44 for "gentlemen and persons engaged in professions," 27 for tradesmen, and 19 for laborers; in Liverpool the figures were 35, 22, and 15; and in Manchester, 38, 20, and 17. "The labouring classes," he wrote, "become old the soonest, and the effects of the unfavourable influences in the adolescent and adult stages is shown in the smaller proportions who attain extreme old age." In the Alsatian textile city of Mulhouse at about the same time, differences in longevity between occupational groups were even sharper, according to contemporary estimates. For the children of manufacturers, merchants, and plant managers, life expectancy was 31.8 years; for those of calico printers, it was 15.0; tailors 7.7; day laborers 7.5; carpenters 5.2; wood engravers 5.1; masons 5.0; bakers 4.9; servants 4.8; shoemakers 4.6; joiners 4.4; spinners 3.9; and weavers and metal workers 3.8. The average for all workers except the calico printers was about 5. Economic position was thus the most important determinant of longevity, affecting it more profoundly than nationality, climate, or location. Although there was an increase in life expectancy during the nineteenth century for all classes, it only helped to reduce the disparity in the average age of death among various strata of society. Substantial differences remained.[22]

The cumulative effect of the demographic changes taking place in Europe after 1750 was not only an unprecedented increase in population but also an explosive growth of overseas emigration. The popular expectations that the rationalization of production aroused could not be satisfied within the economic and institutional framework of the Old World. For millions of people, escape from the constricted environment of the mother country to unbounded new opportunities abroad became an exciting possibility. "The process of settlement and naturalization," wrote the *Democratic Review* of New York in 1852, "together with the freedom of our institutions, and the fertility of our soil, have invited the denizens of the world, wherever assembled, or dispersed, to come among us and become fellow-citizens. And from every degree of latitude and of longitude, and from every isle and continent, under the whole heaven, the flood of emigration has poured in upon the United States. . . . There has been nothing like it in appearance since the encampments of the Roman empire, or the tents of the crusaders." Yet the great "Atlantic Migration" was only in its beginning, a stream about to turn into a deluge. The total number of emigrants from Europe between 1815 and 1914 was about 50 million, but 85 percent of them left after 1871. The sheer magnitude of this modern *Völkerwanderung* dwarfed all the massive movements of population that the world had ever seen.

22. L.-R. Villermé, "Mémoire sur la mortalité en France, dans la classe aisée et dans la classe indigente," *Mémoires de l'Académie royale de médicine*, vol. 1 (1828), "Section de médicine," pp. 75, 81; Great Britain, *Parliamentary Papers* (1842), 26 (*Reports from Commissioners*), "Report to Her Majesty's Principal Secretary of State for the Home Department, from the Poor Law Commissioners, on an Inquiry into the Sanitary Condition of the Labouring Population of Great Britain," pp. 157, 159, 161; Marie-Madeleine Kahan-Rabecq, *L'Alsace économique et sociale sous le règne de Louis-Philippe*, 2 vols. (Paris, 1939), 1:165.

The motivation of the great bulk of those leaving Europe was economic. Political oppression or religious bigotry provided an occasional spur to the outflow, but as a rule such factors played a minor role. It was the prospect of a better livelihood for the emigrant and his family that drew millions of people across the oceans and continents. Gustav von Struve, the German rebel of 1848 who had been forced into exile in the United States because of his republican sympathies, declared upon his return to Europe that "most [emigrants] would prefer to find in the . . . fatherland what they now seek with a great expenditure of time, effort, and money on the other side of the ocean, namely, the freedom to settle down, to marry, and to acquire civic rights, as well as land at cheaper prices."

His assertion is supported by statistical data for the states of south Germany in the period 1848–54 (figure 3.1); they show a close connection between the size of agricultural holdings and the volume of emigration. In those provinces of Bavaria and Württemberg where farms were largest, the rate of emigration was generally lowest. There is no comparable information on farm size in Baden, but if the acreage devoted to potato cultivation is accepted as an index of intensive agriculture and land fragmentation, the same relationship between landholding and emigration becomes apparent. Taking the volume of potato production and the number of emigrants per ten thousand inhabitants in the Mittelrheinkreis as each equal to 100, the figures for the Unterrheinkreis are 95 and 93, for the Oberrheinkreis 53 and 70, and for the Seekreis 28 and 59. The pattern is thus similar to that in Bavaria and Württemberg. The effect of economic conditions on population movements, though not always demonstrable with the same precision, was everywhere direct.[23]

Emigration from Europe began early in the nineteenth century as a trickle, but it soon became a torrent. The figures are at first inexact, but they become more reliable for the years after 1850, as the outflow gained momentum. They show that the increase in emigration was much greater than the increase in population. Werner Sombart has calculated that the number of emigrants from Europe per thousand inhabitants grew from 0.08 annually in 1801–20 to 1.27 in 1851–60, 2.06 in 1881–90, and an extraordinary 4.02 in 1906. Only the outbreak of the First World War kept the curve from climbing even higher.

23. "The Crisis in Europe: Number Two, Intervention of the United States," *Democratic Review* 30 (1852):566; Xavier Lannes, "L'expansion démographique," in *L'Europe du XIXe et du XXe siècle*, ed. Max Beloff, Pierre Renouvin, Franz Schnabel, and Franco Valsecchi, 6 vols. (Milan, 1959–64), 4:871, 876; Gustav Struve, *Diesseits und jenseits des Oceans*, 4 vols. (Coburg, 1863–64), 1:75; Marcus L. Hansen, "The Revolutions of 1848 and German Emigration," *Journal of Economic and Business History* 2 (1929–30): 657–58.

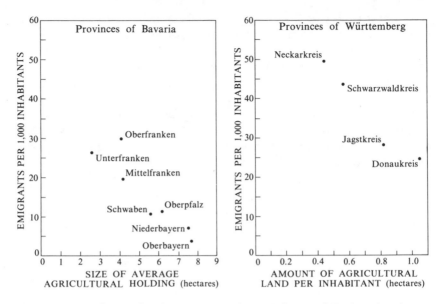

Figure 3.1. Relationship between Landownership and Emigration in South Germany, 1848–54

SOURCE: Marcus L. Hansen, "The Revolutions of 1848 and German Emigration," *Journal of Economic and Business History* 2 (1939–40): 657–58.

The destination of most people who left was the United States. The American share of emigrants crossing the Atlantic varied from about 82 percent in 1866–70 to 61 in 1896–1900. These figures were far ahead of the other leading centers of immigration in the New World: Brazil, whose highest percentage was 21 in 1891–95; Argentina with 17 in 1886–90; and Canada with 11.1 in 1861–65. Of all emigrants in the last prewar decade whose destinations are known, 56 percent went to America, 15 to Asiatic Russia, 11 to Argentina, 6 to Canada, 4 each to Australia and Brazil, and 1 to New Zealand. "In the year ending June 30, 1905," noted Theodore Roosevelt in a message to Congress, "there came to the United States 1,026,000 alien immigrants . . . a greater number of people than came here during the 169 years of our colonial life which intervened between the first landing at Jamestown and the Declaration of Independence."[24]

The sources of the emigration from Europe changed as drastically as

24. Cf. Sombart, *Der moderne Kapitalismus*, 3:384–85; Woodruff, *Impact of Western Man*, pp. 106–9; *International Migrations*, ed. Willcox, 1:172; *The Works of Theodore Roosevelt*, ed. Hermann Hagedorn, 24 vols. (New York, 1923–26), 17:372.

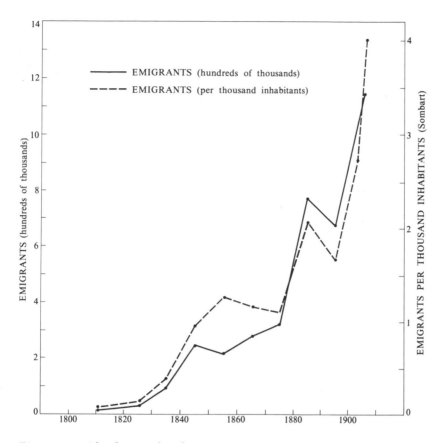

Figure 3.2. Absolute and Relative European Emigration, 1801–1910

SOURCES: Werner Sombart, *Der moderne Kapitalismus: Historisch-systematische Darstellung des gesamteuropäischen Wirtschaftslebens von seinen Anfängen bis zur Gegenwart*, 2d ed., 3 vols. (Munich and Leipzig, 1924–28), 3:385; William Woodruff, *Impact of Western Man: A Study of Europe's Role in the World Economy, 1750–1960* (New York, 1967), p. 106.

its numbers in the course of the nineteenth century. During most of the time, the majority of those leaving came from the north and west, especially the United Kingdom and Germany. Those two countries accounted for 78 and 14 percent of the total in 1846–50, 68 and 22 in 1851–55, 61 and 25 in 1856–60, 64 and 20 in 1861–65, 49 and 24 in 1866–70, 52 and 21 in 1871–75, and 50 and 16 in 1876–80. Combined with the much smaller percentages from Scandinavia and the Low Countries, they easily predominated in the transatlantic flow of population. At the end of the century, however, a sudden shift in the geographic origins of the emigration began to take place. The United Kingdom's share was still considerable: 27 percent in 1891–95, 25 in 1896–1900, 22 in 1901–5, and 24 in 1906–10. The percentages for Germany, however, diminished rapidly from 11 to 4, 3, and finally less than 2. The exodus from Europe was now increasingly fed by the countries of the south and east. Italy, which had accounted for only 5 percent of all emigrants in 1866–70 and 6 in 1871–75, enlarged its share to 31 in 1901–5 and 29 in 1906–10. The percentages for Austria-Hungary rose from 2 and 3 to 19 and 19, and for Russia from 0.1 and 2 to 8 and 7. In the course of only forty years, the national composition of the population outflow had completely changed.

This geographical pattern of the emigration suggests that it was not primarily a movement of the destitute and hopeless. It represented rather a quest for greater opportunity on the part of those who had already emerged from a manorial form of agriculture or the handicraft system of manufacture but who had not yet begun to enjoy the full benefits of economic rationalization. To be sure, there were occasions when the threat of outright starvation drove millions to the New World, as happened during the Hungry Forties. But those were exceptional times. The emigrant was usually a man whose aspirations had risen more rapidly than the means to satisfy them. Consider that 626,000 people left Germany in 1871–80, when that country was just entering the stage of rapid industrialization, while among the rural masses to the south and east, where the standard of living was much lower, the figures were 168,000 for Italy, 58,000 for Russia, and 46,000 for Austria-Hungary. By 1901–10, however, the ratios had been reversed, for Germany, now the dominant economic power on the Continent, had only 274,000 emigrants, whereas Italy had 3,615,000, Austria-Hungary 1,111,000, and Russia 911,000.

The conclusion that the highest rate of emigration generally coincided with a period of incipient economic rationalization is supported by an examination of regional as well as national variations in the flow of population. To take the case of Italy, the number of emigrants per hundred thousand inhabitants in 1876 was much higher in the industrializing north than in the impoverished rural south: 1,247 in Venetia, 1,046 in Piedmont, 588 in Lombardy, and 408 in Liguria, compared to 211 in Basilicata, 112 in Campania, 73 in Calabria, and 45 in Sicily. By 1911–14, however, although there had been a substantial growth in emigration from all parts of the country, the increase was much greater in the restless and embittered south than in the more prosperous north: 3,111 in Venetia, 1,794 in Piedmont, 1,473 in Lombardy, and 638 in Liguria, but 2,510 in Basilicata, 1,811 in Campania, 2,778 in Calabria, and 2,270 in Sicily. The differences in population movement between northern and southern Italy thus paralleled the differences between east and west in Europe as a whole.[25]

The overall effect of emigration was to remove from the Old World millions of people who would otherwise have made increasing demands on its limited material resources. Economic rationalization, despite its great accomplishments, could not satisfy the new aspirations of a growing population no longer willing to accept the hopeless poverty in which the masses had traditionally lived. Passage across the Atlantic became a safety valve for the overcrowded fields and grinding sweatshops of Europe. The distribution of occupations among those coming to the United States makes that clear. Of the non-Jewish emigrants from Poland in 1893–1903, 42 percent were landless peasants, 24 landed peasants, 14 agricultural laborers, 12 city workers, and 8 miscellaneous. In 1913, 34 percent of male Italian emigrants were farm laborers, 31 miners or forest laborers, 14 construction workers, 13 skilled workers, 4 office workers, 1 in the professions, 1 in domestic service, and 1 in household duties or unknown occupations.

Of all Europeans entering the United States between 1899 and 1914 who had been previously employed, the percentage of professionals among Jews was 1 and that of skilled workers 68, for Scots the figures were 6 and 54, for Englishmen 9 and 48, for Frenchmen 9 and 33, for Germans 4 and 30, down to the Rumanians and the Ruthenians at the bottom of the list with 0.2 and 3 and 0.1 and 2 respectively. The average for all nationalities was 2 and 20. During the period 1891–1915, about 35 percent of the alien immigrants into the United States were in domestic service or "general labor," 18 in agriculture, 12 in industry and mining, 4 in transport and commerce, 1 in the liberal professions and public service, and 31 in miscellaneous, unknown, or no occupations. The departure of these semiskilled and unskilled millions meant that there were that many fewer people to feed, clothe, and house in Europe, that many fewer people to intensify economic competition and aggravate social conflict.[26]

The significance of emigration, however, lay not only in the removal of surplus population. The mere knowledge that there was a possibility of leaving the constricted life of the Old World for green new lands overseas

25. *International Migrations*, ed. Willcox, 1:232; Woodruff, *Impact of Western Man*, pp. 106–7; Anna Maria Ratti, "Italian Migration Movements, 1876 to 1926," in *International Migrations*, ed. Willcox, 2:446.

26. V. V. Obolensky-Ossinsky, "Emigration from and Immigration into Russia," in *International Migrations*, ed. Willcox, 2:534; Ratti, "Italian Migration Movements," p. 456; Liebmann Hersch, "International Migration of the Jews," in *International Migrations*, ed. Willcox, 2:491; *International Migrations*, ed. Willcox, 1:217.

was a consolation even to those who never took advantage of it. And then there was the ferment of different customs, ideas, and attitudes brought back by the relative or friend who had been to America. The ratio of returnees from the United States to immigrants rose from 5 percent in 1831–40 and 10 in 1841–50 to 30 in 1881–90, 35 in 1891–1900, and 39 in 1901–7. In all, close to 10 million people went back to Europe between 1886 and 1915.

The historian Arnold Toynbee, writing just as the era of unrestricted population movement was coming to an end, described the impact of the repatriate from America on Greek society:

> His greatest gift to his country will be his American point of view. In the West he has learnt that men of every language and religion can live in the same city and work at the same shops and sheds and mills and switch-yards without desecrating each other's churches or even suppressing each other's newspapers, not to speak of cutting each other's throats; and when next he meets Albanian or Bulgar on Balkan ground, he may remember that he has once dwelt with him in fraternity at Omaha or St. Louis or Chicago. This is the gospel of Americanism, and unlike Hellenism, which spread downwards from the patriarch's residence and the merchant's counting-house, it is being preached in all the villages of the land by the least prejudiced and most enterprising of their sons (for it is these who answer America's call); and spreading upward from the peasant towards the professor in the university and the politician in parliament.[27]

This gospel of Americanism, which millions of emigrants carried back with them to their homeland, was the New World's greatest gift to the Old, helping to change the way of life in Europe during the nineteenth century.

---

27. Walter F. Willcox, "Immigration into the United States," in *International Migrations*, ed. Willcox, 2:89; *International Migrations*, ed. Willcox, 1:196; Nevill Forbes, Arnold J. Toynbee, David Mitrany, and D. G. Hogarth, *The Balkans: A History of Bulgaria, Serbia, Greece, Rumania, Turkey* (Oxford, 1915), pp. 249–50.

4

THE PROCESS OF URBANIZATION

The great movement of population from Europe to America was closely related to a still greater movement of population from country to city motivated by the same search for economic opportunity. The rationalization of production generated a demand for manpower which could only be satisfied by major demographic redistribution. The result was an internal migration that dwarfed the simultaneous migration overseas. The lopsided balance between rural and urban areas, which had remained essentially unchanged since the Middle Ages, was suddenly altered by the rapid growth of cities whose need for labor led to a steady inflow of inhabitants.

The new mobility of population became increasingly apparent after the middle of the nineteenth century, as industrialization spread eastward from its center of origin in the British Isles. The percentage of Prussians born in the town where they were enumerated by the census taker fell from 56.8 in 1871 to 53.4 in 1890. The figures for Austria were 78.7 in 1869 and 63.9 in 1890, for Belgium 70.2 in 1846 and 65.2 in 1890, for the Netherlands 69.09 in 1849 and 65.4 in 1889, and for Switzerland 64.0 in 1850 and 45.9 in 1888. The migration was often only short range, going no farther than a nearby mining town or manufacturing center. Yet there was also a substantial movement to more distant destinations. In Denmark the proportion of those living in their native district declined from 83.15 percent in 1880 to 80.68 in 1890; in France the percentage of those living in their native department dropped from 88.4 in 1866 to 83.2 in 1891; and in Sweden those living in their native *län* fell from 92.8 percent in 1860 to 88.4 in 1880. As for England, by 1871 only 74.04 percent of her people resided in the county in which they had been born.

Toward the close of the nineteenth century, the highest degree of population mobility was recorded in Saxony and the lowest in Norway, Sweden, and Hungary (see table 4.1). Although there are no statistics for the underdeveloped agricultural states of the east and south—Russia, the Balkans, Italy, Spain, and Portugal—the pattern of demographic movement elsewhere suggests that a low level of industrialization tended to inhibit the internal mobility of population. But by the same token, the lack of economic opportunity at home, which reduced domestic migration, encouraged overseas migration. Sweden, for example, where close to 90 percent of the inhabitants in 1880 lived in their native counties, sent proportionately more people to America than any other country except Ireland. The migrant thus did not usually exchange the land of his birth for another European state. Prior to the First World War, only France and Germany had more than a million aliens, and only one person in twenty lived in Europe outside his native country. Those who emigrated preferred to leave the Old World behind them.[1]

The force that determined the direction and intensity of the internal movement of population was industrialization. The expansion of production in the nineteenth century, which required a high concentration of labor, attracted millions of people from farms and villages to the centers of manufacture, mining, and commerce. An examination of demographic growth in several French departments before and after the onset of industrialization illustrates this point. In the period 1821–51, while the number of inhabitants in the country as a whole rose 24.1 percent, in the departments of Nord and Pas-de-Calais, still only on the threshold of a great coal and textile boom, the increase was 27.8 and 10.5. The largely agricultural departments of Aisne and Finisterre actually had a higher rate of growth—21.5 and 27.9—than the average for their northern neighbors. Far ahead were the departments of Seine, chiefly Paris, with 73.0, and Bouches-du-Rhône, which included Marseilles, with 36.6. In the period 1851–81, however, there was a significant change in the demographic distribution. The national population increase was only 5.3 percent, a result in part of the loss of territory after the Franco-Prussian War. The rate of growth in Seine and Bouches-du-Rhône was still the highest, 96.9 and 37.2. But rapidly industrializing Nord and Pas-de-Calais, with 38.4 and 18.2 respectively, were now far ahead of rural Aisne and Finisterre with −0.4 and 10.3. Internal migration from agricultural to industrial regions accounted in large part for this changing pattern of population increase.

The situation in Germany was comparable. Until the middle decades of the nineteenth century, demographic expansion in the farmlands of the east was greater than in the western areas destined to become major centers of industry and mining. In the province of Pomerania, for example, the annual increase was 2.69 percent in 1816–22, 1.45 in 1822–31, 1.64 in 1831–40, 1.41 in 1840–49, and 1.23 in 1849–55. On the other hand, the combined figures for the districts of Arnsberg and Düsseldorf, including the Ruhr coal basin, were 1.16, 1.38, 1.49, 1.18, and 1.61. Thus, only during the 1850s did the western rate begin to surpass the eastern. Thereafter the shift in the distribution of population growth became pro-

1. Adna Ferrin Weber, *The Growth of Cities in the Nineteenth Century: A Study in Statistics* (New York and London, 1899), pp. 248–50, 252; J. J. Spengler, "Population Changes, 1900–1950: Socio-Economic Implications," *Journal of World History* 5 (1960): 937.

Table 4.1. Mobility of Population in Europe, 1875–91

Country or State of Residence at Enumeration	Year	Place of Birth (percentage)		
		County of Residence	Elsewhere in Same Country or State	Different Country or State
Saxony	1885	69.1	20.8	10.1
Prussia	1890	69.7	27.1	3.2
England	1891	71.6	24.5	3.9
Denmark	1890	77.9	18.6	3.5
Austria	1890	80.2	18.1	1.7
France	1891	81.3	16.4	2.3
Switzerland	1888	82.1	11.5	6.4
Norway	1875	87.2	10.7	2.1
Sweden	1880	88.5	11.1	0.4
Hungary	1890	89.2	9.3	1.5

SOURCE: Adna Ferrin Weber, *The Growth of Cities in the Nineteenth Century: A Study in Statistics* (New York and London, 1899), p. 249.

gressively more pronounced, the result largely of internal migration. To illustrate, between 1861 and 1910 the number of inhabitants of four industrial counties in the west—Arnsberg, Düsseldorf, Aachen, and Münster—increased 284 percent, from 1,495,000 to 5,743,000. Most of this rise was clearly due to net immigration because the demographic expansion of the German Empire as a whole was only 83 percent.

Similarly, the population of East Prussia grew 13.2 percent between 1871 and 1910, while that of the Rhine Province grew 99.2. This disparity was primarily the result of the shift of manpower from farming to manufacturing. Whereas East Prussia was losing 18,300 inhabitants annually in the period 1871–1900, the percentage of the native-born in the population of the Rhine Province declined from 93.2 in 1871 to 85.5 in 1905, and the percentage of those born in the east rose from 0.4 to 3.1. The outflow was strongest amid the latifundia beyond the Oder River, where the loss of population through migration was 3.2 million in 1871–1910, almost half the excess of births over deaths. Since there were only about 1 million overseas emigrants during the period, 2.2 million must have left for other parts of Germany.[2]

2. E. A. Wrigley, *Industrial Growth and Population Change: A Regional Study of the Coalfield Areas of North-West Europe in the Later Nineteenth Century* (Cambridge, 1961), pp. 24, 64; Gunther Ipsen, "Die preussische Bauernbefreiung als Landesausbau," *Zeit-*

Even in a small agricultural country like Switzerland at the beginning
of the nineteenth century, there were unmistakable signs of population
movement in response to the onset of industrialization. Salomon Schinz,
a clergyman in the highlands of the canton of Zürich, explained in 1818
the cause of the demographic growth that he saw about him: "Never
would such a mass of people have arisen in these more rugged regions, if
the substantial earnings from factories had not facilitated and promoted
their nourishment and increase, and thereby doubled the size of the
population within half a century. If therefore all these people are to
continue to live here, then such earnings, which had planted them, as it
were, are simply indispensable to them." The economic boom in turn had
led to the familiar problems of rapid demographic expansion: "Even the
middle-class property owners could not subsist without such a livelihood
[from manufacture]. For through expensive purchases, or through the
frequent divisions of properties and the construction of new homes which
thereby became necessary, or through outbidding, a great burden of
indebtedness has accumulated on many landed holdings." The result was
the diminishing importance of farming, as more and more families came
to depend on textile production for their income. "Over 1,360 people in
my parish have to live entirely on earnings from factories. Close to 200
households have no real property, and many have no personal or movable
property, except for their spinning wheel, weaver's loom, or the most
essential furniture and clothing. The poorest people lack even the latter."

The anguished cry of those whose customary way of life was being
destroyed by the movement of population from agriculture to industry
was to be heard over and over again during the nineteenth century.
Pastor Schinz saw in the spread of the factory system the same dangers
against which countless other defenders of the old social order tried to
warn Europe: the decline of the ancestral village, the uncontrolled mobility of labor, the endless quest for profit, the growing dependence on a
capricious capitalistic economy, and the moral deterioration of a society
where wealth accumulates and men decay. But the material needs responsible for the demographic shift were too powerful to be halted by
homilies. The changing religious composition of the town of Wald in the

schrift für Agrargeschichte und Agrarsoziologie 2 (1954):49–50; E. A. Wrigley, Population and History (New York and Toronto, 1969), p. 155; B. R. Mitchell, European His-
torical Statistics, 1750–1970 (London and Basingstoke, 1975), p. 20; Wolfgang Köllmann,
"The Process of Urbanization in Germany at the Height of the Industrialization Period,"
Journal of Contemporary History, 4, no. 3 (1969):64; Erich Keyser, Bevölkerungsge-
schichte Deutschlands, 2d ed. (Leipzig, 1941), p. 424; Hilde Wander, "Migration and the
German Economy," in Economics of International Migration: Proceedings of a Conference
Held by the International Economic Association (London, 1958), ed. Brinley Thomas
(London, 1958), p. 199.

Zürich highlands attested to the magnetic effect of the textile industry on the flow of population. In 1860, when the labor force was still being largely recruited from the community and its surrounding countryside, there were 4,101 Protestants and 197 Catholics. In 1880 the figures were 5,325 and 698 and in 1900, 5,422 and 1,259. As industry increased, the reservoir of manpower on which it drew expanded beyond the Zürich region to more distant and backward Catholic cantons, and even beyond that to Italy. Hence the number of Catholics rose 539 percent, whereas the total number of inhabitants rose only 55 percent. The motivation and the direction of population movement in Switzerland were thus the same as they were in France or Germany.[3]

The shift of economic primacy from farming to manufacturing led logically to the flow of manpower from country to city. Prior to the industrial revolution, most opportunities for livelihood, including many not directly involved in agriculture, were to be found in villages rather than towns. But the mechanization of production resulted in the growing concentration of labor around sources of energy, supplies of raw material, crossroads of trade and shipping, or centers of credit and entrepreneurial expertness. The outcome was an intensive process of urbanization in which cities grew far more rapidly than the population at large. This tendency was global in scope, so that 9.2 percent of all people on earth lived in cities of over twenty thousand by 1900, more than twice the proportion of fifty years before. The degree of urbanization in the economically advanced nations of Europe, however, was far ahead of the world average. As the nineteenth century drew to a close, the percentage of the population living in cities of over twenty thousand was 53.6 in England, 42.4 in Scotland, 30.0 in Saxony, 29.3 in the Netherlands, 26.1 in Belgium, 23.0 in Prussia, 21.9 in Germany, 21.1 in France, and 20.2 in Denmark. Even in the underdeveloped agricultural countries of the south and east, urbanization was greater than in the world as a whole. The figure for Spain was 18.0, Italy 13.3, Austria 12.0, Hungary 11.3, Rumania 10.7, and Portugal 9.2. Of the leading European states, only Russia with a percentage of 7.2 in 1885 was behind the global percentage of 9.2 in 1900.

In most of Western and Central Europe, the rate of urban growth was rapid, as Table 4.2 shows, far more rapid than the rate of demographic growth in general. The movement from country to city became especially

3. Salomon Schinz, *Das höhere Gebirg des Kantons Zürich, und ökonomisch-moralischer Zustand der Bewohner, mit Vorschlägen der Hülfe und Auskunft für die bey mangelnder Fabrik-Arbeit brotlose Uebervölkerung* (n. p., 1818), pp. 8–9; Rudolf Braun, *Sozialer und kultureller Wandel in einem ländlichen Industriegebiet (Zürcher Oberland) unter Einwirkung des Maschinen- und Fabrikwesens im 19. und 20. Jahrhundert* (Erlenbach-Zürich and Stuttgart, 1965), p. 260.

Table 4.2. European Urbanization, 1800–90

	Population in Cities over 10,000 (percentage)			Annual Rate of Concentration in Cities over 10,000 (percentage)	
	About 1800	About 1850	About 1890	1800– 1850	1850– 1890
England	21.3	39.5	61.7	.36	.56
Scotland	17.0	32.2	49.9	.30	.44
Saxony	8.9	13.6	34.7	.14	.52
Belgium	13.5	20.8	34.8	.18	.32
Prussia	7.3	10.6	30.0	.10	.47
France	9.5	14.4	25.9	.10	.29
Denmark	10.9	9.6	23.6		
Austria	4.4	5.8	15.8	.03	.21
Hungary	5.4	9.1	17.6	.07	.21
Russia	3.7	5.3	9.3	.04	.14
Switzerland	4.3	7.3	16.5	.11	.24
Norway	3.3	5.3	16.7	.05	.20

SOURCES: Adna Ferrin Weber, *The Growth of Cities in the Nineteenth Century: A Study in Statistics* (New York and London, 1899), pp. 144–45; Eric E. Lampard, "The Urbanizing World," in *The Victorian City: Images and Realities*, ed. H. J. Dyos and Michael Wolff, 2 vols. (London and Boston, 1973), 1:5.

pronounced after 1850, as industrialization gained momentum on the Continent and the demand for factory labor became more intense. Except for Great Britain, Belgium, and Portugal, the pace of urbanization in Europe during the second half of the nineteenth century was proportionately greater, much greater as a rule, than in the world at large.[4]

The biggest cities, moreover, usually made the biggest gains. The advantage of size meant growing economic opportunity in the metropolis, especially if it was also the seat of government, where the concentration of labor, entrepreneurship, commerce, credit, and intelligence attracted the restless and ambitious from all classes of society. Around 1500 there had been only 6 cities in Europe of over 100,000 inhabitants with a

4. Eric E. Lampard, "The Social Impact of the Industrial Revolution," in *Technology in Western Civilization*, ed. Melvin Kranzberg and C. W. Pursell, Jr., 2 vols. (New York, London, and Toronto, 1967), 1:315; Spengler, "Population Changes," p. 938; Weber, *Growth of Cities*, pp. 144–45; Eric E. Lampard, "The Urbanizing World," in *The Victorian City: Images and Realities*, ed. H. J. Dyos and Michael Wolff, 2 vols. (London and Boston, 1973), 1:5.

combined population of 800,000 or 1.4 percent of the total. In the course of the next three hundred years, the number of large cities rose gradually to 23 with 5.4 million people or 2.8 to 2.9 percent of the total. Then came an explosive growth fed by the industrial revolution, so that by 1850 there were 43 cities of over 100,000 with a combined population of 12.7 million, 4.8 percent of the total, and by 1900 there were 143 cities with 50.1 million or 10.1 percent. The rise of national capitals was particularly rapid. In the course of the nineteenth century, St. Petersburg increased 300 percent, London 340, Paris 345, Vienna 490, Berlin 872, and Budapest 1,256. Yet there were other centers of manufacture, trade, and banking that equaled or even surpassed these rates: Marseilles with 342, Barcelona with 363, Hamburg with 443, Warsaw with 538, Birmingham with 607, Manchester with 617, Cologne with 646, Liverpool with 780, Munich with 1,150, and Leipzig with 1,420. The discovery of coal deposits or metal ores, the construction of textile mills or blast furnaces, the founding of credit institutions or investment banks, the establishment of new trade routes or the expansion of old ones, each had an important effect on the movement of people from village to city.

That the metropolis, especially the national capital, attracted inhabitants of the countryside in large numbers becomes apparent from an examination of the proportion of the population toward the end of the nineteenth century living in its native community. In Sweden the percentage was 92.0 for rural districts, 67.8 for urban districts, and 41.3 for the capital city. In Denmark the figures were 86.8, 75.2, and 55.9; in Belgium 70.4, 59.4, and 57.0; and in Switzerland 60.7, 34.7, and 24.3. In France, where the percentage was about 70.0 for rural districts and 32.4 for Paris, the data for urban districts are unavailable. But in a department like Bouches-du-Rhône, with 83.5 percent of the population residing in a city, only 54.7 percent lived in their native community. Similarly, the English statistics provide no nationwide comparison of demographic mobility in city and country, though there are figures for the proportion of native-born inhabitants in a few of the urban counties: 32.9 percent in Middlesex, 65.5 in London, and 75.9 in Lancashire. The percentage of the native-born in a group of rural counties, on the other hand, was on an average significantly higher: 63.8 in Rutland, 70.0 in Hereford, 82.3 in Suffolk, and 87.6 in Cardigan. The demographic data for Germany show the same trend. In 1907, 92.5 percent of those born in a city were living in a city, but only 69.7 percent of those born in the country were living in the country. The intensity of internal migration was thus much greater in villages than towns.[5]

5. Charles Tilly, "Food Supply and Public Order in Modern Europe," in *The Formation of National States in Western Europe*, ed. Charles Tilly (Princeton, 1975), p. 399; André

The movement of population accounted for a large part, often the major part, of urban expansion in the nineteenth century. Calculations of the relative share of the excess of births, net immigration, and the incorporation of suburbs in the overall growth of several big cities support this conclusion. London is an important exception, for in the period 1852–91 natural increase equaled 84.03 percent of total increase. In Cologne in 1821–90, moreover, the ratios were 34.10, 27.48, and 37.42. But elsewhere the proportional importance of the three factors was significantly different. In Copenhagen in 1801–90, the percentages were 42.98, 57.02, and 0; in Vienna in 1891–90, 20.52, 32.48, and 47.00; in Leipzig in 1801–90, 16.42, 39.70, and 43.88; in Paris in 1821–90, 15.23, 64.21, and 20.56; in Breslau in 1821–90, 15.16, 79.21, and 5.63; and in Munich in 1811–90, 10.59, 72.26, and 17.15. The figures for Berlin and St. Petersburg are incomplete, but in 1801–90 the excess of births accounted for 20.52 percent of total growth in the former and a deficit of −27.81 in the latter. A more limited study of population increase in the seven largest cities of the Austrian Empire between 1881 and 1910 reveals a similar pattern. In Vienna natural growth, that is, the average annual excess of births per thousand inhabitants, was 10.9, whereas actual growth determined by census enumerations but excluding incorporated suburbs was 18.1. The figures were 6.7 and 14.6 for Graz, 5.2 and 15.3 for Trieste and the surrounding area, 9.3 and 20.5 for Prague and its suburbs, 7.8 and 14.0 for Brünn, 10.4 and 20.9 for Lemberg, and 10.4 and 17.0 for Cracow. In Austria as a whole, however, natural growth was greater than actual growth, 10.2 and 8.5, a result of increasing emigration abroad, especially from the rural districts.

The demographic movement from country to city was thus primarily responsible for urbanization in many parts of Europe, although the excess of births in both was as a rule quite substantial. Take Sweden, where the natural increase per thousand inhabitants of the rural population was 12.25 annually in 1851–60, but the total increase was only 9.03, whereas for the urban population the figures were 1.33 and 21.61. In 1861–70 the rates were 11.87 and 5.68 for the former and 6.78 and 21.27 for the latter; in 1871–80, 12.89 and 8.54 compared with 8.08 and 24.40; and in 1881–90, 12.29 and 0.26 compared with 11.33 and 26.22. Statistics for twenty-five large cities in Germany show that in 1861–64 natural increase accounted for an average annual growth of 8.3 per thousand, but net immigration accounted for 27.4. The rates were

Armengaud, "Population in Europe, 1700–1914," in *The Fontana Economic History: Industrial Revolution*, ed. Carlo M. Cipolla (London and Glasgow, 1973), p. 32; Mitchell, *European Historical Statistics*, pp. 76–78; Weber, *Growth of Cities*, pp. 262–63; Wolfgang Köllmann, "Grundzüge der Bevölkerungsgeschichte Deutschlands im 19. und 20. Jahrhundert," *Studium Generale* 12 (1959):387.

4.3 and 17.7 in 1864–67, 6.1 and 22.1 in 1867–71, 10.4 and 21.7 in
1871–75, 12.6 and 12.7 in 1875–80, and 9.9 and 14.3 in 1880–85. In
France the effect of the mobility of population on urban expansion was
even greater. In 1861–65 natural increase accounted for 17 percent and
net immigration for 83 percent of the rise in the number of city residents.
The percentages were 16 and 84 in 1872–76, 3 and 97 in 1876–81, 6
and 94 in 1881–86, and −0.2 and 100.2 in 1886–91. Internal migration
was thus a factor of progressively greater importance in the growth of the
French urban population, until at the end of the nineteenth century it
became the only factor.[6]

The big cities, with their diversified economic structure, expanding
labor market, bustling streets, and bright lights, attracted a disproportionate share of the millions of rustics leaving farms and villages in search
of a better life. Manchester, Marseilles, Cologne, or Prague held out a
greater promise of opportunity and success than Ipswich, Rennes, Greifs-
wald, or Innsbruck. Whereas the proportion of the European population
living in cities increased 39 percent between 1860 and the beginning of
the twentieth century, the proportion in cities of over 50,000 increased
112 percent. The tendency toward urban concentration was even more
pronounced in Western Europe, where those living in cities increased 41
percent during the same period, but those in cities of over 50,000 increased 117 percent. Consider the data on England given in Table 4.3.
Between 1851 and 1911 the proportion of the British population living
in cities rose 56 percent, but the proportion of those in cities of over
100,000 rose 68 percent. Similarly, in France the proportion of the urban
population, defined as those living in communities of over 2,000, grew
84 percent between 1851 and 1910, but the proportion of those in cities
of over 100,000 grew 191 percent.

The most detailed information concerning the effect of internal migration on urban growth comes from Germany, where statistics reveal that
the larger the community, the higher its rate of growth was likely to be.
In 1871, 4.8 percent of the total population lived in big cities of over
100,000, 7.2 in middle-sized cities between 20,000 and 100,000, 11.2 in
small cities between 5,000 and 20,000, and 12.4 in rural towns between
2,000 and 5,000. By 1910 the percentages had changed to 21.2, 13.3,
14.1, and 11.2. The proportion of people in all urban communities had
risen 68.0 percent, but the proportion in big cities had risen 341.7, in
middle-sized cities 84.7, and in small cities 25.9; in rural towns there had
been a decline of 9.7. In other words, there was a close correlation

6. Weber, *Growth of Cities*, pp. 237, 240, 245; William H. Hubbard, "Der Wachs-
tumsprozess in den österreichischen Gross-Städten 1869–1910: Eine historisch-demo-
graphische Untersuchung," in *Soziologie und Sozialgeschichte: Aspekte und Probleme*, ed.
Peter Christian Ludz (Opladen, 1973), p. 390.

Table 4.3. Urbanization in England, 1831–71

| Period | Percentage Change Resulting from Migration | | | |
	London	Other Large Cities	Small Towns	Rural
1831–41	3.25	12.00	−2.02	−4.79
1841–51	8.55	12.12	−2.18	−6.80
1851–61	6.75	7.77	−4.64	−4.64
1861–71	2.78	7.72	−2.11	−4.83

SOURCE: Adna Ferrin Weber, *The Growth of Cities in the Nineteenth Century: A Study in Statistics* (New York and London, 1899), p. 244.

between size and growth. The great metropolis was gaining population more rapidly than the small provincial town, and often at its expense. There were some instances, to be sure, of a national capital like London or Berlin, which had a considerable population before the nineteenth century, growing more slowly than a booming industrial and commercial center like Manchester or Leipzig, which had fewer than 100,000 inhabitants in 1800. Yet by and large growth was proportionate to size, so that the large city generally expanded more swiftly than the small one.[7]

The scope of the internal migration contributing to the growth of an urban community was also to a considerable extent a function of its size. In his "second law of migration," Adna Weber, one of the most perceptive writers of the nineteenth century on urbanization, formulated this principle as follows: "The distance traveled by migrants varies in the same ratio as the magnitude of the city which is their destination. The larger the town, the wider its circle of influence in attracting immigrants; the small city acts as a magnet for the neighboring counties, a large city (100,000+) attracts strangers from other parts or provinces, but only the great capitals exercise an international influence on migration."

In support of this generalization, he adduced statistics from the Austrian census of 1890 (table 4.4). In the country as a whole, 65.2 percent of the population had been born in the community of residence, 15.0 in another community of the same district, 12.8 in another district of the same province, 5.3 in another province, and 1.7 abroad. The percent-

7. Werner Sombart, *Der moderne Kapitalismus: Historisch-systematische Darstellung des gesamteuropäischen Wirtschaftslebens von seinen Anfängen bis zur Gegenwart*, 2d ed., 3 vols. (Munich and Leipzig, 1924–28), 3:387–89; Weber, *Growth of Cities*, pp. 243–44; Armengaud, "Population in Europe," p. 32; Mitchell, *European Historical Statistics*, p. 77.

Table 4.4. Austrian Internal Migration, 1890 Census

Size of Community	Place of Birth (percentage)				
	Community of Residence	Another Community in Same District	Another District in Same Province	Another Province	Abroad
Over 20,000	43.1	1.3	25.8	23.1	7.2
10,000–20,000	46.4	12.2	31.0	7.7	2.7
5,000–10,000	55.6	14.2	21.0	6.7	2.5
2,000–5,000	69.9	13.2	11.9	3.6	1.4
500–2,000	73.5	14.9	8.5	2.3	0.8
Under 500	65.7	21.5	10.0	2.2	0.7
Total	65.2	15.0	12.8	5.3	1.7

SOURCE: Adna Ferrin Weber, *The Growth of Cities in the Nineteenth Century: A Study in Statistics* (New York and London, 1899), p. 260.

ages varied, however, with the size of the community, the percentage of the population of a community born in that community or in another community of the same district being inversely proportional to its size.

Statistical data on the origin of the population of the forty-two largest German cities in 1907 suggest a similar conclusion. There was a rough correspondence between the size of the city and the proportion of its population that had immigrated from another province, state, or country. It becomes clear from Table 4.5 that an approximate correlation existed between the size of the urban community and the distance from which it was able to draw population. Berlin and Hamburg, with their rich opportunities for employment and advancement, attracted more people from more remote regions than Posen and Danzig did. The underlying economic motivation of population movement provided the big city with wider appeal for the mass of migrants than a drowsy provincial town could exert.[8]

Those who left the countryside for an urban community underwent a rapid social and cultural assimilation, soon becoming indistinguishable in tastes or attitudes from those who had been townsmen for generations.

8. Weber, *Growth of Cities*, pp. 259–60; Wolfgang Köllmann, "Industrialisierung, Binnenwanderung und 'Soziale Frage': (Zur Entstehungsgeschichte der deutschen Industriegroszstadt im 19. Jahrhundert)," *Vierteljahrschrift für Sozial- und Wirtschaftsgeschichte* 46 (1959):63–66.

Table 4.5. German Migration to Large Cities, 1907 Occupational Census

| | | Place of Birth (percentage) | | |
	Population	City of Residence	Another Community in Same State or Province	Another German State or Province	Abroad
Posen	139,500	39.7	43.8	15.5	1.0
Danzig	158,000	44.2	35.1	19.8	0.9
Stettin	223,400	35.9	45.1	18.1	0.9
Frankfurt a.M.	341,200	37.6	30.3	29.5	2.6
Munich	533,300	40.5	31.6	23.2	4.6
Hamburg	826,700	48.2	22.2	26.4	3.2
Berlin	2,005,100	40.5	18.0	39.1	2.4
Average of 42 largest cities	280,800	42.4	32.0	22.9	2.7

SOURCE: Wolfgang Köllman, "Industrialisierung, Binnenwanderung und 'Soziale Frage': (Zur Entstehungsgeschichte der deutschen Industriegroszstadt im 19. Jahrhundert)," *Vierteljahrschrift für Sozial- und Wirtschaftgeschichte* 46 (1959):63–65.

At first the transplanted rustic had to content himself with unskilled occupations for which brawn and endurance were the chief qualifications: work in domestic and personal service; in hotels and restaurants; as a postman, truckman, or cabdriver; and occasionally as a laborer in the building trades. But then he began to make his way up the scale of employment, his children usually managed to climb even more rapidly, and within a generation or two, sometimes less than that, the distribution of occupations among the newcomers became comparable to that of the urban population at large.

According to an analysis of the social structure of Karlsruhe in 1895, 82 percent of the immigrants into the city belonged to the lower class, 14 to the middle class, and 4 to the "educated" class. The percentages for their sons, however, were 41, 49, and 10, and for their grandsons 40, 35, and 25. Statistics for Berlin in 1885 show a similar pattern of social and occupational mobility. Immigrants who had been in the capital less than five years made up 21.6 percent of the total population, 29.3 percent of the male working population, 11.7 percent of the male entrepreneurs, and 5.5 percent of the male entrepreneurs with more than five employees. For those who had been residents between five and fifteen years, the percentages were 19.5, 23.7, 24.7, and 18.7; and for those who had been residents for more than fifteen years, they were 16.5, 22.7, 40.9, and 44.6.

A study in 1892 of five hundred village emigrants in England, the great majority of whom went to London, also shows a general movement from less to more skilled occupations and from lower to higher positions on the scale of social respectability. Whereas the number of those in outdoor labor declined from 69.5 to 42.1 percent, those in personal and domestic service increased from 5.8 to 15.8. In the village none had been in a public-service occupation such as soldier or policeman, but in the city 14.5 percent were. Although the percentage of those in the building trades fell from 8.3 to 6.4, those in other industries rose from 7.6 to 9.1. There was a significant increase, moreover, in the proportion engaged in middle-class occupations. The number of retail dealers and innkeepers grew from 7.8 to 9.7 percent, that of clerks from 0.7 to 1.5, and that of professionals such as teachers from 0.3 to 0.9.

The process of urban assimilation became even more intensive after the opening of the twentieth century. That, at any rate, is the conclusion suggested by Wolfgang Köllmann's study of five large German cities in 1907: Munich, Königsberg, Düsseldorf, Chemnitz, and Gelsenkirchen. The native-born inhabitants, whose average percentage of the labor force in each city was 26.2, accounted for an average percentage of 21.8 in such middle-class occupations as entrepreneurs and white-collar employees in industry, mining, commerce, and transportation, civil servants, and members of the learned professions; an average percentage of 29.2 of the workers in industry, mining, commerce, and transportation; and an average percentage of 13.8 of the workers in domestic service. Those born outside the city but in the same province or state accounted for an average percentage of 43.6 of the labor force and average percentages of 48.6, 42.2, and 60.1 in the three occupational categories. Those born in another province or state in Germany accounted for an average percentage of 25.6 of the labor force and average percentages of 26.0, 23.4, and 24.5 in the occupational categories. And those born in a foreign country accounted for an average percentage of 4.6 of the labor force and average percentages of 3.6, 5.2, and 3.1 in the occupational categories. The only significant disproportion between place of birth and nature of employment thus occurred in the small category of domestic servants, where immigrants into the city (most of them recent, no doubt) made up 87.7 percent of the employees, although their share of the entire labor force was 73.8 percent. The big city in the age of economic rationalization, unlike the preindustrial town, was thus expanding rapidly enough to absorb the overflow of population from the countryside without maintaining rigid legal or economic distinctions between natives and aliens.[9]

An examination of the geographic distribution of the growth of cities underscores the close connection between urbanization and industrialization. For the rise of urban centers in Europe after 1800 coincided by and large with the rationalization of production. England, the pioneer in the industrial revolution, was also the first country to experience a massive movement of population from village to city. In the middle of the eighteenth century, the proportion of all inhabitants living in communities of 5,000 or more probably did not exceed 16 percent. But by 1841 the percentage had reached about 60, and in the course of the following decade another 1.8 million people, more than the entire urban population of the 1760s or 1770s, migrated to the big cities. In 1801 the proportion of all inhabitants living in communities of over 20,000 was 16.94 percent; the percentage was 35.0 in 1851 and 53.58 in 1891. During those ninety years more than 20 million people were added to the population of England. But whereas the inhabitants of rural communities, defined as those with less than 5,000, increased from 6.6 million to 9.2 million, the inhabitants of urban communities increased from 2.3 million to 19.8 million. In other words, of the total growth of 20 million, about 17.4 million or more than 80 percent occurred in towns and cities.

In England the most rapid urban increase took place in the first half of the nineteenth century. In this respect her experience differed from that of most countries of Europe, where the major expansion of big cities did not come until after 1850. The difference in the chronology of urbanization reflected a difference in the chronology of industrialization, for whenever mills and mines began to appear, the local population promptly increased. The greatest period in the growth of English urban communities, defined as those with over 2,000 inhabitants in 1871, came during the 1820s and the 1840s, when their decennial increment was 43 and 58 percent higher than that of the nation at large. Thereafter the rate of growth gradually diminished, the percentage of decennial increase dropping from 21.9 in 1851–61 and 28.1 in 1861–71 to 25.6 in 1871–81 and 18.5 in 1881–91. Even in the largest cities of over 100,000, there was a slower increase during the latter part of the century. Between 1800 and 1850 their share of the total population rose 174 percent, but between 1850 and 1910 only 85 percent. In villages and hamlets, in the meantime, an absolute as well as relative decline was occurring. There were approximately 800,000 fewer people living in rural communities in 1891 than in 1851, the result of an internal migration that transformed a

9. Weber, *Growth of Cities*, pp. 389–92; Köllmann, "Industrialisierung," pp. 66–68.

small decennial population increase of 1.88 percent in 1851–61 into a deficit during the decades which followed: −5.86 in 1861–71, −3.84 in 1871–81, and −2.76 in 1881–91. The pattern of urban development thus coincided in general with the pattern of economic development.[10]

Since the expansion of industry in France was far less vigorous, the growth of cities was much less rapid. The rationalization of the economy proceeded at a leisurely pace, so that the demand for labor in urban centers did not increase at the same rate as on the other side of the Channel. In 1801, it has been estimated, the urban population, defined as those living in communities of over 2,000, was 20.5 percent of the total population; in 1836 the percentage was still only 22.2 and in 1851 it was 25.5. The rate of urbanization during the first half of the nineteenth century was thus low, the proportion of residents of cities and towns increasing only 5.0 percent. The pace then quickened, so that the percentage of the urban population rose to 31.1 in 1872 and 37.4 in 1891. During the entire period 1851–91, the proportion of residents of cities and towns increased 11.9 percent, more than twice as rapidly as during the preceding fifty years. The percentage of the urban population reached 42.1 by 1906 and 44.1 by 1911, double the figure for 1801. Cities of more than 20,000 accounted for a disproportionate share of this growth. Whereas their percentage of all inhabitants at the beginning of the nineteenth century was 6.75, by the middle it was 10.6, at the end 21.1, and in 1911 it reached 26.0, a fourfold increase in the course of 110 years, compared to a twofold increase of the urban population as a whole. The initial period of rapid expansion of cities came during the 1850s and 1860s, the time of the Second Empire, coinciding with the breakthrough of mechanized production and railroad construction in France.[11]

Germany demonstrates even more vividly that the factory and the locomotive, the primary forces in the rise of industrialism, were also the transforming agents in the redistribution of population. During the first half of the nineteenth century, while the urban economy was still largely in the hands of the master artisan and small shopkeeper, the proportion of the population residing in cities remained almost stationary. The Prussian statistics, the most complete in the German Confederation, document the demographic equilibrium between town and country, which was in turn a reflection of the economic equilibrium between manufacturing and farming. In the period 1816–58 the urban population grew

---

10. Phyllis Deane, *The First Industrial Revolution* (Cambridge, 1965), p. 260; Weber, *Growth of Cities*, pp. 43–44, 49, 144, 152; Sombart, *Der moderne Kapitalismus*, 3:390.

11. Weber, *Growth of Cities*, pp. 71, 152; J. H. Clapham, *Economic Development of France and Germany, 1815–1914*, 4th ed. (Cambridge, 1966), p. 159.

81.7 percent and the rural population 67.2 percent. The proportion of city residents in the kingdom hardly changed: 25.64 percent in 1834, 26.25 in 1843, 27.72 in 1855, and 29.84 in 1864. In keeping with the general pattern of population growth, however, the big cities were expanding more rapidly than the small ones, and more rapidly still than the population at large. Between 1816 and 1864 urban communities of less than 10,000 increased 55 percent, although their share of all inhabitants fell from 18.2 to 15.3; those between 10,000 and 20,000 increased 303 percent, their share of the total rising from 2.0 to 4.6; those between 20,000 and 30,000 increased 230 percent, their share rising from 0.65 to 1.13; those between 30,000 and 50,000 increased 90 percent, their share rising from 1.54 to 1.6; and those of over 50,000 increased 330 percent, their share rising from 2.77 to 7.5.

The transformation of the German economy after the mid-century, especially after the Franco-Prussian War, produced a corresponding transformation in the distribution of the German population. Although the twenty-five largest cities of the empire in 1890 had only 4.7 percent of all inhabitants in 1819 and still only 6.2 in 1858, by 1880 the percentage had risen to 9.6 and by 1890 to 12.1. All in all, the urban population increased from 36.1 percent in 1871 to 60.1 in 1910. The growth had been roughly proportional to size. The percentage of all inhabitants living in rural towns between 2,000 and 5,000 declined from 12.4 to 11.3, while in cities of over 5,000 it increased from 23.7 to 48.8. Within the latter category, moreover, the larger the population, the larger the growth. Small cities between 5,000 and 10,000 rose from 11.2 to 14.1 percent, medium-sized cities between 10,000 and 100,000 rose from 7.7 to 13.4, and big cities of over 100,000 rose from 4.8 to 21.3. The effect of industrialization on urbanization emerges from these statistics with striking clarity. In the fifty years preceding national unification, while agriculture was still the dominant form of economic activity, the proportion of the population residing in cities remained almost static. In the following forty years, as industrial production expanded at an unprecedented rate, urban communities began to grow with great rapidity. The interconnection of the two processes is unmistakable.[12]

Most other countries in Europe followed the French and German pattern of urbanization rather than the English. That is, their cities grew slowly in the first half of the nineteenth century, while agriculture more or less held its own in the competition with industry. Then, as large-scale manufacture progressively gained the lead, the flow of population to

12. Weber, *Growth of Cities*, pp. 84, 152; *Jahrbuch für die amtliche Statistik des preussischen Staats* 1 (1863):110; Pierre Benaerts, *Les origines de la grande industrie allemande* (Paris, 1933), pp. 152, 157; Köllmann, "Grundzüge der Bevölkerungsgeschichte," p. 389.

urban centers increased, its intensity depending on the availability of remunerative employment.

In Belgium, for example, a trailblazer of the industrial revolution on the Continent, the urban population, defined as those living in communities of over 5,000, reached a substantial 32.6 percent as early as 1846. After growing slowly to 34.8 in 1856 and 36.9 in 1866, it accelerated to 43.1 in 1880 and 47.7 in 1890. The Scandinavian countries began with a much lower level of urbanization, but after the mid-century the spread of manufacture and commerce stimulated the expansion of their cities as well. On the other hand, where the economy did not undergo a significant transformation because of growing industry, the shift in the distribution of inhabitants was likely to be less drastic. To illustrate, the Netherlands, with flourishing commerce and shipping in the eighteenth century, had an urban population of 29.5 percent as early as 1795. Yet there was a slight drop to 26.0 in 1829 and 29.0 in 1849, before a modest rise to 33.5 in 1889 took place.[13] Figure 4.1 summarizes these changes in distribution.

The connection between industrialization and urbanization meant that the proportion of city inhabitants in Europe was generally higher among the economically advanced countries of the north and west than in the tier of underdeveloped agricultural countries in the south and east. Precise comparisons are difficult because the classification of urban and rural communities often varied from state to state, but an approximate ranking of the intensity of urbanization is possible. In the Iberian Peninsula, the percentages of the Spanish population living in cities of over 10,000 was roughly 14.0 around 1820, 16.2 in 1857, and 29.6 in 1887, not far behind Belgium and slightly ahead of France. But in Portugal the figure remained unchanged throughout the nineteenth century, around 12.8 percent. Although there are no comprehensive statistics for Italy prior to national unification, in 1881 the percentage was 20.6.

Farther east in Austria, 4.4 percent of the population around 1800 lived in cities of over 10,000, and 15.8 in 1890. In Hungary the distinction between city and country was based primarily on political status rather than demographic density, and a precise statistical breakdown would in any case be difficult because of the wide extent of territory included in the category of small towns. But it is a reasonable approximation that about 5.4 percent of all inhabitants lived in communities of over 10,000 in 1800–1808, 9.1 in 1850, and 17.6 in 1890. As for Russia, the statistics on urbanization are even less open to comparative analysis than

13. Weber, *Growth of Cities*, pp. 109–11, 113, 115–16; Lennart Jörberg, "The Industrial Revolution in the Nordic Countries," in *The Fontana Economic History: The Emergence of Industrial Societies*, ed. Carlo M. Cipolla (London and Glasgow, 1973), p. 385.

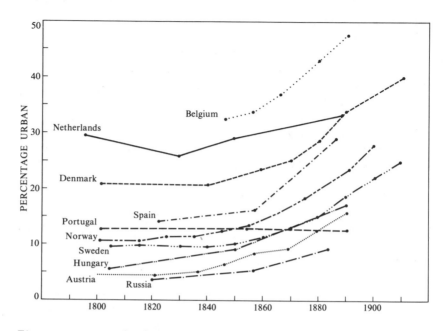

Figure 4.1. Growth of Urban Population in Europe, 1795–1910

SOURCE: Adna Ferrin Weber, *The Growth of Cities in the Nineteenth Century: A Study in Statistics* (New York and London, 1899), pp. 95, 104, 109–11, 113, 115–16, 119–20; Lennart Jörberg, "The Industrial Revolution in the Nordic Countries," in *The Fontana Economic History: The Emergence of Industrial Societies*, ed. Carlo M. Cipolla (London and Glasgow, 1973), p. 385.

in most countries of the south and east. The classification of cities and villages rested on juridical and administrative criteria, so that many rural communities were in fact larger than most urban communities. The best estimate under the circumstances is that 3.7 percent of the population resided in cities of over 10,000 in 1820, 5.3 in 1856, and 9.3 in 1885.

All in all, then, Europe remained a continent of villages rather than cities throughout the nineteenth century. The rural population continued to outnumber the urban, although its lead was steadily diminishing. In 1800 no country except England, Scotland, and the Netherlands had more than 15 percent of its population living in cities of over 10,000, and even fifty years later they had been joined only by Belgium and Spain, if the statistics for the latter are to be trusted. By 1890, on the other hand, every country had risen above the 15 percent level except Bulgaria, Greece, Portugal, Rumania, Serbia, and Sweden. The great spurt in the growth of cities thus came after the mid-century. Yet a vast difference in the intensity of urbanization remained between the economically advanced and economically backward countries. The level that England had reached in 1851, 39.45 percent of the population living in cities of more than 10,000, had been equaled forty years later only by Scotland. At the outbreak of the First World War, the typical European was still a rustic, residing in a community that derived its livelihood primarily from agriculture.

A major shift in the distribution of population had taken place, however, since the Napoleonic Wars; a massive internal migration had upset the equilibrium between town and country. Here and there the city had already gained the upper hand, and it seemed to be only a matter of time before it won ascendancy elsewhere as well. And with the increase in population came political power, economic domination, social esteem, and cultural primacy. Urbanization altered fundamentally the established way of life in Europe.[14]

That was why the rise of cities encountered such widespread hostility among those who commented on its effect on society. It represented a threat to values and institutions that had become deeply rooted through a long historical experience. The hardships arising out of uncontrolled urban expansion—poor nourishment, squalid housing, and inadequate sanitation—shocked contemporary writers who were accustomed to seeing poverty in its traditional rural setting. The British philosopher John S. Mackenzie spoke with grave concern about "perhaps the greatest of all the problems of modern civilisation—the growth of large cities." In urban communities "the physical conditions of health are absent; and the conditions of moral health are often even more so. Men are crowded together in dwellings which in many cases serve the purpose rather of tool-boxes than of homes—boxes, moreover, in which the tool corrodes away. In such places people are, as it has been said, 'born tired.' They are exhausted by the struggle of life before they begin it, and when they do begin it they soon succumb to it."

The German sociologist Georg Hansen was especially disturbed by the unhealthy influence of city life on the young. Since both parents often had to work all day, he wrote, children were generally left to themselves. "But in what an environment! They grow up in the narrow, dirty alleys of the working-class quarters of the big city. Their realm lies within the four walls of a miserable garret or of a gloomy rear building. They have nothing of all those things which arouse joy in a child, which stimulate it to observe and reflect. A tiny bit of sky and here and there a glimpse of the sun, that is their entire share of wide, glorious nature." It was a

14. Weber, *Growth of Cities*, pp. 95, 100, 102, 104, 109, 119–20, 144–45; Roger Portal, "Russie," in *L'Europe du XIXᵉ et du XXᵉ siècle*, ed. Max Beloff, Pierre Renouvin, Franz Schnabel, and Franco Valsecchi, 6 vols. (Milan, 1959–64), 3:269.

disturbing picture of proletarian life in the booming urban communities of the nineteenth century.[15]

Hostility to the city engendered by the juxtaposition of wealth and poverty was frequently intensified by ideological or political considerations. To many radicals, the industrial metropolis embodied those fundamental social injustices that only a collective system of ownership could remedy. In an essay entitled "How We Live and How We Might Live," William Morris argued that urban life epitomized the exploitation of the poor by the rich to which socialism must eventually put an end:

> I feel sure that the time will come when people will find it difficult to believe that a rich community such as ours, having such command over external Nature, could have submitted to live such a mean, shabby, dirty life as we do. And once for all, there is nothing in our circumstances save the hunting of profit that drives us into it. It is profit which draws men into enormous unmanageable aggregations called towns, for instance; profit which crowds them up when they are there into quarters without gardens or open spaces; profit which won't take the most ordinary precautions against wrapping a whole district in a cloud of sulphurous smoke; which turns beautiful rivers into filthy sewers; which condemns all but the rich to live in houses idiotically cramped and confined at the best, and at the worst in houses for whose wretchedness there is no name. I say it is almost incredible that we should bear such crass stupidity as this; nor should we if we could help it. We shall not bear it when the workers get out of their heads that they are but an appendage to profit-grinding, that the more profits that are made the more employment at high wages there will be for them, and that therefore all the incredible filth, disorder, and degradation of modern civilization are signs of their prosperity.[16]

Criticism of urbanization was even more bitter among traditionalists than radicals. The latter could at least reflect that the city, the harsh cradle of the proletariat, was nurturing the future avenger of social injustice. But for the former the rise of urban communities meant the decline of the economic and civic order to which they were committed. It represented the victory of industry over agriculture, of egalitarian restlessness over hierarchical stability. In his classic *Democracy in America*, Alexis de

---

15. John S. Mackenzie, *An Introduction to Social Philosophy* (Glasgow, 1890), p. 101; Georg Hansen, *Die drei Bevölkerungsstufen: Ein Versuch, die Ursachen für das Blühen und Altern der Völker nachzuweisen* (Munich, 1889), p. 211.

16. *The Collected Works of William Morris*, 24 vols. (London, New York, Bombay, and Calcutta, 1910–15), 23:22.

Tocqueville warned that the growth of big cities was a threat to the republican institutions of the United States. "In cities men can hardly be prevented from concerting, from growing angry as a group, from reaching sudden and passionate resolves. Cities form large assemblies, as it were, of which all the inhabitants are members. Their populace exercises a prodigious influence upon the magistrates, and it frequently executes its wishes without their intervention." Thinking of Paris during the preceding fifty years, he concluded that "to subject the provinces to the capital is therefore to place the destiny of the entire empire not only in the hands of a portion of the populace, which is unjust, but also in the hands of a populace acting on its own, which is very dangerous."

The countryside, on the other hand, seemed to embody the civic virtues that traditionalists valued most: loyalty, discipline, patriotism, and moderation. After his retirement from office, Bismarck warned in an interview with a Bavarian newspaperman that "if we do not support our agriculture, then the class which defends us will perish along with the class which feeds us." The peasant was the core of the army; he could endure want and distress, "for he is in close intimacy with the soil, and he has an interest in its preservation out of a simple instinct for self-preservation." The city dweller and factory worker lacked this feeling, since "people cannot be in close intimacy with paving stones and bricks." In short, "without a peasant class there can be no state and no army. The peasant class is the rock on which the phantom ship of social democracy will be dashed to pieces." Those who were alarmed by the spread of egalitarian ideals during the nineteenth century saw in the city the source of opposition to the established order in state and society. They saw in it a challenge to the loyalties and values that the rural community had fostered.[17]

Urbanization also aroused reproach of another sort. It undermined the character of the people, substituting glib cleverness and superficial sophistication for the simple but honest view of life found in the countryside. The resident of the village knew his place and function; his understanding of the relationship of the individual to the community was the natural result of a collective rural experience. In the city, on the other hand, each man tried to outdo the other in an endless pursuit of prestige. The German writer Theodor Fontane described the exhausting quest for social status in Berlin. "It is clear to me," he wrote to a friend, "that as a rule the big city makes people lively, bright, and adroit, but it also makes them shallow and deprives everyone who does not live in seclusion of

17. *Oeuvres, papiers et correspondances d'Alexis de Tocqueville*, ed. J.-P. Mayer, 13 vols. (Paris, 1951–77), 1:291; Otto von Bismarck, *Die gesammelten Werke*, 15 vols. (Berlin, 1924–35), 9:90.

every capacity for higher productivity. . . . The big city has no time for thought and, what is even worse, it also has no time for happiness. What it produces a hundred thousand times over is only the 'hunt for happiness,' which is the same as unhappiness." He mentioned two acquaintances of his, "old gentlemen," privy councillors who "have now been for a very long time everything which they were capable of becoming." Yet "the chase goes on as usual. It can no longer be a question of titles and orders, so that the chase has become an entirely trivial running about to chamber concerts, premières, [and] bazaars where the crown princess will perhaps appear. . . . All of this would be something to laugh at, if it weren't something to cry over."

Even the intellectual stimulation of city life, it was argued, even the broader scope of its education and experience, led to shallow fluency rather than genuine understanding. The English economist J. A. Hobson, for example, surely no hidebound conservative, expressed a common distrust of the character of urban man. He conceded that "the townsman has a larger superficial knowledge of the world and human nature. He is shrewd, alert, versatile, quicker, and more resourceful than the countryman. In thought, speech, action, this superiority shows itself. The townsman has a more developed consciousness, his intelligence is constantly stimulated in a thousand ways by larger and more varied society, and by a more diversified and complex economic environment." Yet the greater knowledge of the world that the urban environment provided was used only for material gain and fatuous amusement. "School instruction [in the city], slightly more advanced than in the country, is commonly utilised to sharpen industrial competition, and to feed that sensational interest in sport and crime which absorbs the attention of the masses in their non-working hours; it seldom forms the foundation of an intellectual life in which knowledge and taste are reckoned in themselves desirable. The power to read and write is employed by the great majority of all classes in ways which evoke a minimum of thought and wholesome feeling." As a result, "scattered and unrelated fragments of half-baked information form a stock of 'knowledge' with which the townsman's glib tongue enables him to present a showy intellectual shop-front," so that city life in general "favours the education of certain shallow forms of intelligence." This was the gist of the contention, heard again and again during the nineteenth century, that although cities might enrich man materially, they debase him spiritually.[18]

18. Theodor Fontane, *Briefe an Georg Friedlaender*, ed. Kurt Schreinert (Heidelberg, 1954), p. 4; John A. Hobson, *The Evolution of Modern Capitalism: A Study of Machine Production* (London and New York, 1894), pp. 338–39.

Finally, urbanization was held responsible for a growing pursuit of pleasure and decline of morality. The metropolis, with its bright lights and gaudy diversions, encouraged self-indulgence; it encouraged a restless chase after ostentatious luxury and sensual gratification. The moderating influence on personal conduct exercised in the village by church, family, and community disintegrated in the city, which was only an aggregate of autonomous individuals held together by nothing more elevated than a common quest for livelihood. This was the view of Johann Heinrich Pestalozzi, the great Swiss educational reformer, who contrasted rural virtue with urban wickedness:

> A people which earns its bread from agriculture and from trade
> in raw domestic products, a people in which many nobles still live
> on their landed property in the simplicity of our old customs, a
> people which has not yet been led beyond the bounds of moderation
> and restraint by the long enjoyment of a more advanced industrial
> system, such a people is in an entirely different position from a
> commercial state, where the enjoyment of harmful industry has
> made seductive pleasures of a thousand sorts indispensable necessities through the force of habit and custom, and has generally diverted the sense of artlessness and innocence in the arrangement
> of domestic duties.[19]

Pestalozzi was defending the pastoral simplicity of Swiss life against the economics and morals of the city. But even in England, the most highly industrialized and urbanized nation in the world, there was a fiery stream of denunciation of large towns, of their corruption, their shamelessness, and their immorality. John Ruskin pronounced judgment against them in the tones of an Old Testament prophet:

> The great cities of the earth, which ought to be the places set on
> its hills, with the Temple of the Lord in the midst of them, to which
> the tribes should go up,—centres to the Kingdoms and Provinces of
> Honour, Virtue, and the Knowledge of the law of God,—have
> become, instead, loathsome centres of fornication and covetousness
> —the smoke of their sin going up into the face of heaven like the
> furnace of Sodom, and the pollution of it rotting and raging through
> the bones and the souls of the peasant people round them, as if they

19. *Pestalozzi's sämtliche Werke*, ed. L. W. Seyffarth, 12 vols. (Liegnitz, 1899–1902), 3:301.

were each a volcano whose ashes broke out in blains upon man and beast.[20]

To such critics, urban life was a slippery downward path leading from faith and spirituality to gross self-gratification. It not only weakened man physically by removing him from air and sunlight to dark, over-crowded factories, but it degraded him morally by teaching that the chief good in life was pleasure. And in the long run, the inward corruption of the individual was bound to lead to the disintegration of the community as well.

Was this indictment of urbanization based on an actual deterioration in the quality of life resulting from the growth of big cities, or was it essentially the response of a society whose values had been shaped in a rural environment to a sudden change in the way people lived and worked? Since much of the criticism of urbanization rested on subjective judgments of intellect and morality, its validity is difficult to determine. But at least the assertion that the villager led a healthier and therefore longer life than the city dweller can be subjected to empirical investigation. Here the evidence suggests that during the early period of urban growth mortality was in fact higher in towns than in the countryside. The sudden influx of population into the big cities contributed to the spread of dirt diseases like typhus and cholera, which were often carried by contaminated water supplies. Vienna obtained an adequate system for distributing water only in 1840, Hamburg in 1848, and Berlin in 1852. In London there were 250,000 cesspools as late as 1850. In such an unhealthy environment, epidemics were a constant menace.

Inadequate housing compounded the problems arising out of inade-quate sanitation. The construction of new dwellings in urban centers usually lagged far behind the increase in the number of inhabitants. In Vienna population increased 42 percent between 1827 and 1847, but housing increased less than 12 percent. Stephen Edward Piper, medical officer of health in Darlington, reported in 1851 on the dreadful over-crowding of the lower classes in his city:

> It is a common occurrence to see a family of 10 or 12 persons congregated in a room of only so many feet square! If the external atmosphere be unwholesome what must be the state of the interior! The air being breathed over and over again is gradually robbed of its oxygen leaving an excess of carbonic acid, thus it becomes vitiated and unfit for respiration. Can we wonder that fever, scrofula and

20. *The Works of John Ruskin*, ed. E. T. Cook and Alexander Wedderburn, 39 vols. (London, 1903–12), 34:205.

consumption should be so prevalent, and so fatal, amongst those who are subject to such harmful influences? How often are medical men called upon to attend these diseases, where the patient is lying amidst poverty, misery and rags, in a low dark damp room where the cheering rays of the sun never enter and where the pure air is unknown![21]

Conditions in other urban communities were no better. The average death rate of Birmingham, Bristol, Leeds, Liverpool, and Manchester, the five largest English cities outside London, rose from 20.7 per thousand in 1831 to 30.8 in 1841; for the period 1841–50 the figure reached 33.1 in Manchester and 39.2 in Liverpool.[22]

Health conditions in the towns, however, began to improve after the mid-century. The initial phase of helter-skelter growth determined solely by considerations of private gain gradually gave way to a more controlled expansion directed by public authority. The introduction of some form of collective supervision over urbanization came usually a generation or two after the beginning of the rapid increase of cities. As a rule, local government was ahead of national government in the adoption of legal measures for the improvement of housing and sanitation. The Borough Police Act of 1844 in Manchester prohibited the further construction of back-to-back dwellings. Liverpool appointed the first medical officer of health in Great Britain in 1847, and by 1860 the city was using municipal funds for the building of houses for the laboring classes. In London the Sewers Act of 1851 provided for the condemnation of unwholesome dwellings and for the inspection of lodgings and homes rented by workers. On the other hand, the first national public health act, and not an effective one at that, came in 1848.

Home construction, moreover, increased until it began to catch up with demographic growth. The English population rose 89 percent between 1821 and 1871, but the number of inhabited houses rose 104 percent, most of the increase occurring in cities. In the course of the nineteenth century, the average number of persons per house in England declined from 5.67 to 5.20. In Germany the growth of population in forty-one towns was less than the volume of residential building during 1871–80, more during 1880–90, equal during the base period 1890–1900, and less again during 1900–1910. By the time of the First World

21. William L. Langer, "Europe's Initial Population Explosion," *American Historical Review* 69 (1963):7 (n. 14); William L. Langer, *Political and Social Upheaval, 1832–1852* (New York, Evanston, and London, 1969), p. 190; C. Fraser Brockington, *Public Health in the Nineteenth Century* (Edinburgh and London, 1965), p. 168.

22. Deane, *First Industrial Revolution*, p. 242.

War, the problems of health and housing created by urbanization were being solved through a combination of public regulation and private enterprise.[23]

This improvement was reflected in the vital statistics of most European countries. At first mortality in the cities, especially the big cities, was substantially higher than that in the rural districts. The figure for Paris in 1821 was 32.6 per thousand, whereas for France as a whole it was 24.3. As late as 1851, the capital was still ahead of the country at large, though by a narrower margin of 26.1 to 23.3. In Sweden during the period 1802–15, the death rate was 41.2 for Stockholm, 30.2 for other towns, and 24.8 for the countryside. In 1816–40 the figures were 45.1, 30.1, and 22.3, and even in 1861–70 a considerable disparity remained: 32.3 for Stockholm, 24.0 for other towns, and 19.3 for the countryside. The hostility toward urbanization was thus based in part on the terrible price in human life that the city exacted during the early period of its growth.

By the end of the nineteenth century, however, the difference in mortality between town and country had greatly diminished, and in some cases the statistics for the former had actually become more favorable. In the Arnsberg district of Germany the death rate in industrial counties in 1894–96 was 20.6 and in nonindustrial counties 19.6; in the Düsseldorf district the figures were 20.3 and 20.6; in the Aachen district 22.2 and 21.8; and in Münster district 22.1 and 21.7. The figures for France given in Table 4.6 show a marked decline in the disparity between urban and rural mortality from 1872–73 to 1900–1902. In Vienna the death rate fell from 60 at the end of the eighteenth century to 23 in 1886–90. The figure for Austrian cities as a whole was 24, whereas for the entire country it was 29. In general, the incidence of infant mortality per thousand live births around 1890 was still a little higher in towns than the national average: 237 to 200 in Germany, 188 to 166 in Belgium, 171 to 166 in France, and 163 to 145 in England. Yet there were also some countries where the urban rate had fallen below the general rate: 239 to 254 in Austria, 158 to 194 in Switzerland, and 195 to 203 in the Netherlands. The city was gradually ceasing to be a pesthole of disease and death.[24]

It remained, however, the home of easy pleasure and lax morality. The high concentration of people in slums and mills led to a depersonalization of human relationships in which private conduct could no longer

23. Deane, *First Industrial Revolution*, p. 219; Llewellyn Woodward, *Age of Reform, 1815–1870*, 2d ed. (Oxford, 1962), p. 599; G. R. Porter and F. W. Hirst, *The Progress of the Nation in Its Various Social and Economic Relations from the Beginning of the Nineteenth Century*, new ed. (London, 1912), p. 91; Ashok V. Desai, *Real Wages in Germany, 1871–1913* (Oxford, 1968), p. 92.

24. Charles H. Pouthas, *La population française pendant la première moitié du XIXe siè-

Table 4.6. Urban and Rural Death Rates in France, 1872–1902

Department	1872–73 (per thousand)		1900–1902 (per thousand)	
	Urban	Rural	Urban	Rural
Nord	25.6	16.2	19.8	18.6
Pas-de-Calais	22.1	21.3	20.2	19.0
Aisne	26.7	18.9	21.9	20.8
Somme	23.4	21.9	21.4	22.0

SOURCE: E. A. Wrigley, *Industrial Growth and Population Change: A Regional Study of the Coalfield Areas of North-West Europe in the Later Nineteenth Century* (Cambridge, 1961), p. 121.

be effectively controlled by community standards. Clergymen, teachers, overseers, relatives, and neighbors, who had exercised a restraining influence on behavior in the village, lost much of their authority in the urban environment. "In the case of the ignorant and immoral worker," observed a French writer in the early nineteenth century, "intelligence is soon extinguished for lack of stimulation and exercise. In the end everything is reduced, so far as he is concerned, to the vegetation of physical life. Without forethought for tomorrow, he wastes in the tavern and in places of debauchery his small daily or weekly earnings." The appetite for vice was gratified by an army of registered prostitutes, about nine thousand in London and thirty-six hundred in Paris during the 1830s, and by an even larger number of occasional prostitutes seeking to supplement their meager earnings as shopgirls or factory employees, so that all in all there may have been as many as eighty thousand women engaged in prostitution in the British capital. So much for Victorian morality. Even more important, city life encouraged a greater freedom in the relations between the sexes based on romantic attachments. The percentage of illegitimate births was therefore consistently higher in town than country, the figures around the mid-century being 14.49 and 5.88 in Belgium, 16.05 and 10.06 in Denmark, 15.13 and 4.24 in France, 7.71 and 2.84 in the Netherlands, 9.80 and 6.60 in Prussia, and 27.44 and 7.50 in Sweden.

cle (Paris, 1956), p. 173; E. F. Heckscher, "Swedish Population Trends before the Industrial Revolution," *Economic History Review*, 2d ser. 2 (1949–50):277; Weber, *Growth of Cities*, pp. 237, 356, 362; Wrigley, *Industrial Growth and Population Change*, pp. 121–22.

The relaxation of behavioral restraints which the urban environment produced was also reflected in a higher crime rate. The impersonality of the city made lawlessness more acceptable, the disparity in wealth made it more defensible, and the ease of concealment made it more tempting. In England the number of indictable crimes per hundred thousand inhabitants in 1894 was 643.6 in seaports, 416.7 in the national capital, 351.8 in manufacturing towns, 182.9 in the agricultural counties of the southwest, and 128.2 in the agricultural counties of the east. In France in 1841–45, 38 percent of those charged with offenses lived in urban communities, although the latter accounted for only about 23 percent of the population; in 1866–70, the percentages were 44 and 31; in 1881–85, 46 and 35. The erosion of traditional patterns of conduct in the city, moreover, led to psychological disorientation. The number of suicides per million inhabitants was 64 for urban communities and 34 for rural communities in Belgium in 1858–60, 283 and 257 in Denmark in 1869–75, 263 and 172 in France in 1883, 66 and 29 in Italy in 1877, 92 and 72 in Norway in 1866–69, 162 and 97 in Prussia in 1869–72, and 167 and 67 in Sweden in 1871–75. The highest rates were recorded in the national capitals: Paris with 472, Stockholm with 440, Copenhagen with 350, Berlin with 191, and Rome with 111. The self-destructive impulse of the emotionally insecure was clearly aggravated by the sense of rootlessness and alienation bred by the city.[25]

And yet urbanization was on the whole a liberating process, altering traditional forms of behavior that had perpetuated social immobility and economic stagnation in the village. The city, with all its vice and crime, with its tinsel brightness and sordid moneygrubbing, nevertheless represented a defiant rejection of the stultifying sameness of rural life. It represented richer experience, broader education, greater opportunity. As the nineteenth century drew to a close, Adna Weber defined this significance of the urban experience. "The influence of the cities," he wrote, "is . . . exerted in favor of liberal and progressive thought. The variety of occupation, interests and opinions in the city produces an intellectual friction, which leads to a broader and freer judgment and a great inclination to and appreciation of new thoughts, manners, and ideals." City life "has brought thinkers into touch with one another, and has stimulated the divine impulse to originate by sympathy or antagonism. As the seat of political power, as the nursery of the arts and

25. Alban de Villeneuve-Bargemont, *Économie politique chrétienne, ou Recherches sur la nature et les causes du paupérisme, en France et en Europe, et sur les moyens de le soulager et de le prévenir*, 3 vols. (Paris, 1834), 1:479; Langer, *Political and Social Upheaval*, p. 195; Weber, *Growth of Cities*, pp. 335, 401–4.

sciences, as the center of industry and commerce, the city represents the highest achievements of political, intellectual and industrial life." To those millions who left ancestral farms to seek their fortune in the big cities of Europe, urbanization held out the promise of a materially and mentally more rewarding way of life.[26]

26. Weber, *Growth of Cities*, p. 439.

Part Two

THE SOCIAL SYSTEM

Of the working classes . . . it may be pronounced certain, that the patriarchal or paternal system of government is one to which they will not again be subject. That question . . . was decided when they were taught to read, and allowed access to newspapers and political tracts. It was decided when dissenting preachers were suffered to go among them, and appeal to their faculties and feelings in opposition to the creeds professed and countenanced by their superiors. It was decided when they were brought together in numbers, to work socially under the same roof. It was decided when railways enabled them to shift from place to place, and change their patrons and employers as easily as their coats. The working classes have taken their interests into their own hands.

John Stuart Mill,
Principles of Political Economy,
1848

5

THE STANDARD OF LIVING

The rationalization of production in industry and agriculture created for the first time the possibility of a humane balance between supply and demand. Throughout history poverty had been accepted as the inescapable condition of most of mankind. People had looked upon this hard reality variously, with poignant regret, pious resignation, or plain indifference. But whatever their attitude, mass privation was regarded as an element of human existence no less inevitable than death itself. "For ye have the poor always with you" was the scriptural affirmation of an experience as old as the organized community. In no respect, therefore, did the nineteenth century introduce a sharper break with the past than in the economic transformation which made it possible, at first more in theory than practice, to satisfy the demand of European society for the basic necessities of life: food, shelter, and clothing. Hitherto the most obvious class difference had been between those to whom hunger and cold were an everyday experience and those to whom they were not. But now the importance of this distinction began to diminish as the output of manufacture and farming rose much faster than population, so that the average standard of living improved as never before. This is the most significant regard in which the years between the fall of Napoleon and the outbreak of the First World War separate an old order of traditional economics from modernity. During that century the outlines of a society of mass consumption began to emerge with increasing clarity, initiating a new period in the history of Europe.

The rise in the volume of output can be traced in considerable detail on the basis of available statistics, with important gaps for the period before 1870 but with growing comprehensiveness thereafter. In England, according to the best estimates, the per capita national product at constant prices increased about 1.5 percent annually in the first half of the nineteenth century, almost doubling between 1801 and 1851. In France national income measured in constant prices rose from 8.47 billion francs in 1810 to 11.35 in 1850, an increase of 34 percent compared with an increase in population of 23 percent. The production of coal in Europe grew 400 percent between 1841 and 1870, with British output rising 220 percent, Belgian 250, French 290, and German 900. In metallurgy, the bellwether industry of the middle decades of the nineteenth century, England retained her dominant position with 258,000 tons of pig iron in 1806, 1.4 million in 1840, and 6.7 million in 1870. Yet the increases in other countries, though on a smaller scale, were also impressive. The production of pig iron in France rose from 198,000 tons in 1824 to 1,178,000 in 1870, a growth of 495 percent compared with the English growth of 379 percent for the period 1840–70. Between 1845 and 1875 the output of pig iron climbed 361 percent in Belgium, 950 in Germany, and 108 in Russia. The statistical data are not always as complete or even as reliable as textbooks on quantification would require. Still, the evidence of a rapid expansion of production is massive enough to be persuasive, if not in all its detail, then at least in its substance.[1]

After the mid-century, the figures become more inclusive, so that estimates of economic development cease to rely so heavily on changes in the performance of a few leading industries. Calculations of national income and national product are now possible with a degree of accuracy hitherto unattainable. They all point to a rapidly rising volume of output in all branches of the economy, indeed, to an increase of such magnitude as to alter completely the traditional balance between supply and demand. This transformation can be measured in part by the usual criteria of industrial growth, given in Table 5.1. During the years 1870–1913, moreover, the production of coal rose 715 percent in Germany, 215 in France, and 161 in England; the percentages for steel in the same period were an unbelievable 9,050 in Germany, 4,600 in France, and 3,750 in England. Indeed, in every branch of industry for which there are statistics, output was expanding at an unparalleled rate.[2]

There are other measures of economic development more sophisticated than mere changes in the level of production, however. Calculations of the rate of growth in product per man-year from the middle decades of the nineteenth century to the First World War show an annual increase of 2.4 percent in Sweden, 2.1 in Denmark, 1.6 in the United Kingdom, 1.5 in Germany, 1.5 in France, 1.3 in Norway, and 0.7 in Italy. Between 1870 and 1913 the gross national product per man-hour rose 193 percent in Denmark, 166 in Germany, 70 in Italy, 232 in Sweden, and 105 in the United Kingdom. Of even greater importance as an index of the standard of living are the statistical data concerning national income.

1. Phyllis Deane, *The First Industrial Revolution* (Cambridge, 1965), pp. 252, 274; Bert F. Hoselitz, "Unternehmertum und Kapitalbildung in Frankreich und England seit 1700," in *Wirtschafts- und sozialgeschichtliche Probleme der frühen Industrialisierung*, ed. Wolfram Fischer (Berlin, 1968), pp. 287–88; B. R. Mitchell, *European Historical Statistics, 1750–1970* (London and Basingstoke, 1975), pp. 20, 25; Pierre Léon, "L'évolution démographique, économique et sociale," in *L'Europe du XIXᵉ et du XXᵉ siècle*, ed. Max Beloff, Pierre Renouvin, Franz Schnabel, and Franco Valsecchi, 6 vols. (Milan, 1959–64), 1:344.
2. David S. Landes, *The Unbound Prometheus: Technological Change and Industrial Development in Western Europe from 1750 to the Present* (Cambridge, 1969), pp. 194–95; Jürgen Kuczynski, *Die Geschichte der Lage der Arbeiter unter dem Kapitalismus*, 38 vols. (Berlin, 1960–71), 4:62–63.

Table 5.1. Expansion of Industry, 1850–73

	Consumption of Coal (thousand metric tons)		Production of Pig Iron (thousand metric tons)		Steam Capacity (thousand horsepower)	
	1850	1873	1850	1873	1850	1869
United Kingdom	37,500	112,604	2,249	6,566	1,290	4,040
Germany	5,100	36,392	212	2,241	260	2,480
France	7,225	24,702	406	1,382	370	1,850
Belgium	3,481	10,219	145	607	70	350

SOURCE: David S. Landes, *The Unbound Prometheus: Technological Change and Industrial Development in Western Europe from 1750 to the Present* (Cambridge, 1969), p. 194.
NOTE: German coal figures are for production.

Here too the evidence that wealth was expanding much more rapidly than population is convincing. Real per capita income in Great Britain, which had risen about 30 percent during 1851–78, increased at a decennial rate of between 17 and 25 percent during 1870–1900, a rate never previously sustained for any appreciable length of time. In the Scandinavian countries, per capita income in fixed prices grew between 1870 and 1910 at a comparable pace: 114 percent in Denmark, 61 in Norway, and 131 in Sweden. All in all, per capita income in fixed prices doubled in northwestern Europe between 1860 and 1913, rising at an annual rate of 1.31 percent. Even for southeastern Europe, the overall percentage of increase was 82 and the annual percentage 1.14. Such estimates are in part no more than informed guesswork, but at least they reflect in a general way an expansion of economic production far greater than in any previous period.[3]

Statistics on industrial growth, however, have only an indirect bearing on changes in the standard of living. Most of the increase in the output of

3. W. A. Cole and Phyllis Deane, "The Growth of National Incomes," in *The Cambridge Economic History of Europe*, 7 vols. (Cambridge, 1941–78), 6:26; Angus Maddison, "Economic Growth in Western Europe, 1870–1957," *Banca Nazionale del Lavoro Quarterly Review* 12 (1959):90; F. H. Hinsley, "Introduction," in *The New Cambridge Modern History*, 12 vols. (Cambridge, 1960–70), 11:4; Lennart Jörberg, "The Industrial Revolution in the Nordic Countries," in *The Fontana Economic History: The Emergence of Industrial Societies*, ed. Carlo M. Cipolla (London and Glasgow, 1973), p. 386; L. J. Zimmerman, "The Distribution of World Income, 1860–1960," in *Essays on Unbalanced Growth: A Century of Disparity and Convergence*, ed. Egbert de Vries (The Hague, 1962), p. 35.

collieries and mills went into capital goods rather than consumer goods. The rising volume of coal fed factories, not men; iron and steel were used to build machines, not to clothe or shelter the poor. Yet there are also figures showing a substantial improvement in the yield of those commodities that contributed directly to the standard of living of the masses. Consider the output of agriculture, whose productivity per male worker rose between 1840 and 1900 by 45 percent in Austria, 50 in Belgium, 35 in France, 190 in Germany, 50 in Italy, 30 in Russia, 75 in Sweden, 90 in Switzerland, and 45 in the United Kingdom. The average percentage for all the countries was 75, equivalent to an annual rate of 0.9. In France the wheat crop grew more than 50 percent between 1815–24 and 1841–50, from 51,719,000 hectoliters to 79,590,000, and the potato crop grew almost 150 percent, from 28,775,000 to 71,329,000 hectoliters. In Germany the average yield of grain per hundred hectares of medium soil climbed from 932.9 hundredweight in 1800–10 to 2,440.8 in 1870–75. In Western Europe the average yield per hectare expanded between 1871–80 and 1901–5 from 10.84 to 12.5 hundredweight of wheat, from 10.90 to 13.97 of rye, from 12.79 to 14.84 of barley, and from 12.37 to 14.06 of oats. Such increases, though less impressive than those for coal, iron, or steel, were directly translatable into a greater availability of food for the inhabitants of Europe.[4]

The development of the textile industry is another measure of the improved standard of living. It is more accurate than mining or metallurgy because it represents an immediate increment in the volume of consumer goods. Here too the pattern of growth points to better material conditions resulting from an increase in output far in excess of the increase in population. Consider the data on the consumption of raw cotton during the first half of the nineteenth century shown in Table 5.2. For Europe as a whole, the figure grew 220 percent between 1821–25 and 1861–66, although then the increase began to slow down in some of the industrially advanced countries: 73 percent in England between 1870 and 1913, 350 in France, and 500 in Germany.

Figures for the consumption of raw wool were climbing at a similar rate, reinforcing the general impression of an expanding volume of consumer goods. In Germany output rose 226 percent between 1816 and 1867, from 11,100 to 36,200 metric tons. In the United Kingdom net imports increased from 7,100 metric tons in 1814 to 73,300 in 1870, more

4. Paul Bairoch, "Agriculture and the Industrial Revolution, 1709–1914," in The Fontana Economic History of Europe: The Industrial Revolution, ed. Carlo M. Cipolla (London and Glasgow, 1973), pp. 472, 484; Landes, Unbound Prometheus, p. 165; Werner Sombart, Der moderne Kapitalismus: Historisch-systematische Darstellung des gesamteuropäischen Wirtschaftslebens von seinen Anfängen bis zur Gegenwart, 2d ed., 3 vols. (Munich and Leipzig, 1924–28), 3:245, 247.

Table 5.2. Consumption of Cotton, 1816–50

Metric Tons

| | 1816 | 1832 | 1850 | Percentage Increase | |
				1816–50	1832–50
Great Britain	40,245	125,634	222,046	452	77
France		33,623	59,273		76
Germany (Zollverein)		2,422	17,117		607
Belgium	1,349	2,435	7,222	435	197

SOURCE: David S. Landes, *The Unbound Prometheus: Technological Change and Industrial Development in Western Europe from 1750 to the Present* (Cambridge, 1969), p. 165.

than 900 percent. In Belgium there was a growth in imports of 1,338 percent between 1840 and 1870, from 2,900 metric tons to 41,700. The curve continued to rise steeply long after the mid-century. Net imports into Austria-Hungary increased 2,945 percent between 1870 and 1913; Belgian imports during the same period increased 257 percent; French consumption climbed 158 percent between 1862 and 1912; German net imports climbed 241 percent between 1881 and 1913; Italian output expanded 83 percent between 1875 and 1910; and net imports into the United Kingdom rose 192 percent between 1870 and 1913. In the course of a hundred years, the production of textiles in Europe had thus multiplied several times.[5]

There is still another index of the standard of living, indirect but significant, that points to growing affluence. The volume and number of accounts in savings banks provide an insight not only into the amount of wealth but into its distribution as well. The statistics on this point are incomplete, yet highly suggestive. In France there was an increase in deposits from 140 million francs in 737,000 accounts in 1847 to 174 million francs in 1,218,000 accounts in 1860, although the average amount in each account declined from 486 to 310 francs. The figures indicate both a growth and a diffusion of affluence. In England the number of bankbooks per thousand inhabitants rose from 8 in 1830 to 45 in 1866, and in Prussia from 16 in 1849 to 48 in 1867. In the canton of Zürich, there were 11,686 accounts totaling 2,153,600 francs in 1835, 43,007

5. Landes, *Unbound Prometheus*, p. 165; Léon, "L'évolution démographique," p. 344; Kuczynski, *Geschichte der Lage der Arbeiter*, 4:62–63; Mitchell, *European Historical Statistics*, pp. 443–45.

accounts totaling 6,222,368 francs in 1853, and 84,584 accounts totaling 19,039,926 francs in 1870. The number of accounts, in other words, grew 624 percent in thirty-five years, and the amount deposited grew 784 percent.

For the rest of Europe, the available statistics deal only with the volume of savings, not their distribution. Still, the evidence of a rapid increase in disposable income in all countries is impressive. In Austria deposits in savings banks rose 512 percent between 1842 and 1869, and another 467 percent between 1870 and 1894. In Belgium there was an increase of 2,580 percent between 1868 and 1888 and 303 percent between 1888 and 1908. In Denmark the volume of savings expanded 5,620 percent during 1849–1913, in France 6,009 percent during 1836–1913, in Germany 23,061 percent during 1838–1913, and in the United Kingdom 7,306 percent during 1820–1913. Even in the backward countries, there was a remarkable growth in the value of bank accounts: 867 percent in Rumania between 1885 and 1913, 777 in Russia between 1880 and 1913, and 426 in Spain between 1890 and 1913. To be sure, these extraordinary increases in savings do not reflect comparable improvements in the standard of living, since they measure not changes in real income but changes in that part of nominal income left after the purchase of the necessities of life. To put it another way, only a minor proportional growth in buying power could lead to a major proportional growth in savings. Yet the rise in the value of bank accounts does indicate in a general way an increase of national wealth.[6]

The distribution of this wealth is as important as its growth in determining fluctuations in the standard of living. A high concentration of the affluence generated by the rationalization of production would mean that for the bulk of the population the struggle for existence remained as pitiless as before. A broad diffusion of its benefits, on the other hand, might lead to a decline of the sharp economic, social, and political distinctions separating the propertied classes from the propertyless. The question is thus of the greatest importance. Unfortunately, the statistical data dealing with it consist largely of bits and pieces, which are sometimes revealing but also often point in opposite directions. In Lille, for example, the "dominant classes," that is, the well-to-do bourgeoisie, increased from 7.06 to 9.07 percent of the population between 1821 and 1873–75, but its share of wealth measured by bequeathed inheritances rose from 57.6 to 89.82 percent. At the same time, although the "popular

6. Charles-H. Pouthas, *Démocraties et capitalisme (1848–1860)* (Paris, 1941), p. 425; Léon, "L'évolution démographique," p. 348; Rudolf Braun, *Sozialer und kultureller Wandel in einem ländlichen Industriegebiet (Zürcher Oberland) unter Einwirkung des Maschinen- und Fabrikwesens im 19. und 20. Jahrhundert* (Erlenbach-Zürich and Stuttgart, 1965), p. 145; Mitchell, *European Historical Statistics*, pp. 688–91.

classes" grew from 62.19 to 67.55 percent of the population, their share of inherited wealth declined from 1.4 to 0.23 percent. An examination of the social structure of Barmen between 1861 and 1907, however, suggests a diffusion rather than a concentration of affluence (table 5.3). Here the figures indicate growing economic opportunity and rising social mobility, a pattern altogether different from that in Lille forty years earlier.

The expanding volume of statistical information in the second half of the nineteenth century made possible a more comprehensive analysis of the distribution of wealth. The study of local conditions could be broadened to include not only national developments but international comparisons as well. In England the introduction of a new tax on inheritance in 1894 revealed that there were only half as many small estates worth between 500 and 1,000 pounds as in France, but there were three times as many estates in excess of 50,000 pounds and four times as many in excess of 200,000 or 250,000 pounds. In addition, the great inequality in wealth, which had hitherto been only surmised or inferred, could now be clearly demonstrated. The young economist Leo George Chiozza Money published a work in 1905 entitled *Riches and Poverty*, which made a deep impression on public opinion, going through ten editions in six years. His conclusion, based on official government statistics, was that *"nearly one-half of the entire income of the United Kingdom is enjoyed by but one-ninth of its population, . . . more than one-third of the entire income of the United Kingdom is enjoyed by less than one-thirtieth of its people,* [and] *about one-seventieth part of the population owns far more than one-half of the entire accumulated wealth, public and private, of the United Kingdom."* Even more important, "the enormous annual income

Table 5.3. Growth of Social Classes in Barmen, 1861–1907

	Number		Percentage Increase
	1861	1907	
Upper bourgeois	336	989	194
Middle bourgeois	534	4,117	671
White-collar employees	606	7,964	1,214
Artisans	1,045	4,772	357
Workers	19,093	51,555	170

SOURCE: Wolfgang Köllmann, *Sozialgeschichte der Stadt Barmen im 19. Jahrhundert* (Tübingen, 1960), p. 104.
NOTE: Middle bourgeois includes merchants and manufacturers of secondary rank, high government officials, and professionals.

of the United Kingdom is so badly distributed amongst us that, out of a population of 43,000,000, as many as 38,000,000 are poor."

The argument, though open to criticism in detail, proved unassailable in substance. To English liberals entering a decade of exciting reform, it sounded a summons to a crusade against social injustice. But was the distribution of wealth in Great Britain at the beginning of the twentieth century significantly different from what it had been a hundred or, for that matter, a thousand years before? To put it another way, did the rationalization of production alter to any substantial extent the historic balance between affluence and want? Simon Kuznets has provided the most systematic answer to this question on the basis of statistics showing the shares in national income of ordinal groups, tax categories, or consuming units in four European states after 1870. Although the data are spotty, they make possible a general evaluation of the effect of the industrial and agricultural revolutions on the distribution of wealth.

The figures do not point to a major shift in the distribution of wealth in the second half of the nineteenth century. They suggest rather that the gap between rich and poor remained by and large unchanged except in Denmark, where a significant decline in the share of the national income going to the most affluent portion of society occurred. Elsewhere, although fluctuations of a few percentage points in one direction or the other were recorded, no substantial alteration in the ratio of the propertied to the propertyless appears to have taken place. The effect of the rationalization of production, in other words, was neither a concentration nor a dispersion of wealth but the maintenance of a traditional pattern of distribution. What changed was the sum total of goods available for consumption, not their apportionment among the various income groups in the community. As output increased, the value of the share in national wealth of each of these groups increased as well. The result was a rise in affluence that did not alter significantly the proportion of rich and poor but did improve the standard of living of both.[7]

It is clear that in the years after 1870 the level of consumption for all social classes grew at a rate that had never before been attained. But what of the period before 1870, when the rationalization of production first began to affect the economy and society of Europe? Here the data are too sparse to permit conclusive generalizations. Only informed guesses are possible, guesses based on literary rather than statistical evidence. To be sure, there was a significant increase in the output of industry and agriculture during the first half of the nineteenth century, but the crucial

7. Alain Plessis, *De la fête impériale au mur des fédérés, 1852–1871* (Paris, 1973), pp. 156–57; Wolfgang Köllmann, *Sozialgeschichte der Stadt Barmen im 19. Jahrhundert* (Tübingen, 1960), p. 104; Elie Halevy, *A History of the English People in the Nineteenth*

Table 5.4. Income Distribution in Europe, 1870–1913

Percentage of Total Received by Various Income Categories

	Top 5 percent	Top 10 percent	Top 20 percent	Lowest 60 percent
Denmark				
1870	36.5	50		
1903	28	38		
1908	30	39	55	31
Prussia				
1875	26		48	34
1896	27		45	
1913	30		50	33
Saxony				
1880	34		56	27
1896	36		57	26.5
1912	33		55	27
United Kingdom				
1880	48		58	
1913	43		59	

SOURCE: Simon Kuznets, *Modern Economic Growth: Rate, Structure, and Spread* (New Haven and London, 1966), pp. 208–9.

question is the distribution of the wealth that they generated. This is precisely the question raised by Phyllis Deane in her account of economic development in England between 1801 and 1851:

> Whether this [growth in national product per head at constant prices] meant a corresponding increase in the average real incomes of the working classes . . . would have depended on the way the increase in the national product was distributed. If the increase in incomes was entirely absorbed by the property-owning classes in the form of profits and rent, and if the increased output of foods and services took the form either of capital goods or of goods and services that were outside the normal budget of the wage-earners, then

Century, 2d ed., 6 vols. (London, 1949–52), 6:276–77; L. G. Chiozza Money, *Riches and Poverty* (London, 1905), pp. 41–43, 72; Simon Kuznets, *Modern Economic Growth: Rate, Structure, and Spread* (New Haven and London, 1966), pp. 208–9.

it is fair to presume that the employed population gained nothing from the process of early industrialization.[8]

The answer has to be sought in a vast body of social literature, contained in government reports, parliamentary records, and private accounts, whose first appearance coincided by and large with the beginnings of economic rationalization. This literature, with only occasional exceptions, presents a grim picture of the life of the lower classes during the initial period of the industrial revolution. But does the depressing recital of hunger, cold, indecent overcrowding, and unremitting toil reflect an actual decline in the standard of living of the mass of the population? Or does it arise out of a spreading conviction that the function of the state should be extended to deal with the problems of human privation? Perhaps poverty in the new urban environment, amid mills and collieries, appeared more terrible or at least more conspicuous than it did as a familiar reality of life in the village. It may even be that the rationalization of production made want, which had in the past been accepted as the natural condition of a great majority of mankind, seem increasingly a remediable social evil that the community should seek to alleviate. In any event, the beginnings of industrialization led to the appearance in every country of books, reports, pamphlets, and articles dealing with the situation of the lower classes. Some of them were simply descriptive, portraying the living conditions of the laboring population. Others had a reformist purpose, suggesting ways in which the hard lot of the poor might be improved. Most were in agreement, however, that the common experience of those employed in manufacture and farming was endless drudgery that provided only the most meager subsistence.

England, the world's leader in the mechanization of industry, was the first country to inspire a substantial body of writing on the way of life of the working class. Starting with the late eighteenth century, official as well as private accounts began to paint a gloomy portrait of widespread privation. The French economist Jean-Baptiste Say, though an admirer of Adam Smith, was disturbed by the effect that unregulated industrial growth was having on British labor. Reporting on a visit to the United Kingdom at the end of the Napoleonic Wars, he spoke with concern about "the great distress of the class which simply lives by day labor alone." A worker, he explained, "depending on the family he has, and despite efforts which are often worthy of the highest recognition, can earn in England only three fourths and sometimes no more than half of his expenditures."

A decade later, the journal of the London Co-operative Society,

8. Deane, *First Industrial Revolution*, p. 252.

founded under the influence of the ideas of Robert Owen, described in greater detail the daily struggle for survival of the lower classes:

> There is scarcely a married working man within the bills of mortality, who is not in arrears with his landlord, his chandler, and his coal merchant. Moreover there is scarcely a working married man within the same limits, whose wardrobe is in his own keeping. *The pawnbroker has it within his grasp in nine cases out of ten.* Few of the working classes occupy more than one room to a family, and the whole contents of such a room is seldom worth more than three pounds at a fair valuation; estimate the duplicates of things pledged at three pounds more, allow three pounds for the threadbare garments of the father of the family, including the tatters on his miserable wife, and children, and we shall have nine pounds as the average capital of each working man in *the state of holy matrimony.* Now out of this nine pounds his debts are to be paid, for instance, *his landlord a quarter's rent, his chandler a month's score,* his hawking linen draper, his doctor, his shoemaker, his taylor, &c. &c. say ten pounds for the whole tribe of clamorous creditors; and we shall find the unhappy man just one pound worse than nothing. This is not an exaggerated statement, an overstrained estimate; experience too fully tells me that I have but faintly described the condition of more than two thirds of all the married operatives in the kingdom.[9]

Other accounts of the life of the lower classes in England during the early years of industrialization are even more poignant, picturing not only chronic indebtedness but near starvation. The reformer Richard Oastler, a well-known Tory radical, testified before a select committee concerning the extreme poverty of the Yorkshire weavers: "There are scores and hundreds of families in the district [around Huddersfield] to whom a piece of flesh meat is a luxury; it does not form a regular article in their daily consumption; they live generally upon porridge and potatoes, and they do not know what it is, many of them, very many of them, to taste flesh meat from year's end to year's end, excepting somebody gives them some. . . . As to their clothing, they are clothed in rags; and their furniture is such, as I am sure I cannot describe, but such as a convict ought not to have."

Conditions in Lancashire were no better, according to a letter published in the *Morning Chronicle*: "In all I visited, eighty-three dwellings

---

9. Jean-Baptiste Say, *De l'Angleterre et des Anglais* (Paris and London, 1815), p. 18; "Address Relative to the Co-operative Community Fund Association," *Co-operative Magazine and Monthly Herald* 1 (1826):309–10.

[in Colne] selected at hazard, they were destitute of furniture, save old boxes for tables, and stools or even large stones for chairs; the beds were composed of straw and shavings. . . . The food was oatmeal and water for breakfast; flour and water, with a little skimmed milk, for dinner; oatmeal and water again, for a third supply, with those who [were] eating three meals a day. . . . I was an eye witness to children appeasing the cravings of the stomach by the refuse of decayed vegetables in the root market." A few miles away in Burnley, "groups of idlers stood . . . haggard with famine . . . their eyes rolling with that fierce and uneasy expression which I have often noticed in maniacs. . . . 'We want not charity but employment,' was their unanimous declaration." Around the mid-century, John Stuart Mill could still maintain that "it is questionable if all the mechanical inventions yet made have lightened the day's toil of any human being. They have enabled a greater population to live the same life of drudgery and imprisonment, and an increased number of manufacturers and others to make large fortunes." The evidence lay all about him, in the mills, collieries, foundries, and sweatshops of early Victorian England.[10]

A sizable literature of social portrayal and protest did not appear in France before the July Monarchy, a generation later than in Great Britain, reflecting the difference in the pace of industrialization of the two countries. Yet even under the Restoration, the Genevan publicist Jean-Charles-Léonard Simonde de Sismondi, an early critic of liberal economics, declared that he had been "deeply moved" by "the cruel sufferings of workers in manufacturing establishments" that he had seen in Italy, Switzerland, and France. He spoke of children forced at the age of six or eight to seek employment in cotton mills, "where they work twelve and fourteen hours in an atmosphere constantly filled with lint and dust, and where they perish of consumption, one after another, before reaching their twentieth birthday." Was economic rationalization, then, only a means for the more effective exploitation of the many by the few? Sismondi rejected this view. "Wealth is desirable in society," he declared, "only because of the well-being which it diffuses among all classes. To the extent that the increase in labor contributes to the increase in this well-being, this labor is itself a national blessing. On the other hand, as soon as we cease to consider those who perform it, but only those who are to enjoy it, it can change into a frightful calamity." He was already

10. Great Britain, *Parliamentary Papers* (1834), 10 (*Reports from Committees*), "Report from Select Committee on Hand-Loom Weavers' Petitions; with the Minutes of Evidence, and Index," p. 280; *Morning Chronicle*, 22 June 1842, p. 7; John Stuart Mill, *Principles of Political Economy with Some of Their Applications to Social Philosophy*, 2 vols. (London, 1848), 2:312.

crossing the dividing line between the description and the reform of social institutions.

Less hortatory but more informative was the detailed account by Louis-René Villermé of the way of life of French textile workers. It appeared in 1840 under the title *Description of the Physical and Moral Condition of the Workers Employed in the Manufacture of Cotton, Wool, and Silk.* Sober and businesslike, it contained a wealth of firsthand information on the standard of living of the urban lower classes during the early period of industrialization. In Lille a family in which the father, mother, and a child between the ages of ten and twelve worked could earn 915 francs annually, but its expenditures for just food and housing were 798 francs. "This is most certainly not enough. If there should be sickness, unemployment, or a little drunkenness, this family will be in the greatest difficulty." In Sedan the usual workday was sixteen hours, with two and sometimes only one hour off for meals and rest periods. There were some factories, to be sure, where the hours were as a rule twelve for men and eight and a half for women, but "the workday is frequently extended beyond this number of hours, and the workers cannot object to it." Around Mulhouse the diet of the operatives varied considerably, depending on their skill, income, and the size of their family. But "vegetables and above all potatoes make up at least three fourths of the nourishment of the largest number. Occasionally a little pork is also part of it." As for housing, Villermé reported, "I have seen . . . some of those wretched lodgings where two families were sleeping each in a corner, on straw thrown on the floor and held in place by two boards. Tatters of a blanket and often a sort of feather mattress disgustingly filthy, that was all that covered up this straw." The concreteness of these pictures of lower-class life gives them an importance equal to the more famous and eloquent appeals for social reform that began to multiply under the July Monarchy.[11]

In Germany detailed data on the standard of living of the working population did not appear before the 1850s or even the 1860s. There had been addresses, complaints, remonstrances, and petitions going back at least a generation, but they were generally richer in pathos than statistics. After the mid-century, however, the literature of social portrayal broadened with the addition of more specific information derived largely from official sources. One of the most revealing was the collection of summarized reports by county commissioners for the years 1858–66, which the Prussian government published. The men who wrote these accounts were

11. J.-C.-L. Simonde de Sismondi, *Nouveaux principes d'économie politique, ou De la richesse dans ses rapports avec la population,* 2 vols. (Paris, 1819), 1:iv–v, 353–54, 358; L.-R. Villermé, *Tableau de l'état physique et moral des ouvriers employés dans les manufactures de coton, de laine et de soie,* 2 vols. (Paris, 1840), 1:27, 44–45, 99–101, 256.

conservative bureaucrats dealing with conditions in towns and villages rather than big cities. But what they had to say was not much different from contemporary descriptions of lower-class life in the great industrial centers. In Lublinitz in Silesia, "families of rural workers hardly earn enough beyond bare subsistence to pay for the cost of celebrating a baptism." Farther west in Neurode, "the hired weavers often work through the whole night, and workers in the spinning and finishing mills work up to 18 hours a day." In Adenau in the Rhine Province, "the chief sources of nourishment of the population at noon and in the evening are potatoes with salt and usually with fat, and in addition black bread and coffee mixed with chicory. Waffles made of oatmeal are frequently a substitute for rye bread. Meat is enjoyed only at church fairs and on holidays." And in Meseritz in the province of Posen, "two thirds of the small handicraftsmen must look for earnings on the side as day laborers because of insufficient employment in their occupation."

Yet not all reports spoke of low wages, long hours, and inadequate nourishment. Here and there a slight rise in the standard of living was recorded, an increase in income or an improvement in diet. "The position of the working classes" in Gladbach near the Dutch border "is not unfavorable," according to the local county commissioner. In Oschersleben in the province of Saxony, "the needs of the workers are in general covered everywhere by their earnings, despite their growing preoccupation with amusements, especially since the scarcity of labor has raised those earnings." In Magdeburg "conditions have become decidedly better, because there is no labor surplus, wage scales are higher, and the winters were mild." Still, a significant improvement in the economic position of the lower classes was the exception, not the rule. Life for the average worker in industry or agriculture remained harsh and insecure. Even the chamber of commerce in Cologne, usually not very sensitive to the needs of labor, conceded in 1858 that "the great increase in wages has only in rare cases led to the transformation of the propertyless into a propertied working class. A special investigation might well reveal in several factory districts that . . . the workers were on an average just as propertyless and even here and there weighed down with a greater burden of indebtedness than ten years ago." The rationalization of production had barely touched the timeless poverty of the masses.[12]

The picture that emerges from these observations of the standard of living of the lower classes is thus essentially the same in all countries. The

12. "Die arbeitenden Classen und die Arbeits- und Lohnverhältnisse," *Jahrbuch für die amtliche Statistik des preussischen Staats* 2 (1867):289, 306, 310, 324, 332, 342; "Jahresbericht der Handelskammer zu Köln für 1857," *Preussisches Handelsarchiv: Wochenschrift für Handel, Gewerbe und Verkehrsanstalten* 2 (1858):260.

sources describe again and again the meager income, endless toil, poor diet, and wretched housing of the working population. But there is still another aspect of industrialization to which the early writers on social conditions repeatedly return: the employment of women and children in manufacturing and mining. Especially in such industries as textiles, where the level of required technical skill was low, the temptation to hire them at wages substantially lower than those paid to men was irresistible. In the manufacture of cotton, wool, linen, and silk in the United Kingdom during the 1830s, according to a contemporary estimate, there were 4,811 boys and 5,308 girls below the age of eleven, 67,203 boys and 89,822 girls between eleven and eighteen, and 88,859 men and 102,813 women above eighteen; all in all, there were 160,873 boys and men and 197,942 girls and women. Women constituted between 56 and 70 percent of the industrial labor force of France in 1838, depending on the department. In Haut-Rhin, a center of textile production, there were 13,000 children in a total of 61,000 wage earners in 1847. Farther east, the ratio of women to men employed in Prussian factories and mines was about 1 to 4 in 1849 and 1 to 5 in 1861. The cotton-spinning mills of the canton of Zürich employed 3,000 workers in 1815, of whom 1,124 were minors. The age distribution of 884 such minors is known: 48 were between seven and nine, 284 between ten and twelve, 406 between thirteen and fifteen, 138 between sixteen and eighteen, and 8 between eighteen and twenty-one. Figures for the labor force of the Zürich cotton industry during the next forty years are given in Table 5.5. They show that the percentage of women rose rapidly, whereas the percentage of children remained steady and then declined.[13]

To many observers this composition of the labor force in industry seemed a serious social evil. It made fathers dependent on the earnings of those whom they should have been supporting. It took mothers away from their duties of child rearing and housekeeping. Worst of all, it meant that children were toiling in mills, amid unhealthy and unwholesome surroundings, when they ought to have been at play or in school. This last problem, the employment of minors in factories and collieries, aroused special concern. A report on the situation in Great Britain maintained that child labor "not only tends to diminish future expectations as to the general sum of life and industry, by impairing the strength and

13. Andrew Ure, *The Philosophy of Manufactures: or, an Exposition of the Scientific, Moral, and Commercial Economy of the Factory System of Great Britain* (London, 1835), p. 481; Régine Pernoud, *Histoire de la bourgeoisie en France*, 2 vols. (Paris, 1960–62), 2:500; Kuczynski, *Geschichte der Lage der Arbeiter*, 18:104; Erich Gruner, *Die Arbeiter in der Schweiz im 19. Jahrhundert: Soziale Lage, Organisation, Verhältnis zu Arbeitgeber und Staat* (Bern, 1968), pp. 113–14.

Table 5.5. Labor Force in the Zürich Cotton Industry, 1827–58

	Men		Women		Children under 16	
	Number	Percentage	Number	Percentage	Number	Percentage
1827	2,000	40	600	12	2,400	48
1842	1,450	29	1,150	23	2,400	48
1858	2,225	37	2,111	35	1,664	28

SOURCE: Erich Gruner, *Die Arbeiter in der Schweiz im 19. Jahrhundert: Soziale Lage, Organisation, Verhältnis zu Arbeitgeber und Staat* (Bern, 1968), p. 114.

destroying the vital stamina of the rising generation, but ... it appears that the children employed in factories are generally debarred from all opportunities of education." A French writer pictured "this multitude of gaunt children, pale and covered with rags, who go barefoot [to the factories in the morning], through rain and mud, holding in their hand or, when it rains, under their clothing, which has been made waterproof by the oil dripping down on them from the looms, the piece of bread which is to nourish them until their return." From Italy came an account of conditions in the Lombard textile mills, where young girls worked in "rooms [which] are often rather damp and poorly protected against changes in the weather. The nature of the work is such as to make a child into a machine or worse than a machine." More than fifteen thousand minors were laboring in the factories, wasting "the flower of life for a daily wage of twenty to twenty-four centesimi, and in a branch of production which provides the country every year with a value of forty-five million Austrian lire." There were many similar descriptions throughout Europe of the employment of children in factories and of the disintegration of the working-class family.[14]

The body of information on the way of life of the masses in the early stages of the industrial revolution is thus vast but incomplete, amorphous, and sometimes contradictory. It points to only one obvious conclusion, and even this obviousness can be misleading. The great bulk of the population lived at a level of meager subsistence, amid toil and squalor, exposed to hunger, cold, disease, and early death. The growing

14. Great Britain, *Parliamentary Papers* (1816), 3 (*Reports from Committees*), "Report of the Minutes of Evidence, Taken before the Select Committee on the State of the Children Employed in the Manufactories of the United Kingdom," p. 140; Villermé, *Tableau de l'état physique et moral*, 2:87–88; Giuseppe Sacchi, "Sullo stato dei fanciulli occupati nelle manifatture," *Annali universali di statistica, economia pubblica, storia, viaggi e commercio* 73 (1842):243–44.

social conscience of the well-to-do in the nineteenth century found these conditions deplorable; to the affluent society of the twentieth, they often appear heartbreaking. But should they be measured by the standards of another class or another age? The pertinent question is whether the standard of living of the masses was declining as a result of the onset of industrialization. Had income been higher, working hours shorter, and housing better fifty or a hundred years earlier on the farm or in the village? There can be no final answer, not only because the evidence is incomplete but also because it consists in part of elements that cannot be weighed and measured. Is grinding labor easier to bear in bright sunlight amid green fields than in the gloomy factories and dirty back alleys of the big city? Is the toil of women and children more tolerable at home in the weaver's cottage or on the crofter's holding, where each member of the family contributes to a collective enterprise, than in mills and mines where father, mother, son, and daughter are often separated from each other for most of the day? These are some of the intangible factors that must be considered in deciding whether the way of life of the lower classes was deteriorating.

It is significant that critics of social conditions in the first half of the nineteenth century did not as a rule speak of a long-term decline in the material conditions of labor—wages, hours, diet, and housing—in contrast to those of the second half of the eighteenth century. There are accounts of the hardships suffered by skilled artisans, especially in the textile trades, whose livelihood was being destroyed by mechanized production. But there are few claims and fewer signs that the factory worker's standard of living after the Napoleonic Wars was substantially lower than the peasant's had been under the ancien régime. Those who deplored the effect of the industrial revolution on the lower classes usually spoke of the loss of independence, decline in self-respect, deterioration of morals, and disruption of the family as the chief evils brought by the new way of life. During the 1830s a writer portrayed nostalgically the vanished Arcadia that had existed in Great Britain before the advent of machinery:

> These were, undoubtedly, the golden times of manufactures, considered in reference to the character of the labourers. . . . Removed from many of those causes which universally operate to the deterioration of the moral character of the labouring man, when brought into large towns—into immediate contact and communion with his fellows, and under the influence of many depressing physical agencies—the small farmer, spinner, or hand-loom weaver, presented as orderly and respectable an appearance as could be wished. It is true that the amount of labour gone through was but small; that the

quantity of cloth or yarn produced was but limited—for he worked by the rule of his strength and convenience. They were, however, sufficient to clothe and feed himself and family decently, and according to their station; to lay by a penny for an evil day, and to enjoy those amusements and bodily recreations then in being. He was a respectable member of society; a good father, a good husband and a good son.[15]

A decade later, however, Friedrich Engels went much farther in a well-known work of social reportage, *The Condition of the Working Class in England*. Contrasting the cruel present with an idyllic past, he portrayed in rosy detail the life of spinners and weavers before the age of mechanization. Competition had been restricted by the limited size of the market. Increases in demand had kept pace with increases in population, "providing employment for all workers," so that they were generally in a position to save a little money and to cultivate a small plot of land in their spare time. The weaver had as much leisure as he wanted, "for he could weave whenever and for as long as he felt like it." He thus "stood in society a step above the present English worker, [leading] an upright and peaceful life in all godliness and respectability." The lower classes had been far better off than they were under the industrial revolution because they did not have to work very hard "and they still earned what they needed." In addition, "they had leisure for healthy work in their garden or field, work which was in itself recreation for them, and they could moreover take part in the recreations and games of their neighbors . . . games [such as] bowling, ball games, etc. [which] contributed to the maintenance of their health and the strengthening of their bodies." As for their children, they grew up in the open country air, "now and then" helping their parents with their work, but "there was no question of a workday of eight or twelve hours." This was the lost paradise of pre-industrial innocence destroyed by the mechanization of production.[16]

But how accurate are such accounts? Paul Mantoux, who early in the twentieth century wrote a masterly study of the origins of the industrial revolution in England, made fun of them, declaring that "a funeral oration could not have been delivered in a more moving or edifying tone." And Herbert Heaton claimed that "the trivial round and common task of the eighteenth-century worker was drab and monotonous, and he would be intensely amused if he could realize the glamour which has been cast . . . over his dreary toil."[17]

15. Peter Gaskell, *The Manufacturing Population of England, Its Moral, Social, and Physical Conditions, and the Changes Which Have Arisen from the Use of Steam Machinery; with an Examination of Infant Labour* (London, 1833), pp. 16, 18.

16. Karl Marx and Friedrich Engels, *Werke*, 39 vols. (Berlin, 1960–69), 2:237–38.

17. Paul Mantoux, *La révolution industrielle au XVIIIe siècle: Essai sur les commence-*

Certainly those arguing before 1850 that the factory was the ruination of the working man were balanced and sometimes outbalanced by those arguing that it raised his standard of living. The latter included such panegyrists of the industrial revolution as Andrew Ure, who maintained that "tens of thousands of old, young, and middle-aged of both sexes, many of them too feeble to get their daily bread by any of the former modes of industry, [are] earning abundant food, raiment, and domestic accommodation, without perspiring at a single pore, screened meanwhile from the summer's sun and the winter's frost, in apartments more airy and salubrious than those of the metropolis, in which our legislative and fashionable aristocracies assemble." Marc Séguin was equally enthusiastic: "The pleasures and conveniences of life which had been reserved for wealth only are now at the disposal of the artisan. A few more steps and they will also be distributed among all classes. . . . Everywhere the most delicate objects of usefulness and luxury are poured into consumption at ever decreasing prices." Even Villermé, cautious and levelheaded as a rule, concluded that the way of life of the lower classes was improving:

> It is good, moreover, that the workers should know that their condition today is better than it has ever been. . . . I have in addition been surprised, when stopping in places which I had visited formerly, to see there workers eating better bread, in footgear where I had seen them barefoot, wearing shoes where I had seen them in wooden clogs, living in houses which were better illuminated, neater, more comfortable, and better furnished than the old ones, in short, to find them in all those places not as I would have always wanted to see them, but in a situation *generally less bad* than twenty or thirty years before.[18]

There are some twentieth-century writers who support this conclusion. The early years of industrialization, they claim, were an age "fond of sickly sentiment," which "sought inspiration for tears in the factories." Many of the social reformers, moreover, were Tories who "for the most part were not only ignorant of the conditions in the factories" but "predisposed to condemn the factory owners" out of class hostility. The industrialists were on the whole "men of humanity." Evidence of the misery of the working population taken from parliamentary inquiries and medical observations is unreliable or inconclusive. Far from reducing

---

ments de la grande industrie moderne en Angleterre (Paris, 1905), p. 47; Herbert Heaton, *The Yorkshire Woolen and Worsted Industries from the Earliest Times up to the Industrial Revolution* (Oxford, 1920), pp. 350–51.

18. Villermé, *Tableau de l'état physique et moral*, 2:346. Cf. Ure, *Philosophy of Manufactures*, pp. 17–18; Marc Séguin, *De l'influence des chemins de fer et de l'art de les tracer et de les construire* (Paris, 1839), pp. ii, v.

the standard of living of the lower classes, these writers maintain, the industrial revolution made possible a substantial improvement. In England during the period 1790–1830, "a greater proportion of the people came to benefit from [factory production] both as producers and as consumers." The decline in the price of textiles meant cheaper clothing. "Boots began to take the place of clogs, hats replaced shawls, at least for wear on Sundays." Clocks and handkerchiefs gradually became articles of general consumption, and the price of tea, coffee, and sugar declined substantially. There were clear signs of "the existence of a large class [of workers] raised well above the level of mere subsistence." The poverty of many people may have remained unabated by the mechanization of production, but "the number of those who were able to share in the benefits of economic progress was larger than the number of those who were shut out from these benefits." And even more important, that number was growing steadily.[19]

The debate goes on and on because the evidence is ambiguous, lending itself to a variety of interpretations. Yet taken as a whole, it does point to a few tentative conclusions. The first generation or two of workers under the industrial revolution experienced no major change in its standard of living as a result of the economic transformation of which it was a part. There were some members of the labor force, especially those in the textile trades, who undoubtedly suffered a decline, as skilled handicraftsmen found themselves unable to compete with machinery. On the other hand, there were others, in metallurgy or engine building, for example, who improved their position as a result of the rationalization of production. For most of them, however, the coming of the industrial revolution made little difference with regard to income, workday, diet, or housing.

This was especially true of those employed in agriculture, who still made up the great bulk of the labor force. Yet even those engaged in manufacture experienced only minor changes in their accustomed level of subsistence. The goods and services generated by early industrialization remained largely inaccessible to them. But the new hardships imposed on the working population by the rationalization of production were less the result of a long-term decline in income than of psychological disorientation. Millions of people who had grown up amid the certainties and traditions of the village or small town were suddenly thrown into an alien environment of factories, shops, tenements, and slums, where the values of rural society soon disintegrated before the hard realities of the

19. W. H. Hutt, "The Factory System of the Early 19th Century," *Economica* 6 (1926):78–85, 88–89; T. S. Ashton, "The Standard of Life of the Workers in England, 1790–1830," *Journal of Economic History*, supp. 9, 1949 (*The Tasks of Economic History: Papers Presented at the Ninth Annual Meeting of the Economic History Association, Rutgers University, New Brunswick, New Jersey, September 9–10, 1949*), pp. 37–38.

urban experience. The outcome was a profound demoralization, which primarily reflected not a change in the standard of living but a change in the way of life.

Such generalizations about the initial effect of the industrial revolution may be open to challenge, but there can be little doubt about what happened subsequently. Within fifty years the standard of living of the lower classes began to rise. The evidence on this point is incontrovertible. Never before had there been such a substantial growth in the income of the labor force in such a short period of time. In Great Britain a working-class family that had earned 20 shillings a week or 52 pounds annually in 1851 was earning 32 shillings a week or 83 pounds annually thirty years later. In France nominal hourly wages rose 58 to 60 percent between 1850 and 1870, and real hourly wages rose 28 percent. In Germany the real annual income of miners grew from 662 marks in 1871 to 1,020 in 1900; in the building trades, the increase was from 394 to 659; and in the iron and steel industry, earnings went from 630 to 885.

Even Jürgen Kuczynski, a Marxian scholar who could never be accused of minimizing the sufferings of labor under industrial capitalism, concedes that the income of the working class improved rapidly after the early stages of economic rationalization. His index of real wages shows an initial period of decline in England after 1789, reflecting the effects of a long war and postwar depression, and then a succession of remarkable gains until the eve of the First World War. In France there was a similar pattern: first a plateau coinciding with the beginnings of the industrial revolution, followed by a vigorous upward movement. Kuczynski's estimates for Germany start at a later period, but they too show a tendency to remain constant at first or even to decline, and then to rise at a rapid pace. Erich Gruner's index of real wages in Switzerland covers only forty-five years, but it follows the same course as wage indexes for the major countries of Western and Central Europe: 64 in 1830, 57 in 1835, 71 in 1840, 72 in 1845, 77 in 1850, 72 in 1855, and then a spurt to 78 in 1860, 80 in 1865, 90 in 1870, and 100 in 1875. It becomes clear that although the income of the lower classes during the nineteenth century may not have increased as much as profits, dividends, or rents, it increased sufficiently to bring about an unprecedented improvement in the standard of living.[20]

The rise in wages of the labor forces was accompanied by a gradual but steady reduction in the workday. During the early period of the industrial revolution, writers on social conditions frequently commented

20. Leone Levi, *Wages and Earnings of the Working Classes: Report to Sir Arthur Bass, M.P.* (London, 1885), p. 53; Léon, "L'évolution démographique," pp. 347–48; Ashok V. Desai, *Real Wages in Germany, 1871–1913* (Oxford, 1968), p. 125; Kuczynski, *Geschichte der Lage der Arbeiter*, 37:111; Gruner, *Arbeiter in der Schweiz*, p. 137.

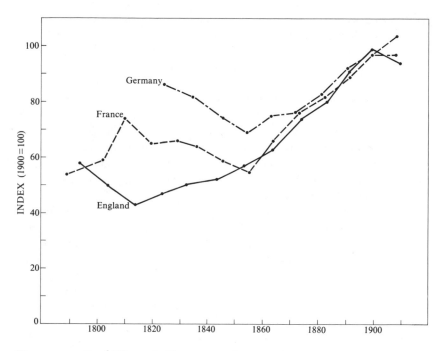

Figure 5.1. Real Wages in Europe, 1789–1914

SOURCE: Jürgen Kuczynski, *Die Geschichte der Lage der Arbeiter unter dem Kapitalismus*, 38 vols. (Berlin, 1960–71), 37:111.

on the exhausting number of hours that workers had to spend in the mills: 12, 14, or 16 were common, six days a week and sometimes even on Sunday. But that began to change little by little after 1850. In England, the pioneer country in this movement, trade unions chipped away at the workweek, slowly reducing it from 60 hours or more to 55, with a half-holiday on Saturday. According to one estimate, the length of the average workweek in British industry declined from 58.8 hours in 1860–69 to 57.1 in 1870–76, 54.3 in 1877–85, 54.3 in 1886–93, 53.5 in 1894–1903, 53.2 in 1904–10, and 53.2 in 1911–13. In Germany the hours of labor varied considerably, but in a few occupations where the workers were well organized, such as the building trades, 10 hours a day had been established as the rule even before the end of the nineteenth century. This then became the goal of the labor force in other industries. Between 1870 and 1913 per capita annual hours fell 19 percent; in 1905–7 alone almost 400,000 workers won reductions averaging 4 hours a week through collective bargaining. By the time of the First World War, 10 hours were the daily norm in more than 60 percent of the factories in Prussia, so that this figure may be taken as typical for the German industrial wage earner.[21]

In France progress was slower, although after 1900 there was legislation providing that the workday of men employed in the same plants as women should not exceed 10 hours. Outside the factories, moreover, in the more demanding forms of labor (at the controls of a locomotive, for example), there was also a tendency to reduce the number of hours to 10. Yet when the twentieth century began, there was still no legal requirement for a day of rest for all workers, and *la semaine anglaise*, a half-holiday on Saturday, was only a remote ideal. In Switzerland, it has been calculated, the workday began to diminish earlier than in France or even Germany. After remaining constant at 14 to 15 hours throughout 1815–40, it fell to between 12 and 14 in 1850, 12 to 13 in 1860, and 11 to 13 in 1870–77. By then the per capita annual hours of labor were declining in most countries, by 19 percent in Denmark, Italy, and Sweden during 1870–1913 and by 6 percent in the Netherlands and Norway during 1900–1913. There are estimates for Europe as a whole, moreover, showing a steady decrease in the average workweek after the middle of the nineteenth century: 84 hours in 1850, 78 in 1870, 69 in 1890, and 60 in 1910. It was all in all an impressive achievement.[22]

The gains of the adult male working population were further enhanced by the decline of competition from the labor of women and children. This was partly a result of the growing supervision of economic conditions by the state, but it also reflected the improved standard of living of the lower classes, which could now make ends meet without the meager earnings of their sons and daughters. In Great Britain the number of children under fourteen employed in transportation fell from 38,439 or 2.7 percent of all workers in 1901 to 27,699 or 1.7 percent in 1911. In mining the number declined from 14,174 or 1.5 percent to 8,670 or 0.7. In the dress industry it went from 12,908 or 1.0 percent to 8,825 or 0.7. And in textiles, where minors had made up almost half of the labor force early in the nineteenth century, there were 57,867 workers under fourteen or 4.8 percent in 1901 and 53,231 or 4.0 percent in 1911. The German statistics deal with children below the age of sixteen rather than

21. Herbert Heaton, "Economic Change and Growth," in *New Cambridge Modern History*, 10:48; Colin Clark, *The Conditions of Economic Progress* (London, 1940), p. 83; J. H. Clapham, *The Economic Development of France and Germany*, 4th ed. (Cambridge, 1966), p. 405; Maddison, "Economic Growth," p. 90; Peter N. Stearns, *Lives of Labor: Work in a Maturing Industrial Society* (New York, 1975), p. 256.

22. Clapham, *Economic Development of France and Germany*, p. 405; Gruner, *Arbeiter in der Schweiz*, p. 131; Maddison, "Economic Growth," p. 90; W. S. Woytinski and E. S. Woytinski, *World Population and Production: Trends and Outlook* (New York, 1953), p. 367.

fourteen, a category that therefore includes many who had already completed the required period of school attendance. The number of such minors employed by industry in 1895 was 691,841 or 7.8 percent of the entire labor force, whereas in 1907 the number was 707,864 or 6.1 percent. In other words, there had been an absolute increase of 2.3 percent but a relative decrease of 1.7.

The employment of women in industrial occupations did not decline to nearly the same extent as that of children. On the eve of the First World War, they continued to make up a substantial part of the labor force: 22.6 percent in Belgium, 33.1 in France, 23.0 in Great Britain, and 18.7 in Germany. Indeed, in some countries their proportion was actually increasing. They accounted for 18 percent of all those employed by German industry in 1882 but 19 percent in 1907. The escalating share of women employees in commerce and transportation was even more striking, rising from 19 to 25 percent. The most rapid growth, however, occurred in agriculture, where, according to official statistics, the percentage of female workers climbed from 31 to 47. The increase is so sharp that the accuracy of these figures has been questioned. But it is clear that as more and more men shifted from husbandry to better paying occupations in manufacture, their wives, sisters, and daughters became a more important source of labor on the peasant's farm or the nobleman's latifundium. As for the women employed in factories and shops, they were now no longer competing with male workers to the same extent as in the early days of industrialization. Their working conditions were increasingly regulated by the state, by measures such as the reduction of their workweek to 56.5 hours in the English textile industry in 1874 or the revision of the German industrial code in 1908, which established a weekly maximum of 60 hours for female employees (subject, however, to numerous exceptions). Legislation of this sort had the effect of diminishing competition within the labor force, improving wages and reducing hours for all workers.[23]

The rising standard of living of the lower classes of Europe was also reflected in the improvement of their diet. The average Frenchman increased his consumption of wine and potatoes during the second half of the nineteenth century by 50 percent, that of spirits by 200 percent, and that of sugar and coffee by 300 percent. Talk about the "black bread of adversity" became metaphorical because even the poor could now afford the white wheat bread that only people of wealth had tasted during the

23. Stearns, *Lives of Labor*, pp. 30, 34–35; Kuczynski, *Geschichte der Lage der Arbeiter*, 18:204; Ephraim Lipson, *The Growth of English Society: A Short Economic History* (London, 1949), p. 358; Clapham, *Economic Development of France and Germany*, p. 405.

Middle Ages. The average German still ate rye bread, by choice rather than necessity, but his consumption of meat grew almost 130 percent between 1860 and 1900. The ratio of the number of calories in his diet to the number required to meet normal needs has been calculated at 75 percent in 1850–54, 90 in 1870–74, 108 in 1890–94, and 118 in 1910–13. In Great Britain the per capita consumption of meat increased between 1880 and 1910 by 20 percent and that of sugar by 33 percent. During 1880–1910, moreover, the average height of men rose about 3 centimeters in Sweden, 2.5 in Switzerland, and 1 in Italy. Near starvation, which had been such a frequent experience of the masses in the preindustrial economy, was giving way before a spreading abundance in which hunger was only a terrible memory.[24]

Even housing conditions, so wretched at the beginning of the nineteenth century, had begun to improve substantially by the end. The statistics for Germany, the most detailed in Europe on this point, are illuminating. The average number of residents in dwellings with only one heatable room declined in 1885–1905 from 3.8 to 3.2 in Berlin, from 3.9 to 3.6 in Hamburg, from 4.1 to 3.4 in Breslau, from 3.9 to 3.5 in Leipzig, from 3.8 to 3.6 in Magdeburg, from 3.5 to 3.4 in Altona, and from 3.5 to 3.0 in Görlitz. In Dresden the proportion of the population living in dwellings with only one heatable room fell between 1880 and 1900 from 48.3 to 37.4 percent, whereas the proportion in dwellings with two heatable rooms rose from 21.9 to 28.4. In Lübeck between 1890 and 1910 the percentage of those in dwellings with one heatable room dropped from 45.0 to 27.0, and those in dwellings with two heatable rooms increased from 24.8 to 31.8.

There is evidence, furthermore, that the housing of the lower classes was becoming not only more spacious but also more comfortable. In Breslau, for example, the number of workers' dwellings grew 60 percent in 1895–1900, but the proportion of workers' dwellings using gas as fuel grew 525 percent. City slums were still squalid and congested. Social critics pointed out that 159,639 people in Berlin in 1880 occupied housing that was classified as "overcrowded," that is, with at least six residents if it consisted of one room or at least ten residents if it consisted of two rooms. In other words, about 14 percent of the population of the capital lived under conditions of poverty that even contemporaries often

24. Clapham, *Economic Development of France and Germany*, pp. 402–3; Walther G. Hoffmann, Franz Grumbach, and Helmut Hesse, *Das Wachstum der deutschen Wirtschaft seit der Mitte des 19. Jahrhunderts* (Berlin, Heidelberg, and New York, 1965), pp. 658–59; Peter N. Stearns, *European Society in Upheaval: Social History since 1750*, 2d ed. (New York and London, 1975), p. 191; Emmanuel Le Roy Ladurie, *Le territoire de l'historien* (Paris, 1973), p. 379.

found shocking. But how much greater had the percentage been only a generation or two earlier.[25]

The most eloquent testimony to the rising standard of living of the lower classes, however, came from the lower classes themselves. The mood of hopelessness and demoralization that they had displayed during the early period of the industrial revolution was being replaced by rising expectations of a well-being to which they had never before aspired. They were gradually turning from the escapism offered by alcohol or millenarian visions of social eschatology to bread-and-butter improvements in their everyday life. A disgruntled old British radical, writing in the 1870s, contrasted his generation's fierce militancy, fed by a sense of desperation, with the frivolity of the younger workers:

> In our old Chartist time, it is true, Lancashire working men were in rags by thousands; and many of them often lacked food. But their intelligence was demonstrated wherever you went. You would see them in groups discussing the great doctrine of political justice . . . or they were in earnest dispute respecting the teachings of Socialism. *Now*, you will see no such groups in Lancashire. But you will hear well-dressed working men talking, as they walk with their hands in their pockets, of "Co-ops" (Co-operative Stores), and their shares in them, or in building societies. And you will see others, like idiots, leading small greyhound dogs, covered with cloth, in a string! They are about to race, and they are betting money as they go! . . . As for their betting on horses—like their masters!—it is a perfect madness.[26]

But appeals for a return to the sterner virtues of the early days of the crusade for labor's rights were largely ignored. They could not overcome the growing complacency voiced by a married couple in the textile industry of Saxony: "We don't want to go back to the good old days. Things are not bad for those working in the factory, compared to what they were." By the time of the First World War, the heroic age of the struggle for social justice was over.

To be sure, the improvement in the standard of living of the lower classes should not be exaggerated. There were pockets of poverty throughout Europe; especially in the south and east, want was often not an exception but the rule. Even in Great Britain at the opening of the twentieth century, the sociologist Benjamin Seebohm Rowntree found that 15 percent of the working population of York lived in "primary"

25. Desai, *Real Wages in Germany*, pp. 26, 28, 123; Heinrich Peus, *Der Wohnungsjammer des Proletariats* (Dessau, 1894), p. 3.
26. *The Life of Thomas Cooper: Written by Himself* (London, 1872), p. 393.

poverty, that is, its earnings were insufficient to obtain "the minimum necessities for the maintenance of merely physical efficiency." Another 28 percent lived in "secondary" poverty, with earnings "sufficient for the maintenance of merely physical efficiency were it not that some portion . . . is absorbed by other expenditure, either useful or wasteful." Yet at the opening of the nineteenth century, 80 percent or more of the working population had lived under similar conditions without arousing either indignation or sympathy among men of property and education. In 1914 hardship remained an everyday experience for the lower classes, but their diet was now better, their workday shorter, their clothing warmer, their housing roomier. The famines and epidemics that had been their lot throughout history were rapidly receding, and ahead loomed in dim outline a society of mass consumption in which not only the necessities but even the amenities of life would be available to all. A revolutionary change in the way of life was taking place in Europe.[27]

27. Robert Wilbrandt, *Die Weber in der Gegenwart: Sozialpolitische Wanderungen durch die Hausweberei und die Webfabrik* (Jena, 1906), p. 126; B. Seebohm Rowntree, *Poverty: A Study of Town Life* (London, 1901), pp. 86–87, 111, 117.

6

THE SPREAD OF LEARNING

The growth of literacy in Europe was a consequence of the industrial revolution second in importance only to the growth of affluence. Access to abstract knowledge had in the past been restricted to a small hieratic group of guardians of the collective intellectual tradition, to priests, scribes, philosophers, teachers, and bureaucrats. At certain times, moreover, familiarity with the arts and letters had been considered a decorous attribute of the dominant class in the community. The well-rounded statesman or warrior, it was felt, ought to be familiar with the high culture of his time; he might even make an occasional contribution to it. This had been the accepted view in ancient Greece and Rome, for example, and in Europe as a whole after the Middle Ages. There was agreement, however, that the instrumentalities of knowledge should not be made available to the bulk of the population. By the time of the industrial revolution, about five thousand years had elapsed since the discovery of the techniques of writing, but throughout that period the masses had been consistently excluded from their mastery. This is not to deny that members of the lower classes sometimes achieved relatively sophisticated levels of technical knowledge through practical experience in skilled crafts such as the construction of ordnance or the smelting of ore. But the ability to transform occupational expertise into a systematic body of knowledge lay beyond them because of their ignorance of reading and writing, the basic tools of abstract learning.

The low level of literacy was in part a function of the marginal economy of the preindustrial era. Society simply lacked the material means for the establishment of a system of education capable of teaching the essentials of knowledge to the entire population. State revenues, derived from the meager surplus that farming and handcrafting could generate, were almost completely absorbed by the expenditures for military security and domestic tranquillity. The cost of waging war and maintaining law and order was so high in relation to government income that little could be spared for social welfare or popular education. Learning, because of its restricted accessibility, thus came to confer status on those who were able to afford it. The ability to read and write became a mark of distinction separating the man of means and position from the common herd. That was why after the Middle Ages literacy came to be regarded as evidence of social rank. Like finer dress or richer diet, like riding or fencing, it served to separate the propertied from the propertyless. With the growing power and scope of central government, more-over, the essential function of the aristocracy became less military and more administrative. This in turn meant that mastery of the martial arts, which had been the chief occupation of the feudal nobility, was increas-ingly complemented by the acquisition of bureaucratic skills needed for the operation of a complex state mechanism. As for the lower classes, their role under royal absolutism remained the same as their role under aristocratic feudalism: the performance of services and the production of goods necessary for the maintenance of a hierarchical social system. Their ignorance, like their poverty, was the inescapable result of an economic system that could provide only bare subsistence for most of humanity.

There was still another factor inhibiting the spread of literacy, how-ever, as important as the lack of material means. It was the general ac-ceptance of the view that education must not be separated from social status or economic function. In other words, the learning imparted to a child should have a direct bearing on his future activity as an adult. Mas-tery of the three Rs was useful to those destined for careers in commerce or finance. Familiarity with the classics, especially Latin, was an essential part of the training of clergymen, lawyers, physicians, and civil servants. Even those whose inherited wealth and position freed them from the need to earn a living could find in ancient languages, philosophy, and literature a form of cultural exclusiveness matching their social distinc-tion. The conspicuous consumption of learning, like sumptuousness in clothing or extravagance in entertaining, provided a cachet of high status. But what would be the point in teaching landless peasants or day laborers to read and write? It would only expose them to ideas that might make them dissatisfied with their station in life. It would only arouse vain hopes and unrealizable expectations leading to disappointment and per-haps even sedition. Since learning meant power, it would be best to with-hold it from those who, by the very nature of human society, were meant to be powerless.

The view that inequality of education was as necessary for the main-tenance of a civilized community as inequality of property was accepted without serious question in the preindustrial age. Not only noblemen, bureaucrats, and well-to-do burghers believed in the class basis of learn-ing, but most social reformers as well agreed that a system of popular education that ignored economic differences would be worse than im-practical; it would be dangerous. The great Voltaire, champion of the En-lightenment, the sworn enemy of ignorance and obscurantism, declared, not in one of his published works, to be sure, but in a private letter: "It seems to me essential that there be ignorant wretches. If you were im-proving an estate, as I am doing, and if you had some plows, you would certainly share my opinion. It is not the unskilled laborer whom we should be educating, but the good bourgeois, the resident of the cities. . . . We should preach virtue to the lowest class of people, but they should not waste their time examining [philosophical questions]. When the populace meddles in reasoning, all is lost." With the exception of Diderot, the philosophes of the eighteenth century accepted the pitiless logic condemning most of mankind to poverty and ignorance that the best of intentions could not overcome. Men of good will should seek to alleviate the distress of the lower classes by the humane treatment of the poor and unfortunate, by the provision of food for the hungry, shelter for the homeless, care for the sick, and work for the unemployed. But to advocate the equality of education would be both futile and risky, as futile and risky as to advocate the equality of property.[1]

The benevolent despots of the eighteenth century were even more cautious in this regard than the benevolent philosophers. Confronted by the intractable problem of translating the theories of the Enlightenment into state policy, they temporized and palliated without challenging the hierarchical structure of society. They willingly accepted the common belief that since only a few could reason and govern, the many had to work and obey. To tamper with the existing distribution of wealth or learning might endanger the entire system of authority of which they were the chief beneficiaries. It would indeed have been unrealistic to expect them to rise above the limitations imposed upon their altruism by obvious self-interest. Their point of view was exemplified by Catherine the Great of Russia, who is reported to have written to the governor of Moscow concerning a proposal for popular education: "We must not in any way provide instruction for the lower class of people. If they were to know as much as you and I, *Monsieur le maréchal*, they would no longer want to obey us, as they obey us today." The authenticity of this letter has been questioned by Kazimierz Waliszewski, the well-known biographer of the empress. But even he concedes that it accurately reflects her beliefs, at least in the later years of her reign, after the French Revolution had convinced her that it was only a short step from reform to sedition. The other rulers of Europe faced the same dilemma, how to alleviate the economic and educational privation of the masses without diminishing their social and political subordination, and they came to the same conclusion. It was better to leave the established order unchanged than to innovate at the risk of subversion.[2]

1. *Oeuvres complètes de Voltaire*, 52 vols. (Paris, 1877–85), 44:256; Lawrence Stone, "Literacy and Education in England, 1640–1900," *Past & Present*, no. 42 (1969), p. 86.
2. Kazimierz Waliszewski, *Le roman d'une impératrice: Catherine II de Russie d'après ses mémoires, sa correspondance et les documents inédits des archives d'état* (Paris, 1893), p. 494.

Even in England, with a long history of vigorous representative institutions, where two revolutions in the seventeenth century had demonstrated that defiance of established authority was not incompatible with national greatness, there was profound suspicion of popular education. Here too men of property generally believed that the spread of literacy among the masses would breed dissatisfaction with existing social conditions. As late as 1807, Davies Giddy, who afterward became president of the Royal Society, warned in the House of Commons against the democratization of learning:

> For, however specious in theory the project might be, of giving
> education to the labouring classes of the poor, it would, in effect, be
> found to be prejudicial to their morals and happiness; it would teach
> them to despise their lot in life, instead of making them good
> servants in agriculture, and other laborious employments to which
> their rank in society had destined them; instead of teaching them
> subordination, it would render them factious and refractory . . . ; it
> would enable them to read seditious pamphlets, vicious books, and
> publications against Christianity; it would render them insolent
> to their superiors; and, in a few years, the result would be, that the
> legislature would find it necessary to direct the strong arm of power
> towards them, and to furnish the executive magistrates with much
> more vigorous laws than [are] now in force.[3]

Throughout Europe the ignorance of the masses seemed to be the safeguard of a rigid social structure resting on a static agrarian economy.

On the eve of the industrial revolution, therefore, the bulk of the adult population of Europe was still illiterate. As late as 1850, the percentage of those who could not read was between 55 and 60, and the percentage of those who read poorly, hardly understanding what they were reading, was around 30. Such figures are only approximations, to be sure, but if anything, they underestimate the extent of functional illiteracy. The method usually employed to determine literacy prior to the nineteenth century rests on the proportion of bridegrooms and brides signing the marriage register or contract. For the period after 1815, this information is often supplemented with data on army recruits and prison inmates, the only significant samples of the population available as a rule before regular national censuses began. Here too the distinction between literacy and illiteracy depends almost entirely on the ability to sign one's name. But to what extent should this ability be equated with an effective mastery of the tools of learning? Does a signature on a marriage deed or a muster roll reflect the capacity to read a newspaper, write a letter, solve a

3. Great Britain, *Parliamentary Debates*, 1st ser. (1803–20), 9:798–99.

problem in long division, or understand the state and society of which the individual is a part? The information on this point is spotty, but it suggests that many of those able to write their name had reached a level of literacy only a step or two above out-and-out illiteracy.

Consider the statistical data on a group of 754 recruits conscripted in Mecklenburg-Schwerin in 1852, data that are illuminating because they provide a more sophisticated measure of literacy than the mere ability to sign a document. Of the 754, only 21 were illiterate in the strict sense, that is, they were unable to read. But among the remaining 733, there were 106 who could only name the letters of words and 330 who read poorly. For 636 of the recruits, there is also information concerning the ability to write: 215 could not write at all, 285 wrote a little, and only 136 wrote well. Finally, all 754 were tested on their knowledge of arithmetic, the results showing that 402 could not do sums, 254 had difficulty with them, and no more than 98 received a rating of "good." All in all, according to the report, although only 21 recruits or 3 percent were illiterate, 381 or 51 percent had received inadequate schooling and were at best semiliterate.

The conclusion suggested by this information is supported by the less detailed data on a much larger group of Prussian recruits in 1851–52, which reveal that, out of a total of 50,191, only 2,412 or 5 percent had not received any education, but 10,106 or 20 percent had received "inadequate school training," that is, they could read only printed letters and their skill in writing was described as "little." In other words, the usual definition of literacy as the ability to sign one's name includes a large number, often a half or more, of those whose mastery of the three Rs was so inadequate that they should properly be classified as functional illiterates. They, no less than the millions who could not read at all, were condemned by their ignorance to a life of endless poverty without hope of improvement.[4]

This point should be kept in mind when considering the statistics on literacy in Europe before the industrial revolution. They show that in some of the western countries literacy had approached the 50 percent mark by the end of the eighteenth century and in a few cases had even exceeded it. There had been a steady growth of adult male literacy in England, for example, from about 25 percent in 1600 to perhaps 45 percent in 1675. By 1750 the percentage had risen to 53, and in 1800 it

4. Carlo M. Cipolla, *Literacy and Development in the West* (Harmondsworth, Baltimore, and Ringwood, 1969), pp. 55, 71, 115; "Statistische Uebersicht über den Grad der Schulbildung der im Jahre 1851–2 in die Königlich Preussische Armee eingestellten Ersatzmannschaften aus den Preussischen Landestheilen," *Mittheilungen des statistischen Bureau's in Berlin* 6 (1853):219, 221, 223–24.

was 65. These figures, to be sure, are only extrapolations from samples taken at various times in different parts of the kingdom. An examination of some 15,000 marriage entries in nearly 40 town and country parishes shows that in 1754–62 about 51 percent of the combined total of bridegrooms and brides could write their name, and in 1799–1804 the percentage was only a little higher, 54. Another study of 17 country parishes and chapelries in the East Riding of Yorkshire yields similar results: 51 percent in 1754–60 and 57 percent in 1791–1800. There was a substantial difference, however, between the rates of male and female illiteracy. According to a sample of 274 parishes (out of some 10,000 in all of England), which produced about 1,300 marriages annually in the late 1750s and about 2,900 in the late 1830s, the percentage of women able to sign their name was a little less than 40 in the middle of the eighteenth century, but it then climbed slowly, rising to just above 50 by 1840. The percentage of men, on the other hand, remained fairly constant at 60 or close to it throughout the period 1750–1800 before it increased to around 67 in 1840.

In Scotland the growth of adult male literacy was even more rapid than in England. The rate was only about 15 percent in 1600, a figure substantially below the English percentage, but then came a powerful surge that continued without interruption for two hundred years: 33 percent in 1675, 55 in 1720, 75 in 1750, 81 in 1775, and an extraordinary 88 in 1800, far ahead of England. The reasons for this remarkable spread of education in a country that was economically backward and socially immobile are still not clear. The role of Calvinism, with its emphasis on book learning and casuistical reasoning, was undoubtedly important, but whether it alone can explain the swift increase in the literacy of the lower classes remains an open question. In any case, there can be no doubt that the eighteenth century was a period of unparalleled intellectual flowering among the Scots, extending from literature, philosophy, and economics to the ability of the common people to read and write.[5]

Although the level of literacy on the Continent was generally below that of Great Britain, it was rising at a steady pace along much of the Atlantic seaboard. Adult male literacy in France, by one estimate, stood at about 16 percent in 1600, 29 around 1688, perhaps 35 in 1750, 47 around 1788, and 54 around 1805. According to another estimate, whereas only some 25 percent of newlyweds could sign their name in 1686–90, the percentage had risen to between 40 and 45 a hundred years later in 1786–90. There were significant differences, however, between

5. Stone, "Literacy and Education," pp. 120–21; Cipolla, *Literacy and Development*, pp. 62–63; R. S. Schofield, "Dimensions of Illiteracy, 1750–1850," *Explorations in Economic History* 10 (1973):445–46.

various regions of the country. In the north, in such provinces as Artois, Flanders, and Picardy, the rate of literacy among men during the last decades of the ancien régime was about 50 percent, but in Auvergne, Languedoc, and Provence in the south the percentage was no more than approximately 13. Equally important were the differences between male and female literacy. François Furet and Jacques Ozouf have calculated that the proportion of bridegrooms signing the marriage deed reached 47.0 percent in 1786–90 and 54.3 in 1816–20, but for brides the figures were only 26.8 and 34.7.

The statistical information on the Low Countries is less detailed, but there can be no doubt that a substantial increase in literacy occurred during the seventeenth and eighteenth centuries, especially in the Netherlands. Samples of newlyweds in Amsterdam show that 63 percent could sign their name as early as 1729–30, and by 1780 the percentage had risen to 74. In the Dutch villages and hamlets, the literacy rate must have been well below that in the great commercial and financial metropolis, but Carlo Cipolla, after surveying conditions throughout the Continent, concludes that "by about 1700, the Netherlands and England were possibly the two most literate countries in Europe." In Belgium, on the other hand, only 49 percent of the army recruits in 1843 could read or write, and as late as 1856 the approximate rate of adult literacy was 50 to 55 percent. As for the Scandinavian countries, although all writers agree that they were among the best educated in the world, hard data for the period before the middle of the nineteenth century are difficult to find. By 1850, however, adult literacy in Sweden may have been as high as 90 percent, and in 1874 the proportion of illiterates among Swedish army recruits was only 2 percent.[6]

In Central Europe there was greater disparity in the levels of popular education. In some parts the rate of literacy equaled or surpassed that achieved in the British Isles. Prussia in particular, with a tradition of discipline, frugality, and hard work, had created even before the advent of industrialization a system of popular education that, like military conscription, was designed to produce a nation of loyal and industrious subjects. Foreign observers spoke of it with admiration, envy, and sometimes a touch of uneasiness. During the 1830s the French philosopher Victor Cousin described Prussia as "that classic country of barracks and schools, of schools which civilize the people, and of barracks which defend them," and the English writer Edward Bulwer-Lytton referred to her

---

6. Stone, "Literacy and Education," pp. 120–21; Cipolla, *Literacy and Development*, pp. 61, 63–64, 71, 91, 115, 117–18; Hugh M. Pollard, *Pioneers of Popular Education, 1760–1850* (London, 1956), p. 9; François Furet and Jacques Ozouf, "Literacy and Industrialization: The Case of the *Département du Nord* in France," *Journal of European Economic History* 5 (1976):17; E. J. Hobsbawm, *The Age of Revolution, 1789–1848* (Cleveland and New York, 1962), p. 136.

as "that country in which, throughout the whole world, education is the most admirably administered."

The Prussian literacy rate was certainly impressive. The percentage of army recruits who had received no schooling was only 10.17 in 1838–39, 8.97 in 1839–40, 9.08 in 1840–41, and 8.20 in 1841–42. Yet here too there were significant regional variations. Whereas the overall rate of illiteracy among conscripts fell to 6.88 percent in 1842–43, it was 36.58 in Posen and 12.02 in East and West Prussia but 0.60 in the province of Saxony and 1.39 in Brandenburg. It is clear, moreover, that many of those classified as literate were in fact functionally illiterate. In addition to the 10.40 percent of army recruits from East and West Prussia in 1851–52 who had received "no school training," there were the 45.29 percent who had received "inadequate school training," that is, they were only able to read printed letters and write a little. In Posen the percentages were 20.67 and 31.31, in Pomerania 0.93 and 22.67, and in Westphalia 2.11 and 19.39. In "that classic country of barracks and schools," as in most countries, the system of popular education lagged behind the system of military training.

There were other parts of Central Europe where literacy, at least in the technical sense, was widespread before the coming of the industrial revolution. In Switzerland the economic importance of the independent peasants and skilled artisans contributed to the growth of basic learning. In the region of Geneva, marriage registers around 1800 reveal that about 90 percent of newlyweds in towns and about 60 percent in the countryside could sign their name. Such data, though only a local sample, support the view accepted by most writers that "Switzerland was one of the most literate countries in Europe." But there is no conclusive evidence until the second half of the nineteenth century, when statistics on army recruits show that in 1879 only 6 percent were illiterate. In the Austrian Empire, on the other hand, there was considerable disparity between regions as well as nationalities. The ability to read and write was quite common in the Alpine crown lands; according to the census of 1890, the rate of illiteracy in the Tyrol and Vorarlberg among those who had passed their fiftieth birthday was just 10 percent. But among the south Slavs, many of whom lived in the Habsburg monarchy, literacy in 1827 was less than 0.5 percent, and even around 1870 no more than 1 percent of the army recruits from Dalmatia were literate. By one estimate, the rate of adult literacy for the empire as a whole was between 55 and 60 percent in 1851, but as late as 1867 only 34 percent of all conscripts could read or write, well below half the percentage in Prussia or Switzerland.[7]

7. Victor Cousin, *Rapport sur l'état de l'instruction publique dans quelques pays de l'Allemagne, et particulièrement en Prusse*, 2 vols. (Paris, 1832), 1:17; Edward Lytton Bulwer, *England and the English*, 2 vols. (London, 1833), 1:252; [Heinrich Karl Wilhelm Berg-

The lowest rate of literacy, however, was to be found in the backward agrarian states extending in the south and east from the Iberian Peninsula across Italy and the Balkans to Russia. Here a privileged landed aristocracy, a servile impoverished peasantry, a stagnant urban economy, and a weak middle class constituted in combination a towering obstacle to the development of primary education. In Spain the percentage of literacy was 5.96 in 1803, 9.21 in 1841, and 19.27 in 1860, although the figures were probably at least 5 percent higher for the adult population. In Portugal there appear to have been barely eight thousand children attending school after the Peninsular War. The Italian figures vary considerably from region to region. In 1858 Piedmont and Liguria, the most developed provinces economically, had an adult illiteracy rate of 61 percent, but for the island of Sardinia the figure was 92. As early as 1740, there were 60 bakers in Turin out of 79 who could sign their name, and by 1796 the proportion had risen to 70 out of 72. Yet this was an exceptional achievement, for in 1871 the rate of literacy among the inhabitants of the Piedmontese capital who had passed their nineteenth birthday was still under 75 percent. During the 1770s a work published in Venice declared matter-of-factly that "the peasants . . . do not know how to read nor do they know how to write a word." Tuscany had an adult illiteracy rate of about 80 percent in 1841, probably close to the national average. According to the census of 1871, 69 percent of all Italians above the age of five were illiterate, but the percentage ranged from 54 in the north to 75 in the central region, 84 in the south, and 86 in the islands.

The highest illiteracy rate in Europe, with the exception of the Balkans for which there are few hard data, was recorded in Russia. Judging from the statistical information concerning persons over sixty years of age in the 1890s, at most 1 boy out of 6 and 1 girl out of 14 acquired an elementary education in the rural communities around the middle of the nineteenth century. According to an estimate that Heinrich Berghaus published in 1845, no more than 7 percent of the Russian population could read and write. This figure is generally supported by Carlo Cipolla, who calculates the rate of adult literacy around 1850 at between 5 and 10 percent. But not until statistics on army recruits began to appear during the 1870s, reflecting primarily the level of education of men from the countryside, could conjecture and extrapolation be replaced by comprehensive data. At that time the national percentage of literacy stood at

haus], *Statistik des Preüssischen Staats: Versuch einer Darstellung seiner Grundmacht und Kultur, seiner Verfassung, Regierung und Verwaltung im Lichte der Gegenwart* (Berlin, 1845), pp. 219, 222; "Statistische Uebersicht über den Grad der Schulbildung," pp. 219, 221; Cipolla, *Literacy and Development*, pp. 64, 71–72, 115, 117–18; Hobsbawm, *Age of Revolution*, p. 136; idem, *The Age of Capital, 1848–1875* (New York, 1975), p. 192.

21, although there was a vast disparity between the province of Livonia on the Baltic with 95 and the province of Ufa along the Urals with 7. The rate then rose slowly, exceeding 30 percent only in 1889, as the country entered a period of rapid economic rationalization nurtured by the state.[8]

To summarize, Europe was to a large extent a continent of total or functional illiterates before the industrial revolution. The level of popular education, to be sure, varied from region to region, being higher in prosperous countries than it was in impoverished ones, higher in urban than in rural communities, and higher among Protestants than among Catholics. Along the Atlantic seaboard, moreover, there had generally been a steady growth of literacy since at least the beginning of the seventeenth century. Yet nowhere had the lower classes acquired a sufficient mastery of the fundamentals of learning to formulate a systematic challenge to the existing distribution of wealth, status, and authority. The industrial revolution, by creating for the first time a society that was literate in the broad sense, made it possible to alter the traditional relationship between the propertied and the propertyless classes. The mechanization of production generated the resources needed to provide primary education for the masses. The preindustrial marginal economy, which had barely been able to feed the laboring population, much less educate it, was replaced by an industrial surplus economy capable of supporting a national system of elementary schooling. No longer did the role of the state have to be restricted to the primal functions of police and warfare. Government was now able to expand the scope of its activity, improving the welfare of its subjects by founding hospitals, supporting orphanages, establishing poorhouses, and, most important, building classrooms. The endless cycle of poverty and ignorance, each reinforcing the other, could finally be broken.

The industrial revolution, however, did more than create the economic basis for popular education; it provided a powerful practical motivation for its growth. Technological progress meant that in the long run the labor force had to attain a level of learning well above that which had sufficed on a village farm or in the artisan shop. The ability to read instructions, write reports, or add fractions became essential for the effective operation of the complex machinery that played an increasingly important part in the economic process. With time, therefore, the rationalization of manufacture and farming led to the growth of schooling

8. Stanley G. Payne, *A History of Spain and Portugal*, 2 vols. (Madison, 1973), 2:482; Cipolla, *Literacy and Development*, pp. 63–64, 81, 83, 115; Hobsbawm, *Age of Revolution*, p. 136; Arcadius Kahan, "Determinants of the Incidence of Literacy in Rural Nineteenth-Century Russia," in *Education and Economic Development*, ed. C. Arnold Anderson and Mary Jean Bowman (Chicago, 1963), p. 298; [Berghaus], *Statistik des Preüssischen Staats*, p. 221.

among the masses, schooling intended only to produce trained workers but also having far-reaching social and political consequences.

This aspect of the industrial revolution has been obscured because in the early stages it sometimes had exactly the opposite result, that is, it led to a decline in the literacy rate of the laboring population, particularly in Great Britain. The level of technological skill required in textiles and mining, the first industries to feel the impact of mechanization, was initially so low that not only did book learning seem to the lower classes even more remote from workaday reality than before but the large-scale employment of children had the effect of removing them from the school-house to the mill or colliery. In a survey of the beginnings of the industrial revolution in England, Michael Sanderson makes this point forcefully: "The assumption that a literate labour force was relevant for the economy as a whole at this time is open to question in light of available evidence. The probable increase in literacy [in the first half of the eighteenth century] may have helped the onset of industrialization but once the process began levels of literacy deteriorated. According to all the evidence it was extremely low and did not rise in [Lancashire] although it remains one of the classic instances of rapid industrial growth. It would seem that the greater the industrialization the worse the effects for education."

There are admittedly ample data to support this generalization. Nowhere in England was the number of illiterates at the beginning of the nineteenth century greater than in Middlesex and Lancashire, the two industrial centers of the country. The proportion of school attendance in the former was 1 out of 24 and in the latter 1 out of 21. According to a report in 1804, "Since the establishment of the cotton mill, the poor people are tempted by the earnings of their children to neglect their being taught to read." A clergyman complained in 1815 about "the almost unconquerable indifference of parents in general and their neglect of forcing regular attendance at school and frequently detaining [their children] at home for household purposes," as well as "their habit of sending the boys to work, such as can, and the girls to lace-making." Even after the mid-century, a commission inquiring into the state of popular education heard from one of its members: "It can hardly be a matter of surprise that, when three children in a family, above eight years old, can double the weekly income of the house, parents should withdraw the children from school." The demand for unskilled labor during the early years of industrialization had no doubt a depressing effect on the level of education.[9]

9. Michael Sanderson, "Literacy and Social Mobility in the Industrial Revolution in England," *Past & Present*, no. 56 (1972), p. 89; Cipolla, *Literacy and Development*, p. 102;

Yet it is also clear that even in those early years there were occupations requiring a degree of expertness that only schooling could make attainable. Testifying in 1824 before a select committee, an engineer declared that "I have found, from the mode of managing my business, by drawings and written descriptions, a man is not of much use to me unless he can read and write; if a man applies for work, and says he cannot read and write, he is asked no more questions, but he is informed that I cannot employ him." With the growing sophistication and complexity of industrial techniques, the need for an educated work force became increasingly apparent. The attraction of inexpensive child labor was soon overshadowed by the demand for skilled workingmen. When the government finally introduced a bill in 1870 to establish a national system of elementary education, William Edward Forster, vice-president of the Privy Council, explained to the House of Commons why it had become so important to end illiteracy among the lower classes: "Upon the speedy provision of elementary education depends our industrial prosperity. It is of no use trying to give technical teaching to our citizens without elementary education; uneducated labourers—and many of our labourers are utterly uneducated—are, for the most part, unskilled labourers, and if we leave our work-folk any longer unskilled, notwithstanding their strong sinews and determined energy, they will become overmatched in the competition of the world." Technological progress and economic rivalry thus generated a need for popular education that overcame the fear among men of property concerning the use that the masses might make of learning.

Russian statistics at the turn of the twentieth century clearly suggest that in the long run literacy was important for industrialization, enhancing the profits of capital and the wages of labor. They are especially illuminating because Russia was one of the few countries in which detailed data on the level of education of the work force began to appear at a time when a substantial part of it was still illiterate. Direct comparisons can thus be made between the earnings of literates and illiterates employed in the same industry.

The figures reveal that workers who could read and write received consistently a higher wage than those who could not. In a sample of about 3,500 workers in Nikolaev in 1895–96, the proportion of literates among the skilled workers was 75 percent, but among the unskilled it

---

Elie Halevy, *A History of the English People in the Nineteenth Century*, 2d ed., 6 vols. (London, 1949–52), 1:533; Stone, "Literacy and Education," pp. 76, 116; Great Britain, *Parliamentary Papers* (1861), 21, pt. 2 (*Reports from Commissioners*, 7, pt. 2), no. 2794-II, "Reports of the Assistant Commissioners Appointed to Inquire into the State of Popular Education in England," p. 149.

was only 49 percent. Locksmiths, metal workers, and carpenters, who had the highest literacy rate, earned the highest daily wage; on the other hand, boilermakers and blacksmiths, with the lowest literacy rate, received the lowest wage. The advantage of the literates, moreover, increased with the amount of education they had received. Those with one year of schooling earned 2 percent more than the illiterates, those with two years 5 percent more, three years 14 percent, four years 16 percent, five years between 18 and 19 percent, and six years 20 percent. Another study of some 3,000 weavers in the Tver district in 1902 disclosed that, depending on their age, literate male workers earned 7 to 14 percent more than illiterates; for female workers the differential ranged between 6 and 21 percent. Finally, a survey of 69,000 textile workers in the Moscow district in 1912 demonstrated once again that literates received higher wages than illiterates, their advantage increasing from 15 percent for the 20–25 age group to 35 percent for the 46–50 age group. The industrial revolution clearly provided an economic incentive for the growth of education; as a result, general literacy became a profitable as well as practicable goal of society for the first time.[10]

But there was still another way in which economic rationalization furthered the spread of learning, more important even than the need for a literate labor force. Revolutionary changes in production during the nineteenth century generated a massive shift of population from country to town, from the pieties and devotions of the village to the deracinated individualism of the city. The influence of the traditional bearers of authority—squires, clergymen, overseers, mayors, and constables—could not be exercised in the impersonal urban environment. New forms of social control had to be found to rule the behavior of the lower classes, which were increasingly inaccessible to the prescriptions of a rural code of conduct. The governments and elites of Europe, therefore, began to see in the school an instrument for the inculcation among the masses of those virtues of restraint and submissiveness that the country church and the manor house could no longer nourish. Industrialization and urbanization consequently had the effect of furthering popular literacy as a means of maintaining class differences, not reducing them. Its purpose was stability rather than liberation. François Guizot, minister of public instruction in France during the 1830s, dwelt on this point in one of his early works. Although primary schooling was desirable, too much education "inspires among young people of the lower classes scorn for their

10. Great Britain, *Parliamentary Papers* (1824), 5 (*Reports from Committees*, 2), no. 51, "First Report from Select Committee on Artizans and Machinery," p. 25; Great Britain, *Parliamentary Debates*, 3d ser. (1830–91), 199:465; Arcadius Kahan, "Russian Scholars and Statesmen on Education as an Investment," in *Education and Economic Development*, ed. Anderson and Bowman, pp. 5–8.

equals and distaste for their position which . . . no longer let them be satisfied with a laborious and obscure existence."[11]

That was why the advocates of elementary instruction for the laboring population emphasized again and again that they were not proposing to educate the poor to the point of making them dissatisfied with their station in life. The English writer Hannah More, who had established Sunday schools in the Mendip Hills mining district, hastened to explain that her system of education for the children of farmers and workers was designed to make them industrious and obedient. "My plan of instruction is extremely simple and limited," she reassured the bishop of Bath and Wells in 1801. "They learn, on week-days, such coarse works as may fit them for servants. I allow of no writing for the poor. My object is not to make fanatics, but to train up the lower classes in habits of industry and piety." In 1819 the *Edinburgh Review* commented favorably on the school for abandoned children founded by the Swiss reformer Philipp Emanuel von Fellenberg at Hofwyl near Bern because "the boys never see a newspaper, and scarcely a book; they are taught, *viva voce*, a few matters of fact, and rules of practical application. The rest of their education consists simply in inculcating habits of industry, frugality, veracity, docility, and mutual kindness." Only after the middle of the century did the accepted view of the instruction suitable for the lower classes become more generous. In 1861 the report of the Newcastle Commission in Great Britain declared that the duty of the teachers "consists in preparing the children of the poor for their future life by appropriate religious and moral discipline, by teaching them to write, to read their own language with interest, and with an intelligent perception of its meaning, and to perform common arithmetical operations." Even this was considerably more than had been conceded fifty years before.[12]

Schools seemed especially important as means of training an obedient labor force willing to accept the hardships of life in a spirit of resignation. The *Edinburgh Review* acknowledged in 1826 that the country was going through "a most trying season of distress"; consequently, "the sufferings of the poor have been, in many districts, as severe as in the worst times of the late war, or the still more depressed state of industry which attended the first years of the peace." And yet nowhere had there been any of "those outrages" that, "in former times, were the constant

11. François Guizot, *Essai sur l'histoire et sur l'état actuel de l'instruction publique en France* (Paris, 1816), pp. 6–7.

12. *The Letters of Hannah More*, ed. R. Brimley Johnson (London, 1925), p. 183; "Tracts on M. de Fellenberg's Establishments at Hofwyl," *Edinburgh Review, or Critical Journal* 32 (1819):492; Great Britain, *Parliamentary Papers* (1861), 21, pt. 1 (*Reports from Commissioners*, 7, pt. 1), no. 2794-I, "Report of the Commissioners Appointed to Inquire into the State of Popular Education in England," p. 133.

accompaniments of sudden and general want of employment." The reason was clear. "It is not too much, surely, to bestow upon the progress of education a portion of the praise which so salutary an improvement is fitted to call forth. Men have been attending more than formerly to the cultivation of their minds: The refinement of their taste, and the softening of their feelings, has been one consequence; the habit of reflecting more upon their best interests, has been another."

Sometimes workers would recognize that the education their children were receiving was designed to make them acquiesce in their economic and social subordination. A Manchester cotton spinner named Thomas Daniel charged in 1832 before a committee considering the regulation of child labor that the schooling of the lower classes had become a weapon in the struggle between employers and employees:

> I think the instructions given at those Sunday-schools are for the very purpose of making those children as humble and as obedient to the wishes of the manufacturers as possible. In fact there was an instance not more than two or three years ago, when there was a great turn-out of spinners in Manchester, in which the visitors used language, showing that those children that were thrown out of employment ought not, and it was a great sin for them, to withstand their employers; that they ought to be subject to them, and ought to go to work, while at the same time they were taking one-half the bread out of their mouths.[13]

Yet protests against the underlying values of popular education could not overcome a deep-rooted conviction that education was a function of class, so that what children of the working population were taught should prepare them for a life of hard work and willing obedience. A classic formulation of this argument appeared in 1866 in a report of the Manchester and Salford Education Aid Society:

> The first need of society is order. If order is to be produced in men and women, what kind of preparation for it is that which leaves the children as wild as young ostriches in the desert? When for the first ten or twelve years of life there has been no discipline, either of mind or body—when cleanliness and comfort have been unknown—when no law of God or man has been considered sacred, and no power recognised but direct physical force—is it to be expected that they will quietly and industriously settle down in mills, workshops,

13. *Edinburgh Review, or Critical Journal* 45 (1826–27):195–96; Great Britain, *Parliamentary Papers* (1831–32), 15 (*Reports from Committees*, 11), no. 706, "Report from the Committee on the 'Bill to regulate the Labour of Children in the Mills and Factories of the United Kingdom': with the Minutes of Evidence, Appendix and Index," p. 327.

warehouses, or at any trade, or in the orderly routine of any family, to work continuously, day by day, from morning till evening, from Monday till Saturday? The expectation is absurd. Continuous labour and sober thought are alike impossible to them.[14]

The purpose of popular education, then, was to make "continuous labour and sober thought" an ingrained habit among the lower classes.

In the second half of the nineteenth century, the growth of mass suffrage reinforced the movement for mass schooling. The diffusion of political rights created a need to train loyal citizens, just as the rationalization of economic techniques created a need to train skilled operatives. In 1867, when the franchise was being extended in Great Britain to the urban workers, Robert Lowe declared in Parliament that "before we had intrusted the masses—the great bulk of whom are uneducated—with the whole power of this country we should have taught them a little more how to use it, and not having done so, this rash and abrupt measure having been forced upon them, the only thing we can do is as far as possible to remedy the evil by the most universal measures of education that can be devised." He went on, in a famous passage that has been quoted, requoted, and misquoted in a thousand textbooks: "I believe it will be absolutely necessary that you should prevail on our future masters to learn their letters," for "from the moment that you intrust the masses with power their education becomes an absolute necessity." In short, "you have placed the government in the hands of the masses, and you must therefore give them education."

The slogan that "we must educate our masters" began to echo throughout Europe as one country after another broadened the franchise, creating for the first time a mass electorate. One of the main purposes of primary schooling was now to teach the lower classes to make proper use of their new civic rights and to be patriotic in their loyalties, modest in their hopes, reasonable in their expectations, and restrained in their demands. It was the function of the school to help insure that the changing form of political authority did not alter the underlying economic and social realities.[15]

This was basically why a system of popular education supported and directed by the state began to emerge in most countries in the course of the nineteenth century, especially after 1850. In the Habsburg monarchy the Hungarian government, immediately after gaining autonomy under the Ausgleich of 1867, ordered that every community should maintain an elementary school. Austria introduced similar legislation in 1869. In

14. *Second Report of the Manchester and Salford Education-Aid Society: 1866* (Manchester, 1866), p. 13.
15. Great Britain, *Parliamentary Debates*, 3d ser. (1830–91), 188:1549.

Great Britain the Forster Elementary Education Act of 1870, three years after the enfranchisement of the urban working class, provided that new schools must be established at the expense of the taxpayers in any locality where there were not enough for all children. In Prussia an ordinance promulgated as early as 1819 organized the elementary schools of the kingdom, creating the most highly developed system of primary education in Europe. Then in 1872, following the introduction of manhood suffrage in the German Empire, the Prussian schools were further consolidated and nationalized. The Netherlands in 1878 and Belgium in 1879 extended their system of public instruction. In France the Guizot Law of 1833 had required every community to maintain an elementary school. It was reinforced during the early 1880s by the Ferry Laws, which provided for a free and secular primary education.

Obligatory school attendance without tuition accompanied the growth of public instruction, for the authorities recognized that it was precisely those least able to pay for their education who needed it most, both to improve their economic skills and to shape their political attitudes. To be sure, the establishment of an effective system of free compulsory schooling required more than a stroke of the pen. Laws imposing the obligation to provide elementary instruction for all children were passed in 1857 in Spain and 1877 in Italy, but they proved largely unenforceable in an environment of poverty and indifference. On the other hand, in Switzerland the new constitution of 1874 requiring all children to attend a cantonal school had an important effect on the level of education of the lower classes. In England compulsory school attendance, left at first to the discretion of local boards, was extended in 1876 and became general in 1880. An act of 1891, moreover, rapidly reduced the number of schools charging tuition so that within a few years virtually all elementary instruction became free. In France fees were abolished in the state primary schools in 1881, and in 1882 school attendance became a legal requirement for all children between six and thirteen. Even in the Netherlands, where public education developed more slowly, compulsory schooling was introduced in 1901.[16]

The result of all these measures was an unprecedented increase in the number of children receiving primary instruction. According to E. J. Hobsbawm's estimate, whereas the population of Europe grew 33 percent between 1840 and the 1880s, school attendance grew 145 percent.

16. Carlton J. H. Hayes, *A Generation of Materialism, 1871–1900* (New York and London, 1941), pp. 83, 173; Robert Ulich, *The Education of Nations: A Comparison in Historical Perspective*, rev. ed. (Cambridge, Mass., 1967), pp. 113, 157; Halevy, *History of the English People*, 5:143–44; Georges Weill, *L'éveil des nationalités et le mouvement libéral (1815–1848)* (Paris, 1930), p. 359; Maurice Baumont, *L'essor industriel et l'impérialisme*

In one country after another, the proportion of inhabitants found in the classroom began to rise rapidly, often approaching the 18 percent mark, the approximate point at which, depending on the age distribution of the population, virtually all children are obtaining some schooling (see table 6.1). All in all, the percentage of those receiving primary instruction at least doubled in the course of the nineteenth century. The most rapid increases were recorded in England, France, Austria-Hungary, Italy, Spain, Portugal, and Russia. If other countries like Germany, Switzerland, the Low Countries, and the Scandinavian states made less impressive gains, that was generally because they had attained a relatively high level of popular education before industrialization. By the end of the nineteenth century, the only European countries that had not yet exceeded the 10 percent level were Portugal, Russia, and the small impoverished states of the Balkan peninsula: Serbia, Bulgaria, Rumania, and Greece. Illiteracy remained a serious problem on the Continent, especially in the underdeveloped agricultural countries of the south and east, but that was largely because most adults had not had the educational opportunities that were now open to their children and grandchildren. For those born in the last few decades before the First World War, universal primary schooling was, or at least was becoming, a reality.[17]

The rising level of expenditures for education reflected the determination of the governments of Europe to create a system of schooling capable of turning out skilled workers as well as patriotic citizens. The rationalization of the economy made it possible to increase vastly the revenues that the state could devote to the construction of school buildings, the training of teachers, the purchase of instructional materials, and the support of the bureaucracy needed to operate a complex public system of elementary education. Total expenditures are hard to calculate, partly because the statistical data on the cost of schooling remained incomplete until at least the middle of the nineteenth century but also because the cost was covered from several sources: national treasuries, local taxes, church contributions, and tuition fees. Yet the estimates for the leading states of Europe show an impressive relative as well as absolute increase in the share of national income committed to public education.

---

colonial (1878–1904), 2d ed. (Paris, 1949), p. 500; David Thomson, "The Transformation of Social Life," in The New Cambridge Modern History, 12 vols. (Cambridge, 1960–70), 12:54.

17. Hobsbawm, Age of Capital, p. 95; Richard A. Easterlin, "A Note on the Evidence of History," in Education and Economic Development, ed. Anderson and Bowman, pp. 426–27; Peter Lundgreen, Bildung und Wirtschaftswachstum im Industrialisierungsprozess des 19. Jahrhunderts: Methodische Ansätze, empirische Studien und internationale Vergleiche (Berlin, 1973), p. 81.

Table 6.1. European School Enrollments, 1830–87

| | Percentage of Population in School | | | |
	1830	1850	1878	1887
England	9	12	15	16
France	7	10	13	15
Austria-Hungary	5	7	9	12–13
Italy	3		7	11
Spain	4		8	11
Portugal		1		5
Russia		2	2	3
Germany	17	16	17	18
Switzerland	13		15	18
Low Countries	12		16	
Netherlands		13		14
Belgium		12		11
Scandinavia	14		14	
Denmark		14		12
Norway		14		13
Sweden		13		15

SOURCE: Richard A. Easterlin, "A Note on the Evidence of History," in *Education and Economic Development*, ed. C. Arnold Anderson and Mary Jean Bowman (Chicago, 1963), p. 426.

In France per capita national product in constant prices rose 14 percent between 1860 and 1880, from 350 to 400 dollars, and another 50 percent between 1880 and 1900, from 400 to 600 dollars. But the share of gross domestic product spent for schooling grew much more rapidly, from 0.4 percent in 1860 to 0.9 in 1880 and 1.3 in 1900, so that expenditures for education in proportion to income more than tripled in forty years, whereas per capita national product less than doubled. The British figures on the cost of public instruction are less detailed, but they show the same tendency to expand more rapidly than the economy as a whole, with their share of gross national product climbing from 0.9 percent in 1880 to 1.3 in 1900. Finally, the statistics for Germany reinforce the conclusion that the states of Europe were investing a growing part of their wealth in primary schooling. Here the percentage of net national product devoted to instructional purposes rose from 1.0 in 1860 to 1.6 in 1880 and 1.9 in 1900. The German rate of increase in the second half of the nineteenth century thus lagged behind the French or English, but only because in the first half the country had been spending proportionately more on education than its western neighbors. Although by 1900 its lead had diminished as other governments made strenuous efforts to catch up, it still remained substantial.[18]

The investment of public resources in primary instruction on such a vast scale was justified by its proponents not only as a means of producing an enlightened citizenry and a disciplined labor force but also as an instrument for maintaining political and social stability. The elementary school became the principal institution through which the established order sought to preserve the status quo. In addition to the three Rs, it taught allegiance to king and country, respect for church and state, and submission to landlord and millowner. The values propagated in the classrooms of Europe were defined as early as the 1830s by the *Quarterly Journal of Education* in England: "The labouring classes . . . should, first of all, be made acquainted with the motives which have induced every society emerging from barbarism to establish the rights of property; and the advantages resulting from its establishment, and the necessity of maintaining it inviolate, should be clearly set forth." Moreover, "the circumstances that give rise to those gradations of rank and fortune that actually exist ought also to be explained: it may be shown that they are as natural to society as differences of sex, of strength, or colour . . . and that . . . equality . . . violently and unjustly brought about could not be maintained for a week."

The well-known reformer James Phillips Kay-Shuttleworth warned that failure to educate the lower classes properly would play into the hands of demagogues and rabble-rousers eager to stir up the passions of the poor and ignorant. "The operative population constitutes one of the most important elements of society," he wrote, "and when numerically considered, the magnitude of its interests and the extent of its power assume such vast proportions, that the folly which neglects them is allied to madness. If the higher classes are unwilling to diffuse intelligence among the lower, those exist who are ever ready to take advantage of their ignorance; . . . if they will not endeavour to promote domestic comfort, virtue, and knowledge among them, their misery, vice, and prejudice will prove volcanic elements, by whose explosive violence the structure of society may be destroyed."

A generation later, Robert Lowe described in greater detail what was generally meant by promoting "domestic comfort, virtue, and knowl-

18. Lundgreen, *Bildung und Wirtschaftswachstum*, p. 77; Albert Fishlow, "Levels of Nineteenth-Century American Investment in Education," *Journal of Economic History* 26 (1966):432–33.

edge" among the masses. In a speech to the House of Commons in 1861, he emphasized the social and economic doctrines that an elementary education ought to inculcate:

> I really think that the schoolmaster should be taught some political economy in these days of strikes; so that the person who is looked up to as an authority next to the clergyman in his village should be able to give some sensible opinion on those melancholy contests about wages; and if he knows a little less of the wars of the Roses, or of the history of the heresies in the early Church, and more of the principles which regulate the price of labour, and should be able to impress on his hearers the doctrine that wages do not depend on the will of a master, but have a law of their own to regulate them, I think his ability in that respect would be very serviceable.[19]

Such were the expectations of the men who helped establish the national systems of public education in Europe during the nineteenth century.

They were met only in part, however. The greatest success of the new program of primary schooling for the lower classes lay in the rapid decline of illiteracy. For the first time in history, the masses began to acquire the basic tools of learning. In some countries the process was virtually completed by the time of the First World War; in others it still had a long way to go. But everywhere the progress that had been made in only a few decades was impressive (figure 6.1).

In England the percentage of men unable to sign their name fell from about 30 in 1850 to 1 in 1911; that of women fell from about 45 to 1. The fastest rate of improvement was among those leaving school after 1870 or marrying after 1885, a measure of the effectiveness of the Forster Elementary Education Act. In France adult male illiteracy also decreased sharply from about 40 percent in 1850 to 5 in 1900. The percentage of illiterates among army recruits in Prussia went from 9 in 1841 to 1 in 1887. According to the national census of Italy, the proportion of the population over the age of five unable to read or write diminished from 69 percent in 1871 to 38 in 1911. In Spain the percentage of illiterates in the entire population dropped from 76 in 1860 to 68 in 1887; for those above the age of ten the decrease was from 61 percent in 1887 to 50 in 1910. The illiteracy rate among army recruits in the Austrian Empire fell from 66 percent in 1867 to 22 in 1894. Even in Russia, two-thirds of the army recruits in 1913 were able to read.

19. "Reasons for Establishing a Public System of Elementary Instruction in England," *Quarterly Journal of Education* 1 (1831):217; James Phillips Kay, *The Moral and Physical Condition of the Working Classes Employed in the Cotton Manufacture in Manchester* (London, 1832), p. 72; Great Britain, *Parliamentary Debates*, 3d ser. (1830–91), 164:723.

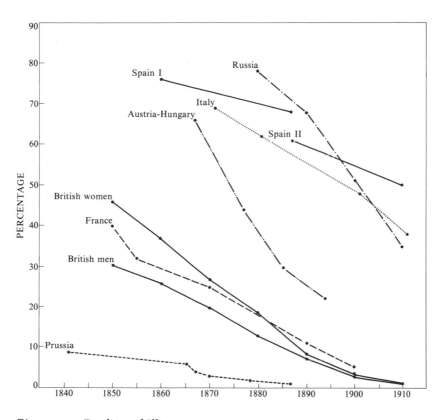

Figure 6.1. Decline of Illiteracy, 1841–1911

SOURCES: Carlo M. Cipolla, *Literacy and Development in the West* (Harmondsworth, Baltimore, and Ringwood, 1969), pp. 117–18, 127–28; Arcadius Kahan, "Determinants of the Incidence of Literacy in Rural Nineteenth-Century Russia," in *Education and Economic Development*, ed. C. Arnold Anderson and Mary Jean Bowman (Chicago, 1963), p. 367; R. S. Schofield, "Dimensions of Illiteracy, 1750–1850," *Explorations in Economic History* 10 (1973): 442; Lawrence Stone, "Literacy and Education in England, 1640–1900," *Past & Present*, no. 42 (1969), p. 120.
NOTE: The figures for Spain I cover the entire population; for Spain II, the population above age 10.

It is clear, moreover, that the most rapid growth of basic learning occurred after the middle of the nineteenth century. Although the level of literacy climbed steadily for the entire population of Europe, its rise was most striking among those who reached school age after the establishment of the national systems of public education, as shown in Figure 6.2. By the time of the First World War, general literacy had already been reached by some countries such as Germany and England, and its

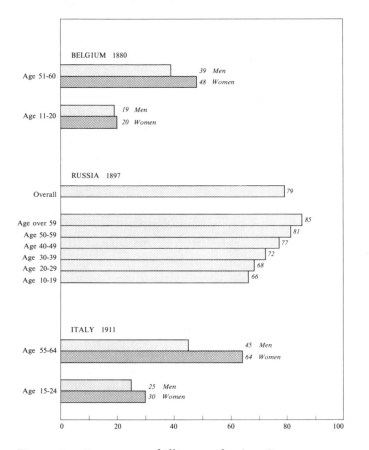

Figure 6.2. Percentage of Illiterates by Age Group

SOURCE: Carlo M. Cipolla, *Literacy and Development in the West* (Harmondsworth, Baltimore, and Ringwood, 1969), pp. 93–94; Arcadius Kahan, "Determinants of the Incidence of Literacy in Rural Nineteenth-Century Russia," in *Education and Economic Development*, ed. C. Arnold Anderson and Mary Jean Bowman (Chicago, 1963), p. 367.

achievement in the others, even in Italy, Spain, or Russia, seemed certain within another two or three generations.[20]

Yet the statesmen and educators responsible for this swift spread of popular learning regarded their success with mixed feelings. Their assumption had been that the ability to read and write would have a mollifying effect on the masses, that it would tame their passions and restrain their hopes. "The spectacle of hundreds of industrious individuals,"

20. Schofield, "Dimensions of Illiteracy," p. 443; Stone, "Literacy and Education," p. 120; Cipolla, *Literacy and Development*, pp. 90–91, 93–94, 117–18, 127–28; Arcadius

wrote one reformer in 1825, "who have finished the labours of the day, congregating together in a spacious apartment, listening with mute admiration to the sublime truths of philosophy, is truly worthy of a great and enlightened people." Yet the growth of literacy did not in fact turn workers and peasants into devoted admirers of the sublime truths of philosophy. It gave rise instead to cultural tastes and interests altogether different from those that had inspired the movement for mass education.

The new system of primary schooling, to be sure, vastly increased the reading public of Europe. As the lower classes mastered the alphabet, the book trade began to reflect the ascending curve of literacy. Between about 1830 and 1880 the average number of works published annually grew from 1,000 to 6,000 in Great Britain, from 5,000 to 7,000 in France, and from 6,000 to 15,000 in Germany. In 1848 there had been close to four hundred major European libraries with over 16 million volumes. By 1880 the number of libraries had multiplied more than twelve times and the number of volumes had almost doubled. Whereas fewer than 500 magazines and reviews had appeared in England in 1861, the figure rose to 638 in 1871, 1,097 in 1881, 1,778 in 1891, and 2,328 in 1900. The most significant increase, however, was in the number of newspapers. In Prussia there were 845 in 1824 and 2,127 in 1869. Circulation in the German Empire climbed from 519,798,000 in 1885 to 1,431,706,000 in 1900 and 1,878,283,590 in 1910. England had 267 newspapers in 1821, 472 in 1842, 1,102 in 1861, 1,886 in 1881, and 2,491 in 1900. All in all, there were approximately 6,000 European newspapers in the period 1866–82 and twice that many by the end of the century. At first this increase resulted from the expansion of a middle-class readership, but as the cost of publication continued to decline with the mechanization of printing and the repeal of newspaper taxes, a mass circulation became economically possible for the first time. The penny press and then the halfpenny press began to attract lower-class readers whose tastes and interests shaped a different kind of journalism. The *Daily Mail* and *Daily Express* in London, the *Matin* and *Petit journal* in Paris, the *Neueste Nachrichten* and August Scherl's *Lokal-Anzeiger* in Berlin—such were typical examples of the new popular newspapers fostered by the spread of literacy.[21]

Kahan, "Social Structure, Public Policy, and the Development of Education and the Economy in Czarist Russia," in *Education and Economic Development,* ed. Anderson and Bowman, p. 367.

21. James Scott Walker, *An Essay on the Education of the People* (London, 1825), p. 45; Cipolla, *Literacy and Development*, pp. 106, 110; Michael Wolff and Celina Fox, "Pictures from the Magazines," in *Victorian City: Images and Realities*, ed. H. J. Dyos and Michael Wolff, 2 vols. (London and Boston, 1973), 2:575; Werner Sombart, *Die deutsche Volkswirtschaft im neunzehnten Jahrhundert und im Anfang des 20. Jahrhunderts*, 4th ed. (Ber-

Their rise helped to hasten the decline of an ancient lower-class sub-culture that had flourished in the agrarian, illiterate community of the preindustrial age. The village superstitions, customs, and ceremonials, the folk myths and old wives' tales descending in the form of oral tradition from generation to generation, began to yield to new interests that primary education stimulated among the masses of an urbanizing, industrializing society. The established newspapers and journals, attuned to the tastes of a staid bourgeoisie, dispensing civic enlightenment and moral uplift, could not attract the half-educated lower classes that sought an escape from the drabness of everyday existence in shocking revelation or violent crime. In his *New Grub Street* published in 1891, George Gissing described through the bumptious would-be newspaper editor Whelpdale the outlook of the emerging yellow press, which appealed primarily to a semiliterate proletarian readership:

> No article in the paper is to measure more than two inches in length, and every inch must be broken into at least two paragraphs. . . . Let me explain my principle. I would have the paper address itself to the quarter-educated; that is to say, the great new generation that is being turned out by the Board schools, the young men and women who can just read, but are incapable of sustained attention. People of this kind want something to occupy them in trains, and on 'buses and trams. As a rule they care for no newspapers except the Sunday ones; what they want is the lightest and frothiest of chit-chatty information—bits of stories, bits of description, bits of scandal, bits of jokes, bits of statistics, bits of foolery. Am I not right? Everything must be very short, two inches at the utmost; their attention can't sustain itself beyond two inches.[22]

The garish preoccupations of yellow journalism were a far cry from the proper literary tastes that educational reformers at the beginning of the century had wanted primary schooling to nurture among the masses.

They would have been even more disturbed, however, to discover that popular education, intended to insure maintenance of the established order, frequently led to its complete rejection. They had hoped that the three Rs would transform peasants and workers into miniature landlords and businessmen who accepted the inevitability of social distinctions and economic inequalities. This expectation did not prove entirely false because the primary school did assiduously preach loyalty to the status quo. The readiness of the masses of Europe to march into battle after the

lin, 1923), p. 412; Friedrich Heer, *Europa: Mutter der Revolutionen* (Stuttgart, 1964), p. 532.

22. George Gissing, *New Grub Street*, 3 vols. (London, 1891), 3:232–33.

outbreak of the First World War was a measure of its effectiveness. Yet there were also those, and their number was growing, who recognized that the educational system was designed to persuade the poor to acquiesce in their poverty. The Chartist leader William Lovett expressed in his autobiography the attitude of many who challenged the social doctrines propagated in the classrooms of every country: "While a large portion of the hawks and owls of society were seeking to perpetuate that state of mental darkness most favourable to the securing of their prey, another portion, with more cunning, were for admitting a sufficient amount of mental glimmer to cause the multitude to walk quietly in the paths they in their wisdom had prescribed for them."

A socialist journal in London launched an even more bitter attack on the primary-school curriculum. It denounced the indoctrination of children, in the guise of elementary education, with the values of an acquisitive society:

> Every item which receives attention is so prepared for administration to a submissive and patient race of children that it is nothing short of marvellous that any of them, when they become adults even, break away from the old rut of submissive obedience. The commercial spirit of greed and gain is fostered in every possible way. A successful man is picked out and held up as an example worth imitating. If they are taught proportion sums the problems are put in this way: If I purchase an article for three farthings and sell it for a penny what per cent. profit should I make on an invested capital of £100? . . . The elementary education given to-day in our Board schools does no more than prepare the minds of the children for their patient obedience to the domination of a proud and haughty middle and upper class. The spirit of competition . . . is encouraged; the grab-all, grasping idea of "profit" is held up as an ideal to be striven for; the individual, personal, selfish doctrine of "get on, honestly if possible, but get on," is rammed and jammed down the children's throats, but not a single word or hint of the advantage of co-operative association for the welfare of all is ever breathed.[23]

How shocking would such a denunciation have seemed to the Kay-Shuttleworths and Robert Lowes throughout Europe who had insisted years before that "we must educate our masters" so that they would not in fact seek to become masters.

23. *The Life and Struggles of William Lovett, in His Pursuit of Bread, Knowledge, and Freedom; with Some Short Account of the Different Associations He Belonged to, and of the Opinions He Entertained* (London, 1876), p. 134; H. W. Hobart, "Education: I. Elementary," *Justice: The Organ of the Social Democracy*, 30 June 1894, p. 3.

Experience showed that learning could not be made permanently subservient to any social order or economic system. It had a revolutionary dynamic that was sooner or later bound to transcend the interests of those who had made it generally accessible only in order to preserve the class structure of their community. Once the masses learned to read and write, there could be no effective control over what they thought. Sometimes elementary education shaped them into loyal supporters of king and country, defenders of church and state. Sometimes it only made them devotees of the scandal sheet and the pulp magazine. And sometimes it taught them that the differences between the haves and have-nots known by every society were not eternal. They could, indeed they should, be ended by a new social order founded on equality and justice. As a speaker declared at a meeting of English workers in 1832, "Their rulers, unfortunately for themselves, had taught them to read, and they now knew there was no actual superiority between man and man." Mass schooling, like mass production, made possible a liberation of the lower classes of Europe whose subservience had historically been rooted in poverty and ignorance.[24]

24. *Poor Man's Guardian*, 7 April 1832, p. 339.

7

ECONOMIC OPPORTUNITY AND

CLASS MOBILITY

The industrial revolution produced a major shift in the distribution of occupations and incomes in Europe. Under the old agrarian order, the ability to move laterally from one branch of the economy to another or vertically from one class of society to another had been severely restricted by the inelasticity of the system of production. People had remained confined to the livelihood in which they had been born and trained because there was little opportunity to find more gainful employment in a different occupation requiring a different skill. The laws of many countries on the Continent upholding social distinctions and occupational demarcations—prohibitions, for example, against the acquisition of noble land by commoners or against the practice of a manual trade by aristocrats—were not primarily responsible for the rigidity of class and property. Rather, they reflected the fact that this rigidity had already become accepted as an inescapable reality. But the rationalization of the economy led to a break with the past, creating the opportunity for large numbers of people to leave the occupation that had been traditional in their family for more remunerative work far from the place of their birth. The result was a vast internal migration, economic as well as geographic, from country to city and from husbandry to manufacture. Accompanying this change in the pattern of occupations came a corresponding change in the pattern of classes as a new distribution of employment and wealth began to undermine the traditional structure of the community. Here was the most significant social consequence of the industrial revolution.

The shift in the choice of livelihoods is easier to trace than the change in the relationship of classes because the available statistical data measure occupation more readily than status. There can be no doubt that a major redistribution in the relative importance of the various branches of the economy took place in the course of the nineteenth century. A rapid change was most apparent in Western and Central Europe. During the 1880s the sociologist Charles Booth calculated the sharp decline since 1851 in the proportion of the employed population of England engaged in agriculture and fishing, as opposed to the rise in manufacture, mining, building, and transport. A more recent estimate by Phyllis Deane and W. A. Cole covering a longer period of time underscores the diminishing share of agriculture, forestry, and fishing in the British national income and the growing importance of industry, commerce, and finance. In France the shift of economic primacy from farming to manufacturing was less pronounced but just as apparent so that the pattern on both sides of the Channel was very much alike.[1]

Even more drastic was the change in the distribution of occupations in Central Europe. The process of industrialization reached its highest intensity in Germany, where in the course of a single lifetime a primarily agricultural nation became transformed into the most developed center of manufacture on the Continent. As Table 7.2 shows, in Prussia the proportion of the population dependent on farming fell by half between 1843 and 1907, whereas the percentage in industry, commerce, and transportation doubled. In Saxony, which became even more industrialized than Prussia, the rate of occupational change was higher still. Figures for Germany as a whole prior to national unification are only approximations, but thereafter they are taken from the official censuses of the empire. They reveal a marked decline in agriculture and a corresponding rise in manufacturing, trade, transportation, and the professions. Even in Great Britain, change in the pattern of employment was not as rapid or intense.[2]

The decline in the importance of farming and the rise of manufacture and trade can be traced in varying detail in almost every country of Europe. Simon Kuznets has put together a highly useful compilation of data on the distribution of national product in a number of states, and although there is a clear distinction between national product and occupational structure, changes in the composition of the former provide a rough measure of changes in the latter. According to his figures, agriculture in the Netherlands, where it had been declining even before the nineteenth century, produced only 16 percent of national income in 1913; industry's share was 33 and services accounted for 51. In Denmark agriculture's percentage of net domestic product in current prices fell from 47 to 29 between 1870–74 and 1905–9. In Norway its share of gross domestic product dropped from 34 percent in 1865 to 24 in 1910,

1. Charles Booth, "Occupations of the People of the United Kingdom, 1801–81," *Journal of the Statistical Society* 49 (1886):324; Phyllis Deane and W. A. Cole, *British Economic Growth, 1688–1959: Trends and Structure* (Cambridge, 1962), p. 291; J. Mayer, "La croissance économique française: La structure de l'économie française à trois époques éloignées: 1788, 1845, 1885," in *Income and Wealth*, 3d. ser., ed. Milton Gilbert (Cambridge, 1953), p. 91.

2. Werner Sombart, *Die deutsche Volkswirtschaft im neunzehnten Jahrhundert und im Anfang des 20. Jahrhunderts*, 4th ed. (Berlin, 1923), pp. 422–23; *Statistisches Jahrbuch für den Preussischen Staat* 9 (1911):46; Karl von Langsdorff, *Die Landwirthschaft im Königreich Sachsen und ihre Entwickelung in den Jahren 1876 bis einschl. 1879* (Dresden, 1881), p. 46.

Table 7.1. Changing Pattern of the Economy in Great Britain and France, 1788–1901

England (Booth)

	Percentage of Labor Force	
	1851	1881
Agriculture and fishing	21.1	11.8
Manufacture, mining, building, and transport	46.3	47.9

Great Britain (Deane and Cole)

	Percentage of National Income		
	1801	1851	1901
Agriculture, forestry, and fishing	32.5	20.3	6.1
Manufacture, mining, and building	23.4	34.3	40.2
Trade, transport, and income from abroad	17.4	20.7	29.8
Housing	5.3	8.1	8.2

France (Mayer)

	Percentage of Population		
	1788	1845	1885
Agriculture	75	62	49
Industry	10	18	25
Commerce and services	8	6	12

SOURCES: Charles Booth, "Occupations of the People of the United Kingdom, 1801–81," *Journal of the Statistical Society* 49 (1886): 324; Phyllis Deane and W. A. Cole, *British Economic Growth, 1688–1959: Trends and Structure* (Cambridge, 1962), p. 291; J. Mayer, "La croissance économique française: La structure de l'économie française à trois époques éloignées: 1788, 1845, 1885," in *Income and Wealth*, 3d ser., ed. Milton Gilbert (Cambridge, 1953), p. 91.

whereas that of industry rose from 21 to 26 and that of services, including transport and communication, from 45 to 50. In Sweden, where the percentage of gross domestic product attributable to agriculture fell from 39 to 35 between 1861–65 and 1901–5, industry's percentage rose from 17 to 38.

Table 7.2. Changing Pattern of the Economy in Germany, 1843–1907

Prussia

| | Percentage of Population | | | |
	1843	1882	1895	1907
Agriculture	61	44	36	29
Industry	23	34	39	43
Commerce and transportation	2	10	11	13

Saxony

| | Percentage of Population | | | |
	1849	1861	1871	1875
Agriculture and forestry	32	25	16	15
Industry, mining, and metallurgy	48	52	52	53
Commerce and transportation	5	6	10	9

Germany

| | Percentage of Population | | |
	1882	1895	1907
Farming, fishing, forestry, horticulture, and animal husbandry	43	36	29
Industry, mining, metallurgy, and construction	36	39	43
Commerce and transportation	10	12	13
Army, court, church, bureaucracy, and professions	5	6	6

SOURCES: Werner Sombart, *Die deutsche Volkswirtschaft im neunzehnten Jahrhundert und im Anfang des 20. Jahrhunderts*, 4th ed. (Berlin, 1923), pp. 422–23; *Statistisches Jahrbuch für den Preussischen Staat* 9 (1911): 46; Karl von Langsdorff, *Die Landwirtschaft im Königreich Sachsen und ihre Entwickelung in den Jahren 1876 bis einschl. 1879* (Dresden, 1881), p. 46.

Changes in the source of wealth and the distribution of employment were less drastic in the south and east, where the industrial revolution arrived slowly and late. Since economic information is in part a function of economic development, the statistical data for this region are not as detailed as for Western Europe. In Italy, however, the proportion of national income derived from agriculture declined from 55 to 47 percent between 1861–65 and 1896–1900, whereas industry rose from 20 to 22 and services from 25 to 31. Russia remains an enigma with regard to the occupational pattern, as in so many other respects. Yet although the established facts are tantalizingly few, they are not without significance. It has been determined that 74.6 percent of the labor force in 1897 was employed in agriculture, 9.3 in manufacturing industry, 4.6 in private service, 3.8 in commerce, 1.6 in transport, and 0.4 in mining. The figures suggest a country still in the initial stage of transition from an agrarian to an industrial economy. But the proportion of those engaged in husbandry must have been even greater around the middle of the nineteenth century, judging from the fact that the urban population increased from less than 10 percent to about 15 between 1863 and 1914. By the time of the First World War, Russia was going through an early phase of economic rationalization that countries farther west had experienced fifty or even a hundred years before.[3]

The shift of the primary source of livelihood away from agriculture toward industry, however, did not lead to a major redistribution of wealth. The lack of detailed information on the pattern of incomes in preindustrial society makes generalization difficult, but statistics for the nineteenth century do not indicate a substantial diffusion of affluence. Since real income was rising for all classes, thanks to the industrial and the agricultural revolution, the general standard of living improved, especially after 1850. Yet the distance between those at the top of the ladder and those at the bottom remained by and large undiminished, and it may even have grown wider.

Although the bits and pieces of data on this point are too scattered to be conclusive, they at least do not suggest a more even apportionment of wealth. Indeed, the information supplied by tax returns in England around the mid-century indicates a growing disparity (figure 7.1). In the space of ten years, the number of fortunes producing an income below 500 pounds increased 7 percent and the number producing an income below 1,000 pounds 9 percent. But the higher the position on the scale of affluence, the more rapid its rate of growth. Thus, fortunes with incomes between 5,000 and 10,000 pounds rose 31 percent and those with incomes above 50,000 pounds 142 percent. Prussia displayed the same tendency. Between 1852 and 1873 the number of taxpayers with an income below 1,200 marks increased 22.8 percent, those with an income

3. Simon Kuznets, *Modern Economic Growth: Rate, Structure, and Spread* (New Haven and London, 1966), pp. 88–93; W. H. Parker, *An Historical Geography of Russia* (Chicago, 1968), pp. 282–83, 314–15.

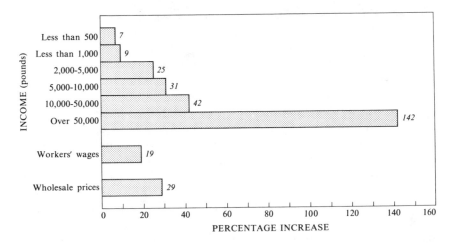

Figure 7.1. Growth of English Fortunes Yielding an Annual Income,
1850–60

SOURCE: Charles-H. Pouthas, *Démocraties et capitalisme (1848–1860)* (Paris, 1941),
p. 393.

between 1,200 and 3,000 marks 75 percent, and those with an income
above 3,000 marks 125.7 percent.

Conditions admittedly varied from place to place and sometimes from
decade to decade. In Breslau the number of people in the low income
category, those with 900 marks annually or less, declined from 95.2 percent of all inhabitants in 1858 to 88.2 in 1900 and 79.5 in 1910. Yet
Werner Sombart concluded early in the twentieth century that the distribution of wealth in Germany had not changed significantly as a result of
economic rationalization: "Is [the bulk of the population] differently
structured in any substantial way with regard to its income relationships
than a hundred or fifty years ago? To put it another way, the question is:
do as many people per thousand have an income of 300–400 marks,
500–600, and so forth today as then? I am almost inclined to answer:
yes, the distribution today is approximately the same. In any case, substantial shifts are not demonstrable, and have also probably not occurred."

The same generalization could be made even more safely about England, where in 1911–13 some 32,000 people, constituting 0.2 percent of all people age twenty-five or over, owned capital in excess of
25,000 pounds apiece and controlled 41.3 percent of all capital, whereas
16,382,500 people, constituting 87.4 percent of all people age twenty-
five or over, owned a capital of less than 100 pounds apiece and controlled 8.5 percent of all capital. Only 0.9 percent of the entire popula-

tion age twenty-five or over, those with a capital of at least 5,000 pounds, owned 65.4 percent of all capital. The concentration of property in Great Britain at the time of the First World War could hardly have been less than during the Napoleonic Wars, and it may well have been greater.[4]

But although there was relatively little downward movement of wealth from higher to lower income categories, there was very substantial sideways movement from country to city and from agriculture to industry. In almost every part of Europe, the proportion of national income derived from farming and fishing was declining in relation to that derived from manufacture and trade. By 1860–61 the per capita national income of the employed population of France earned in industrial occupations already exceeded that earned in agricultural occupations by almost 4 percent. In England in 1867 farm income totaled 140 million pounds, manufacturing income 300 million, and income from services 274 million. Indeed, the change in the major sources of wages and salaries in Great Britain in the course of the nineteenth century provides a measure of the shift in the center of wealth from fields to factories. In 1801 agriculture, forestry, and fishing accounted for 25.0 percent of wages and salaries; manufacturing, mining, and building for 22.1; and trade and transport for 10.1. By 1851 the percentages had become 16.1, 37.3, and 15.1; and by 1901 a complete transformation in the pattern of income sources had taken place: 5.3, 41.6, and 23.3 percent.

Another case in point is Prussia, where in 1910 the income tax from taxpayers in the income category between 9,500 and 30,500 marks produced revenue totaling 24.9 million in the cities and 4.8 million in the country. In the category of taxpayers with an annual income between 30,500 and 100,000 marks, the cities produced 19.2 million in revenue and the country 4 million. And in the highest category, comprising taxpayers with an income of over 100,000 marks a year, the cities produced 21.6 million and the country 5.3 million. In other words, the amount of taxes paid on annual incomes in excess of 9,500 marks was almost five times greater in urban than in rural communities, although the population in the former was less than twice as great as in the latter. The decline in the importance of land as a source of wealth could also be seen in the cities themselves, where real estate became a progressively less valuable form of proprietorship with the advance of industrialization. In Bordeaux, for example, which still depended primarily on trade and shipping for its livelihood, landed property accounted in 1873 for 40.37 percent of the wealth transmitted by inheritance, although the percentage was

4. Charles H. Pouthas, *Démocraties et capitalisme, 1848–1860* (Paris, 1941), p. 393; Sombart, *Die deutsche Volkswirtschaft*, pp. 430–31; Mark Abrams, *The Condition of the British People, 1911–1945: A Study Prepared for the Fabian Society* (London, 1946), p. 110.

20.56 in the category of very large fortunes in excess of 500,000 francs. But in Lille, the great textile center, real estate constituted only 31.43 percent of all inherited wealth. Land clearly was in retreat before other categories of property.[5]

This change in the dominant form of ownership had profound implications for the distribution of authority and status in society. It meant that the landed aristocracy, whose privileged position had been based on its control of the major source of affluence, was now losing economic primacy to the urban bourgeoisie. The consequence was a growing discrepancy between the apportionment of wealth and the apportionment of power. Those whose ascendancy rested on noble birth began to fear that their predominance was being undermined by an economic process depriving them of the means to maintain their position in society. In 1800 the aristocracy still controlled almost 20 percent of the annual production of Great Britain; by 1850 it was less than 10. On the Continent the change in the pattern of wealth was less rapid, but there could be little doubt that here too the distribution of material advantages was gradually shifting. The prospects before the nobility were gloomy, full of phantoms of forgotten loyalty and vanishing piety, charged with premonitions of popular insurrection, mob rule, and bloody Jacobinism.

The sense of doom haunting many aristocrats was intensified by their numerical weakness. The landholding patriciate had always been a narrow elite proud of its exclusiveness. Its primacy had depended on control of the source of wealth and mastery of the technique of warfare. That was why its situation became so precarious in an age of mechanized industries and mass armies. How could a small class of highborn landowners retain its social eminence in an industrializing, urbanizing, liberalizing Europe? In most countries it made up 1 percent of the population or less. In Bavaria there were only 1,384 noble families in 1822 so that not even 1 inhabitant in 900 was a member of the aristocracy. The ratio of Polish nobles in Galicia to the rest of the population was 1 to 68. In Bohemia there were 1,400 commoners for every aristocrat. In Hungary the proportion of noblemen was much higher; they constituted around 5 percent of the population in 1837. Most of them lived in modest circumstances, however, a vast difference in income and status separating the small provincial landlords from the great magnates.

5. Pierre Léon, "L'évolution démographique, économique et sociale," in *L'Europe du XIXe et du XXe siècle*, ed. Max Beloff, Pierre Renouvin, Franz Schnabel, and Franco Valsecchi, 6 vols. (Milan, 1959–64), 1:346–47; Deane and Cole, *British Economic Growth*, p. 152; Sombart, *Die deutsche Volkswirtschaft*, pp. 395, 468; Pierre Guillaume, "Essai sur la composition et la répartition de la fortune bordelaise au milieu du XIXe siècle d'après les déclarations de mutation après décès de l'année 1873," *Revue d'histoire économique et sociale* 43 (1965):331–32, 351.

The Russian aristocracy was also above average in size, but not by much. According to official statistics, hereditary nobles in 1875 numbered 653,000 and personal nobles 374,000 in a population of 77.7 million. Altogether, including state officials, they made up close to 1.5 percent of all inhabitants. In Germany aristocratic rank was more difficult to attain. In 1860 there were about 250,000 members of the nobility, both hereditary and newly created; they constituted less than 1 percent of a population of 35,567,000. Close to 142,000 aristocrats lived in Prussia, making up about 0.8 percent of the population; many of them belonged to the Junker caste that played such an important role in the political, military, and economic life of the kingdom. Membership in the nobility of Sweden was even more restricted; during the 1850s there were only 11,000 aristocrats in a population of more than 4 million, not quite 0.3 percent. This exclusiveness of the European patriciate, which it had guarded with jealous vigilance during the preindustrial era of rigid social stratification, became a serious weakness in an age of economic change and political reform.[6]

The size of the bourgeoisie is more difficult to determine. For one thing, it was a social rather than legal designation so that, unlike the aristocracy, there are no official registers of those belonging to it. For another, it was a much less homogeneous group because it was dependent economically on a variety of businesses and occupations. Its members had in common only a level of personal income, a position in the social hierarchy, and an attitude toward others and toward themselves. The easiest but crudest way to measure its extent is by its wealth. In the case of Great Britain, where the middle class was one of the largest in Europe, this would mean that those categorized as bourgeois were among the approximately 100,000 taxpayers in 1801 and 340,000 in 1848 earning more than 150 pounds annually. Out of a population of 21 million at the mid-century, there were about 1.5 million people, including dependents, whose income classification was above that of the lower classes. This proportion is roughly comparable to the 12.6 percent of all inhabitants in England age twenty-five or over who had a capital of 100 pounds or more in 1911–13. Obviously, not all of them belonged to the bourgeoisie because members of the nobility were also included in this category of wealth. But most of them did. Thus, according to this method of computation, the middle class constituted less than 5 percent of the population

6. Peter N. Stearns, *European Society in Upheaval: Social History since 1750*, 2d ed. (New York and London, 1975), p. 94; Eugene N. Anderson and Pauline R. Anderson, *Political Institutions and Social Change in Continental Europe in the Nineteenth Century* (Berkeley and Los Angeles, 1967), p. 24; B. R. Mitchell, *European Historical Statistics, 1750–1970* (London and Basingstoke, 1975), p. 20.

at the beginning and less than 10 percent at the end of the nineteenth century.

These estimates do not differ widely from those reached by E. J. Hobsbawm, who used life-style rather than income level as the measure of class. The 674,000 female "general domestic servants" employed in Great Britain in 1851 would be more than the number of middle-class households, but the approximately 50,000 cooks, 50,000 housemaids, or 50,000 housekeepers would no doubt be less. Thus, including all dependents, bourgeois families made up about 10 percent of the population, a figure close to that obtained by the calculation of tax or capital classifications. It is in general conformity, moreover, with the percentages for the city of Barmen in 1861 given by Wolfgang Köllmann in Table 7.3. All in all, 10.4 percent of the population belonged to the middle class, roughly the same figure as in Great Britain. By 1907, however, the situation had changed significantly. A total of 24.6 percent was now in the middle class.[7]

In her study of British industrialists between 1850 and 1950, Charlotte Erickson uses a different categorization. According to her calculations, 1,213,851 people or 18.3 percent of the male labor force in Great Britain around the mid-century belonged to the middle class. Yet almost a fourth of them were farmers, and at least a fourth were managers, bookkeepers, clerks, and salesmen, people employed in respectable but frequently underpaid white-collar occupations. The census of 1851 also found 20,000 landed proprietors and more than 10,000 "independent gentlemen" among them but only 11,000 "masters" with more than ten employees and 12,500 professionals. Business decisions involving significant economic risk were made as a rule by employers and administrators in industry, commerce, and banking, a group numbering about 300,000. Most of these had modest incomes, but a few were rich enough to be included among the 4,000 men in the kingdom earning more than five thousand pounds a year.[8]

This category of entrepreneurs did not grow as rapidly during the nineteenth century as the white-collar labor force, especially in private employment. For example, although the population of Germany increased 35.7 percent between 1882 and 1907, the number of white-collar

7. E. J. Hobsbawm, *The Age of Revolution, 1789–1848* (Cleveland and New York, 1962), pp. 300–301; Abrams, *Condition of the British People*, p. 110; Mitchell, *European Historical Statistics*, p. 24; Wolfgang Köllmann, *Sozialgeschichte der Stadt Barmen im 19. Jahrhundert* (Tübingen, 1960), pp. 103–4.

8. Charlotte Erickson, *British Industrialists: Steel and Hosiery, 1850–1950* (Cambridge, 1959), p. 234; Phyllis Deane, *The First Industrial Revolution* (Cambridge, 1965), pp. 264–65; W. L. Guttsman, *The British Political Elite* (London, 1965), p. 19; Hobsbawm, *Age of Revolution*, p. 300.

Table 7.3. Composition of the Middle Class of Barmen, 1861–1907

	Percentage	
	1861	1907
Upper bourgeois	1.4	1.4
Businessmen of secondary rank, high government officials, and professionals	2.2	5.7
White-collar employees and government officials of middle rank	2.5	11.0
Handicraftsmen, shopkeepers, and small manufacturers	4.3	6.6
Total	10.4	24.6

SOURCE: Wolfgang Köllmann, *Sozialgeschichte der Stadt Barmen im 19. Jahrhundert* (Tübingen, 1960), p. 104.

workers increased from 116,000 to 615,000 or 430 percent in industry, from 87,000 to 379,000 or 338 percent in commerce, and from 247,000 to 683,000 or 174 percent in the postal, telegraph, and railroad systems. In government service, however, the number increased from 258,000 to 391,000 or only 51 percent.

Growth in the learned professions was not much greater than in the category of the decision-making and risk-taking entrepreneurs. Those classified by the British census of 1851 as doctor, lawyer, professor, or "other educated person following miscellaneous pursuits" made up a proportionately very small group. There were only 16,000 lawyers, not including judges, and 1,700 law students; 17,000 physicians and surgeons and 3,500 medical students and assistants; fewer than 3,500 architects; and about 1,300 "editors and writers." This narrow professional elite was increasing at a rate that hardly surpassed that of the population at large. In England between 1851 and 1881, the number of inhabitants grew 44.9 percent and that of employed males 38.0 percent, but the number of those in law grew 35.4 percent, in medicine 32.7, in literature and science 321.1, in education 83.9, and in religion 45.8. The five professions together grew 52.2 percent, exceeding the general population increase but with law and medicine lagging behind. Even those employed in administration, who could largely be classified as professionals, grew 46.1 percent, just about equaling the national average.

On the Continent the percentages were generally different; in particular, the increase in the proportion of lawyers was usually greater than in Great Britain. Look at the figures for Moscow, for example, in Table 7.4.

Table 7.4. Number of Professionals in Moscow, 1840–97

	1840	1882	1897
Lawyers	24	500	652
Educators	182	5,000	5,900
Medical workers	615	2,000	3,178
People in "the arts"	410	1,500	2,900
Total	1,231	9,000	12,630

SOURCE: Michael Pushkin, "The Professions and the Intelligentsia in Nineteenth-Century Russia," *University of Birmingham Historical Journal* 12 (1969–70):88.

Yet despite their rapid growth, professionals remained a tiny minority of the population of a city with 365,000 inhabitants in 1850–51, 748,000 in 1880, and 989,000 in 1900–1901.[9]

Any general conclusion concerning the size of the European bourgeoisie drawn from such a vast, disparate, and not always comparable body of information should be advanced with caution. Not only are the statistical data scattered and incomplete, but there is no agreement even on the composition of the bourgeoisie. Significant differences persist regarding the social groups to be included, whatever the criterion used to determine class boundaries: income, occupation, or way of life. Yet the question is too important to be avoided; it demands an answer, however tentative. On the whole, then, it appears that the middle class during the nineteenth century made up between 5 and 20 percent of the population, depending on time and place. The percentage was near the upper limit in the industrially advanced countries of the north and west, and closer to the lower limit in the largely agricultural countries of the south and east. The propertied classes, including the aristocracy, constituted less than a fifth of all inhabitants, usually much less.

It follows that the lower classes made up 80 percent or more of the population of Europe. They were divided in varying proportions between husbandry, manufacture, trade, and services, and had in common only the experience of poverty and hardship. In England at the beginning of

9. A. R. L. Gurland, "Wirtschaft und Gesellschaft im Übergang zum Zeitalter der Industrie," in *Propyläen Weltgeschichte*, ed. Golo Mann, Alfred Heuss, and August Nitschke, 12 vols. (Berlin, Frankfurt, and Vienna, 1960–65), 8:333; Hobsbawm, *Age of Revolution*, p. 194; H. J. Perkin, "Middle-Class Education and Employment in the Nineteenth Century: A Critical Note," *Economic History Review*, 2d ser., 14 (1961–62):128; Michael Pushkin, "The Professions and the Intelligentsia in Nineteenth-Century Russia," *University of Birmingham Historical Journal* 12 (1969–70):88; Mitchell, *European Historical Statistics*, p. 77.

the twentieth century, 5 percent of wages and salaries were earned in agriculture, 42 in industry, 23 in commerce, and 10 in domestic service. In Germany at the same time, 29 percent of the population depended on agriculture, 43 on industry, 13 on commerce, and 13 on domestic service and hired labor. In Russia, on the other hand, agriculture still provided employment for 75 percent of the work force, industry for 9, commerce and transportation for 5, and private service for 5. The figures on the distribution of occupations among all inhabitants of a country approximate very closely the figures for the lower classes alone.[10]

The changing pattern of employments, incomes, and riches aroused in many noblemen a profound resentment of the bourgeoisie. They saw their position in state and society being undermined by parvenus, by moneygrubbing businessmen and scribbling litterateurs cunningly embracing the gospel of careers open to talent. Their fears for the future were reflected in the numerous diatribes that defenders of the old order directed against those daring to challenge established tradition. In his *profession de foi*, the long memorandum of 15 December 1820 that Metternich submitted to Alexander I of Russia, the Austrian statesman denounced middle-class troublemakers who were threatening the political foundations of the Restoration. It was the same in France, Germany, Italy, or Spain, he insisted. Everywhere "the agitated classes are those of men of wealth—true cosmopolites insuring their profits at the expense of any order of things whatsoever—of paid state officials, men of letters, lawyers, and those in charge of public education." As for the source of the mounting danger, it could be "fully defined in one single word: presumption," presumption in questioning the existing structure of status and authority.

In 1860 the *Berliner Revue*, a conservative Prussian journal, denounced the unhealthy ambition of rich, educated social climbers in terms similar to those Metternich had used forty years before. Who, it asked rhetorically, makes up the "new bourgeoisie" that seeks to become the "new nobility" in every country of Europe? "The answer is provided by the membership list of the lower house of the legislature, in France as well as in Italy, in Germany as well as in Prussia. In first place ahead of everyone else are those who have acquired a higher academic education by attending a secondary school and a university, but who have remained virtually strangers to the actual realities of life, in other words, men of abstract education which is instructive about everything and nothing." This meant above all "the judicial officials, the administrative officials, to a considerable extent the clergy, the physicians, the scholars, the teachers

10. Deane and Cole, *British Economic Growth*, p. 152; Sombart, *Die deutsche Volkswirtschaft*, pp. 422–23; Parker, *Historical Geography of Russia*, p. 283.

at the higher levels, the lawyers, and similar people." In addition, there were those "who have acquired a modern scholarly education, and whose spiritual sensitivity has been diminished to the extent that their intellect has been trained, in other words, the engineers, the higher technicians, the men of letters, especially the Reformed Jews of the press, and others of that sort." And finally there were "the bigger merchants, manufacturers, artificers, managers, [and] noble landowners who have given up the old traditions." The long catalog of villains included not only all the elements of the bourgeoisie but its occasional allies in the other classes of society as well.

Most aristocrats feared, however, that warnings and denunciations would not halt the decline that the changing economy seemed to make inevitable. A new era was beginning, and the values of a hierarchical social system now had to confront the ideals of competition and equality. The long domination of the landed patriciate of Europe appeared to be ending. "Our century is the age of movement, just as the preceding century was that of enjoyment and contemplation," wrote Baron Victor von Andrian-Werburg, a prominent Austrian politician, during the 1840s. "We are no longer allowed to continue to live, comfortably enjoying life, in the position which birth and circumstances have allotted to us, like a good-natured oyster in its bed. A general stir, a restless striving is the characteristic quality of our time, and in this general commotion everyone wants to and must find his place." After the opening of the twentieth century, the conservative party leader Ernst von Heydebrand und der Lasa, the "uncrowned king of Prussia," sounded even more pessimistic. He confessed to a liberal member of the Reichstag that time was against him and his class: "After all, the future belongs to you; the masses will assert themselves and deprive us, the aristocrats, of our influence. This current can only be slowed down for a while by a strong statesman. In any case, we do not want to give up our position voluntarily. But if you force us, then you will have what you want." The prospects before the nobility were profoundly disheartening.[11]

The bourgeoisie, on the other hand, could look to the future with confidence. The rationalization of the economy was steadily increasing its share of wealth, influence, and status. It appeared to be only a matter of time before a moneyed elite would replace the landed nobility as the dominant group in society. In England the *Westminster Review* declared as early as 1824 that the middle class "is the strength of the community.

11. *Aus Metternich's nachgelassenen Papieren*, ed. Richard Metternich-Winneburg, 8 vols. (Vienna, 1880–84), 3:404, 411–12; "Das Haus der Abgeordneten," *Berliner Revue: Social-politische Wochenschrift* 20 (1860):434; [Victor von Andrian-Werburg], *Oesterreich und dessen Zukunft*, 3d ed., 2 vols. (Hamburg, 1843–47), 1:48–49; Hermann Pachnicke, *Führende Männer im alten und neuen Reich* (Berlin, 1930), p. 63.

It contains, beyond all comparison, the greatest proportion of the intelligence, industry, and wealth of the state. In it are the heads that invent, and the hands that execute; the enterprise that projects, and the capital by which these projects are carried into operation." Specifically, "the merchant, the manufacturer, the mechanist, the chemist, the artist, those who discover new arts, those who perfect old arts, those who extend science; the men in fact who think for the rest of the world, and who really do the business of the world, are the men of this class. . . . It is this class which gives to the nation its character."

Yet the bourgeoisie's claim to political power in virtue of its talent and wealth was being frustrated, it maintained, by highborn sluggards whose domination of the state rested on privileges acquired by a feudal caste in bygone ages of oppression. All the built-up resentment of the ant for the grasshopper, of the self-made man for the noble prodigal, came pouring out in the attack by Joseph Chamberlain, businessman-turned-politician, against the aristocratic leader of the Conservatives in England. "Lord Salisbury," he inveighed in a speech in Birmingham in 1883, "constitutes himself the spokesman of a class—of the class to which he himself belongs, who toil not neither do they spin (great cheering), whose fortunes, as in his case, have originated by grants made in times gone by for the services which courtiers rendered kings (renewed cheers), and have since grown and increased while they have slept by levying an increased share on all that other men have done by toil and labour to add to the general welfare and prosperity of the country." The change in the distribution of wealth engendered by the industrial revolution led logically to demands for a corresponding change in the distribution of power. To rich and ambitious men on the make, it was intolerable that the right to decide affairs of state was in the hands of an aristocracy whose dominant position rested not on ability but birth. Throughout the nineteenth century, they fought to remove the obstacles, legal and traditional, that stood in the way of their acquisition of political primacy.

In this struggle the bourgeoisie was heartened by the conviction that history was on its side, that sooner or later hereditary class prerogative would give way to a system of authority in which talent was the only requirement of power. This was the belief of Pierre Paul Royer-Collard, leader of the "doctrinaires" in the French legislature who supported moderate constitutionalism. He maintained in 1819 that "the influence of the middle class is a fact, a mighty fact to be reckoned with . . . capable of resisting the blows of its opponents. The centuries have prepared the way for it; the revolution has proclaimed it. It is to this class that the new interests belong. Its security cannot be disturbed without imminent danger to the established order." The destiny of the bourgeoisie, more and more of its members concluded, was to replace the aristocracy at the apex of the social pyramid, to dominate political life as completely as it dominated economic life. But there would be a fundamental difference between the old feudal nobility of warriors and landowners and the future patriciate of money and ability. During the Revolution of 1848 in Germany, Joseph Schneider of Vienna, a member of the Frankfurt Parliament, explained that difference: "I am certainly aware that we will always have an aristocracy of wealth and that we will always have an aristocracy of intellect, human nature unfortunately being what it is. But those, gentlemen, are natural aristocracies to which all may aspire and to which all may ascend. An aristocracy of birth, however, is never natural and neither is it necessary." Since achievement rather than birth was to be the criterion of social distinction, the classless nobility that the bourgeoisie hoped to establish would be accessible to all men of merit.[12]

But did the nineteenth century in fact witness the rise of "natural aristocracies," based on wealth and intellect, "to which all may aspire and to which all may ascend"? There was at least a widespread belief that economic opportunities were broadening and class barriers diminishing, perhaps not as much as in the New World but certainly more than at any previous time in Europe. It crops up over and over again in the works of publicists, economists, and even writers of fiction. In 1855, for example, in the novel *North and South*, Elizabeth Gaskell's self-made millowner, John Thornton, describes how the beginnings of industrialization made it possible for men of low birth but high ability to rise to the top: "Raw, crude materials came together; men of the same level, as regarded education and station, took suddenly the different positions of masters and men, owing to the motherwit, as regarded opportunities and probabilities, which distinguished some, and made them far-seeing as to what great future lay concealed in that rude model of Sir Richard Arkwright's." The ascent from rags to riches, or at least from poverty to comfort, became possible for all, depending only on dedication and hard work: "It is one of the great beauties of our system, that a working-man may raise himself into the power and position of a master by his own exertions and behaviour; that, in fact, every one who rules himself to decency and sobriety of conduct, and attention to his duties, comes over to our ranks; it may not be always as a master, but as an overlooker, a cashier, a bookkeeper, a clerk, one on the side of authority and order." Here was the European version of the Horatio Alger creed, the creed of shoeshine boy to bank president, of careers open to talent.

Many writers dealing with everyday realities also maintained that class

12. "Literary Education," *Westminster Review* 1 (1824):68–69; J. L. Garvin and Julian Amery, *The Life of Joseph Chamberlain*, 4 vols. (London, 1932–51), 1:392; Amable Guillaume Prosper Brugière de Barante, *La vie politique de M. Royer-Collard: Ses discours et*

exclusiveness was becoming less rigid and movement across social boundaries more common. In his *Subjection of Women* published in 1869, John Stuart Mill declared that "human beings are no longer born to their place in life, and chained down by an inexorable bond to the place they are born to, but are free to employ their faculties, and such favourable chances as offer, to achieve the lot which may appear to them most desirable." This was essentially a restatement of the position taken by the imaginary John Thornton in the preceding decade. Even after the cruel experience of the First World War, Werner Sombart remained convinced that opportunities for self-improvement, for advancement from worker to manufacturer or from clerk to banker, were increasing. "If we consider first of all the area of recruitment of entrepreneurship within a given portion of the population, in other words, if we consider its social origins," he wrote in his history of modern capitalism, "then the most important characteristic of our epoch can be identified as a far-reaching democratization of leadership. The leading men in economic life arise out of constantly broadening and therefore constantly deepening strata of the population." It was the last echo of nineteenth-century social optimism, still reverberating on the eve of the crash of 1929.[13]

To be sure, the belief in movement up the ladder of success by virtue of determination and hard work was not entirely based on myth. There were cases of men who had ended up as industrialists or financiers after starting out as mill hands or shop assistants. A study of the Lancashire textile industry in 1912 examined a random selection of 63 employers in cotton weaving who responded to a letter of inquiry. Forty-eight or 79 percent of them belonged to the "first generation," a category consisting of "employers, managers and others . . . who have themselves risen from the operative classes or from classes earning no more than operatives." In a manufacturing city of 100,000 inhabitants, the social backgrounds of 139 employers owning 93,400 looms were investigated. Eighty-eight or 63 percent of them belonged to the "first generation" and owned 49 percent of the looms; 44 percent of the looms were in the hands of other private businesses and the remaining 7 percent belonged to public companies. Cotton spinning, on the other hand, was largely controlled by limited-liability companies; here the study focused on the class origins of

ses écrits, 2 vols. (Paris, 1861), 1:456; Germany, *Stenographischer Bericht über die Verhandlungen der deutschen constituirenden Nationalversammlung zu Frankfurt am Main*, ed. Franz Wigard, 9 vols. (Frankfurt am Main, 1848–49), 2:1313.

13. [Elizabeth Cleghorn Gaskell], *North and South*, 2 vols. (London, 1855), 1:124, 126; John Stuart Mill, *The Subjection of Women* (London, 1869), pp. 29–30; Werner Sombart, *Der moderne Kapitalismus: Historisch-systematische Darstellung des gesamteuropäischen Wirtschaftslebens von seinen Anfängen bis zur Gegenwart*, 2d ed., 3 vols. (Munich and Leipzig, 1924–28), 3:19.

members of the boards of directors. In one representative district, it found that 33 out of 45 respondents or 73 percent belonged to the "first generation"; in another well-known center of spinning, 38 out of 45 or 84 percent were in this category. The proportions were thus similar to those in cotton weaving.

Although these data support the thesis of social mobility, they also suggest that there was a progressively more rigid limitation on upward movement. An inquiry covering twenty mills in a town where spinning was the principal industry found that 67 percent of the assistant managers, with a salary between 100 and 150 pounds, belonged to the "first generation," but the percentage for managers, with a salary between 200 and 800 pounds, was 42, and that for managing directors, the highest classification, only 13. In other words, the crossing of class boundaries was easiest from the upper level of lower-class occupations to the lower level of middle-class occupations. The higher a position on the scale of income and status, the more difficult it was to attain for those at the bottom.[14]

Even this cautious appraisal of the opportunities for social advancement in the nineteenth century may be too optimistic. After studying conditions in Lancashire in the early stage of industrialization, Michael Sanderson maintains that class boundaries were becoming more rigid. His examination of literacy levels and occupational patterns leads him to a somber conclusion:

> In an eighteenth-century commercial society unaffected by the development of the cotton factory industry, the possibility of social mobility for the educated son of a labourer was vastly greater than in the 1830s in a society considerably affected by such industrialization, even when both societies were within the same county. Moreover by any criteria the Lancashire of the 1830s could not be regarded as having anything more than a very low degree of social mobility with over half of its young men making no change of occupation from that of their fathers and with three-quarters of its literate young men either making no change from the parental occupation or sinking into a less literate one than their fathers held. This is simply not consistent with an interpretation of the industrial revolution that sees it as demanding more literacy, creating more literate jobs and drawing an increasingly educated labour force up the social scale into them.[15]

14. S. J. Chapman and F. J. Marquis, "The Recruiting of the Employing Classes from the Ranks of the Wage-Earners in the Cotton Industry," *Journal of the Royal Statistical Society* 75 (1911–12):296–97.

15. Michael Sanderson, "Literacy and Social Mobility in the Industrial Revolution in England," *Past & Present*, no. 56 (1972), pp. 101–2.

Focusing on the system of education in England during the initial phase of industrialization, Nicholas Hans also concludes that "the gulf between the wealthy employers of labour and the proletarian factory hands and miners of the Victorian Era was deeper than the ha-ha ditch which separated the squire from the farmer and wider than the distance between the merchant and the craftsman of the eighteenth century." All in all, "social mobility in the eighteenth century was greater than in the middle of the nineteenth." This picture is vastly different from that presented in the study of Lancashire on the eve of the First World War.

It may be, of course, that there was a substantial increase of social mobility in Europe between the middle of the nineteenth century and the beginning of the twentieth, but there is little evidence to support such a contention. On the contrary, the experience of the industrial city of Bochum in Westphalia suggests a continuing high rigidity of class boundaries (table 7.5). In a random sample of 1,117 adult males, about a tenth of the total, almost 80 percent of the unskilled or semiskilled workers in 1880 were still unskilled or semiskilled in 1901; in the category of skilled or artisanal workers, the position of more than 60 percent remained unchanged; and in the category of nonmanual occupations, almost 97 percent were still in that classification twenty-one years later. Only about a tenth of those in the lower strata of manual occupations and about a fourth of those in the upper strata were able to gain entry into nonmanual occupations, usually into positions at the bottom of that category.

The economic, educational, and psychological barriers to movement across class boundaries were also transmitted from one generation to the next. Consider Table 7.6, which gives a sample of 697 men marrying in Bochum in 1900, comparing their occupations with those of their fathers. All in all, 87.8 percent of the sons of manual workers were themselves manual workers. Many had risen within the hierarchy of working-class occupations, but the position of most had remained unchanged or had even declined. Only about 1 in 8 had succeeded in climbing from manual into nonmanual occupations. Indeed, the proportion of the bridegrooms of 1900 who had managed to cross the boundaries of their class was smaller than that of their fathers during the preceding two decades.[16]

It becomes apparent that the rationalization of the European economy was of greatest benefit to those who already enjoyed important material and social advantages. To put it another way, men of means in the nineteenth century were likely to be the sons of men of means. Depending on their skill in exploiting the opportunities open to them, they were sometimes able to enlarge substantially the wealth they had inherited. But the

16. Nicholas Hans, *New Trends in Education in the Eighteenth Century* (London, 1951), p. 210; David Crew, "Definitions of Modernity: Social Mobility in a German Town, 1880–1901," *Journal of Social History* 7 (1973–74):53, 61.

Table 7.5. Social Mobility in Bochum, 1880–1901: Extent of Movement among Occupational Categories

| | | Occupation in 1901 (percentage) | | |
		Unskilled or Semiskilled	Skilled or Artisanal	Nonmanual
	Unskilled or semiskilled	78.8	9.3	11.9
Occupation in 1880	Skilled or artisanal	15.5	60.9	23.6
	Nonmanual	3.2	0.0	96.8

SOURCE: David Crew, "Definitions of Modernity: Social Mobility in a German Town, 1880–1901," *Journal of Social History* 7 (1973–74): 53.

Table 7.6. Intergenerational Mobility in Bochum, 1900

| | Sons' Occupations (percentage) | | | |
| | Manual | | | |
Fathers' Occupations	Lower Skill Level	Same Occupation or Same Skill Level as Father	Higher Skill Level	Non-manual
Unskilled or semiskilled				
Miners		54.2	27.1	19.0
Factory workers		65.8	28.1	5.9
Skilled workers and artisans				
Metalworkers	23.3	66.6		10.0
Building and construction	39.2	43.1		17.6
Food, drink, and clothing	31.3	56.3		12.5
Wood, leather, and luxury	29.1	54.1		16.6

SOURCE: David Crew, "Definitions of Modernity: Social Mobility in a German Town, 1880–1901," *Journal of Social History* 7 (1973–74): 61.

meteoric rise from rags to riches was an exception. According to one estimate, 70 percent or more of the 189 millionaires in Great Britain who died between 1858 and 1879 must have been descended from at least one generation of affluence and probably from several. More than half of them were landowners. Even in the heroic age of English industrialism between 1750 and 1850, before the mounting cost of mechanization began to shift primacy in production from the manufacturer to the financier, self-made entrepreneurs were a distinct minority. A survey of 132 prominent industrialists revealed that only about a third were sons of workers or small farmers, whereas two-thirds came from families already engaged in business and often simply enlarged the enterprises that they had inherited.

After the middle of the nineteenth century, the preponderance of the well-to-do in industry became even more pronounced, especially in the older, more established branches. A detailed study of the social background of British steel manufacturers in the period 1875–95 shows that, when they began their careers, 31 percent of their fathers were partners, owners, or directors in the same industry; 15 were partners, owners, or directors in another industry; 8 merchants or bankers; 13 landowners or farmers; 15 professional men; 4 senior managers or agents; 3 retail tradesmen; 4 clerks, foremen, salesmen, or bookkeepers; 4 independent craftsmen; 1 employed skilled workers; and 2 unskilled or semiskilled workers. All told, 86 percent of the steel manufacturers came from the aristocracy and the upper strata of the bourgeoisie, 11 from the lower strata of the bourgeoisie, and 3 from the working class.

The parliamentary inquiry of 1867–68 concerning scientific instruction in the English school system provided significant information on the social and economic background of manufacturers and managers in industry as a whole. It reported that "the smaller manufacturers and managers . . . have either risen from the rank of foremen and workmen . . . or else they are an offshoot from the class of smaller tradesmen, clerks, &c." As for "the proprietors and managers of great industrial undertakings," there were "not unfrequent cases where these persons also have risen from the rank of artizans. . . . More generally, however, the training of the capitalists, and of the managers of their class, has been that of the higher secondary schools; followed in rare, though in more recent years less unfrequent, instances, by a course of more or less systematic scientific instruction in colleges." The education of most of the large-scale entrepreneurs suggests a level of income and status well above that of the working class.[17]

17. E. J. Hobsbawm, *The Age of Capital, 1848–1875* (New York, 1975), p. 146; Reinhard Bendix, *Work and Authority in Industry: Ideologies of Management in the Course of Industrialization* (New York and London, 1956), pp. 24–25; Erickson, *British*

The situation in Germany was similar. Men from well-to-do families tended to dominate industry and finance, especially after the initial pioneering stage of economic rationalization. In his study of about 200 industrialists in the period from 1800 to the beginning of the 1840s, Heinz Sachtler found that 61 percent came from a working-class or petty bourgeois background; 28 percent from intermediate groups such as merchants, artisans, and civil servants of middle rank; and 11 percent from the upper strata of society, including nobility, clergy, and leading civil servants. On the other hand, of the approximately 400 industrialists studied in the period from the early 1840s to the early 1890s, only 21 percent were of working-class or petty bourgeois origin, 65 percent came from the intermediate groups, and 14 percent came from the upper strata. Using similar data, Derk Visser examined a selected group of 34 German business leaders born before 1830; he discovered that the social origin of no more than 7 could be described as either "lower-middle" or "farmer." Of the 37 born in 1830–68, moreover, 10 were "lower-middle," "lower," or "farmer."

But the most solid and systematic work on the social background of the German business world has been done by Hartmut Kaelble, who concludes that 67 percent of 235 entrepreneurs in the period 1800–1870 came from the "upper strata," that is, from families of high officials, army officers, university or secondary school teachers, clergymen, lawyers, physicians or pharmacists, landowners, and, most important, entrepreneurs; 31 percent came from the "middle strata," including first of all handicraftsmen, shopkeepers, and innkeepers, and then farmers, government officials of intermediate rank, white-collar workers, and elementary school teachers; none came from the "lower strata," made up of workers, minor officials, and servants. In the years 1871–1914, the corresponding percentages for the 297 entrepreneurs studied were almost exactly the same: 67, 33, and 0. Kaelble's work on conditions in Berlin, moreover, suggests that the chances for newcomers were diminishing after the middle of the nineteenth century. Of 58 businessmen surveyed in the period before 1836, 86 percent were founders of their enterprises and 14 percent were heirs; in the period 1836–50, the percentages for 65 businessmen were 72 and 28; and in the period 1851–73, the percentages for 74 businessmen were 43 and 57. The opportunity for rapid economic advancement, largely restricted to members of well-to-do families, was becoming even narrower with the passage of time.[18]

Industrialists, pp. 11–12; Great Britain, Parliamentary Papers (1867–68), 15 (Reports from Committees, 10), no. 432, "Report from the Select Committee on Scientific Instruction; together with the Proceedings of the Committee, Minutes of Evidence, and Appendix," pp. v–vi.

18. Heinz Sachtler, Wandlungen des industriellen Unternehmers in Deutschland seit Be-

The chief barrier to lower-class movement into the ranks of industrialists or financiers was the lack of capital, experience, and personal contact. Formal education was not a major factor because most entrepreneurs preferred to receive their training in the mill or countinghouse rather than the classroom. In his autobiography, Robert Owen recalled that "the manufacturers [at the end of the eighteenth century] were generally plodding men of business, with little knowledge and limited ideas, except in their own immediate circle of occupation." In the case of the learned professions, on the other hand, inadequate schooling was a serious obstacle to the upward mobility of sons of working-class families. Even in the most advanced countries, the educational system was such that the masses received only elementary instruction without much prospect for advanced training. Of the men born in Prussia in 1800–1809, 18.08 percent received no schooling at all, and 78.83 percent received between one and eight years. For those born in 1847–56, the percentages were 6.97 and 87.51, and for those born in 1887–97, 0 and 90.42. The proportion of men without any education thus declined in the course of the nineteenth century from almost a fifth to none, but the proportion of those with more than an elementary education increased at a much lower rate from 3.09 to 9.58 percent.

Of the 3,589,248 male pupils going through the required period of formal instruction in Prussia in 1911, 91.74 percent were in public elementary schools, which meant that they would normally go to work at the age of fourteen; 3.24 percent were in public or private middle schools, which prepared them for white-collar occupations; and 5.02 percent were in preparatory or secondary schools providing the academic training required for ultimate admission to the professions. Public expenditures per student, moreover, varied with the exclusivity of the category of instruction: 64 marks in public elementary schools, 169 in public middle schools and higher schools for girls, 336 in secondary schools for boys, 849 in universities, and 1,145 in institutes of technology. Class rigidity in the educational system thus reflected and reinforced class rigidity in the economic system.[19]

ginn des 19. Jahrhunderts: Ein Versuch zur Typologie des Unternehmers (Berlin, 1937), pp. 7, 24; Derk Visser, "The German Captain of Enterprise: Veblen's Imperial Germany Revisited," Explorations in Entrepreneurial History, 2d ser., 6 (1968–69):314–15; Hartmut Kaelble, "Sozialer Aufstieg in Deutschland, 1850–1914," Vierteljahrschrift für Sozial- und Wirtschaftsgeschichte 60 (1973):52–53; idem, Berliner Unternehmer während der frühen Industrialisierung: Herkunft, sozialer Status und politischer Einfluss (Berlin and New York, 1972), p. 55.

19. The Life of Robert Owen: Written by Himself, with Selections from His Writings and Correspondence (London, 1857), p. 37; Peter Lundgreen, Bildung und Wirtschaftswachstum im Industrialisierungsprozess des 19. Jahrhunderts: Methodische Ansätze, empirische Studien und internationale Vergleiche (Berlin, 1973), pp. 92, 111; idem, "Industri-

In other countries the proportion of the population receiving more than elementary schooling was no higher, and sometimes it was considerably lower. The number of pupils in the state lycées in France doubled between 1809 and 1842, but even then it did not exceed 19,000. The total of those receiving a secondary education around the mid-century was about 70,000. Their ratio to all children of the same age rose during the period 1842–64 from 1 in 35 to 1 in 20, but in the conscript classes of the 1840s only 1 man in 93 was a graduate of a secondary school, and in the early 1860s the proportion was still 1 in 55 or 60. In Great Britain at about the same time, 25,000 boys were attending the 225 private institutions curiously miscalled "public schools," but by 1909 the total number of those receiving secondary instruction in English educational establishments of various kinds was 174,000. Around 1850 some 20,000 pupils out of a population of 68 million attended secondary schools in Russia, whereas in Prussia, with a population of 16.3 million, close to 62,000 pupils were in secondary schools. Yet even in countries with the most advanced system of education, only about 5 percent of those receiving elementary instruction on the eve of the First World War went on to a secondary school.

Institutions of higher learning were even more exclusive. At the beginning of the nineteenth century, there were not many more than 1,500 students in all of the Prussian universities, only about a fourth of the number enrolled at the University of Paris in 1789. In Russia university attendance totaled some 1,700 in 1825, although by 1848 the figure had nearly tripled to 4,600. At the mid-century, there were probably no more than 40,000 university students in all of Europe, and the number thirty years later was not substantially greater. Excluding students of theology, Germany was in first place at the end of the 1870s with almost 17,000, then came Italy and France with between 9,000 and 10,000 each, and then Austria with about 8,000. The enrollments in institutions for the training of engineers and technicians were even lower. The famous École polytechnique in Paris, a hotbed of political discontent under the Restoration, had only 1,581 students during the entire period 1815–30. The École des ponts et chaussées graduated 800 civil engineers between 1820 and 1850, and the École des mines 120 mining technicians. The Bauakademie in Berlin during the same time trained 1,000 civil engineers for government service, and the Gewerbe-Institut 1,000 technicians for private industry. The figures kept growing, to be sure. By 1908–9 the German universities had 46,632 students, more than all of Europe sixty

alization and the Educational Formation of Manpower in Germany," *Journal of Social History* 9 (1975–76):68.

years before. But even then they constituted less than 0.1 percent of the population.[20]

The academic training required for admission to the learned professions thus had the effect of largely excluding members of the lower classes. The French ministry of education conducted a survey of the social background of students in secondary schools in 1864–65. Of the 12,605 cases investigated, 11.8 percent of the fathers were government employees; 18.2 professionals or semiprofessionals; 17.0 landowners or rentiers; 12.3 peasant proprietors; 12.9 businessmen in either commercial or industrial enterprises; 16.5 men in lower-middle-class occupations such as white-collar jobs or commercial employments; 7.8 workers (6.1 skilled and 1.7 unskilled); and 0.2 agricultural laborers. This pattern resembles that of the students entering the gymnasium in Bochum between 1876 and 1906. At the beginning of this period, the sons of factory owners and other leading businessmen made up 7.7 percent of the total and at the end 1.9; sons of professionals increased from 4.4 to 13.5; sons of high-level administrators in government service or private enterprise also grew from 3.3 to 14.4; sons of low-level administrators decreased from 26.4 to 24.1; sons of skilled manual workers rose slightly from 5.5 to 6.7; and sons of unskilled manual workers rose even less from 3.3 to 3.8. Educational opportunities for children of lower-class background were thus expanding at the end of the nineteenth century, but not very rapidly. They made up 8.8 percent of the entering class in 1876 and 10.5 percent thirty years later.

Sometimes the sons of workers did succeed in moving into middle-class occupations, though usually at the lower levels in white-collar jobs or subordinate technical employments. At the provincial industrial school in Potsdam in 1822–23, the social background of nineteen out of twenty students is known: seventeen were children of handicraftsmen and two were children of government officials. Figures for the middle 1860s show that the industrial schools in Saarbrücken, Trier, Koblenz, Iserlohn, Hagen, and Elberfeld still had a majority, though less one-sided, of sons of skilled artisans. The fathers of 60 percent of the graduates were handi-

20. Hobsbawm, *Age of Revolution*, p. 135; idem, *Age of Capital*, pp. 94–95; Edward C. Mack, *Public Schools and British Opinion since 1860: The Relationship between Contemporary Ideas and the Evolution of an English Institution* (Westport, 1971), p. 118; Erich Keyser, *Bevölkerungsgeschichte Deutschlands*, 2d ed. (Leipzig, 1941), p. 404; Lundgreen, *Bildung und Wirtschaftswachstum*, pp. 136–37, 152; Stearns, *European Society in Upheaval*, p. 116; Friedrich Paulsen and Rudolf Lehmann, *Geschichte des gelehrten Unterrichts auf den deutschen Schulen und Universitäten vom Ausgang des Mittelalters bis zur Gegenwart: Mit besonderer Rücksicht auf den klassischen Unterricht*, 3d ed., 2 vols. (Berlin and Leipzig, 1919), 2:696.

craftsmen; merchants, manufacturers, and business managers made up 24 percent; and government officials accounted for 12 percent. In the more prestigious Gewerbe-Institut in Berlin, on the other hand, less than a third of the students came from families of skilled artisans. Handicraftsmen and white-collar workers constituted 31.7 percent of the fathers; merchants, manufacturers, and business managers 28.3; government officials and army officers 24.4; and men in the professions and in miscellaneous occupations 15.6. Finally, among the graduates of institutes of technology, which provided the equivalent of a university education, the proportion of sons of manual workers was still smaller. Of those living in Berlin in 1907, 23 percent came from families belonging to the "upper strata," 64 percent from the "middle strata," and 5 percent from the "lower strata." The sons of handicraftsmen, retailers, and innkeepers, who were classified as members of the "middle strata," accounted for 33 percent of the total, whereas the percentages for the sons of minor government officials, workers, and servants, who made up the "lower strata," were 4, 1, and 0.

The number of children of manual workers in the other learned professions was proportionately even less. Among university students of philology from Württemberg preparing in the period 1887–1900 for careers as teachers in secondary schools, 17 percent were sons of handicraftsmen, retailers, and innkeepers; 3 percent were sons of minor government officials; and 1 percent were sons of workers. Among university students of medicine from Württemberg in the period 1876–1900, 10 percent were sons of handicraftsmen, retailers, and innkeepers; 2 percent were sons of minor government officials; and there were no sons of workers. Thus, the higher the status of a profession, the less the chance that a member of the lower classes could enter it.[21]

Economic rationalization, it becomes clear, did not provide a ladder to success by which those at the bottom of the scale could rise in significant numbers to positions at the top or even in the middle. It created instead an escalator carrying all classes of society to ever higher levels of production and consumption without altering substantially the distance between them. Only at the very summit, in the ranks of the dominant elite in economics and politics, was there a significant change in social composition, and here the change was quite different from what had been expected. The uneasy forebodings of aristocratic landowners proved to be too

21. Patrick J. Harrigan, "The Social Origins, Ambitions, and Occupations of Secondary Students in France during the Second Empire," in *Schooling and Society: Studies in the History of Education*, ed. Lawrence Stone (Baltimore and London, 1976), p. 210; Crew, "Definitions of Modernity," p. 64; Peter Lundgreen, *Techniker in Preussen während der frühen Industrialisierung: Ausbildung und Berufsfeld einer entstehenden sozialen Gruppe* (Berlin, 1975), pp. 96–97, 120; Kaelble, "Sozialer Aufstieg in Deutschland," pp. 58–60.

gloomy, and the rosy expectations of bourgeois businessmen turned out to be too optimistic. What actually occurred in the course of the nineteenth century was not the replacement of an agricultural by an industrial patriciate but the amalgamation of the two into a new aristocracy combining the status of the one with the wealth of the other. To be sure, at first there had been violent confrontations between nobility and bourgeoisie in the revolutionary movements of the early 1820s, the early 1830s, and especially the late 1840s. But then the armed struggle became gradually transformed into a peaceful process of social integration that could be seen throughout Europe, though sometimes only in faint outline. Still obscure in the backward agricultural regions of the south and east, this process was clearly apparent in the economically developed countries of the north and west.

The assimilation of the upper bourgeoisie into the nobility was most advanced in England, where it had been going on for a long time. Most British peerages were only about a hundred years old, being based to a large extent on success in entrepreneurship or achievement in the military and diplomatic service. Of the aristocratic members of the House of Commons in 1841–47, 15 percent were active businessmen and 35 percent had at least some business connection as directors of banks, insurance companies, railroad lines, or public utilities. Yet the up-and-coming bourgeois generally lacked assurance, breeding, and education; he lacked the gracious life-style and sense of superiority of the nobleman; he felt himself to be awkward and provincial. "Traders have no bond of union, no habits of intercourse," wrote the economist and publicist Walter Bagehot in 1867. "Their wives, if they care for society, want to see not the wives of other such men, but 'better people,' as they say—the wives of men certainly with land, and possibly with titles."

The self-made businessman therefore did not seek to displace the aristocrat but to identify with him through imitation, schooling, intermarriage, and ennoblement. According to the report submitted to a parliamentary commission in 1868, "When his fortune is made, when his income begins to exceed a thousand or two per annum, he suddenly expands from the chrysalis into the butterfly, turns from the class out of which he has risen, and strives to attach himself to that composed of the older manufacturing families, or if it be possible, even to the landed gentry. The first step to this is to send his children away from home to a boarding school, nominally to get rid of the dialect, but really to get rid of their cousins, to form genteel connexions, and acquire manners more polished than those of home." By the end of the century, a new British elite had emerged combining the wealth of the bourgeoisie with the prestige of the nobility. Of the 670 members of the House of Commons elected in 1895, almost 250 were manufacturers, merchants, directors, mineowners, brewers, and bankers. Most of the others, moreover, whether barristers, officers, or gentlemen of leisure, were bound by close ties to the world of business. Members of the gentry in particular were unable to live on their rents and had to rely on the money they made in the city. The bourgeoisie was even invading the House of Lords itself, the citadel of blue blood and high birth. Of the approximately 200 men who were admitted to the nobility between 1886 and 1914, some 70 represented the new wealth of the industrial revolution and another third had risen in the professions or in government service. Barely 25 percent came from established landed families, which had formerly provided the largest proportion of new peers.[22]

The social integration of the middle and upper classes has not been studied to the same extent in France as in England, but there are close similarities between the two countries. In his perceptive analysis of French society since 1848, Theodore Zeldin found that by the end of the nineteenth century "the bourgeoisie adopted many of the ideals associated with the aristocracy. Though they praised work, their ideal was also to live off a private income, to have a house in the country, and divide their time between it and the town in exactly the same way as the aristocracy." More than that, "their attitude to commerce was aristocratic. They adopted aristocratic attitudes towards social status." The aristocracy for its part "did not disdain to work in the bourgeois civil service: the departments of finance and justice and the army were particularly smart. The aristocracy joined the bourgeoisie in business and industry, particularly banks, insurance, railways, mines and steel." In 1902, 30 percent of the directors of railway companies and 23 percent of the directors of large steel and banking companies were noblemen.[23]

Even in Germany, where in the past social barriers between bourgeois and aristocrat had been more rigid than in Western Europe, a synthesis of the two classes into a new elite of wealth and status was clearly in the making. A study of the men who gained entry into or advancement within the Prussian nobility shows that the proportion of those whose fathers had been businessmen or bankers rose from 9.56 percent in 1871–79 to 16.99 in 1880–93, 21.95 in 1894–1905, and 24.58 in 1906–14. It is

22. William L. Langer, *Political and Social Upheaval, 1832–1852* (New York, Evanston, and London, 1969), pp. 7–8, 48; Walter Bagehot, "The English Constitution: No. VI, The House of Commons," *Fortnightly Review* 4 (1866):275; Great Britain, *Parliamentary Papers* (1867–68), 28, pt. 8 (*Reports from Commissioners*, 13, pt. 8), no. 3966-VIII, "Schools Inquiry Commission, Vol. 9: General Reports by Assistant Commissioners—Northern Counties," pp. 752–53; Elie Halevy, *A History of the English People in the Nineteenth Century*, 2d ed., 6 vols. (London, 1949–52), 5:15–16; F. M. L. Thompson, *English Landed Society in the Nineteenth Century* (London and Toronto, 1963), p. 294.

23. Theodore Zeldin, *France, 1848–1945*, 2 vols. (Oxford, 1973–77), 1:17, 405.

equally significant, however, that the proportion of those entering or advancing in the Prussian nobility who were themselves businessmen or bankers was considerably smaller, rising from 6.54 percent in 1871–79 to 7.28 in 1880–93, 14.39 in 1894–1905, and 14.49 in 1906–14. In other words, many of the men ascending from the bourgeoisie to the aristocracy were abandoning the occupations of their fathers, turning instead to the more "genteel" pursuits of bureaucrats, officers, land-owners, or simply gentlemen of leisure. Growing intermarriage was an-other measure of the integration of wealth and status. In 1800–1829 only 26 percent of the wives of noblemen in Lower Saxony were of non-noble birth, but by 1860–89 the percentage had increased to 42. Noble-women were also marrying into nonnoble families in greater numbers so that 43 percent of the Prussian generals in the First World War who had been born commoners had aristocratic wives.

Soon after the opening of the twentieth century, Werner Sombart—at that time still the daring academic radical—clearly perceived the process of integration taking place at the apex of the social pyramid:

> It has remained the highest goal of our bourgeoisie to become Junkers, that is, to be ennobled and, so far as possible, to assume a seigneurial way of thinking and a knightly mode of conduct. But thereby the feudal class undergoes a continuous process of rejuve-nation. It constantly receives new reinforcements from bourgeois circles which it rapidly assimilates. In the process of interbreeding between gentry and bourgeoisie, the former always proves in our country to be the stronger element. Its daughters marry members of their own class, while its sons introduce new blood into that class by marrying rich heiresses. But the bourgeois who have become rich seek to forget their origins as soon as possible and to dissolve in the landed aristocracy or at least in feudal landownership.[24]

Fifty years later, in an attempt to determine why the growing acquisition of noble estates by middle-class proprietors did not lead to a democra-tization of the landlord class, Hans Rosenberg confirmed this analysis. He discovered that "bourgeois owners of noble estates became arch-conservative haters of democrats, who often behaved more like Junkers than the old Prussian landed aristocracy." In Germany, as in most other countries on the Continent, the strong hostility between nobility and

---

24. Lamar Cecil, "The Creation of Nobles in Prussia, 1871–1918," *American Historical Review* 75 (1969–70):778–80; Keyser, *Bevölkerungsgeschichte*, p. 416; Nikolaus von Pre-radovich, *Die Führungsschichten in Österreich und Preussen (1804–1918): Mit einem Aus-blick bis zum Jahre 1945* (Wiesbaden, 1965), p. 162; Sombart, *Die deutsche Volkswirt-schaft*, p. 470.

bourgeoisie at the beginning of the nineteenth century was being transformed at the end into a tacit partnership. The propertied classes, both noble and nonnoble, were coalescing into a new patriciate determined to defend its position against the growing demand of the propertyless millions for a greater share of wealth and authority in Europe.[25]

25. Hans Rosenberg, "Die Demokratisierung der Rittergutsbesitzerklasse," in *Zur Geschichte und Problematik der Demokratie: Festgabe für Hans Herzfeld*, ed. Wilhelm Berges and Carl Hinrichs (Berlin, 1958), p. 471.

8

THE EMERGENCE OF THE

LABOR QUESTION

The shift of primacy in the European economy from husbandry to manufacture meant that the labor force became increasingly transformed from an agricultural into an industrial proletariat. The peasant masses gradually turned into factory operatives whose new way of life engendered new interests and attitudes. At first the great internal migration from village to city created among those it uprooted a sense of profound alienation from which only occasional dissipation offered escape. That was why so many of the early observers of the industrial revolution commented on the drunkenness and immorality of the urban working class. But after a generation or two, this feeling of rootlessness began to give way to a renewed self-awareness, a growing recognition of common problems and collective goals. Little by little, a rudimentary social consciousness developed among the early factory workers.

In the preindustrial society of villages and hamlets, concerted action by the masses had been infrequent and sporadic. They had led lives of isolation, intensified by economic decentralization and functional illiteracy, so that an organized struggle in behalf of their class was usually impossible. Peasant wars and rebellions attest that at times the village population could use force effectively in defense of its interests. Yet such efforts were always hampered by a parochialism fostered by the economic system.

The industrial revolution imposed on the labor force discipline and a class consciousness. It meant that large numbers of people were living and working in close proximity, exchanging hopes and ideas, and acquiring common purposes, outlooks, and interests. There was a fundamental difference between the cowed, ignorant rustics of the old economic order and the restless, disaffected operatives of the factory system. By the middle of the nineteenth century, many writers were expressing their uneasiness at the growing strength of the factory proletariat created by economic rationalization. For example, after a trip through Lancashire in 1842, W. Cooke Taylor felt disturbed by the emergence of what he perceived to be a powerful new social class:

> As a stranger passes through the masses of human beings which
> have been accumulated round the mills and printworks . . . he

206 · The Social System

cannot contemplate these "crowded hives" without feelings of anxiety and apprehension almost amounting to dismay. The population, like the system to which it belongs, is NEW; but it is hourly increasing in breadth and strength. It is an aggregate of masses, our conceptions of which clothe themselves in terms that express something portentous and fearful . . . as of the slow rising and gradual swelling of an ocean which must, at some future and no distant time, bear all the elements of society aloft upon its bosom, and float them—Heaven knows whither. There are mighty energies slumbering in these masses. . . . The manufacturing population is not new in its formation alone: it is new in its habits of thought and action, which have been formed by the circumstances of its condition, with little instruction, and less guidance, from external sources.[1]

Here was a consequence of the industrial revolution as momentous as the increase in production or the growth of cities.

Economic rationalization also fostered in the urban laboring population of Europe a uniformity of outlook and purpose, a class solidarity far greater than the peasant masses had displayed during the preindustrial era. Robert Mohl, liberal politician and professor of political science at Heidelberg, concluded in the 1850s: "We all know now that the common condition of these millions [of factory workers] has also produced among them a community in the way of life extending far beyond the boundaries of the individual state, a community in the attitudes toward life, in interests and passions, a uniformity in morals and vices, and the same behavior toward other groups in the population." The similarity of the economic experiences of the industrial workers, he went on, had led to a similarity of beliefs and aspirations, in short, to a distinct new social class: "Through this uniqueness [of the urban proletariat], which is so widespread, an entirely new element has entered public life . . . quite independent of the form of the state, and until now touched only very superficially by the laws of the state." Although Germany was still on the threshhold of industrialization, many observers could already see in the distance a militant industrial proletariat, embittered by hardship and ready to challenge the distribution of wealth and authority under the existing order.

In France, which had a more highly developed economy in the first half of the nineteenth century, the growth of industrial labor was even more striking. Countess Marie de Flavigny d'Agoult, better known for

1. W. Cooke Taylor, *Notes of a Tour in the Manufacturing Districts of Lancashire; in a Series of Letters to His Grace the Archbishop of Dublin* (London, 1842), pp. 4–6.

her liaison with Franz Liszt than for her literary and political writings, spoke in her recollections of the July Monarchy about "an important part of the common masses which . . . had come to form a class apart, as it were, a nation within the nation." A special term had even been coined for those employed in factories and mines. "People were beginning to call [them] by a new name: the industrial proletariat." The emergence of this new social class could be seen in many countries of Europe, its rate of growth depending on the pace of industrialization. Petitions, demonstrations, strikes, and riots by workingmen were familiar in England during the early Victorian era or in France under Louis Philippe, but they were a rarity in Germany before 1848, and in Austria, Russia, and the Balkans they were virtually unknown. Still, the rise of the industrial proletariat aroused even in agricultural states an apprehension far out of proportion to its size. Not only did it represent an implicit threat to established authority, but there was a general recognition that the development of the economy was bound to increase its strength.[2]

The apprehension of the propertied classes was intensified by a rudimentary ideology that the urban masses began to formulate in the attempt to improve their position in society. Many of the basic ideas of socialism could already be discerned in the rhetoric of the incipient labor movement during the early decades of the nineteenth century. There was first of all the concept of a paradise lost, a golden age when each man had a respected place and a secure livelihood until industrial capitalism reduced the worker to a slave of the machine. Consider the attack on economic rationalization that appeared in 1832 in a Manchester labor periodical, the *Union Pilot, and Co-Operative Intelligencer*:

> Could inspiration have unfolded to our fathers, who now moulder in their graves, the calamities which the invention of machinery was to bring upon their descendants;—could they have obtained but a faint glimmering of the havoc it has made upon the independence, the physical energies, and moral habits of Englishmen, what would they have thought, or how would they have acted? Would they have sung the praises of those who unintentionally were the authors of the pestilence; would they have permitted "*improvements*," which have been a scourge to the country, to overwhelm the health and happiness of the people? Oh, no! Unless we greatly err in our estimation of the spirit of our forefathers, they would have raised up the standard of humanity, and under its sacred banners, have fought

2. Robert Mohl, "Gesellschafts-Wissenschaften und Staats-Wissenschaften," *Zeitschrift für die gesammte Staatswissenschaft* 7 (1851):40; Marie de Flavigny d'Agoult [Daniel Stern], *Histoire de la révolution de 1848*, 2d ed., 2 vols. (Paris, 1862), 1:7.

against *"improvements"* which have been, and are at this moment, the curse of the country.[3]

Many factory workers believed that the root of the problem lay in the growing accumulation of riches by a small group of industrial capitalists, to whom private gain was more important than the common good. Shortly after the Napoleonic Wars, an open letter by a British journeyman cotton spinner declared that "these evils to the men have arisen from that dreadful monopoly which exists in those districts where wealth and power are got into the hands of the few, who, in the pride of their hearts, think themselves the lords of the universe." Yet the source of wealth was not capital but labor, according to an article appearing at the same time in a radical London journal: "Of the four staple manufactures, namely, cotton, linen, cloth, and iron, perhaps, on an average, the raw material does not constitute one-tenth of their value, the remaining nine-tenths being created by the labours of the weaver, spinner, dyer, smith, cutler, and fifty others, employed in different departments. The labours of these men form the chief article of traffic in this country." By "trading in the blood and bones of the journeymen and labourers of England," the merchants had piled up their riches and the country had reaped its glory and importance.[4]

Finally, there was a widespread conviction in the early labor movement that existing political institutions were only an instrument for the perpetuation of inequality in wealth and power. A few years after the passage of the Reform Bill of 1832 in England, a parliamentary committee investigating conditions among the handloom weavers asked John Scott, a representative chosen by textile workers in Manchester and Salford, whether "the working classes [are] better satisfied with the institutions of the country since the change has taken place." The answer was straightforward: "I do not think they are. They viewed the Reform Bill as a measure calculated to join the middle and upper classes to Government, and leave them in the hands of Government as a sort of machine to work according to the pleasure of Government." A profound distrust of established authority lay behind the repeated attempts of industrial workers to alter the structure of government: the Chartist demonstrations in Great Britain or the strikes and riots in France, for example. Sometimes the urban masses saw in political reform the key to a solution of economic questions. Manhood suffrage in particular, by giving the lower classes a greater voice in public policy, seemed to hold out the promise of a more just distribution of national income. At other times the emphasis was on

3. *Union Pilot, and Co-Operative Intelligencer*, 17 March 1832, p. 105.
4. *Black Dwarf*, 30 September 1818, p. 624; "An Appeal to the Public in Favour of the Working Classes," *Gorgon*, 12 September 1818, p. 129.

social reform, usually the interposition of the state in the relationship between employer and employee so as to insure a decent livelihood for all. In any case, the working-class movement from its beginnings regarded the existing system of government as only a tool of the propertied for the exploitation of the propertyless.

That was why reformers who hoped to solve the "social question," as it came to be known, by conciliation found the task so thankless. To most industrialists, they were do-gooders who, with the best of intentions, would only make a bad situation worse. To most workers, on the other hand, they were manipulators seeking to appease the lower classes with big promises and small concessions. Francis Place, a self-made businessman who had risen from poor apprentice to proprietor of a highly successful tailor's shop, complained that his efforts during the 1820s to repeal the Combination Laws against trade unions in England were hampered by the unrealistic demands of factory operatives. "The workmen were not easily managed," he wrote. "It required great care and pains and patience not to shock their prejudices. . . . They were filled with false notions, all attributing their distress to wrong causes, which I, in this state of the business, dared not attempt to remove. Taxes, machinery, laws against combinations, the will of the masters, the conduct of magistrates, these were the fundamental causes of all their sorrows and privations." According to him, their exaggerated hopes arose from ignorance of the hard realities of economics. "All expected a great and sudden rise of wages when the Combination Laws should be repealed; not one of them had any idea whatever of the connection between wages and population. I had to discuss everything with them most carefully, to arrange and prepare everything." Others were less patient. Peter Gaskell declared during the 1830s that lower-class organizations "form an 'imperium in imperio' of the most obnoxious description." The industrial revolution was thus creating conditions for a bitter struggle between the propertied and the propertyless classes.[5]

The ideology of the labor movement in this struggle was shaped in part by the teachings of a group of social theorists, most of them men of education and means, who recognized the transformation of the class structure resulting from the rationalization of the economy. These "utopian" socialists sought above all to analyze the growing importance of capital

5. Great Britain, *Parliamentary Papers* (1835), 13 (*Reports from Committees*), "Report from Select Committee on Hand-Loom Weavers' Petitions; with the Minutes of Evidence, and Index," p. 181; Graham Wallas, *The Life of Francis Place, 1771–1854* (London, New York, and Bombay, 1898), pp. 213–14; Asa Briggs, "The Language of 'Class' in Early Nineteenth-Century England," in *Essays in Labour History: In Memory of G. D. H. Cole, 25 September 1889–14 January 1959*, ed. Asa Briggs and John Saville (London and New York, 1960), p. 63.

and labor in the changing society of the nineteenth century. They argued that the landed aristocracy, whose primacy had rested on agriculture, was ceasing to be the dominant class. Its place was being taken by entrepreneurs, financiers, technologists, and scholars—people whose importance derived from function rather than status. In his famous "parable" that appeared in 1819, Henri Saint-Simon asks his readers to assume that France has suddenly lost her greatest scientists, poets, painters, musicians, engineers, businessmen, and agriculturists, "totaling all in all the three thousand leading scholars, artists, and artisans" and including "farmers, manufacturers, merchants, bankers, and all the clerks or workers they employ." As the result of such a loss, "the nation would become a body without a soul," it would immediately decline to "a state of inferiority vis-à-vis nations to whom today it is a rival." At least a generation would have to pass before France could recover from such a disaster.

Consider now another supposition, Saint-Simon goes on, namely, that all the men of genius in the arts, the sciences, and the trades remain alive but that France loses simultaneously all the members of the king's family, all the officers of the crown and ministers of state, all the marshals, cardinals, archbishops, bishops, and judges, and in addition "the ten thousand richest landowners among those who live like noblemen." Such a calamity would certainly grieve most Frenchmen "because they are good, because they could not regard with indifference the sudden disappearance of such a large number of their countrymen." Yet this loss of "the thirty thousand individuals reputed to be the most important in the state" would cause sorrow for sentimental reasons only since "no political misfortune to the state would result from it, [and] it would be very easy to fill the places which became vacant." These two contrasting hypothetical situations with which Saint-Simon opens his *Organisateur* were only a literary device to dramatize the profound change that he saw taking place in the social structure of Europe. But the point was well taken, so well taken that the author was prosecuted for his presumption, although in the end the jury returned a verdict of not guilty.[6]

In their study of the effect of the industrial revolution, however, the utopians went beyond an analysis of the rise and fall of social classes. They saw in the rationalization of the economy an opportunity to put an end to mass privation, an opportunity that was being frustrated by the concentration of the means of production in the hands of a small capitalist elite. They maintained that the progress of technology, far from improving the position of labor, had actually widened the gulf separating rich from poor. The Prussian civil servant and agricultural engineer Lud-

6. *Oeuvres de Saint-Simon & d'Enfantin précédées de deux notices historiques*, 47 vols. (Paris, 1865–78), 20:17–21.

wig Gall maintained during the 1820s that "the earth produces more food and clothing than would be needed to feed and clothe twice as many people as are living at the present time, and it is not true that such a shocking gap between the condition of the lowest and the upper classes has always existed." In fact, "this gap has grown larger from year to year with every advance of the arts and science, which have been of benefit only to the upper strata." The basic reason for the disparity in the distribution of wealth was "the worthlessness of human energy in relation to money, which rules everything"; it was the system of laws and values by which the fruits of labor went to those who exploited it, not to those who performed it. The great task facing modern society, then, was to reapportion property in such a way that the effects of the industrial revolution would be a blessing rather than a curse to most of mankind.

The contrast between what the human condition is and what it should be was a pet theme of the utopian socialists. They taught that the happiness of the society of the future would be as great as the misery of the society of the present. "All the sacred books agree in proclaiming that man is the king of creation," preached Victor Considérant, leader of the Fourierist school. "Such is indeed his destiny. But I ask you, does man today deserve to bear this glorious title? What sort of king is this, covered with rags, devoured by hunger and disease, who comes to display his sores and his misery in public places? I do not recognize there the king of the earth! The prophecies have not been realized." Man is still only an outcast; "the condition of animals is better and often nobler than his." But that would change. Before Considérant's listeners rose visions of human redemption and triumph. "Let all nations combine, let all peoples unite and organize in the unity of a great family. Let man make use of his arms and his intelligence for the general cultivation of the globe, instead of devastating it. Let him take complete possession of his domain, and let him apply the riches which are produced TO THE HAPPINESS OF ALL. Then he will be able to call himself king of creation!" Here was a glimpse of the New Jerusalem to which all mankind would some day ascend.[7]

There was something religious about the tone in which utopian socialism portrayed the future of society. At the end of a long road of sorrow lay the community of saints, the promised land, the terrestrial paradise. Here the exploitation of the weak by the strong would come to an end because differences of class and property would cease to exist. Not only

7. Ludwig Gall, *Was könnte helfen? Immerwährende Getraidelagerung, um jeder Noth des Mangels und des Ueberflusses auf immer zu begegnen, und Credit-Scheine, durch die Getraidevorräthe verbürgt, um der Alleinherrschaft des Geldes ein Ende zu machen* (Trier, 1825), pp. 5, 9–10; Victor Considérant, *Exposition abrégée du système phalanstérien de Fourier*, 3d ed. (Paris, 1846), pp. 50–51.

would the barriers between rich and poor crumble, but the very concepts of wealth and poverty would vanish. The sufferings of the masses were the price of their salvation. The men who described this eschatology were more than reformers; they were seers and prophets. "*A spirit of combination has grown up among the working classes, of which there has been no example in former times,*" declared Bronterre O'Brien, a radical Irish publicist who later became prominent in the Chartist movement. "The object of it is the sublimest that can be conceived, namely—*to establish for the productive classes a complete dominion over the fruits of their own industry.*" But that was not all. "An entire change in society—a change amounting to a complete subversion of the existing 'order of the world'—is contemplated by the working classes. They aspire to be at the top instead of at the bottom of society—or rather that there should be no bottom or top at all!" Thus, the goal of the labor movement was not a reversal of the roles of oppressor and oppressed but the elimination of oppression as such.[8]

The society of the future, however, would do more than improve the material well-being of mankind; it would make possible a transformation of human character itself. The end of privation would lead to virtue, wisdom, and a higher standard of conduct. Faith in the perfectibility of man, in the capacity of social circumstances to affect private actions, was at the heart of the doctrine of the utopians. It found its loftiest expression in Robert Owen's *New View of Society*: "On the experience of a life devoted to the subject I hesitate not to say, that the members of any community may by degrees be trained to live *without crime, without punishment, without idleness, and without poverty*; for each of these is the effect of error in the various systems prevalent throughout the world. *They are all the direct consequences of ignorance.*" Man's nature, far from being immutable, "is without exception universally plastic." With proper training, "THE INFANTS OF ANY ONE CLASS IN THE WORLD MAY BE READILY FORMED INTO MEN OF ANY OTHER CLASS." It followed that society could shape the behavior of its members by controlling the physical and psychological environment. "ANY CHARACTER, FROM THE BEST TO THE WORST, FROM THE MOST IGNORANT TO THE MOST ENLIGHTENED, MAY BE GIVEN TO ANY COMMUNITY, EVEN TO THE WORLD AT LARGE, BY APPLYING THE PROPER MEANS; WHICH ARE TO A GREAT EXTENT AT THE COMMAND AND UNDER THE CONTROUL, OR EASILY MADE SO, OF THOSE WHO POSSESS THE GOVERNMENT OF NATIONS." The battle for social justice would thus do more than put an end to privation;

8. *Poor Man's Guardian*, 19 October 1833, pp. 333–34.

it would lead to a new humanity, wise and noble, rising to greater heights of achievement.[9]

But how was today's cruel struggle for existence to be transformed into the blessedness of tomorrow? To most utopian socialists, the answer lay in the innate philanthropic instincts of man, who would surely seek to create a better society once he had been shown the injustices of the existing one. Their writings are full of ingenious schemes by which a collective system of property could swiftly and painlessly replace individual ownership. There were blueprints and specifications for cooperatives, communities, colonies, settlements, phalansteries, and social workshops. The details varied, but they all envisioned a new form of economic and social organization characterized by a concern for common good rather than private gain.

Take the views of Ferdinand Lassalle, founder of the first socialist political party in Europe. Although he came a generation after the heyday of the utopians, he remained closer to them in spirit than to his contemporary Karl Marx. Social justice, he remained convinced, could be achieved by stratagems and tricks, by sleight of hand, by pulling a rabbit out of the hat. "The abolition of the profit of the entrepreneur in the most peaceful, legal, and simple manner, in that the working class through voluntary associations organizes itself as its own entrepreneur . . . that is the only true improvement in the position of the working class, the only one meeting its just claims, the only one which is not illusionary," he declared in his *Open Reply to the Central Committee*. "But how?" he then asked, and promptly answered his own question: "It is the business and task of the state to make this possible for you . . . to offer you the means and the opportunity for this self-organization and self-association of yours. . . . Once again, then, the free individual association of the workers, but the free individual association made possible by the supporting and furthering hand of the state, that is the only way out of the wilderness open to the working class."

And how could the government be persuaded to allow itself to be used for the establishment of socialism? Here too the answer was simple: "The working class must be organized as an independent political party, and must make the general, equal, and direct suffrage the watchword and banner expressing the principle of this party. The representation of the working class in the legislative bodies of Germany, only this can satisfy its legitimate interests in regard to politics. To open a peaceful and

9. Robert Owen, *A New Vision of Society: or, Essays on the Principle of the Formation of the Human Character, and the Application of the Principle to Practice*, 3 vols. (London, 1813), 1:9; 2:35–36; 3:85.

legal agitation for it with all legal means is and must be the program of the workingmen's party."

Once the proletariat won a majority in parliament, the rest would be easy. It would not take much—only about a hundred million talers—to establish a network of factories owned by labor that could destroy the system of private ownership.

> You may ask now: "Where are we to get these hundred million?" Gentlemen, I of course will not and cannot explain here a long financial theory to you. But I must make you cast a fleeting glance at how easy, yes, how ridiculously easy it would be to obtain these hundred million without the poor peasant . . . needing to hand over one pfennig out of his pocket for this purpose. I raise the question: "On what do the banks depend which issue bank notes? On what," I say, "depends the profitability of such an enterprise?" On nothing other than the following:
>
> When a bank, for example, puts a hundred million in its vaults, it can now issue 400 million in bank notes, and this depends simply on the fact established by experience that never will more than a fourth of the bank note holders appear at the same time to exchange their notes for cash. On this simple axiom, on this fact established by experience, all banks throughout Europe which issue bank notes depend. This is a fact of society, a fact lying in the nature of all men. No one has made this fact, neither Peter nor Christopher nor William. It is an elementary law of society, just as there are elementary laws of nature.[10]

Such were the nostrums and panaceas with which many of the early defenders of labor hoped to cure the ills of mankind.

By the middle of the nineteenth century, most of the basic ideas of socialism—the class struggle, the labor theory of value, the concept of surplus value, the concentration of capital, the progressive impoverishment of the proletariat, and the economic interpretation of history —had already been formulated or at least foreshadowed by various working-class organizations and by the utopian school. On this hodgepodge of visions, hypotheses, and cure-alls, Marx imposed a discipline that transformed their humanitarian nebulousness into a coherent system of thought. The application of a rigorous dialectic to the amorphous speculations of the pioneers of socialism is his most important contribution to the labor movement.

The emancipation of the proletariat from capitalism, he taught, did

10. Ferdinand Lassalle, *Gesammelte Reden und Schriften*, ed. Eduard Bernstein, 12 vols. (Berlin, 1919–20), 3:47, 69–70, 88, 252–53.

not depend on exhortation and preachment. It would come because of its logical inevitability, because the laws of history made no other outcome of the class struggle possible. Its advent was not contingent on human volition or individual action. Man could influence but could not determine the elemental process of transition from one form of economy and society to another. Through tricks and stratagems, the capitalists might cling to power a little longer; through courage and determination, the workers might achieve their liberation a little sooner. But whatever they did, the juggernaut of the dialectic would move on relentlessly toward its predestined goal. "No social order ever disappears until all the productive powers for which there is room within it have been developed, and new, higher relations of production never appear until the material conditions for their existence have matured in the womb of the old society," declares the preface to the *Critique of Political Economy.* "Therefore mankind always takes up only such problems as it can solve, for if we look at the matter more closely, we shall always find that the problem itself arises only when the material conditions for its solution are already present or are at least in the process of formation." The fact that the labor question has emerged in modern society is itself proof that the world has the means to solve it.[11]

Marx differed from the utopian socialists in still another important respect, namely, the method to be employed for the overthrow of capitalism. They had generally believed that education and example could shape society, that cooperative workshops and communities could change a private into a public system of ownership. They envisioned the peaceful establishment of a collective economy through the piecemeal dismantlement of the existing structure of property. A few of them, Philippe Buonarotti and August Blanqui, for example, did advocate the use of force, but for them it was essentially an expression of the hatred felt by the oppressed for the oppressor. To Marx, on the other hand, force was the impersonal instrument of change in society, of the dialectical process in history.

As early as 1847, he had written in the *Poverty of Philosophy* that only in an order of things where there are no classes and no class antagonism will social evolutions cease to be political revolutions. Until then, the last word of social science on the eve of any general reconstruction of society will always be "struggle or death; bloody war or extinction." In the *Communist Manifesto* the following year, he spoke of a "covert civil war" that goes on within existing society until "it breaks out into open revolution, and through the violent overthrow of the bourgeoisie, the proletariat establishes its domination." The ultimate goal, he declared,

11. Karl Marx and Friedrich Engels, *Werke,* 39 vols. (Berlin, 1960–69), 13:9.

could only be attained through the forcible destruction of all existing social conditions. "Let the ruling classes tremble before a communist revolution." In the first volume of *Capital*, which appeared in 1867, Marx still maintained that "force is the midwife of every old society pregnant with a new one. It is itself an economic power." And in 1878 Engels, reflecting Marx's views as well as his own, asserted in the *Anti-Dühring* that violence is "the tool with which the social movement forces its way through, shattering inert, withered political forms."

Yet it is also clear that the emphasis on force gradually diminished in the writings of Marx and Engels as they began to perceive the possibility of achieving socialism by political means. The concept of revolution never disappeared from their thought or rhetoric, but it became less central to their strategy. As early as 1852, Marx had written in an article in the *New York Daily Tribune* that universal suffrage meant political power for the British working class since the proletariat formed the great majority of the population. Twenty years later, in a speech reporting on the congress of the First International at The Hague, he was more explicit: "We know that the institutions, customs, and traditions of the various countries must be considered, and we do not deny that there are countries like America, England, and, if [Dutch] institutions were better known to me, I would perhaps also add Holland, where the workers can reach their goal in a peaceful way."

After Marx's death, as the political system of Europe became progressively more democratic, Engels also began to acknowledge that the road to socialism did not always have to be violent. In his commentary in 1891 on the Erfurt program of the German Social Democratic party, he argued that an old social order might be transformed peacefully into a new one in those countries where the popular representation had concentrated all power in its hands, where "we can do constitutionally what we want to, as soon as we have a majority of the people behind us," that is, "in democratic republics like France and America, or in monarchies like in England." Shortly before his death in 1895, he came out with his clearest statement in support of a socialist strategy of education rather than violence. He still repeated the familiar shibboleths of his youth, asserting that "the right to revolution is indeed generally the only *real* 'historic right.'" But more significant was his advice not to exercise it. "The time for surprise attacks, for revolutions carried out by small conscious minorities at the head of unconscious masses is over," he wrote. "Where a complete transformation of the social structure is at stake, the masses themselves must be involved, they themselves must first understand what is at stake, what it is they should be fighting for. The history of the last fifty years has taught us that. But for the masses to understand what has to be done takes long, persevering work, and it is precisely in this work that we are now engaged." The caution of the grand old man stood in stark contrast to the impetuosity of the young firebrand half a century earlier.[12]

The means by which capitalism was to be overthrown thus remained ambiguous in the teachings of socialism. They oscillated between force and education, between revolution and reform. On the whole, the emphasis shifted slowly toward a strategy employing parliamentary methods. As the labor movement gained in size and strength, the equivocal position of Marxism on this point encouraged militancy in language but moderation in deed. Although doubts remained regarding the means to be used for the emancipation of the working class, there was at least agreement that only in a socialist society would the full development of mankind become possible. First, however, there had to be a period of transition, a season in purgatory. Here lie the more arcane realms of socialist theory. The working class, having finally gained control of the state by force or persuasion, must now use its power to destroy the last remnants of capitalism. For the enemy is stubborn; he will not yield easily to the victors; he will go on plotting and intriguing. Not only that, but the yoke of oppression that the proletariat had to endure has left its mark on social attitudes and institutions. Therefore, even after the overthrow of the old order, force will have to be used for a time to extirpate its last vestiges. "Between capitalist and communist society lies the period of revolutionary transformation from the one into the other," writes Marx in the *Critique of the Gotha Program.* "Corresponding to it there is also a period of political transition in which the state can be nothing other than *the revolutionary dictatorship of the proletariat.*"

And then? Marx and Engels begin to grope for words to describe what life will be like after the final triumph of socialism. There is something pentecostal, something chiliastic, about the way they depict the ultimate destiny of mankind. Like Dante, they are at their best in portraying the inferno. Their account of paradise, on the other hand, is all luminous radiance and ineffable blessedness. "The intervention of state power in social relations becomes superfluous in one area after another, and then ceases on its own," declares the *Anti-Dühring.* "The government of persons is replaced by the administration of things and the direction of the processes of production. The state is not 'abolished,' *it withers away.*" This is the most recondite of the concepts in the Marxian canon, the hardest to grasp, the trickiest to interpret.

Yet the vagueness of socialism regarding the remote future was a theoretical rather than practical weakness. Its appeal to the working class lay in the promise to end economic exploitation by collective action. What it

12. Ibid., 4:182, 473, 493; 8:344; 18:160; 20:171; 22:234, 523–24; 23:779.

taught about the hereafter was less important than what it had to say
about the here and now. Beneath its dialectical armor, Marxism was an
indignant protest against human suffering, an outburst of rage at the
disparity between what society is and what it ought to be. The French
sociologist Émile Durkheim recognized its emotional undercurrent. "It is
passion which has been the inspiration of all these systems," he wrote.
"What has given birth to them and what constitutes their strength is
thirst for a more perfect justice, is pity for the wretchedness of the working class, is a vague feeling of uneasiness which torments contemporary
societies. . . . Socialism is not a science, a sociology in miniature. It is
a cry of pain, and sometimes of anger, uttered by men who feel most
keenly our collective malaise." Here is the psychological wellspring of the
Marxian tradition.[13]

There was another tradition, however, that sought to achieve the same
objective by a different method. Socialism appealed primarily to those
workers in whom the experience of factory discipline had bred an acceptance of rational but impersonal organization. To them, the homogeneity
of the labor force resulting from the industrial revolution was a weapon
to be used in the struggle against exploitation. But there were also workers who rejected the faceless anonymity of large-scale social movements
in which the individual was submerged beneath the mass. Skilled artisans
threatened with economic extinction as a result of mechanized production or mill hands recently recruited from the tightly knit village community were often reluctant to become part of the gray proletarian army
with which Marx hoped to defeat the existing system. They sought not to
use the institutions created by capitalism for the overthrow of capitalism
but to destroy those institutions themselves as inherently evil. Their aim
was a return to a simpler but richer preindustrial way of life, where there
had been less material advantage and greater emotional satisfaction. They
were most numerous in countries where industrialization had not yet
eroded the diversified structure of small-town life, in Italy, Spain, and
Russia, for example, or in parts of Switzerland and France. Here anarchism became an important rival of socialism.

The most important theoretical difference between the two lay in their
attitude toward government. Both agreed that eventually all oppressive
authority must vanish so that men might live in freedom and justice. But
the socialists maintained that the state could be destroyed only through
the state, that is, before political power withers away, it has to be used
for the extirpation of capitalism. To the anarchists, on the other hand,
the only outcome of an attempt to employ coercive means to achieve

13. Ibid., 19:28, 20:262; Émile Durkheim, *Le socialisme: Sa définition, ses débuts, la
doctrine saint-simonienne*, ed. Marcel Mauss (Paris, 1928), p. 6.

emancipatory ends would be that the means would themselves become the ends. That was the assumption behind the attack on government in any form launched by Pierre-Joseph Proudhon, the most talented of Marx's radical opponents. In his *General Idea of Revolution in the Nineteenth Century*, he delivers a blistering assault:

> To be GOVERNED is to be—in every deed, in every transaction, in every movement—noted, registered, recorded, docketed, stamped, measured, marked, assessed, patented, licensed, authorized, recommended, admonished, hindered, reformed, rebuked, corrected. It is to be—under the pretext of public benefit and in the name of the general interest—subject to taxation, drilled, fleeced, exploited, monopolized, embezzled, squeezed, hoaxed, robbed. Then—at the least resistance, at the first word of complaint—it is to be repressed, fined, vilified, annoyed, encircled, abused, beaten, disarmed, garrotted, imprisoned, shot, machine-gunned, judged, condemned, deported, sacrificed, sold, betrayed, and on top of everything, mocked, ridiculed, insulted, dishonored. That is government, that is its justice, that is its morality![14]

It makes little difference whether a state is an autocratic empire like Russia or a democratic republic like Switzerland. All governments are equally corrupted by the constraining power they use to repress the individual in the name of society. They are distinguishable only by the extent to which they attempt to disguise their despotism. In *The Bears of Bern and the Bear of St. Petersburg*, Michael Bakunin maintains that the instincts of those who make or execute laws are diametrically opposed to the instincts of those who have to obey them. The former, however democratic their intentions, regard the rest of society in the way a guardian regards his ward. But there can be no equality between guardian and ward. "Whoever speaks of political power speaks of domination." Where domination exists, there must necessarily be a group that is dominated. Those who are dominated naturally hate those who dominate them, and those who dominate must necessarily repress those subject to their domination. "Such is the eternal history of political power, ever since that power was established in the world." According to Bakunin, it follows that any system of authority, whatever its political philosophy, is of necessity tyrannical. "If tomorrow we established a government and a legislative council, a parliament, composed exclusively of workers, those workers, who today are firm democratic socialists, would the day after tomorrow become resolute aristocrats, bold or timid worshippers of the

14. *Oeuvres complètes de P.-J. Proudhon*, new ed., 9 vols. (Paris, 1923–59), 3:344.

principle of authority, oppressors and exploiters." The evil influence of power will corrupt any man and any institution.[15]

There are clear antidemocratic implications in the position that the collective political will cannot be trusted to defend the collective social interest. They lie close to the surface of much of the radical thought of the nineteenth century, but nowhere are they more apparent than in anarchism. The latter rests squarely on the assumption that the entire mechanism of democratic politics—free speech, manhood suffrage, secret ballot, responsible government—is only a clever device to create the illusion among the masses that they can achieve the transformation of society peacefully, when in fact they are simply being distracted from the essential task of revolution. Proudhon declares openly that "I do not believe in the slightest, and for good reason, in that divinatory intuition of the multitude which enables it to discern at first glance the merit and the honor of candidates. Examples abound of persons elected by acclamation who, on the platform where they were presenting themselves to the gaze of the elated people, were already preparing the plot for their treachery. The people in their election meetings scarcely encounter one honest man for every ten rascals." And it is to these people, he goes on, "ignorant about everything which concerns them," that we talk of "sovereignty, legislation, government!" In order to "entertain their minds and divert them from the revolution, we speak to them of politics and fraternity!"

Bakunin shares the conviction that democracy is a fraud. How naive to think that once legislative and executive power emanate directly from universal suffrage, they become a pure expression of the will of the people leading to liberty and prosperity. How blind. "All the falsehood of the representative system rests on the fiction that a government and a legislature arising out of popular elections are absolutely bound or are even able to represent the real will of the people." Even those who are the most militant democrats or the most fiery rebels while they are part of the governed become cautious conservatives as soon as they climb to power. Yet it would be a mistake to attribute their shift of allegiance simply to treachery. Its main cause is the change in perspective and position. Bakunin's conclusion is that *we must completely abolish, in principle as well as in fact, everything which is called political power. For as long as political power exists, there will be those who dominate and those who are dominated, masters and slaves, exploiters and exploited.*" It is not the form but the essence of authority that makes it despotic.[16]

Since capitalism can never be overthrown by parliamentary methods, force remains the only weapon for the liberation of society. On this point

15. Michel Bakounine, *Oeuvres*, 6 vols. (Paris, 1907–13), 2:38–39.
16. *Oeuvres de Proudhon*, new ed., 3:210, 248; Bakounine, *Oeuvres*, 2:37, 39.

the anarchists are not far from theoretical agreement with the socialists. But for the latter violence is at best a stern historical necessity, whereas for the former it is a means of purification, emancipating and regenerating mankind. Sometimes it almost ceases to be an instrument and becomes the object, desirable for its own sake. Bakunin in particular is a fiery prophet of destruction as the inescapable precondition of a just society. "Let us therefore put our trust in the eternal spirit which destroys and annihilates only because it is the unfathomable and eternally creative source of all life," he wrote in 1842. "The urge to destroy is at the same time a creative urge." During the political upheaval at the end of the decade, he repeated the call for violence: "The revolution . . . is the power, it is the right, it is the truth, it is the salvation of the present time, it is the only practice which leads to what is good and successful. There is no prudence, no wisdom, no policy outside it. It is the only prudence, wisdom, policy, and everything which leads to the goal. . . . Trust the revolution!" A generation later, Peter Kropotkin, another Russian anarchist in exile, prophesied the coming of a regenerating violence that would uproot the corrupt world of capitalism. "Those who desire the triumph of justice," he wrote in the *Words of a Rebel*, "understand the need for a revolutionary storm which will sweep away all this rottenness, vivify with its breath the hearts which are numb, and bring to humanity the devotion, self-denial, and heroism without which a society becomes debased, degraded, decayed." At times the anarchists sounded as if they were more inspired by the prospect of destroying the old order than by that of creating a new one.[17]

They differed from the socialists not only in their uncompromising insistence on violence but also in the way violence was to be employed in the revolutionary process. They believed that the broad masses had been rendered incapable by their social experience of waging a hard, unremitting struggle against their oppressors. How could the man in the street—impoverished, ignorant, brutalized, and cowed—see through the stratagems of those in power? The anarchists fell back on an earlier, conspiratorial, elitist concept of revolution, the concept of the Carbonari in Italy or the Decembrists in Russia. To be sure, the masses must at some point become involved in the war against the established order, but victory depends ultimately on a small group of dedicated soldiers whose courage and intelligence would prove to be the decisive factor. Bakunin concedes that the army of the revolution can only be the

17. Michael Bakunin [Jules Elysard], "Die Reaction in Deutschland," *Deutsche Jahrbücher für Wissenschaft und Kunst* 5 (1842): 1002; Michael Bakunin, *Aufruf an die Slaven* (Köthen, 1848), pp. 27–28; Pierre Kropotkine, *Paroles d'un révolté* (Paris, 1885), p. 280.

people themselves. But there is also the need for "a kind of revolutionary general staff," made up of dedicated, energetic, and intelligent men without ambition or vanity, who are above all sincere friends of the people and who have the ability to serve as intermediaries between the revolutionary idea and the popular instincts. The number of such men does not have to be very large. "For the international organization in all of Europe a hundred firmly and resolutely united revolutionaries are enough. Two to three hundred revolutionaries will be enough for the organization of the largest country." Thirty years after Bakunin's death, his Italian disciple, Errico Malatesta, made the same point: "It is certain that in the present state of society, where the great majority of men, crushed by poverty and stupefied by superstition, lie in abasement, human destiny depends on the action of a relatively inconsiderable number of individuals." To most anarchists, the key to a successful revolution was not the organized activity of the masses but the heroic deed of a man or a group.[18]

Their strategy for waging the class struggle may have been less disciplined than that of the socialists, but their vision of life after the overthrow of capitalism was more concrete and vivid. The new society would be based on natural, spontaneous associations shaped by human need, not by government coercion. As Proudhon explained in his *Political Contradictions*, every time men, accompanied by their wives and children, assemble in one place, consolidate their dwellings and fields, develop diverse industries, establish neighborly relations with one another, and, whether they like it or not, impose on themselves a state of solidarity, they form a natural group that soon becomes a city or a political organism, affirming its identity in its unity, its independence, its life, and its autonomy. Such free communities would form the foundation on which the society of the future would be built.

Once the old order was overthrown, the rest would fall into place very easily. In the *Conquest of Bread*, there is a charming artlessness about the way Kropotkin describes what will happen on the day after the downfall of capitalism:

> Without waiting for anyone's leave, those citizens will probably
> go and find their comrades who are living in slums, and will say to
> them quite simply: "This time, comrades, it is really the revolution.
> Come this evening to such and such a place. The entire neighbor-
> hood will be there; we are going to redistribute apartments. If you

18. *L'alliance de la démocratie socialiste et l'association internationale des travailleurs: Rapport et documents publiés par ordre du congrès international de La Haye* (London and Hamburg, 1873), p. 132; Errico Malatesta, *L'anarchie* (Paris, 1907), p. 56.

are not satisfied with your hovel, you can choose one of the five-room apartments which are available. And once you have moved in, that will be the end of it. The people in arms will talk to anyone who may want to come and evict you from it."[19]

In the anarchist eschatology, as in the Christian, the meek eventually inherit the earth.

The rise of various schools of radical thought in Europe during the nineteenth century was evidence that the working class had found an ideology expressing its needs. After a generation or two of painful readjustment from the traditions of village life to the complexities of the industrial experience, the urban masses began to see themselves as participants in a fundamental historical process that would ultimately fulfill their hopes. The formation of socialist parties was a sign of this growing political consciousness of the proletariat. Ferdinand Lassalle led the way in 1863 with the founding of the General German Workingmen's Association, which united in 1875 with its younger Marxian rival, the Social Democratic Workingmen's party. In 1879 Pablo Iglesias established the Socialist Workingmen's party of Spain; Jules Guesde's Workingmen's party emerged in France in 1882; and Henry Mayers Hyndman's Democratic Federation adopted a socialist program in 1883, becoming the Social Democratic Federation a year later.

Then came a flood of party formations, reconciliations, splits, and reunions. The Norwegian socialists established a national organization in 1887, the Austrians and the Swiss in 1888, and the Swedes in 1889. The Labor party of Italy, founded in 1885 with both socialist and anarchist members, was dissolved a year later by the government, but a successor Labor party reemerged in 1892 with a Marxian program. The Socialist party of Holland was organized in 1878 by Ferdinand Domela Nieuwenhuis; after it fell apart in the course of a struggle over anarchism, a new Social Democratic League committed to orthodox socialist doctrine was established in 1889. Although the Belgian Labor party formed in 1885 under the influence of César de Paepe did not embrace Marxism in every detail, it was close enough to be acceptable to the other socialist parties. In the course of the next two decades, working-class political activity began in the backward countries of Eastern Europe. Socialist parties came into existence in Poland and Finland in 1892. As early as 1883, a handful of Russian exiles in Switzerland, among them G. V. Plekhanov and P. B. Axelrod, formed the Emancipation of Labor Group, but in Russia itself socialism became an organized force only after the

19. *Oeuvres de Proudhon*, new ed., 17:237; Pierre Kropotkine, *La conquête du pain* (Paris, 1892), p. 105.

founding of the Social Democratic party in 1898. By the opening of the twentieth century, the labor movement was spreading through the Balkan peninsula, reaching Croatia and Slavonia in 1894, Slovenia in 1896, Dalmatia in 1902, Serbia in 1903, and Bosnia, Herzegovina, Rumania, and Greece in 1909. No city on the Continent was too remote or too provincial to have its socialist club and its socialist newsletter.[20]

The increase in the size of the socialist parties was as striking as the increase in their number. The following that they attracted cannot always be determined by counting the ballots on election day or the members paying dues because many governments tried to control radicalism by restrictions on voting and organizing. But there is enough information on the labor movement in those countries of Western and Central Europe where political activity was relatively free to conclude that it had become a powerful force by the time of the First World War. The German Social Democratic party was a model for the rest of the world, with 534,000 members in 1907, 837,000 in 1911, and 1,086,000 in 1914. Its strength at the polls was even more impressive, rising from 1.5 million votes in 1890 to over 2 million in 1898 and 4 million in 1912. The two French socialist parties, the Parti socialiste de France and the Parti socialiste français, got about 400,000 votes each in 1902, but in 1914, after joining forces, they received almost 1.4 million. The Labor party in Great Britain, with 376,000 members around the time of its founding in 1900, had 1,895,000 about a decade later in 1912. And in Belgium the socialists gained 350,000 votes as early as the election of 1894, roughly a fourth of the total.

As the franchise spread, the labor movement acquired ever greater representation in the parliaments of Europe. In Austria the law of 1907 establishing equal manhood suffrage enabled the socialists to increase the number of mandates from 10 to 87. In Italy the candidates of the far left received only 200,000 ballots in 1900. However, the electoral reform of 1912, which almost tripled the number of eligible voters, made it possible for the orthodox socialists to increase their seats in parliament from 25 to 52; the reformist socialists got 18 and the independents, leaning mainly toward syndicalism, 7 or 8. Even in Russia, after the Revolution of 1905, political groups representing the urban and rural working class—social democrats, social revolutionaries, laborites, and populists—managed to win 40 percent of the seats in the first Duma. At the outbreak of hostilities in 1914, parties speaking in behalf of the labor movement controlled 28 percent of the parliamentary mandates in Germany, 25 in Norway,

20. G. D. H. Cole, *A History of Socialist Thought*, 5 vols. (London and New York, 1956–65), 2:95, 207, 244, 425–26; 3:421; Dimitrije Djordjević, *Revolutions nationales des peuples balkaniques*, 1804–1914 (Belgrade, 1965), pp. 223–24.

20 in Belgium, 17 in France, 10 in Italy, 9 in the Low Countries, and 6 in England.[21]

The growth of trade unions was a more sensitive measure of the class consciousness of the masses than the growth of socialist parties. Not only did the workers of Europe generally receive the right to organize before they received the right to vote, but social and psychological pressures against their participation in a labor association were not as great as those against their participation in a political party. For one thing, even the most rugged individualist among employers agreed that it was better for a mill hand to seek higher wages and shorter hours than the overthrow of capitalism. For another, the workers themselves were more attracted to organizations dealing with bread-and-butter issues than to those promising the salvation of mankind. The most important restrictions on the formation or activity of labor unions were repealed in 1866 in Belgium, 1869 in Germany, 1870 in Austria, 1871 and 1875 in England, 1872 in the Netherlands, 1884 in France, 1905 in Finland and Poland, and 1906 in Russia. At first the growth of organized labor was steady but unspectacular. In Great Britain the number of workers represented at the meetings of Trades Union Congress fluctuated from 455,000 in 1876 to 381,000 in 1880 and 500,000 in 1885 before climbing sharply to 1,593,000 in 1890 and, according to the official statistics that became available around that time, about 2 million in 1900. In Germany union membership rose from 300,000 in 1886 to 850,000 in 1900, and in France it rose from 140,000 in 1890 to 589,000 in 1901. Then, after the opening of the twentieth century, came a decade of extraordinary growth so that by 1912 Germany had 3,754,000 organized workers, Great Britain 3,281,000, France 1,027,000, Italy 972,000, Austria 693,000, Belgium 231,835, the Netherlands 189,000, Denmark 139,000, Switzerland 131,000, Sweden 122,000, Hungary 112,000, and Spain 100,000. For Europe as a whole, the number of trade unionists on the eve of the First World War was in the neighborhood of 11 million.[22]

21. Douglas A. Chalmers, *The Social Democratic Party of Germany: From Working-Class Movement to Modern Political Party* (New Haven and London, 1964), p. 11; Carlton J. H. Hayes, *A Generation of Materialism, 1871–1900* (New York and London), p. 187; Robert Schnerb, *Le XIXᵉ siècle: L'apogée de l'expansion européenne (1815–1914)*, 4th ed. (Paris, 1965), p. 529; Cole, *History of Socialist Thought*, 3:351, 540, 725–26; James Joll, *The Second International, 1889–1914* (London, 1968), p. 149; G. D. H. Cole, *British Working Class Politics, 1832–1914* (London, 1941), p. 306; Maurice Crouzet, *L'époque contemporaine: A la recherche d'une civilisation nouvelle*, 4th ed. (Paris, 1966), p. 14.

22. Herbert Heaton, *Economic History of Europe* (New York and London, 1936), p. 717; Robert C. Binkley, *Realism and Nationalism, 1852–1871* (New York and London, 1935), p. 115; Jürgen Kuczynski, *Die Geschichte der Lage der Arbeiter unter dem Kapitalismus*, 38 vols. (Berlin, 1960–71), 24:230–31; F. H. Hinsley, "Introduction," in *The New Cambridge Modern History*, 12 vols. (Cambridge, 1960–70), 11:14–15; J. H.

This figure, far surpassing the combined membership of the socialist parties, approached the total of socialist votes cast on election day. To be sure, even in the economically most advanced countries, the proportion of organized workers in the industrial labor force was substantially less than half. Although most unions adopted a radical political ideology, usually a form of socialism but sometimes anarchism or syndicalism, there was a significant minority seeking nothing more for its members than an improved economic position within the existing system. For example, out of a total labor force of more than 7 million in France, only 1 million were organized; of these, only about six hundred thousand belonged to the militant Confédération générale du travail. Yet the proportion of unionized workers was rising steadily, and their readiness to employ collective force was becoming more apparent. An increase in the frequency and intensity of strike activity attested to the growing assertiveness of labor. Usually it occurred in the struggle for a higher standard of living, but at times it was also employed as a political weapon for the broadening of the franchise or the granting of a constitution, as in Belgium in 1893, Sweden in 1902, Russia in 1905, and Austria in 1907. Labor unrest began to spread with special rapidity after the opening of the twentieth century so that by 1912 the number of strikers in Great Britain was 793 percent greater than in 1899, in Germany 300, in Belgium 78, and in France 34. There were timid souls among the propertied classes who half expected to wake up one morning amid riots, barricades, and bloody street battles.[23]

Yet by a curious paradox, the growing strength of the labor movement was also a growing weakness. Its militancy in the early days had been a reflection of its sense of desperation. Surrounded by what appeared to be insurmountable obstacles, it had been forced to fall back on apocalyptic visions of class struggle and proletarian dictatorship. As it gained power, however, it began to see other paths to victory, less violent, less painful. Indeed, the ultimate goal of a classless society became gradually obscured by the immediate purpose of reducing class distinctions and injustices. In the process of preparing the masses for revolution by raising their standard of living, the labor movement taught them to value the means more than the ends. Why squander energies on some future Armageddon when they could be used here and now to gain higher wages, shorter hours,

Clapham, *The Economic Development of France and Germany, 1815–1914*, 4th ed. (Cambridge, 1966), p. 273; Werner Sombart, *Der moderne Kapitalismus: Historisch-systematische Darstellung des gesamteuropäischen Wirtschaftslebens von seinen Anfängen bis zur Gegenwart*, 2d ed., 3 vols. (Munich and Leipzig, 1924–28), 3:690.

23. Joll, *Second International*, p. 131; Francis W. Coker, *Recent Political Thought* (New York and London, 1934), pp. 237–38; Peter N. Stearns, *Lives of Labor: Work in a Maturing Industrial Society* (New York, 1975), p. 314.

warmer clothing, better housing? The same expansion of economic opportunity making possible the peaceful coexistence of aristocracy and bourgeoisie was also making possible the peaceful coexistence of bourgeoisie and proletariat. The most striking evidence of this tendency was the rise of heterodox groups within socialism—revisionists, possibilists, independents, laborites, and Fabians—that advocated the use of piecemeal reform for the achievement of social justice. Even the orthodox majority that condemned the gradualist heresies was, without realizing it, increasingly under their influence. The bigger the party, the greater its influence, and the larger its parliamentary representation, the less likely it was to risk all its gains on a throw of the revolutionary dice.

The comfortable underlying assumptions of the reformist wing of socialism were expressed with style by Sidney Webb in the *Fabian Essays in Socialism*:

> Slice after slice has gradually been cut from the profits of capital, and therefore from its selling value, by socially beneficial restrictions on its user's liberty to do as he liked with it. Slice after slice has been cut off the incomes from rent and interest by the gradual shifting of taxation from consumers to persons enjoying incomes above the average. . . . Almost every conceivable trade is, somewhere or other, carried on by parish, municipality, or the National Government itself without the intervention of any middleman or capitalist. . . . The State in most of the larger industrial operations prescribes the age of the worker, the hours of work, the amount of air, light, cubic space, heat, lavatory accommodations, holidays, and mealtimes; where, when, and how wages shall be paid; how machinery, staircases, lift holes, mines, and quarries are to be fenced and guarded; how and when the plant shall be cleaned, repaired, and worked. Even the kind of package in which some articles shall be sold is duly prescribed, so that the individual capitalist shall take no advantage of his position. On every side he is being registered, inspected, controlled, and eventually superseded by the community. . . . The economic history of the century is an almost continuous record of the progress of Socialism.[24]

Most socialist parties officially rejected the revisionist position, to be sure. At its congress in Amsterdam in 1904, the Second International condemned reformism by a vote of 25 to 5, with 12 abstentions. But it was significant that those who opposed the motion or abstained from voting came largely from countries with liberal political institutions. Aus-

24. Sidney Webb, "The Basis of Socialism: Historic," in *Fabian Essays in Socialism*, ed. G. Bernard Shaw (London, 1889), pp. 31, 47, 49.

tralia cast 2 votes against, France 1, Norway 1, and Great Britain 1; the abstentions included the Belgians, Swiss, Swedes, Danes, and Argentines. On the other hand, the strongest support for orthodoxy came from countries where, with the possible exception of Italy, the socialists were least likely to achieve power by parliamentary methods. The largest socialist party in Europe, the German Social Democrats, had already denounced revisionism a year earlier at the national congress in Dresden. Yet its bold rhetoric about "our twice-tested and victorious tactics based on the class-struggle" only served to disguise a Fabian policy. The small band of desperate revolutionaries of thirty years before had become a mass organization directed by a huge bureaucratic apparatus, plump and satisfied, which was almost as frightened by the thought of violence as the bourgeois politicians. Its drift toward reformism was apparent not only in avowed revisionists like Eduard Bernstein but even in old established leaders like Wilhelm Liebknecht who boasted of their orthodoxy. "They have learnt the art of electioneering thoroughly, and have turned their backs on the barricade and taken to the ballot box," wrote George Bernard Shaw about the German socialists. "Liebknecht still covers every compromise by a declaration that the Social-Democrats never compromise." This was the path that most socialist parties in Europe were following.[25]

The original uncompromising fervor of the labor movement could still be found here and there, especially where the political environment bred a sense of powerlessness among those seeking to change the established system. Their weakness, however, was not a result of their militancy; their militancy was a result of their weakness. In Russia, for example, Lenin, confronted by the oppressiveness of czarism, became a proponent of unremitting class warfare. But the revolution, he argued, could not be left to the spontaneous activity of the masses. In *What Is to Be Done?*, published in 1902, he fell back on the elitist, antidemocratic concept of insurrection implicit in Proudhon and Bakunin. He insisted that the history of all countries shows that the working class, relying on its own efforts, is able to develop only a "trade-union consciousness," that is, the conviction that it is necessary to form unions, fight the employers, and seek to force the government to adopt labor legislation. The struggle for fundamental change must therefore be directed by a nucleus of dedicated radicals. Only "a small, compact core of the most reliable, experienced, and hardened workers," with representatives in the principal districts connected to the organization of the revolutionaries by rules of strict secrecy, can perform the function of a trade union in a manner serving

25. Cole, *History of Socialist Thought*, 3:46, 48, 54; Joll, *Second International*, p. 104; G. Bernard Shaw, "Socialism at the International Congress," *Cosmopolis* 3 (1896):667.

the real interests of the labor movement. Conspiracy, in other words, is the chief weapon with which socialism must oppose autocracy.

As for the anarchists, unable to undermine the loyalty of the peasant masses to traditional values, unable to compete with the socialists for the allegiance of the industrial workers, they had to rely more and more on isolated deeds of heroic terrorism or on ecstatic visions of ultimate liberation. A few carried out sensational but pointless assassinations: that of President Sadi Carnot of France in 1894, Prime Minister Antonio Cánovas del Castillo of Spain in 1897, Empress Elisabeth of Austria in 1898, King Umberto I of Italy in 1900, and President William McKinley of the United States in 1901. Others drafted fanciful plans by which the working class could wage a relentless but successful struggle for a better social order. For example, the French syndicalist theoretician Georges Sorel maintained in his *Reflections on Violence* that since "strikes have engendered in the proletariat the noblest, deepest, and most moving sentiments which it possesses," there is "only one single force which can produce today that enthusiasm without whose effect no morality is possible at all, and that is the force resulting from propaganda in favor of the general strike." Once a general strike occurred, "something powerful, new, and unblemished will remain amid the total ruin of institutions and morals, namely, that which constitutes, properly speaking, the soul of the revolutionary proletariat. That will not be swept away in the general collapse of moral values." And even if it never occurred, at least its mystique would sustain the ardor of the masses. "When we take our place in this realm of myths, we are safe against all refutation." For many anarchists, the road to revolution thus ended in a cabalistic never-never land of symbols and incantations.[26]

And what about the workers themselves? Did the leadership thwart their militant zeal, as the left wing maintained, or did it merely reflect their growing moderation? The evidence suggests that the rising standard of living was making it possible for the established order to assimilate the lower classes by improving their position within the existing social structure. The radicalism of the industrial proletariat had always derived from material need more than from theoretical conviction. Julius Vahlteich, who had become active in the German labor movement during the 1860s, recalled long afterward that "our knowledge in the field of economics was small. We knew nothing about constant and variable capital, and we were not initiated in the profoundest mysteries of capital formation. But we knew very well that capital and the capitalists were our enemies, and we also knew that we could overcome them only through the develop-

26. V. I. Lenin, *Collected Works*, 45 vols. (Moscow, 1963–70), 5:375, 459; Georges Sorel, *Réflexions sur la violence* (Paris, 1908), pp. xxxvii, 95–96, 252–53.

ment of power, that is, through organization." In his autobiography, Will Thorne, member of the Social Democratic Federation, founder of the National Union of Gas Workers and General Laborers, and eventually Labor M.P., described conditions in England fifteen years later in almost exactly the same terms: "The system we lived under at that time, the poverty and hardships the workers had to endure—the hard work and long hours, and the tender age at which we were thrown into the industrial battle field—made us rebels. [But] the economic and industrial system of capitalism, in which production was for the purpose of profits, and not for use, was a mystery of which we knew nothing."

By the opening of the twentieth century, however, the improvement in the material condition of the lower classes had the effect of eroding their militancy. To most workers, contract negotiations with the employers began to seem more important than the overthrow of capitalism. A German metalworker expressed this growing proletarian practicality in his statement of what he hoped to get out of the struggle for social justice: "You know, I never read a social democratic book and rarely a newspaper. I used not to occupy myself with politics at all. But since I got married and have five eaters at home I have to do it. But I think my own thoughts. . . . We really do not want to become like the rich and refined people. There will always have to be rich and poor. We would not think of altering that. But we want a better and more just organization at the factory and in the state."

Despite the rise of political consciousness among the masses, European society on the eve of the First World War was generally moving not toward class conflict but toward class compromise and accommodation. An idealistic radical like William Morris found this very disturbing. He wondered in 1893 "whether in short the tremendous organization of civilized commercial society is not playing the cat and mouse game with us Socialists. Whether the Society of Inequality might not accept the quasi-socialist machinery above mentioned, and work it for the purpose of upholding that society in a somewhat shorn condition, maybe, but a safe one. That seems to me possible, and means . . . the workers better treated, better organized, helping to govern themselves, but with no more pretence to equality with the rich, nor any more hope for it than they have now." He had perceived the direction in which the labor movement of Europe was heading.[27]

27. Julius Vahlteich, "Das Leipziger Zentralkomitee und Ferdinand Lassalle," in *Die Gründung der deutschen Sozialdemokratie: Eine Festschrift der Leipziger Arbeiter zum 23. Mai 1903* (Leipzig, 1903), p. 20; Will Thorne, *My Life's Battles* (London, 1925), pp. 46–47; Stearns, *Lives of Labor*, p. 149; *The Collected Works of William Morris*, 24 vols. (London, New York, Bombay, and Calcutta, 1910–15), 23:267.

Part Three

THE STRUCTURE OF POLITICS

Le gouvernement quitte les mains de ceux
qui possèdent pour aller aux mains de
ceux qui ne possèdent pas, de ceux qui ont
un intérêt matériel à la conservation de la
société à ceux qui sont complètement dé-
sintéressés d'ordre, de stabilité, de conservation. . . . Peut-être, dans la grande loi du
changement des choses d'ici-bas, pour les
sociétés modernes, les ouvriers sont-ils ce
qu'ont été les Barbares pour les sociétés
anciennes, de convulsifs agents de dissolution et de destruction?

Edmond de Goncourt, Journal, 1871

9

CIVIC IDEOLOGIES AND

SOCIAL VALUES

A profound change occurred in Europe during the nineteenth century in the way people regarded the institutions of government. Traditionally they had been viewed as the temporal manifestation of a hierarchical principle of authority that was sacred in character. The royal will had to be obeyed for the same reason that the divine will had to be obeyed, because in the eternal scheme of things the submission of man to those above him was essential for the effective functioning of the social system as a whole. The prevailing theories of government—the divine right of kings or the timeless constraints of the social contract, for example—were exercises in moral philosophy rather than a popular legitimation of the power of crowned heads. There was something academic about them; they suggested a lecture platform, a classroom rather than a fundamental public debate. In the age of benevolent despotism, most people simply accepted the existing structure of authority as immutable. To challenge the prerogative of the monarch was to question the very foundation on which the community rested. Except in England, France, Switzerland, and the Low Countries, discussion of the basic problems of state and society rarely rose above the level of abstract theory. Royal power remained what it had always been, a system of coercion from which there was no appeal except through petition or prayer. It did not have to justify itself; it simply was.

The French Revolution had the effect of undermining not only the accepted institutions of government but also the beliefs on which they depended. Authority became desanctified and demythologized. It was shown that the royal prerogative, far from being hallowed, could be defied with impunity. Law and order had been maintained under a republic as strictly as under a monarchy; the national interest had been defended in the name of the people with even greater effectiveness than in the name of the crown. The thaumaturgical qualities of the monarchical principle evaporated during the fiery ordeal of twenty-five years of insurrection and war.

What came after the downfall of Napoleon was a system of authority resembling that in effect before 1789 but lacking the unquestioning popular acceptance based on belief in its sanctity. Under the Restoration, the political process had to assume rationality or at least the semblance of rationality in order to prevail in the marketplace of creeds. Rival civic ideologies began to emerge in public life that were designed to express the interests of economic groups and social classes in the form of timeless laws of government. The society of the nineteenth century, shaped by the experiences of industrialization and urbanization, could not accept the heavenly justification of royal authority that had appeared so persuasive in a preindustrial age. New political theories appeared, defining the needs of a particular time and place as the eternal imperatives of human progress. The men who formulated them did not always belong by birth or station to those elements of society whose interests they were defending. To give an obvious example, only a handful of the socialist theoreticians came from the working class. It is also clear that the ideological systematizers did not deliberately disguise the special interests they represented; as a rule, they believed in what they were preaching. But the social implications of their doctrines could be clearly recognized in the following that they attracted. The class composition of the support given to them is the best guide to their class predisposition.

The most important of the emerging ideologies in the first half of the nineteenth century was liberalism, which expressed the aspirations of the new middle class being created by the industrial revolution. Many of those whose political influence or social status was not in keeping with their material affluence or intellectual achievement found in it a justification for their view of state and society. As the rationalization of the economy shifted the distribution of wealth, liberalism gained strength in the political conflicts of Western and Central Europe. It succeeded in winning followers in all classes, but the bulk of its support came from less than 10 percent of the population; it came from the social strata between the landed aristocracy and the urban and rural proletariat. That was why its opponents charged it with being a stalking-horse by which the bourgeoisie hoped to exploit the rest of the community. Julius Fröbel, for example, a German publicist who had evolved from radical firebrand to cautious bureaucrat, declared in the 1860s that "liberalism, moreover, which currently plays a dominant role in the life of European peoples and states, is by no means to be understood as the system of popular freedom in general, but as a system in the special interest of quite specific elements of society which are assembled in the commercial and industrial middle class."[1]

The liberals, of course, denied that they were primarily interested in advancing the interests of men of property and education. They were defending the rights of every citizen, regardless of wealth or status. But they

---

1. Julius Fröbel, *Theorie der Politik, als Ergebniss einer erneuerten Prüfung demokratischer Lehrmeinungen*, 2 vols. (Vienna, 1861–64), 1:258.

also maintained that the general welfare could best be entrusted to the bourgeoisie, the class whose talent and achievement were a token of trustworthiness and responsibility. In Great Britain Henry Peter Brougham drew a distinction between the mob and the people. The former, ignorant and greedy, represented the worst instincts of the masses. The latter, on the other hand, included all those whose industriousness had created the material basis of a civilized community. "If there is a mob, there is the people also," he argued. "I speak now of the middle classes—of those hundreds of thousands of respectable persons—the most numerous and by far the most wealthy order in the community . . . who are also the genuine depositaries of sober, rational, intelligent, and honest English feeling."

According to the liberals, the bourgeoisie should play a dominant role in public affairs because its influence would be exercised in behalf of all men and all classes. Thomas Babington Macaulay maintained in 1829 that the "middling orders" were among the "natural representatives of the human race." In some things their interest might be opposed to that of their poorer contemporaries, but "it is identical with that of the innumerable generations which are to follow." In 1842 François Guizot made a similar point in a speech before the French legislature, arguing that the well-to-do bourgeois voter sought not only his own advantage but also the advantage of the man who had less property and income. "He does not exclude him; he represents him, he protects him, he covers him; he experiences and defends the same interests." If the middle class was not the nation, it was at least the spokesman for the nation. It was the tireless defender of its vital interests. In Germany in 1865, the journal of the liberal Nationalverein reminded its readers of the many benefits that the bourgeoisie had bestowed on the proletariat: "The highest degree of ignorance or dishonesty is really required to overlook the fact that the classes engaged in manual labor owe to the educated and well-to-do middle class, that is, to the liberal party, everything which they have gained with respect to civic justice and civic freedom since the days of serfdom and the most brutal police rule." The interest of the bourgeoisie was thus inseparable from the interest of the people; the growing influence of one was bound to promote the welfare of the other.[2]

The most important contribution of liberalism to political theory, how-

2. *Speeches of Henry Lord Brougham, upon Questions Relating to Public Rights, Duties, and Interests*, 4 vols. (Edinburgh, 1838), 2:600; [Thomas Babington Macaulay], "Mill's Essay on Government: Utilitarian Logic and Politics," *Edinburgh Review, or Critical Journal* 49 (1829):184; François Guizot, *Histoire parlementaire de France: Recueil complet des discours prononcés dans les chambres de 1819 à 1848*, 5 vols. (Paris, 1863–64), 3:556; "Die Fortschrittsparthei und der Socialismus," *Wochen-Blatt des Nationalvereins*, 6 April 1865, p. 6.

ever, lay not in its identification of the needs of the middle class with those of society but in its definition of a sphere of human activity immune to the authority of government. The traditional inseparability of the private from the public experience, the identification of personal and civic action, was challenged for the first time. An autonomous realm of thought and deed began to emerge, protected against royal authority and popular sovereignty alike. The most eloquent defender of this new concept of individualism was Benjamin Constant, the leading French liberal theoretician under the Restoration. Reacting against the claim of Napoleon to represent the will of the people, he declared: "There is, on the contrary, a part of human existence which remains of necessity individual and independent, and which is by right beyond all social authority. Sovereignty exists only to a limited and relative extent." The jurisdiction of the state stops at the point where the independence of individual existence begins. "Society cannot exceed its competence without being usurpative; the majority cannot do so without being factious." The approval of the people does not in any way justify acts in violation of inalienable private rights. Whenever any authority commits such acts—"regardless of whether it is an individual or a nation; it could be the entire nation minus the individual whom it oppresses"—it is to that extent acting illegally.

The liberals thus posited two realms of human experience, public and private, personal and collective, each judged by different standards, each governed by different principles. Individual rights were not earned or acquired; they were the inheritance of every man. Their scope was defined by Guizot under two headings: first, "the right not to be subjected to any injustice whatever on the part of anyone without being protected against it by public authority," and second, "the right to dispose of our individual existence according to our will and interest, in so far as it does no harm to the individual existence of others." These rights are "personal, universal, and equal for all." They are the possession of everyone because they derive from "equality in the civil order and in the moral order." They are "inherent in humanity, and no human being can be deprived of them without iniquity and disorder." Their recognition by the state redounds to the "honor of modern civilization." Armed with them, each man can pursue his interests secure against the arbitrary intervention of government or society. The experience of the French Revolution and the Napoleonic era had taught the liberals that tyranny could be exercised by the crowd as well as the crown. Their task therefore became to find a juste-milieu between autocracy and anarchy, between royal despotism and mob rule. They opposed the danger of government oppression by creating a sphere of personal freedom beyond the jurisdiction of political authority. This freedom would act as a counterweight to the power of government, whether government was exercised through an absolute monarchy or a popular democracy.[3]

Yet the same logic that led the liberals to a system of private rights protecting the individual against oppression by the state also led them to a realm of public rights that could be exercised only by an elite of intelligence and wealth. They believed that the best form of government was a constitutional monarchy, in which the power of the king was limited by the authority of parliament. The system of political representation, however, must never be allowed to become an instrument of mob rule. How could the man in the street—impoverished, exhausted, often illiterate—be expected to display the discernment and independence required of the intelligent voter? Was he not likely rather to fall prey to any demagogue who promised him the moon? That was why the liberal Prussian businessman and politician David Hansemann wrote in 1830 that although state authority should indeed rest on majority rule, "by majority we are never to understand one determined by counting heads, but rather the true strength of the nation, which, while it is also to have no interest other than that of the numerical majority, yet differs essentially from it, since by its better education, greater insight, and its property it has a larger stake in the maintenance of a stable, vigorous, and good government." Thirty years later, Herbert Spencer was also drawn by his commitment to individual rights to favor the restriction of political rights. "Men who are ready to render up their private liberties to the despotic rulers of trades-unions," he wrote on the subject of parliamentary reform, "seem scarcely independent enough rightly to exercise political liberties. Those who so ill understand the nature of freedom, as to think that any man or body of men has a right to prevent employer and employed from making any contract they please, would almost appear to be incapacitated for the guardianship of their own claims and those of their fellow citizens." In his resolve to protect freedom in one sphere of human action, he was prepared to curtail it in another.

It becomes clear that the liberals sought not to destroy the elite structure of politics but to make it more accessible to men of intelligence and means. They accepted the traditional belief that the masses, condemned by their position in the community to ceaseless toil, were incapable of exercising civic rights responsibly. Their wild passions would always drive them to utopian schemes of social equality, leading in the final outcome to revolution, chaos, and dictatorship. The state needed an

3. Benjamin de Constant, *Collection complète des ouvrages publiés sur le gouvernement représentatif et la constitution actuelle de la France, formant une espèce de cours de politique constitutionelle*, 4 vols. (Paris and Rouen, 1818–20), 1:178; Guizot, *Histoire parlementaire*, 3:307–8.

aristocracy made up of people who had the wealth, education, and leisure to consider public issues objectively and dispassionately. This aristocracy, however, must not become a closed caste based on hereditary status. It must remain open to ambition and talent, assimilating those who could prove their ability by the possession of property. Each man, regardless of birth or background, should be tested in the crucible of economic competition. Let the noble wastrel sink into the ranks of the proletariat, the position to which his improvidence had condemned him, and let the unpolished but gifted commoner rise by his efforts to the very top. Out of the relentless strife of private interests would emerge a new patriciate whose eminence reflected its achievement. Thus, the bourgeoisie of the nineteenth century, molded by the experience of the industrial revolution, transformed its class aspirations into immutable laws of Providence.[4]

The distinction between individual deed and collective action, between private and public rights, served the economic needs as well as the political interests of the middle class. It established a category of entrepreneurial decisions that were declared to be beyond the scope of government regulation. Did not a man have the same right to do what he liked in his business as to read what he liked in his newspaper or profess what he liked in his church? Did not the same principle of individualism that protected him against the political oppression of the masses also protect him against their economic tyranny? Since differences in material possessions were as natural as differences in civic rights, any attempt by the state to reduce them was bound to have an adverse effect on society as a whole. Indeed, privation was a spur to industriousness; without it, the chief motivation for labor would disappear. That was why poverty performed a positive function in the eternal scheme of things. The inequality of property is by no means a misfortune, declared Karl Braun before the Reichstag of the North German Confederation. "On the contrary, I affirm that the equality of property and its immutability would be the greatest misfortune which could befall the world." If every man had exactly as much property as every other, and each knew that he could not increase that property, then anyone willing to work would be a fool. "The inclination toward *dolce far niente* is a tendency very deeply implanted in the hearts of all of us, and we can overcome it only for compelling reasons, whether it be the stimulus of hunger or the ethical motives of family, community, and state."

This theme appears over and over again in the economic writings of liberalism. Mass privation, harsh though it admittedly appeared, was

4. *Rheinische Briefe und Akten zur Geschichte der politischen Bewegung 1830–1850*, ed. Joseph Hansen, 2 vols. (Essen and Bonn, 1919–42), 1:17; [Herbert Spencer], "Parliamentary Reform: The Dangers and the Safeguards," *Westminster Review* 73 (1860):269.

essential for the maintenance of a disciplined and industrious labor force. To eliminate it, even if that were possible, would only undermine the willingness of the proletariat to undertake the unremitting toil that is essential for the progress of society. Provide the worker with three meals a day, give him a warm coat to put on his back, add a room or two to house his family, and you destroy his incentive for going into the mill or the mine. Most liberals believed that the ambition of the common man did not extend beyond the basic necessities. Once society guaranteed them, he would sink into a life of indolence and dissipation. Even the *Edinburgh Review*, which advocated so many improvements in the political system of Great Britain, remained convinced of the futility of social reform. "Poverty," it declared, "is the natural, the primitive, the general, and the unchangeable state of man; and . . . as labour is the source of wealth, so is poverty of labour. Banish poverty, you banish wealth. . . . Indigence may be provided for—mendicity may be extirpated; but all attempts to extirpate poverty can have no effects but bad ones." Such were the hard inescapable laws of laissez-faire economics.[5]

To the lower classes, then, liberalism could offer only the austere doctrines of rugged individualism and self-denial. It may have been difficult for many workers to accept the circular reasoning that they must remain poor because they had no capital, and they could not acquire capital because they were poor. Yet according to the theoreticians of free enterprise, it was better to face even this harsh reality than to indulge in visionary schemes of social reconstruction that could only impoverish the propertied without enriching the propertyless. The best course for the man who had no means was to live within his income, save his pennies, and slowly inch up the ladder of success. In an article concerning the "so-called labor question," John Prince-Smith, an Englishman who had become leader of the liberal school of economics in Germany, wrote that "the conscientious economist thus has only the one old advice in dealing with more general economic hardships," namely, "work and save!" Let poverty provide the spur and let the advantage enjoyed by the well-to-do inspire the lower classes so that they may take at least the first steps "on the road to salvation from economic want"; so that they may finally make possible what they have so far not accomplished in a thousand years of succeeding generations, that is, to save something beyond what is needed for the daily necessities of life; so that they may become "economically and spiritually" better endowed. "*Only he who puts something away will advance economically.*"

5. Germany, *Stenographische Berichte über die Verhandlungen des Reichstages des Norddeutschen Bundes: I. Legislatur-Periode, Session 1869*, 3 vols. (Berlin, 1869), 1:121; "The New Poor Law," *Edinburgh Review, or Critical Journal* 63 (1836):501.

Yet most liberals recognized that the common man, even if he led a life of the most Spartan simplicity, was not likely to rise above the working class. Human talents were too rare and material goods too few to enable any but a small minority to enjoy a life of comfort. The rest must simply accept the fact that the laws of economics condemned mankind to toil and hardship. The dramatist Silvio Pellico, who paid for his belief in a liberal and united Italy with ten years in prison, preached to the masses the virtue of pious resignation. It is true, he wrote in the *Duties of Men*, that in human society merit is not always justly rewarded. He who works hard is often so modest that he does not strive for recognition; he is often overshadowed or even defamed by aggressive men of little ability who seek to surpass him. "Such is the world, and in this respect we cannot hope that it will change."

It was especially important to recognize the futility of egalitarian political and economic doctrines: "Enlightened ideas which should be spread among the ignorant people of the low class are those which will preserve them from error and exaggeration . . . which will keep them from wild and foolish ideas of anarchy or plebeian government, which will teach them to practice with religious dignity the obscure but honorable occupations to which Providence has called them, and which will persuade them that social inequality is necessary." The liberals refused to compromise with doctrines of popular sovereignty or manhood suffrage. Their rigid logic concerning the oligarchical nature of society led them to reject any flirtation with the masses. They remained convinced that the irrefutability of what they believed would prevail in the long run against popular but false teachings about the equality of men and classes.[6]

Liberalism, however, was not the only middle-class ideology to emerge during the nineteenth century. Many members of the bourgeoisie, especially the lower bourgeoisie—writers, journalists, lawyers, teachers, physicians, engineers, clerks, managers, shopkeepers, and small businessmen—looked to the egalitarian political tradition of the sans-culottes in France, the tradition of democracy. They would not accept the stern liberal dogmas condemning most people to poverty and powerlessness. They maintained rather that the distinctions of class and property separating men from one another should be subordinated to a common concern for the welfare of society as a whole. Differences of wealth or education would no doubt always exist, but they could be mitigated by the reformist policy of a wise government. The democrats—in some

6. John Prince-Smith, "Die sogenannte Arbeiterfrage," *Vierteljahrschrift für Volkswirthschaft und Kulturgeschichte* 2, no. 4 (1864):193; Silvio Pellico, *Dei doveri degli uomini, discorso ad un giovane* (Paris, 1834), pp. 63–64, 112–13.

countries they were also known as republicans or radicals—refused to believe in the innate and unalterable incapacity of the lower classes. On the contrary, the peasant or the worker could become a responsible citizen, sacrificing his private interest for the common good. There were elemental energies slumbering in the masses, energies capable of deeds of extraordinary valor. After all, did not the Jacobin republic in France defy the combined might of monarchical Europe?

At bottom the teachings of democracy rested on a mystical faith in the virtue and wisdom of the common man. "The prominent and principal feature which has always struck me the most in my long study of the people," declared the historian Jules Michelet, "is that amid the disorders of destitution and the vices of misery, I have found among them a richness of sentiment and a goodness of heart very rare in the wealthy classes." The masses have "the faculty of devotion and the power of sacrifice"; they have the quality that is "the closest to heroism." Intellectual superiority, proceeding partly from education, "can never be put in the balance against this sovereign faculty." As for the argument that the lower classes lack foresight, that they are guided by blind impulse, "even if the observation were just, it by no means does away with the equally noticeable unremitting devotion and indefatigable sacrifice which are so often exemplified by hard-working families, a devotion which is not exhausted even by the total sacrifice of one life, but which often continues from one to another for several generations." The altruism and courage so often displayed by the poor in their daily existence justified a rejection of the traditional oligarchical system of rule. The most effective government was the most representative government; it was a form of authority in which all those affected by the laws of the community participated in their enactment.[7]

The democrats recognized that they were attempting to overcome a deep-seated belief in the civic incapacity of the common man. Yet they also felt that time was on their side, for history had entered a new phase of human development with the French Revolution. The throne and all its institutions of repression and discrimination were increasingly on the defensive. They might still repel attacks against the established system, but they could not maintain it indefinitely. The republic is not yet ripe but it will embrace all of Europe within a century, wrote Victor Hugo in his *Journal of a Revolutionary of 1830*. It means that society is its own sovereign, protecting itself by means of a national militia, judging itself by means of the jury system, administering itself by means of local authority, and governing itself by means of the body of voters. "The four

7. Jules Michelet, *Le peuple* (Paris, 1846), pp. xviii–xix.

limbs of monarchy—the army, the judiciary, the administration, and the peerage—are for this republic only four troublesome excrescences which will soon atrophy and die."[8]

No barrier of inalienable rights protected the individual against the collective will of the people. Private interest was subordinate to public interest; civic concerns took precedence over personal concerns. Government must be strong in order to correct the accumulated wrongs and oppressions of history. Yet power should be justified not only by its lofty purpose but also by its popular origin. Only an authority responsible to all had the right to command the obedience of all. That was why manhood suffrage was so important to the democrats; it distinguished them from the liberals more sharply than any other political doctrine. To the argument that the common man was too ignorant to exercise the franchise intelligently, they responded that he had a profound concern for the well-being of society as a whole, a concern that arose directly out of experience. Who knew better the evil consequences of arbitrary rule and caste privilege? The masses were interested in good government because they were so familiar with bad government.

Describing the civic beliefs of the "Parliamentary Radicals" in England during the 1830s, John Stuart Mill wrote that "they are the only party in politics who have, to any degree, common objects with the working classes. They are the only party who are not overflowing with groundless dread, and jealousy, and suspicion of them. They are the only party who do not in their hearts condemn the whole of their operative fellow-citizens to perpetual helotage, to a state of exclusion from direct influence on national affairs." On the contrary, he went on, they look forward to a time when the whole adult population will have an equal voice in the election of the members of Parliament. "Others believe this and tremble; *they* believe it, and rejoice; and instead of wishing to retard, they anxiously desire, by national education and the action of the press, to advance this period, to hasten this progress. . . . Their principle of government is, until Universal Suffrage shall be possible, to do everything for the good of the working classes, which it would be necessary to do if there were Universal Suffrage." The political ideal of petty-bourgeois radicalism, then, was the Jacobin republic of 1793, secure against monarchical tyranny, governed by a popularly elected legislature, defended by a citizen army, scorning the obscurantism of an established church, and rejecting traditional class distinctions and privileges. Free institutions would make free men able to develop their civic and economic

8. Victor Hugo, *Oeuvres complètes*, ed. Jeanlouis Cornuz, 38 vols. (Lausanne, 1966–68), 38:104–5.

talents without regard for birth or wealth. This was the guiding vision of democracy.[9]

It differed from liberalism in its attitude not only toward authority but toward property as well. The liberals regarded untrammeled possession as the foundation of social existence, more important even than freedom of speech or liberty of worship. The democrats, on the other hand, felt that proprietorship should be supervised and regulated by government in consonance with the general welfare. They were not socialists, to be sure. The inequality of property seemed to them inevitable and indeed desirable. Economic initiative would atrophy if it did not receive a suitable reward in the form of affluence. But the difference between rich and poor should be controlled; it should be kept within bounds. The distance separating the propertied from the propertyless must not become so wide as to threaten the stability of society.

Corporate wealth in particular was a danger to democratic institutions. During the July Monarchy, in the course of a debate in the chamber concerning railroad construction, the radical poet Alphonse de Lamartine spoke of "the incompatibility of true, progressive liberty with the existence of corporations in a state or in a civilization." Their tyranny is the most hateful because it is the most enduring; it is "the tyranny with a thousand heads, a thousand lives, a thousand roots; the tyranny which can be neither broken nor killed nor extirpated." It is the most deceptive form that oppression has ever assumed in order to crush the individual and the general interest. Free government is no more immune to the influence of corporations than any other government. They insinuate themselves everywhere—in the press, in public opinion, and in political bodies, where they find mercenaries and auxiliaries. "Do we not see the entire country oppressed in its agriculture or its commerce by these collective interests of a small number of ironmasters, millowners, and manufacturers, who were once upon a time given the privilege of subsidies, of rights which protect them alone, and which are ruinous to everyone else?" Sixty or eighty ironmasters tyrannize the entire country with impunity. "You, the supporters of freedom and of the liberation of the masses, you, who have destroyed feudalism with its tolls and its rights of transit and its boundaries and its posts, you are going to let [the railroad companies] shackle the people and wall in their territory with the feudalism of money. No, never has a government, never has a nation created a power beyond its control, derived from money, exploitation, and even politics, which is more menacing and usurpative." It could have been one

9. [John Stuart Mill], "Parties and the Ministry," *London and Westminster Review* 28 (1837–38):10.

of Proudhon's thundering denunciations of the capitalistic system.

Or take the views of Giuseppe Mazzini, prophet of a democratic Italian republic embodying the ideals of national freedom and social justice. Writing in 1860 in a chapter of his *Duties of Man* dealing with the "economic question," he boldly condemns the shortcomings of the existing system of class relations. The disparity of wealth in the community derives from oppression legitimized by law and history. The system of property is badly constituted because the origin of its distribution at present lies as a rule "in conquest, in the violence by which, in times remote from ours, certain invading peoples or classes took possession of lands and of fruits of labor not their own." More than that, "the bases of the distribution of the fruits of labor earned by the owner and the worker do not rest on a just equality proportionate to the labor itself." Since property confers on its possessor political and legislative rights denied to workers, it tends to become monopolized by the few and inaccessible to the many. Finally, the system of taxation perpetuates the concentration of wealth in the hands of the propertied, "burdening the poor classes and depriving them of any chance to save money." To Mazzini and to most democrats, exploitation was not the price but the abuse of material progress. It was an evil that the government of a free state must seek to remedy. The political equality of men could only be maintained by their social equality, that is, by the elimination of poverty, ignorance, suffering, and oppression. Popular sovereignty resting on a wide distribution of civic rights required an economic system in which the disparity of property had been reduced to a tolerable level.[10]

The democrats shrank, however, from the ultimate logic of their own reasoning. They would not accept the conclusion that the maintenance of class distinctions must lead to the perpetuation of class conflicts. They continued to hope that the difference between the propertied and the propertyless could be sublimated in a common struggle for the ideals of a free government and a just society. The system of private ownership must remain inviolate. Its abuses should of course be eliminated; its weaknesses would have to be corrected. To establish full economic equality, however, would destroy business initiative; the result would be the impoverishment of all classes. What was needed was an equality of opportunity, not of property. To Michelet the do-nothing nobleman living on his inherited wealth was a parasite, but the self-made bourgeois busily amassing profits deserved the gratitude of society for contributing to its welfare. "If the rich man is industrious, he is a saint. I revere him." And

10. Alphonse de Lamartine, *La France parlementaire (1834–51): Oeuvres oratoires et écrits politiques*, ed. Louis Ulbach, 4 vols. (Paris, 1864–65), 2:116–17; Giuseppe Mazzini, *Scritti editi ed inediti*, 100 vols. (Imola, 1906–43), 69:122–23.

Mazzini made it clear that his criticism of the established system of economic relations was not meant to call in question the institution of private ownership: "But if, instead of correcting the shortcomings and slowly modifying the constitution of property, you should seek to abolish it, you would be suppressing a source of wealth, emulation, and activity, and you would resemble the savage who cut down the tree in order to gather the fruit. We must not abolish property because today it is the possession of the *few*. We must open the way by which the *many* can acquire it." In the free community of the future, distinct social classes separated by differences of possession would remain in existence, but the distance between them would be reduced by the reforming hand of a government deriving its authority from the people.[11]

There were times, moreover, when the democrats were troubled by private doubts about the masses, on whose natural virtue they had built their theories of state and society. Why were they so stubbornly preoccupied with petty details of everyday life, with increasing their wages by a few pennies, with reducing their workweek by an hour or two? Why did they remain so indifferent to the lofty ideals that men who had only their best interests at heart were preaching to them? During the constitutional conflict in Prussia in the early 1860s, Franz Ziegler confessed to Lassalle his disappointment with the lower classes for failing to support the struggle against Bismarck: "Our fatherland, all of Germany, and many other nations besides are struggling at this moment for the most sacred rights of man. The fight is far from over; the entire earth watches it in suspense. Yet here come the workers and say: 'What do we care about honor, freedom, or self-government! The belly! Help us, O state! He who does not want to provide for our belly cannot become deputy!'" Beneath the idealization of the people in most democratic writings lurked an uneasy suspicion of their ignorance, crudeness, materialism, and undisciplined strength. Essentially, democracy offered to the masses a form of government in which selfless men of enlightened views would do for them what they themselves would want to do if they knew what was best for them.[12]

A paternalistic concern for the common man was also voiced by the defenders of the old order. Those still loyal to the traditional form of authority—courtiers, bureaucrats, officers, landowners, churchmen— saw in theories about the rights of man and the sovereignty of the people mere abstractions derived from bloodless logic rather than living reality.

11. Jules Michelet, *Histoire du XIXe siècle*, 3 vols. (Paris, 1875–76), 1:133; Mazzini, *Scritti*, 69:123.

12. Ferdinand Lassalle, *Nachgelassene Briefe und Schriften*, ed. Gustav Mayer, 6 vols. (Stuttgart and Berlin, 1921–25), 5:104.

They were the work of bourgeois doctrinaires who, seeking only to advance their class interests, drafted constitutions and bills of rights without regard for the cumulative experience of society. The outcome was bound to be insurrection, chaos, and ultimately some form of tyranny. Men are not alike, and the differences between them cannot be legislated away by a stroke of the pen. To the concept of an inalienable freedom inherent in the individual or the collective, conservatism opposed the idea of a pulsating, vital tradition formed by life itself. Established institutions are not simply the product of some lawmaking process, to be shaped and twisted at will by those in authority. They reflect attitudes, feelings, beliefs, instincts, and, yes, prejudices. They are organic in character, growing and responding to a changing historical environment. They cannot be drastically altered to fit a textbook theory of perfection any more than the organs of the body can be drastically altered by the surgeon's knife. Any attempt to do so will only lead to distortion, not improvement. Political and social traditions demonstrate by the very fact of their existence that they satisfy a profound human need. They provide the community with a guide to collective behavior that must not be sacrificed to the philosophical dogmas of the constitution makers.

The basic principles of the conservative ideology emerged even before the nineteenth century in a country that was already irrevocably committed to liberalism. Edmund Burke, the most brilliant intellectual defender of the status quo, challenged the political theories of the philosophes during the heyday of the Enlightenment. "A nation is not an idea only of local extent, and individual momentary aggregation; but it is an idea of continuity, which extends in time as well as in numbers and in space," he declared in 1782 in a speech concerning the system of representation in the House of Commons. "And this is a choice not of one day, or one set of people, not a tumultuary and giddy choice; it is a deliberate election of the ages and of generations; it is a constitution made by what is ten thousand times better than choice, it is made by the peculiar circumstances, occasions, tempers, dispositions, and moral, civil, and social habitudes of the people, which disclose themselves only in a long space of time." And then came the classic legitimation of the established order as the embodiment of a collective intelligence: "The individual is foolish; the multitude, for the moment, is foolish, when they act without deliberation; but the species is wise, and, when time is given to it, as a species it always acts right."

Eight years later in his *Reflections on the Revolution in France*, Burke again advanced the argument for the conservative principle with an eloquence and persuasiveness that have never been surpassed:

> Society is indeed a contract. Subordinate contracts for objects of
> mere occasional interest may be dissolved at pleasure—but the state

ought not to be considered as nothing better than a partnership agreement in a trade of pepper and coffee, calico or tobacco, or some other such low concern, to be taken up for a little temporary interest, and to be dissolved by the fancy of the parties. It is to be looked on with other reverence; because it is not a partnership in things subservient only to the gross animal existence of a temporary and perishable nature. It is a partnership in all science; a partnership in all art; a partnership in every virtue, and in all perfection. As the ends of such a partnership cannot be obtained in many generations, it becomes a partnership not only between those who are living, but between those who are living, those who are dead, and those who are to be born. Each contract of each particular state is but a clause in the great primaeval contract of eternal society, linking the lower with the higher natures, connecting the visible and invisible world, according to a fixed compact sanctioned by the inviolable oath which holds all physical and all moral natures, each in their appointed place.[13]

For the next hundred years, in every part of Europe, the defenders of the old order found solace in those words. They provided the justification for a traditional form of authority in a world increasingly transformed by new methods of production and new forms of wealth. They supported Pope's reassuring conclusion that whatever is, is right. They asserted the validity of historical experience against abstract right.

This meant that conservatism continued to advocate a hierarchical structure of politics in a society experiencing the leveling effects of industrialization. It denied that all men of talent and accomplishment are equally qualified for a position of leadership. Life itself imposes on individuals and groups differences in civic function derived from differences in economic achievement and social tradition. According to the German jurist and politician Friedrich Julius Stahl, the eternal law of aristocracy "is not restricted to counts and barons." It governs all classes and occupations, distinguishing the peasant proprietor from the small cottager, the master guildsman from the journeyman, the freeman of a borough from the mere city resident, and the clergyman from a member of the congregation. The basis of a "true aristocracy" is the belief that people are important not only as individuals, being therefore all equal, but as "representatives of a thing, of a property, of an occupation." Only to the extent that they have duties and obligations do they possess rights and powers.

Although in theory the principle of hierarchy cut across class lines, in

13. *The Works of the Right Honourable Edmund Burke*, 8 vols. (London, 1868–72), 2:368–69; 6:146–47.

fact there could be little doubt who its chief beneficiaries were. In his *Philosophy of Law*, Hegel speaks of a social group possessing "natural morality," which has "the ownership of land for its basis." Since, as a result of entailment, "its property is independent of the property of the state and the uncertainty of business, independent of the desire for profit and the instability of ownership in general, independent of the favor of governmental authority and the favor of the multitude," it is more properly constituted for political rank and importance than other groups. British peers, Prussian Junkers, and Hungarian magnates must have rejoiced at this flattering description, assuming that they read the great philosopher.[14]

On the other hand, conservatism was generally hostile toward the middle class. Men of great wealth but low birth tended to suffer from overweening political ambition. They sought to subvert the time-honored institutions of the nation, to replace a natural, organic relationship between individuals and groups with the paper prescriptions of a written constitution. Wherever the bourgeoisie comes to power, wrote the *Berliner Revue*, it promptly reveals its civic ineptitude. It promulgates new laws designed to dissolve the traditional bonds of society, but it can never find a vital, enduring principle of authority because it lacks judgment and experience. "It knows what to do on the stock market, in the exchange of money, in administration, and in police work; it excels in literature and has almost exclusive possession of the press." It lacks positive ideas in politics, however, since it is inherently incapable of understanding them. For this reason, it provides a form of government that is most hateful to the people. In dealing with the common man, it displays only arrogance and ignorance. It is indifferent to the real needs of the community.

There are good reasons for this civic incapacity of the middle class. The production and distribution of goods may be essential for the amassing of wealth, but they do not provide the experience needed for the effective government of a nation. Only prudent judgment and calm confidence arising out of the possession of inherited property, especially landed property, can produce a stable system of authority. As for manufacturers, bankers, and merchants, they merely try to apply to the administration of a country the same huckstering tricks that have proved successful in the world of business. "As far as capitalism is concerned, the state is a large industrial establishment, a sort of joint-stock association calculated to produce the highest net profit possible," declared the politi-

14. Friedrich Julius Stahl, *Die gegenwärtigen Parteien in Staat und Kirche* (Berlin, 1863), p. 311; Georg Wilhelm Friedrich Hegel, *Sämtliche Werke*, ed. Hermann Glockner, 26 vols. (Stuttgart, 1949–59), 7:415.

cal scientist Johann Carl Glaser. "The state officials are the managers, and the head of state is the president of the firm, whether he directs it in a republic simply as the agent of the stockholders, or in a monarchy as the principal of the business, on the analogy of a limited-liability company. In any case, he is responsible to the stockholders for his management of the business, or he must provide a security in the form of responsible ministers." Behind the new theories of paper freedom, representative government, and ministerial responsibility lurked a lust for power, seeking to replace the organic ties of social responsibility with a mechanistic individualism. The bourgeoisie was by nature the enemy of all legitimate authority.[15]

And what about the masses? What should be their role in the struggle of the upper and the middle classes? Here the attitude of the conservatives was ambivalent, torn between confidence in the submissive loyalty of the common man and fear of his vast strength. There was general agreement, however, that allowing the peasant and the worker to decide questions of public policy would prove disastrous. Many noblemen shared the gloomy foreboding of the marquis de La Mole in Stendhal's *Red and the Black*, who predicted that in fifty years' time not a single king would be left—only presidents of republics. And with the disappearance of the monarchy, priests and gentlemen would disappear as well. Nothing would be left but candidates paying court to unwashed majorities. The same hostility toward the democratization of politics resounded in the speech in 1848 of the Pomeranian Junker Adolf von Thadden-Trieglaff. He denounced the view that there should be "one elector for approximately 10,000 pounds of human flesh (including human bones)" and that "perhaps 40,000 hundredweight of these substances" should provide one member of parliament. It could have been the speech of a Constant or Guizot.

But although the masses were not qualified to play a decisive role in government, they could be used to maintain in power those who were. Count Joseph de Villèle, leader of the ultraroyalists in France and prime minister under Charles X, wrote to his father that the proletariat had been under the influence of the aristocracy ever since the beginning of the world, whereas the middle class, envied by the former and hostile to the latter, had made up the revolutionary party of society in all states. Therefore, "if you want the first class to sit in your assemblies, have it elected by the auxiliaries whom it has in the last class. Descend as low as you can and thus annihilate the middle class, which is the only one you have to

15. "Das Haus der Abgeordneten," *Berliner Revue: Social-politische Wochenschrift* 20 (1860):435; Johann Carl Glaser, "Die Arbeiterfrage und die Parteien," *Jahrbücher für Gesellschafts- und Staatswissenschaften* 5 (1866):114.

fear." Defenders of the old order in the nineteenth century followed this basic political strategy.[16]

In return for the support of the masses, conservatism offered them an agrarian, hierarchical, anticapitalistic ideology combining the denunciation of laissez-faire economics with a defense of private property. Since most traditionalists did not derive their livelihood from mills, mines, or banks, they could afford to deplore the disruptive social effects of industrialization. They could bewail the concentration of property in the hands of a grasping plutocracy while millions of peasants and workers hungered. Speaking through the character of Montesinos in his *Colloquies*, Robert Southey declared that "a people may be too rich; because it is the tendency of the commercial, and more especially of the manufacturing system, to collect wealth rather than to diffuse it. Where wealth is successfully employed in any of the speculations of trade, its increase is in proportion to its amount; great capitalists become like pikes in a fishpond, who devour the weaker fish; and it is but too certain that the poverty of one part of the people seems to increase in the same ratio as the riches of another." The language of Tory reformism could at times sound surprisingly like the rhetoric of the socialist movement.

Yet the two were separated by a fundamental difference regarding the institution of private property. The conservatives may have denounced the malefactors of great wealth, but they did not denounce great wealth as such. What they opposed was a particular form of financial gain derived from a specific category of economic activity. The man whose affluence depended on the ownership of a factory, colliery, store, or bank was suspect. He was likely to be tightfisted and moneygrubbing, without education or breeding, and quick to challenge established loyalties and institutions. But the man whose money came from a hereditary landed estate was in an entirely different situation. His way of life engendered respect for the rights of all classes as well as recognition of their obligations. It endowed him with the qualities of leadership and dedication essential for the progress of a nation.

Although the conservatives often spoke of the need to regulate the rights of ownership, they resolutely opposed any attempt to abolish those rights. To them private property was as sacred as to the most ardent bourgeois liberal. That is why they could offer the lower classes little beyond a paternalistic concern for their welfare. The shortcomings of the capitalistic system should be acknowledged and mitigated, but they must not be eliminated by eliminating the system itself. The limitations of the

---

16. Prussia, *Verhandlungen des zum 2. April 1848 zusammenberufenen Vereinigten Landtages*, ed. Eduard Bleich (Berlin, 1848), p. 99; *Mémoires et correspondance du comte de Villèle*, 5 vols. (Paris, 1888–90), 1:489–90.

traditionalist reform program are illustrated by the memorandum that the historian Leopold von Ranke submitted to King Frederick William IV of Prussia during the Revolution of 1848. "Under certain conditions the state ought to organize labor and perhaps recognize the right to work, yet it must also respect private enterprise. We may well agree that the state in times of peace should provide employment under military supervision for those workers especially who are physically fit for service in war." Just as the character of the army was formerly transformed from that of an unruly crowd into a disciplined body, so the activity of manual workers should now be regulated. "We could create labor cohorts for the many necessary public works, the control of rivers, the reclamation of lands, etc., etc. Political rights, on the other hand, could be granted the propertyless only to a very small extent, just as the Roman republic formed out of the entire mass of proletarians only one century entitled to vote in a total of 193." The lower classes were to receive sympathy, encouragement, assistance, and guidance, but they were to remain the lower classes.[17]

In its struggle to maintain the established structure of authority, conservatism generally received the support of the churches, both Catholic and Protestant. Throughout the history of Europe, an established faith had been considered essential for the preservation of order in society. Only a divine sanction of the existing distribution of wealth and power could reconcile the poor to their poverty and the oppressed to their oppression. This does not mean that the propertied classes regarded religion cynically, using it as a means of social discipline without accepting its moral teachings. As a rule, they sincerely believed in its principles and doctrines. But their readiness to accept what it had to say about the afterlife was enhanced by what it had to say about this life.

The function of religious faith as a bulwark of the existing social order was not a subject that statesmen and publicists avoided. On the contrary, they discussed it openly and at great length. Just as the school was expected to inculcate the virtues of loyalty and obedience, so the church was expected to provide support for the status quo as man's lot on earth. Napoleon I, always the cold-blooded skeptic, asked: "How are we to have order in a state without a religion?" Society cannot exist without the inequality of fortunes, and the inequality of fortunes cannot exist without religion. When one man is dying of hunger beside another who is satiated, it is impossible for the former to accept the difference in their position unless there is an authority that tells him: "God wishes it thus;

17. Robert Southey, *Sir Thomas More: or, Colloquies on the Progress and Prospects of Society*, 2 vols. (London, 1829), 1:193–94; Leopold von Ranke, *Sämmtliche Werke*, 54 vols. (Leipzig, 1867–90), 49–50:597–98.

there must be poor and rich in the world; but afterward, during eternity, the distribution will be different."

There were many others who emphasized the role of religion as a defender of political and social stability. The English agricultural reformer Arthur Young urged Parliament at the end of the eighteenth century to build more churches and send more clergymen to those districts where the lower classes were concentrated because "the true christian will never be a leveller; will never listen to French politics, or to French philosophy." During the Second Republic in France, Adolphe Thiers, the quintessential liberal since the days of the Restoration, spoke of "the very good and very wholesome religious influence, which is, far more than any other perhaps, capable of giving birth to that useful resignation to what I call the conditions of society, the conditions for all men." Especially after a period of social upheaval—following the Revolution of 1848 or the Paris Commune, for example—religion appeared essential for the protection of the established order. Even Ernest Renan, who had scandalized the devout during the 1860s with his life of Jesus, recommended less than a decade later that the church should be entrusted with the education of the masses. "Do not interfere with what we [rationalists] teach and what we write," he suggested to the clergy, "and we will not question your control over the people. Do not challenge our position in the university and in the academy, and we will leave the country school to you in its entirety." The alliance of church and state in Europe thus rested on a common opposition to lower-class radicalism.[18]

The readiness of established religion to defend the status quo was not simply a result of the support it received from the public treasury or of the government supervision to which it was in varying degrees subject in all countries. The social structure of authority in the church resembled that in the state because there were close bonds of class affinity and family relationship between the dominant groups in each. Background was as important for advancement in the spiritual life as it was in the secular. At the death of George III in 1820, there were twenty-seven Anglican bishops in England and Wales; eleven were members of the aristocracy, eleven had been tutors in aristocratic families, and five had ties of friendship or patronage with the upper classes. Even the ordinary clergymen, recruited to a large extent from sons of the landed gentry or the well-to-do bourgeoisie, generally led the life of comfortable country squires.

Hartmut Kaelble has compiled more detailed data on the social com-

18. *Autour de Bonaparte: Journal du comte P.-L. Roederer, ministre et conseiller d'état* (Paris, 1909), pp. 18–19; Arthur Young, *An Enquiry into the State of the Public Mind amongst the Lower Classes: and on the Means of Turning It to the Welfare of the State; In a Letter to William Wilberforce, Esq. M.P.* (London, 1798), pp. 21–23, 25; *Discours par-*

position of the German clergy during the nineteenth century (table 9.1). These data do not provide a correlation between social status and clerical rank, but there is in general ample evidence that throughout Europe there were proportionately more aristocrats among bishops than among curates and more men of means among professors of theology than among country pastors.[19]

That was why the views of the church on social and economic questions were usually indistinguishable from those of the state. Both defended the same interest; both upheld the same orthodoxy. Take the sermon that Bishop Edward Stanley preached in 1839 to a congregation of workers who supported Chartism:

> Some there are who will tell the poor that the rich are their enemies, and that the poor have, therefore, a right to combine, and take, by force, property from those that are richer than themselves, since all were created by the same God equal. But though all alike are in one sense equal, that is, that the blessings of immortality are provided alike for all, yet it should also be remembered that the Bible tells us, that it is the same God which maketh rich and maketh poor; that from the earliest times in every nation of the known world, there were graduations of rank, and degrees of wealth: that in the parable of the talents, one has ten talents committed to him, another has five, another two, another one. The inequality of goods and earthly possessions appears to be as much a part of God's providence as the differences between one man's bodily strength and faculties and another's; in fact, in proportion as some are more industrious, more talented, or from various other causes, some must be richer, and some must be poorer, and the great lesson to be learned is, with every one of these talents, whether it be one, or five, or ten, to do our master's work therewith—never forgetting that, from him who has ten committed to his charge much is required, that from him who has but one, in like manner an obedient, right, and faithful use of that one is as solemnly demanded; and to this end, as St. Paul tells us, we must learn in whatever station of life in which our lot is cast, to be content.[20]

lementaires de M. Thiers, ed. Marc Antoine Calmon, 16 vols. (Paris, 1879–89), 8:618–19; Ernest Renan, _La réforme intellectuelle et morale_ (Paris, 1871), pp. 98–99.

19. Georges Weill, _L'éveil des nationalités et le mouvement libéral (1815–1848)_ (Paris, 1930), pp. 189–90; Hartmut Kaelble, "Sozialer Aufstieg in Deutschland, 1850–1914," _Vierteljahrschrift für Sozial- und Wirtschaftsgeschichte_ 60 (1973):63–64.

20. _A Sermon Preached in Norwich Cathedral, on Sunday, August 18th, 1839, by the Right Reverend the Lord Bishop of Norwich, before an Assembly of a Body of Mechanics Termed Chartists_ (London, 1839), p. 7.

Table 9.1. Social Origins of German Clergymen in the Nineteenth Century

	Period	Number	Strata (percentage)		
			Upper	Middle	Lower
Württemberg Protestant clergymen	1834–1896	2,024	46	47	1
Prussia Protestant theology students	1887–1900	5,769	37	61	1
Württemberg Catholic priests	1825–1901	1,724	4	90	4
Augsburg diocese Catholic priests	1804–1917	4,160	4	86	6
Prussia Catholic theology students	1887–1900	2,195	8	87	4

SOURCE: Hartmut Kaelble, "Sozialer Aufstieg in Deutschland, 1850–1914," *Vierteljahrschrift für Sozial- und Wirtschaftgeschichte* 60 (1973): 63.
NOTE: Upper strata include high government officials, army officers, large landowners, entrepreneurs, and professionals. Middle strata include artisans, small businessmen, farmers, middle government officials, white-collar workers, and teachers. Lower strata include workers, servants, and low government employees.

No statesman, conservative or liberal, could have defended the established social system with greater conviction.

The attitude of the church toward the lower classes was not uniform, to be sure, any more than that of society as a whole. Especially after 1850, a Christian socialist movement emerged that sought to reconcile the teachings of religion with the interests of the masses. The names of its leaders became well known in the nineteenth century, names like Wilhelm Emanuel von Ketteler and Philippe-Joseph-Benjamin Buchez among the Catholics or Frederick D. Maurice and Friedrich Naumann among the Protestants. Charging that the established faith had in the past merely provided a spiritual sanction for existing institutions, they fought to transform it into an instrument of social justice. "For a century all legislation has been framed in favor of capital, to assure its rights, to give it every possible opportunity for organization," argued Albert de Mun, "while it has done nothing or almost nothing to guarantee the rights of labor and give it the means to defend them."

Some of the reformers even began to flirt with secular radicalism, echoing many of the demands of the socialist movement. According to Percy Dearmer, for whom devotion to God was synonymous with devotion to the proletariat, "if you are a Christian, and love your rich neighbour as yourself, you will do all you can to make him poorer. For if you believe in the Gospel, you know that to be rich is the very worst thing that can happen to a man." Yet the advocates of social change remained a vocal but small minority within the church. Even at their most militant, they could only offer the masses a little more security and dignity in a world in which class disparities would remain as sharp as ever. Their vision of a just economic order could not compete with that of the socialists.[21]

Church attendance therefore diminished steadily as industrialization began to nurture new attitudes and beliefs among the urban proletariat. For the first time in the history of Europe, a substantial part of the lower classes turned away from established religion. Skepticism had been common, even fashionable, among the educated and propertied in the eighteenth century. In the nineteenth century, however, people of means generally accepted the teachings of the church, at least outwardly, and it was the workers of the cities who became increasingly secular in outlook.

This trend was not reflected in any substantial increase in the number of formal withdrawals from the church. Any man officially labeled a freethinker faced not only a difficult psychological break with tradition but social and economic reprisal as well. In Saxony in the period 1876–98, only 4.2 percent of the children of Protestant parents were not baptized, and in the period 1877–1900 only 7.4 percent were not confirmed. Between 1909 and 1914 the number of people in all of Germany withdrawing from the Protestant churches fluctuated between 13,000 and 20,000 annually; in the Netherlands in 1909 the total of those in all denominations who had formally abandoned their religion was 291,000. A growing indifference toward Christianity was apparent in the declining attendance at services, however, especially in the big cities. A survey of ninety-six Protestant churches in Berlin conducted in 1914 suggested that at best 4.3 percent of the 2,190,000 members went to Sunday worship. In Dresden around 1900, about 3.5 percent of the 300,000 Lutherans attended morning services. In 1902–3 an inquiry into the extent of religious observance in London showed that although the population had increased by 500,000 during the previous fifteen years, the number of practicing Christians had decreased by 150,000, so that only 16 percent

21. *Discours et écrits divers du comte Albert de Mun*, ed. Charles Alexandre Geoffroy de Grandmaison, 7 vols. (Paris, 1888–1904), 5:324; Percy Dearmer, *Christian Socialism, Practical Christianity* (London, 1897), p. 12.

of all Londoners still observed the teachings of their church. In the course of the nineteenth century, a society that was essentially indifferent to religion began to emerge in Europe.[22]

It is also clear that the attitude toward faith was largely a class characteristic. For the most part, the aristocracy, the bourgeoisie, and the peasantry remained loyal to the church, at least in appearance, but the urban proletariat became openly skeptical. As early as the 1840s, the economist Jérôme-Adolphe Blanqui reported that the religious spirit was "quite rare" among French workers. He had questioned the millowners, the clergy, and the workers themselves on this subject and had become convinced that they generally went to church very little after their first communion. They respected the priests but did not listen to them much. In his description of life in London about fifty years later, Charles Booth observed that "as regards certain religious developments, class conditions seem paramount. [For] the great bulk of those of rank and station amongst our people, ... devotional expression is, as a rule, cold and unemotional, but with no class is religion more completely identified with duty." On the other hand, "the great section of the population, which passes by the name of the working classes, lying socially between the lower middle class and the 'poor,' remains, as a whole, outside of all the religious bodies." The organized church as a bulwark of the established order was losing its effectiveness.[23]

The decline in the influence of religion was part of a broad process of change affecting all political and social institutions as a result of the expanding role of the masses in public life. At the end of the Napoleonic Wars, the power of the crown, nobility, bureaucracy, and clergy was still unchallenged in most countries. Only England, France, Scandinavia, the Low Countries, and some of the secondary German states had begun to impose constitutional limitations and parliamentary restraints on the traditional forms of authority. The general direction of civic development during the nineteenth century, however, was from conservatism through liberalism to democracy. By the time of the First World War, almost every nation was committed to the appearance, if not the reality, of popular

22. Kenneth Scott Latourette, *Christianity in a Revolutionary Age: A History of Christianity in the Nineteenth and Twentieth Centuries*, 5 vols. (New York and Evanston, 1958–62), 2:76; Heinrich Hermelink, *Das Christentum in der Menschheitsgeschichte: Von der französichen Revolution bis zur Gegenwart*, 3 vols. (Tübingen and Stuttgart, 1951–55), 3:157 (n. 1), 191; *Kirchliches Jahrbuch für die evangelischen Landeskirchen Deutschlands* (1914), p. 527; Elie Halevy, *History of the English People in the Nineteenth Century*, 2d ed., 6 vols. (London, 1949–52), 5:380.

23. Jérôme-Adolphe Blanqui, *Des classes ouvrières en France, pendant l'année 1848* (Paris, 1849), p. 210; Charles Booth, *Life and Labour of the People in London*, 3d ser., 7 vols. (London, 1902), 7:394–95, 399.

government. Not only the advanced industrial countries of the north and west but the backward agricultural states of the south and east had broadened the franchise to the point where workers and peasants could take part in elections. There were of course some exceptions. Hungary, for example, remained a feudal stronghold right down to 1914. But even in the Iberian Peninsula, Italy, Austria, and Russia, all or at least most men had the right to vote. Europe witnessed for the first time the emergence of a system of mass politics, a system under which the man in the street received in theory the power to decide questions of public policy.

This profound transformation of the class basis of the political process aroused grave concern among the educated and well-to-do. Some feared that the domination of the masses would mean an end to scientific and technological progress. For example, the British jurist and historian Henry Sumner Maine declared: "If for four centuries there had been a very widely extended franchise and a very large electoral body in this country, there would have been no reformation of religion, no change of dynasty, no toleration of Dissent, not even an accurate Calendar. The threshing-machine, the power-loom, the spinning-jenny, and possibly the steam engine, would have been prohibited. . . . The gradual establishment of the masses in power is of the blackest omen for all legislation founded on scientific opinion." To the Swiss cultural historian Jacob Burckhardt, on the other hand, the danger of democracy lay in its indifference to intellect and spirit. "Which classes and strata will hereafter be the real bearers of learning?" he wondered anxiously. "Which will hereafter provide the scholars, artists, and poets, the creative personalities? Or is everything perhaps to become mere business, like in America?" Yet the fear of the consequences of a democratization of civic life was exaggerated. The dominance of elites and oligarchies remained as much a reality in the nineteenth century as in the eighteenth. It was forced, however, to assume the form of popular politics in which the lower classes appeared to play a decisive role in the determination of state policy.[24]

24. Henry Sumner Maine, *Popular Government: Four Essays* (London, 1885), p. 98; Jacob Burckhardt, *Gesammelte Werke*, 10 vols. (Basel, 1955–59), 4:149.

10

THE FUNCTIONS OF GOVERNMENT

The great increase in wealth resulting from the rationalization of the economy enabled the states of Europe to assume a new role in the development of their society. Government had traditionally been expected to perform two essential functions: the protection of frontiers against foreign attack and the suppression of domestic disorder. As a result, the resources of the public treasury were devoted primarily to the military establishment because maintenance of external security and preservation of internal stability were entrusted to the same authority, the armed forces. Thus, during the reign of Frederick the Great of Prussia, between 70 and 80 percent of the known public expenditures of the kingdom went for military purposes. The distribution of the costs of government in other countries was not very different. Even in Great Britain, where geography provided much of the security that Continental states had to seek in large standing armies, total expenditures in 1765 were 12,016,000 pounds, of which the armed forces received 51 percent, interest on the debt 40, and civil government 9.

British budgets became far larger by the end of the Napoleonic Wars, but the ratio between civil and military expenditures did not change substantially. There was still nothing for poor relief or education, nothing for local administration or justice, nothing even for local police. In 1814, out of a total budget of close to 112 million pounds, civil expenditures (including the courts, the mint, the civil list, allowances to the royal family, salaries, bounties, and miscellaneous services) accounted for only 4 percent. The navy's share, on the other hand, was 20 percent and that of the army and ordnance 34. Finally, subsidies to the Allied Powers took 9 percent and interest on the public debt amounted to 34. Throughout Europe the resources of the public treasury were largely absorbed by the requirements of security.[1]

Yet government in the preindustrial era was not content merely to protect its citizens against incursion or lawlessness. It also sought to regulate their economic and social activity in such a way as to preserve a

1. Knut Borchardt, "The Industrial Revolution in Germany, 1700–1914," in *The Fontana Economic History: The Emergence of Industrial Societies*, ed. Carlo M. Cipolla (London and Glasgow, 1973), p. 87; Witt Bowden, Michael Karpovich, and Abbott Payson Usher, *An Economic History of Europe since 1750* (New York, 1937), p. 246; Elie Halevy, *A History of the English People in the Nineteenth Century*, 2d ed., 6 vols. (London, 1949–52), 1:357–58.

hierarchical class structure in which each man had his assigned place and permanent occupation. The authorities defined the relationship between peasant and landlord, master and journeyman, producer and consumer, and creditor and debtor. They even tried to shape the general development of agriculture, industry, commerce, and finance. This was no passive government, content with the role of a policeman on the corner. It was a forceful instrument of policy attempting to regulate the details of public and even private life. It dealt not only with the conditions of business and employment but even with the particulars of housing, clothing, and nourishment. The scope of its activity was limited only by its lack of resources. Unable to maintain a large bureaucracy on a modest income, it had to rely extensively on local officials and notables who were often too busy or indifferent to enforce the law with vigor.

To be sure, the purpose of government regulation in the preindustrial era was not to transform but to uphold the social system, not to diminish but to perpetuate class distinction. Its ideal was stability rather than change. Yet the fact that the state had actively sought to insure the material well-being of its citizens reminded men in the nineteenth century that government could become a means for the attainment of the collective goals of the community. Whether it should play a significant role in molding society, however, remained a subject of dispute. The *Edinburgh Review* advocated a far-reaching reorganization of public life, complaining that the nation was not doing enough to promote reform. "Great as have been the improvements in our social institutions," it declared in 1835, "Europe has not yet achieved in any of her states the blessed triumph of a paternal government. The events which now agitate England indicate her distance from so glorious a consummation." But only twenty years later, writing about the ancien régime in France and the great revolution that followed, Alexis de Tocqueville maintained that the state had become the instrument of centralization and uniformity, destroying the rich variety of preindustrial life: "The princes . . . all seek, within their domains, to destroy immunities and to abolish privileges. They intermingle ranks, they equalize conditions, they substitute civil servants for the aristocracy, uniform rules for local rights, and the unity of government for the diversity of powers." Was this the same Europe that remained so far removed from the "blessed triumph of a paternal government"?[2]

In an important respect, it was not. The difference of opinion regarding the role of government arose in part out of a clash of civic temperaments, a clash between the belief that the community must promote the

2. "The British Scientific Association," *Edinburgh Review, or Critical Journal* 60 (1834–35):364; *Oeuvres, papiers et correspondances d'Alexis de Tocqueville*, ed. J.-P. Mayer, 12 vols. (Paris, 1951–70), vol. 2, pt. 1, p. 86.

general welfare and the fear that strong rule meant oppressive rule. Yet there was more to it than that, for the function of the state began to change significantly after the middle of the nineteenth century. In the first half, a reaction against government regulation coincided with the ideological primacy of liberalism. The industrial revolution had created a powerful motive for rejecting the principle of state control by which the old order had sought to maintain a static economic system. After 1815 a vigorous agitation, supported largely by the middle class, began to urge the restriction of government in both politics and business. "But what is this true mission of the state, considered from the economic point of view?" asked Karl Braun. "Nothing other than legal protection for person and property in domestic affairs, and the development of power in foreign policy, which is beneficial to individuals and to society as a whole." The state as such has no economic mission, his argument ran. We must be content if it merely ceases to take a hostile attitude toward the development of the economy. "To be sure, the state was still obliged until now to act in many areas of public commerce as a business manager for economic and civic society, so long as the latter did not have enough strength and judgment to do so everywhere on its own. But that, after all, always is and remains a temporary expedient, and we must always strive for its elimination."

After the mid-century, however, especially after 1870, this insistence on free enterprise began to give way gradually to a cautious advocacy of state intervention in the struggle of economic interests. The spread of democracy meant that the lower classes were now playing an increasing role in the political life of Europe. Proletarian demands for an improvement in the position of labor through government action could no longer be ignored. The authorities recognized that the extension of civic rights to the masses could prove dangerous without a rise in their standard of living; there was a widespread fear that they might take by force what they did not get by persuasion. The growth of trade unions was a clear warning that the urban working class expected a larger share in the affluence of society. And beyond the trade unions loomed the specter of revolution, the specter of socialism or anarchism. There were still many who defended the austere doctrines of laissez-faire, but they were now being increasingly challenged by the advocates of state regulation. Barely a generation after Karl Braun had urged the end of government tutelage over the economy, another German publicist, Adolph Wagner, recommended its extension as a means of attaining social justice. "State socialism must therefore undertake two tasks, which indeed are closely connected with one another: to raise the lower, the working classes as such at the expense of the upper, the propertied classes, and deliberately to restrict the excessive accumulation of wealth among certain groups and members of the propertied." To achieve this goal, government would have to exercise an even higher degree of control than it did in the pre-industrial era.[3]

The new activist state of the nineteenth century, however, differed from that of the eighteenth in that its purpose was not merely to maintain a traditional balance between social interests and economic pursuits. It now sought to raise the standard of living of the lower classes, regulate the condition of labor, limit the employment of women and children, supervise housing construction, promote public sanitation, provide free elementary instruction, and even protect the worker against sickness, old age, and unemployment. The growth of public expenditures clearly reflects this revolutionary change in the goals of the state. The proportion of national income absorbed by the government budget remained constant or increased slowly until about 1870. The savings made possible by the reduction of economic and social regulation were offset by the rising costs of a standing army based on conscription, a central bureaucracy that increasingly replaced local functionaries and notables, and an emerging system of primary schooling for the lower classes. Yet the growth in the expense of government was at first gradual and moderate.

Take the case of France, where state expenditures as a percentage of gross agricultural and industrial product actually declined in the first half of the nineteenth century. During the years 1803–12, a period of uninterrupted warfare extending over most of the Continent, the figure was 13.6 percent. But in the peacetime decade 1825–34, it fell to 11.5 and remained low throughout the next forty years, reaching 12.8 in 1845–54 and 13.5 in 1865–74, less than the percentage at the time of the Napoleonic Wars. The statistics for Prussia around the mid-century reinforce the impression of a steady but restrained increase in the cost of government. The population of the kingdom grew 16 percent between 1851 and 1865, but the national income increased 42 percent and the state budget 56. It is apparent, moreover, that the distribution of government revenue among the various categories of public need remained largely unchanged. The Prussian armed forces received 28 percent of budgetary appropriations in 1851 and 29 in 1865; education accounted for 3 percent at the beginning and 2 at the end of the period; and the share going to penal and correctional institutions was 1 and 1. The figures do not suggest any significant shift in the objectives of state policy.

After about 1870, however, there was a striking increase in the propor-

---

3. Carl Braun, "Staats- und Gemeinde-Steuern, im Zusammenhange mit Staats-, Heeres-, Kommunal- und Agrarverfassung," *Vierteljahrschrift für Volkswirthschaft und Kulturgeschichte* 4, no. 2 (1866):16–17; Adolf Wagner, "Finanzwissenschaft und Staatssozialismus," *Zeitschrift für die gesamte Staatswissenschaft* 43 (1887):718.

tion of national income absorbed by the cost of government. It coincided with the spread of democracy and the assumption by the state of an obligation to improve the quality of life. The statistics tell the same story in almost every country (figure 10.1). In the case of France, the available data are not strictly comparable to those for the other nations, but the ratio of state expenditures to gross agricultural and industrial product grew from 13.5 percent in 1865–74 to 18.8 in 1885–94. Although it then declined to 14.7 in 1905–13, the figure remained higher than that for any regime prior to the Third Republic. Only in countries like Italy, which turned to the task of social reform slowly and reluctantly, did government consumption as a percentage of gross national product fail to grow significantly. According to the estimates provided by Werner Sombart, public revenues or expenditures for Europe as a whole rose from $3.00 per capita in 1786 to $9.40 in 1880, an average annual increase of $0.07, whereas between 1880 and 1907–8 they rose from $9.40 to $15.80, an average annual increase of $0.23.[4]

Changes in the size of the civil service followed a similar pattern, that is, an initial moderate expansion to about the mid-century and then an unprecedented explosive growth until the First World War. Even Italy conforms to this generalization. On the eve of national unification in the late 1850s, there were close to 63,000 public employees, but some forty years later the total of civil servants and members of learned professions such as law and medicine reached 640,000. The number of higher officials in the Prussian ministries nearly tripled between 1821 and 1901. According to one calculation, the percentage of government workers in the labor force rose in Germany from 9.3 in 1895 to 10.6 in 1907, and in Great Britain it rose from 5.8 in 1901 to 6.9 in 1911. According to another, the ratio of German state and community employees to the population as a whole went from 0.47 percent in 1882 to 0.56 in 1895 and 0.63 in 1907. These were remarkable rates of increase.

The growth of local government was especially rapid, often exceeding the growth of central government. The city of Turin employed about 30 people in 1824 and more than 650 in 1869. Mannheim had 48 municipal officials in 1870 and 717 in 1905, a ratio of 1 official to 825 inhabitants

4. Gabriel Ardant, "Financial Policy and Economic Infrastructure of Modern States and Nations," in *The Formation of National States in Western Europe*, ed. Charles Tilly (Princeton, 1975), p. 221; W. G. Hoffmann and J. H. Müller, *Das deutsche Volkseinkommen, 1851–1957* (Tübingen, 1959), pp. 86–87; Leopold Clausnitzer, *Geschichte des preussischen Unterrichtsgesetzes*, 2d ed. (Berlin, 1891), p. 260; Simon Kuznets, *Modern Economic Growth: Rate, Structure, and Spread* (New Haven, 1966), pp. 236–39; Werner Sombart, *Der moderne Kapitalismus: Historisch-systematische Darstellung des gesamteuropäischen Wirtschaftslebens von seinen Anfängen bis zur Gegenwart*, 2d ed., 3 vols. (Munich and Leipzig, 1924–28), 3:487.

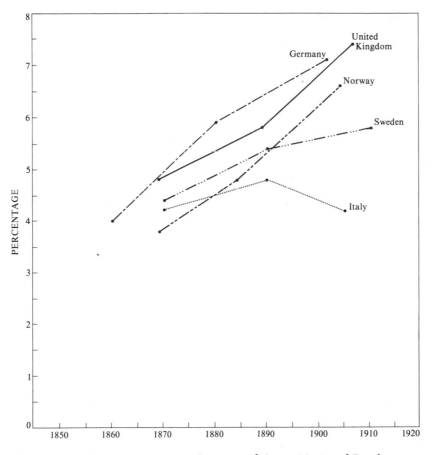

Figure 10.1. Government Consumption of Gross National Product, 1851–1920

SOURCE: Simon Kuznets, *Modern Economic Growth: Rate, Structure, and Spread* (New Haven and London, 1966), pp. 236–37.

in the beginning and 1 to 216 at the end. In 1890 there were 650 municipal officials and 1,150 municipal workers in Leipzig, whereas in 1908 the corresponding figures were 1,940 and 2,560. The percentage of city employees among all inhabitants thus rose from 0.5 to 0.9. A similar trend was apparent in Great Britain. The civil service of the central government increased from 50,000 in 1881 to 79,000 in 1891, 116,000 in 1901, and 162,000 in 1911, a growth of 224 percent in thirty years. The number of employees of local government rose a little more slowly, from 21,000 in 1881 to 25,000 in 1891, 37,000 in 1901, and 64,000 in 1911, a growth of 205 percent. For the opening decade of the twentieth century, however, the pattern was reversed: employment by central government increased 40 percent, and that by local government 73 percent. These changes in the growth rates of the bureaucracy reflect the rising involvement of the state in everyday life.[5]

The steady decline in the proportion of public expenditures going for military purposes was further evidence of new attitudes and expectations concerning the state. The functions of internal and external security, which had in the past been regarded as primary, were forced to yield to a growing demand for government action in the enhancement of private life. In Great Britain the personnel of the armed forces, including their civilian employees, accounted for about 85 percent of the entire public labor force in 1851; by 1914 the percentage had fallen to 55. The national budget rose from 132 million pounds in 1901 to 196 million in 1913, an increase of 48 percent. But whereas the share assigned to the civil services rose from 18 to 28 percent, the share of the fighting services fell from 46 to 38.

In Germany total government employment grew about 47 percent between 1882 and 1895, from 1,265,190 to 1,855,184, and about 45 percent between 1895 and 1907, from 1,855,184 to 2,692,379. This rate of increase was faster than that of the labor force as a whole, which rose 17 percent in 1882–95 and 27 in 1895–1907. The share of all government employees allotted to the armed forces, however, dropped from 36 percent in 1882 to 34 in 1895 and 24 in 1907. By comparison, rapid growth occurred in the categories of health and sanitation; postal, telegraph, and telephone systems; public transportation; and water, gas, and electric utilities. The new functions of government thus required a constantly rising proportion of public revenue and employment. On the eve of the First World War, by one estimate, there were 73 public officials for every ten thousand inhabitants in England, 126 in Germany, 176 in France, and 200 in Belgium.[6]

As for the performance of the European bureaucracy in the early years of its expansion, it was at best uneven. The problems created by indus-

5. Eugene N. Anderson and Pauline R. Anderson, *Political Institutions and Social Change in Continental Europe in the Nineteenth Century* (Berkeley and Los Angeles, 1967), pp. 167, 410 (n. 11); John P. Cullity, "The Growth of Governmental Employment in Germany, 1882–1950," *Zeitschrift für die gesamte Staatswissenschaft* 123 (1967):211; Jürgen Kuczynski, *Die Geschichte der Lage der Arbeiter unter dem Kapitalismus*, 38 vols. (Berlin, 1960–71), 14:184; Halevy, *History of the English People*, 6:262.

6. Wolfram Fischer and Peter Lundgreen, "The Recruitment and Training of Administrative and Technical Personnel," in *Formation of National States*, ed. Tilly, p. 463; R. C. K. Ensor, *England, 1870–1914* (Oxford, 1936), p. 526; Cullity, "Governmental Employment in Germany," pp. 202–4; Anderson and Anderson, *Political Institutions*, p. 167.

trialization, urbanization, demographic growth, and the rising tide of popular expectations had to be solved by men without training or experience in the economic and social complexities that faced them. No wonder that their level of achievement was so low. Early in the twentieth century, Henri Chardon, a leading authority on the administrative system of France, admitted in an open reply to a disgruntled taxpayer that the ineffectualness of local government was deplorable:

> You write to me, sir, that no public service functions properly in your town. There is no distribution of water; a few wells are open in public places for one hour in the morning and one hour in the evening. You are not supposed to draw from them except for nourishment, which makes it illegal for you to wash. The watercourse, moreover, passes below the cemetery; no one would dare think of drains. The streets are foul, illumination is rudimentary, the hospital is unsanitary, and typhoid is permanent in the poor neighborhoods. The schools are periodically decimated by scarlet fever and the croup. There is no hygiene, there is little poor relief, and the police force is ridiculous. Yet the municipal budget is exhausted, and the town is overflowing with officials who do not appear to be idle. What are they doing? Where is the money going? You are incensed. Compose yourself, sir. Almost all of France is in the same situation. If you will examine coolly the sum total of our public services, you will find everywhere an incredible disparity between effort and result. You will also find everywhere that an enormous expenditure is necessary in order to obtain in the end a service which is more or less normal.[7]

The classic complaints of modern society concerning the ineffectualness and wastefulness of the bureaucracy are as old as the bureaucracy itself.

The low efficiency of so many public employees in Europe around 1900 was in part a result of their lack of preparation. Civil servants had been taught to deal with the routine of a laissez-faire state. Only after 1850, and often much later than that, were they confronted by the intricacies of municipal sanitation, factory regulation, elementary schooling, mass transportation, and the water, gas, and electricity system. Until then the scope of activity of the government bureaucracy had been limited by restrictive doctrines concerning the proper relationship between public authority and private enterprise. To the mercantilists and cameralists of the eighteenth century, economics had still been largely an empirical investigation of the behavior of individuals and groups in the

7. Henri Chardon, *Le pouvoir administratif* (Paris, 1911), pp. 75–76.

pursuit of their material interest. In the writings of the classical school that followed, it became a deductive discipline whose laws ostensibly possessed the same degree of certitude as the natural sciences. The conclusion to which they seemed to point with an inescapable logic was that the well-being of society depended on unrestrained entrepreneurship. Thus the needs of a distinct class at a particular period became universalized into a decalogue beyond time and space.

The parallel between economics and physics, chemistry, or mathematics appears again and again in the polemical literature of laissez-faire. The French scholar Ambroise Clément wrote around the middle of the nineteenth century: "We are convinced that [political economy] is sufficiently advanced today to leave no legitimate doubt concerning its essential principles, and that the truths expressed by these principles will not be shaken by subsequent research or discovery, any more than the elements of geometry or the laws of universal gravitation have been shaken by the work of Lagrange or Laplace. We believe that we can affirm that of all the sciences which have man or society for their subject, political economy is the most positive and the least incomplete."

Prince-Smith sounded equally confident in his affirmation of the irrefutability of classical economics. "Do you then first ask the dyer whether the chemist is right in his assertions?" he argued. "Do you ask the locomotive fireman whether the mechanic's computation of the size and strength of a boiler is correct?" There is no need even to raise such questions. "And why not? Is it perhaps because chemistry, physics, and statics are based on experience? So is economics, just as completely. Or is it because the principles of the technicians prove true in practice every time? This is also the case, to an equally high degree, with the principle of economics." To be sure, that principle is seldom applied and almost never in its pure form. "But where it was applied, its blessed results have always and without exception become apparent." There was a charming artlessness about the way liberal economists sought to clothe their predilections and predispositions in the mantle of scholarly infallibility.[8]

What they taught helped bring about a major change in the role that government played in the life of the community. Their doctrines undermined the supervision of business activity by public authority for the purpose of maintaining social stability. In its place they advocated the principle, favorable to the private exploitation of economic rationalization, that the state should allow unrestrained competition to determine

8. Ambroise Clément, "Introduction," in *Dictionnaire de l'économie politique*, ed. Charles Coquelin and Gilbert-Urbain Guillaumin, 2d ed., 2 vols. (Paris, 1854), 1:xiv; *Die Verhandlungen des Vierten Congresses deutscher Volkswirthe zu Stuttgart am 9., 10., 11. und 12. September 1861* (Stuttgart, 1861), p. 29.

individual and collective status in the community. Their teachings were spread by an army of journalists, publicists, exegetes, and popularizers, who provided the reading public with a superficial grasp of the intricacies of classical economics. In a review of Southey's *Colloquies* in 1830, Macaulay wrote: "It is not by the intermeddling of . . . the omniscient and omnipotent State, but by the prudence and energy of the people, that England has hitherto been carried forward in civilisation." The nation now looks with hope to the same prudence and energy. "Our rulers will best promote the improvement of the people by strictly confining themselves to their own legitimate duties—by leaving capital to find its most lucrative course, commodities their fair price, industry and intelligence their natural reward, idleness and folly their natural punishment—by maintaining peace, by defending property, by diminishing the price of law, and by observing strict economy in every department of the state."

The defenders of laissez-faire acknowledged that a society in which the relationship of man to man was determined by the clash of material interests could be cruel. Still, for those who lost out in the universal struggle for gain, there was no recourse but the charity of the more fortunate. They had no title to support, no right of survival. Malthus, the most ruthless logician of the dismal science, stated this position with brutal frankness in the second edition of his *Essay on the Principle of Population*: "A man who is born into a world already possessed, if he cannot get subsistence from his parents on whom he has a just demand, and if the society do not want his labour, has no claim of *right* to the smallest portion of food, and, in fact, has no business to be where he is. At nature's mighty feast there is no vacant cover for him." Even Malthus shrank from the pitilessness of this formulation; the passage does not appear in subsequent editions. Yet its import was tacitly accepted by the advocates of free enterprise as a hard but inescapable consequence of human progress.[9]

To them, suffering was the price of achievement; some must hunger so that others may prosper. But on balance, they argued, the advantages of free enterprise for society as a whole far outweighed the hardships that it imposed on the incompetent or the unlucky. Look at the enormous economic advances of mankind since the beginning of the industrial revolution. Would they have been possible under a system of government regulation of profits, wages, and conditions of labor? Would the genius

9. [Thomas Babington Macaulay], "Southey's *Colloquies on Society*," *Edinburgh Review, or Critical Journal* 50 (1829–30):565; T. R. Malthus, *An Essay on the Principle of Population; or, a View of Its Past and Present Effects on Human Happiness; with an Inquiry into Our Prospects respecting the Future Removal or Mitigation of the Evils Which It Occasions*, 2d ed. (London, 1803), p. 531.

of a Richard Arkwright or George Stephenson have flowered without the promise of enrichment for men of talent? Would mass production have been achieved without the elimination of countless small shops employing inefficient tools and wasteful methods? By a providential law of economics, individual misfortune became transformed into collective well-being, and out of the cruel conflict of private ambitions emerged the greatest happiness of the greatest number. Here was the miracle of free enterprise, if we would only recognize it.

The happy process by which privation turns into prosperity and suffering into joy is the theme of a work published by Frédéric Bastiat in 1850 under the suggestive title *Economic Harmonies*. In an introduction addressed to the young people of France, he declares confidently that "the social problem . . . whatever may be said about it, is easy to solve. Interests are harmonious,—therefore the solution lies entirely in the word LIBERTY." The rest of the book is one long elaboration of this sanguine proposition. Competition, so often portrayed as the law of dog-eat-dog, in fact mitigates the conflict among individuals and classes. "We should consider it as the principle of a just and natural equalization." It holds in check the egoism of personal interest, curbing its greediness and at the same time spurring its activity. "We should bless it as the most striking manifestation of the impartial solicitude of God for all His creatures." It could admittedly appear hard at times. "I certainly do not deny, I do not disregard, and I deplore, as others do, the sufferings which competition inflicts on men." Yet is that a reason for closing our eyes to the good that it produces? "Competition, I believe, is, like all the great laws of nature, indestructible." There have been efforts to suppress it, especially by the "*levée en masse* of all the modern reformers." But "if they were crazy enough, they were not strong enough" to achieve their purpose. The teachings of classical economics were on the march to ultimate victory.[10]

They encountered considerable opposition on the way, however. The appearance of Adam Smith's *Wealth of Nations* late in the eighteenth century initiated a fundamental debate in Europe regarding the legitimate purposes of public policy. The advocates of free enterprise were met by the argument that individualism in economic conduct would weaken the ability of government to defend the national interest against other governments. It might even upset the balance between occupations and classes on which the stability of society depended. Especially in countries whose industry was still undeveloped and whose domestic production was in no position to resist foreign competition, there were loud demands for protection by the state. During the 1840s Friedrich List reflected the views of many German businessmen confronting the British colossus. In his *National System of Political Economy*, he gave classic expression to

10. Frédéric Bastiat, *Harmonies économiques* (Paris, 1850), pp. 23, 422, 450.

the contention that economic goals must not be divorced from political purposes. Pointing directly to England, he wrote: "A nation which through protective duties and restrictions on navigation has developed its manufacturing power and its navigation to such a degree that no other nation is able to engage in free competition with it can do nothing shrewder than throw away this ladder to its greatness, preach to other nations the benefits of free trade, and confess penitently that it has hitherto wandered in the path of error, only now discovering the truth."

Yet the teachings of liberal economics, List went on, are imbued with the spirit of cosmopolitanism and materialism, for they deal only with private enterprise in interaction with humanity in the abstract. They ignore a central fact: between man and mankind stands the nation, with its distinctive language and literature; its peculiar origin and history; its unique customs, habits, laws, and institutions; its claims to existence, independence, perfection, and permanence; and its separate territory. It is a society united by a thousand ties of spirit and interest into one independent whole; it stands in opposition to other societies of a similar kind. Under existing world conditions, it can defend its independence only by its own energies and resources. State policy should therefore subordinate the freedom of the individual to the security of the aggregate. The political needs of the nation must take precedence over the economic interests of the citizen.

Many conservative noblemen and bureaucrats expressed similar opinions, particularly in the backward agricultural states of the south and east. They continued to advocate the supervision of the economy by the state in order to maintain armed strength and class stability. M. M. Speransky, the influential adviser of Alexander I, reported to the czar in 1803 that although the principle of laissez-faire was sound, "in Russia, perhaps, some qualifications should be made." When national industry, strengthened by time and circumstances, reaches its full maturity, it can and should be allowed to proceed on its own. But in its early beginnings, when it is not yet able to consolidate its enterprises, before experience has clearly shown its prospects, so long as many areas of the economy are still unknown, the government has the obligation to guide it, to show where its advantage lies, to promote it through encouragement, "and even,—where there is lack of capital—to give it subsidies." There were unmistakable echoes of mercantilist theory in such views. They reflected the preindustrial belief that the state should regard economic activity as the handmaid of national policy, to be directed in accordance with the requirements of military effectiveness and social equilibrium.[11]

11. Friedrich List, *Schriften, Reden, Briefe*, 10 vols. (Berlin, 1927–35), 6:209, 372; Marc Raeff, *Michael Speransky: Statesman of Imperial Russia, 1772–1839* (The Hague, 1957), p. 53.

But other arguments against freedom of enterprise rested on entirely different assumptions. They advanced the novel view that the state must become an instrument of class justice, that it must protect the poor and oppressed against the rich and powerful. Reform rather than stability in the relationship between the propertied and the propertyless should become the object of government policy. Such was the position of those who favored not the preservation but the transformation of the established social order. One example would be the utopian socialists; another, the theorists and publicists who advocated a reorganization of industrial society without proposing the abolition of private property. Sismondi argued during the 1830s that the process of economic rationalization had upset the balance between capital and labor, enabling a few to become rich at the expense of the many. "The intermediate classes," he maintained, "have disappeared; the small proprietors and the small farmers of the countryside and the small master craftsmen, the small manufacturers, and the small shopkeepers of the city have been unable to withstand the competition of those who control vast enterprises. There is no longer room in society for anyone except the big capitalist and the man who works for wages. We have seen the frightfully rapid growth of a formerly almost unknown class of men who have absolutely no property." There were grave problems of economic injustice and social conflict in this growing polarization of the class structure.[12]

The most poignant appeals against the theories of liberal economics, however, came from those who were directly threatened by industrialism. For about seventy-five years, the governments of Europe continued to receive pleas for help from countless handicraftsmen and shopkeepers whom the factory system was depriving of their livelihood. For example, the wool combers of Barnstaple in Devonshire submitted to Parliament in 1794 a petition complaining of the effects of mechanization on their trade:

> The Petitioners have hitherto been considered as useful Members of the Community, who, by their Industry and Manual Labour, have provided for themselves with as little Assistance from Parochial Bounty as any Class of Manufacturers of their Numbers within these Kingdoms, but beg Leave to state to the House, that, by the Invention and Practice of a Machine for combing of Wool, which diminishes Labour to an alarming Degree, the Petitioners entertain serious and just Fears that themselves and their Families will speedily become a useless and heavy Burthen to the State. . . . It appears to the Petitioners that One Machine only, with the Assis-

---

12. J. C. L. de Sismondi, "De la richesse territoriale," *Revue mensuelle d'économie politique* 2 (1834):124.

tance of One person and Four or Five Children, will perform as much Labour as Thirty Men in the customary Manual Manner. . . . In Consequence of the Introduction of the said Machine, the great Body of Woollen Manufacturers will almost immediately be deprived of their Business and Employ, the whole Trade will be engrossed by a few powerful and wealthy Adventurers, and after short Competition, the surplus Profits arising from the Annihilation of Manual Labour will be transferred into the Pockets of the Foreign Consumers. . . . It is with the most heartfelt Sorrow and Anguish the Petitioners anticipate that fast approaching Period of consummate Wretchedness and Poverty.[13]

Compare this with the speech of a master artisan before a congress of German handicraftsmen meeting in Cologne in 1864: "We have shown our opponents that the system of industrial freedom is false and unjust. We have shown that it is a reprehensible doctrine to determine the value of human labor on the basis of supply and demand. A man must be able to be a man; humane interests must be cherished and protected." Or listen to the attack on financial speculation by another master artisan in 1869 in Halle at a gathering of handicraftsmen from north Germany: "The stock exchange is displaying the greatest activity; it is a hothouse which grows poisonous plants to the detriment of the nation as a whole. . . . If business life, commerce, art, and industry are the moral side of livelihood, then the swindle of the stock exchange constitutes its immoral side, the prostitution of enterprise. And I will allow myself, gentlemen, to add besides that gambling on the stock exchange is the cancerous sore of all popular well-being." Many of those whose way of life was being destroyed by economic rationalization thus formulated a crude but incisive critique of laissez-faire capitalism, condemning in particular its concept of labor as a mere commodity whose value depends on the impersonal forces of the marketplace.[14]

The long debate between supporters and opponents of classical economics was finally decided during the middle decades of the nineteenth century. Never before or since has Europe believed so confidently in the beneficence of rugged individualism. There was an excited feeling among liberal politicians and publicists that the superstitions of the past were being swept aside at last. Human enterprise would now be free to create a better life for mankind, secure against the interference of guilds, governments, and traditions. The first major triumph of laissez-faire came in

13. Great Britain, *Journals of the House of Commons*, 49 (1794), p. 21.

14. *Der dritte deutsche Handwerkertag zu Cöln vom 26. bis 28 September 1864* (Aachen, 1864), p. 6; *Der vierte norddeutsche Handwerkertag zu Halle a. d. S., am 20., 21. und 22. September 1869* (Halle, 1870), p. 38.

international commerce with the sharp reduction of tariff duties. It rested on the conviction that the free exchange of goods would encourage each nation to engage in those forms of economic activity most suited to its skills and resources. As a result, consumers throughout the world would profit from the most efficient organization of production. David Ricardo defended this position with compelling logic in his *Principles of Political Economy and Taxation* of 1817. Under a system of free trade, he argued, every country will devote its capital and labor to the employments that are most beneficial to its producers. "This pursuit of individual advantage is admirably connected with the universal good of the whole." By stimulating industry, rewarding ingenuity, and using intelligently the powers bestowed by nature, it distributes labor most effectively and most economically. By increasing general output, moreover, it diffuses general well-being and "binds together by one common tie of interest and intercourse, the universal society of nations throughout the civilized world." The result is bound to be a higher standard of living for all.

Liberal economics, however, sought to justify its teachings by their moral superiority as well as their financial advantage. They would do more than insure greater efficiency in the production of goods; they would serve a higher spiritual purpose. The free exchange of commodities would reduce friction among nations by increasing their interdependence. The danger of armed conflict among them would diminish as they recognized how much they needed each other, how much the advantage of one was the advantage of all. Mankind might be witnessing the dawn of an age of peace, about which philosophers had long dreamed. Richard Cobden, leader of the fight in England against the corn laws imposing protective duties on imported grain, declared during the 1840s: "I see in the Free-trade principle that which shall act on the moral world as the principle of gravitation in the universe,—drawing men together, thrusting aside the antagonism of race, and creed, and language, and uniting us in the bonds of eternal peace." John Stuart Mill was also convinced that free trade would eliminate the cause of strife among nations. "It is commerce which is rapidly rendering war obsolete," he wrote. "It may be said without exaggeration that the great extent and rapid increase of international trade, in being the principal guarantee of the peace of the world, is the greatest permanent security for the uninterrupted progress of the ideas, the institutions, and the character of the human race." The demands of a vigorous middle class seeking outlets for its manufactured goods thus became transmuted in the writings of liberal economists into moral imperatives deciding the destiny of mankind.[15]

15. *The Works and Correspondence of David Ricardo*, ed. Piero Sraffa and M. H. Dobb, 10 vols. (Cambridge, 1951–55), 1:133–34; Richard Cobden, *Speeches on Questions of*

The initial victory of free trade was won in England, which had the least to fear and the most to gain from unrestrained commercial competition. Nonetheless, the repeal of the corn laws was an impressive achievement because industrial interests prevailed not against small handicraftsmen and shopkeepers but against a powerful landed aristocracy that opposed the importation of foreign foodstuffs. After a long struggle between what one free trader called "30,000 landowners and 26,000,000 of men," the protective duties on grain were abolished in 1846. Most other tariffs soon followed. By 1870 there were only seventeen dutiable commodities, of which sugar, tea, wine, spirits, and tobacco produced 90 percent of the customs revenue. Although net imports had increased 400 percent since the early 1830s, income from the duties they paid had risen only 30 percent, not merely because the number of levies diminished but also because their average rate declined from 35 to less than 10 percent.

The movement for freedom of commerce spread from the British Isles to the Continent. On the eve of repeal of the corn laws, Cobden had predicted to his countrymen: "There will not be a tariff in Europe that will not be changed in less than five years to follow your example." The prophecy did not prove entirely accurate, but there was a substantial decrease in tariff rates in many countries during the next two or three decades. Napoleon III in particular became a vigorous advocate of tariff reduction in a country that, partly out of habit, partly out of necessity, had been staunchly protectionist. During the latter part of his reign, France concluded a number of important commercial treaties lowering import duties—with England in 1860, with Belgium in 1861, and with Prussia in 1862. The Netherlands eliminated tariffs almost completely between 1845 and 1877, and Belgium abolished her corn laws in 1850. Under Bismarck the Prussians entered into liberal trade agreements with the Belgians in 1863 and 1865 and with the British and Italians in 1865. Cavour introduced greater freedom of commerce in Sardinia, and even Russia, whose tariff walls were the highest in Europe, began cautiously to reduce her customs duties. "This cluster of trade agreements," writes David Landes concerning the 1860s, "is unique in economic history."

Freedom of navigation was a logical complement to freedom of commerce. Prohibitions against foreign shipping that had originated in the age of mercantilism began to disappear during the middle years of the nineteenth century. As usual, England led the way. The navigation laws had been designed to restrict water transportation within the British Empire to British vessels. They were removed at the same time as the corn

---

Public Policy, ed. John Bright and James E. Thorold Rogers, 2 vols. (London, 1870), 1:362–63; John Stuart Mill, *Principles of Political Economy with Some of Their Applications to Social Philosophy*, 2 vols. (London, 1848), 2:120.

laws and for essentially the same reason. The famine in Ireland during the Hungry Forties forced the government to suspend them in order to facilitate the importation of foreign grain, and in 1849 the suspension became permanent except for coastal navigation. Even this exception came to an end in 1854. Other maritime nations promptly followed the example of the United Kingdom. The Dutch navigation laws, for instance, were repealed between 1850 and 1855. At the same time, restrictions and levies imposed on important international waterways were gradually lifted. Passage through the Sound and the Belts connecting the North Sea with the Baltic became free in 1857. River tolls were abolished on the Danube in the same year, on the Rhine and the lower Elbe in 1861, on the Scheldt in 1863, and on the upper Elbe in 1863 and 1870. The shipment of goods among the nations of Europe was now easier than ever before.[16]

The advantages that economic liberalism brought industrialists and financiers were even greater than those enjoyed by merchants and shippers. Indeed, the wishes of the entire business community found an increasingly attentive and sympathetic hearing in government circles. As early as 1829, the *Circular to Bankers* in Great Britain had declared that "every Administration has, for twenty years past, considered the Custom-House, the Excise, the merchants and manufacturers of Lancashire; and the merchants, loan-contractors, and money-dealers, in London; as the whole of the political world." The people in government, it went on, *"now watch the operations in London, of the great money machine, with as much solicitude as a projector watches the motion of the most essential parts of an ingenious invention, upon which he has staked his fame and fortune."* It may have been an exaggeration to say that the authorities regarded business interests as the whole of the political world, but they believed them to be of major importance.

Their concern for manufacturers and bankers became apparent in the wave of legislation facilitating the incorporation of business enterprises. Its purpose was to substitute a general registration procedure for the special authorization required of companies seeking the advantages of limited liability. The Congress of German Economists, a pillar of laissez-faire orthodoxy, claimed that it was a mistake to insist on a state concession for the formation of joint-stock companies because the bureaucracy

16. *Manchester Times*, 27 October 1838, p. 3; Herbert Heaton, "Economic Change and Growth," in *The New Cambridge Modern History*, 12 vols. (Cambridge, 1960–70), 10:38; Cobden, *Speeches*, 1:360; David S. Landes, *The Unbound Prometheus: Technological Change and Industrial Development in Western Europe from 1750 to the Present* (Cambridge, 1969), p. 200; Herbert Heaton, *Economic History of Europe* (New York and London, 1936), pp. 675–76; Charles H. Pouthas, *Démocraties et capitalisme (1848–1860)* (Paris, 1941), p. 231.

was in no position to judge the needs and problems of industry. Many of the European governments, eager to encourage economic expansion, agreed. In England a series of acts between 1855 and 1858 granted limited liability upon registration under certain conditions, and in 1862 a new comprehensive measure made it generally available. In France the law of 1863 created the *société à responsabilité limitée*, a true limited-liability corporation, but restricted its size until a new measure in 1867 removed the last controls. In 1869 the liberal provisional government of Spain adopted the French law of 1867 almost word for word. Finally, the North German Confederation in 1870 and Belgium in 1873 followed the example of London and Paris.

During those same years, the remaining restrictions on industrial competition imposed by artisan guilds, which were still active in Central and Eastern Europe, fell. In Germany the long struggle for *Gewerbefreiheit*, the right of the citizen to engage in any occupation or business, was finally won—in the Austrian crownlands in 1859, in most German states during the early 1860s, and in the North German Confederation in 1869. Sweden, which had abolished the handicraft corporations in 1846, introduced complete industrial freedom in 1864. Denmark repealed the old guild laws in 1849 and 1857. Russia, most of which had never known a corporative artisan system, destroyed its last remnants in the Baltic provinces in 1866.[17]

Of particular significance to financiers and bankers was the removal of the limitations on interest rates. An agrarian society, suspicious of most forms of moneyed wealth, had maintained these since the Middle Ages. In the industrializing nineteenth century, however, usury laws appeared to spokesmen for business interests as relics of a bygone time of economic darkness. Karl Braun spoke with amused condescension about those who "have the firm conviction that we can by means of 'laws,' that is, by means of commandments or prohibitions manufactured in a constitutional law factory, make bread bigger, tastier, and cheaper, or the interest rate lower, or the trades prosperous, or freight costs everywhere uniformly cheap." In Great Britain the usury laws, which generally had been evaded anyway during periods of tight credit, were repealed in 1854. Holland followed in 1857, Belgium in 1865, and the North German Confederation in 1867. In 1857 the Bank of France received the right to set its discount rate at more than 6 percent, and this privilege was

17. *Circular to Bankers*, 19 June 1829, p. 379; *Verhandlungen des eilften Kongresses deutscher Volkswirthe in Mainz am 1., 2., 3. und 4. September 1869* (Berlin, 1870), pp. 45–46; Rondo E. Cameron, *France and the Economic Development of Europe, 1800–1914: Conquests of Peace and Seeds of War* (Princeton, 1961), p. 35; Landes, *Unbound Prometheus*, pp. 197–98; Pouthas, *Démocraties et capitalisme*, pp. 234–35, 390–91; E. J. Hobsbawm, *The Age of Capital, 1845–1878* (New York, 1975), p. 36.

later extended by judicial interpretation to all banking houses. In short, by 1870 the governments of Europe had largely cleared away the legal obstacles to industrial capitalism with which earlier centuries had sought to perpetuate an agrarian economic system.[18]

Yet the ebb tide of laissez-faire was as rapid as the flood had been. No sooner was state regulation of economic activity largely eliminated after a long and bitter struggle than a movement began for its return in a different form. The unceasing conflict of interests and classes, it turned out, did not always produce the greatest happiness of the greatest number. There were victims as well as victors, and the victims were sometimes strong enough to induce government to intervene in their behalf. The most drastic shift of opinion occurred within the business community itself, which had fought so doggedly for rugged individualism. The crash of 1873 and the following depression converted most industrialists from free trade to protectionism. Similarly, the quickening flow of grain from the New World to the Old persuaded many landowners, who had traditionally favored low tariffs, that their survival depended on a change in commercial policy. A powerful alliance of business and agricultural interests soon prevailed in every country of Europe except a handful of laissez-faire stalwarts. The twenty-five or thirty years of declining customs duties initiated by the repeal of the corn laws in England were followed by about forty years of rising rates. The vision of a continent bound together by ties of commercial interdependence which made military conflict unlikely dissolved in the latter decades of the nineteenth century.

The retreat from free trade was led by countries so backward economically that their industries could not hold their own in international competition. The tariff rates of Russia rose about 50 percent in 1876, when a new law required payment of duties in gold instead of the depreciated paper currency. In 1877 Spain established two sets of customs, one for countries that granted her most-favored-nation status and another for those that did not. In Italy, where the Piedmontese industrialists sought greater protection, the government introduced a rate increase in 1878, although its extent was limited by commercial treaties that were still in force. That same year a new tariff in the Dual Monarchy established an uneasy compromise between the agrarians of Hungary, who still favored free trade, and the manufacturers of Austria, who wanted security against foreign competitors.

In 1879 the protectionist trickle turned into a torrent when Germany, now the greatest economic power on the Continent, adopted a higher tariff in response to demands from the Junker landowners of the east and

18. Braun, "Staats- und Gemeinde-Steuern," p. 18; Phyllis Deane, *The First Industrial Revolution* (Cambridge, 1965), pp. 208–9; Landes, *Unbound Prometheus*, p. 198.

the wealthy industrialists of the west, an unbeatable combination. This was a signal to the remaining waverers to start abandoning free trade. France, never entirely happy with the commercial policies of Napoleon III, substituted specific for ad valorem duties in 1881, raising rates on many manufactured imports, especially woolens. For the next decade, customs in Europe multiplied and leapfrogged as each nation tried to defend its manufacturing and farming against what it considered unfair competition. Even Switzerland departed from a long-standing policy by introducing protective duties in 1891. A year later France adopted the Méline tariff, which raised the rate on most agricultural products other than grain by about 25 percent. At the opening of the twentieth century, only Great Britain and the Netherlands were still loyal to free trade, while Belgium and the Scandinavian countries were slowly moving toward protectionism. Elsewhere economic nationalism had already triumphed. The average ad valorem equivalent of customs duties on the principal manufactures exported from the United Kingdom in 1904 was 25 percent in Germany, 27 in Italy, 34 in France, 35 in Austria, and 131 in Russia. Although businessmen and agriculturists had argued after the Napoleonic Wars that government regulation of commerce was an unwarranted intrusion, they were maintaining a hundred years later that it had become an urgent necessity.[19]

This economic nationalism of the period after 1870 was not a new phenomenon in Europe. It represented rather the reemergence in a modified form of the mercantilistic principles of the absolutist monarchs, who had sought to strengthen the material resources of their state by prescription so as to compete more effectively with other states. The commercial policies advocated by a Friederich List or Félix-Jules Méline were not fundamentally different from those espoused by a Thomas Mun or Jean-Baptiste Colbert. There was another aspect of economic life, however, in which the state assumed a completely new function during the nineteenth century. For the first time, it began to regulate the relationship between capital and labor for the purpose of mitigating the poverty and exploitation of the working class. This was a radical departure. In the preindustrial age, the economy had been too weak to enable government to protect the citizen against extreme privation. But the growth of affluence resulting from the rationalization of production now enabled the community to raise the standard of living of the propertyless without under-

19. Bowden, Karpovich, and Usher, *Economic History of Europe*, pp. 617–18, 621–22; Carlton J. H. Hayes, *A Generation of Materialism, 1871–1900* (New York and London, 1941), pp. 205–7; Cameron, *France and the Economic Development of Europe*, pp. 39–40; J. H. Clapham, *The Economic Development of France and Germany, 1815–1914*, 4th ed. (Cambridge, 1966), pp. 182, 322; Heaton, *Economic History*, pp. 676–77.

mining the source of wealth of the propertied. A new concept of public authority began to emerge, a revolutionary insight that the state could be an important instrument for the assertion of individual need against collective indifference. Government was a two-edged sword that might become a weapon of the masses in the struggle for a more humane society. The utopian socialists had been the first to recognize fully the philanthropic potentialities of the state, but after 1870 many defenders of the established system also began to maintain that it must solve the social question or be destroyed by it.

This does not mean that laissez-faire was suddenly abandoned in a drastic shift of public opinion toward the welfare state. Far from it. There were scholars and publicists who continued to spread its doctrines right up to the First World War. In 1887 the eminent historian Ernest Lavisse, writing pseudonymously, published a primer for the elementary schools of France entitled *Little Stories for Learning about Life*. In one of the tales, an old shoemaker refutes the arguments of a young man confused by socialist propaganda; he recites the familiar catechism of rugged individualism: "I say that what we must recommend to the worker above all is labor, order, and thrift. Thereby we rise. Not all at once, of course. My father had nothing; I have something; my children, if they do as I do, will double or triple what I shall leave; my grandchildren will be gentlemen. This is how we rise in society." Such lessons continued to be taught in the school system and in the popular press of Europe.

Now, however, there were also those—and their number was growing —who maintained that society must not allow economic competition to degenerate into a struggle to the death. The state should seek to establish a fair balance between weak and strong, between rich and poor. The men who advocated far-reaching social reform were motivated by various considerations. Some were dedicated idealists like Johann Jacoby, a restless firebrand from East Prussia who began his political career as a middle-of-the-road liberal and ended it more than thirty years later as a member of the socialist party. In 1870, while still in the camp of bourgeois democracy, he declared in a speech to the voters of Berlin that a truly moral life of the community must rest on the principles of equality and fraternity. It followed that "the founding of the smallest association of workers will be of greater value for the future cultural historian than the day of the battle of Sadowa!"

Other proponents of social reform were inspired by less lofty considerations. To them, concession was the only alternative to class war. If the workers could not improve their position under the established system, they would listen to the blandishments of radicals and subversives. Arthur James Balfour, leader of the Conservatives in the House of Commons, explained in a speech in Manchester in 1895 that social legislation was not merely to be distinguished from socialist legislation but was its most direct opposite and its most effective antidote. Socialism would never gain control of public opinion among the working class or among any other classes if those who wielded the collective forces of the community showed themselves willing to ameliorate every legitimate grievance and put society "upon a firmer and more solid basis." The imperatives of idealism thus combined with the calculations of self-interest to produce a persuasive argument that the state could no longer afford to be content with the role of policeman on the corner. It had to become an instrument of social justice.[20]

An important step in this direction was the legalization of combinations of employees for the purpose of collective bargaining with employers. After the mid-century, the governments of Europe began to repeal laws that had kept workers from attempting to improve their economic position by organizing. Until then trade unions had been regarded as dangerous associations, futile yet insubordinate, whose activities must be restricted to prevent serious harm to the economy. During the 1830s Harriet Martineau observed, in a work of popularization designed to make the complexities of classical economics comprehensible to the general public, that "combinations of labourers against capitalists (whatever other effects they may have) cannot secure a permanent rise of wages unless the supply of labour falls short of the demand;—in which case, strikes are usually unnecessary. Nothing can permanently affect the rate of wages which does not affect the proportion of population to capital." More than that, wrote the *Edinburgh Review* at the same time, trade unions were no longer content merely to seek "the establishment or maintenance of a fixed rate of wages in a particular employment." Now their spokesmen often assumed a higher tone. "They proclaim war against capitalists in general and hold out the grand project of dividing profits among that class of producers which at present furnishes labour and receives wages,—a project which of course implies a complete social as well as political revolution." To allow free scope to such subversive organizations was sure to invite class warfare.

But during the latter decades of the nineteenth century, the state began to accord a grudging recognition to their activities. For one thing, the size of the industrial labor force grew so rapidly that it was increasingly difficult to enforce the prohibition against combinations. Workers were forming fraternal orders and benefit societies. Although these groups generally remained within the letter of the law, they performed many of

20. Ernest Lavisse [Pierre Laloi], *Petites histoires pour apprendre la vie* (Paris, 1887), p. 100; Johann Jacoby, *Gesammelte Schriften und Reden*, 2d ed., 2 vols. (Hamburg, 1877), 2:354; *Times* (London), 17 January 1895, p. 10.

the functions of trade unions, legally, semilegally, and sometimes illegally. Would it not be better to allow what could not be suppressed anyway? Many reformist bureaucrats and politicians also found it awkward to uphold the right of citizens to organize for the realization of political goals while denying them the same right for the achievement of economic goals. Laws against combinations of employees began to seem anachronistic in an age that boasted of its growing democracy.

Finally, there was a widespread feeling that trade unions would give the worker an illusion that he was doing something to improve his position but would not actually change the existing distribution of material advantages. The laws of economics would prove stronger than the rhetoric of labor organizations. The democratic *Volks-Zeitung* in Berlin argued in 1864 that trade unions should be legalized, provided that freedom of occupation and freedom of movement were introduced at the same time. For the mobility of labor would counteract the effect of strikes by insuring an ample supply of strikebreakers. "We shall see how [the right to organize] will lose its ostensible dangerousness as soon as the two other demands are met." Even though he was in sympathy with the labor movement, Albert de Mun declared in the French legislature in 1883 that trade unions, regardless of their right to strike, would "not give [the workers] what they lack above all: security for their future, stability in their position, and steady advancement in their occupation." Most of those who supported the repeal of prohibitions against combinations did so not in the expectation that it would change much but that it would change little.[21]

The result was the gradual legalization of the establishment and activity of trade unions in most countries of Europe—in Belgium and the North German Confederation during the 1860s, in Austria, Great Britain, and the Netherlands during the 1870s, in Spain and France during the 1880s, and in Finland, Poland, and Russia during the 1900s. Yet those who had assumed that the right of workers to organize would have only a minor effect on the relations between capital and labor were mistaken. The number of employees joining trade unions increased rapidly, and although it did not reach even half of the industrial work force in any country, it usually included the most skilled, productive, and energetic members. By the effective use of collective bargaining, they often forced employers to grant concessions that would have been unthinkable before

---

21. Harriet Martineau, *Illustrations of Political Economy*, 25 vols. (London, 1832–34), vol. 7, *A Manchester Strike: A Tale*, p. 135; "Trades'-Unions and Strikes," *Edinburgh Review, or Critical Journal* 59 (1834): 341–42; *Volks-Zeitung*, 24 June 1864, p. 1; *Discours et écrits divers du comte Albert de Mun*, ed. Charles Alexandre Geoffroy de Grandmaison, 7 vols. (Paris, 1888–1904), 3:76.

the legalization of combinations. Some workers even established links with workers in the same industry in foreign countries, starting with the International Miners' Federation in 1890, which brought together representatives from labor organizations in England, France, Germany, and Austria. Twenty years later, there were twenty-eight international trade-union secretariats with a combined affiliation of more than 6 million members, between 55 and 60 percent of all organized workers. The labor movement had now become a major force in the economic life of Europe.[22]

The state, however, was not content merely to allow employees to defend their interests collectively in dealing with employers. It also proceeded to intervene directly in one of the most sensitive areas of the economic process, the condition of employment. Within a generation or two after the onset of industrialization, it began to limit the work of women and children, the first victims of entrepreneurial exploitation. Its efforts frequently encountered the resistance of those who, for a variety of reasons, maintained that government supervision of labor relations, however well-intentioned, would do more harm than good. There were business organizations like the chamber of commerce in Altena in Westphalia, which declared that "many an honest worker, who now rejoices in the good fortune, for which he has so endlessly yearned, of a piece of property and a certain affluence, owes this solely and exclusively to the advances of industry, which offered him the opportunity to free his children . . . from idleness and lazy dawdling, and to use the wages of their labor wisely in the best interest of the family."

There were also laissez-faire politicians, like Kirkman Finlay in the British Parliament, who worried that "those poor children would be thrown upon the world without means of support," and who "put it to the House, whether . . . it was prepared to legislate upon the subject—to regulate free labour, and to interpose between the father and his child?"

And then there were the workers themselves, who often saw in government regulation only the lost earnings of their sons and daughters. Take the petition from forty-four heads of families in the canton of Zürich against a proposal to prohibit the employment of schoolchildren in the spinning mills. Should not every citizen who is under the same government, they asked, have as much right and freedom as every other citizen? And if my neighbor, who has a weaver's shop in his cellar, is free to em-

22. Heaton, *Economic History*, p. 717; F. H. Hinsley, "Introduction," in *The New Cambridge Modern History*, 12 vols. (Cambridge, 1960–70), 11:14–15; Gustav Stolper, Karl Häuser, and Knut Borchardt, *The German Economy, 1870 to the Present* (New York, Chicago, San Francisco, and Atlanta, 1967), p. 49; F. S. L. Lyons, *Internationalism in Europe, 1815–1914* (Leyden, 1963), pp. 157–58.

ploy his children in winding and weaving, why should not my children have a chance to earn a schilling in the spinneries as well?[23]

Despite all these arguments, the governments of Europe started to impose restrictions on employment with regard to age and sex. There was special concern that the exploitation of the young would lead to the growth of a work force that was illiterate, unskilled, debilitated, and insubordinate. "Nor if young boys are imperfectly educated, or prematurely overworked, can they become vigorous and intelligent artisans" is how the London *Times* put it. "To employ women and children unduly is simply to run in debt with Nature." Starting in the middle decades, there was an outpouring of labor legislation, which soon spread across all of Europe. England led the way with the factory act of 1833—after earlier measures had proved inadequate because they had remained unenforced—which forbade the employment of children under nine in most textile mills and limited the number of hours that those between nine and thirteen could work to nine a day or forty-eight a week. In 1839 a cabinet order in Prussia prohibited the labor of children under nine in manufacturing establishments and restricted the working day of those under sixteen to ten hours. According to the French law of 1841, children under eight were not to be employed in establishments with machinery or with more than twenty workers, those between the ages of eight and twelve were to work no more than eight hours a day, and those between twelve and sixteen were to work no more than twelve hours. In Lombardy the government in 1843 declared it illegal for factory owners to hire minors under nine. And in Switzerland, where labor legislation was at first left to the cantons, a federal law of 1877 prohibited night work for young people between fourteen and eighteen.

Regulation of the employment of women began a little later for essentially the same reason. The increasing sophistication of technology made cheap but unskilled labor less important for industrial growth. Society could now afford to place new emphasis on the promotion of family life among the lower classes, on the proper upbringing of children and a higher standard of personal morality. One government after another adopted measures restricting female labor on the same lines as child labor. In 1842, for example, Great Britain prohibited the employment of women in mines; in 1844 it established for them a maximum workweek of sixty-nine hours; and in 1847, 1850, 1853, and 1874, it introduced

23. "Jahresbericht der Handelskammer des Kreises Altena für 1856 und 1857," *Preussisches Handelsarchiv: Wochenschrift für Handel, Gewerbe und Verkehrsanstalten* 2 (1857):675; Great Britain, *Parliamentary Debates*, 1st ser. (1803–20), 38:369; Rudolf Braun, *Sozialer und kultureller Wandel in einem ländlichen Industriegebiet (Zürcher Oberland) unter Einwirkung des Maschinen- und Fabrikwesens im 19. und 20. Jahrhundert* (Erlenbach-Zürich and Stuttgart, 1965), pp. 116–17.

a limit of ten hours a day for female employees in the textile mills. In France the law of 1892 prescribed a workday of eleven hours for women and the law of 1900 prescribed ten hours. So it went in other countries as well.

Male workers benefited from such legislation. There were first of all indirect advantages because many industrial establishments could not operate economically without the participation of the women and children on their work force. Thus, restrictions meant to apply to some came to apply to all. But more directly, the reasoning that justified protection for women and children could also be used to vindicate protection for men. Should they not also be defended by the state against economic oppression and exploitation? More and more countries agreed that they should. The Swiss law of 1877 limited the workday of all employees to eleven hours. In England the law of 1909 established a maximum of eight hours a day for miners, the first measure directly regulating the workday of adult males. The state even sought to determine wages as well as hours with the introduction in 1912 of a minimum rate of pay in the British collieries.[24]

More than that, some governments began to move cautiously beyond the supervision of industrial conditions toward the establishment of social security. Not only would the worker be protected against exploitation during the period of employment, but he would be secure against privation during the period of unemployment. Insurance funds, supported by contributions from the public treasury as well as from employers and employees, were to guarantee a minimum income to the urban working class in times of need. This was the most radical departure from classical economics, whose theoreticians had stressed that the only way to improve the position of the masses was self-help. In the second edition of his *Economic Harmonies*, Bastiat had written that retirement funds for workers should be supported only by workers, that they should be voluntary, and that "it is most unjust and antisocial to make the classes which remain excluded from the benefits contribute to them by taxation, that is, by force."

Yet only a generation later, the logic of laissez-faire, however plausible

24. *Times* (London), 4 March 1867, p. 9; Heaton, *Economic History*, pp. 697–99; Theodore S. Hamerow, *Restoration, Revolution, Reaction: Economics and Politics in Germany, 1815–1871* (Princeton, 1958), p. 19; Bowden, Karpovich, and Usher, *Economic History of Europe*, p. 486; Kent Roberts Greenfield, *Economics and Liberalism in the Risorgimento: A Study of Nationalism in Lombardy, 1814–1848* (Baltimore, 1934), p. 145; Lyons, *Internationalism in Europe*, p. 141; Achille Viallate, "La France économique de 1870 à nos jours," in *Histoire générale du IVᵉ siècle à nos jours*, ed. Ernest Lavisse and Alfred Rambaud, 12 vols. (Paris, 1893–1901), 12:783; Peter N. Stearns, *European Society in Upheaval: Social History since 1750*, 2d ed. (New York and London, 1975), p. 208.

or persuasive, was in retreat before the exigencies faced by statesmen anxious to preserve social stability. The embattled Bismarck, struggling in vain to halt the spread of socialism, told the Reichstag in 1889: "If we have 700,000 small pensioners, who draw their pensions from the empire, among precisely those classes which do not otherwise have much to lose and which believe erroneously that under a change they can gain a great deal, then I consider it a tremendous advantage. . . . If you can provide us with this benefit of more than half a million small pensioners in the empire, you will teach . . . the common man to regard the empire as a beneficent institution." Such was the usual reasoning of those who established the social security systems of Europe.

The Germans pioneered with their comprehensive program of insurance against sickness in 1883, accident in 1884, and old age and invalidity in 1889. Austria introduced accident insurance in 1887 and sickness insurance in 1888. Denmark adopted the German system between 1891 and 1898, and Belgium between 1894 and 1903. Italy established accident and old-age insurance in 1898. In a constitutional amendment of 1890, Switzerland authorized the federal government to organize a social security program. Insurance against accidents was also introduced in Norway in 1894, England in 1897, France in 1898, Spain and the Netherlands in 1900, Sweden in 1901, and Russia in 1903. Great Britain adopted a broad program of social security later than many of the Continental countries. But when it finally came, it was the most advanced in the world, providing old-age pensions in 1908 and limited insurance against unemployment in 1911, an entirely new departure. Not only was participation in these programs obligatory for both employers and employees, but in some cases, in Germany and England, for example, the public treasury contributed to the payments. For the first time in history, the community recognized in principle an obligation to protect the citizen against destitution, not as a matter of charity but of right. By the time hostilities began in the summer of 1914, Europe had crossed the threshold of the welfare state.[25]

---

25. Bastiat, *Harmonies économiques*, 2d ed. (Paris, 1851), p. 398; Otto von Bismarck, *Die gesammelten Werke*, 15 vols. (Berlin, 1924–35), 13:403; Hayes, *Generation of Materialism*, p. 214; Theodor Schieder, "Political and Social Developments in Europe," in *The New Cambridge Modern History*, 12 vols. (Cambridge, 1960–70), 11:265; Stearns, *European Society in Upheaval*, pp. 208–9.

11

THE ENFRANCHISEMENT OF THE MASSES

Of all the political and social reforms introduced in Europe during the nineteenth century, none represented a sharper break with the past than manhood suffrage. Never before had any sizable community been able to sustain a form of government in which civic equality was granted to every adult male regardless of class, property, or education. Even in France the revolutionary experiment with a mass franchise in 1792 was abandoned by the constitution of 1795. The exclusion of the lower classes from participation in the political process was everywhere regarded as essential for stable government. The purpose of the state was precisely to maintain economic and social distinctions, which were believed to be timeless and ineradicable. It would thus be absurd to rely on civic equality to defend class inequality; it would be a contradiction. Adam Smith had declared that "civil government, so far as it is instituted for the security of property, is in reality instituted for the defence of the rich against the poor, or of those who have some property against those who have none at all." This view had been accepted as a truism of political theory. To allow the masses to participate in the determination of state policy was to open the door to chaos; it was to invite the fox to guard the henhouse. The result was sure to be anarchy leading to tyranny.[1]

Yet after 1815 the enfranchisement of the lower classes gradually became a reality. The right to elect members of the legislature was broadened little by little until most European countries had extended it to virtually all adult male citizens by the time of the First World War. The result was a political revolution, accomplished generally without violence. Not only did the propertyless receive the suffrage for the first time, but as a consequence the nature of the civic process itself changed drastically. The system of elite politics, in which men of means controlled affairs of state directly, gave way to one of mass politics, in which a highly complex structure of party organizations, publications, conventions, and campaigns became essential for the maintenance of influence over government. As early as 1834, Chateaubriand complained that Europe was rushing toward democracy. The people had become their own masters. Having reached their majority, sighed the aging writer, they were claiming that they no longer needed guidance. "The most impudent doctrines

1. Adam Smith, *An Inquiry into the Nature and Causes of the Wealth of Nations*, 2 vols. (London, 1776), 2:320.

concerning property, equality, and liberty are being proclaimed day and night in the presence of monarchs, who tremble behind a triple line of unreliable soldiers. The flood of democracy will overtake them." There were countless other traditionalists who worried about the future of their society as the suffrage was extended lower and lower in the community, as the electorate grew, as the political process became democratized. They watched in apprehension, while the masses gained what appeared to be a decisive influence in the determination of public affairs.

By the time war broke out in July 1914, the enfranchisement of the masses had been largely completed. A few countries still clung to a restricted suffrage, but their number was rapidly diminishing, so it appeared to be only a matter of time before they too succumbed to the democratic tide. On the eve of the war, Stanley Leathes, one of the editors of *The Cambridge Modern History*, surveyed the contemporary world scene: "In Europe itself one of the most remarkable features of the most recent period has been the steady advance of democracy." Since it had been practically unknown before the French Revolution, he continued, the universal acceptance of representative democracy among European nations constituted a "striking revolution," accomplished in many cases without any violent convulsion. Manhood suffrage was on the march, spreading from the industrialized states of the west toward the eastern oligarchies and autocracies. "Its adoption in Hungary is under consideration. In Russia, in spite of periodic reactions, there seems to be an advance in the same direction. Even Turkey is making the democratic experiment. If it succeeds, every country in Europe, not even excepting Russia, will have recognised to some extent the democratic principle."

Moreover, all the self-governing European communities beyond the seas had adopted democratic government, Leathes pointed out. Some observers even looked forward to its adoption in British India and Egypt, not to mention the attempt to introduce it in the Ottoman Empire. "But few would assert with confidence that democracy was suited to Asiatics; in spite of the example of Hayti, none perhaps would venture to propose its general application to the communities of African negroes." It was a European invention and was probably only suited to the "European race and European culture." Yet that was unfortunate, for in every country where the constitution is democratic, "representative institutions afford a means, however imperfect, for the expression of popular sentiments; they act as a real check on the executive authorities and exercise a modifying influence upon older national institutions and customs." They stand guard over Europe against political tyranny.[2]

2. François René de Chateaubriand, "L'avenir du monde, fragment politique," *Revue des deux mondes*, 3d ser., 2 (1834):232–34; Stanley Leathes, "Modern Europe," in *The Cam-*

The enfranchisement of the masses, the most important result of the victory of democracy, was all the more remarkable because throughout the nineteenth century most politicians and publicists continued to fear the effects of manhood suffrage. All the time-honored arguments concerning the ignorance and corruption of the mob were enlisted in defense of oligarchical authority. Opposition to a broad franchise was especially vigorous among the conservatives and the liberals, who, however much they may have differed regarding the best system of government, at least agreed that it must be elitist in nature. Both remained convinced that people without property or education were incapable of exercising civic rights intelligently.

Indeed, they believed that the common man preferred not to be troubled with decisions concerning affairs of state. Thomas Carlyle, who was closer in spirit to the landed patricians of the Continent than to the bourgeois reformers of Victorian Britain, voiced a common conservative conviction that what the masses wanted was not to lead but to be led, to be led by men of greater wisdom and experience:

> What are all popular commotions and maddest bellowings, from Peterloo to the Place-de-Grève itself? Bellowings, *in*articulate cries as of a dumb creature in rage and pain; to the ear of wisdom they are *in*articulate prayers: "Guide me, govern me! I am mad, and miserable, and cannot guide myself!" Surely of all 'rights of man,' this right of the ignorant man to be guided by the wiser, to be, gently or forcibly, held in the true course by him, is the indisputablest. Nature herself ordains it from the first; Society struggles toward perfection by enforcing and accomplishing it more and more. If Freedom have any meaning, it means enjoyment of this right, wherein all other rights are enjoyed. . . . In Rome and Athens, as elsewhere, if we look practically, we shall find that it was not by loud voting and debating of many, but by wise insight and ordering of a few that the work was done. So is it ever, so will it ever be.[3]

According to the conservatives, the distribution of civic rights should reflect the inherent inequality of men as clearly as the distribution of property rights.

The liberals also adhered to the elite principle of authority, although they maintained that talent rather than birth was the true measure of political capacity. They too believed that the man in the street wanted to be told what to do; he wanted to obey the decisions of government, not

bridge Modern History, ed. A. W. Ward, G. W. Prothero, and Stanley Leathes, 14 vols. (Cambridge and New York, 1902–12), 12:5–7.

3. Thomas Carlyle, *Chartism* (London, 1840), pp. 52–54.

make them. How could someone whose life had been spent in toil and hardship be expected to master the complexities of statecraft? As the Bourbon Restoration began in France, Benjamin Constant defined the liberal position on the system of voting. Those whom poverty keeps in eternal dependence, he asserted, are no more enlightened than children on public affairs, nor are they more interested than foreigners in national prosperity, whose elements they do not understand and whose advantages they share only indirectly. "Property alone," by providing leisure for reflection and judgment, "makes men capable of exercising political rights." Thus, the masses could reasonably expect order, justice, defense, and even solicitude from the state, but not participation in the shaping of its policy.

The condemnation of manhood suffrage appears repeatedly in the writings of middle-of-the-road political theorists throughout Europe. The Italian philosopher Antonio Rosmini-Serbati, who played a significant role in the Risorgimento as a spokesman for liberal Catholicism, wrote in 1848 that "the universal vote is the same in its consequences as the equalization of all property; it is the agrarian law which in our time ends in communism. . . . What was the proximate and efficient cause of the revolution of '89? It was the vote bestowed on persons and not on things." The views of the liberal Swiss jurist Johann Kaspar Bluntschli were similar. In his *Theory of the Modern State* of 1876, he declared that the right to vote in the state and for state purposes is not a natural right of man but a state right, a right derived from the state and serving the state. It does not exist outside the state and should not exist against the state. "The voters exercise this right not as men but as citizens." Since the ability to vote intelligently is the essential precondition for the right to vote, it follows that "without political education there should be no political freedom and no political suffrage." To give the franchise to classes that are obviously incompetent and unfit would mean suicide for the state. On this point all liberals were in agreement.[4]

The position of the democrats on the suffrage question was more equivocal. In principle they were committed to the enfranchisement of all men without regard for status or wealth. After all, the lower classes embodied the popular will to which they assigned ultimate authority in all civic issues. They therefore fought for the enfranchisement of the common man with courage, often at considerable political and even personal risk. Their faith in his capacity to govern himself must be ac-

4. Benjamin de Constant, *Collection complète des ouvrages publiés sur le gouvernement représentatif et la constitution actuelle de la France, formant une espèce de cours de politique constitutionelle*, 4 vols. (Paris and Rouen, 1818–20), 1:138–39; Antonio Rosmini-Serbati, *Opere edite e inedite*, 49 vols. (Rome, Milan, and Padua, 1934–77), 24:181; J. C. Bluntschli, *Lehre vom Stat*, 3 vols. (Stuttgart, 1875–76), 3:421–22, 425.

knowledged. Yet the fact remains that the democrats believed in him in the abstract rather than in his concrete coarseness and griminess. The lower classes should be given the right to vote so that they could elect to office men of greater wisdom who had their best interests at heart. But what if they turned instead to unscrupulous demagogues and rabble-rousers or to glib reactionaries who knew how to play on their prejudices? The democrats had to wrestle constantly with the fear, voiced in private more often than in public, that the common man might use the franchise against them, ungrateful for all that they were trying to do for him.

John Stuart Mill epitomizes the dilemma of those who sought to give the masses the right to shape government policy without the risk that they might use it unwisely. In 1835, as a young reformer still in his twenties, he had been confident that the people would use the suffrage to put in power men of patrician background but plebeian sympathy, in short, men like himself:

> It is not necessary that the Many should themselves be perfectly wise; it is sufficient, if they be duly sensible to the value of superior wisdom. It is sufficient if they be aware, that the majority of political questions turn upon considerations of which they, and all persons not trained for the purpose, must necessarily be very imperfect judges; and that their judgment must in general be exercised rather upon the characters and talents of the persons whom they appoint to decide these questions for them, than upon the questions themselves. They would then select as their representatives those whom the general voice of the instructed pointed out as the *most* instructed; and would retain them, so long as no symptom was manifested in their conduct of being under the influence of interests or of feelings at variance with the public welfare.[5]

But when Mill wrote his *Considerations on Representative Government* twenty-six years later, his tone was significantly different; it had become more cautious, more disillusioned. The spread of radical ideas among the lower classes of England and the success of Napoleon III in establishing a plebiscitary autocracy in France had aroused in him a fear of the tyranny of the majority. He still declared boldly that no arrangement of the suffrage can be satisfactory in which any person or class is peremptorily excluded. The right to vote must be open to all persons of full age who desire to obtain it. But at the same time he grumbled about "the natural tendency of representative government, as of modern civilization, . . . towards collective mediocrity." Changes in the system of

5. [John Stuart Mill], "Rationale of Representation," *London Review* 1 (1835):348–49.

election only intensified this tendency by placing the principal power in the hands of classes more and more below the highest level of instruction in the community.

How then is good government to be reconciled with a mass franchise? After wrestling with this problem, Mill comes to a conclusion with which many conservatives would have agreed. It is clear to him that the right to vote must be denied to those who cannot read, write, and perform the common operations of arithmetic. But more than that, until there shall have been devised and until public opinion is willing to accept some mode of plural voting, which will assign to education a degree of superior influence sufficient to counteract the numerical might of the least educated classes, for so long the benefits of manhood suffrage cannot be obtained "without bringing with them, as it appears to me, a chance of more than equivalent evils." Most democrats were less candid about their doubts concerning a popular franchise, but they too pondered and agonized over the contradiction between the wisdom that the masses were supposed to possess in theory and the ignorance that they so often displayed in practice.[6]

Even the socialists had no easy answer to the problem. To be sure, they proclaimed their belief in a fundamental reconstitution of society by which the proletariat would be able to control its own political and economic destiny. But the masses that would create a new era of justice for mankind tomorrow were not necessarily the same masses that were groaning under the yoke of capitalism today, sunk in ignorance and prejudice. Before they could fulfill their high mission, they would have to be educated and enlightened, freed from the superstitions instilled by the old order. That was why the attitude of socialism toward manhood suffrage was so divided. To Ferdinand Lassalle, a popular franchise was the key to the emancipation of the working class; only by using it effectively could the proletariat force the state to become an instrument of its deliverance. To Louis-Auguste Blanqui, on the other hand, manhood suffrage under existing conditions would simply be an obstacle to the victory of the progressive forces in the community. For fifty years, he argued in the spring of 1848, only the counterrevolution has been talking to France. The press, muzzled by financial requirements, has been unable to penetrate beneath the upper levels of society. The education of the masses has been conducted solely by oral instruction, "which has always belonged and still belongs to the enemies of the Republic." The well-known leaders of the vanquished reactionary parties, chiefly in the countryside, are the only ones who attract the attention of the people, whereas

6. John Stuart Mill, *Considerations on Representative Government* (London, 1861), pp. 145–46, 159–60, 171–72.

"the men devoted to the democratic cause are almost unknown to them." How wise is it, then, to entrust the destiny of society to an ignorant and misguided electorate?[7]

The "scientific" socialists were as ambivalent in their attitude toward manhood suffrage as the utopians. What they wrote for publication was as a rule favorable to a mass franchise, which would theoretically make it possible for the proletariat to intensify the agitation for its liberation. In their private correspondence, however, there were frequent expressions of doubt, frequent fears that the lower classes could be misled by false promises and minor concessions into supporting the reaction. In a letter written in 1868, for example, Marx criticized Lassalle's reliance on manhood suffrage. The latter had tried to combine the idea of state assistance to producer cooperatives advanced by the utopian socialist Philippe-Joseph-Benjamin Buchez with the demand of the Chartists for the enfranchisement of the lower classes. But he had overlooked the fact that conditions in Germany were different from those in England. He had overlooked the lessons of the Second Empire in France concerning manhood suffrage. "What I am saying here after the event I told Lassalle to a large extent before, when he came to London in 1862 and invited me to join him at the head of the new movement."

Engels was even more explicit. In 1865, while the constitutional conflict raged in Prussia and the air was full of rumors that Bismarck was about to introduce manhood suffrage, he published his views in a pamphlet dealing with the German situation: "As long as the rural proletariat is not drawn into the movement [opposing the reaction], the urban proletariat . . . cannot and will not accomplish anything, and the general direct franchise is not a weapon for the proletariat but a snare." Only the politicization of the masses, especially in the countryside, could transform the ballot into a support of the working class in the struggle against capitalism.[8]

As for the anarchists, their commitment to a conspiratorial strategy of revolution led logically to a condemnation of the entire apparatus of parties, functionaries, publications, demonstrations, and elections by which socialism sometimes hoped to overthrow the system of private ownership. They saw in all the talk about the enfranchisement of the masses a diversion from the only effective means of destroying capitalism, namely, an unceasing struggle by a dedicated elite of revolutionaries. Bakunin described manhood suffrage as "a grand illusion," which had

7. Ferdinand Lassalle, *Gesammelte Reden und Schriften*, ed. Eduard Bernstein, 12 vols. (Berlin, 1919–20), 3:47, 88–89; Maurice Dommanget, *Auguste Blanqui et la révolution de 1848* (Paris and The Hague, 1972), pp. 53–54.

8. Karl Marx and Friedrich Engels, *Ausgewählte Briefe* (Berlin, 1953), pp. 246–47; idem, *Werke*, 39 vols. (Berlin, 1960–69), 16:74.

led to the defeat of the radical party in many cantons of Switzerland and to its demoralization in all. The advocates of a mass franchise had only been fooling themselves when they promised the people to achieve liberty by means of the ballot box. Their mistake had led to nothing except bitter disappointment, for though their intentions had been honorable, their tactics had been hopelessly wrongheaded.

But the most violent denunciation of manhood suffrage came from Proudhon, who saw in it something even worse than an ineffectual means of expressing the popular will, namely, a device for distorting and frustrating it. The mass franchise, he declared during the Revolution of 1848, is only a clever scheme for making the masses say not what they think but what others want them to say. Indeed, "the surest means of making the people lie is to establish universal suffrage," for it rests on a sort of atomic theory by which the lawmaker, incapable of letting the community speak in the unity of its essence, invites the citizens to express their opinions individually, the way the Epicurean philosopher explains thought, will, and intelligence by combinations of atoms. "As if out of the addition of any quantity of franchises whatsoever the general idea could ever emerge, the idea of the people!" A determination of the popular will was not to be reached by simply counting heads. It had to take into account feelings, instincts, interests, and longings; it could be attained only by those who knew intuitively what the masses really needed and wanted.[9]

Both right and left thus had grave doubts about the civic capacity of the common man, the former because he was too radical, the latter because he was not radical enough. As a result, all the constitutions and election laws in Europe during roughly the first half of the nineteenth century, and many of those in the second half as well, excluded the lower classes from voting or at least minimized their political influence. They did this by a variety of devices restricting the suffrage so that men of means would dominate the electorate. The franchise was made contingent on the ownership of property, payment of taxes, headship of a household, or membership in one of the elite social, economic, educational, or ecclesiastical corporative bodies of the country. Sometimes a combination of these requirements was employed. The relative size of the electorate thus varied from state to state, depending on the stringency of the qualifications for voting. Of the constitutions promulgated in Western and Central Europe before 1848, the French charter of 1814 was one of the most restrictive. It required the payment of three hundred francs in

9. Michel Bakounine, *Oeuvres*, 6 vols. (Paris, 1907–13), 2:36–37; *Oeuvres complètes de P.-J. Proudhon*, 34 vols. (Paris, 1865–76), 17:19, 153.

direct taxes as a condition of the suffrage so that fewer than 100,000 men were eligible in a population of about 30 million. The Spanish constitution of 1812, on the other hand, gave the right to vote to every householder, a provision that most political writers at the time regarded as very democratic, indeed too democratic. All the franchise systems in force during the Restoration, however, sought in various ways to bar from the polls the politically unreliable elements of society: the poor, the ignorant, the restless, the lowly.

Yet even these restrictions did not appear to offer sufficient protection, so that several additional safeguards were introduced. The first was the establishment of an upper house of the legislature, whose function was to counteract reformist zeal on the part of the lower. The qualifications for membership varied considerably, but they generally involved a higher social and economic status than was required for election to the second chamber.

In France during the Restoration, the king could appoint as many peers as he liked with either lifetime or hereditary tenure, each with a seat in the upper house. The Piedmontese Statuto of 1848, which became the constitution of a united Italy, gave the ruler the right to choose members of the senate from several categories of men in an important position in national life, including "persons who by their services or eminent merit have done honor to the country." The Spanish constitution of 1876 conferred membership in the upper house on three groups: first, sons of the king and the heir apparent, archbishops, grandees with a yearly income of sixty thousand pesetas from landownership, captains general, admirals, and high government officials; second, senators appointed by the crown for life from those who could meet the property or salary qualifications; and finally, men elected "by the corporations of the state and by the larger taxpayers," that is, by the nine archbishoprics, the six royal academies, the ten universities, the Economic Societies of the Friends of the Country, and the electoral colleges made up of "members of the provincial deputations, and of representatives chosen from among the municipal councillors and largest taxpayers of the several towns and municipal districts."

The Austrian Herrenhaus was established under a constitutional system originating in the October Diploma of 1860. In 1891 it included 21 archdukes, 66 hereditary peers, and 125 life members (among the latter were 4 princes, 48 counts, 22 church dignitaries, and assorted barons, generals, bankers, professors, and lawyers). In Russia the council of the empire formed in 1906 consisted of a variable number of men. The clergy elected 6, the provincial zemstvos 1 each, the assemblies of the nobility 18, the Imperial Academy of Science and the universities 6, and the

Council of Trade and Commerce together with the committees of commerce and boards of trade 12; the czar also reserved the right to appoint a number equal to the elected members.

To be sure, not all upper houses were weighted so heavily in favor of property and status. The Belgian constitution of 1831, considered in its day the most liberal in Europe, established a senate whose members were elected in part directly by the voters and in part by the provincial councils, each of which could choose two to four members, depending on the number of inhabitants it represented. The Dutch constitution of 1887 provided for the election of senators by the provincial estates. Under the Norwegian constitution of 1814, the Storting as a whole simply chose a quarter of its members to serve as an upper house, the rest then forming the lower. On the other hand, the French senate under the Third Republic was elected indirectly by colleges made up of members of the chamber of deputies, members of the general councils of the departments and the councils of the arrondissements, and delegates chosen by the municipal councils.

In short, the legislative system in almost every country was designed to inhibit reformist tendencies in the lower house by countervailing political, economic, social, and geographical forces represented in the upper house. As Guizot put it, the latter was to perform the function of a body "on a level with the government, living customarily within its sphere, knowing its needs, imbued by its spirit, having the same general interests as it does, but without the personal interests and passions which animate the government in its struggle against the democratic element." It was to serve as a balance wheel of the political mechanism.[10]

There were still other devices for protecting the established order against the dangers of a broad franchise. Until well after the middle of the century, the system of public voting in Europe enabled men of means to exert a restraining influence on the voters, especially in the rural districts. A villager who cast his ballot against the wishes of the landlord was inviting reprisal when time came to renew a loan or extend a lease. Even in the city, where social relations were more impersonal, an employer on election day could intimidate many of his employees. In other words, the method of polling made it easier for those who had an interest in the preservation of the status quo to oppose those who were trying to change it. That is at least one reason why the stronghold of conservatism was almost always the countryside, where deference by the lower to the upper classes remained a deep-rooted tradition.

10. Eugene N. Anderson and Pauline R. Anderson, *Political Institutions and Social Change in Continental Europe in the Nineteenth Century* (Berkeley and Los Angeles, 1967), pp. 56–58; François Guizot, *Histoire parlementaire de France: Recueil complet des discours prononcés dans les chambres de 1819 à 1848*, 5 vols. (Paris, 1863–64), 1:315.

The defenders of public voting, to be sure, advanced other arguments in defense of their position, most of them plausible, all of them sincere. In the course of a discussion of this question in the Prussian legislature, the conservative leader Hermann Wagener maintained that a secret vote leads to intimidation and fraud: "Look also at America. . . . People stand at the ballot box with revolvers and daggers, and force those who are voting in secret to show their ballots to the bystanders." The liberal deputy Georg Beseler came to the same conclusion by a different reasoning. He conceded with some reluctance that secret voting offers greater protection against improper influence over elections. Public voting, however, provides intangible advantages that outweigh its palpable shortcomings: "It is more in keeping with the moral dignity of a free people, and . . . is generally closer in every respect to the Germanic principle of publicity." Even John Stuart Mill, a champion of democracy, argued that voting must be open to public scrutiny since it is a public function. In any political election, he declared, the voter is under an absolute moral obligation to consider the interest of the community, not his private advantage, and to give his vote to the best of his judgment, exactly as he would be bound to do if he were the sole voter and the outcome depended on him alone. This being admitted, it is at least a prima facie consequence that the duty of voting, like any other public duty, should be performed under the eye and criticism of the public because everyone has an interest in its performance and a good reason to consider himself wronged if it is not performed honestly and carefully.

Yet there was still another calculation behind all these arguments. It was almost never openly discussed but was confined to private conversation or correspondence. It appears, among other places, in the diary of the German writer and diplomat Theodor von Bernhardi:

> The proper influence of social position, of education, and of higher insight and intelligence ceases under secret voting, and in its place comes the improper influence of the basest political agitation. For let us make no mistake about it. We will then not be the ones who will lead the great uneducated mass. It will be the worst individuals, the most dangerous elements of civil society who will then gain an entirely incalculable influence. For no man of honor knows the wretched tricks which are required to produce an effect on the masses, and if he did know them, he would not use them. The sense of his own personal dignity does not allow him to do so. . . . The need for secret voting is at bottom always a sign of unhealthy conditions.[11]

11. Stein Rokkan, "The Comparative Study of Political Participation: Notes toward a Perspective on Current Research," in *Essays on the Behavioral Study of Politics*, ed. Austin

Here lay the nub of the opposition to the confidentiality of the ballot.

This was also why, throughout the nineteenth century, most political writers objected to the payment of salaries to members of the legislature. It would reduce the lawmaker to a mere paid employee of the electorate, they argued; it would make him less independent in dealing with conflicting material interests; it would sway his judgment and weaken his impartiality. Politics should be left to people who have the means for withstanding the temptations to which those in authority are always exposed. There was a widespread assumption that the man of wealth was immune to the danger of identifying his private interest with the public interest because he had already achieved economic security. Baron Georg von Vincke, one of those highborn politicians who dominated parliamentary life in Europe during the early stages of constitutional government, boasted in the Prussian chamber of deputies that never in his life had he sought the position of a representative; he had never issued a single declaration to the voters; he had never received from them an address expressing confidence or nonconfidence. He had always refused to permit it. "I believe that, with respect to my voters, I am thus in a completely independent position."

The conviction that a system of elite politics resting on birth and wealth was the surest guarantee of sound government underlay the practice in almost all countries of requiring members of the legislature to serve without salary. The only important exception was France under the Second Empire, an example used repeatedly by political writers elsewhere to vindicate the principle of nonremuneration. Payment to lawmakers, the argument went, makes them pliant tools in the hands of an unscrupulous government. The legitimist *Volksblatt für Stadt und Land* in Germany attacked the idea of placing the government of a country in the hands of an assembly elected by counting heads and composed of people "paid a daily wage." It was "the craziest chimera" ever imagined. "In general, payment for the representation of a country makes sense only when someone wants to make use of it in the Napoleonic sense as a convenient instrument of despotism."

Conservatives, however, were not the only ones to oppose the remuneration of legislators. In England the liberal Brougham wrote in his *Political Philosophy* that nothing could be "more speculative or less practical" than the suggestion of "some extreme reformers" to pay mem-

---

Ranney (Urbana, 1962), p. 75; Prussia, *Stenographische Berichte über die Verhandlungen der durch die Allerhöchste Verordnung vom 27. Dezember 1860 einberufenen beiden Häuser des Landtages: Haus der Abgeordneten,* 7 vols. (Berlin, 1861), 2:654, 656; Mill, *Considerations on Government,* p. 193; *Aus dem Leben Theodor von Bernhardis,* 9 vols. (Leipzig, 1898–1906), 2:72–73.

bers of the legislature for their services, as was done in ancient times. "The only result of this would be a considerable increase in bribery." And John Stuart Mill, with his unique talent for using a democratic logic to arrive at an undemocratic conclusion, defended the principle of non-remuneration as a bulwark against dishonest politics. If legislators were paid, "the occupation of a member of parliament would . . . become an occupation in itself; carried on, like other professions, with a view chiefly to its pecuniary returns, and under the demoralizing influences of an occupation essentially precarious." It would become an object of desire to "adventurers of a low class." Those in office, he went on prophetically, and the many more trying to get into office would be incessantly bidding to attract or retain the support of the voters "by promising all things, honest or dishonest, possible or impossible, and rivalling each other in pandering to the meanest feelings and most ignorant prejudices of the vulgarest part of the crowd." In their resolve to resist any radical tendencies of the electorate, the opponents of legislative salaries overlooked the fact that the determination of public policies by private interests occurs as easily under elite as under mass politics.[12]

Finally, the techniques employed to counteract an excess of reformism included direct influence and pressure by those in authority. The prevailing view in the nineteenth century was that the state had a duty to instruct the voters regarding their interests, to warn them against rabble-rousers and protect them against agitators. After all, they were being bombarded by the conflicting arguments of a bewildering variety of political movements—conservative, liberal, democratic, socialistic. Was it not proper, then, for government, the embodiment of the collective will, to provide civic enlightenment? The minister of the interior was usually entrusted with the delicate task of manipulating the electorate. In a circular to the prefects following the coup of 2 December 1851 in France, Charles de Morny declared that when a man has made his fortune by labor, industry, or agriculture, improving the lot of his workers and making noble use of his wealth, he makes a better legislator than what is by general agreement called a politician. Morny's successor, Jean-Gilbert-Victor de Persigny, was more explicit. How great would be the perplexity of the French people, he wrote, without the intervention of the government. It is therefore important that the authorities enlighten the voters on the subject of the elections. "The people must be prepared to distinguish who are the friends and who are the enemies of the govern-

---

12. Prussia, *Verhandlungen des Landtages: Haus der Abgeordneten* (1861), 3:1440; Anderson and Anderson, *Political Institutions*, p. 54; *Volksblatt für Stadt und Land*, 30 April 1862, p. 1; Henry Brougham, *Political Philosophy*, 3 vols. (London, 1846), 3:73; Mill, *Considerations on Government*, p. 210.

298 · The Structure of Politics

ment which they have just established." Pierre-Jules Baroche, who served successively as minister of the interior, minister of foreign affairs, and president of the state council, said simply that "universal suffrage, left without guidance to contend with local passions, might become a real danger." It was to counter this danger that the state established the system of official candidates.

The situation in Central Europe was similar. From the beginning of German parliamentarism in the early days of the Restoration, princes and ministers had not hesitated to influence the electorate in favor of those who supported the established order. After the victory over the Austrians in 1866, Bismarck acted in accordance with accepted tradition when he set out to insure approval at the polls of the new order that had just been founded by blood and iron. His instructions to subordinates were full of suggestions on how to manipulate votes and voters. He spoke of "the arrangement, consolidation, or division of the election districts"; he sought to determine "that method of voting which holds out the prospect of the most favorable result for us"; but he also warned that "any influence must be exercised with care, avoiding notice." He advised the governor of Schleswig-Holstein not to exert so much pressure on the voters "that it makes the freedom of the elections appear doubtful." At the same time, "your Excellency will not want to hesitate to have suitable candidates recommended by the authorities and officials." He wrote to the minister of the interior that "we must put up government candidates," wondering whether "the moment has not come when the instruction of the people through the official gazettes regarding the North German Confederation seems desirable." The ministry should also direct local officials to "reject and oppose on principle only the incorrigibles, who . . . refuse to cooperate with the government in any way. On the other hand, where a [moderate] liberal or nationalist candidate has the prospect of winning a majority, they should not come out against him." Such were the contrivances and devices that helped Bismarck win his great victory at the polls early in 1867.

Even in Great Britain, with its long tradition of parliamentary government, many men in public life held that the political education of the electorate should not be left to the biased rhetoric of parties and politicians. The authorities had a duty to instruct the voters concerning the great issues of state policy on which law and order depend. When the constitutional conflict was beginning in Prussia during the early 1860s, Lord Augustus Loftus, the English minister in Berlin, told Bernhardi that it was "wrong that . . . the elections have been left entirely alone, and that the government has refrained from swaying them in any way." The authorities should try to exercise influence at the polls. "That happens in all constitutional countries and is part of the game." There was something faintly incongruous about a British diplomat offering advice to Prussian politicians on how to pressure voters and manipulate elections.[13]

All this evidence points to the conclusion that throughout the nineteenth century most men in public life continued to look upon manhood suffrage with profound distrust. It seemed to open the way to demagogues and malcontents, to Napoleons and Caesars. It posed a threat to the accepted values of politics and economics in Europe. It was unfamiliar and unpredictable, unsettling and unreliable. This much is clear. But how can we then account for the fact that, despite all these reservations and fears, the suffrage broadened steadily until the narrow oligarchies of the Restoration had largely been transformed into popular democracies by 1914? What persuaded those in authority to act against their convictions by giving the ballot to the man in the street? This is a crucial question.

The answer appears to be that most of the politicians who introduced the mass franchise regarded it as the lesser of two evils. Sometimes open revolution, as in France in 1848 or in Russia in 1905, left them no choice but to grant the vote to the lower classes. To do otherwise might lead to more fighting in the streets, to chaos, radicalization, and socialism. In most countries, however, manhood suffrage came not as the result of violence but in response to the possibility or threat of violence. The growing demands of labor organizations, trade unions, democratic movements, and socialist parties gradually persuaded the governments of Europe that the enfranchisement of the masses had become inevitable and that the only choice was whether it would come from above through reform or from below through insurrection. The former was obviously preferable. By granting what could not be withheld, the established order might control and tame manhood suffrage, perhaps even emasculate it. Thus, the extension of the voting franchise to the lower classes was intended to preserve the existing distribution of property and power, not displace it. It was to provide the appearance of a democratization of society without its substance.

All these calculations appear clearly in the arguments for manhood suffrage advanced by the well-known politician Hermann Schulze-Delitzsch, a lifelong democrat who pioneered in the establishment of credit unions and consumer cooperatives in Germany. To begin with, he maintained, the enfranchisement of the masses is a matter of simple justice; it is the logical corollary of the principle of the equality of all men before the law.

13. Charles-H. Pouthas, *Démocraties et capitalisme (1848–1860)* (Paris, 1941), p. 414; Albert Thomas, "Napoleon III and the Period of Personal Government (1852–59)," in *Cambridge Modern History*, ed. Ward, Prothero, and Leathes, 11:294; Otto von Bismarck, *Die gesammelten Werke*, 15 vols. (Berlin, 1924–35), 6:97, 181, 215, 238; *Aus dem Leben Bernhardis*, 4:229.

Yet more than that, a broad franchise will have the effect of safeguarding the established social system: "I say to you, gentlemen, that I and my friends demand the same universal, direct, and equal suffrage . . . as the only permanent and effective weapon against these socialistic projects! Only by granting complete equality of rights will you have the weapon to oppose effectively the socialistic leveling of the outward fortunes of life, which nature did not want and which will never be realized."

But might a broad franchise not lead to a political system in which the propertyless predominated over the propertied? Might it not alter in a fundamental way the traditional relationship between economic interests and social classes? Schulze-Delitzsch had no fears on that score. No one ever recognized more clearly the ineffectualness of equality in politics without equality in property and status. "Great social interests like an important social position will automatically prevail," he reassured his listeners, "and . . . the general suffrage without a property requirement is perhaps the most suitable means to establish these interests, to the extent that they are justified. The man who occupies an important position, who stands at the head of an important industrial establishment, the man who by his intelligence surpasses a great part of his fellow citizens, the proprietor of a large estate . . . you will not deprive him of his altogether justifiable influence over many of his fellow citizens, whatever system of voting you establish. Those are powers in life which assert themselves of their own accord." Thus, to many advocates of manhood suffrage, the enfranchisement of the masses was not only the lesser of two evils. It was also an effective safeguard against the danger of true democracy. It was a device by which society could maintain the semblance of civic equality without its reality. It made possible the perpetuation of oligarchical rule in the guise of representative government. Its ultimate effect, far from being revolutionary, was often intended to be conservative.[14]

More than that, the lower classes could be used as a support of the status quo in the perpetual struggle of parties and ideologies. Manhood suffrage did not have to lead to radical schemes of social reconstruction; it could serve to strengthen the existing form of authority against its adversaries. The peasant masses in particular, conservative in their tradition and submissive in their piety, might easily be led to vote in favor of the legitimate order. All that would be required to manufacture popular support for the government at the polls would be some minor economic concessions, a few appeals from the clergy, a little pressure from the bureaucracy, and perhaps a bit of gerrymandering or stuffing of ballot boxes. Napoleon III demonstrated that manhood suffrage could help es-

14. Hermann Schulze-Delitzsch, *Schriften und Reden*, ed. Friedrich Thorwart, 5 vols. (Berlin, 1909–13), 4:415, 632.

tablish an authoritarian regime. His success, especially during the 1850s, in maintaining a plebiscitary dictatorship with the support of the lower classes revealed the possibilities inherent in what came to be known as "Bonapartism." Most traditional statesmen, liberal as well as conservative, shrank from what they regarded as the unscrupulousness and recklessness of those who were ready to unleash the masses in the hope that they would be able to control them. But after the mid-century, a new generation of government leaders—opportunistic, realistic, pragmatic— began to seek the support of the lower classes in order to escape from the political impasses in which they were entangled.

In the spring of 1865, when his foreign policy was encountering stubborn resistance throughout Germany, Bismarck confided to a Hanoverian diplomat that "I do not want . . . lawyers to be elected, but loyal peasants. . . . I do not wish to provide support for democracy with the election law which I have devised and which is designed for the masses. If I, for example, could send here in Prussia 100 workers from my estate to the ballot box, then they would outvote every other opinion in the village to the point of destroying it. This is what I hope to achieve with the help of the landowners in [Schleswig-Holstein]." Such calculations and expectations led other statesmen during the next fifty years to broaden the suffrage, giving the lower classes the right to vote in the hope that they could be manipulated into supporting the government at election time. The mass franchise seemed to offer a way out to politicians in multinational states torn by ethnic conflicts or in industrializing countries frightened by demands for social reform. Behind these extensions of the ballot was the assumption that the common man, especially the peasant, would remain loyal to the established order and would thus swamp the small educated minority seeking fundamental change. The strategy was successful enough, at least in the short run, to persuade many radicals, the anarchists in particular, that manhood suffrage was only an artifice designed to forestall a basic reorganization of the community. And it is also evident that the political leaders responsible for the introduction of manhood suffrage generally expected it to serve not as an instrument of social reconstruction but as a bulwark against it.[15]

This expectation appears repeatedly in various parts of Europe as the right to vote expanded in the course of the nineteenth century. Great Britain was the early model for the Continent in the process of enfranchisement because its parliamentary institutions and experiences were the oldest. As the Napoleonic Wars drew to a close, the English system of representative government began to spread along the Atlantic and the

15. William von Hassell, *Geschichte des Königreichs Hannover*, 2 vols. (Bremen and Leipzig, 1898–1901), vol. 2, pt. 2, p. 247.

Mediterranean coasts, providing a common pattern for the constitutions adopted in Sicily, Spain, France, and the Netherlands. All of these, as well as the ones introduced in Central and Eastern Europe during the early years of the Restoration, maintained restrictions on the franchise, often in the form of property requirements. Of the various election systems in force after the return of peace, the British suffrage, even with its many limitations and exclusions, was the most liberal. In 1831 England and Wales had about 435,000 eligible voters in a population of close to 14 million so that not quite 1 person out of every 30 had the ballot. The Continental constitutions, on the other hand—the Swedish of 1809, the Norwegian of 1814, the Dutch of 1815, the French of 1830, and the Belgian of 1831—all maintained a narrower franchise requirement than the county forty-shilling freehold that had been in force in Great Britain for about four hundred years, even narrower than the franchise requirement in all but the rottenest of the rotten boroughs.

Many Englishmen proudly regarded their political system as an exemplar of enlightened government for the rest of the world. The House of Commons, declared one member, "is the only constituent body that ever existed, which comprehends within itself, those who can urge the wants and defend the claims of the landed, the commercial, the professional classes of the country; those who are bound to uphold the prerogatives of the Crown, the privileges of the nobility, the interests of the lower classes, the rights and liberties of the whole people." Indeed, "it is the very absence of symmetry in our elective franchises which admits of the introduction to this House of classes so various [and] opens the door to the admission here of all talents, and of all classes, and of all interests." To those who were the beneficiaries of the oligarchical system of rule in Great Britain, it seemed to possess all the virtues of well-founded civic authority.[16]

For this reason, the Reform Bill of 1832 extending the suffrage encountered bitter resistance. Yet the measure was modest enough. In the counties it granted the franchise to long-term leaseholders of land with an annual value of ten pounds as well as to short-term leaseholders of land with an annual value of fifty pounds; in the boroughs the franchise was given to those who occupied a house or shop with an annual rental of ten pounds. The number of eligible voters rose to nearly 653,000, an increase of about 50 percent. Even after passage of the bill, however, the ratio of population to electorate was still 30.19, although by 1865 it fell

16. Elie Halevy, A History of the English People in the Nineteenth Century, 2d ed., 6 vols. (London, 1949–52), 1:101; J. A. Hawgood, "Liberalism and Constitutional Developments," in The New Cambridge Modern History, 12 vols. (Cambridge, 1960–70), 10:192; G. D. H. Cole, British Working Class Politics, 1832–1914 (London, 1941), p. 4; Great Britain, Parliamentary Debates (Commons), 3d ser. (1830–91), 2:1108–9.

to 22.04 as the improvement in the standard of living enabled more men to qualify for the ballot. England remained an oligarchy in which the aristocracy now shared political power with the bourgeoisie more evenly. Of greater importance in its practical consequences than the extension of the suffrage was the redistribution of seats, which increased the representation of the populous towns and counties at the expense of the smaller boroughs.

Still, to the opponents of the bill, it represented the beginning of a process that must end in mob rule and social upheaval. They warned that once the inviolability of the established political order had been compromised, there would be no end of attempts to tinker with and improve the system of government. These fears, not altogether unjustified, help explain the gloomy premonition of the politician and writer John Wilson Croker concerning the Reform Bill of 1832: "No King, no Lords, no inequalities in the social system; all will be levelled to the plane of the petty shopkeepers and small farmers; this, perhaps, not without bloodshed, but certainly by confiscations and persecutions." The struggle over passage of the measure was followed with great interest on the Continent as well for there was a widespread feeling that an extension of the suffrage in Great Britain would have an important effect on political developments in the rest of Europe. In one of his last writings, part of which was published posthumously, Hegel warned that the bill would bring about a significant change in the structure and function of Parliament. The lower classes would begin to exert influence over the legislative process because an opposition party that was unable to achieve power by other means "could be misled into seeking its strength among the people, and then bringing about not reform but revolution." That was the great danger.[17]

The apprehensions of the opponents of the bill were epitomized by Tocqueville a few years later in what he called "one of the most invariable rules governing societies," namely, that once a country begins to tamper with the property requirement for voting, the process cannot stop short of manhood suffrage. But at first Great Britain appeared determined to resist further efforts to extend the franchise. The Chartist agitation of the 1830s and 1840s for the right of all men to vote was violent but fruitless.

17. Cole, *British Working Class Politics*, pp. 4–5; William O. Aydelotte, "A Data Archive for Modern British Political History," in *The Dimensions of the Past: Materials, Problems, and Opportunities for Quantitative Work in History*, ed. Val R. Lorwin and Jacob M. Price (New Haven and London, 1972), p. 341; *The Croker Papers: The Correspondence and Diaries of the Late Right Honourable John Wilson Croker, LL.D., F.R.S., Secretary to the Admiralty from 1809 to 1830*, ed. Louis J. Jennings, 3 vols. (London, 1884), 2:113; Georg Wilhelm Friedrich Hegel, *Sämtliche Werke*, ed. Hermann Glockner, 26 vols. (Stuttgart, 1949–59), 20:xvii, 518.

Benjamin Disraeli could declare in his *Sybil* that "since the passing of the Reform Act the altar of Mammon has blazed with triple worship. To acquire, to accumulate, to plunder each other by virtue of philosophic phrases, to propose an Utopia to consist only of WEALTH and TOIL, this has been the breathless business of enfranchised England." There was little room for political reform amid this wild scramble for wealth.

Twenty years later, however, came another major extension of the suffrage. It was partly a response to renewed pressure from trade unions and labor organizations, but even more important, it resulted from an effort by each of the two dominant parties, deadlocked in an endless battle for office, to win a decisive victory with the aid of the lower classes. The Reform Bill of 1867 went farther than either the Liberals or the Conservatives had wanted to go, but each had helped make the proposed measure progressively more generous in the hope of embarrassing the other until the final outcome far exceeded the wishes of either. Its most significant provision was the enfranchisement in the boroughs of all adult males who owned or rented a house on which they paid the poor rate or who occupied lodgings worth ten pounds in annual rental unfurnished. It almost doubled the number of eligible voters in England and Wales from 1,057,000 to 1,995,000, the increase coming largely from the urban working class. To Carlyle the result was bound to be total disaster. He fulminated against "traitorous Politicians, grasping at votes," and against "the calling in of new supplies of blockheadism, gullibility, bribeability, amenability to beer and balderdash." He denounced the principle of "any man equal to any other; Quashee Nigger to Socrates or Shakspere; Judas Iscariot to Jesus Christ;—and Bedlam and Gehenna equal to the New Jerusalem." The old man could only groan in despair about "poor Mankind." Great Britain had crossed the threshold of democracy.[18]

The last step toward a mass suffrage came in 1884 with the adoption of the third Reform Bill, which extended to the counties the same voting requirements already introduced in the boroughs. The result was the enfranchisement of the agricultural laborers and an increase in the number of eligible voters in England and Wales from 2,618,000 to 4,381,000. The ratio of population to electorate now dropped from 11.50 to 6.54. This was still not manhood suffrage. The requirement of ownership or rental of a dwelling as a condition of voting meant that between a third and a fourth of all adult males was denied the franchise. On the eve of the First World War, there were about 7.7 million voters in the United King-

18. *Oeuvres, papiers et correspondances d'Alexis de Tocqueville*, ed. J.-P. Mayer, 12 vols. (Paris, 1951–70), 1:56; Benjamin Disraeli, *Sybil; or the Two Nations*, 3 vols. (London, 1845), 1:69; Cole, *British Working Class Politics*, pp. 5, 29; Thomas Carlyle, "Shooting Niagara: and After?" *Macmillan's Magazine* 16 (1867):321, 323–24.

dom out of a total of 12 million men. Those who remained without a ballot were not only lunatics, prisoners, and paupers but also those who did not own or rent their place of residence: a servant occupying a room in his master's house, for example, or a son living with his father. Still, even with these significant disfranchisements, there could be no doubt that the lower classes now had a decisive voice in determining the outcome of elections.[19]

In other European countries, however, the system of voting had become by the end of the nineteenth century more democratic than that of Great Britain. During the great revolution, France had pioneered in the establishment of manhood suffrage, for in the election of the Convention in 1792 all adult males had been eligible to vote. This unrestricted franchise had remained in force, at least on paper, until the formation of the Directory in 1795. Napoleon had reintroduced manhood suffrage in 1799, but in a form so convoluted and controlled that its obvious purpose was to provide a facade of popular approval for an essentially autocratic regime. The Bourbon Restoration was more restrictive but at least more honest. It made the payment of three hundred francs in direct taxes a condition of the franchise so that there were no more than about 90,000 eligible voters in the entire country, 1 person out of every 300. The July Monarchy more than doubled the electorate by lowering the suffrage requirement to two hundred francs in direct taxes. Yet the number of those who could qualify for the ballot still ranged between 180,000 and 240,000. This narrow oligarchy, even narrower than that in England before the Reform Bill of 1832, dominated parliamentary life. Marx could write derisively that "the July Monarchy was nothing but a joint-stock company for the exploitation of the French national wealth, whose dividends were distributed among ministers, chambers, 240,000 voters, and their adherents."

The Revolution of 1848 reestablished manhood suffrage in France, this time for good. The proclamation of the Second Republic meant a return to the system of voting introduced by the First Republic. The overthrow of Louis Philippe thus resulted in the sudden enlargement of the electorate from fewer than 300,000 to 9,395,000. The subsequent establishment of the Second Empire, like that of the First, signified that for the time being a democratic franchise would be used to legitimize an autocratic government. With the gradual liberalization of the regime during the 1860s, however, the votes of the lower classes began to exert a growing influence over state policy. The formation of the Third Republic therefore reinforced a tendency that had already been gaining strength under Napoleon III. The election laws of 1871 and 1875 gave about

19. Cole, *British Working Class Politics*, pp. 5–6, 81–82; Aydelotte, "Data Archive," p. 341; Halevy, *History of the English People*, 6:442–43.

10 million men the right to vote. According to figures compiled at the end of the century, the French electorate was proportionately the largest in Europe. No less than 27 percent of the population had the franchise. This meant that virtually all adult males could qualify for the ballot.[20]

In France manhood suffrage was historically rooted in both the Jacobin and the Bonapartist traditions, with the former predominating. In Germany the situation was reversed. The democratic movement was weak and the socialist movement nonexistent before the 1860s so that the state constitutions adopted prior to national unification almost invariably maintained a requirement of wealth or status as a condition of voting. In Prussia the election law of 1849, which was incorporated into the constitution of 1850, did establish manhood suffrage. The voters, however, were divided into three classes based on the payment of direct taxes and weighted in such a way that the propertied were easily able to outvote the propertyless. In the elections held between 1849 and 1863, an average of 4.73 percent of the adult males belonged to the first class, 13.26 to the second, and 82.01 to the third. Since each class elected an equal number of members to the electoral colleges, which in turn elected the members of the legislature, less than a fifth of the voters could defeat the other four-fifths. Under such an arrangement, manhood suffrage posed no threat to the established political and social system.

Yet when national unification was achieved in Germany in 1866–71, the method adopted for electing the Reichstag was more democratic than anywhere else in Europe. In state elections money and position continued to predominate, but in federal elections every adult male had an equal vote, regardless of property. Manhood suffrage, however, came not because of a demand by the lower classes for civic emancipation but as the result of cold calculation by those in power. The constitutional conflict in Prussia had convinced Bismarck that a restricted system of voting only helped the liberal bourgeoisie compete with crown and aristocracy for primacy in the state. The rural masses, on the other hand, were still loyal to monarchical authority. Manhood suffrage would thus make it possible to defeat the opposition with the aid of the votes of millions of faithful

20. Régine Pernoud, *Histoire de la bourgeoisie en France*, 2 vols. (Paris, 1960–62), 2:312, 417, 423; Guillaume de Bertier de Sauvigny, "French Politics, 1814–47," in *New Cambridge Modern History*, 9:364; Georges Weill, *L'éveil des nationalités et le mouvement libéral (1815–1848)* (Paris, 1930), pp. 102–3; Albert Malet, "La France: La monarchie de juillet de 1830 à 1847," in *Histoire generale du IVe siècle à nos jours*, ed. Ernest Lavisse and Alfred Rambaud, 12 vols. (Paris, 1893–1901), 10:378; Karl Marx and Friedrich Engels, *Werke*, 39 vols. (Berlin, 1960–69), 7:14; Charles Seignobos, "La révolution de 1848 et la réaction en France, 1848–1852," in *Histoire générale*, ed. Lavisse and Rambaud, 11:13; Oron J. Hale, *The Great Illusion, 1900–1914* (New York, Evanston, and London, 1971), p. 196; Anderson and Anderson, *Political Institutions*, p. 319.

peasants. "May I indeed express it as a conviction based on long experience," Bismarck tried to persuade Alexander II of Russia in the spring of 1866, that "the artificial system of indirect and class elections is much more dangerous, since it hinders the contact of the highest authority with the healthy elements which form the core and the mass of the people." In a country with conservative traditions and a loyal disposition, he went on, "the general franchise, by eliminating the influence of the liberal bourgeois classes, will also lead to monarchical elections." Such were the motives behind the introduction of a democratic form of voting in Germany.[21]

After 1870 the other nations of Europe also began to move toward a mass franchise. Fortified by the growth of the great national systems of elementary education designed to inculcate loyalty to traditional institutions, relying on an expanding body of social legislation to reconcile the lower classes to the established order, encouraged by the success of France, Germany, and England in harmonizing a democratic suffrage with political stability, the large agrarian states of the south and east gradually extended the vote to the lower classes. In Italy the Statuto of 1848 had established such a high property qualification for the ballot that at first only about 2 percent of the population had the right to vote. The reform of 1882 reduced the voting age from twenty-five to twenty-one, the income tax requirement from forty to nineteen lire, and the qualifying amount of schooling to two years so that the number of eligible voters rose from 600,000 to 2 million, close to 7 percent of the population. Only in 1912, however, did the government, hoping to counter the spread of radicalism with the ballots of the peasant masses, give the franchise to all men over twenty-one who could read and write, to those who had fulfilled their military obligation, and to all other male citizens who had reached the age of thirty. This meant virtually complete manhood suffrage.

In Austria the system of elections introduced piecemeal during the 1860s and early 1870s provided for the division of the eligible voters into four classes: large landowners, chambers of commerce and industry, cities and towns, and rural communities. The number of deputies to be elected by each class was distributed in such a way that in 1891 there were 63 voters in the first class for each member of the legislature representing it, 27 in the second class, 2,592 in the third, and 10,918 in the fourth. More than two-thirds of the adult male population, moreover, were entirely excluded from the franchise. In 1896 a new election law created a fifth class composed of all men over twenty-four (including

21. Theodore S. Hamerow, *The Social Foundations of German Unification, 1858–1871*, 2 vols. (Princeton, 1969–72), 1:297–98; Bismarck, *Werke*, 5:457.

those who already had the ballot in one of the other four), which received the right to elect 17 percent of the members of the legislature. Only in 1907 did the authorities, seeking to allay the nationality conflict by an appeal to the loyalty of the lower classes, establish equal manhood suffrage.

As for Russia, her traditional system of autocracy remained untouched until defeat in the war against Japan and the outbreak of a revolution forced the government to agree to a national representation. A law of 24 December 1905 established the franchise for the election of the Duma. Though unequal and indirect, it nonetheless approached manhood suffrage because the authorities continued to believe that the peasant masses remained faithful to the established order. After this expectation proved false, however, the Stolypin ministry sharply curtailed the right to vote by the law of 16 June 1907.[22]

Several of the smaller states of Europe had introduced manhood suffrage much earlier. In Spain, where the electorate had remained below 3.5 percent of the population through most of the century, manhood suffrage was introduced temporarily between 1868 and 1876 and was then established permanently in 1890. In Belgium, "the republic with a crown," a restricted franchise subjected 5.5 million people to the will of 116,000 eligible voters paying over forty-two francs in direct taxes. But a campaign against it by the democratic and socialist parties led to the introduction of manhood suffrage in 1893. A unique system of plural voting, however, gave additional ballots to heads of families, owners of property, and holders of diplomas of higher education. There were 853,000 men with one vote, 293,000 with two, and 223,000 with three. In the Netherlands a revision of the "fundamental law" in 1887 reduced the property requirement for the franchise sufficiently to double the number of eligible voters from 140,000 to 300,000, and another reduction in 1896 doubled it again to 700,000. More than half of the adult males now had the suffrage.

The most significant extension of the right to vote, however, took place in the Scandinavian countries. In 1898 the Norwegian Storting established manhood suffrage, the logical culmination of a deep-rooted democratic tradition in a country largely free of landed aristocrats and

22. Charles Tilly, Louise Tilly, and Richard Tilly, *The Rebellious Century, 1830–1930* (Cambridge, Mass., 1975), pp. 95–97; Anderson and Anderson, *Political Institutions*, pp. 320, 333; Félix Ponteil, "L'évolution politique de l'Europe," in *L'Europe du XIXe et du XXe siècle*, ed. Max Beloff, Pierre Renouvin, Franz Schnabel, and Franco Valsecchi, 6 vols. (Milan, 1959–64), 3:19–20; Louis Eisenmann, "L'Autriche-Hongrie depuis 1871," in *Histoire générale*, ed. Lavisse and Rambaud, 12:193–94; Maurice Baumont, *L'essor industriel et l'impérialisme colonial (1878–1904)*, 2d ed. (Paris, 1949), pp. 485–86; Hale, *Great Illusion*, p. 199; Donald W. Treadgold, *Twentieth Century Russia* (Chicago, 1959), pp. 79, 107.

big businessmen. Sweden followed this example in 1907. But it was Finland that made the great breakthrough in the European system of voting in the twentieth century. In November 1905, at the height of the revolutionary turmoil that threatened the czarist regime, the Finnish diet adopted a new constitution extending the franchise to all women as well as men at the age of twenty-four. At first Nicholas II hesitated to give his approval, but in the summer of 1906 he finally yielded. Woman suffrage became a reality for the first time. Nine years later, in June 1915, Denmark also introduced a constitution that established universal suffrage, men and women having the right to vote on the same terms. Europe had entered a new stage in its political development.[23]

As it became apparent that a mass franchise was not incompatible with stable government, the safeguards erected against its effects began to relax. The most obvious example was the introduction of secret voting in one country after another: Sweden in 1866, Germany in 1867, Great Britain in 1872, France in 1875, Belgium in 1878, Norway in 1884, and Denmark in 1901. The readiness and ability of the upper chamber to challenge the decisions of the lower gradually diminished. For instance, France eliminated the position of lifetime senator in 1884, and the Parliament Act of 1911 in England restricted the authority of the House of Lords to veto legislation. Even salaries for members of parliament were cautiously introduced, in Germany in 1906, in the United Kingdom in 1911, and in Italy in 1912.

When the question of manhood suffrage first arose in the constituent Reichstag of the North German Confederation in 1867, the historian Heinrich von Sybel declared that the establishment of a mass franchise has always meant the beginning of the end for any form of parliamentarianism. It can produce desirable results, he warned, only when "tigers and wolves feed on bran and play with sheep and lambs." Yet forty years later, elite politics, which were the rule in Europe throughout history, had been largely replaced by mass politics based on organized parties, election campaigns, popular journalism, and democratic suffrage. The tigers were grazing beside the sheep and the wolves were playing with the lambs. Or so at least it seemed.[24]

23. Stanley G. Payne, *A History of Spain and Portugal*, 2 vols. (Madison, 1973), 2:464, 474, 489, 494; Baumont, *L'essor industriel*, p. 495; Albert Métin, "Les royaumes de Belgique et des Pays-Bas depuis 1870," in *Histoire générale*, ed. Lavisse and Rambaud, 12:253–55; G. D. H. Cole, *A History of Socialist Thought*, 5 vols. (London and New York, 1956–65), 3:678, 688, 699, 706.
24. Rokkan, "Comparative Study of Political Participation," p. 75; Germany, *Stenographische Berichte über die Verhandlungen des Reichstages des Norddeutschen Bundes im Jahre 1867*, 2 vols. (Berlin, 1867), 1:427.

12

THE NATURE OF AUTHORITY

The social and political reforms introduced during the nineteenth century persuaded many contemporaries that they were witnessing the beginning of a fundamental change in the distribution of power. They began to believe that the narrow oligarchies that had traditionally monopolized lawmaking in the community were about to be replaced by a popular form of government. Now that the propertyless were receiving the right to vote on the same basis as the propertied, it would surely be only a matter of time before changes in the structure of authority reflected changes in the structure of politics. How could it be otherwise? In the past an undemocratic form of rule had been the logical result of an undemocratic form of suffrage. But since civic power was now passing into the hands of the masses, it was reasonable to expect a corresponding shift in the system of legislation and administration. The transformation of the process of voting was seemingly bound to lead to a transformation in the making and enforcing of laws.

Each successive political reform was therefore greeted by supporters and deplored by opponents as the beginning of a reconstruction of state and society. When the establishment of county councils in Great Britain in 1888 transferred the administration of rural districts from centrally appointed justices of the peace to locally elected boards, the prime minister complained that critics of the bill were describing it as "a great revolutionary measure," as "upsetting the arrangements of centuries," and as "the dethronement of squirearchy." When in 1893 the government introduced the parish councils bill, which provided for self-government in the smallest units of local administration, a speaker in the House of Commons declared that the measure was needed because most clergymen "had allied themselves time out of mind with the squire and the privileged classes in the attempt to rule full-grown men against their will, to order them about like children, and to check the least symptom of independence." The agricultural laborers looked forward to the adoption of the bill "as a means of independence, as giving them the hope and prospect of standing on more equal terms with those who, from time out of mind, had borne rule over them." In short, "the hereditary right to dominate in civil and social matters would, as far as its legal basis was concerned, be rudely shaken by the legislation now before the House." The death duties in the budget of 1894 introduced by Sir William Harcourt, chancellor of the exchequer, were described as meaning ruin for the agricultural landowners, who had in the past played such an important role in the politics of the nation. There appeared to be no way in which the old order could survive the rising tide of reform generated by the transformation of economy and society.[1]

The enfranchisement of the masses appeared to have special importance. Once the common man got the right to vote, would he not insist on the adoption of laws ending the domination of birth and wealth? Would he not use his authority to improve the position of the lower classes? And would this not mean a redistribution of power among economic and social interests? Here was the reason why the debates concerning each extension of the suffrage were so full of dire misgivings and buoyant hopes.

During the discussion of the first Reform Bill in England, Michael Thomas Sadler, the Tory social reformer, warned that the destruction of the influence enjoyed by the great property owners would have the most serious consequences. It would prepare the way for those agrarian struggles that had long disturbed and finally destroyed Rome; it would prepare the way for spoliations similar to those recently witnessed "in a neighbouring country, where property, bereft of its political influence, lost its rights, and only served to mark out its possessors to certain destruction." The same fear was expressed by Viscount Cranborne, later marquess of Salisbury and prime minister of Great Britain, during the debate concerning the second Reform Bill. On most questions of state policy, the workers would probably vote soberly and reasonably, he told the House of Commons. "But if ever you come to a question between class and class—if ever you come to a question where the interests of one class are, or seem to be, pitted against those of another, you will find that all those securities of rank, wealth, and influence in which you trust are mere feathers in the balance against the solid interest and the real genuine passions of mankind." A decade after the adoption of the third Reform Bill, Harcourt wrote Lord Rosebery, who had just become prime minister, that the enfranchisement of the lower classes had made inevitable a confrontation between rich and poor: "You desire to avert the 'cleavage of classes'—The hope on your part is natural, but you are too late. 'The horizontal division of parties' was certain to come as a consequence of household suffrage. The thin edge of the wedge was inserted, and the cleavage is expanding more and more every day." Where would it all end?[2]

The reaction to the establishment of equal manhood suffrage in Ger-

1. Great Britain, *Parliamentary Debates*, 3d ser. (1830–91), 329:929; ibid., 4th ser. (1829–1908), 18:124–25; F. M. L. Thompson, *English Landed Society in the Nineteenth Century* (London and Toronto), p. 325.

2. Great Britain, *Parliamentary Debates*, 3d ser. (1830–91), 3:1536, 188:1532; A. G. Gardiner, *The Life of Sir William Harcourt*, 2 vols. (London, Bombay, and Sydney, 1923), 2:284.

many in 1867 was similar. There was the same fear that the masses would reject law and order, that class resentments would become more intense, that the traditional foundations of authority would totter, and that the way would be open to radical experiments. On the eve of the elections to the constituent Reichstag of the North German Confederation, the influential *Grenzboten* in Leipzig wrote that manhood suffrage gave the lower elements of the population and the mass of the voters such a decisive influence over politics that the nation faced the most far-reaching changes in the daily press and in the organization of parties. "We will from now on have great popular assemblies, processions, mass demonstrations, and the inciting and winning over of the crowd." Many a politician will look back with longing from the stormy sea of the future to the "quiet inland lake" of the restricted suffrage. Candidates must give up the "proud modesty" with which they once faced the voters and must not shrink from days of scandal, rotten apples, and perhaps even street riots.

Ten years later, the liberal politican Hans Viktor von Unruh expressed a similar concern in his memoirs. The level of popular education is such, he maintained, that the lower stratum can read and write, absorbing the contents of the writings of agitators. But it is still far from knowing how to think and judge independently. It can therefore be very easily misled, especially under the impression of seeming successes, such as the election of Social Democrats to the Reichstag. The lower stratum of voters, however, if you include the countryside, is by far the most numerous. The class of those who work with their hands and of all those who live from hand to mouth outweighs the number of the well-to-do and educated so decidedly that the poorer class needs only to become conscious of the power that the general and equal suffrage bestows upon it to win the elections in both city and country, excluding those who are educated and in a better position. "Therefore we can foresee with certainty that in time the general and equal suffrage will lead to a majority of the lower strata of voters and of their leaders in the Reichstag, unless we succeed in creating a remedy in some effective fashion." In the meantime, the nation faced a terrible danger.[3]

Not all observers feared the consequences of an enfranchisement of the masses. Some expected it to introduce a new era in the history of mankind, an age free of injustice and oppression. In 1833 John Arthur Roebuck, member of the small radical faction in Parliament, declared that if, as heretofore, the majority of mankind were content to be a slumbering

---

3. "Das preussische Abgeordnetenhaus," *Die Grenzboten* 26 (1867), no. 1, pp. 3–4; *Erinnerungen aus dem Leben von Hans Viktor von Unruh*, ed. Heinrich von Poschinger (Stuttgart, Leipzig, Berlin, and Vienna, 1895), p. 148.

mass, an inert and utterly inactive body, then the selfish policy of attempting to continue the present situation might possibly be defended. But this was not the case. The business of government was not and could no longer be the affair of a small minority. "Within these few years a new element has arisen, which now ought to enter into all political calculations. The multitude—the hitherto inert and submissive multitude—are filled with a new spirit—their attention is intently directed towards the affairs of State." They were now taking an active part in their own social concerns. "However unwilling persons may be to contemplate the fact, any one who will calmly and carefully watch the signs of the times, will discover . . . that the hitherto subject many are about to become paramount in the State." The effect on the structure of authority was sure to be of far-reaching importance.

In Germany the believers in democracy had to defend their position with greater caution, especially during the reactionary 1850s. Georg Gottfried Gervinus, professor at Heidelberg, wrote in his *Introduction to the History of the Nineteenth Century* that society stood on the threshold of a new golden age. Individualism, the self-awareness of the personality, had become so powerful in men that it would modify political concepts and institutions. It would dissolve the closed corporations, the states within the state; it would eliminate all caste and class differences. The striving for the equality of all relations, for the freedom of man toward man, was necessarily involved in this self-awareness of the personality.

> But political equality, if it is not the expression of equal oppression under despotism, requires the rule of the popular will in accordance with the decision of the majority. It postulates a government which is not founded on the illusion of divine right, but on necessity. It calls for legislation resting on the requirements of society, concerning which the people themselves as a whole judge. Everything in our time is pressing forward jointly and irresistibly, in accordance with these democratic concepts, forms, and classifications of state and society, as if the powers of destiny worked directly to give form and substance to a historic idea.[4]

Even this convoluted language, no doubt incomprehensible to the great multitude, was enough to cost Gervinus his position at the university.

Yet the fears of the traditionalists and the hopes of the democrats concerning the consequences of political reform were equally exaggerated. The most striking aspect of the enfranchisement of the masses was how little effect it actually had on the structure of authority. The old

4. Great Britain, *Parliamentary Debates*, 3d ser. (1830–91), 20:144–45; G. G. Gervinus, *Einleitung in die Geschichte des neunzehnten Jahrhunderts* (Leipzig, 1853), pp. 168–69.

order showed itself far more skillful in retaining power than either its supporters or its opponents had imagined. It clung to its position with stubborn tenacity, now relying on the ingrained attitude of deference on the part of the masses, now assimilating the most successful elements of the bourgeoisie, now posing as the champion of the poor and oppressed. By 1914 the social background of the wielders of authority within the political system had been significantly modified, reflecting more and more a partnership between the middle and upper classes. But the masses were excluded from positions of leadership almost as completely as in 1815. In Giuseppe di Lampedusa's brilliant historical novel *The Leopard*, Tancredi, the young aristocratic careerist, tells his conservative uncle, the prince of Salina, that in order to retain power the nobility will have to adjust to the new conditions that the national unification of Italy is about to create. "If we want things to stay as they are, things will have to change," he shrewdly suggests. Such was the strategy followed by the ruling classes of Europe in response to the challenge confronting them.

The system of political authority, though assuming new forms, remained largely a preserve of the old and new aristocracy, that is, of those whose eminence rested on background and those whose eminence rested on ownership. That was the gist of the criticism by G. D. H. Cole and William Mellor directed against the reform movement of the period before the First World War. Expounding the principles of guild socialism, they wrote: "The crowning discovery of the nineteenth century was that democratic government made no difference to the life of the ordinary man. Nominally self-governing, he remained in bondage." As for the reasons for the ineffectualness of the enfranchisement of the masses, "economic power is the key to political power. Political democracy has been unmeaning because it has reflected the power of an economic aristocracy." Here was a profound insight into the nature of change in the power structure of Europe. It suggested that the imposition of an egalitarian political system on a society of oligarchical wealth and hierarchical status might lead to corrections and improvements but could not create a democratic community.[5]

This does not mean that the dominant minority in the nineteenth century was the same as in the eighteenth. The landed aristocracy gradually recognized that changes in the principal sources of wealth made it advantageous to assimilate the more successful and ambitious elements of the bourgeoisie. In the process of coalescence, however, the old nobility retained the upper hand, not in the possession of property, to be sure, but in status, prestige, way of life, and symbol of superiority. The

5. G. D. H. Cole and William Mellor, *The Meaning of Industrial Freedom* (London, 1918), pp. 2, 40.

children of even the richest industrialists or bankers were generally eager to exchange the middle-class attitudes and beliefs adopted by their fathers during the rise to the top for the grand airs and manners of the aristocracy of birth. Title, land, family, and background continued to play a major role in politics and society at the same time that their importance in the economy was declining. "And you see," Archdeacon Grantley says in Trollope's *Last Chronicle of Barset*, "land gives so much more than rent. It gives position and influence and political power, to say nothing about the game." Even among those who championed democracy, status counted. Roebuck wrote in 1836 that "it is of great importance in this wealth-loving aristocratic country to have among [the members of the House of Commons courageous enough to say and do what is right] a *rich* man, of good standing and *rank*." The habits of deference to the nobility, fostered by centuries of hierarchical rule, were hard to overcome.

The role of the aristocrat in political life was actually more secure in those countries where he was willing to share his power with the bourgeois. In Russia the system of autocracy was under attack throughout the nineteenth century by a succession of radical groups: Decembrists, Populists, Social Democrats, and Social Revolutionaries. Before the achievement of national unification in Germany, there were periodic confrontations between the upper and middle classes, during the revolutionary movement of 1848–49, for instance, or during the Prussian constitutional conflict of 1862–66. In England, on the other hand, the Reform Bills democratizing the franchise did nothing to weaken the popular attitude of esteem for noble birth and manner. On the contrary, they made possible the continuing political influence of the aristocracy long after its economic power had dwindled.

Thomas Erskine May, who for forty years held a variety of administrative positions in Parliament, declared during the early 1860s that "we see nearly the same families still in the ascendant." Deprived in great measure of their direct influence over the legislature, he went on, their general weight in the country and in the councils of state had suffered little diminution. Notwithstanding the more democratic tendencies of recent times, rank and station had still retained the respect and confidence of the people. "When the aristocracy had enjoyed too exclusive an influence in the government, they have aroused jealousies and hostility; but when duly sharing power with other classes, and admitting the just claims of talent, they have prevailed over every rival and adverse interest; and,— whatever party has been in power,—have still been the rulers of the state."

At the same time, Walter Bagehot was describing Great Britain as "a deferential community" in which "the mass of the English people yield a deference rather to something else than to their rulers. They defer to what we may call the *theatrical show* of society. A certain state passes before them; a certain pomp of great men; a certain spectacle of beautiful women; a wonderful scene of wealth and enjoyment is displayed, and they are coerced by it." In the introduction to the second edition of his *English Constitution*, which appeared a few years after the Reform Bill of 1867, he conceded that "the middle class element has gained greatly by the . . . change, and the aristocratic element has lost greatly." Yet noble birth continued to play a major role in public life. "I doubt if there has ever been any [country] in which all old families and all titled families received more ready observance [than in Great Britain] from those who were their equals, perhaps their superiors, in wealth, their equals in culture, and their inferiors only in descent and rank." Political authority was thus changing much more slowly than the economic system or the social structure.[6]

The domination of civic life by men of wealth and birth was reinforced by the failure of the masses to participate effectively in public affairs, partly as a result of ignorance, partly as a result of indifference. The typical peasant or worker, spending his days in tedious toil, semiliterate or often illiterate, with only a vague idea concerning the nature of government, was incapable of wresting power from the well-to-do classes by a calculated use of the ballot. Especially in the agrarian states of the south and east, where the rural masses were too absorbed in eking out a living to read newspapers or attend meetings, politics became a monopoly of people of means. Of one hundred Serbian army recruits examined around 1909, all knew who the half-legendary Marko Kraljević was and ninety-eight had heard of Miloš Obilić, another medieval folk hero. But only forty-seven were able to identify Peter I, the reigning monarch of the country. In his *Virgin Soil* of 1893, the Bulgarian novelist Khristo Dimitrov Maksimov wrote that the peasant has only the vaguest idea about his nation's transition from servitude to independent life. For him it matters little whether he pays his tax to Akhmed or Ivan. In fact, Ivan is often more distasteful to him than Akhmed because Akhmed could be more easily fooled or bribed. Akhmed did not take his son off as a soldier, whereas Ivan does. Akhmed was naive and spoke Turkish, but Ivan is to all appearances a Christian like him and speaks Bulgarian, yet exacts more from him than Akhmed did. The meaning of state, rights,

6. *Life and Letters of John Arthur Roebuck*, ed. Robert Eadon Leader (London and New York, 1897), p. 81; Thomas Erskine May, *The Constitutional History of England since the Accession of George the Third, 1760–1860*, 2 vols. (London, 1861–63), 1:137; Walter Bagehot, "The English Constitution: No. II, The Pre-requisites of Cabinet Government, and the Peculiar Form Which They Have Assumed in England," *Fortnightly Review* 1 (1865):325–27; idem, *The English Constitution*, new ed. (London, 1872), pp. xxiv, xxviii.

and duties for the peasant adds up to no more than the payment of taxes and the conscription of his son as a soldier.

A generation later, a Rumanian writer, Constantin Rădulescu-Motru, offered another gloomy assessment of Balkan politics. The introduction of progressive reform in the country had only served as a facade for favoritism and corruption, he wrote. The state had established universal suffrage, but with ballot stuffing. It had ruined rural households in order to increase credit institutions, but it had not permitted free competition among them, favoring some—those belonging to the party in power—and attacking others—those belonging to its adversaries. It had encouraged national industry, not for the benefit of the rural population but for the benefit of the politicians. It had centralized the administration, not in the hands of a trained bureaucracy but in those of the party and its supporters. "In a word, we have aped the European bourgeoisie in form, but at bottom we have persisted in the sycophantic habits of the past." Thereby political life had become a hopeless turmoil.

In his description of popular civic attitudes in Spain in 1881, the educator R. Torres Campos emphasized the sheer lack of interest on the part of the lower classes. The indifference of many people to voting and taking part in public affairs; the ease with which the voters did one thing as readily as another, without understanding the importance of what they were undertaking in casting their ballots; the resistance to paying any kind of tax and the refusal to regard taxes as an obligation; the theory that distinguished between fraud perpetrated against the administration and fraud perpetrated against a private person; "the lack, in short, of integrity, independence, and morality with regard to the state"—such were the vices of the existing customs, which the political education of the people would have to suppress.[7]

Even in the economically more advanced countries of Western and Central Europe, interest in the political process remained low, especially in the early decades. Auguste Romieu, a subprefect under the July Monarchy, complained about the incompetence and apathy of those chosen to administer public affairs in the towns and villages. "The laws are simply unknown in those places," he maintained. "I could name a list of mayors who do not even cut the pages of the *Bulletin des lois*, a growing collection in some old trunk where it is resting, a reserve for gun wadding."

7. L. S. Stavrianos, "The Influence of the West on the Balkans," in *The Balkans in Transition: Essays on the Development of Balkan Life and Politics since the Eighteenth Century*, ed. Charles Jelavich and Barbara Jelavich (Berkeley and Los Angeles, 1963), p. 211; Vivian Pinto, "The Civic and Aesthetic Ideals of Bulgarian Narodnik Writers," *Slavonic and East European Review* 32 (1953–54):357; Henry L. Roberts, *Rumania: Political Problems of an Agrarian State* (New Haven, 1951), pp. 115–16; Yvonne Turin, *L'éducation et l'école en Espagne de 1874 à 1902: Libéralisme et tradition* (Paris, 1959), p. 49.

More than that, "there are communities in [Brittany] where only three or four inhabitants out of a thousand know how to read. It has also happened that for sixteen years in succession the municipal council of one of these communities has not met, although it was supposed to meet in required sessions, and that the budgets for each period have been drawn up by the mayor and then signed at home by those of the members who knew how to scrawl their names." How much greater must have been the civic ignorance of the man in the street?[8]

To be sure, interest in politics increased after the mid-century. In Germany during the 1850s and 1860s, the total number of those who participated in such activities as voting, signing petitions, and attending mass meetings was somewhere between 1 million and 2 million, less than a third of the adult male population. After the achievement of national unification and the establishment of equal manhood suffrage, however, participation rose significantly as the result of political acclimatization on the part of the lower classes. In the Reichstag elections of 1871, 50.7 percent of the eligible voters went to the polls; between 1874 and 1884 the percentage ranged from 56.1 to 63.1, averaging 60.1; and between 1887 and 1912 it ranged from 67.7 to 84.5, reaching an average of 76.1. In many state elections within the German Empire, moreover, there was also a substantial increase in voter participation. In Bavaria, for example, it rose from 31.2 percent in 1893 to 81.9 in 1912. Even in Spain the proportion of eligible voters appearing at the polls was surprisingly high. Under the restricted suffrage that prevailed in the early years of constitutionalism, the rate of participation fluctuated between 75.85 percent in 1840 and 51.75 in 1867. That was not unexpected because only men of means and education had the franchise. It was more remarkable, however, that in the first Spanish elections by manhood suffrage late in 1868 some 70 percent of the eligible voters cast their ballots, exceeding the 64 percent reached the previous year in the first elections by manhood suffrage in the North German Confederation.[9]

Yet the growing participation of the lower classes in the political process through ballots, petitions, and meetings, a trend greeted by enthusiastic reformers as evidence of the progressive democratization of public affairs, did not alter the fact that ultimate control of power remained in the hands of an oligarchy. The enfranchisement of the masses demonstrated that the right to vote did not in itself insure popular direction of

8. Auguste Romieu, "De l'émancipation des communes," Revue de Paris, 2d ser., 5 (1833), no. 3, pp. 149–50.

9. Theodore S. Hamerow, The Social Foundations of German Unification, 1858–1871, 2 vols. (Princeton, 1969–72), 1:301–2, 363–65; 2:281, 324; Thomas Nipperdey, Die Organisation der deutschen Parteien vor 1918 (Düsseldorf, 1961), pp. 38–39, 91 (n. 1); Stanley G. Payne, History of Spain and Portugal, 2 vols. (Madison, 1973), 2:464, 474.

politics. The conduct of government was so complex that only those who had education and leisure could undertake it. The lower classes were effectively excluded from the determination of state policy because they had neither the training nor the affluence for a full-time commitment to civic leadership. They could increasingly choose between opposing political elites made up of members of the aristocracy and the bourgeoisie. More than that, those elites would at times introduce economic or social reforms of benefit to the masses. But such reforms were almost invariably the result of a decision by an oligarchy of means and status responding philanthropically or expediently to the demands of the lower classes. Politics during the nineteenth century, as in every preceding century, remained a monopoly of dominant minorities.

There were many writers who recognized this continuation of oligarchical rule within the framework of popular government. In his *American Commonwealth* of 1888, James Bryce calculated that in Great Britain the total number of those who "may fairly be called professional or Inner Circle politicians" was no more than 3,500. It included about 100 members of the House of Lords, 670 members of the House of Commons, some 280 editors, managers, and chief writers on the leading newspapers, perhaps 450 candidates for Parliament, and approximately 2,000 persons "who in each constituency devote most of their time to politics," for instance, secretaries of politicial associations and registration agents.

The concentration of power may have been greater in England than in most other countries, but observers everywhere agreed that the political process was to a large extent controlled by a small minority drawn from the well-to-do classes. In the first volume of his *Principles of Practical Politics* published in 1853, August Ludwig von Rochau had advocated calculating self-interest as the only means of achieving national unification in Germany. But in the second volume of 1869 he sounded disillusioned, although his political objectives had now been achieved by precisely the strategy he had urged: "The general suffrage then does not in any way alter the fact that among us the hundreds, now as before, have much greater weight than the thousands, and that elections even under the freest system will certainly not turn out in the spirit of the great mass, but in the sense of small minorities." The law decreeing that the affluent few always lead the indigent many seemed to him inexorable.[10]

In fact, a closer examination of the agencies by which political power was exercised in Europe does suggest that the elite nature of authority

10. James Bryce, *The American Commonwealth*, 3 vols. (London and New York, 1888), 2:395; [August Ludwig von Rochau], *Grundsätze der Realpolitik, angewendet auf die staatlichen Zustände Deutschlands*, 2 vols. (Stuttgart and Heidelberg, 1853–69), 2:14.

did not change as a result of the enfranchisement of the lower classes. It reveals rather that the old oligarchical system was becoming more flexible, admitting to positions of civic importance the most wealthy, talented, and ambitious among those who had hitherto been excluded from the direction of public affairs.

Take the British House of Commons, where the process of amalgamation between the old elite of status and the new elite of means was most apparent. In 1831 a Tory spokesman had warned that "in a Reformed Parliament, when the day of battle came, the country Squires would not be able to stand against the active, pushing, intelligent, people who would be sent from the manufacturing districts. . . . The field of coal would beat the field of barley." This fear proved greatly exaggerated. In the House elected in 1830, according to contemporary estimates, 62 members represented the East India interest, 35 the West India interest, and 33 were bankers. In the House elected in 1835, the figures were 35, 14, and 35, and in the one elected in 1837 there were altogether 97 businessmen, including 29 bankers, 26 merchants, and 14 manufacturers. The percentage of "aristocrats," that is, Irish peers, baronets, and sons of peers and baronets, hardly declined from 33 in 1831 to 31 in 1865, whereas members of the gentry by descent and other relations of aristocrats actually increased from 34 percent in 1841–47 to 45 in 1865. The percentage of manufacturers, merchants, and bankers remained virtually unchanged, with 24 in 1831 and 23 in 1865. Wealth continued to be the key to civic power, and the *Economist* could write in 1864 that "the career of politics, instead of being thrown open to the nation, is confined to a very limited class, the Premier has to choose among five thousand men instead of half a million. . . . If matters advance in the same direction a little longer, England will be governed by Peers' sons and men with 20,000 £ a year."

The representation of industry and commerce in Parliament began to grow rapidly only in the last decades of the century. Landowners and rentiers declined from 32 percent of the membership in 1874 to 16 in 1885, but men in the professions rose from 24 to 32 and those in business from 24 to 38. About 250 out of 670 members of the House of Commons elected in 1895 were businessmen of various sorts—manufacturers, merchants, bankers, directors of companies, mineowners, and brewers. Many of the others also had close ties to the world of business, although they preferred to be considered landowners.

Indeed, by now the interpenetration of rural and urban wealth was so far advanced as to form the basis for a new elite of status and affluence sharing common attitudes, beliefs, manners, and customs. Of the members of Parliament elected in 1906, 33 percent of the Liberals and 51 percent of the Conservatives had attended one of the exclusive public schools; 36 percent in each party had studied at Oxford or Cambridge; 24 percent of the Liberals and 51 percent of the Conservatives were "gentlemen" or officers in the armed forces; 41 percent of the former and 25 percent of the latter were businessmen; and 23 percent of the former and 16 percent of the latter were barristers or solicitors. On the other hand, only 2 percent of the Liberals were trade unionists, and there were none among the Conservatives. The figures suggest that the most significant change in civic life in a hundred years was the progressive *embourgeoisement* of politics, by which men of recent wealth were admitted to the power elite of the nation. The lower classes remained almost as effectively excluded from positions of authority at the end of the nineteenth century as at the beginning.[11]

After the Napoleonic Wars, even the House of Lords, the stronghold of the grand aristocracy, became increasingly open to people of common birth but uncommon wealth. There had been only 153 peers at the time of the Glorious Revolution of 1688 and 174 at the death of George II in 1760. Under George III and George IV, the number almost doubled to 326; between the accession of Queen Victoria in 1837 and the death of Palmerston in 1865, it rose again from 385 to 400. Yet as early as 1833, Edward Bulwer-Lytton commented on the increasingly plutocratic character of the peerage. "The sordid and commercial spirit of our aristocracy may be remarked in the disposition of its honours," he complained. "It is likely enough that there will soon be a numerous creation of Peers:—in France, such a creation would be rendered popular and respectable, by selecting the most distinguished men of the necessary politics;—*here*, neither the minister nor the public would ever dream of such a thing—we shall choose the *richest men*!"

What would he have said fifty years later, when the trickle of bourgeois affluence into the House of Lords became a flood? During the Melbourne ministry in 1837–41, only 3 percent of the new peers were associated with commerce and industry. Under the Disraeli ministry of 1874–80, the percentage was 8; under Gladstone and Rosebery in 1892–95, it was 35; and under Campbell-Bannerman and Asquith in 1905–11, it reached 40. Not counting members of the royal family, about two hundred men entered the British nobility for the first time between 1886 and 1914. Of this number, some seventy represented the new wealth of the industrial revolution. Another third came from the professions, especially law, and from service in diplomacy, the colonies, or the armed forces. Barely a

11. Great Britain, *Parliamentary Debates*, 3d ser. (1830–91), 5:580, 614; Elie Halevy, *A History of the English People in the Nineteenth Century*, 2d ed., 6 vols. (London, 1949–52), 3:62; 5:15–17; W. L. Guttsman, *The British Political Elite* (London, 1965), pp. 41, 82, 90; "Mr. John Stuart Mill upon the Increase of Corruption," *Economist*, 16 April 1864, p. 480.

fourth headed established landed families, which had formerly been the backbone of the peerage. Two-thirds of the new lords, moreover, had performed political service, either in the cabinet or in the Commons alone. Within this group, a third came from the landed classes, a fifth from the professions, and the rest from the world of industry and commerce. Yet it is also significant that a list prepared in 1909 by one of the British journals included among the thirty-five bankers in the House of Lords a duke of Buccleuch and a marquis of Ailesbury, whereas among the thirty-nine "captains of industry" were the duke of Abercorn and the duke of Argyll. In other words, the interpenetration process of the upper and middle classes involved not only the adoption of aristocratic manners and attitudes by the bourgeoisie but also the pursuit of bourgeois occupations and interests by the aristocracy.[12]

On the Continent the change in the social composition of the legislatures was less striking. In Prussia landowners and government officials constituted a permanent majority of the members of the lower house. The boundary between the two groups was not always clear because many bureaucrats also owned estates and many landed proprietors had formerly served in the bureaucracy. But the percentage of landowners increased steadily from 17.4 in 1849 to a high point of 39.3 in 1899 before decreasing to 31.4 in 1912. The number of state officials, on the other hand, rose from 36.8 percent in 1849 to a peak of 49.7 in 1855; it then began to diminish, falling to 21.2 in 1912. The percentage of merchants, industrialists, and manufacturers remained relatively stable throughout the period, fluctuating between a low of 4.3 in 1855 and a high of 10.2 in 1904. The proportion of the old aristocracy in the chamber, that is, of those whose families had been noble at least a hundred years, was also generally constant: 18 percent in 1862, 19 in 1878, 26 in 1890, 23 in 1909, and 21 in 1918. It is significant that virtually all of the legislators were owners of property or members of the professions. The category of "other occupations" declined from 2.3 percent in 1849 to 0.9 in 1879 before disappearing from the list; "no indication or imprecise indication of occupation" accounted for 3 percent in 1849 and 0 after 1889. There were no workers, no artisans, no clerks, and no peasants.

A comparison of the social composition of the Prussian legislature (figure 12.1), which was elected by a franchise weighted in favor of wealth, with that of the German Reichstag (figure 12.2), which was elected by equal manhood suffrage, reveals no major differences. Birth,

12. Halevy, *History of the English People*, 6:308–9, 311; E. L. Bulwer, *England and the English*, 2 vols. (London, 1833), 2:193 (n. *); Ralph E. Pumphrey, "The Introduction of Industrialists into the British Peerage: A Study in Adaptation of a Social Institution," *American Historical Review* 65 (1959–60):9; Thompson, *English Landed Society*, p. 294.

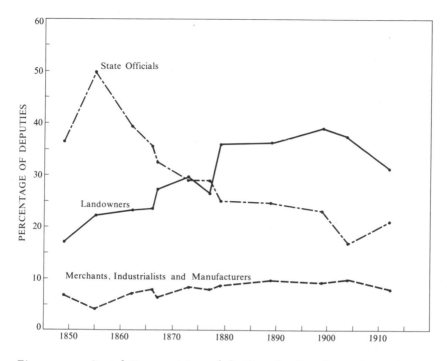

Figure 12.1. Social Composition of the Prussian Landtag, 1849–1912

SOURCE: Louis Rosenbaum, *Beruf und Herkunft der Abgeordeneten zu den deutschen und preussischen Parlamenten 1847 bis 1919* (Frankfurt am Main, 1923), pp. 29–30, 63.

affluence, and education predominated in both, though in different proportions. The two largest groups in the Reichstag were at first the same as in the Landtag: landowners and civil servants. The former accounted for less than a third but more than a fourth of all members until the election of 1912, when their percentage dropped to 18. The number of state officials, on the other hand, diminished steadily from 25.9 percent in 1871 to 9.1 in 1912. Merchants, industrialists, and manufacturers began with 8.0 percent in 1871, reached their peak in 1887 with 17.4, and then declined again to 11.9 in 1912. The greatest relative increase was in the category of writers and journalists, a reflection of the growing professionalization and democratization of political activity. Their percentage went from 1.6 in 1871 to 6.8 in 1893 and 14.2 in 1912. Handicraftsmen, workers, and white-collar employees achieved an impressive relative increase but an insignificant absolute increase: 0.3 percent in 1871, 1.1 in 1877, 0.8 in 1881, 1.3 in 1887, 5.0 in 1893, 6.0 in 1903, and 3.5 in 1912.

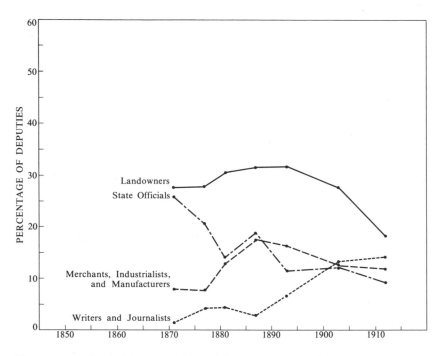

Figure 12.2. Social Composition of the German Reichstag, 1871–1912

SOURCE: Louis Rosenbaum, *Beruf und Herkunft der Abgeordeneten zu den deutschen und preussischen Parlamenten 1847 bis 1919* (Frankfurt am Main, 1923), pp. 23–24, 62.

An examination of the educational background of the Reichstag reinforces the view that equal manhood suffrage had little effect on the participation of the lower classes in the lawmaking process. A study of the members of the various liberal parties represented in the federal legislature between 1884 and 1912 shows that, out of a large sample of 422 men, 5.0 percent had not gone beyond an elementary and continuation school and another 3.1 percent had attended an elementary and trade or vocational school. On the other hand, 10.0 percent had attended a business or industrial school; 3.8 had attended a secondary school without completing their studies; 7.1 had completed their studies at a secondary school but had not gone on to a university; 63.3 had attended a university; and 30.1 had received the doctorate. An analysis of the level of education of the members of the Reichstag thus points to the same conclusion as an analysis of the distribution of occupations. The democratization of the forms of political activity did not lead to the exercise of political power by the lower classes. To be sure, the proportion of the nobility in the federal legislature declined from 40 percent in 1871 to 31 in 1887 and 14 in 1912. But its place was being taken not by workers or peasants but by members of the bourgeoisie who, as in England, were forming the basis of a new elite of birth and wealth.[13]

The preservation of an oligarchical structure of authority can also be seen in the system of administration. The people who enforced the laws, like the people who made them, continued to be men of background, education, and means. If anything, the higher bureaucracy was more selective than the national legislature about whom it admitted to the corridors of power. Certainly the tenacity with which the nobility continued to cling to such strategic positions as cabinet seats and diplomatic appointments is impressive. Many contemporaries recognized that upper-class control of administration meant upper-class influence over government. Matthew Arnold declared in 1861 in the introduction to his *Popular Education of France* that "the aristocracy of England . . . still, indeed, administers public affairs; and it is a great error to suppose, as many persons in England suppose, that it administers but does not govern. He who administers, governs, because he infixes his own work and stamps his own character on all public affairs as they pass through his hands; and, therefore, so long as the English aristocracy administers the commonwealth, it still governs it." Yet there were unmistakable signs, he went on, that leadership by the aristocracy based on the acquiescence of the majority of the nation in its right to lead was nearly over. That acquiescence, the tenure by which it held power, was fast giving way. "The superiority of the upper class over all others is no longer so great; the willingness of the others to recognise that superiority is no longer so ready."[14]

He correctly gauged that a change in the class structure of the administrative system was approaching, but he exaggerated its pace and intensity. Of 103 British cabinet members between 1830 and 1868, 56 were great territorial lords or their sons; 12 were country gentlemen, that is, lesser landowners; 21 came from the mercantile and administrative patriciate, most of them rentiers; and only 14 were *hommes nouveaux* with no family background, largely lawyers. As late as 1859, Bagehot could write that "the series of cabinet ministers presents a nearly unbroken rank of persons who either are themselves large landowners, or are connected closely by birth or intermarriage with large landowners." Between

13. Louis Rosenbaum, *Beruf und Herkunft der Abgeordneten zu den deutschen und preussischen Parlamenten 1847 bis 1919* (Frankfurt am Main, 1923), pp. 23–24, 29–31, 34, 62–63; Nikolaus von Preradovich, *Die Führungsschichten in Österreich und Preussen (1804–1918): Mit einem Ausblick bis zum Jahre 1945* (Wiesbaden, 1965), pp. 155–57; Joachim H. Knoll, *Führungsauslese in Liberalismus und Demokratie: Zur politischen Geistesgeschichte der letzten hundert Jahre* (Stuttgart, 1957), p. 174.

14. *The Works of Matthew Arnold*, 15 vols. (London, 1903–4), 10:7.

1868 and 1886, approximately between the adoption of the second Reform Bill and the passage of the third, the aristocracy continued to predominate over the bourgeoisie in the cabinets, though by a smaller margin of 27 to 22. Only in the period 1886–1916 did the number of bourgeois members equal the number of aristocrats, 49 each. Now, moreover, men of working-class background, 3 of them, appeared in the cabinet for the first time. The center of power was thus moving away from the landed nobility, but gradually and grudgingly. Under Disraeli in 1874, there had been 7 aristocrats and 5 bourgeois in the cabinet; under Gladstone in 1880, the figures were 8 and 6; under Balfour in 1902, they were 9 and 10; and under Campbell-Bannerman in 1906, 7 and 11, with 1 member of proletarian origin, an unprecedented occurrence. Although the shift was clear, it was taking place much more slowly than Matthew Arnold had anticipated.

On the Continent the social composition of the cabinets generally displayed the same tendency toward a decrease in the proportion of upper-class members, without altering the control over positions of authority by an elite of birth and wealth. There are no data on the Austrian ministry of the early 1860s, when the constitutional system was first established, but the members of the state council, leading bureaucrats charged with reviewing measures passed by the legislature before they were submitted for royal approval, were all noble, though 5 of the 7 had a bourgeois background. In 1878, 4 out of 10 ministers were aristocrats; in 1897, 6 out of 9; in 1908, 2 out of 13; and in 1918, 3 out of 14. In Hungary, a semifeudal monarchy dominated by the great landowners, the percentage of noblemen in the ministry was consistently higher: 100 in 1878 and 1897, 80 in 1908, and 53 in 1918. As in England in 1867 and 1884 or in Austria in 1907, the democratization of the suffrage had the effect of hastening the admission of commoners to the cabinets of Europe. The maintenance of a restricted franchise, on the other hand, generally coincided with a high rate of aristocratic participation in the ministries, as in Hungary. In either case, the nobility continued to play a central role far out of proportion to its size or even its wealth, and the lower classes remained almost completely excluded from cabinet positions. In this respect, the form of government, oligarchical or democratic, appeared to make little difference.[15]

The same pattern of class origins emerges from an examination of important administrators in Central Europe. Of the 22 leading bureaucrats in the Austrian Empire in 1829, 16 were members of the established nobility and 6 came from recently ennobled or bourgeois families; in

15. Guttsman, *British Political Elite*, pp. 38, 78–79; [Walter Bagehot], "Parliamentary Reform," *National Review* 8 (1859):233; Preradovich, *Die Führungsschichten in Österreich und Preussen*, pp. 60–61.

1847 the figures were 16 and 4; in 1878 they were 8 and 10; and in 1908 they were still what they had been a generation earlier, 8 and 10. In Prussia the aristocracy continued to control local administration outside the self-governing cities of the kingdom. In 1888–91, 62 percent of those appointed provincial governors, 73 percent of those appointed district superintendents, and 62 percent of the county commissioners in office were noble. Twenty years later, the situation was essentially the same. Eleven out of 12 provincial governors, 23 out of 37 district superintendents, and 268 out of 481 county commissioners came from aristocratic families. The higher the position on the scale of importance and prestige, moreover, the more likely it was to be held by a man of noble descent. Of the 612 councillors in the ministry of the interior in 1911, 473 were commoners; of the 506 assessors, 311 were commoners. At these lower levels of the bureaucracy, the ratio between nobles and nonnobles was the reverse of that at the upper levels.

But what about the positions that were becoming open to nonnobles? What was the class origin of those commoners who were now able in increasing numbers to gain admission to the administrative system? Specifically, how many of them were sons of the urban or rural proletariat who had managed to rise within the civil service thanks to the democratization of political life? The most detailed answer is provided in Hartmut Kaelble's study of social mobility in Central Europe during the nineteenth century. In a sample of 73 Bavarian government officials in the period 1836–50, only 1 percent could be categorized as coming from the "lower strata," that is, from families whose father was a worker, a servant, or a clerk. In 1851–75 the percentage was 3 for a sample of 96; in 1876–1900 it was 2 for a sample of 113; and in 1901–14 it was 0 for a sample of 145. In Westphalia the ratio was even more lopsided. There was not a single member of the "lower strata" in a sample of 355 during the entire period 1836–1914. In Baden, on the other hand, 5 percent of the 1,653 government officials surveyed for the years 1901–14 were of proletarian origin. The great majority of those employed in the administration of the state in all parts of Germany came from the "upper strata," from families of high officials, army officers, university or secondary school teachers, clergymen, lawyers, physicians and pharmacists, landowners, and entrepreneurs. Their preponderance on the eve of the First World War was almost as great as on the eve of the Revolution of 1848.[16]

The diplomatic service and the officer corps in particular remained

16. Preradovich, *Die Führungsschichten in Österreich und Preussen*, pp. 39–41, 111–12, 114; J. C. G. Röhl, "Higher Civil Servants in Germany, 1890–1900," *Journal of Contemporary History* 2 (1967), no. 3, p. 116; Hartmut Kaelble, "Sozialer Aufstieg in Deutschland, 1850–1914," *Vierteljahrschrift für Sozial- und Wirtschaftsgeschichte* 60 (1973):54–55.

strongholds of the nobility despite the onset of the age of mass politics. Aristocratic background was almost a prerequisite for appointment to a leading embassy of the German Empire. During the 1890s the only envoys of bourgeois origin out of a total of 30 were those in Peru, Venezuela, Colombia, and Siam. According to a member of the Reichstag in 1914, the higher positions in the foreign service were held by 8 princes, 29 counts, 20 barons, 54 untitled noblemen, and only 11 commoners. A more systematic examination reveals that 11 of the leading Prussian diplomats in 1829 belonged to the established nobility and 11 to recently ennobled or bourgeois families; in 1847 the figures were 20 and 9; in the new imperial diplomatic service of 1878 they were 23 and 14; and in 1909 they were 28 and 17. In Austria-Hungary the division of prominent diplomats between members of the established nobility and members of the new nobility and the bourgeoisie was roughly the same: 20 and 9 in 1829, 22 and 9 in 1847, 16 and 10 in 1878, and 22 and 16 in 1908. It is striking how inflexible these ratios remained despite the constitutional and political changes taking place during the nineteenth century.[17]

The officer corps could not maintain the same exclusivity in an age of mass armies and technological warfare. The demand of the armed forces for trained leadership grew so rapidly that the aristocracy was no longer able to satisfy it from within its own ranks. An influx of nonnoble members into the officer corps became unavoidable. But although commoners gradually came to form a majority of all officers, aristocrats often retained control over the most important positions in the military establishment.

Take the Prussian officer corps. In 1817, shortly after the war against Napoleon, it had 4,138 noble and 3,367 nonnoble members; in 1818 the figures were 3,828 and 3,350; and in 1819 they were 3,605 and 3,053. In 1860, on the eve of the struggle for national unification, the preponderance of the aristocracy was even more striking: 65 percent of all officers. By 1913, on the other hand, the ratios had become reversed as the result of a steady expansion in the size of the army. Now only 30 percent of the officers were noble. The aristocracy, however, was more successful in maintaining its position within the higher ranks of the armed forces. Of the Prussian generals and colonels, 86 percent were noble in 1860, 61 in 1900, and 52 in 1913. Among second lieutenants in the infantry, by contrast, 62 percent were commoners in 1873 and 78 in 1909. At the outbreak of the First World War, only about a fourth of the captains, first lieutenants, and second lieutenants came from aristocratic families. Since the nobility was not large enough to meet the rising need

17. Rudolf Morsey, *Die oberste Reichsverwaltung unter Bismarck* (Münster, 1957), p. 246; Preradovich, *Die Führungsschichten in Österreich und Preussen*, pp. 23–25, 100–102.

for officer candidates, it had to open the doors of the army leadership wider and wider to sons of the bourgeoisie. But it generally managed to keep control over the more strategic positions within the army: the upper levels of command, the elite guard and cavalry regiments, and the general staff, whose personnel was still 60 percent aristocratic in 1906 and 50 percent in 1913.

In most of the other states of the German Empire, the proportion of the officer corps recruited from the bourgeoisie was significantly greater than that in Prussia, but the obstacles to the admission of members of the lower classes were equally high. In 1811 there were 902 noble officers and 1,341 nonnoble officers in the Bavarian army; in 1853 the figures were 1,181 and 2,554; in 1872 they were 1,333 and 5,070; and in 1893 they were 1,122 and 7,390. The percentage of aristocrats in the officer corps thus declined from 40 to 32, 21, and 13. Yet as late as 1904, 50 percent of the officers in the higher positions and 50 percent of the members of the general staff were noble, whereas the percentage was only 4 in the foot artillery regiments, engineer battalions, and transport troops. In Saxony the aristocracy accounted for 71 percent of the officers in 1808, 57 in 1828, 61 in 1848, 43 in 1868, 44 in 1888, and 15 in 1908. There are no detailed statistics for Württemberg, but the officer corps, which at the beginning of the nineteenth century was almost entirely noble in the ranks above lieutenant, had a substantial number of non-noble captains by the time of the wars of 1866 and 1870–71. Thereafter the bourgeoisie acquired a growing preponderance, except in a few old and exclusive grenadier, dragoon, and uhlan regiments.

Alfred von Waldersee, later chief of staff of the imperial army, was one of many aristocratic officers of the old school who worried about what he described in 1877 as "the inundation of the officer corps by the aristocracy of money." It remained his hope that "the officer class, as a class in its own right, will distance itself more from the other classes." This was all the more important, he explained, because society was moving toward an unavoidable struggle of the propertyless against the propertied. "We will soon need an army, small and well-paid, which will shoot down the *canaille* without hesitation, as soon as it is demanded."

To be sure, the expectation that the officer corps could retain its aristocratic character in an age of industrialism was unrealistic. Yet if the role of status as the key to a military career was diminishing, that of wealth remained unchanged. An examination of the social origins of those attending officer candidate schools in Germany in 1912 reveals a solid array of affluence, background, and education. Of those surveyed, 40 percent had fathers who were higher government officials, clergymen, lawyers, physicians, and professors; 25 percent of the fathers were themselves officers; 15 percent were merchants and factory owners; 8 percent were landowners; 5 percent were minor government officials and non-commissioned officers; 2 percent were lessees of estates; and 6 percent were engaged in miscellaneous private occupations. This last category might have included a few workers and peasants.[18]

The officer corps in other countries of Europe was going through a similar transformation. That is, a growing proportion of its members was of bourgeois origin, especially at the lower levels of command, but the barriers to the acceptance of sons of the laboring classes remained largely insuperable. In France the percentage of general officers with the aristocratic *de* before their surname was already no more than 25 by 1898, and it continued to decline steadily as a result in part of the purge of monarchists from the army after the Dreyfus affair. In the Austrian and later the Austro-Hungarian army, the same process was occurring more slowly: in 1804, 92 percent of the leading generals came from the old established nobility; in 1816, the percentage was 81; in 1829, it was 88; in 1847, 93; in 1859, 90; in 1878, 48; in 1897, 72; in 1908, 41; and in 1918, 25.

In Russia the guards and many of the cavalry regiments remained a preserve of the aristocracy. Of those attending the elite cadet schools from which the former usually selected their officers, 60 percent belonged to the hereditary nobility and another 28 percent were sons of personal nobles, usually members of the officer corps. In the army as a whole, however, the situation was rapidly changing. The shift in the social composition of one of the typical military schools in Moscow illustrates what was happening to the officer corps at large. In the late 1860s, 81 percent of those enrolled came from the hereditary nobility and 9 from the personal nobility. In the late 1870s, about 45 percent were from the hereditary nobility, 33 from the personal nobility, 13 from the bourgeoisie, and 11 from the clergy. By the end of the 1880s, only 12 percent were sons of hereditary nobles, 57 of personal nobles, 16 of bourgeois, and 5 of peasants. Finally, at the beginning of the First World War, 9 percent were sons of hereditary nobles, 28 of personal nobles, 28 of bourgeois, and 19 of peasants. Even more revealing, by 1912 only 48 percent of those attending the academy of the general staff were hereditary nobles. The class structure of the officer corps in Russia thus conformed in general to the pattern established in the other states of Europe.[19]

18. Karl Demeter, *Das deutsche Offizierkorps in Gesellschaft und Staat, 1650–1945*, 2d ed. (Frankfurt am Main, 1962), pp. 12, 22, 26–28, 30–31, 37, 44, 46, 53; Preradovich, *Die Führungsschichten in Österreich und Preussen*, pp. 151–53; Gerhard Ritter, *Staatskunst und Kriegshandwerk: Das Problem des "Militarismus" in Deutschland*, 4 vols. (Munich, 1954–68), 2:360 (n. 24).

19. Correlli Barnett, "The Education of Military Elites," *Journal of Contemporary History* 2 (1967), no. 3, p. 27; Preradovich, *Die Führungsschichten in Österreich und Preus-*

It becomes clear from all these data that the exercise of authority in the nineteenth century remained concentrated in the hands of an oligarchy of birth and wealth. Within this oligarchy there was a pronounced shift in the center of gravity from the aristocracy to the bourgeoisie. Yet the two dominant minorities, notwithstanding their occasional clashes, were gradually fusing to form a new patriciate combining the manners and traditions of one with the riches and energies of the other. This alliance of status and affluence continued to predominate in the legislatures, cabinets, administrative systems, and armed forces of Europe. The proletariat, on the other hand, despite its improving standard of living, rising level of literacy, and growing acquisition of the franchise, remained largely excluded from positions of authority. Why? Why did the lower classes, which were now increasingly in a position to decide who would govern them, fail to choose men of their own experience and background? To put it more broadly, why was the democratization of the political process insufficient to produce a democratization of the political elite?

The answer appears to lie in the continuation of a concept of civic leadership derived from a preindustrial hierarchical society. More than that, the belief that men in authority must have an advanced education in order to master the complexities of government served to disqualify 95 percent or more of the adult male population. Yet the training provided in the secondary schools and universities was largely irrelevant to the practical problems of administration and statecraft. It represented rather the ritualization of scholarship; it reflected the belief that learning should be not a guide to action but a token of status. The curriculum of the institutions of secondary and higher education was exclusive precisely because of its impracticality. It did not train students for civic life. It helped instead to maintain the socially discriminatory function of advanced study, whose conspicuous consumption and conspicuous waste had the effect of separating the haves from the have-nots. The emphasis on a knowledge of Greek, Latin, philosophy, and mathematics clearly served this purpose. "The ostensible function of studying the classics," writes Lawrence Stone perceptively, "was—and is—to preserve and foster the humanistic values of the ancient world." With time, however, "the latent function of the classics had grown in importance, namely the reservation of higher culture as the distinctive monopoly of a social élite. . . . By the middle of the nineteenth century this latent function had emerged into the open." In short, the acquisition by the masses after

---

sen, pp. 56–58; Raymond L. Garthoff, "The Military as a Social Force," in *The Transformation of Russian Society: Aspects of Social Change since 1861*, ed. Cyril E. Black (Cambridge, Mass., 1960), p. 326.

1850 of the external means for achieving power was not accompanied by the inner conviction that they could in fact exercise it effectively. They remained subject to feelings of inadequacy and attitudes of deference derived from their long historical experience of subordination.[20]

There were some observers who conceded that the content of advanced learning had little relevance for civic affairs. In any case, many students mastered it only superficially, and many more forgot most of what they had learned soon after leaving the school or the university. Yet what mattered were the attitudes, beliefs, and habits they acquired, the friendships they formed, and the manners they assumed. A British educator early in the twentieth century provided a classic defense of the exclusive system of secondary education in his country: it may not inculcate academic excellence but it builds character. "A boy when he leaves a Public School at the age of eighteen will very likely imagine that Michelangelo was a musician, or that Handel wrote comic verse. He will be unable to tell you the difference between rates and taxes. He will not know the name of the present French Premier or the names of the battles in the Russo-Japanese War." But here is the nub of the argument: "He can get in a Public School what he could not get anywhere else in any country. . . . He will learn self-reliance, and will acquire certain other moral qualities—a sense of duty and fellowship, a knowledge of how to command and to obey. . . . He will learn the Public School Tradition."

Compare this confidence in the capacity for leadership acquired by those attending a secondary school with the account in H. G. Wells's autobiography of the patient resignation and cheerful submissiveness fostered by the primary schools to which the children of the propertyless went: "In spirit, form and intention they were inferior schools, and to send one's children to them . . . was a definite and final acceptance of social inferiority. The Education Act of 1871 [sic] was not an Act for common universal education, it was an Act to educate the lower classes for employment on lower-class lines, and with specially trained, inferior teachers who had no university quality." The most important civic virtue taught in such schools was the acceptance by the common man of the judgment of his betters.[21]

The role of education in maintaining an oligarchical structure of authority was reinforced by various other influences and institutions that shape the way people see themselves and others. Newspapers, journals,

20. Lawrence Stone, "Literacy and Education in England, 1640–1900," *Past & Present*, no. 42 (1969), p. 86.

21. Francis R. G. Duckworth, *From a Pedagogue's Sketch-Book* (London and Leipzig, 1912), pp. 12–14; H. G. Wells, *Experiment in Autobiography: Discoveries and Conclusions of a Very Ordinary Brain (since 1866)* (London, 1934), p. 93.

books, lectures, and sermons taught the familiar lesson that learning, wealth, and status are the essential qualifications for an intelligent use of power. To allow the *profanum vulgus* to exercise authority is to invite chaos and tyranny. Religion in particular rivaled learning as an intellectual mainstay of the status quo. A reformist clergyman in Great Britain admitted during the 1890s that "the Church is mostly administered and officered by the classes; her influential laity belong almost wholly to the classes; she is doing a great and growing work amongst the masses; but the deep sympathies of the clergy with the poor as such are largely obscured to the eyes of the masses by the fact that social rank and social position secured by wealth and tradition still count for so much in her service, both amongst clergy and laity." In short, the experience of the nineteenth century demonstrated that the legal right of the lower classes to vote was not enough to bring about a democratization of authority. A complex of beliefs, attitudes, and habits deeply ingrained in men's minds had to be overcome before manhood suffrage could effect the diffusion of political power that its advocates had expected from the introduction of a mass franchise. In the political process, what people think they can do is more important than what they in fact have the right to do.[22]

The failure of the democratization of politics to alter in any basic way the oligarchical structure of authority strengthened the belief of many European social thinkers that the lower classes were by their very nature—by their mental makeup even more than their material position—doomed to be subordinate to an intelligent, aggressive, affluent minority. Here was an inescapable truth of the human condition, they maintained, that neither the rationalization of the economy, the redistribution of wealth, the transformation of society, nor the democratization of politics could alter. The surface manifestations of power might change; the reality beneath would always remain the same. "The *demos* in the sense of an unorganized mass never 'administers' by itself in larger groups," wrote the brilliant German sociologist Max Weber. "It is administered, and only changes the way of selecting the dominant leaders of the administration and the measure of influence which it or, more correctly, other circles of people from its midst are capable of exercising over the content and direction of administrative activity through the supplement of so-called 'public opinion.'" There was a tone of profound pessimism and hopelessness concerning the political process in such writings. They suggested that civic justice was a mirage that men could seek but never reach.

The classic country of disenchanted political realism was Italy, where

22. T. C. Fry, "Church Reform and Social Reform," in *Essays in Aid of the Reform of the Church*, ed. Charles Gore (London, 1898), p. 303.

the fiction of civic equality confronted the truth of civic inequality in its most pitiless starkness. Here, in the land of Machiavelli and Guicciardini, of rapacious condottieri and ambitious princes, of a hardheaded Renaissance skepticism regarding statecraft, flourished a school of writers who gave definitive expression to the inevitability of oligarchy in society. According to Gaetano Mosca, there is one fact concerning any political organism that is so obvious as to be apparent to everyone. "In all societies—from those which are least developed, which have barely reached the dawn of civilization, to those which are most numerous and most cultivated—there are two classes of people, one made up of the rulers and the other of the ruled. The former, which is always the less numerous, performs all political functions, monopolizes power, and enjoys the advantages derived from power." Vilfredo Pareto came to the similar conclusion that a form of government in which the "people" express their "will" without factions, intrigues, or cliques, assuming that they have a will (the quotation marks are his), exists only as the pious wish of theorists.

The most poignant expression of civic fatalism, however, the most sensitive to the injustice of social oppression and yet the most pessimistic about the possibility of democratic government, appeared in the work of Robert Michels, a German by birth but an Italian by choice: "The majority of human beings, predestined by the cruel fatality of history, [are] forced to bear patiently the domination of a small minority in their midst, and to serve merely as the pedestal for the power of oligarchy." This discouragement concerning the effectualness of civil reform reflected the failure of the nineteenth century to bring about a genuine political emancipation of the lower classes. It echoed the folk wisdom of the worldly French proverb that the more things change, the more they remain the same.[23]

23. Max Weber, *Grundriss der Sozialökonomik: Wirtschaft und Gesellschaft* (Tübingen, 1922), p. 667; Gaetano Mosca, *Elementi di scienza politica* (Rome, 1896), p. 60; Vilfredo Pareto, *Trattato di sociologia generale*, 2 vols. (Florence, 1916), 2:619; Robert Michels, *Zur Soziologie des Parteiwesens in der modernen Demokratie: Untersuchungen über die oligarchischen Tendenzen des Gruppenlebens* (Leipzig, 1911), p. 376.

Part Four

Der Krieg als der Zustand, in welchem
mit der Eitelkeit der zeitlichen Güter und
Dinge, die sonst eine erbauliche Redensart
zu seyn pflegt, Ernst gemacht wird, ist
hiermit das Moment, worin die Idealität
des Besonderen ihr Recht erhält und
Wirklichkeit wird;—er hat die höhere
Bedeutung, dass durch ihn, wie ich es
anderwärts ausgedrückt habe, "die sittliche
Gesundheit der Völker in ihrer Indifferenz
gegen das Festwerden der endlichen
Bestimmtheiten erhalten wird, wie die
Bewegung der Winde die See vor Fäulniss
bewahrt, in welche sie eine dauernde Ruhe,
wie die Völker ein dauernder oder gar ein
ewiger Friede versetzen würde."

Georg Wilhelm Friedrich Hegel,
Grundlinien der Philosophie des Rechts,
1821

13

THE PATTERN OF DIPLOMACY

The rationalization of the economy, though affecting the states of Europe in so many different ways, had little direct influence on the conduct of international relations. It may have revolutionized the way people earned their livelihood; it may have transformed the relationship between social classes and occupational groups; it may have produced an alteration in the form, if not the essence, of the political process. But the diplomatic system resting on the interaction of some twenty sovereign states—six of them Great Powers; two of them, Spain and Turkey, intermediate states; and the rest small states—remained essentially unchanged. The same men with the same background and training were running the foreign offices after 1815 as before, the same ends were being pursued, the same means were being employed. A Richelieu or a Kaunitz might have been horrified to see what European society had become by the time of the First World War, but they would have felt quite at home in the chancelleries and ministries where the crucial diplomatic questions were being decided.

In a survey of the international relations of Europe at the turn of the twentieth century, William L. Langer commented on the unchanging outlook of the leading diplomats:

> One cannot study this period without marvelling at the exuberance and optimism which went hand in hand with recklessness and confidence in the conduct of foreign affairs. It was taken for granted that the world was marked out by Providence for exploitation by the European white man and that the principle of every man for himself and the devil take the hindmost was natural law. In the writings of the statesmen and in the writings of journalists there is very little trace of deeper understanding. The rise of Japan, the Adua disaster, the Boxer rising, none of these epoch-making events really opened the eyes of Europe. Even Lord Salisbury could see in the world nothing but a few virile nations and a large number of dying nations. The basic problem of international relations was who should cut up the victims.[1]

1. Robert Ensor, "Political Institutions in Europe: Political Issues and Political Thought," in *The New Cambridge Modern History*, 12 vols. (Cambridge, 1960–70), 12:73; William L. Langer, *The Diplomacy of Imperialism, 1890–1902*, 2d ed. (New York, 1951), p. 797.

Changing a few words here and there, he might just as well have been writing about Europe at the time of the War of the Spanish Succession or the partitions of Poland.

Yet the industrial revolution did have a subtle but significant effect on international relations in that it supported the forces of stability. The nineteenth century was a period of relative peace, greater than any the Continent had known in some fifteen hundred years since the barbarian invasions of the Roman Empire. The rapid economic expansion after 1815 clearly contributed to this age of tranquillity, diverting public and private energies from the pursuit of conquest to the acquisition of profit. It offered an alternative to war as a means of acquiring affluence. Why expend effort on the achievement of military domination when the same effort invested in industrial or financial enterprise could bring a greater return with less risk? Here is the key to the era of stability that lasted through most of the nineteenth century.

The boundaries of Europe drawn up at the Congress of Vienna remained almost unchanged for forty years. Only the independence of Belgium and Greece distinguished the map of 1815 from that of 1855. Then came a period of sixteen years of intermittent wars, bloody but short, the most important outcome of which was the emergence of a united Germany and a united Italy. It was as if the diplomatic system established after the defeat of Napoleon could no longer withstand the strains and pressures of maintaining the status quo. But by 1871 the process of readjustment had been completed, and Europe returned to another forty-three years of tranquillity during which there were crises and conflicts—in the Balkans in 1877–78 and 1912–13, for example—but when no two Great Powers were at war with one another. The Continent thus enjoyed peace for more than eighty of the ninety-nine years between Waterloo and the Marne. When was the last time it had known such a prolonged period of stability?

This remarkable achievement was not the result of some new theory or technique of statecraft. On the contrary, as the century progressed, a new diplomacy of ideology was increasingly replaced by the more traditional diplomacy of expediency and *raison d'état*. The long period of incessant warfare in Europe between 1792 and 1815 had invested international conflict with a theoretical justification that the dynastic wars of benevolent despotism had neither sought nor needed. Since at least the Peace of Westphalia, nations had fought for reasons of pure self-interest, for the commerce of the New World and India or for rich territories like Silesia and the Austrian Netherlands. After the outbreak of the French Revolution, however, statecraft and warfare also began to reflect fundamental differences concerning the purposes of government, differences between freedom and stability, natural rights and historic traditions, social equality and hereditary status. The conception of diplomacy as an instrument of purposes transcending mere expediency continued under the Restoration, first in the Quadruple Alliance between the victors over Napoleon and later, especially after 1830, in the two opposing camps—England and France on one side, Russia, Prussia, and Austria on the other—which continued to confront one another until the Crimean War brought about a realignment of the Great Powers.

The issues dividing them were partly those of national self-interest and partly those of political ideology. In one camp were the countries where constitutional government had prevailed over royal absolutism, where liberal theories of state and society were in the ascendant. Their separation from the eastern autocracies of the Continent, wrote Palmerston during the 1830s, "is not one of words, but of things; not the effect of caprice or of will, but produced by the force of occurrences. The three and the two think differently, and therefore they act differently." The great object of policy, he explained to the British minister in Madrid, "ought now to be to form a Western confederacy of free states as a counterpoise to the Eastern league of the arbitrary governments." An alliance of England, France, Spain, and Portugal would form a political and moral power in Europe capable of holding Metternich and Nicholas I in check. "We shall be on the advance, they on the decline; and all the smaller planets of Europe will have a natural tendency to gravitate towards our system." Such was the diplomatic design of the leading liberal statesmen of Europe.

Public opinion in the west, especially bourgeois public opinion, supported this conception of a confederacy of free nations opposing the tyranny of the east. In 1832 the *Edinburgh Review* published a spirited defense of the policy of backing the constitutional movement throughout the Continent: "It is vain to deny that two great antagonist principles now divide Europe—freedom and despotism. They are to be seen contending from Lisbon to St Petersburgh; and we meet them in every political question. England and France are on the one side, Prussia and Russia on the other." The differences between them raised the danger of armed conflict, to be sure. Yet if the supporters of freedom remained firm, the others would be forced to back down. "The absolutes can carry their ends only by war; from which they are now restrained by a sense, if not of weakness, certainly of that which is akin to it, insecurity. The best security of the liberals is in tranquillity; and in their strength, therefore, lies peace." The threat of force in defense of liberty, as they defined it, was the weapon with which the nations of the west confronted those of the east in every part of the Continent, in Belgium, Italy, Poland, the Iberian Peninsula, and the German Confederation.[2]

2. *Lord Melbourne's Papers*, ed. Lloyd C. Sanders (London, 1889), p. 339; Charles Webster, *The Foreign Policy of Palmerston, 1830–1841: Britain, the Liberal Movement*

But the conservative powers had their theories of state and society no less than the liberals. They too believed that statecraft should be motivated by more than expediency, that it should seek to serve moral as well as material purposes. They differed from the west, however, in their formulation of those purposes. Not liberty but order, not abstract constitutional rights but concrete historical traditions provided the only basis for a stable social system. Had not the events of the French Revolution and the Napoleonic era demonstrated that? Now that the forces of sedition had been defeated, the monarchs of Europe must work together to oppose their revival. The danger was omnipresent. It lurked in the extravagant expectations and unrealizable hopes that liberal ideas nourished. On one side of the ideological struggle was the overweening ambition to cast aside the eternal restraints of civilized human existence; on the other was a courageous acceptance of the need for established authority. The duty of the state was to defend the legitimate rights of every class and every interest in society, maintaining a balance between collective stability and individual liberty. Respect for everything that exists, wrote Metternich in 1820, freedom for every government to look out for the well-being of its own people, a league of all governments against factions in all the states, scorn for the meaningless words that have become the rallying cry of the seditious, respect for the progressive development of institutions in legal ways, refusal on the part of every ruler to give aid to the adherents of a party in whatever disguise they may be masked—such are the ideas of the great monarchs. "The world can be saved if they put them into effect; it is lost if they do not."

It was clear to the conservatives that the danger of subversion was too great to be dealt with by each government independently. The forces of revolution were international in scope; what began as domestic unrest in one country would, if left to fester, grow into an insurrectionary epidemic infecting all countries. Is this not precisely what happened after 1789? The rulers therefore had the duty of forming an alliance for the maintenance of established authority, intervening to suppress sedition in any nation whose government was unable or unwilling to do so. Statesmen must not regard the outbreak of revolution in a neighboring country as purely an internal affair, any more than they can regard the outbreak of fire in a neighbor's house as purely an internal affair. The Great Powers in particular should establish an alliance or confederation to oppose subversive movements wherever they might appear. Since the western constitutional monarchies refused to form part of an international police force, the three autocracies of the east would have to work alone for the

---

and the Eastern Question, 2 vols. (London, 1951), 1:390; "History, Present Wrongs, and Claims of Poland," Edinburgh Review, or Critical Journal 55 (1832):264.

preservation of the status quo. In his political testament of 1 December 1827, Frederick William III of Prussia urged the crown prince to maintain harmony among the Great Powers. "Above all, Prussia, Russia, and Austria should never separate from one another." Differences of ideology between the western and eastern powers were admittedly reinforced by differences of interest. For example, the opposing policies of England and Russia concerning the Ottoman Empire helped intensify their disagreements concerning the form and function of government. But until the mid-century, principle was often as important as expediency in determining the diplomacy of the Great Powers.[3]

The Crimean War finally put an end to the alignments based on ideology, although there had been signs for some time of growing tension within each camp. Consider the rivalry between Austria and Prussia during the Revolution of 1848. It was the outbreak of hostilities in the Balkans in 1853, however, that revealed unmistakably that a new political age was beginning. The decision of Austria to support the western powers in the struggle against Russia, initially by diplomatic means and then by the threat of force, destroyed the unity of the eastern autocracies and initiated a period of growing antagonism between Vienna and St. Petersburg that culminated sixty years later in a world conflict. The effect of the Crimean War was felt throughout Europe in the new crisscrossing of agreements and alliances formed on the basis of *raison d'état* pure and simple. It represented a return to the diplomacy of the eighteenth century in all its unabashed self-interest. No sooner were hostilities over than France and Russia began to cooperate in the Balkans and in Italy in opposition to Austria. On the eve of the Seven Weeks' War, Prussia concluded an alliance with the liberal Italian kingdom. In the late 1860s, France and Austria drew close together out of common distrust of the designs of Berlin. And when the Franco-Prussian War broke out in the summer of 1870, British public opinion supported Bismarck because of deep suspicion of Napoleon III. Ideology had simply ceased to be a significant factor in the diplomacy of Europe.

For many men in public life, liberals as well as conservatives, this abandonment of the statecraft of principle was hard to accept. They continued to believe that relations between states should be based on more than the interaction of collective egoisms. Governments should be guided by enduring principles of truth, justice, and international morality. To these men the new primacy of *Realpolitik* was a tragedy. Edwin von Manteuffel, adjutant general to King William I of Prussia, wrote

3. *Aus Metternich's nachgelassenen Papieren*, ed. Richard Metternich-Winneburg, 8 vols. (Vienna, 1880–84), 3:416; F. R. Paulig, *Friedrich Wilhelm III., König von Preussen (1770 bis 1840)* (Frankfurt an der Oder, 1905), p. 349.

despairingly in the spring of 1865: "All European alliances are broken. The system on which the European balance rested has been violently shaken or has, properly speaking, already collapsed. Revolutionary tendencies have gained power in all states. The movements against the old Europe and the old dynasties which began with the year 1789 find support in a great part of mankind. . . . These crises must lead to a great European war or to socialist revolutions which will overthrow the present dynasties." To those who believed in the politics of principle, in foreign as well as domestic affairs, the diplomatic developments between the Crimean War and the Franco-Prussian War represented the end of an era of stability on the Continent.[4]

Europe was to enjoy another forty years of peace, however, for the conflicts of the mid-century helped release many of the tensions and dissatisfactions that had been weakening the status quo. A new equilibrium became possible. Yet the situation after 1871 was significantly different from the one that had existed before 1853. The most important change was German unification, which created a powerful new state combining military and economic preponderance with political inexperience. As a result, the traditional distribution of power on the Continent became profoundly altered.

When hostilities began in 1870, the neutral countries generally favored Prussia over France in the belief that Napoleon III had provoked the conflict. Once they ended, however, many observers recognized that they had witnessed a diplomatic revolution. After the capitulation of Paris, Sir Robert Peel expressed in the House of Commons a deep concern about what was happening: "I must say I look on the unification of Germany as a great peril to Europe. . . . We have at this moment the unification of Germany under a military despotism. Can that be for the good of Europe? It cannot be for the good of Europe that there should be a great military despotism in Germany, built up on the ruin and destruction of France." Disraeli was even more deeply perturbed. "This war represents the German Revolution, a greater political event than the French Revolution of last century," he said. Not a single principle in the management of the foreign affairs of Great Britain, accepted by all statesmen for guidance up to six months ago, existed any longer. There was not a diplomatic tradition that had not been swept away. "You have a new world, new influences at work, new and unknown objects and dangers with which to cope, at present involved in that obscurity incident to novelty in such affairs. . . . What has really come to pass in Europe? The balance of

4. Rudolf Stadelmann, *Das Jahr 1865 und das Problem von Bismarcks deutscher Politik* (Munich and Berlin, 1933), p. 80.

power has been entirely destroyed." To the statesmen of other countries, the German Empire appeared to be a diplomatic sphinx, powerful yet inscrutable, posing a riddle that they vainly tried to solve.[5]

The change in the position of Austria as a result of the wars of the mid-century was also of far-reaching significance. The Habsburg empire had traditionally been both an eastern and a central European state, for much of its history even a western European state. The loss of its possessions in the Low Countries and on the upper Rhine in the aftermath of the French Revolution had ended its role on the Atlantic seaboard, but it continued to play an important part in Italian as well as German affairs. Although it had long had a vital interest in the Balkans, that interest had been counterbalanced by an orientation toward other parts of the Continent until the middle of the nineteenth century. After 1871, however, Austria found herself confronted in the northwest by a united Germany and in the southwest by a united Italy. Thereafter she was forced to seek in the east an outlet for energies and ambitions that had formerly been directed toward Central Europe. The result was a fundamental readjustment of Vienna's diplomatic policy.

Its new goal was described in 1872 by Count Gyula Andrássy, foreign minister of the Dual Monarchy, as follows: "We have been thrown out of Germany, and that is good. We have lost Italy, and have thereby become stronger. We do not want to annex anything, but we want to have peace, to defend our vital interests, which are threatened with regard to our Slavic population." The Christian peoples of the Ottoman Empire, he continued, should develop in association with the power closest to them. That is Austria, which cannot allow herself to be outflanked. "It is best for Europe that we, who can never have Pan-Slav tendencies, protect and develop the Slavic states in Turkey in order to fulfill in due time the civilizing mission which Turkey perhaps cannot accomplish." This emphasis on expansion to the southeast meant that the Habsburg monarchy was likely to come into conflict with Russia, whose interest in the Balkans was equally intense. Consequently, a rivalry sprang up between the two conservative empires that had been so closely allied under the Restoration. As the Ottoman state continued to weaken, the question of who would gain control over its European possessions became increasingly urgent. To Vienna its solution promised not only compensation for defeat in Germany and Italy but also an opportunity to check by a display of strength the separatist tendencies of minority nationalities within the Dual Monarchy. To St. Petersburg it held out the prospect of realizing a manifest destiny: expansion into the Balkans, conquest of Constanti-

5. Great Britain, *Parliamentary Debates*, 3d ser. (1830–91), 204:81–82, 404–5.

344 · International Relations

nople, access to the Mediterranean, protection of the Orthodox faith, and liberation of the Slavic peoples. A compromise between such contradictory objectives became progressively more difficult.[6]

The foreign policy of Great Britain was also undergoing a momentous change. Throughout most of the nineteenth century, it had been an axiom of English statesmen that they must protect Turkey against Russia because it was better to have a weak and compliant state in control of the Straits than a strong and aggressive one. Not even the most obvious evidence of the inability of the Ottoman Empire to achieve political stability or military effectiveness was enough to persuade the British to abandon Constantinople. They continued to maintain that they could bring about reforms in Turkey that would make her capable of resisting both Russian expansionism and Christian separatism. Palmerston had written in 1839 that "as to the Turkish empire, if we can procure for it ten years of peace under the joint protection of the five Powers, and if those years are profitably employed in reorganizing the internal system of the empire, there is no reason whatever why it should not become again a respectable Power. . . . All that we hear every day of the week about the decay of the Turkish empire, and its being a dead body or a sapless trunk, and so forth, is pure and unadulterated nonsense." The determination of the English to restrain Russia continued to grow with time; by the late 1870s, they were holding a line from Constantinople through Persia and Afghanistan to Peking, opposing the ambitions of St. Petersburg in Asia as well as Europe.

This attitude began to change late in the century. The introduction of the iron vessel in oceanic shipping made the routes to the New World and the East Indies safer so that the interest of Great Britain in the commerce of the Black Sea declined. As American grain and Asian rice became more easily available, the Turkish straits began to seem less important. The acquisition of control over the Suez Canal Company and Egypt shifted the emphasis of English diplomacy toward the eastern Mediterranean, the Red Sea, and the Persian Gulf. Thus the European possessions of the Ottoman Empire lost much of their significance. In addition, developments in the Balkans after the Congress of Berlin of 1878 suggested that the rise of independent Christian states in that region need not necessarily lead to its domination by St. Petersburg. Events in Bulgaria during the late 1880s in particular seemed to indicate that there was a basic clash of interest between the democratic nationalism of the Balkan peoples and the authoritarian policy of czarist Russia. By the end of the century, Lord Salisbury, the British prime minister, was criticizing those who had sup-

6. *Denkwürdigkeiten des Botschafters General v. Schweinitz*, 2 vols. (Berlin, 1927), 1:297.

ported "as a political faith" the independence and integrity of the Ottoman Empire. "If we had only listened to the Emperor Nicholas when he
spoke to Sir Hamilton Seymour [in 1853 about the need to partition
Turkey], what a much pleasanter outlook would meet us when we contemplate the continent of Europe." According to the German ambassador
in London, the prime minister was considering "the most ample satisfaction" for Russia in the Near East, including Constantinople "avec tout ce
qui s'ensuit." This was a complete about-face of British foreign policy.[7]

The change in the attitude of England toward the Ottoman Empire
must be seen as part of a broader reorientation of her diplomacy. During
most of the nineteenth century, she had pursued a strategy of "splendid
isolation," which meant not an indifference to what was happening on
the Continent but a free hand to intervene only when a vital national
interest justified intervention. Thus London repeatedly played an important part in European affairs—in Belgium, in the Iberian Peninsula, in
Italy, and above all in the Ottoman Empire—but on the basis of a specific objective rather than a general commitment. After the disintegration
of the Quadruple Alliance in the early 1820s, the avoidance of entangling
alliances became as much an axiom of British foreign policy as of American. This position began to change only after 1880, when English statesmen grew increasingly uneasy about their isolation in a Europe dominated by the alliances of the other Great Powers. The Boer War finally
persuaded Britain that she must align herself directly or indirectly with
one of the diplomatic combinations on the Continent. As early as 1887,
however, Salisbury expressed the fear that "if, in the present grouping of
nations, which Prince Bismarck tells us is now taking place, England was
left out in isolation, it might well happen that the adversaries, who are
coming against each other on the Continent, might treat the English
Empire as divisible booty, by which their differences might be adjusted;
and, though England could defend herself, it would be at fearful risk and
cost." This calculation altered the assumptions of the foreign policy of
British statesmen, leading them to abandon the diplomacy of the free
hand in favor of an alignment with one of the Continental powers.[8]

The international tensions generated by changes in the statecraft of the

7. Henry Lytton Bulwer, *The Life of Henry John Temple, Viscount Palmerston*, 3 vols.
(London, 1870–74), 2:298–99; Hajo Holborn, *The Political Collapse of Europe* (New
York, 1965), pp. 72–74; *British Documents on the Origins of the War, 1898–1914*, ed.
G. P. Gooch and Harold Temperley, 11 vols. (London, 1926–38), 6:780; *Die grosse Politik
der europäischen Kabinette, 1871–1914: Sammlung der diplomatischen Akten des Aus-
wärtigen Amtes*, ed. Johannes Lepsius, Albrecht Mendelssohn Bartholdy, and Friedrich
Thimme, 40 vols. (Berlin, 1922–27), 10:23.

8. *The Letters of Queen Victoria*, 3d ser., ed. George Earle Buckle, 3 vols. (London,
1930–32), 1:272.

leading countries were aggravated by an important new factor in diplomatic relations: nationalism. Although its intellectual roots went back to the eighteenth century and beyond, it was only after 1815 that national as opposed to dynastic or religious loyalty began to play a crucial part in the politics of all Continental states. Whether nationalism in the age of the industrial revolution was in fact a destabilizing force of greater magnitude than commercial competition or colonial rivalry in the age of mercantilism had been remains an open question. Its emergence as the cohesive principle of the collective existence of the peoples of Europe may have made the maintenance of peace among them more difficult, but the span of almost a hundred years of relative tranquillity in diplomatic relations after Waterloo does not support such a proposition. The evidence remains at best inconclusive.

Yet as soon as hostilities broke out in the summer of 1914, historians began to argue that nationalism had been a primary factor in bringing about the conflict. Thus, in his important pioneer work on the origins of the First World War, Sidney Bradshaw Fay listed it as the third of his five "underlying causes of the war," putting it behind "the system of secret alliances" and "militarism" but ahead of "economic imperialism" and "the newspaper press." In its chronic form of Pan-Germanism, Pan-Slavism, and revanche, he contended, nationalism had nourished hatred between Germany and her two neighbors to the east and west. It had worked in curious and devious ways. It had assisted happily in the unification of Germany and Italy, but it had also disrupted the Ottoman Empire and had threatened to disrupt the Habsburg monarchy. In its virulent form, it had contributed for a century to a series of wars for liberation and unity in southeastern Europe. It had been an important factor in the Balkan situation, leading directly to the immediate occasion of the First World War. In short, it had to bear a large share of the responsibility for the tragedy of Sarajevo.[9]

Throughout the nineteenth century, however, many defenders of nationalism had maintained that it would lead to harmony rather than discord among the peoples of Europe. By putting an end to the domination of one over another, it would make possible their peaceful coexistence. War was a result not of the expression but the repression of national loyalty. Mazzini, the prophet of the Risorgimento, had written in 1859 that "your first duties—first at least in importance—are . . . toward Humanity. You are *men* before you are *citizens* or *fathers*. If you do not embrace the whole human family in your love . . . you betray your law of life and you do not comprehend the religion which will bless

9. Sidney Bradshaw Fay, *The Origins of the World War*, 2 vols. (New York, 1928), 1:32–49.

the future." In a less oracular vein, the French scholar Antonin Debidour argued some thirty years later in the conclusion of his well-known diplomatic history that any people that succeeds in forming an independent or autonomous state in accordance with its traditions, language, customs, and religion promotes more than its own well-being and the prosperity of its neighbors. Having satisfied its most cherished desire, it no longer has to seek the realization of that desire by continuing the plots, insurrections, and wars that have been for too long a cause of uneasiness and disturbance to all of Europe. And since it has become strong and capable of gaining respect, it will no longer be a helpless prey over which its neighbors quarrel incessantly, sword in hand. "Thereby it will make at least one cause of war disappear." To many believers in nationalism, then, the lesson of history was that its triumph would diminish the danger of armed conflict.[10]

More than that, nationalism was regarded as an essential condition of political freedom. Only on a continent in which the subordination of one people to another had come to an end would the domination of one class over another cease as well. For those who battened on the oppression of aliens would not shrink from enslaving their own countrymen as well. Liberty was all of a piece; its establishment in internal affairs could not be secured apart from its introduction in foreign relations.

Take the argument of that staunch democrat Georg Gottfried Gervinus in defense of the unification of Germany. Her destiny, he wrote, had until now seemed to be that of other divided nations such as Judea, Greece, and modern Italy, namely, to form a cosmopolitan people whose achievements lay in the realm of the intellect. Through religious freedom during the Reformation and spiritual freedom during the literary renaissance of the eighteenth century, she had led Europe to the threshold of political freedom. She could now assume the importance previously held by France. But she would not play the role of a conquering state, any more than England had done. "The object of her statecraft could be nothing other than to dissolve everywhere the dangerous, unitary great states into federations, which would combine the advantages of great and small states, and which would offer a more secure guarantee to general freedom and to the peaceful diffusion of all kinds of education." Such was the lofty mission of Germany.

Even in Great Britain, where political consolidation had been achieved long before, there was a widespread feeling that under modern conditions freedom was a function of unity, that the one remained unattainable

10. Giuseppi Mazzini, *Scritti editi ed inediti*, 100 vols. (Imola, 1906–43), 69:59; Antonin Debidour, *Histoire diplomatique de l'Europe depuis l'ouverture du congrès de Vienne jusqu'à la cloture du congrès de Berlin (1814–1878)*, 2 vols. (Paris, 1891), 2:566.

without the other. John Stuart Mill reasoned that "one hardly knows what any division of the human race should be free to do, if not to determine, with which of the various collective bodies of human beings they choose to associate themselves. . . . It is in general a necessary condition of free institutions, that the boundaries of governments should coincide in the main with those of nationalities." Until the middle decades of the nineteenth century, it was an accepted view that unity was the logical corollary of liberty.[11]

Yet from its beginnings nationalism displayed tendencies suggesting that its spread might aggravate rather than allay the problem of maintaining stability in international relations. It was impossible to make political boundaries coincide with cultural, ethnic, or linguistic divisions, especially in Eastern Europe. The distribution of peoples in this region was so confused and the intensity of their antagonisms so profound that whatever frontiers were drawn, disgruntled minorities were bound to remain on one side or the other.

As a result, even the cultural nationalism of the Restoration period often assumed a tone of bitter hostility toward alien neighbors. During those years there were numerous examples of a literary patriotism that bordered on literary chauvinism. In the prologue to his sonnet sequence *The Daughter of Slava*, to give one illustration, the Slovak poet Jan Kollár expresses a profound resentment of the Germans, who have usurped what rightfully belongs to the Slavs. Before his weeping eyes stretches the land, once the cradle of his people, now their grave. From the banks of the Elbe to the plains of the Vistula, from the foaming waves of the Danube to the Baltic, the harmonious sounds of the Slavic tongue once resounded. But hatred has stifled them. And who committed this odious crime? The shame is yours, raging Germany! Your hand is stained by this accumulation of crimes. Only he who knows how to respect the liberty of others is worthy of liberty himself. The poet's eye searches for Slavs on Slavic soil and finds none. They were the first to awaken life in the north; they taught men to embark on the sea and seek rich shores beyond the waves; they extracted metals from the bowels of the earth; others among them taught laborers to break the still infertile soil with a plow and make it bear golden harvests. And what has been your reward, o my people, for your kindnesses and your lessons? A perfidious neighbor has slipped into the house and thrown heavy chains around the neck of the sovereign. The gods themselves have fled. Only the earth has remained faithful; the forests, the rivers, the walls of the villages and towns have not disowned their Slavic names. But the soul has vanished.

11. G. G. Gervinus, *Einleitung in die Geschichte des neunzehnten Jahrhunderts* (Leipzig, 1853), pp. 179–81; John Stuart Mill, *Considerations on Government* (London, 1861), pp. 289, 291–92.

The spirit of such writings—and they could be found in all parts of the Continent—suggested that the victory of nationalism was likely to lead to an aggravation rather than a mitigation of diplomatic tensions. The incompatible national objectives of the peoples of Europe could not all be realized by peaceful means. In their more extreme form, they were attainable only through force. This became clear during the Revolution of 1848 when the "springtime of peoples," which had been greeted as the fraternal movement of oppressed nationalities, turned into a conflict among irreconcilable patriotic movements. At the spectacle of German nationalists fighting Danish and Polish nationalists, Austrian nationalists marching against Italian and Czech nationalists, Hungarian nationalists shooting at Croatian nationalists, even the most sanguine believers in self-determination began to sense that it might not lead to peace and freedom after all. John Stuart Mill, though continuing to uphold the right of every people to political unity, now spoke disapprovingly of "the feelings which make men reckless of, or at least indifferent to, the rights and interests of any portion of the human species, save that which is called by the same name and speaks the same language as themselves." He had watched "with . . . regret, not to say disgust, . . . the evidence which recent events have afforded, that in the backward parts of Europe, and even (where better things might have been expected) in Germany, the sentiment of nationality so far outweighs the love of liberty, that the people are willing to abet their rulers in crushing the liberty and independence of any people not of their own race and language." The vision of a European community of nations, united, contented, living side by side in peace and mutual respect, began to pale amid the strife of contending peoples.[12]

After the mid-century, moreover, nationalism became more conservative, more willing to seek its objectives through the established political system. It gradually assimilated the ideas of authoritarian government, the teachings of biology about the struggle for existence, and the doctrines of racism regarding the genetic inequality of peoples or groups of peoples. Now it spoke not only of its mission to liberate but also of its duty to prevail. Even in those states where political unity was firmly established, many men became convinced that in the society of nations, as in that of individuals, the primal law is the survival of the fittest. In a book on international politics published in 1886, the Russian sociologist I. A. Novikov reflected this new view of relations among peoples. Societies are organisms, he wrote, conforming to the laws of biology. Nature is a vast field of carnage. There is conflict between living creatures every

---

12. Ernest Denis, *La Bohème depuis la Montagne-Blanche*, 2 vols. (Paris, 1903), 2:149–50; [John Stuart Mill], "The French Revolution of 1848, and Its Assailants," *Westminster Review* 51 (1849):17.

second, every minute, without truce or respite. It takes place first between separate individuals, then between collective organisms—tribe against tribe, state against state, nationality against nationality. "No cessation is possible; to live is to struggle." The subordination of the less fit organism, whether individual or collective, to the more fit represents justice in nature, an incorruptible but implacable justice knowing no pity yet giving to each impartially the place due to his merit. The struggle for existence determines this place, and international politics is thus "the art of conducting the struggle for existence between social organisms."

By the beginning of the twentieth century, the ideal of the state as a servant of humanity, which had inspired many early writers on nationalism, had been largely replaced by the concept of political egoism as the law of nature. Force was more than a legitimate means of achieving diplomatic objectives; it was a manifestation of vigor and greatness, it was a good per se. Only through force could a state defend its interests against other states; only through force could it win submission in a world dominated by the strong. "In every nation of Europe from England and France to Russia and Turkey," wrote the British classicist Gilbert Murray, "the same whisper from below the threshold sounds incessantly in men's ears. 'We are the pick and flower of nations: the only nation that is really generous and brave and just. We are above all things qualified for governing others: we know how to keep them exactly in their place without weakness and without cruelty. . . . Every unprejudiced observer admits that our territories ought to be enlarged. . . . The excellence of our rule abroad is proved in black and white by the books of our explorers, our missionaries, our administrators and our soldiers, who all agree that our yoke is a pure blessing to those who bear it. It is only those envious and lying foreigners who dare to dispute the fact.'" A Europe governed by such concepts was in growing danger of diplomatic and military conflict.[13]

Yet nationalism, despite its universal appeal, was not impervious to differences of social class or economic interest. Its most ardent followers came generally from the ranks of the bourgeoisie, for both material and psychological reasons. To begin with, political consolidation meant bigger markets, bigger enterprises, bigger earnings, in short, economic opportunity. But more than that, the middle classes of Europe, whose loyalty to throne and altar had weakened in the course of the nineteenth century, found in nationalism a substitute faith capable of arousing the same devotion that tradition and religion had once inspired.

13. J. Novicow, *La politique internationale* (Paris, 1886), pp. 152–53, 235–36, 242; Gilbert Murray, "National Ideals; Conscious and Unconscious," *International Journal of Ethics* 11 (1900–1901):21.

Other groups in society, though responding to appeals to national pride, did not yield to them as completely because other ideals competed for their allegiance. The peasant masses continued to cling to the civic and religious values rooted in the life of the village. Many industrial workers, inspired by the vision of a classless society, were loyal to the international proletariat rather than the national state. To some conservative aristocrats—landowners, soldiers, courtiers, and bureaucrats—the supreme civic virtue remained not ethnic but dynastic fidelity. And to countless devout Christians, Catholics more than Protestants, the interests of the church outweighed the interests of the nation.

Manifestations of opposition to nationalism were therefore almost as numerous and varied as those of support. The anarchist Proudhon, defender of the proletariat against bureaucratic centralization, believed that distinct polyglot ethnic groups were a source of strength in society. It was not at all bad for the fraternity of nations, he declared in his pamphlet on the treaties of 1815, that there should be Flemings, Germans, Italians, and Basques in France. The intermingling of nationalities teaches the people that "justice like religion is above language, creed, and appearance." After the achievement of national unification in Italy, the peasantry of the south continued to resist the new order by what was officially labeled brigandage but was actually civil war. At one point a secessionist government was even established in Palermo in opposition to the one in Turin. In Sicily and Naples as a whole, popular resistance to political consolidation cost more lives than all the wars of the Risorgimento together. Only a few months after the proclamation of the Kingdom of Italy in 1861, the former Sardinian prime minister Massimo d'Azeglio wrote that "at Naples we overthrew a sovereign in order to set up a government based on universal suffrage. And yet we still to-day need sixty battalions of soldiers to hold the people down, or even more, since these are not enough."

There were also many men of position and wealth who opposed nationalism. Legitimist statesmen and politicians in particular saw in it a threat to the multinational dynastic states containing ethnic and linguistic minorities within their borders. The Russian foreign minister Karl Robert von Nesselrode wrote during the Revolution of 1848 that nationalist doctrines, whose authors have not considered carefully enough the consequences for the interests of their own country, are the negation of history and would lead logically to the overthrow of the entire world. "There is not a single state, monarchical or republican, which they would leave standing in its present form." A principle providing guidance only to absurdity cannot be invoked by cabinets acting in earnest. The only just and rational principle is the one that has been recognized until now, namely, "the state of territorial possession as defined by treaties."

The most incisive and telling critique of nationalism, however, came from the British Catholic historian Lord Acton, who in 1862 defended the constructive role of diversity and multiplicity in the community. "The combination of different nations in one state is as necessary a condition of civilised life as the combination of men in society," he maintained. "Inferior races are raised by living in political union with races intellectually superior. Exhausted and decaying nations are revived by the contact of a younger vitality. Nations in which the elements or organisation and the capacity for government have been lost, either through the demoralising influence of despotism, or the disintegrating action of democracy, are restored and educated anew under the discipline of a stronger and less corrupted race. This fertilising and regenerating process can only be obtained by living under one government." Here was the sharpest argument of those who continued to reject the doctrines of nationalism.[14]

The odds were on the other side, to be sure, because the principle of self-determination was steadily gaining support. Yet the danger to the stability of Europe arising out of the changing diplomatic position of the Great Powers and the increasing intensity of national conflicts did not lead to a period of prolonged hostilities. On the contrary, despite the succession of wars around the mid-century, the ninety-nine years from Waterloo to the Marne were an era of unprecedented tranquillity. The ability of the system of international relations to resolve diplomatic differences without recourse to arms encouraged a belief that Europe stood on the threshold of an age of perpetual peace. Writers in past ages had drafted grand designs for maintaining stability in foreign affairs, but these had been generally dismissed as the utopian schemes of well-meaning visionaries. Only in the nineteenth century did an organized international peace movement emerge, preaching that strife was not the natural condition of relations among states, that harmony was the wave of the future.

This belief was propagated by writers, academics, publicists, jurists, and even some politicians. Tennyson's lines in "Locksley Hall" about a future when "the war drum throbbed no longer, and the battle flags were furled / In the Parliament of Man, the Federation of the world" have been quoted and requoted countless times since they first appeared in 1842. Less familiar but almost as eloquent was Victor Hugo's address at the second international peace congress in Paris in 1849. He prophesied

14. *Oeuvres complètes de P.-J. Proudhon*, new ed., 19 vols. (Paris, 1923–59), 17:380; Denis Mack Smith, "The Italian Peasants and the Risorgimento," *Pubblicazioni dell'Istituto Italiano di Cultura di Londra* 3 (1954):28; Harold Acton, *The Last Bourbons of Naples (1825–1861)* (London, 1961), p. 523; Victor L. Tapié, "La Russie et l'Europe," in *L'Europe du XIXe et du XXe siècle*, ed. Max Beloff, Pierre Renouvin, Franz Schnabel, and Franco Valsecchi, 6 vols. (Milan, 1959–64), 2:859; [J. E. E. D. Acton], "Nationality," *Home and Foreign Review* 1 (1862):17–18.

that a day will come when nations will throw away their weapons, when war between Paris and London, St. Petersburg and Berlin, or Vienna and Turin will seem as impossible and absurd as war between Rouen and Amiens or Boston and Philadelphia today. A day will come "when there will no longer be fields of battle other than markets opening to commerce and minds opening to ideas." The words were greeted with enthusiastic applause.[15]

It was more surprising that many men in public life, men who had direct experience with affairs of state (most of them liberals), believed that conflict among peoples, which had characterized human society throughout history, was subsiding or even ending. In the parliaments and cabinets of Western Europe particularly, there was growing optimism regarding the peaceful settlement of international disputes. In 1849 Richard Cobden urged in the House of Commons that "we should enter into mutual engagements with other countries, binding ourselves and them, in all future cases of dispute, which cannot be otherwise arranged, to refer the matter to arbitration." He claimed to speak in the name of those who had "an abhorrence of war," specifically, the numerous portion of the middle classes and the great bulk of the working classes. "Unless you can adopt some such plan as I propose—unless you can approach foreign countries in a conciliatory spirit, and offer to them some kind of assurance that you do not wish to attack them, and receive the assurance that you are not going to be assailed by them—I see no necessary or logical end to the increase of our [military] establishments; for the progress of scientific knowledge will lead to a constant increase of expenditure." There was no limit to such expenditure but the limit of taxation, and that, he added in all innocence, the country has nearly reached. His plan for the arbitration of international disputes, he wrote to a friend, did not "imply the belief in the millennium, or demand your homage to the principles of non-resistance." It was realistic and reasonable.[16]

Guizot was more hard-boiled than Cobden could ever be, more distrustful, more ruthless. The clash of interests and the struggle of classes seemed to him the natural law of social existence. Yet he too adopted an Isaian tone in his memoirs, predicting that the future of mankind would bring growing harmony among governments and peoples. The progress of civilization and rational public opinion would not eliminate human passions, he conceded, and consequently the spirit of conquest, propaganda backed by armed force, and rigid dogma would always have their

15. Victor Hugo, *Oeuvres complètes*, ed. Jeanlouis Cornuz, 38 vols. (Lausanne, 1966–68), 31:288–89.

16. Great Britain, *Parliamentary Debates*, 3d ser. (1830–91), 106:54, 61–62, 68; John Morley, *The Life of Richard Cobden*, 2 vols. (London, 1881), 2:44.

place and play their part in the foreign policy of states. But Guizot was also certain that those forces were no longer in harmony with the customs, ideas, interests, and instincts of the present day. The extent and vigor of industry and commerce; the need for general prosperity; the frequent, easy, rapid, and regular communication among peoples; the invincible desire for free association, examination, discussion, and publicity—all these developments in modern society exercised a powerful influence against military or diplomatic fantasies in foreign policy. "We may smile, not without reason, at the language and the childlike confidence of the 'Friends of Peace' and the 'Peace Societies.' All the great aspirations, all the great hopes of mankind have their dreams and their simpletons, their days of failure and of disappointment." But societies were indeed changing, and foreign as well as domestic policy was forced to change with them.[17]

Not even the wars of the mid-century were enough to shake the confidence of those who believed in the ultimate triumph of peace. In the fall of 1870, after Sedan had surrendered and the siege of Paris had begun, William E. Gladstone, the prime minister of England, reaffirmed his faith in an anonymous article in the *Edinburgh Review*. Neither the recklessness of Napoleon III nor the ruthlessness of Bismarck had weakened his conviction that eventually, in some mysterious, providential way, right makes might. In his view, the conflict on the Continent did not discredit reliance on moral force. If anything, it reinforced the need for a peaceful solution to international disputes. "Certain it is," he maintained, "that a new law of nations is gradually taking hold of the mind, and coming to sway the practice, of the world; a law which recognises independence, which frowns upon aggression, which favours the pacific, not the bloody settlement of disputes, which aims at permanent and not temporary adjustments; above all, which recognises as a tribunal of permanent authority, the general judgment of civilised mankind. It has censured the aggression of France; it will censure, if need arise, the greed of Germany." Sooner or later, then, the verdict of enlightened world opinion would replace recourse to arms as the accepted way of settling international controversies.[18]

The confidence of those who maintained that an era of peace was about to begin rested in part on the belief that diplomacy had found a new instrument for dealing with disputes: the "Concert of Europe." There was a growing consensus among states, the argument went, that

17. François Guizot, *Mémoires pour servir à l'histoire de mon temps*, 8 vols. (Paris and Leipzig, 1858–67), 6:8–9.

18. [W. E. Gladstone], "Germany, France, and England," *Edinburgh Review, or Critical Journal* 132 (1870):304.

could be determined by conferences and congresses and that constituted a collective judgment to which all governments would have to bow. This method of resolving diplomatic differences of opinion would end the reliance on armed force. And since the Concert of Europe had in fact been instrumental in bringing about a peaceful solution of several international problems during the nineteenth century, especially those involving the Ottoman Empire, there was surely reason to hope that it would become progressively more effective in the future.

The British in particular professed great faith in its efficacy. During the 1890s Salisbury, head of the ministry, called it the "federation of Europe"; George Nathaniel Curzon, undersecretary of state for foreign affairs, referred to it variously as the "cause of peace," the "Committee of the Privy Council of Europe," the "Cabinet of nations," and the "greatest advance in international law and even international ethics that this century has seen." Not all politicians shared this view, however. One member of the House of Commons characterized the Concert as "nothing better than a group of greedy, selfish, pitiless, heartless Powers." But to Curzon this was outrageously unfair. "It is very easy to denounce the Concert of Europe," he declared indignantly. "But is it politic, I ask, is it just, and is it wise? . . . If you had an alternative I could understand it. Denounce the Concert if you have something to set up in their place, but you come here barren of any policy—with your mouths full of denunciation and your brains empty of suggestion."

Yet the Concert of Europe was effective only in settling issues that the Great Powers were willing to settle. It did not create a consensus; it reflected a consensus that had already been reached. Where a peaceful compromise appeared preferable to a military confrontation, it could bring the parties to the conference table to work out a reasonable accommodation. But where there was no basic agreement to begin with, where the differences were so profound that they could not be reconciled, the Concert was no more useful than other techniques of diplomacy. Bismarck, always the hardheaded realist, had no illusions about a coming age of harmony among nations. To him the Concert was only a forum where diplomats sought to disguise selfish aims in selfless rhetoric. He wrote in 1876 that he had invariably found the word "Europe" in the mouths of politicians who demanded something from other powers that they did not dare claim in their own name. And in his memoirs twenty years later, he spoke with scorn about "philanthropic hypocrisy" and about "the luminous haze" with which many people invested such catchwords of the western powers as "humanity" or "civilization." Even Salisbury, disappointed at the outcome of the international crisis over Crete, was forced to admit in 1897: "I am afraid the upshot of our experience . . . is that the Concert of Europe is too ponderous a machine for daily use."[19]

The stability of international relations during the nineteenth century, then, was the result not of a new diplomatic method but of a new economic environment in which the advantages of power seemed attainable without the risks of war. There is no doubt that the improvement of communication and transportation made it easier for statesmen to concert their policies, attend conferences and congresses, and attempt to reach an accommodation. But the course of foreign affairs since 1914 suggests that an increasing facility for the exchange of diplomatic views is not of itself enough to mitigate the danger of conflict. At best it reveals more accurately the state of mind of those who determine policy, their view of national interests and international obligations. Throughout most of the nineteenth century, the leaders of Europe believed that their legitimate objectives could be attained by peaceful means, although there were important exceptions in the case of the German Confederation, the Italian Peninsula, and the Ottoman Empire. War became less frequent and less prolonged than it had been in the preindustrial age largely because collective energies and ambitions were diverted to the new opportunities created by economic rationalization. Wealth and power could now be achieved through investments rather than conquests, through factories rather than bayonets. This was the basic reason for the abatement of armed conflict after 1815, not the Concert of Europe.

Many writers recognized that increasing material interdependence was exercising a subtle but important moderating influence on foreign relations. In his study of the problem of war in economic thought during the nineteenth century, Edmund Silberner enumerates an impressive list of liberal publicists who predicted that the spread of the industrial revolution, especially international commerce, would eliminate the fundamental cause of hostility among states. The list includes David Ricardo, John Ramsay MacCulloch, and Richard Cobden in Great Britain; Jean-Baptiste Say, Frédéric Bastiat, Henri Dameth, and Michel Chevalier in France; Gustav Mevissen, John Prince-Smith, and Victor Böhmert in Germany; and Émile de Laveleye in Belgium. They all believed, in Bastiat's words, that war arises out of economic isolation and exclusiveness: "Let the peoples be permanent markets for one another, let their relations be such that they cannot be broken without inflicting on them the double disadvantage of privation and glut, and they will no longer need those

19. *Malcolm MacColl: Memoirs and Correspondence*, ed. George W. E. Russell (London, 1914), p. 282. Cf. Langer, *Diplomacy of Imperialism*, p. 381; Great Britain, *Parliamentary Debates*, 4th ser. (1892–1908), 48:993; 49:26, 30, 45–46; *Times* (London), 5 April 1897, p. 9; *Die grosse Politik*, 2:88; Otto von Bismarck, *Die gesammelten Werke*, 15 vols. (Berlin, 1924–35), 15:316–17.

powerful navies which ruin them, those large armies which crush them. The peace of the world will not be endangered by the whim of a Thiers or a Palmerston, and will disappear for lack of nourishment, resources, motives, pretexts, and popular sympathy." In other words, a transformation of the economy was sure to lead to a transformation of diplomacy as well.

Liberal economists were not the only ones to examine the effect of the industrial revolution on international relations. There were others, representing a diversity of ideologies and interests, who studied the question. Most of them came to the same conclusion, however. Friedrich List, the foremost theoretician of protectionism, believed that a clearer insight into the nature of wealth and industry was leading the wiser heads of civilized nations to the conviction that colonization offered a richer and safer field for their productive powers than wars or restrictions on trade. According to the democrat Hermann Schulze-Delitzsch, the spread of wealth and education among the masses would make them less inclined to risk in combat their goods and lives, their laboriously acquired possessions of property and culture. For people feel bound to one another by the true solidarity of economic and humane interests. In view of the international nature of modern commerce, disruption caused by war cannot be restricted to those immediately involved; it must affect the entire world market. Saint-Simon taught that waging war in order to promote trade is self-defeating because trade can neither be won nor preserved by arms. It is the reward of industry and is maintained by industry. All wars are thus harmful for they hinder production and injure commerce.

But no one expressed more sonorously than Tennyson the view that economic progress would make armed conflict obsolete. In the "Ode Sung at the Opening of the International Exhibition" of 1862, he hailed the dawn of a new age of peace in Europe:

> O ye, the wise who think, the wise who reign,
> From growing Commerce loose her latest chain,
> And let the fair white-wing'd peacemaker fly
> To happy havens under all the sky,
> And mix the seasons and the golden hours;
> Till each man find his own in all men's good,
> And all men work in noble brotherhood,
> Breaking their mailed fleets and armed towers,
> And ruling by obeying Nature's powers,
> And gathering all the fruits of earth and
> crown'd with all her flowers.[20]

20. Edmund Silberner, *The Problem of War in Nineteenth Century Economic Thought* (Princeton, 1946), pp. 19–20, 59, 61, 82–83, 98, 100, 139, 200–201, 220, 227–28;

Only toward the end of the century did this general assessment of the role of economic rationalization in international relations begin to change. As the pioneering era of industrial capitalism drew to a close, as the period of rugged individualism and unlimited opportunity gave way to corporative consolidation and monopolized enterprise, the belief emerged that the development of commerce was aggravating relations among states, which would not and indeed should not hesitate to go to war to retain their markets. This represented a return to the attitudes of the age of mercantilism, the age of military conflict over trade and colonization. In 1896 an anonymous writer signing himself "a Biologist" published a relentless analysis of foreign affairs in the London *Saturday Review*. He argued that the growing economic rivalry between Germany and Great Britain must end in an armed struggle. In all parts of the earth, in every pursuit, in commerce, in manufacturing, in exploiting other races, the English and the Germans jostle each other, he asserted. If every German were wiped out tomorrow, every English trade and pursuit would immediately expand. If every Englishman were wiped out tomorrow, the Germans would gain in proportion. "Here is the first great racial struggle of the future: here are two growing nations pressing against each other, man to man all over the world. One or the other has to go; one or the other will go."

In time the argument became more inclusive and more sophisticated, touching on the ultimate effect of industrialization on statecraft. In 1910 General Ian Hamilton, who five years later commanded the British troops at Gallipoli, defined in starkest terms the relationship between trade and diplomacy: "Commerce is the leading idea and first interest of the modern State; and so soon as a Government is faced by the alternative of seeing some millions of workers lose their livelihood through unemployment or of losing a few thousand lives in battle, it will quickly know how to decide." This was still not the accepted view. Only on the left, among anarchists, socialists, and militant democrats, was it generally assumed that big business by its very nature had to employ armed force to maintain its interests. Public opinion at large continued to believe that industrialization was contributing to the preservation of peace. Yet now there were also those, still a minority but growing in number, who argued that armed struggle or peaceful decline was the only choice that life offered the state in a pitiless dog-eat-dog world.[21]

Joseph Hansen, *Gustav von Mevissen: Ein rheinisches Lebensbild, 1815–1899*, 2 vols. (Berlin, 1906), 2:546; Victor Böhmert, *Freiheit der Arbeit!; Beiträge zur Reform der Gewerbegesetze* (Bremen, 1858), pp. 160–61; Frédéric Bastiat, *Sophismes économiques* (Paris, 1846), p. 129; Hermann Schulze-Delitzsch, *Schriften und Reden*, ed. Friedrich Thorwart, 5 vols. (Berlin, 1909–13), 1:582.
21. A Biologist, "A Biological View of Our Foreign Policy," *Saturday Review of Politics,*

But to what extent did public opinion, particularly the opinion of the business community, affect the policies pursued by politicians and diplomats? To put it more broadly, were the needs engendered by economic rationalization able to influence in any substantial way the conduct of statecraft? The evidence on this point is ambiguous. A case can easily be made for the contention, advanced by many writers on the left, that the state was becoming an instrument for the protection of the interests of industrial capitalism. There are numerous statements by political leaders, notably in Great Britain, that one of the main functions of government is to encourage the initiative of entrepreneurs and financiers. Peel declared during the early 1840s that tariff reductions offered a better guarantee of peace than political treaties because the interests of commerce are permanent and must be defended by all administrations, regardless of political party. Palmerston was even more explicit. It is the business of the government, he wrote at about the same time, to open and secure the roads for the merchant.

Some seventy years later, only a few weeks before the outbreak of the First World War, Sir Edward Grey stated that "I regard it as our duty, wherever *bona fide* British capital is forthcoming in any part of the world, and is applying for concessions to which there are no valid political objections, that we should give it the utmost support we can, and endeavour to convince the foreign government concerned that it is to its interest as well as to our own to give the concessions for railways and so forth to British firms who carry them out at reasonable prices and in the best possible way." In 1903 Lord Lansdowne actually refused to submit to Parliament the correspondence between the government and the great financial houses regarding the Baghdad railway: "The occasions upon which the British Government finds itself in such confidential communication with the representatives of that great organism which we are in the habit of describing as the City, are of rare occurrence. . . . But I do say that when those occasions arise, and when those confidential communications take place, it should be on the clearest possible understanding that the confidence which is given and received is respected from beginning to end."

More revealing than the words were the policies and deeds of the English statesmen. Consider the flood of financial laws, commercial treaties, and diplomatic or military interventions in other countries designed to promote the interests of the business community. The Opium Wars in China and the Don Pacifico affair in Greece are familiar examples of the service that statecraft rendered to economics. British diplomats would

lecture foreign statesmen on the beauties of liberal government, the in-
iquities of the slave traffic, and the advantages of free trade. Consuls
were permitted to serve in a private capacity as agents for bondholders,
to hold funds for their account, and to participate in the management of
monopolies and customs. Downing Street remained officially aloof from
such activities, but its representatives were busy negotiating concessions
that would bring dividends to the investors and commissions to themselves. Under such circumstances, it was hard to tell where government
policy ended and business enterprise began.[22]

There are also many instances, however, in which politicians and diplomats not only refused to bow to the wishes of merchants and financiers
but imposed their own will on them. During the invasion of Spain in
1823, for example, the French prime minister Villèle wrote to the com-
mander of the army, the duke of Angoulême, concerning the possibility
of obtaining the financial assistance of the Rothschilds. "Banking and
commerce are friends of peace," he warned, "but they would like to have
it always, even at the expense of honor. Yet with a counterweight such as
the sentiments of *Monseigneur*, there is no fear of letting those gentlemen
interfere." Canning's position in 1824 regarding international loans was
that "assistance would in no case extend to the claiming as from Government to Government, the discharge of a debt due by a Foreign Government to an individual British subject." The same Palmerston who
sometimes argued that the government must open the door for the businessman maintained at other times that the businessman must not em-
broil the government in diplomatic complications. "If the principle were
to be established as a guide for the practice of British subjects, that the
payment of . . . loans should be enforced by the arms of England," he
declared in 1847, "it would place the British nation in the situation of
being always liable to be involved in serious disputes with foreign Governments upon matters with regard to which the British Government of
the day might have had no opportunity of being consulted."

Indeed, there were numerous occasions when the government expected
the economic activities of the business community to serve the political
interests of the state. In Germany it was common for the ministry to
direct the financiers to conform their lending policies to diplomatic needs.
In 1902 the chancellor wrote that the head of the banking house of
Mendelssohn & Co. in Berlin should under no circumstances be per-

22. Vernon John Puryer, *International Economics and Diplomacy in the Near East: A
Study of British Commercial Policy in the Levant, 1834–1853* (Stanford, Calif., and London, 1935), p. 184; Webster, *The Foreign Policy of Palmerston*, 2:750–51; Great Britain,
Parliamentary Debates (Commons), 5th ser. (1909–), 64:1446; ibid., 4th ser. (1892–1908),
121:1344; Leland Hamilton Jenks, *The Migration of British Capital to 1875* (New York
and London, 1927), pp. 119–20.

mitted to place "his private interest over the state interest" in negotiating a loan with the Russians. "His Majesty will be glad to exert moral and other pressure on Mendelssohn in the indicated direction, and he will not be trifled with, if the latter opposes the course of our policy." In 1909 a partner in the Diskonto-Gesellschaft, one of the leading German banks, testified that "often it is our own Government that imposes the duty upon us, under all circumstances, to cultivate good relations with Brazil, East Asia, Chile, or Argentina, in as much as these are countries that still constitute a neutral ground and which, unless we look out, will be wrested from us without ceremony by the English and Americans."

In a letter to the Paris stock exchange in 1873, the French minister of finance stated that it was necessary for him and the minister of foreign affairs to judge, one from the point of view of the treasury, the other from the point of view of political interest, whether there was any reason for opposing the official listing of foreign government securities. Even the British cabinet did not hesitate to pressure the financiers in London into withdrawing from the Baghdad railway project in 1903. The bankers had agreed among themselves that the English, the French, and the Germans would each take 25 percent of the stock and have eight seats on the board of directors. Why Downing Street decided to veto the plan is still not entirely clear, but its ability to exercise a decisive influence over the City in this enterprise is beyond dispute.[23]

It thus becomes apparent that the business community did not control diplomacy any more than diplomacy controlled the business community. Rather, the two coexisted in an informal partnership, their symbiosis resting on common interest and purpose, and increasingly on common background, education, and attitude. Sometimes one or the other would gain the upper hand, but usually they worked together, adopting the same policies because they sought the same objectives. In examining their interrelationship, the economist Jacob Viner concluded after the First World War that "the bankers seem to have been passive, and in some cases unwilling, instruments of the diplomats." Not only that, the former in general "seem to have been pacifically inclined, and to have been much more favorably disposed than were their governments to international coöperation and reconciliation." The formulation may be

23. *Mémoires et correspondance du comte de Villèle*, 5 vols. (Paris, 1888–90), 4:276; Jenks, *Migration of British Capital*, p. 118; Great Britain, *Parliamentary Debates*, 3d ser. (1830–91), 93 (1847), 1299; *Die grosse Politik*, 18:45; National Monetary Commission, *German Bank Inquiry of 1908–9: Stenographic Reports*, 2 vols. (Washington, D.C., 1910–11), 2:249; Herbert Feis, *Europe, the World's Banker, 1870–1914: An Account of European Foreign Investment and the Connection of World Finance with Diplomacy before the War* (New Haven, 1930), p. 120; Parker Thomas Moon, *Imperialism and World Politics* (New York, 1926), pp. 245–48.

somewhat exaggerated, but there can be no quarreling with his summa-
tion: "For the claim sometimes made that the bankers exercised a controlling influence over pre-war diplomacy, the available source material
offers not the slightest degree of support." It is clear, moreover, that the
nineteenth century was a period of tranquillity not because the techniques
of diplomacy had changed but because fundamental national needs could
generally be satisfied by peaceful means. Statecraft reflects the dominant
interests, values, and attitudes of society. In the preindustrial age, it
reflected those of kings and noblemen or traders and shippers. After the
industrial revolution, it began to reflect those of manufacturers, bankers, investors, and entrepreneurs, who required international stability in
order to pursue the task of economic rationalization.[24]

24. Jacob Viner, "International Finance and Balance of Power Diplomacy, 1880–1914,"
Southwestern Political and Social Science Quarterly 9 (1928–29):450–51.

14

THE SYSTEM OF WARFARE

Although the transformation of the economy during the nineteenth century did not alter the method of conducting diplomacy, it did alter the method of waging war. The great danger facing Europe after 1815 was not the frequency of international conflict, which in fact declined, but its growing capacity for devastation. To put it another way, although the techniques for maintaining stable relations among states remained unchanged, the consequences of their failure became much more serious. The same processes of efficiency and organization that led to such extraordinary achievements in the production and distribution of goods could also be applied with deadly effect to the destruction of life and property. This was the constant threat hanging over European society in the age of the industrial revolution.

The most obvious change in the system of warfare resulting from economic rationalization was a rapid increase in the size of the armed forces. For the first time since the decline of the city-states of antiquity, it became possible to establish a mass army in which all able-bodied citizens were theoretically required to serve. This represented a basic alteration in the source and structure of military manpower. As combat techniques improved and costs increased in the preindustrial era, war began be be waged by professional rather than citizen armies. The economy was simply too primitive to support more than a few thousand soldiers with the arms necessary for success on the battlefield. Armies were thus small, and their capacity to inflict losses on the enemy remained limited. After the Middle Ages, the growth of the economy made possible a significant expansion of the armed forces, but even the largest of them had remained a tiny fraction of the entire population.

According to the estimates in Quincy Wright's massive study of war, armies in the sixteenth century rarely exceeded 20,000 to 30,000 men. In the seventeenth century, as the population of Europe returned to roughly the level it had reached under the Roman Empire, about the same proportion was under arms, 0.3 percent. The new national armies often numbered 50,000 or 60,000, but the normal size was 19,000 in the Thirty Years' War and 40,000 in the wars of Louis XIV. During the eighteenth century, the forces led by Marlborough, Prince Eugene, and Frederick the Great sometimes totaled 80,000 or even 90,000, although the forces in the wars waged by Prussia were more generally 47,000. In short, the growing costliness of military operations had the effect of professionalizing the armed forces to the point where the waging of war ceased to be the duty of the citizen and became the occupation of a small warrior caste.[1]

To Adam Smith, standing on the threshold of the industrial revolution, it was clear that the increasing expense of waging war had the inevitable result of decreasing the relative size of the armed forces. In primitive societies, he wrote, "among nations of hunters" and "among nations of shepherds," every man is a warrior. Indeed, because such a society is accustomed to a wandering life even in time of peace, the entire community, including old men, women, and children, easily takes the field in time of war. As the economy becomes more complex, however, the proportion of the population able to participate in military operations steadily declines. In agricultural communities, where the mobility of the population is limited by the need to tend the crops, only men of military age, between a fourth and a fifth of all inhabitants, can engage in warfare. The others must remain at home to take care of the farm chores. Even the young men are able to take part in a military campaign only after planting is finished and before harvesting has begun. Otherwise the economy will suffer serious damage.

Finally, "the number of those who can go to war, in proportion to the whole number of the people, is necessarily much smaller in a civilized than in a rude state of society." For in a civilized society in which soldiers are maintained entirely by the labor of those who are not soldiers, the number of the former can never exceed what the latter can support over and above supporting themselves and the administrators of government and law. Thus, although 20 to 25 percent of the people considered themselves soldiers in the agricultural city-states of ancient Greece, it is generally calculated that no more than 1 percent can be employed as soldiers in a civilized nation of modern Europe without ruin to the country.

It follows, Smith reasons, that the first duty of the sovereign, that of defending society against the violence and injustice of other societies, grows more and more expensive as the society advances in civilization. "The military force of the society, which originally cost the sovereign no expence either in time of peace or in time of war, must, in the progress of improvement, first be maintained by him in time of war, and afterwards even in time of peace." The great change in the art of war introduced by the invention of firearms has further increased the cost of both training a body of soldiers in peacetime and employing them in wartime because their weapons and munitions have become much more expensive. But Smith shrewdly observes that this costliness of firearms has shifted the military balance between the opulent and civilized nations on the one

1. Quincy Wright, *A Study of War*, 2 vols. (Chicago, 1942), 1:232–33.

hand and the poor and barbarous ones on the other. In ancient times the former found it difficult to defend themselves against the latter. In modern times the latter find it difficult to defend themselves against the former. "The invention of fire-arms, an invention which at first sight appears to be so pernicious, is certainly favourable to the permanency and to the extension of civilization." The mechanization of armed conflict, in other words, is making possible the expansion of Europe.[2]

Yet within twenty years after Smith had advanced his generalization that the technological improvement of warfare meant that a progressively smaller proportion of the population would be employed in its pursuit, events proved him wrong. He had failed to recognize that the industrialization of the economy, which was only beginning in his day, would make possible a rapid relative increase in the size of the armed forces, reestablishing the citizen armies that had disappeared two thousand years before. As national wealth began to grow faster than the expense of supporting a small professional military establishment, an expansion of the number of men under arms became possible. The French were the first to make or, more accurately, to stumble on this discovery. The *levée en masse* of 1793, designed to cope with the danger facing the young Jacobin republic, was a piece of desperate improvisation that turned out to be a brilliant success. It showed for the first time that a rising economy in the early stages of the industrial revolution could maintain a citizen army that was more than a match for professional troops. During the Napoleonic Wars, the normal size of the opposing forces marching into battle was about 84,000, almost 80 percent greater than they had been fifty years earlier during the campaigns of Frederick the Great. Indeed, there were some military engagements in which the French committed as many as 200,000 soldiers, and at times they could mobilize close to 1 million men, more than 3 percent of the entire population. The long-term decline in the relative size of the armed forces of the European states had suddenly become reversed.

Under the Restoration, the liability of all able-bodied young men for military service was generally maintained, at least in theory, as a result of the experience of the previous twenty-five years. But in practice it was almost invariably weakened by numerous provisions for exemption or substitution. The long period of peace between the Congress of Vienna and the Crimean War encouraged the view that the task of national defense could be left largely to professional soldiers. The middle classes in particular, busily amassing wealth in industry or finance and half-convinced that an era of permanent peace was around the corner, were

2. Adam Smith, *An Inquiry into the Nature and Causes of the Wealth of Nations*, 2 vols. (London, 1776), 2:291–92, 294–95, 297, 312–13.

reluctant to accept the disruption of civilian pursuits entailed by military service. Adolphe Thiers, a leading figure in French political life for nearly half a century, declared in 1848 that "the society where everyone is a soldier is a barbaric society." It is in the interest of the state to have merchants, lawyers, doctors, and notaries, "and for that it is necessary that the education of men destined for those careers not be interrupted or made impossible by general conscription." In the case of the lower classes, the situation was of course entirely different. "We observe generally in our countryside that every man from the fields who leaves the army, who has spent seven years in the service, comes back stronger, more moral, and better instructed."

The educated and well-to-do thus generally managed to avoid military service altogether, but even among the propertyless the draft was enforced sporadically and capriciously. England continued to rely entirely on a professional army. In Prussia, which adhered to the principle of general conscription more closely than any other country, about a third of the able-bodied young men received no military training around the mid-century because there was no room for them under the established organization of the armed forces. Yet despite that, the total figure for the standing armies of Europe in 1858 has been estimated at 2,675,000 compared with 300,000 in the Roman Empire at the time of Augustus. The population of the former was five times greater than that of the latter, but the armed forces were nine times greater. Thus, even under the system of semiprofessional armies prevailing on the Continent before 1871, the rationalization of the economy made it possible almost to double the relative size of the military establishment.[3]

The outcome of the Franco-Prussian War hastened the conversion of almost all European states to the practice of general conscription. It seemed to prove that an army composed largely of professionals, such as the French had, was no match for one in which all able-bodied men were required to serve. As a result, universal military service, introduced by Austria as early as 1868 in the wake of the Seven Weeks' War, was adopted in rapid succession by France in 1872, Japan in 1873, Russia in 1874, and Italy in 1875. By the opening of the twentieth century, almost all nations except Great Britain and the United States had accepted the concept of the citizen army.

This meant a sharp increase not only in the size of the standing armies but also in the size of the total forces that could be raised in times of

3. Wright, *Study of War*, 1:233; B. R. Mitchell, *European Historical Statistics, 1750–1970* (London and Basingstoke, 1975), p. 20; *Discours parlementaires de M. Thiers*, ed. Marc Antoine Calmon, 16 vols. (Paris, 1879–89), 8:167–69, 172; Gordon A. Craig, *The Politics of the Prussian Army, 1640–1945* (Oxford, 1955), pp. 139, 145.

national emergency. Those who had completed their period of military training with a line regiment—the term usually varied from two to five years—were enrolled in a reserve unit that remained subject to active service under a plan for general mobilization. As this system became progressively more efficient, an industrialized nation was able to enlist close to 10 percent of its citizens in the armed forces in time of war. For example, the Germans in 1914 had a peace establishment of about 850,000 soldiers out of a population of 65 million, but in the event of hostilities almost 5 million trained men were available for service. The French had a peace establishment of over 800,000 out of a population of 39 million, but in wartime more than 3.5 million men could be called up. Such an intensive concentration of military manpower was unprecedented in modern history.[4]

To be sure, not every country could conscript an equally high proportion of its citizens. A great deal depended on the level of economic development and the effectiveness of the administrative system. With a population of approximately 160 million, Russia had a peacetime strength of less than 1.5 million and a wartime strength of approximately 6 million trained men. About 50 percent of those liable for conscription in Russia at the beginning of the twentieth century were excused, ostensibly for reasons of family obligation or hardship; in Italy the percentage was 37. The real reason, however, was the lack of financial resources to train all those reaching military age. On the other hand, exemption from the draft was rare in France, with a more highly developed economy, because the only way in which the country could maintain an army capable of opposing the Germans effectively was by training a much higher proportion of the population for military service. Around 1900 only 3.0 percent of the able-bodied male population of Italy between the ages of twenty-one and sixty was in the armed forces; in Austria-Hungary the percentage was 3.4, in Russia 4.4, in Germany 4.8, and in France 5.8. The result of these variations in the rate of conscription was that the proportion of trained soldiers, including the reserves, in the total able-bodied adult male population ranged from 21 percent in Russia and Austria-Hungary to 24 in Italy, 36 in Germany, and 41 in France.

Differences in the degree of industrialization and the intensity of recruitment could thus counterbalance differences in the size of population to a considerable extent. The German general staff calculated at the

4. Oron J. Hale, *The Great Illusion, 1900–1914* (New York, Evanston, and London, 1971), pp. 21–22; Carlton J. H. Hayes, *A Generation of Materialism, 1871–1900* (New York and London, 1941), pp. 20–21; Archibald Percival Wavell, "Armed Forces and the Art of War: 2. Armies," in *The New Cambridge Modern History*, 12 vols. (Cambridge, 1960–70), 12:257; Mitchell, *European Historical Statistics*, p. 20; Theodore Zeldin, *France, 1848–1945*, 2 vols. (Oxford, 1973–77), 2:886–87.

beginning of 1913 that, in the event of a European war, Germany would be able to send at once 1,545,000 men into the field against 1,449,000 in France, 460,000 in Russia on the German frontier, 127,000 in Great Britain, and 90,000 in Belgium. France, with a population less than two-thirds that of Germany and with only 7.8 million men of service age compared to 15 million, could mobilize a military force almost equal to that of the Germans. But at what cost! In 1910 about 10,000 men fully qualified for service were not called to the colors in Germany, but in France there were no such exemptions. The Germans classified 83,000 men as only conditionally suitable for service, whereas the French drafted most men in this category. In 1911 the German government conscripted 53.1 percent of those liable for military duty; the French government conscripted 83.0. The balance of military power on the Continent thus reflected not only the distribution of population and resources but also the ability and willingness to employ them for purposes of war.[5]

The resurgence of citizen armies in the nineteenth century altered the spirit as well as the technique of armed conflict. Just as mass suffrage transformed the structure of politics, so mass conscription transformed the nature of warfare. In the era of professional armies, war had been waged without regard for ideological justification. The soldier had fought because that was his business. There was no need to vindicate a military struggle by portraying it as a contest between good and evil or between justice and lawlessness. The will of the sovereign—his thirst for glory, his desire for territory, his appetite for wealth—was warrant enough for a declaration of hostilities.

To be sure, the religious wars from the middle of the sixteenth century to the middle of the seventeenth had been inspired at least in part by an ideological consideration, the maintenance of the true faith. But the destructiveness of that long succession of bitter conflicts only strengthened the conviction among the statesmen of Europe that wars waged for self-interest, for *raison d'état*, were far preferable to those fought for some cosmic ideal. They were less likely to be ruinous and brutal; they were less likely to provoke fanaticism and hatred. The kaleidoscopic changes in the combinations and alignments of the Great Powers during the eighteenth century reflected an aversion to conflicts of ideology. Yesterday's enemies became today's friends; today's allies could become tomorrow's adversaries. Professional armies practiced war without passion, out of a sense of pride and discipline. Armed struggle appeared to be part of the

5. Mitchell, *European Historical Statistics*, pp. 23, 26; Wavell, "Armed Forces: Armies," p. 257; Gerhard Ritter, *Staatskunst und Kriegshandwerk: Das Problem des "Militarismus" in Deutschland*, 4 vols. (Munich, 1954–68), 2:346 (n. 15), 351 (n. 6); Alfred Vagts, *A History of Militarism: Civilian and Military*, rev. ed. (New York, 1959), pp. 217–18.

eternal scheme of things; it was a deadly game that nations had always played and always would play. Only soldiers really understood its rules and complexities. As for civilians, they need not trouble themselves about it, except to pay the taxes that made it possible.

This concept of war began to change with the rise of citizen armies. As conscripted civilians increasingly replaced professional soldiers in the armed forces of Europe, it became necessary to justify international conflict in terms that public opinion could accept. It was no longer enough to appeal to the professional pride of the military or to demand unquestioning obedience to the will of the sovereign. The technical conduct of hostilities had to be reinforced by ideals, convictions, passions, and fears shared by the broad masses of the population. In other words, war became democratized. And this in turn meant that the formation of an alliance, a declaration of war, and the conclusion of peace, matters that had once been the exclusive concern of governments, could no longer be left to the cold calculation of *raison d'état*. International conflict had become more intense, more uncompromising.

This change in the nature of armed struggle did not of course occur all at once. After the popular wars of the French Revolution and the Napoleonic era, military affairs seemed to return to the familiar pattern of professionalism. Yet there were some observers, even in the early years of the Restoration, who recognized that the old order could not be permanently reestablished. The leading military theorist of the period, Carl von Clausewitz, wrote in his classic work on international conflict that war in 1793 suddenly became once again an affair of the people, an affair of those who consider themselves citizens of the state. Under Napoleon the new French mass army easily defeated the professional armies of the other states until they too were forced to adopt the principle of general military service. "Thus since Bonaparte war has . . . assumed an entirely different character, or rather it has come much closer to its true character, to its absolute perfection."

Helmuth von Moltke, the greatest strategist of the nineteenth century, who pioneered in adapting the technological advances of the industrial revolution to the operations of a modern army, was even more explicit. In his history of the Franco-Prussian War written during the 1880s, he declared that a new age of mass armed conflict had begun: "Gone are the times when small armies of professional soldiers took the field for dynastic goals, to seize a city or a piece of land and then move into winter quarters or conclude peace." The wars of the present, he explained, summon entire nations to arms. There is hardly a family that is not affected. "It is generally no longer the ambition of princes which threatens peace, but the mood of the people, uneasiness about internal conditions, and the activity of parties, especially of their leaders. . . . The great struggles of

recent times have arisen against the wish and will of those who govern."
He had recognized that changes in the method of warfare were bringing
about changes in its spirit.[6]

The rise of mass armies, moreover, meant that the social function of
the armed forces became altered. The old order had maintained a sharp
distinction between military and civilian life. Soldiers constituted a distinct warrior caste, separated from other groups in the community by a
unique way of life. Indifferent to the interests and ideals of the bourgeoisie and the proletariat alike, it had been designed specifically to
defend the hierarchical structure of society. Its purpose was to safeguard
security at home as well as abroad, to oppose the domestic enemies of the
status quo no less than the foreign. Indeed, Richard Cobden maintained
in the House of Commons as late as 1851 that "the armies of the Continent are not kept up by the Governments for the sake of meeting foreign
enemies, but for the purpose of repressing their own subjects."

With the emergence of armies made up of citizen soldiers, however, it
became doubtful whether the armed forces would in the future continue
to function as a warrior caste apart from the rest of the community. To
put it another way, the democratization of warfare created the possibility
that conscripted civilians might choose to defend the interests not of the
ruling class but of their own. Would not the peasant in arms feel closer to
the peasant in the village than to the landowner who was his officer?
Even more likely, would not the industrial worker infected with radical
ideas spread disaffection in the ranks? The principle of universal military
service was clearly a two-edged sword.[7]

That was why many politicians and soldiers of the old school regarded
general conscription with deep distrust. They saw in it a radical doctrine
akin to manhood suffrage. For a military system that imposed uniformity
of obligations implied uniformity of rights. As early as 1808, the German
statesman and historian Barthold Georg Niebuhr, opposing "an equality
which arouses the indignation of the true friend of freedom," maintained
that "such a system of conscription . . . must lead to the brutalization
and degeneration of the entire nation, to general coarseness, and to the
destruction of culture and of the educated classes." Seventy years later,
Alfred von Waldersee, at that time chief of staff of a Prussian army corps,
expressed privately the conviction that "we will soon abandon the system
of general military obligation." A class conflict between rich and poor
was becoming unavoidable so that "only a professional army can prevent

6. *Hinterlassene Werke des Generals Carl von Clausewitz über Krieg und Kriegführung*,
10 vols. (Berlin, 1832–37), 3:116–18; *Gesammelte Schriften und Denkwürdigkeiten des
General-Feldmarschalls Grafen Helmuth von Moltke*, 8 vols. (Berlin, 1891–93), 3:1.
    7. Great Britain, *Parliamentary Debates*, 3d ser. (1830–91), 117:916.

the total collapse of all existing social institutions." Since every state on the Continent is threatened by socialism, he expected, "in accordance with the natural law of recurrence," a general return to the system of professional armies, although he conceded that the idea was "somewhat extravagant." To him the military advantages of a mass army were outweighed by its social dangers.[8]

Yet the same considerations that made the draft suspect to some conservatives made it acceptable to some radicals. To be sure, the left generally regarded the military establishment with hostility. In the mass army, whose recruits were conscripted from the proletariat but whose officers came from the ruling classes, it saw an instrument for the defense of the existing economic system. The armed forces embodied the evils of militarism, helping to perpetuate a half-feudal, half-capitalistic form of society. There were a few radicals, however, some of them quite prominent, who perceived in the draft a means of changing established political and social institutions. As the lower classes obtained arms, as soldiers ceased to be hired mercenaries and became conscripted workers and peasants, they would become capable of more effective resistance against their oppressors. Just as manhood suffrage appeared to many socialists to be an instrument for gaining power peacefully, so general conscription appeared to a few to be an instrument for gaining it by force.

In 1891 Friedrich Engels, now near the end of his life, described the draft as more important than the franchise in the struggle for socialism. The main strength of German social democracy, he wrote, does not by any means lie in the number of its voters. A man becomes a voter in Germany at the age of twenty-five, but a soldier at twenty. Since the younger generation provides the most numerous recruits for the socialist party, it follows that the armed forces are becoming more and more infected with socialism. "Around 1900 the army, once the most Prussian element of the country, will be socialist in its majority. That is coming as inescapably as a decree of fate."

Equally sanguine was the assessment of citizen armies in 1911 by the French socialist Jean Jaurès, whose assassination at the outbreak of the First World War saved him from discovering how unrealistic his expectations had been. In his view, the democratization of military recruitment would promote the maintenance of peace, not the pursuit of war. With workers and peasants making up the bulk of the armed forces, the ruling classes would hesitate to provoke a conflict contrary to the interests of the proletariat. "To make the mobilization of the army mean the mobili-

8. *Die Briefe Barthold Georg Niebuhrs*, ed. Dietrich Gerhard and William Norvin, 2 vols. (Berlin, 1926–29), 1:494–95, 500; Ritter, *Staatskunst und Kriegshandwerk*, 2:360 (n. 24).

zation of the nation itself will render it more difficult for governments to entertain ideas of adventure." To be sure, if a people is attacked by states seeking pillage or diversion from domestic difficulties, that would justify a national war. All citizens must therefore understand "the necessity and the beauty of the military obligation," which should serve one "sublime" object: "THE PROTECTION OF NATIONAL INDEPENDENCE FOR THE FREE EVOLUTION OF SOCIAL JUSTICE." But once all nations recognize the crucial distinction between armaments for defense and armaments for aggression, "there will be a new era in Europe," an era of "high hope for justice and peace." These words, so full of idealistic exuberance, written on the eve of the most devastating war Europe had ever known, have a poignant ring.[9]

The vast increase in the size of the military establishment was only one aspect of the transformation of warfare. The other was the progressive mechanization of weapons and equipment, that is, the application of technological innovation to the instrumentalities of conflict among states. The same techniques that increased the output of goods could be used to increase the destructiveness of war. Consequently, the capacity of the armed forces to inflict casualties and damages on the enemy grew more rapidly than their size because each of their members could now function with greater effectiveness. The breech-loading rifle was a deadlier firearm than the muzzle-loading musket; heavy siege guns moving by rail had a longer range than light artillery drawn by horses. But in addition, as the materiel required for the waging of war became more complex and therefore more expensive, the cost of national defense increased faster than the number of men under arms. By the end of the nineteenth century, there was much talk in liberal and radical circles about the crushing burden of armaments and the pernicious economic consequences of the arms race. Some writers were even predicting that all states would eventually be ruined unless a way was found to reduce military competition among them. Europe, it was argued, simply could not afford the price of rationalized warfare.

The best example of an increase in the cost of national defense beyond the increase in the number of men under arms was provided by the naval establishments. More than any other tool of combat, warships were a weapon whose price bore little relationship to the size of the personnel it required. It was the technological sophistication, not the manpower involved, that demanded a heavy commitment of financial resources. Thus, the growing conviction among military planners that naval strength was

9. Karl Marx and Friedrich Engels, *Werke*, 39 vols. (Berlin, 1960–69), 22:251; Jean Jaurès, *L'organisation socialiste de la France: L'armée nouvelle* (Paris, 1911), pp. 273–74, 649–50, 674.

a key to national defense meant a steadily rising appropriation of public revenues for the armed forces.

During the 1870s the Great Powers, still digesting the lessons taught by the Franco-Prussian War, emphasized the growth and improvement of land armies. The British spent only about 50 million dollars annually on their navy, the French not quite 38, the Russians 11, the Germans 9, and the Italians 6. The crisis in the Balkans at the end of the decade, however, raised the possibility of an international conflict in which naval operations might play an important part as they had during the Crimean War. This would be even more likely if a clash arose over competing interests in Persia, India, or the Far East. Russia therefore hastened to increase naval construction, building strong bases at Odessa and Vladivostok and raising her expenditure for the fleet in 1886 to almost 19 million dollars. France, facing the danger of hostilities with England over Egypt or Burma, enlarged her naval budget to 40 million dollars in the same year. Even Italy, financially and militarily the weakest of the Great Powers, spent 30 million dollars on her fleet in 1888.

England's response was to embark on an ambitious program of naval expansion designed to maintain her position as the leading sea power. In 1888 a committee of three admirals, appointed to report on the fleet maneuvers of that year, expressed the view that "no time should be lost in placing the British navy beyond comparison with that of any two powers." Lord George Hamilton, first lord of the admiralty, at once approved this proposed "two-power standard," putting through Parliament in 1889 a naval defense act that provided for the addition to the fleet within five years of seventy vessels totaling 318,000 tons. By 1890 English naval expenditures had jumped to more than 86 million dollars.

The overall result, however, was only an intensification of the game of naval leapfrog that the armaments race was now forcing all the Great Powers to play. Both France and Russia promptly increased their expenditures for the fleet by a million dollars each. In 1890 Leo von Caprivi, Bismarck's successor as chancellor of Germany, obtained the approval of the Reichstag for increasing the naval budget to more than 22 million dollars. Until then the German navy had been relatively small. At the same time, an American naval board recommended to Congress the formation of a fleet of one hundred vessels, twenty of which should be first-class battleships. Soon afterward, the Japanese entered the competition with a warship construction program of their own. By the opening of the twentieth century, the British were spending 130 million dollars annually on their navy, the French 63, the Russians 43, the Germans 38, and the Italians 23. "For a growing people," maintained Prince Adalbert, head of the Prussian fleet, "there is no prosperity without expansion, no expansion without an oversea policy, and no oversea policy without a navy."

This was the credo of the navalism that helped shape the theories of warfare during the decades preceding the First World War.[10]

Its chief prophet was Alfred Thayer Mahan, an American naval officer and historian, whose most influential works appeared in the early 1890s. The burden of his teachings was that naval power holds the key to national security. Control of the seas and the acquisition of colonies are inseparably connected, forming the foundation for the strength and wealth of a state. "The influence of the government will be felt in its most legitimate manner in maintaining an armed navy, of a size commensurate with the growth of its shipping and the importance of the interests connected with it." But even more significant than the size of the navy are the institutions of a country "favoring a healthful spirit and activity, and providing for rapid development in time of war by an adequate reserve of men and ships and by measures for drawing out that general reserve of power." Although it is true that an unexpected attack may cause a nation disaster in one quarter, the superiority of naval power will prevent such a disaster from becoming general or irremediable. History has given sufficient proof of this. "England's naval bases have been in all parts of the world; and her fleets have at once protected them, kept open the communications between them, and relied upon them for shelter."

Indeed, the experience of Great Britain since the middle of the seventeenth century provided irrefutable evidence of the importance of sea power. Especially in the wars of the French Revolution and the Napoleonic Empire, naval supremacy proved to be the one force strong enough to withstand the dynamism of the new citizen armies. "Upon it depended the vigorous life of the great nation which supplied the only power of motive capable of coping with the demoniac energy that then possessed the spirit of the French." Control over the ocean, the chief strength of England, furnished her with two principal weapons: naval superiority, which the course of the war soon developed into supremacy, and money. By the mastery of the sea, Mahan continued, by the destruction of the French colonial system and commerce, by her persistent enmity to the spirit of aggression that was incarnate in the French Revolution and personified by Napoleon, and by her own sustained and unshaken strength, she drove the enemy into the battlefield of the Continental System, where his final ruin was certain. For the privations that it had imposed on the peoples of Europe turned them against France. Thus, "it was not by attempting great military operations on land, but by controlling the sea, and through the sea the world outside Europe, that both the first and the

---

10. Hayes, *Generation of Materialism*, pp. 238–41; H. W. Wilson, "The Growth of the World's Armaments," *Nineteenth Century* 43 (1898):710; Mary Evelyn Townsend, *The Rise and Fall of Germany's Colonial Empire, 1884–1918* (New York, 1930), p. 57.

second Pitt insured the triumph of their country in the two contests where either stood as the representative of the nation." The lesson of this experience for the conduct of war was obvious.[11]

The extent to which the Great Powers learned this lesson can be measured by the rise in their appropriations for the fleet. This component of the overall defense budget was growing most rapidly, not only because of an increase in personnel but also because of an increase in the technological complexity of materiel. Look at the changes in the expenditure for the armed forces of Great Britain between 1880 and 1910. Naval manpower grew 191 percent, from 45,000 to 131,000, whereas the standing army grew only 38 percent, from 322,000 to 445,000 men. Yet the difference in the budgetary increases for the two branches of the armed services was even more striking: 296 percent for the navy, from 51 to 202 million dollars, and 84 percent for the army, from 75 to 138 million dollars. The pattern in Germany, which relied on land forces to a far greater extent than England, was similar. Naval personnel grew 729 percent in the period 1880–1910, from 7,000 to 58,000 men, and naval appropriations 836 percent, from 11 to 103 million dollars, whereas army personnel grew 52 percent, from 419,000 to 636,000 men, and army appropriations 124 percent, from 91 to 204 million dollars.

Even those countries that did not pursue sea power with the same determination raised their budgets for the fleet more rapidly than for the army. In France between 1880 and 1910, the increase in naval manpower was 40 percent and in naval expenditure 72 percent, whereas the percentages were 42 and 65 for the land forces. In Italy the increase in naval manpower was 88 percent and in naval expenditure 356 percent, whereas army personnel increased 46 percent and army appropriations 98 percent. Austria-Hungary enlarged the personnel of her fleet by 150 percent and its budget by 250 percent, whereas the personnel of the army grew 71 percent and its budget 18 percent. The percentages in Russia were 140 and 147 for the navy and 60 and 105 for the army. In short, all the Great Powers embraced the new theories of navalism, though with varying degrees of commitment and enthusiasm.

Yet the army remained the mainstay of national defense in almost every country. Both history and geography suggested that the outcome of a war would probably be determined to a greater extent by land operations than by sea operations. Control of the ocean might prove decisive in the long run, especially in the event of a military stalemate, but in order to organize a victorious campaign against the enemy, it was essential to have

11. A. T. Mahan, *The Influence of Sea Power upon History, 1660–1783* (Boston, 1890), pp. 82–83; idem, *The Influence of Sea Power upon the French Revolution and Empire, 1793–1812*, 2 vols. (Boston, 1892), 2:381, 386, 400–402.

superior armies. Of the international conflicts fought since the downfall of Napoleon, only the Crimean War could be said to have depended significantly on naval power. At the outbreak of hostilities in 1914, therefore, the lion's share of the defense budget was still going to the army rather than the navy. In Germany the land forces received 80 percent of total military appropriations, in France 69, in Italy 65, in Austria-Hungary 79, and in Russia 73. Only in England was the distribution substantially different. When the First World War began, she was spending 62 percent of her defense budget on the fleet, although as recently as 1890 the army had been getting 56 percent. Of the combined defense budgets of all the Great Powers of Europe in 1914, the land forces accounted for 68 percent. Most military planners on the Continent continued to regard them as the key to victory.[12]

The growing costliness of national defense was the subject of a great public debate in the years before Sarajevo. Critics of the military establishment complained about the tax burden imposed by the armaments race, partly because they believed that large armies and navies encouraged conflict among nations, partly because they perceived that the increase in defense expenditures helped maintain the social importance of the landed aristocracy, which provided a large part of the officer corps. But to what extent were their arguments economically justified? Were appropriations for national defense in fact rising so swiftly as to sap the productive energies of Europe?

At first glance, the increase in the cost of security does appear rapid enough to support the contention of those who maintained that the civilian standard of living was being sacrificed to support a bloated military establishment. Although the estimates vary to some extent, they all agree that there was only a modest rise in the outlay for defense from the middle to the last quarter of the nineteenth century, but that then the curve began to climb. In the twenty-five years between 1858 and 1883, according to the London *Economist*, the totals grew from 462 to 793 million dollars for Europe as a whole, a rate of 72 percent (see table 14.1). Only in Germany and Italy, the two countries that achieved national unification during this period, did military expenditures more than double. During the next thirty years, however, between 1883 and 1913, the total outlay for defense grew 198 percent, from 793 to 2,365 million dollars. Germany was far in the lead, but the figures for Great Britain, France, and Russia nearly tripled as well. Only by contrast does the rise in Austria-Hungary and Italy seem moderate.

Estimates of the per capita cost of armaments, however, point to a

12. Wright, *Study of War*, 1:670–71; A. J. P. Taylor, *The Struggle for Mastery in Europe, 1848–1918* (Oxford, 1954), pp. xxvii–xxviii.

Table 14.1. Estimates by the London Economist of Total Military Expenditures, 1858–1913

	1858	1883	Millions of Dollars Percentage Change, 1858–1883	1913	Percentage Change, 1883–1913
Great Britain	112	136	21	375	176
Germany	24	97	304	487	402
France	92	151	64	399	164
Russia	92	175	90	448	156
Austria-Hungary	54	63	17	117	86
Italy	10	58	480	141	143
Other European Countries	78	112	44	398	255
Total	462	793	72	2,365	198

SOURCE: P. Jacobsen, "Armaments Expenditure of the World," *Economist*, 19 October 1929, Armaments Supplement, p. 3.

lower rate of expansion because in most countries the population was also growing at a steady pace. Yet it is clear that the increase in the expenditure for national security far outstripped the increase in the number of inhabitants. Jürgen Kuczynski's figures on the per capita outlay for the army and navy in Germany show a rise from 2.65 dollars in 1890 to 3.07 in 1895, 3.59 in 1900, 3.96 in 1905, 4.70 in 1910, and 7.91 in 1913, a steep 198 percent in twenty-three years. According to the calculations of Quincy Wright, moreover, the growth in the per capita cost of defense during the period 1880–1910 amounted to 110 percent in Great Britain, 59 in France, 84 in Germany, 94 in Italy, and 20 in Russia. Only in Austria-Hungary was there a slight decline of 1 percent. For all the Great Powers combined, his statistics indicate a rise of 52 percent, from 2.38 to 3.62 dollars. These data suggest, then, that the armaments race before the First World War was indeed imposing an increasingly heavy burden on the population of Europe.[13]

Yet when the cost of security is measured not by its nominal value or

13. P. Jacobsen, "Armaments Expenditure of the World," *Economist*, 19 October 1929, Armaments Supplement, p. 3; Jürgen Kuczynski, *Die Geschichte der Lage der Arbeiter unter dem Kapitalismus*, 38 vols. (Berlin, 1960–71), 4:18; Wright, *Study of War*, 1:670–71.

its ratio to population but by its relationship to productivity, a different pattern begins to emerge. Precise estimates are difficult because of the incompleteness or unreliability of statistics on the growth of wealth in the nineteenth century. The available information, however, points to a much more gradual increase in the burden of armaments. The most detailed figures on national income, that is, "the total value of the commodities and services produced by the people comprising the nation in a year or the total received by them for engaging in economic activities," are those for England and Germany. They show that in the former the percentage of national income spent for defense rose from 2.0 in 1870 to 2.3 in 1880 and 1890, 3.1 in 1900, 3.6 in 1910, and 3.4 in 1914, an increase for the entire period of 70 percent, whereas the increase in per capita defense expenditure for the same years was 128 percent. These estimates are generally supported by the calculation of military appropriations as a percentage of the British gross national product: 2.4 in 1890; 2.9 in 1895; a jump to 6.9 in 1900, the time of the Boer War, but then a drop back to 3.2 in 1905; 3.5 in 1910; and 3.7 in 1913.

The figures for Germany show an even slower rise in the relative cost of armaments. Military expenditures as a proportion of national income stood at 2.6 percent in 1875. They fell to 2.5 in 1880, 1885, and 1890, climbed to 2.8 in 1895 and 1900, climbed again to 2.9 in 1905 and 1910, and then reached 3.1 in 1912. Only in 1913, the last prewar year, was there a sudden spurt to 4.5. Thus, for the entire period 1875–1912, the increase in relation to economic growth was only 19 percent compared with a nominal per capita increase of 127 percent. Even the inclusion of 1913 in the calculation raises the relative increase to 73 percent, whereas the per capita increase then comes to 234 percent.

For most of the other states of Europe, the statistical information is less complete; in some cases there are only tantalizing bits and pieces. Yet the available data reinforce the impression that economic growth did not lag far behind defense appropriations, at least in the industrially advanced countries. In France, for example, the ratio of military expenditure to national income rose from 3.6 percent in 1880 to 4.0 in 1910, but per capita cost rose from 4.22 dollars to 6.70. In Italy, on the other hand, the gross national product grew only 45 percent between 1880 and 1910, whereas military expenditure grew 144 percent and per capita cost 94 percent. Here the increase in the burden of armaments remained far ahead of the increase in wealth.[14]

14. Wright, *Study of War*, 1:669–71; Alan T. Peacock and Jack Wiseman, *The Growth of Public Expenditure in the United Kingdom* (Princeton, 1961), p. 190; Kuczynski, *Geschichte der Lage der Arbeiter*, 14:184; Bert F. Hoselitz, "Unternehmertum und Kapitalbildung in Frankreich und England seit 1700," in *Wirtschafts- und sozialgeschichtliche Prob-*

It is demonstrable, nevertheless, that the rise in the cost of defense in poor as well as rich countries was on the whole no greater than the rise in the cost of other public services. In other words, when examined in the light of the total increase in government activities and expenditures, the burden of armaments remained relatively stable. Military appropriations before the First World War were growing on an average at the same rate as civilian appropriations. Take the proportion of the national budget committed to defense needs around the turn of the twentieth century (figure 14.1). In Great Britain, except for the wartime years 1899–1902, the percentage remained almost unchanged. To be sure, there were some countries, like France and Italy, in which the share of state expenditures assigned to the armed forces was rising more swiftly. But there were others in which the ratio was actually declining. In Germany, for example, where most civilian functions of government were left to the states, the portion of the federal budget spent on armaments fell from 75 percent in 1880 to 51 in 1890, 44 in 1900, and 43 in 1910. There was also a substantial drop in Russia and Austria-Hungary. For all the Great Powers of Europe combined, the proportion remained remarkably stable; 29 percent in 1880, 29 in 1890, 27 in 1900, and 28 in 1910.

What all these figures suggest is that the increase in the cost of defense was part of a general increase in the cost of government. As the state began to broaden its old responsibilities and assume new ones—instruction, transportation, law enforcement, public health, and social welfare, in addition to national security—its need for revenue rose. Yet the share of its income allotted to the military establishment did not grow very rapidly in the aggregate. In the economically advanced countries of Western and Central Europe, moreover, the overall increase in state expenditure did not substantially exceed the increase in national wealth. In the more backward countries of the east and south, the scope of government activity did expand more rapidly than the value of goods and services so that the burden of taxation was becoming heavier. This, however, was primarily a result not of the armaments race but of a general enlargement of state functions. The proportion of the national income spent on defense, ranging from 3 to 6 percent in 1914, was probably no bigger than in the preindustrial era, and it may well have been smaller. There can be no doubt that warfare was becoming more destructive and therefore more dangerous, but not because of a relative growth in military expenditure. The decisive factor was the increase in the size of military

leme der frühen Industrialisierung, ed. Wolfram Fischer (Berlin, 1968), p. 287; Angus Maddison, "Economic Growth in Western Europe, 1870–1957," Banca Nazionale del Lavoro Quarterly Review 12 (1959):85.

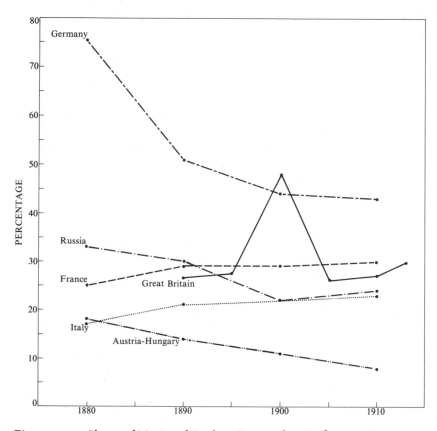

Figure 14.1. Share of National Budget Devoted to Defense, 1880–1913

SOURCE: Quincy Wright, *A Study of War*, 2 vols. (Chicago, 1942), 1:670–71; Alan T. Peacock and Jack Wiseman, *The Growth of Public Expenditure in the United Kingdom* (Princeton, 1961), p. 186.

manpower and in the efficiency of military weaponry made possible ultimately by the rationalization of the economy.[15]

This does not mean, of course, that the cost of national security was the same in all countries. There were important disparities in the financial resources assigned to the support of the armed forces. Yet it is clear that these disparities derived not from differences of civic ideology or governmental system but from differences of economic growth and demographic development. That is, the need to be prepared for an armed conflict with one or more of the Great Powers imposed on all of them, democratic and

15. Peacock and Wiseman, *Growth of Public Expenditure*, p. 186; Wright, *Study of War*, 1:670–71.

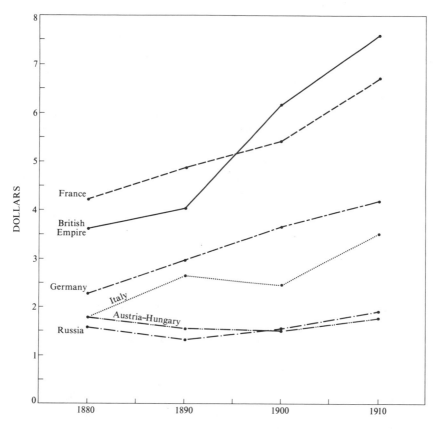

Figure 14.2. Per Capita Expenditure for Defense, 1880–1910

SOURCE: Quincy Wright, *A Study of War*, 2 vols. (Chicago, 1942), 1:670–71.

conservative states alike, the same burden of maintaining a costly military establishment. Their ability and willingness to support it depended on their wealth and population (see figure 14.2). Thus Great Britain, relying on a large fleet rather than a conscript army for her security, had consistently either the largest or the second largest per capita expenditure for national defense in Europe, according to Quincy Wright's calculations. France, seeking with a static population to match the military strength of growing Germany, competed with Great Britain for first place. Russia and Austria-Hungary, on the other hand, populous but with a largely agrarian economy, were at the bottom of the list. Italy was in the middle range, and Germany, though often criticized at home and abroad as the embodiment of saber-rattling militarism, was only in third place.

Yet when the commitment of financial resources to military purposes is

measured in relation to national wealth rather than by per capita appropriation for the armed forces, a different picture emerges. Then the development of the economy rather than the size of the population becomes
the decisive factor. By this method of calculation, the backward countries
of the east and south had to bear the heaviest burden of armaments. At
the outbreak of the First World War, 6.3 percent of the national income
in Russia and 6.1 percent in Austria-Hungary was being spent on defense, but in Great Britain the figure was 3.4 and in France 4.8. Italy was
able to keep her percentage down to 3.5 only by maintaining the smallest
armed forces among the Great Powers, forces even smaller than Great
Britain's. As for Germany, she continued to occupy an intermediate position with 4.6 percent, though her army was the strongest in Europe. Of
course, militarism cannot be measured solely by the size and costliness of
armaments. Attitudes, beliefs, values, and assumptions must also be considered. Yet it is apparent that all the states of Europe, whatever their
view of the role of the military in state and society, were committing
more of their wealth and manpower to national security in order to cope
with an increasingly complex system of warfare.[16]

Did people in the nineteenth century recognize that they were threatened by a new form of international conflict in which technological progress was intensifying the destructive capacity of armaments? It seems
that many of them did, particularly those who regarded war not as an
escape from the humdrum of everyday life but as a deadly struggle in
which the very survival of the state might be at stake. The financier and
economist Jan Gotlib Bloch, the "Polish Rothschild," wrote in his massive analysis of modern warfare at the end of the 1890s that "we have
often had an opportunity to converse with military men of different nationalities, and everywhere we have found the conviction that in a future
war very few of them would reach their objective." With a smokeless
field of battle, increasing accuracy of fire, the general practice of trying to
kill the enemy officers first, and the obligation to set an example to the
rank and file, they had little chance of returning home safe and sound.
"The times are past when an officer, rushing ahead, would lead his men
and make a breach in the enemy ranks with a bold bayonet charge, or
when a squadron, seeing an unsupported enemy battery, would gallop
against it, saber the gunners, and spike the cannons or throw them into a
ditch. Courage is necessary today no less than in the past; it is even more
necessary. But it is the courage of tenacity, of sacrifice, and no longer the
courage of scenic heroism. Combat has assumed an aspect more mechanical than knightly." To make matters worse, Bloch concluded, the

16. Wright, *Study of War*, 1:670–71; Taylor, *Struggle for Mastery*, pp. xxviii–xxix.

economic losses caused by armed conflict would be far greater than those experienced in the past.

Friedrich Engels was even more perceptive. In 1887, in his introduction to a pamphlet by Sigismund Borkheim, he described a coming international conflict in uncannily prophetic terms:

> No war is any longer possible for Prussia-Germany except a world war, and indeed a world war of an extent and violence which have hitherto never been imagined. Eight to ten million soldiers will kill one another, and in the process they will strip all of Europe bare, as no swarm of locusts has ever done. The devastations of the Thirty Years' War will be compressed into three or four years and spread over the entire Continent. There will be famine, pestilence, and a general brutalization of the armies as well as the masses of the population. There will be a hopeless confusion of our artificial machinery in commerce, industry, and credit, ending in general bankruptcy. There will be a collapse of the old states and of their traditional state wisdom to the point where crowns will be rolling on the pavement by the dozen, and no one will be found to pick them up.[17]

Although he conceded that it was impossible to foresee how this future war would end and who would be the winner, Engels remained confident that the general exhaustion resulting from the conflict would establish the conditions for the final victory of the working class. His thinking may have been wishful, but his insight was remarkably sharp. Through the apparent solidity of political and economic institutions in the late nineteenth century, he discerned the devastated Europe of 1918.

To many other observers, however, it seemed that increasing destructiveness was making war improbable or even impossible. It might have been easy, they reasoned, for princes and statesmen to embark on military adventures when all they had to lose was some disputed province and a few thousand soldiers. But when an international conflict threatened victor and vanquished alike with enormous casualties and a breakdown of the entire economy, would they not hesitate? The very fact that modern combat was becoming so risky would have a deterrent effect, making the preservation of peace more likely.

This conviction appears repeatedly in various comments on the changing nature of war and international relations. The Italian economist Gerolamo Boccardo maintained as early as the 1850s that men were

17. Jean de Bloch, *La guerre*, 6 vols. (Paris, 1898–1900), 6:212–13, 232; Marx and Engels, *Werke*, 21:350–51.

substituting the maxim "war will kill war" for the ancient proverb "war feeds war." In other words, when the means of killing, mining, bombarding, and destroying had reached the peak of perfection—a point rapidly being approached—war would become almost impossible. The Swedish industrialist and pacifist Alfred Nobel, the inventor of dynamite, also believed that the growing deadliness of armaments would make military conflict unthinkable. "My factories will perhaps put an end to war even sooner than your congresses," he told Bertha von Suttner, a leader of the peace movement, in 1892. "On the day when two army corps can annihilate one another in a second, all civilized nations will surely recoil and disband their troops." In the chapter on contemporary Europe appearing in *The Cambridge Modern History* only a few years before Sarajevo, the British educator Stanley Leathes was confident that on the whole the existence of vast armaments made for peace. The consequences of war would be felt in every household, and statesmen as well as nations shrank from the thought of a conflict between forces so immense. "The nations appear to desire peace, and, if they desire it, they may perhaps retain it." Since the cost of victory was now almost as insupportable as the cost of defeat, countries would be forced to avoid an armed struggle out of sheer self-preservation.[18]

The idea that war was becoming so terrible that it would soon cease appealed primarily to those who wanted it to cease, that is, liberal politicians, scholars, intellectuals, reformers, and pacifists. Yet even those who believed that conflict was a natural condition of relations among states concluded that it would be less prolonged in the future because it would be less bearable. Hostilities might be costly and devastating, but at least they would be of short duration. None of the major European wars between 1815 and 1914 had lasted more than a few months, except the Crimean War. In that conflict the logistical problem of conducting military operations between combatants who were a thousand miles apart helped explain the unusual length of the struggle. Yet ordinarily nations could not endure the social and economic strain of a long period of combat.

In 1903 Ferdinand Foch, at that time a lieutenant colonel who had been on the staff of the École supérieure de guerre, sought to demonstrate in a book on military operations that in the future wars would have to be short. The armies that are set in motion, he wrote, are not armies of pro-

---

18. Gerolamo Boccardo, *Dizionario della economia politica e del commercio*, 4 vols. (Turin, 1857–61), 2:140; Bertha von Suttner, *Memoiren* (Stuttgart and Leipzig, 1909), p. 271; Stanley Leathes, "Modern Europe," in *The Cambridge Modern History*, ed. A. W. Ward, G. W. Prothero, and Stanley Leathes, 14 vols. (Cambridge and New York, 1902–12), 12:7–8.

fessionals. They are armies of civilians belonging to all the occupations and all the ranks of society, torn away from their families. These occupations, societies, and families cannot do without them indefinitely. "War brings inconvenience; under its conditions life everywhere comes to a halt. The consequence is that it cannot last a long time."

Six years later, Alfred von Schlieffen, former chief of staff of the German army, made the same point in an article on the nature of warfare in the present time. "The Russo-Japanese War has demonstrated that a simple frontal attack against the enemy may very well succeed despite all difficulties." Yet its effectiveness even under the best of circumstances is limited. To be sure, the enemy is forced back, but after a while he renews his resistance. The campaign drags on. However, long wars are unendurable at a time when the existence of the nation depends on the uninterrupted progress of commerce and industry. "A strategy of attrition cannot be pursued, when the support of millions of men requires the expenditure of billions of marks." The only way out is "a decisive and annihilating success."[19]

Since the wars of the future would be short, it followed that victory was contingent on rapidity of mobilization and attack. There was no time for cautious maneuvers or delaying tactics. Everything depended on the first blow. It was ironic that Émile-Auguste-Cyprien Driant, who fell at Verdun four years later in the greatest battle of attrition of modern times, assured the Chamber of Deputies in 1912 that "the victorious army will be the one which, scorning reserves and fortresses, will leap first at the throat of the adversary and will immediately gain the moral superiority which forces events. And nothing tells us, gentlemen, that for that we will need hundreds of thousands of men. The first great battle will decide the entire war, and wars will be short." It would therefore be essential to throw all available resources into combat at once. The more violent war is, the shorter it is and the longer are periods of peace, maintained General Henri Bonnal, a former commandant of the École supérieure de guerre. "War on the Napoleonic model, therefore, marks progress for mankind." Since the decision on the battlefield would be reached quickly, it was all the more important to conduct military operations with a ruthlessness that would help insure the enemy's defeat by demoralizing him. Charles Ross, an officer in the British army, wrote that "war is a relapse into barbarism. . . . There is no chivalry in war save that which forbears to spare; no morality save that which ends quickly. . . . Atrocities are the last resource of strategy in its efforts to force an

19. Ferdinand Foch, *Des principes de la guerre: Conférences faites à l'École supérieure de guerre* (Paris and Nancy, 1903), pp. 36–37; Alfred von Schlieffen, *Gesammelte Schriften*, 2 vols. (Berlin, 1913), 1:17.

enemy to his knees." According to this reasoning, anything that shortens war serves the interests of mankind; cruelty becomes an act of kindness and wholesale killing is really a means of saving lives.[20]

Only here and there did some military analyst, more perceptive than the others, foresee that the next war would be long and exhausting, testing the national will to the breaking point. An article appearing in a Swiss journal maintained that "we must envision [the defensive battle of the future] as aligning face to face two human walls, almost in contact, separated only by the size of the danger, and this double wall will remain almost unchanged despite the wish to advance by one side as well as the other, despite the efforts which they will exert to achieve this. . . . The end of the purely defensive war of the future will therefore be a result of external circumstances."

Jean-Baptiste Montaigne, a colonel in the French army, argued similarly that the battle of the future would assume the features and borrow the methods of a war of siege. The perfection of technique, the force of materiel, and the abundance of supplies, combined with the perseverance and tenacity of the fighting men, would play the principal role. It would no longer last days or weeks but entire months. This would be a war of engineers, a triumph of scientific warfare. "It is quite possible that the great battle of nations will degenerate into a barbaric battle of attrition, in which victory will go to the people which will be in a better position to feed the struggle, which will be able to throw the last soldier into the furnace. The battle will be decided by exhaustion." Such prophecies were unusual, however; they were visions of a few lonely Cassandras. The accepted view remained that military conflict would become shorter and rarer; it might even disappear altogether.[21]

This miscalculation of the effect of technological change on the conduct of warfare was understandable. The military analysts underestimated the extent to which the rationalization of the economy would enable society to support the burden of total conflict because they were misled by experience. In the nineteenth century, armed struggle among nations had become less common and less intense. A study of the wars fought since the Middle Ages by the eleven leading states of Europe—France, Austria, Great Britain, Russia, Prussia, Spain, the Netherlands, Sweden, Denmark, Turkey, and Poland—shows that the average length

20. France, *Annales de la chambre des députés, 10me législature: Débats parlementaires, session extraordinaire de 1912*, 2 vols. (Paris, 1913), 1:690; Henri Bonnal, *La vie militaire du maréchal Ney, duc d'Elchingen, prince de la Moskowa*, 3 vols. (Paris, 1910–14), 1:286; Charles Ross, *Representative Government and War* (London, 1903), pp. 4, 8.

21. Emile Mayer [Emile Manceau], "Quelques idées françaises sur la guerre de l'avenir," *Revue militaire suisse* 47 (1902):403, 409; Jean-Baptiste Montaigne, *Vaincre: Esquisse*

of each war during the period 1100–1900 was 2.4 years. It declined from 3.5 in the twelfth century to 1.8 in the thirteenth; it rose to 2.1 in the fourteenth, 2.4 in the fifteenth, and 2.9 in the sixteenth; it declined again slightly to 2.7 in the seventeenth and eighteenth; and then it fell dramatically to 1.4 in the nineteenth, the lowest figure in eight hundred years. Was it not reasonable to assume that it would continue to diminish?

According to the estimates of the sociologist Pitirim Sorokin, moreover, the percentage of war casualties, both killed and wounded, in the population of Europe as a whole equaled 0.2 in the twelfth century, 0.5 in the thirteenth, 0.8 in the fourteenth, 1.0 in the fifteenth, 1.5 in the sixteenth, 3.7 in the seventeenth, and 3.3 in the eighteenth, but only 1.5 in the nineteenth. Thus the relative losses of the citizen armies based on conscription were less than half what the professional armies of the ancien régime had suffered. In addition, Sorokin prepared an index of the intensity of war in eight major countries: France, Austria, Great Britain, Russia, Germany, Spain, the Netherlands, and Italy. Based on the duration of the conflict, the size of the forces engaged, the number of killed and wounded, the number of states involved, and the proportion of combatants to the total population, this index shows a sharp drop in the nineteenth century to a level lower than any since the late Middle Ages. The figures per million inhabitants are 18 in the twelfth century, 24 in the thirteenth, 60 in the fourteenth, 100 in the fifteenth, 180 in the sixteenth, 500 in the seventeenth, 370 in the eighteenth, and 120 in the nineteenth. No wonder that in the years before the First World War so many people believed that the frequency of international conflict was declining and its severity diminishing. Their optimism seemed to be supported by history and statistics alike.[22]

Yet they were tragically mistaken. Although war had become less common after 1815, its power to inflict death and destruction was growing rapidly. The danger to the established political and economic system of Europe arising out of the changing nature of international conflict was primarily the result not of an increase in armed forces or military budgets but of the rising capacity for devastation made possible by modern technology. War may not have been as frequent as in the preindustrial era, but its effect on society could be far more disruptive. What made the situation especially dangerous was that the idea of armed struggle was somehow appealing to many men. It aroused a sense of excitement, pur-

d'une doctrine de la guerre basée sur la connaissance de l'homme et sur la morale, 3 vols. (Paris and Nancy, 1913), 2:159–60.

22. Wright, Study of War, 1:226–27, 237, 654–56; Pitirim A. Sorokin, Social and Cultural Dynamics, 4 vols. (New York, 1937–41), 3:304–34, 340–51.

pose, sacrifice; it offered an escape from the comfortable but dull routine of everyday life. The *Spectator* of London wrote during the 1890s:

> There is a certain fear of war everywhere, due to a perception of the vast scale on which it must be fought, and the terrible reduction in the chances of escape which the new weapons will ensure, but nevertheless there is hardly a nation which is without the feeling that if war came life would be brighter, more vivid, more like the dreams which fill the brains of youth. . . . A new generation after thirty years of peace is very like a public school which takes to the battle called football with delight, because in it the latent savagery and thirst for deep excitement can be innocently expended.[23]

This mood helped plunge Europe into the abyss eighteen years later.

23. "The Appetite for War," *Spectator*, 15 February 1896, pp. 235–36.

15

THE ZENITH OF IMPERIALISM

That bellicosity held in check in Europe by the destructiveness of modern warfare could find a safe outlet overseas, for the nineteenth century witnessed the climax of the imperialist movement initiated four hundred years before by the great voyages of exploration. Beginning with isolated, hesitant attempts to find precious metals, raw materials, or a water route to the Far East, it culminated during the years before Sarajevo in the political domination of almost the entire world. By 1914 the states of Western and Central Europe had about 84 percent of the earth's land surface under their control. But this historic process of expansion, suddenly reversed after the First World War, was not an uninterrupted sequence of incursions and acquisitions. It proceeded by fits and starts, first gathering speed, then slowing down, sometimes regarded with enthusiasm, at other times with indifference. The successive stages of imperialism reflected to a large extent the internal conditions of the states of Europe, their political purposes and economic needs, their social tensions and civic beliefs. Overseas policies thus cannot be understood apart from domestic problems and goals.[1]

The first great wave of imperialism, led by the Spaniards and the Portuguese, who were then joined by the Dutch, the French, and the English, began to ebb in the second half of the eighteenth century. Even before the wars of independence in North and South America between 1775 and 1825, some writers maintained that colonies were a source of expense without corresponding benefit. Like children growing up in the parental home, they were sooner or later bound to strike out on their own. It was useless for the mother country to try to dissuade them or retain them by force. Whatever she did, the outcome would be the same. Anne-Robert-Jacques Turgot, the famous French economist and statesman, declared as early as 1748 that "colonies are like fruits which cling to the tree until they have received sufficient nourishment from it. Then they detach themselves from it, germinate, and produce new trees." Such is the lesson of history, he added prophetically. "Carthage did what Thebes had done and what some day America will do."[2]

1. Grover Clark, *A Place in the Sun* (New York, 1936), pp. 31–32; idem, *The Balance Sheets of Imperialism: Facts and Figures on Colonies* (New York, 1936), p. 6.
2. *Oeuvres de Turgot et documents le concernant*, ed. Gustave Schelle, 5 vols. (Paris, 1913–23), 1:141.

The outbreak of revolution in the New World a generation later served to confirm this analysis. But although the most valuable British and Spanish colonies succeeded in winning their independence, the separation had no adverse effect on the mother country. England in particular entered a period of unprecedented economic growth during precisely the decades that followed the loss of her chief possessions in America. There was seemingly no need to seek conquests overseas when handsome profits could be earned right at home by building railroads, establishing factories, or digging mines. Besides, the steady reduction of tariff barriers in Europe beginning with the 1840s suggested that the world was entering an era of free trade, in which the advantages of colonial expansion could be obtained without the burdens of political control. The acquisition of overseas possessions, which had formerly been justified by the teachings of mercantilism, began to appear less important in an age of economic liberalism.

That is why the political rhetoric of the middle years of the nineteenth century is so full of assertions that colonies are a hindrance rather than a help to the mother country. Especially in Great Britain, still the greatest imperialist power in the world, statesmen and publicists vied with each other in thinking up reasons for opposing imperialism. Sir Henry Parnell, a prominent Whig politician, maintained that "the possession of the Colonies affords no advantages which could not be obtained by commercial intercourse with independent states," and thus "the number of them should be greatly reduced." The *Westminster Review* described overseas acquisitions as "impediments to commerce, drawbacks on prosperity, pumps for extracting the property of the many for the benefit of the few, the strong holds and asylums of despotism and misrule." The historian and educator Goldwin Smith, a leading advocate of the dismemberment of the empire, offered a more detailed critique of the colonial system. There was a time, he wrote in a letter to the London *Daily News*, when the universal prevalence of commercial monopoly made it worthwhile to hold colonies in dependence for the sake of controlling their trade. But that time is gone. "Trade is everywhere free, or becoming free; and this expensive and perilous connexion has entirely survived its sole legitimate cause." England should recognize the change that has come over the world.

On the eve of a new wave of expansion in 1870, the prime minister himself, Gladstone, reiterated in Parliament the view that Turgot had advanced a century before: "If you look back to the history of the colonial connection between European and trans-Atlantic possessions you find that it is the nature of those possessions to grow, and so to grow as to alter essentially, in obedience to laws stronger than the will of man, the conditions of their relation to the countries with which they were originally connected, until they arrive at that stage of their progress in which separation from the mother country inevitably takes place." That Gladsone, the quintessential mid-Victorian liberal, should regard the dissolution of Britain's colonial empire with equanimity is understandable. But it is surprising that his great rival Disraeli, the future spokesman for a revived imperial pride, was of the same opinion. "These wretched Colonies will all be independent, too, in a few years," he wrote in 1852, "and are a millstone round our necks." As late as 1866, he was still arguing that England should exercise power and influence in Asia, consequently in Eastern Europe, and consequently also in Western Europe. "But what is the use of these colonial deadweights which *we do not govern*? . . . Leave the Canadians to defend themselves; recall the African squadron; give up the settlements on the west coast of Africa; and we shall make a saving which will, at the same time, enable us to build ships and have a good Budget." On the colonial question there appeared to be little difference between him and Gladstone.[3]

With the 1870s, however, came a sharp reaction against the anti-imperialist attitudes of the era of economic liberalism. Colonies began to seem important to states resolved to find a place in the sun; they came to be regarded as preconditions or manifestations of national greatness. In a world in which the strong were destined to rule over the weak, it was now argued, overseas expansion provided a sign of political might and cultural vigor. Only the timid would shrink from the task of spreading their influence over other parts of the globe. This revival of imperialism was connected with the turn away from free trade, the increase of diplomatic tension, and the acceleration of the armaments race in Europe. As early as 1879, the German historian Leopold von Ranke, a venerable octogenarian whose political attitudes had been formed fifty years before during the Restoration, was writing about "the genius of the Occident . . . the spirit which . . . is filling far-off continents with colonies," the spirit which, "steadfast, multiform, unapproachable, is subduing the world, armed irresistibly with weapons and science."

By the end of the nineteenth century, the subjugation of the earth was virtually complete. Lord Salisbury, the prime minister of England, could still express a vague uneasiness about what was happening. "We have been engaged in drawing lines upon maps where no white man's foot has ever trod," he said at a Mansion House dinner. "We have been giving away mountains and rivers and lakes to each other, only hindered by the

---

3. Henry Parnell, *On Financial Reform* (London, 1830), pp. 249–50, 253; "Financial Reform," *Westminster Review* 12 (1830):403; *Daily News* (London), 30 January 1862, p. 2; Great Britain, *Parliamentary Debates*, 3d ser. (1830–91), 200:1900–1901; William Flavelle Monypenny and George Earle Buckle, *The Life of Benjamin Disraeli, Earl of Beaconsfield*, 6 vols. (London, 1910–20), 3:385; 4:476.

small impediment that we never knew exactly where the mountains and rivers and lakes were." Most men, however, did not share his misgivings. To them it was no more than right that the nations of Europe should further their material well-being at the expense of non-European societies. According to the London *Saturday Review*, the flag has followed the Bible and trade has followed the flag—in the Transvaal, at the Cape, in central Africa, in India and the East, in the islands of the South Seas, and in the far northwest. "Is there a mine to exploit, a railway to build, a native to convert from breadfruit to tinned meat, from temperance to trade gin, the German and the Englishman are struggling to be first." Such was the stern law of life.

Europeans began to take it for granted that the rising standard of living of the Occident could only be maintained by their domination over distant territories and alien peoples. Those who opposed the new imperialism—and there were some who did—ran the risk of being charged with showing greater concern for the welfare of dark-skinned natives than that of their own countrymen. For this reason, many politicians rushed to climb on the bandwagon of colonial expansion. By 1899 Cecil Rhodes, the imperialist supreme, could declare with satisfaction that criticism of overseas acquisition had now been silenced:

> All thoughts of a Little England are over. They are tumbling over
> each other, Liberals and Conservatives, to show which side are
> the greatest and most enthusiastic Imperialists. The people have
> changed, and so do all the parties, just like the Punch and Judy show
> at a country fair. The people have found out that England is small,
> and her trade is large, and they have also found out that other
> people are taking their share of the world, and enforcing hostile
> tariffs. The people of England are finding out that "trade follows the
> flag," and they have all become Imperialists. They are not going to
> part with any territory. And the bygone ideas of nebulous republics
> are over. The English people intend to retain every inch of land they
> have got, and perhaps, sir, they intend to secure a few more inches.[4]

This spirit of exultant imperialism appears repeatedly in the political rhetoric of many public figures.

But how much reality was there behind this rhetoric? Granted that politicians and publicists painted dazzling pictures of national bliss to be

---

4. Leopold von Ranke, *Sämtliche Werke*, 54 vols. (Leipzig, 1867–90), 43–44:518–19; Gwendolen Cecil, *Life of Robert, Marquis of Salisbury*, 4 vols. (London, 1921–32), 4:323; "England and Germany," *Saturday Review of Politics, Literature, Science and Art*, 84 (1897):278; F. Verschoyle [Vindex], *Cecil Rhodes: His Political Life and Speeches, 1881–1900* (London, 1900), p. 642.

found through conquest on far-off continents. Did governments in their day-to-day conduct manifest the same enthusiasm? Most of the older writers on imperialism agree that they did, that the actions of statesmen largely paralleled their words. Thus the anti-imperialist arguments of the era of economic liberalism both affected and reflected anti-imperialist policies. For instance, in the two decades following Lord Durham's famous report on British North America in 1839, which recommended a large measure of autonomy for the Canadian colonies, England granted responsible self-government not only to Canada but also to New South Wales, South Australia, Victoria and Tasmania, New Zealand, Cape Colony, and Queensland. Since many Englishmen considered autonomy to be a first step toward independence, its spread has been taken as proof of the growing influence of the opponents of colonialism.[5]

It seemed even more apparent that the revival of imperialist ideas in the last quarter of the nineteenth century must have contributed to that last feverish outburst of territorial acquisitiveness. According to the computations of Grover Clark, after close to four centuries of colonial expansion, the nations of Western and Central Europe in 1878 controlled about 67 percent of the total land surface of the world. During the next three or four decades, the percentage rose to over 84. The partition of Africa, the second largest continent, was the most striking achievement of this new surge of imperialism. Prior to 1875 the states of Europe had acquired less than 10 percent of its territory. By 1895 they had acquired all but 10 percent; out of the small remainder, the Sudan and the Boer republics were swallowed up in the next decade. But there were also other parts of the globe where the colonial powers succeeded in enlarging their domination. Between 1876 and 1900, for example, their possessions in Polynesia grew from 57 to 99 percent of the total area and those in Asia rose from 52 to 57 percent.

All in all, during the thirty years following the Franco-Prussian War, the British annexed 4.25 million square miles with 66 million inhabitants, the French 3.5 million square miles with 26 million inhabitants, the Germans 1 million square miles with 13 million inhabitants, the Russians 500,000 square miles with 6.5 million inhabitants, the Dutch 116,000 square miles with 10.7 million inhabitants, and the Belgians, or rather the king of the Belgians, 900,000 square miles with 8.5 million inhabitants. Although less successful, the Italians, with 185,000 square miles and 750,000 inhabitants, and the Portuguese, with 77,000 square miles and 5.2 million inhabitants, did not do badly either. Surely there was a world of difference between this wild scramble for overseas posses-

5. Parker Thomas Moon, *Imperialism and World Politics* (New York, 1926), p. 15.

sions in the second half of the nineteenth century and the anti-imperialist attitudes that had predominated in the first half.[6]

Yet recently two British scholars, John Gallagher and Ronald Robinson, have challenged the accepted view that there were two distinct phases in the colonial movement, an anti-imperialist phase before 1871 and a pro-imperialist one after. They have argued persuasively, though not without iconoclastic zeal, that imperialism was all of a piece. Its methods may have differed with time; its objectives were always the same. Those who speak of an ebb and flow in the expansion of Europe, they maintain, confuse rhetoric with reality. Their argument, provocative and ingenious, appeared originally in 1953 in an article in the *Economic History Review*. Restricting their generalizations to Great Britain, the authors advanced here for the first time their theory of a continuous as opposed to a discontinuous imperialism. It is based on two considerations. First of all, even during the period of the so-called reaction against colonial expansion, England continued to enlarge her overseas possessions. Gallagher and Robinson cite a number of territories, some rather obscure, that the British occupied or annexed: New Zealand, the Gold Coast, Labuan, Natal, the Punjab, Sind, and Hong Kong between 1841 and 1851; and Berar, Oudh, Lower Burma, Kowloon, Lagos, "the neighbourhood of Sierra Leone," Basutoland, Griqualand, and the Transvaal between 1851 and 1871, not to mention new colonies established in Queensland and British Columbia. "For all the extensive anthologies of opinion supposedly hostile to colonies," they ask rhetorically, "how many colonies were actually abandoned?"

Then their logic shifts. Even if we agree that there was a new wave of colonial acquisition after 1871, they now say, this represents a change only in the means of imperialism, not the ends. That is, throughout the nineteenth century England preferred to protect her economic interests overseas by "informal techniques," by the unhindered pursuit of trade and investment without administrative control. Only when it became difficult to maintain a commercial connection without exercising political authority did the government in London agree to colonial annexation. As a rule, it sought to enjoy the advantages of exploitation without the burdens of ownership. It is thus erroneous to contend, as earlier writers have done, that in the first half of the nineteenth century the basic policy

6. Clark, *Place in the Sun*, pp. 31–32; idem, *Balance Sheets of Imperialism*, pp. 5–6; Carlton J. H. Hayes, *A Generation of Materialism, 1871–1900* (New York and London, 1941), pp. 236–38; Werner Sombart, *Der moderne Kapitalismus: Historisch-systematische Darstellung des gesamteuropäischen Wirtschaftslebens von seinen Anfängen bis zur Gegenwart*, 2d ed., 3 vols. (Munich and Leipzig, 1924–28), 3:65; Jürgen Kuczynski, *Die Geschichte der Lage der Arbeiter unter dem Kapitalismus*, 38 vols. (Berlin, 1960–71), 33:149.

of Great Britain overseas was "trade not rule," whereas in the second half rule became more important than trade. The correct formulation should be: "trade with informal control if possible; trade with rule when necessary." According to Gallagher and Robinson, this recognition of the underlying continuity of English colonial policy disposes of the over-simplified orthodox interpretation based on a superficial discontinuity. "One principle then emerges plainly: it is only when and where informal means failed to provide the framework of security for British enterprise . . . that the question of establishing formal empire arose." The manifestations of imperialism may have changed; the motivations remained the same.[7]

This argument deserves careful consideration; it corrects what has clearly been an overemphasis on the disparity between the earlier and the later period in the colonial movement. There is supporting empirical evidence that in fact the acquisition of colonies was pursued during the supposedly anti-imperialist phase with almost as much vigor as during the subsequent pro-imperialist phase. Grover Clark's figures suggest that in the years 1801–78 the states of Western and Central Europe extended their control over the earth's surface at an average rate of 216,000 square miles annually; in the years 1878–1914, they extended it at an average rate of 240,000 square miles annually. The rate of expansion thus increased about 11 percent. The difference is significant but not nearly as significant as earlier interpretations of imperialism had led us to believe. It becomes apparent that before 1871 colonial rhetoric lagged behind colonial policy, whereas after 1871 it ran ahead. To this extent, the Gallagher and Robinson thesis is a healthy corrective.[8]

But as for their contention that the motivation of imperialism remained essentially uniform, that the methods of imperialism may have changed without changing the ends, this is to some extent a question of semantics, perhaps even metaphysics. The distinction between formal and informal methods is so fundamental that it ceases to be a difference of degree and becomes one of kind. Gallagher and Robinson may believe that the imperialisms imposed on China and the Congo or on Turkey and India were basically the same. But the Chinese and the Congolese, the Turks and the Indians thought otherwise. There were a thousand ways in which the life of native peoples under the indirect domination of Europe differed—for the better, most of them would have said—from the life of those who were directly subject to colonial rule. There is no denying that outright annexation often meant an improvement in sanitation, a decline

7. John Gallagher and Ronald Robinson, "The Imperialism of Free Trade," *Economic History Review*, 2d ser. 6 (1953–54):2–4, 12–13.
8. Clark, *Place in the Sun*, pp. 30, 32; idem, *Balance Sheets of Imperialism*, pp. 5–6.

in mortality, a reduction in illiteracy, and sometimes a rise in the standard of living. But it also meant a loss of self-respect, a confusion of values, a sense of bewilderment, and a feeling of demoralization, in short, cultural and psychological disintegration. Those under indirect European control were also exposed to it, but not nearly to the same degree. To minimize these differences as merely categories of "formal" and "informal" imperialism is itself an oversimplification.

More than that, if the English after 1871 were only pursuing the same objectives by different methods, what about those nations that had few or no colonial possessions before the middle of the nineteenth century? What about the French or, even more to the point, what about the Germans, the Italians, and the Belgians? Surely they could not have been informally but actively pursuing a colonial policy at a time when they had no colonies and when they made no effort to acquire any. Yet they too embraced the theories of imperialism more or less simultaneously with the English and ostensibly for the same reasons. The arguments advanced in Paris or Berlin or Rome to justify overseas expansion were indistinguishable from those advanced in London. Admittedly, what statesmen profess in defense of their statecraft is not always what actually motivates them. A distinction must be made between the plausible and the real reasons for government policy. Yet the fact that so many politicians in so many countries were saying the same thing at the same time about colonial possessions suggests that a fundamental change in the attitude toward imperialism was taking place.

The rhetoric of overseas expansion emphasized first of all the material advantages that would accrue to the mother country. The most important of these was economic well-being. One statesman after another assured his countrymen that imperialism meant an extension of trade, an increase of wealth, and a rise in the standard of living. Gallagher and Robinson classify Joseph Chamberlain with those British statesmen who accepted the scramble for Africa after 1888 as "a painful but unavoidable necessity." Yet Chamberlain spoke in 1894 without evidence of pain about "the necessity for using every legitimate opportunity to extend our influence and control in that great African continent which is now being opened up to civilisation and to commerce." Experience teaches that trade follows the flag, he argued, so that in commercial questions the colonial connection has a powerful effect on the balance of profit and loss. "Is there any man in his senses who believes that the crowded population of [the British Isles] could exist for a single day if we were to cut adrift from us the great dependencies which now look to us for protection and assistance, and which are the natural markets for our trade?" Were it possible tomorrow to reduce the British Empire by a stroke of the pen to the dimensions of the United Kingdom, at least half of the population would starve.

That a British politician should seek to vindicate the expansion of England's established colonial empire is not surprising. However, the same language was used by many Continental statesmen to justify a new policy of imperialism on which their country was embarking. Robinson and Gallagher maintain that "Bismarck and Ferry . . . had no solid belief in African empire; indeed they sneered at the movement as something of a farce." But there are no sneers about African colonies to be found in the speeches of that archimperialist Jules Ferry. On the contrary, they over-flow with a conviction that overseas possessions represent the difference between prosperity and decline for France. Listen to his address of 28 July 1885 before the Chamber of Deputies concerning Madagascar. "For rich countries, colonies are among the most advantageous investments of capital," he declared. "I think that France, which has always had an excess of capital and which has exported considerable amounts of it abroad . . . has an interest in considering this side of the colonial question." But there is yet another, more important aspect to the issue. "For countries like ours, which are by the very nature of their industry dependent on a large export trade, the colonial question is essentially a question of markets. . . . From this particular point of view, which is of the greatest importance, considering the time in which we find ourselves and the crisis which all European industries are experiencing, the establishment of a colony means the creation of a market." The assertion that economic stability depends on colonial expansion appears repeatedly in his public statements. Does this sound like a politician who has no solid belief in African empire?

Or consider the attitude of Bismarck, who had encouraged the export of German industrial products to overseas markets but had hesitated to engage in direct annexation. A new period of depression beginning in the early 1880s persuaded him to embrace a program of out-and-out imperialism. In justifying this change of policy before the Reichstag in March 1885, he employed arguments similar to those Ferry advanced in the French legislature four months later. The inhabitants of the coastal colonies in Africa might not become large consumers of manufactured goods, he conceded, but branch offices of domestic commercial firms established there would serve as middlemen for the sale of German wares in the interior. This was not all. "If part of the cotton and the coffee which we import into our country were grown on German soil overseas, would that then not be an increase of German national wealth?" He hoped that some day German miners would be able to earn a comfortable living exploiting the metal deposits of southwest Africa. "Our colonial

398 · International Relations

efforts are means for the development of German shipping and German export, and the acquisition and establishment of colonies is indeed nothing more than an additional means of developing German shipping, German navigation, and German economic life." This was a central theme of his defense of overseas expansion. It was the same logic by which Chamberlain, Ferry, and a thousand other politicians in all parts of Europe were trying to defend the new wave of imperialism.

Although the expectation that overseas possessions would contribute to national wealth was an important motive in the scramble for colonies, this does not mean that financiers, industrialists, and merchants were primarily responsible for initiating and sustaining the colonial agitation. Those who reject an economic interpretation of imperialism have shown that the business community preferred to trade with and invest in areas over which its government had no political control. Robinson and Gallagher, as well as many others, emphasize that no more than about a sixth of the credit that the United Kingdom accumulated abroad between 1815 and 1880 was placed in the British possessions. "Even by 1913, something less than half of the £3,975,000,000 of foreign investment lay inside the Empire. Similarly, in no year of the century did the Empire buy much more than one-third of Britain's exports." The proportions for the other colonial powers of Europe were even smaller. That is only one aspect of the situation, however. The expectation of economic rewards is as powerful a motive as the economic rewards themselves. It is clear that most businessmen remained skeptical about the financial gains to be derived from the colonies; bankers, manufacturers, and traders were not as a rule ardent imperialists. But there were countless others—politicians, publicists, economists, academics, professionals, shopkeepers, and clerks —who were convinced that their country would be left behind in the competition for wealth unless it acquired overseas possessions. In this sense economic motivation played a central role in the imperialism of the late nineteenth century.[9]

There were also other material considerations figuring prominently in the rhetoric of the colonial movement. At a time when emigration was providing an outlet for the surplus population of Europe, colonies seemed to offer a way of reducing demographic pressure without sacrificing the economic and military advantages of an abundant source of manpower. Those countries supplying large numbers of migrants to the

9. Gallagher and Robinson, "Imperialism of Free Trade," pp. 5, 12; Joseph Chamberlain, *Foreign & Colonial Speeches* (London, 1897), pp. 26, 132, 202; R. E. Robinson and John Gallagher, "The Partition of Africa," in *The New Cambridge Modern History*, 12 vols. (Cambridge, 1960–70), 11:593; *Discours et opinions de Jules Ferry*, ed. Paul Robiquet, 7 vols. (Paris, 1893–98), 5:195–96; Otto von Bismarck, *Die gesammelten Werke*, 15 vols. (Berlin, 1924–35), 13:11–14, 18.

New World—especially the United Kingdom, Germany, and Italy—saw in imperialism a solution to the problem of how to avoid the loss of inhabitants. As Adolf Marschall von Bieberstein, the foreign minister of the German Empire, told the Reichstag in 1897: "Our interest remains therefore undiminished in trying to keep these [emigrants] German, and in seeing to it . . . that they remain loyal to their emperor and their nation, and that their activity is made useful to the mother country."

No one dwelt on this aspect of the colonial movement more eloquently than the nationalist historian Heinrich von Treitschke. In a series of lectures on politics, which he gave regularly at the University of Berlin from 1874 until shortly before his death in 1896, he emphasized how important the question of emigration was for the future of the nation: "After all, the entire position of Germany depends on how many million people will speak German in the future." What benefit has Germany derived from the fact that thousands of her best sons have turned their back on the fatherland because they could not find a livelihood in their native country? The emigrant himself may still feel a natural bond to Germany, but his children and certainly his grandchildren cease to be Germans. Although on an average more cultured than the Americans, they are soon assimilated by the people among whom they live. How much precious strength has Germany thus lost through emigration. The labor and capital of the emigrants are gone forever. And yet they could have offered their native country enormous financial advantages. Imperialism was the only answer. "The result of our next successful war must be, if possible, the acquisition of some sort of colony," for it is quite conceivable that a nation without colonies, however strong, will some day cease to belong to the Great Powers of Europe.[10]

Strategic considerations also appear regularly in the literature of the imperialist movement. The navalists in particular contended that overseas possessions, by facilitating the maintenance of a far-flung fleet, were essential for national security. The reasoning on this point was circular, some writers insisting that colonies were necessary for the support of the navy, others teaching that the navy was indispensable for the acquisition of colonies. Imperialists and navalists were natural allies; indeed, they were frequently the same people preaching the same doctrine of national expansion. In his discussion of the elements of sea power, Mahan himself spoke of "the maintenance of suitable naval stations, in those distant parts of the world to which the armed shipping must follow the peaceful vessels of commerce." The protection of such stations depends either on

10. Germany, *Stenographische Berichte über die Verhandlungen des Reichstags: IX. Legislaturperiode, IV. Session 1895/97*, 8 vols. (Berlin, 1896–97), 7:5191; Heinrich von Treitschke, *Politik: Vorlesungen gehalten an der Universität zu Berlin*, ed. Max Cornicelius, 2 vols. (Berlin, 1897–98), 1:123–24.

direct military force, as do Gibraltar and Malta, or on a surrounding friendly population, as the American colonists once were to Great Britain and the Australian colonists now are. "Such friendly surroundings and backing, joined to a reasonable military provision, are the best of defences, and when combined with decided preponderance at sea, make a scattered and extensive empire, like that of England, secure." History has proved this. Great Britain's naval bases have been established in all parts of the world; her fleets have protected them, kept open the communications between them, and relied on them for shelter. "Colonies attached to the mother-country afford, therefore, the surest means of supporting abroad the sea power of a country."[11]

Imperialism offered still another practical advantage that was rarely mentioned by its apologists. It diverted the attention of the community from social injustice at home to colonial expansion abroad. It channeled political dissatisfactions and economic resentments into foreign adventures and overseas conquests. It helped alleviate the danger of class conflict by creating a common national purpose directed against distant and alien peoples. Harassed politicians coping with the tensions in society created by industrial growth could always find a convenient distraction in the scramble for colonies.

The statesman Giovanni Giolitti writes in his memoirs that the ruling classes during the early 1890s became fearful of the incipient socialist agitation when public opinion in Italy was disturbed by banking scandals. A colonial venture seemed to offer a welcome diversion. "But ventures undertaken in such circumstances," he adds with a sigh, "become really adventures, and generally they have an unfortunate result." This was the road that led to the disaster at Adua.

A decade earlier, Bismarck's turn to colonial expansion was also influenced by the need to counter domestic discontent. Hans-Ulrich Wehler has made a careful study of this aspect of the German chancellor's statecraft. He concludes that imperialism was a means of integrating a society torn by class differences, whereby the enthusiasm for colonies and crude Anglophobic nationalism could be manipulated as crisis ideologies for purposes of political advantage. It defended the traditional social and power structures of the Prusso-German state and shielded them not only from the turbulent effects of industrialization but also from the movements toward parliamentarization and democratization. In short, "social imperialism performed its most important function for the time being as a policy of diversion in the continuity of the 'revolution from above,' retarding the process of social and political emancipation."

The most explicit statement of this diversionary effect of the colonial

11. Mahan, *Influence of Sea Power, 1660–1783*, pp. 82–83.

movement came from Cecil Rhodes on the occasion of his visit to England in 1895. According to the journalist William Thomas Stead, the growing dissatisfaction of the proletariat convinced him that overseas expansion was the only alternative to class warfare:

> Last night I went down to a meeting of the unemployed in the East End [of London]. . . . The wild speeches, which were nothing but semi-articulate wails for bread, and the hungry look on the faces of those present, gave me a bad turn. . . . My great idea is the solution of the social problem, which, being interpreted, means that in order to keep your forty millions here from eating each other for lack of other victuals, we beyond the seas must keep open as much of the surface of this planet as we can for the overflow of your population to inhabit, and to create markets where you can dispose of the produce of your factories and of your mines. The Empire, I am always telling you, is a bread-and-butter question. If you have not to be cannibals, you have got to be Imperialists.[12]

There were many other politicians who believed that colonies could alleviate social conflict or at least create the illusion that they could alleviate it. They could reduce the tension between parties, interests, and classes by a promise of riches overseas from which all would profit. This was the tranquilizing function of imperialism.

And then there were the intangible motivations—psychological needs, emotional yearnings, irrational fears, subconscious aversions—that the colonial movement satisfied or expressed. The mystique of imperialism is more difficult to analyze than its material incentive, but it is just as important. Take the many devout Christians who saw in overseas expansion a means of converting the heathen. Or the idealists and patriots who regarded it as an opportunity to spread culture on earth, assume the white man's burden, enlighten the "lesser breeds without the Law," or fulfill a sacred *mission civilisatrice*. The imperialist rhetoric is rich in invocations of lofty ideals: dedication, perseverance, courage, and self-sacrifice.

As early as the 1850s, the *Economist* was describing railways in India as "a widely civilising influence," as an important part of "the very principles of secular government which, without any touch of intentional proselytism, have struck so effectually at the rapidly decomposing structure of native superstition." Forty years later, the German explorer Karl

---

12. Giovanni Giolitti, *Memorie della mia vita*, 2 vols. (Milan, 1922), 1:133; Hans-Ulrich Wehler, "Bismarck's Imperialism, 1862–1890," *Past & Present*, no. 48 (1970), p. 153; idem, *Bismarck und der Imperialismus* (Cologne and Berlin, 1969), p. 500; W. T. Stead, *The History of the Mystery: A Sequel to Blastus, the King's Chamberlain* (London, 1897), pp. 10–11.

Peters vividly portrayed the blessings that the colonial movement would bring to eastern Africa. A German population will dwell on the healthful heights, the standard-bearer of German life and civilization in the Dark Continent. In the lower regions, which today are only sparsely inhabited, a dense black population will be settled, "secure and happy under the protection of our flag, enjoying the fruits of its own labor under the sign of the cross." The German language, moreover, will predominate among the natives. Peters's vision of things to come culminated in a rhapsodic effusion:

> The reward which beckons is great and worthy of the ambition of a nation striving to get ahead. If Germany succeeds in gaining it, she will enrich herself materially and ideally, and at the same time she will achieve the greatest triumph which the genius of history can bestow on the civilized nations of this earth: to elevate an inferior and languishing race and draw it into the stream of vital human development. Only through such practical activity which impresses its own stamp on large parts of the earth's surface will the German people earn the last palm offered by Providence to the ambition of entire nations: to participate directly in the ennoblement of the human race as a whole. A people which thus enlists in the service of the highest tasks of world history will experience in its own soul something of the proud satisfaction which the earth spirit in *Faust* expresses in the sublime words:
> "Thus at Time's humming loom 'tis my hand prepares
> The garment of Life which the Deity wears!"[13]

Even this flight into the empyrean was surpassed by the English historian John Adam Cramb, who wrote during the Boer War that the cause of Great Britain was in some mystical sense the cause of God Himself. Advancing day by day irresistibly across the veldt of Africa, her army brings with it not the rack or the dungeon but the assurance of England's unbroken might. It brings her devotion to the ideal that has exercised a conscious sway over the minds of three generations of her sons and quickened in the blood of the unreckoned generations of the past "—an ideal, shall I say, akin to that of the prophet of the French Revolution, Diderot, '*élargissez Dieu!*'—to liberate God within men's hearts, so that man's life shall be free, of itself and in itself, to set towards the lodestar of its being, harmony with the Divine." Have nobler words ever been used for such ignoble purposes?[14]

13. "Indian Railways," *Economist*, 25 July 1857, p. 810; Karl Peters, *Das deutschostafrikanische Schutzgebiet* (Munich and Leipzig, 1895), pp. 418–19.

14. J. A. Cramb, *Reflections on the Origins and Destiny of Imperial Britain* (London, 1900), p. 24.

But to its apologists imperialism was more than the fulfillment of a civilizing mission. It also meant the realization of a biological destiny. In an age increasingly influenced by concepts of evolution and race, the superiority of the white over the black, brown, or yellow man was simply taken for granted. It was the result of a fundamental law of nature. Darwin himself had declared in 1881: "The more civilized so-called Caucasian races have beaten the Turkish hollow in the struggle for existence. Looking to the world at no very distant date, what an endless number of the lower races will have been eliminated by the higher civilized races throughout the world."

A systematic application of the teachings of Darwinian biology to the conflict of states and cultures appeared first in Walter Bagehot's *Physics and Politics*, which was originally published between 1867 and 1872 as a series of articles in the *Fortnightly Review*. Here he posited a law that "those nations which are strongest tend to prevail over the others; and in certain marked peculiarities the strongest tend to be the best." In illustrating this law, Bagehot chose to ignore recent struggles among European states: the Crimean War, the Italian War, the Seven Weeks' War, or the Franco-Prussian War. He preferred to dwell on "such differences as exist between the Aryan, the Turanian, the negro, the red man, and the Australian." It was obvious to him that the first of these was destined to rule over the others. He declared regretfully that "the experience of the English in India shows—if it shows anything—that a highly civilised race may fail in producing a rapidly excellent effect on a less civilised race, because it is too good and too different." The political domination of the white man was thus rooted for all time in his genetic superiority.

The idea that the colonial powers are only asserting their biological heritage appears repeatedly in the speeches and writings of the imperialists. Lord Rosebery, a prominent advocate of overseas expansion, expressed it in an address in Adelaide in 1884. On the "British race," he said, whether in Great Britain or the United States or the colonies or wherever it may be, rest the highest hopes of those who try to penetrate the dark future or who seek to raise and better the patient masses of mankind. Each year the power and the prerogative of that race appear to increase; each year it seems to fill more and more of the world. Joseph Chamberlain expressed the same belief even more forcefully in 1887 at the annual dinner of the Toronto board of trade. Amid the cheers of his audience, he spoke of the greatness and importance of the destiny reserved for the "Anglo-Saxon race," for that proud, persistent, self-asserting, and resolute stock, which no change of climate or condition can alter and which is infallibly destined to be the predominant force in the future history and civilization of the world. Treitschke's views sound almost mild by comparison. All he taught in his lectures was that colonization had become a factor of enormous importance for the future of the world because on it would depend the extent to which each nation will participate in the domination of the world by the "white race."

Underlying the assumption of the European's biological right to rule mankind was an intricate pattern of racial attitudes and stereotypes disseminated by schools, newspapers, magazines, and books—stereotypes such as the inscrutable Oriental, the childlike Negro, the treacherous Indian, the wily Levantine, the Dark Continent, the Yellow Peril, the Fuzzy-Wuzzies, and "never the twain shall meet." They helped make the process of colonial expansion seem natural and justifiable.[15]

Finally, imperialism was closely connected with the rising tide of nationalism in Europe, with the idea that the acquisition of territory was evidence of strength and vitality quite apart from its material benefit. The importance of a country could be measured by the number of people subject to its rule or by the size of the area appearing on a map of the earth in its particular color. That is why there was so much criticism in Italy of the Cairoli government, which had come out of the Congress of Berlin with "clean hands" but without a single piece of the defenseless Ottoman Empire. Its conduct had been petty and narrow-minded, wrote the scholar and politician Ruggero Bonghi, because the nation had not felt itself capable of assuming "a position, a role, a mission in the world." The economist Paul Leroy-Beaulieu, a leading French imperialist, declared in 1882 in the preface to the second edition of his well-known book on overseas expansion that "colonization is a question of life and death for France. Either France will become a great African power, or in a century or two she will be only a secondary European power; she will count for about as much in the world as Greece or Rumania counts in Europe." And then there was the querulous statement in 1897 by Bernhard von Bülow, the newly appointed foreign minister of Germany, who gave classic expression to the imperialist mystique: "We do not want to put anyone in the shade, but we also demand our place in the sun." Colonies had become symbols of virility, energy, and power. They were desirable not only because of their tangible advantages: they were desirable in themselves.[16]

15. *The Life and Letters of Charles Darwin, Including an Autobiographical Chapter*, ed. Francis Darwin, 3 vols. (London, 1887), 1:316; Walter Bagehot, *Physics and Politics; or, Thoughts on the Application of the Principles of "Natural Selection" and "Inheritance" to Political Society* (London, 1872), pp. 43, 136, 145; The Marquess of Crewe, *Lord Rosebery* (New York and London, 1931), p. 149; Chamberlain, *Speeches*, p. 6; Treitschke, *Politik*, 1:124.

16. Ruggero Bonghi, *Il Congresso di Berlino e la crisi d'Oriente* (Milan, 1878), pp. 182–83; Paul Leroy-Beaulieu, *De la colonisation chez les peuples modernes*, 2d ed. (Paris, 1882), pp. viii–ix; Germany, *Stenographische Berichte über die Verhandlungen des Reichstags: IX. Legislaturperiode, V. Session 1897/98*, 3 vols. (Berlin, 1898), 1:60.

This entire complex of changing attitudes and beliefs concerning imperialism is dismissed by Robinson and Gallagher as irrelevant to the basic motivation of colonial expansion. The chief partitioners of the 1880s, they write, had no grand imperial design behind what they were doing. They felt no need for colonies in Africa, and in this they reflected the indifference of all but the lunatic fringe of European business and politics. The pride and pomp of African empire did not suit the popular taste until the process of partition was almost over. Only after Africa lay divided and allotted at the end of the nineteenth century did public opinion in Europe embrace the mythology of empire.

But if the politicians, businessmen, publicists, and the broad masses of Europe were indifferent to colonies, why did they rush to partition the world with such eagerness? Here Robinson and Gallagher advance their "excentric" theory of imperialism. To understand its incentives and policies, we must look not at what was happening in Europe but at what was happening in the colonies themselves. Tensions along the frontiers between colonial and noncolonial areas led to the steady expansion of the former. Thus the collapse of the khedive's regime in Egypt and the Islamic revival in the Sudan compelled the English to advance into tropical Africa. Similarly, the new commercial importance of the Transvaal and the intransigence of Boer nationalism led to the expansion of Great Britain in southern Africa. In its final formulation, now applied to European imperialism as a whole, the Robinson and Gallagher thesis falls back on the recondite language of mathematics and physics: "There was the Eurocentric circle of industrial strategy making varying intersections with circles centered in the implacable continuities of African and Asian history. Imperialism, especially in its time scale, was not precisely a true function of either circle. It was in many ways excentric to both. It should be emphasised that the Afro-Asian crises which evoked imperialism were often not essentially the products of European forces but of autonomous changes in African and Asian domestic policies. Changing over to a mechanical analogy, imperialism was in another sense the 'centre of mass' or resultant of both circles."

Does this sound much more convincing than the old "Eurocentric" interpretation of the colonial movement? If the British were drawn into the scramble for African territory by developments in Egypt, the Sudan, and the Boer republics, what about the French, the Germans, the Italians, and the Belgians? And what about that vast literature preaching the importance of overseas acquisition? Was it no more than the howling of a lunatic fringe? And was the partition of Africa then only "a remarkable freak"?

To be sure, Robinson and Gallagher have made a significant contribution to the historical understanding of imperialism. They have shown that the traditional distinction between an earlier anti-imperialist period and a later pro-imperialist period in the nineteenth century is to a considerable extent artificial. They have shown that colonial expansion cannot be understood solely in terms of the interests, policies, and attitudes of the states of Europe. Developments within and beyond the colonies were also of major importance. But their thesis suffers from a hunger for originality, originality at almost any cost. It is too eager to refute the conventional wisdom. In its resolve to be different, it sometimes sacrifices good judgment and common sense for the sake of a paradox or an aphorism. What Robinson and Gallagher have to say is not altogether satisfying. As E. H. Carr has observed in the *Times Literary Supplement*: "The writers seemed so frightened of being taken for disciples of Marx, Hobson or Lenin that they were unable to produce any coherent analysis of imperialism, British or other, and were content to depict a series of empirical, often rather muddled, responses to successive crises. The ultimate impression left on the mind of the reader is not so far removed from the old Victorian adage that the British Empire was acquired in a fit of absence of mind." He has a point.[17]

Certainly the contention that the mythology of imperialism was only an afterthought, which did not find widespread acceptance until the partition of the world had been completed, does not stand up. On the contrary, there was a vast popular literature supporting the colonial movement as early as the 1870s and 1880s. That many conservatives embraced its teachings was to be expected, although many others argued that national greatness must be achieved on the Continent, not overseas. More surprising is the extent to which liberals and democrats succumbed to the spell of imperialism. Men who had spent a lifetime defending the right of Europeans to personal liberty and representative government began to clamor for the subjugation of Africans and Asians.

Take Mazzini, the champion of national freedom not only for Italy but for Germany, Hungary, and Poland as well. He described colonial expansion in 1871 as a "splendid movement" for which his country, "an early and a mightier colonizing power in the world" than any other state, was eminently qualified. "In the inevitable movement summoning Europe to civilize the African regions, . . . Tunis, key to the central Mediterranean, . . . obviously belongs to Italy. Tunis, Tripoli, and Cyrenaica form a part

17. Robinson and Gallagher, "Partition of Africa," 11:593–95; Ronald Robinson, John Gallagher, and Alice Denny, *Africa and the Victorians: The Climax of Imperialism in the Dark Continent* (New York and London, 1961), pp. 465–68; Ronald Robinson, "Non-European Foundations of European Imperialism: Sketch for a Theory of Collaboration," in *Studies in the Theory of Imperialism,* ed. Roger Owen and Bob Sutcliffe (London, 1972), p. 139; E. H. Carr, "The View from the Arena," *Times Literary Supplement,* 7 March 1975, p. 246.

—a most important part because of its proximity to Egypt and, through Egypt and Syria, to Asia—of that African zone which truly belongs to the European system as far as the Atlas Mountains." The flag of Rome once flew on the peaks of those mountains when, after the defeat of Carthage, the Mediterranean was called "Mare nostro." The Italians were masters of this entire region until the fifth century. "Today the French are eying it, and if we do not have it, they will soon have it." It could have been Crispi or Giolitti speaking.[18]

Even more surprising is the discovery of a rich imperialist tradition on the far left, among the socialists and anarchists. It emphasized, of course, that the justification of overseas expansion was the improvement of the natives, not the enrichment of the colonizers. But is this really much different from the familiar platitudes concerning the white man's burden? Among Charles Fourier's papers, unpublished at the time of his death in 1837, are fragments dealing with the subjugation of Africa, especially Algeria and Morocco, and the incorporation of China and Japan in Russia. Although the rulers of Europe had squabbled for centuries over miserable provinces like Luxembourg or Finland, he complained, they never devised a plan "for the systematic conquest of the barbarian empires." Proudhon declared that all races and nations have a right to freedom as the common heritage of their humanity. Yet the Caucasian differed from the others in "the beauty of his face and the elegance of his figure" as well as "the superiority of his physical, intellectual, and moral strength." This inequality had to be recognized. "All that we of the superior race have to do with regard to our inferiors is to raise them to our level, and to try to improve, strengthen, teach, and ennoble them."

Marx himself saw in the colonial movement a painful but unavoidable step in the gradual evolution of mankind toward socialism. Thus the French conquest of Algeria represented historical progress because the bourgeois, with his civilization, industry, order, and relative enlightenment, was preferable to the feudal lord or the marauding robber in a barbarian state of society. He and Engels believed that the Chinese nation, "with all its overbearing prejudice, stupidity, learned ignorance and pedantic barbarism," was engaged in a popular struggle against European domination. Yet it seemed to him as if history first had to make the people of China addicted to opium before it could raise them out of their "hereditary stupidity." As for India, it was sad to see countless industrious, patriarchal social groups disorganized and dissolved, their members losing the ancient form of civilization as well as the hereditary means of subsistence. British policy was actuated only by the "vilest interests." But the real question was: "Can mankind fulfil its destiny

18. Giuseppi Mazzini, *Scritti editi ed inediti*, 100 vols. (Imola, 1906–43), 92:167–68.

without a fundamental revolution in the social state of Asia? If not, whatever may have been the crimes of England, she was the unconscious tool of history in bringing about that revolution." The old order had to be destroyed so that a new one could be built.[19]

The scramble for overseas possessions in the last quarter of the nineteenth century only intensified the feeling on the left that colonies as objects of capitalist exploitation were bad, but as beneficiaries of socialist humaneness they might be good. The moderate wing in particular became convinced that it would be a mistake to reject imperialism out of hand. Eduard Bernstein, the father of revisionist socialism in Germany, wrote that, although the value and prospect of overseas possessions should be carefully weighed, although the treatment of the natives and the administrative system as a whole should be closely supervised, there was no reason to regard colonies as something to be rejected a priori. "The decisive question here is not whether but how. . . . In an extreme case the higher culture has also the higher right. Not conquest but cultivation of the soil provides the historically valid claim to its use."

The idea that the strong have a right to rule over the weak for the benefit of mankind appears even more starkly in the writings of the Fabian Socialists. During the Boer War, George Bernard Shaw defended Great Britain's policy in South Africa by precisely this argument. "The fact remains," he maintained, "that a Great Power, consciously or unconsciously, must govern in the interests of civilization as a whole; and it is not to those interests that such mighty forces as gold-fields, and the formidable armaments that can be built upon them, should be wielded irresponsibly by small communities of frontiersmen." Until the federation of the world becomes an accomplished fact, we must accept the most responsible imperial federations available—the British Empire, for example —as a substitute.

Gradually more and more socialists, many of them close to Marxism, began to find reasons for defending the acquisition of colonies, provided of course that the methods and purposes were right. Jean Jaurès, the most brilliant orator of the French labor movement, spoke favorably in the Chamber of Deputies in 1903 about "a policy of discreet penetration in Morocco." The government should show the Moslems that France, far from being an exploiter nation, will help them enjoy the benefits of civilization by stockpiling food in order to meet the danger of famine, by reviving ancient native handicrafts, and by building schools, infirma-

19. *Publication des manuscrits de Charles Fourier*, 4 vols. (Paris, 1851–58), 1:285–90; *Oeuvres complètes de P.-J. Proudhon*, new ed., 19 vols. (Paris, 1923–59), 7:177–79; *Northern Star, and National Trades' Journal*, 22 January 1848, p. 7; Karl Marx and Friedrich Engels, *Werke*, 39 vols. (Berlin, 1960–69), 9:96, 132–33; 12:214.

ries, and railroads. The result would be "the moral occupation" of the Moroccan state.

At its congress in Stuttgart in 1907, the Second International itself came close to approving a socialist form of imperialism. Its committee on colonies came in with a majority resolution stating: "In view of the fact that socialism wants to develop the productive energies of the entire globe and to raise all peoples to the highest level of culture, the congress does not in principle reject every colonial policy, since such a policy can have a civilizing effect under a socialist regime." The motion was rejected 127 to 108, with 10 abstentions, but the representatives from the leading colonial powers were overwhelmingly in favor. The German, Dutch, and Belgian delegations supported it unanimously; the English delegation was for it 14 to 6 and the French 12 to 10. Only the Italian delegation opposed it 11 to 4. The resolution was defeated by the combined votes of the Americans, Argentines, Australians, Bulgarians, Finns, Hungarians, Japanese, Norwegians, Poles, Rumanians, Russians, Ruthenians, Serbs, and Spaniards. Still, it was now becoming possible for a socialist to favor a colonial policy without serious risk of excommunication.

This does not mean that the imperialists of the left can be simply lumped with those of the right. The socialists were always among those concerned for the welfare of the native peoples; they advocated a higher standard of living for them, better education, better housing, better health care. In this respect they differed significantly from the colonialists who were motivated solely by considerations of profit, demography, strategy, or race. But although their imperialism was moderate and humane, it was imperialism just the same.[20]

Many socialists, moreover, supported the vigorous anti-imperialist movement that resisted the growing agitation in Europe for overseas possessions. It drew its strength largely from the left wing, from those uncompromising enemies of the established order who saw in colonial expansion only the insatiable rapacity of capitalist society. As the Second International became progressively more reformist, they intensified their opposition to any collaboration with the class enemy. Most of them came from countries where the labor movement was too weak to win concessions from the government, and their unyielding hostility to the existing system was thus partly an expression of their sense of powerlessness.

20. Eduard Bernstein, *Die Voraussetzungen des Sozialismus und die Aufgaben der Sozialdemokratie* (Stuttgart, 1899), pp. 149–50; *Fabianism and the Empire: A Manifesto by the Fabian Society*, ed. Bernard Shaw (London, 1900), pp. 23–24; France, *Annales de la chambre des députés, 8ᵐᵉ législature: Débats parlementaires, session extraordinaire de 1903*, 2 vols. (Paris, 1904), 1:623–24; *Internationaler Sozialisten-Kongress zu Stuttgart, 18. bis 24. August 1907* (Berlin, 1907), pp. 24–25, 34, 38–39.

Rosa Luxemburg, for example, whose political radicalism had emerged out of the inhospitable soil of eastern Poland, wrote a seminal study in 1913 on the concentration of capital. According to her theory, imperialism is the political manifestation of the process of capital accumulation in its competitive struggle for the remainder of the noncapitalist world environment that has not yet been seized. But the more violently, energetically, and thoroughly it effects the decline of noncapitalist cultures, the more rapidly it cuts the ground from under capital accumulation. It is "a historic method for prolonging the existence of capital," yet it is also "the surest means of placing objectively a limit to its existence in the shortest way possible." The tendency toward this ultimate end of capitalist development becomes palpable in forms that make the final phase of capitalism a period of catastrophe.

Three years later, exiled in Zürich while the First World War was raging about him, Lenin offered the classic Marxian analysis in his *Imperialism, the Highest Stage of Capitalism*. Monopoly, oligarchy, the striving for domination, the exploitation of an increasing number of small nations by a handful of rich and powerful ones—all these have given birth to the distinctive characteristics of imperialism, "which compel us to define it as parasitic or decaying capitalism." What emerges prominently as one of the tendencies of imperialism is the "rentier state," the "usurer state," in which the bourgeoisie lives increasingly on the proceeds of capital exports by "clipping coupons." Capitalism is growing more rapidly than before, but this growth is becoming uneven, and its unevenness is particularly apparent in the decay of the countries that are richest in capital.

The socialist opponents of imperialism often received important support from bourgeois democracy. Indeed, the most widely read attack on the colonial movement, influencing the great Marxian critiques, came in 1902 from the English economist John Atkinson Hobson. He first presented in a systematic fashion many of the arguments that Luxemburg and Lenin were to employ in the following decade, clearly anticipating them in the contention that "the chief economic source of Imperialism has been found in the inequality of industrial opportunities by which a favoured class accumulates superfluous elements of income which, in their search for profitable investments, press ever farther afield." The influence of investors and their financial managers on state policy produces a national alliance of other vested interests that are threatened by movements of social reform. The adoption of imperialism thus serves the double purpose of securing private material benefits for favored classes of investors and traders at the public cost and sustaining the general cause of conservatism by diverting public energy and interest from domestic agitation to external employment. But whereas to the Marxists the colonial movement was a logical expression of the capitalist system, to Hobson it was a distortion of the public interest that could be corrected by the democratic process. "The power of the imperialist forces within the nation to use the national resources for their private gain, by operating the instrument of the State," he concluded, "can only be overthrown by the establishment of a genuine democracy, the direction of public policy by the people for the people through representatives over whom they exercise a real control." Here was the fundamental difference between the socialist and the democratic critics of imperialism.

Then there were those who opposed the colonial movement for humanitarian reasons. They recoiled from the abuse, oppression, destruction, and suffering that it was inflicting on weak and uncomprehending peoples overseas. Wilfrid Scawen Blunt, the British diplomat, traveler, poet, and publicist, was an eloquent representative of this ethical anti-imperialism. In an entry in his diary on 22 December 1900, he expressed a feeling of outrage and shame at the way the nations of the West were behaving in distant parts of the globe:

> The old century is very nearly out, and leaves the world in a pretty pass, and the British Empire is playing the devil in it as never an empire before on so large a scale. We may live to see its fall. All the nations of Europe are making the same hell upon earth in China, massacring and pillaging and raping in the captured cities as outrageously as in the Middle Ages. The Emperor of Germany gives the word for slaughter and the Pope looks on and approves. In South Africa our troops are burning farms under Kitchener's command, and the Queen and the two Houses of Parliament, and the bench of bishops thank God publicly and vote money for the work. The Americans are spending fifty millions a year on slaughtering the Filipinos; the King of the Belgians has invested his whole fortune on the Congo, where he is brutalizing the negroes to fill his pockets. The French and Italians for the moment are playing a less prominent part in the slaughter, but their inactivity grieves them. The whole white race is revelling openly in violence, as though it had never pretended to be Christian. God's equal curse be on them all! So ends the famous nineteenth century into which we were so proud to have been born.[21]

Many other men of principle regarded the wild race to carve up the earth with a very uneasy conscience.

Yet they generally managed to suppress their doubts, reassuring them-

21. Rosa Luxemburg, *Die Akkumulation des Kapitals: Ein Beitrag zur ökonomischen Erklärung des Imperialismus* (Berlin, 1913), pp. 423–24; V. I. Lenin, *Collected Works*, 45

selves that what the Occidental might find unbearable, the Oriental, with his entirely different mentality, considered proper or at least natural. Their view of native peoples as less intelligent and sensitive than Europeans was a defense mechanism that made the injustices of the colonial movement acceptable. To Bagehot all "savage nations" were alike; they lacked distinctiveness and individuality. "When you have seen one Fuegian, you have seen all Fuegians—one Tasmanian, all Tasmanians. . . . A savage tribe resembles a herd of gregarious beasts." An English businessman who had settled in the Ottoman Empire found the Turks a little puzzling, even after he had lived in the country for fifty years: "The Oriental mind is so very differently constituted to ours that it is impossible to fathom it completely at all times." It is strange how little Europeans, even scholars interested in ethnic and cultural diversities, understood civilizations other than their own. The *Anthropological Review* in Great Britain wrote that the type of the Negro is "foetal" and that of the Mongol is "infantile." In accordance with this principle, it found that their government, literature, and art were also infantile. "They are beardless children, whose life is a task, and whose chief virtue consists in unquestioning obedience." The native was simply too different in his outlook to respond properly to European norms of conduct.

Although in Western eyes the peoples of Asia and Africa appeared primitive and immature, "half-devil and half-child," they also had the natural charm of playful youngsters or household pets. "To know the simple, unsophisticated tiller of the soil in the village is to love him," said a Scotsman who went out to India early in the twentieth century. "He is wonderfully contented despite his illiteracy, poverty and low standard of living." But like youngsters or pets, they had to be supervised, directed, and restrained; they had to be taught discipline in their own interest. "They are only Asiatics," explained Sherard Osborn, a British naval officer who had participated in the capture of Canton in 1857. "Treat them as children; make them do what we know is for their benefit, as well as our own, and all difficulties with China are at an end." Oppression was thus a means of liberation, and harshness really meant kindness. The explorer and novelist Winwood Reade, though trying hard to understand alien societies, concluded that "the great Turkish and Chinese Empires, the lands of Morocco, Abyssinia, and Thibet, will be eventually filled with free, industrious, and educated populations. But those people will never begin to advance until their property is rendered secure, until they enjoy the rights of man; and these they will never obtain except by

vols. (Moscow, 1963–70), 22:300; J. A. Hobson, *Imperialism: A Study* (New York, 1902), pp. 381–83; Wilfred Scawen Blunt, *My Diaries: Being a Personal Narrative of Events, 1888–1914*, 2 vols. (New York, 1921), 1:375–76.

means of European conquest." There was clearly a cultural imperialism that facilitated and justified the political imperialism of the nineteenth century.[22]

Europeans were equally shortsighted in the way they regarded the future of the colonial movement. It seemed to them that they were building for the ages, that the possessions they were acquiring overseas would insure the strength and prosperity of their nation for generations to come. Yet even when the scramble for colonies was in full swing, there were unmistakable signs of growing resistance to the white man's domination in various parts of the world. The defeat of the Italians at Adua in 1896 and of the Russians at Tsushima in 1905—even the costly British victory in the Boer War—indicated that the period of easy conquests was drawing to a close. Less than a century after the last wave of imperialism began, the great colonial empires had disintegrated, leaving behind them a heritage of resentment and bitterness.

What other movement of such evanescence ever created an illusion of such durability? Now it serves only as a reminder of the human capacity for self-deception. The material advantages supposed to result from colonial expansion have been shown to be spurious. Statistics have long since demolished the argument that colonies would provide a rich field for commerce and investment. The trade of France with her colonies was just a little over 10 percent of her total foreign trade in 1894–1903 and just a little over 11 percent in 1904–13. No more than 600 to 800 million dollars out of a total of close to 10 billion dollars invested abroad by the French had gone to the colonies. Germany's trade with her colonies was 48 million dollars or 0.2 percent of total foreign trade in 1894–1903, whereas her expenditures on the colonies were 38 million dollars. In the next decade, trade with the colonies increased 281 percent, but expenditures increased 434 percent, now exceeding the value of the trade. To make matters worse, only about 12 percent of the total foreign holdings of German investors were in the colonies. As for the Italian overseas possessions, they accounted for 0.2 percent of the foreign trade of the mother country in 1894–1903 and 0.8 percent in 1904–13.

For that matter, Great Britain, with the largest and richest of the colonial empires, found a more attractive field for commerce and investment in foreign countries. Her trade with the dominions, protectorates,

22. Bagehot, *Physics and Politics*, pp. 100–101; J. William Whittall, *Frederick the Great on Kingcraft: From the Original MS., with Reminiscences and Turkish Stories* (London, New York, and Bombay, 1901), p. 165; "Race in Legislation and Political Economy," *Anthropological Review* 4 (1866):120; David Clouston, *From the Orcades to Ind* (Edinburgh and London, 1936), p. 21; Sherard Osborn, *The Past and Future of British Relations in China* (Edinburgh and London, 1860), p. 15; Winwood Reade, *The Martyrdom of Man* (London, 1872), p. 504.

and colonies more than tripled in the sixty years preceding the First World War, but so did her trade with the rest of the world. The share of total trade derived from the overseas possessions thus remained almost constant: 26 percent in 1854–63, 25 percent in 1894–1903, and 27 percent in 1904–13. Less than half of the 19 billion dollars of her foreign investments, moreover, were within the empire in 1913. It is clear that political control had little to do with the flow of goods and capital.

There was still less basis for the other material benefits that imperialism was alleged to bring. The great mass of emigrants from Europe preferred a new life under an alien flag in the Americas to their own nation's possessions in Africa or Asia. In 1914 there were only twenty thousand Germans (including officials, soldiers, missionaries, and traders) in all of the colonies, but about sixty thousand were living on the island of Manhattan alone. Of the 13 million Italians who left the mother country between 1881 and 1915, fewer than fifty-six thousand settled in the colonies. Even in the British Isles, almost 70 percent of those who left between 1812 and 1914 went outside the empire. Life in the overseas possessions appealed most to those who could make a career and a living administering them. The observation that the "British Empire is a gigantic system of outdoor relief for the British governing classes," attributed variously to James Mill and John Bright, was not without a measure of truth.

And what about the military security that colonies were supposed to provide by supporting a strong fleet? They did nothing to avert the defeat of Germany in the First World War or of Italy in the Second World War. Nor did they do much to alleviate social tensions and class conflicts. In 1914 disaffection from the established order was as great in the colonial nations as it was in the noncolonial ones. Expansion overseas was thus built on myths and illusions, deceptions and miscalculations.[23]

Yet imperialism did leave an important heritage, a heritage that its proponents had neither sought nor foreseen. It helped create one world, blurring the distinction between East and West, between the white and the colored man, between Europeans, Americans, Africans, and Asians. The most obvious manifestation of this process was the emergence of a world-wide economic system. At the opening of the twentieth century,

23. Clark, *Place in the Sun*, pp. 87–88, 134–35, 153–54, 162, 164–66; Oron J. Hale, *The Great Illusion, 1900–1914* (New York, Evanston, and London, 1971), pp. 6, 9; Jonathan Hughes, *Industrialization and Economic History: Theses and Conjectures* (New York, 1970), p. 190; Gallagher and Robinson, "Imperialism of Free Trade," p. 5; Carlo M. Cipolla, "Four Centuries of Italian Demographic Development," in *Population in History: Essays in Historical Demography*, ed. D. V. Glass and D. E. C. Eversley (London, 1965), p. 586; Mary Evelyn Townsend and Cyrus Henderson Peake, *European Colonial Expansion since 1871* (Chicago, Philadelphia, and New York, 1941), pp. 599–600.

James Bryce spoke of the growing material interdependence of the nations of the earth: "It is hardly too much to say that for economic purposes all mankind is fast becoming one people. . . . Such an event opens a new stage in World-history, a stage whose significance has perhaps been as yet scarcely realized either by the thinker or by the man of action." Brooks Adams had made a similar point in his prophetic *Law of Civilization and Decay*: "Even now factories can be equipped almost as easily in India, Japan, and China, as in Lancashire or Massachusetts, and the products of the cheapest labour can be sold more advantageously in European capitals, than those of Tyre and Alexandria were in Rome under the Antonines."

But more important than the diffusion of European methods of production was the diffusion of European concepts, attitudes, and beliefs. The Hungarian traveler and orientalist Ármin Vámbéry wrote in 1906 that present-day Europe in its restless, bustling activity would take good care not to let the East relapse again into its former indolence. "We forcibly tear its eyes open; we push, jolt, toss, and shake it, and we compel it to exchange its world-worn, hereditary ideas and customs for our modern views of life." Yet this Europeanization of the world also meant that colonial peoples were learning to use the weapons and ideas of their masters for their own liberation. The British historian Charles H. Pearson saw as early as the 1890s what was likely to happen in the twentieth century: "We were struggling among ourselves for supremacy in a world which we thought of as destined to belong to the Aryan races and to the Christian faith; to the letters and arts and charm of social manners which we have inherited from the best times of the past. We shall wake to find ourselves elbowed and hustled, and perhaps even thrust aside by peoples whom we looked down upon as servile, and thought of as bound always to minister to our needs." The enduring legacy of imperialism lay not in the controls and coercions but in the technologies and ideologies that it spread over the earth. Here was its true importance.[24]

24. James Bryce, *The Romanes Lecture, 1902: The Relations of the Advanced and the Backward Races of Mankind* (Oxford, 1902), p. 9; Brooks Adams, *The Law of Civilization and Decay: An Essay on History* (London and New York, 1895), p. 291; Arminius Vámbéry, *Western Culture in Eastern Lands: A Comparison of the Methods Adopted by England and Russia in the Middle East* (London, 1906), p. 2; Charles H. Pearson, *National Life and Character: A Forecast* (London and New York, 1893), p. 85.

16

THE END OF AN ERA

The nineteenth century appears in retrospect as a singularly attractive age. Political tensions and military rivalries notwithstanding, there was still a community of institutions, ideas, and values among the states of Europe that two world wars have now destroyed. In 1914 a man could travel from one end of the Continent to the other without a visa or even a passport, except in Russia and Turkey. There was no need for currency declarations or travelers checks; the universal acceptance of the gold standard meant that the money of any country could be easily exchanged for that of any other. A Londoner deciding on the spur of the moment to leave for Paris, Rome, Berlin, or Vienna could start on his journey an hour later with only his luggage and a handful of bank notes. Goods moved across frontiers almost as easily as people, for despite the spread of protectionism, tariffs were not yet a serious obstacle to commerce. The United Kingdom remained committed to free trade. Although the other governments were gradually increasing their customs duties, there was not much difference between the average British rate of 5.7 percent levied on imports for revenue and the French rate of 8.2 percent or the German rate of 8.4 percent levied for protection. Only in Russia, where the tariff reached 35 percent, did the state impose a real barrier against the importation of goods. Not since the days of the Pax Romana had Europe known such freedom of movement, personal as well as economic.

The traveler in those days, moreover, found an underlying homogeneity of attitudes and interests wherever he went. To begin with, all people who were educated had received roughly the same form of education. They had all read the same philosophers, mastered the same languages, ancient and modern, and puzzled over the same problems in algebra and geometry. There was even a common tongue in which they could all converse, French, used every day by the diplomats, but familiar also to anyone who had attended a lycée, a gymnasium, or a "public school." Men of means and education not only shared the same body of knowledge, but also subscribed to a set of beliefs, attitudes, and loyalties that characterized the dominant classes in all parts of Europe. A Russian officer, a British politician, a French banker, and a German industrialist had more in common with each other than any one of them had with a Russian peasant, a British worker, a French shopkeeper, or a German handicraftsman. For most people the accident of birth still determined the position they held in the community; they generally knew their place and they generally accepted it. The social dissatisfactions resulting from equality of opportunity had not yet destroyed the hierarchical structure of class and status. The tacit acceptance of inherited distinctions in wealth and rank was being undermined by radical new doctrines, to be sure, but so far the established order did not appear to be in serious danger. It would take a major catastrophe to overthrow it.[1]

The nineteenth century, however, was more than an age of order and stability. It was also an age of change and reform that altered Europe more fundamentally than any previous period. When the Napoleonic Wars ended, society was still closer in spirit and structure to the era of monarchical absolutism or even to the Middle Ages than to the world of industrialization and democracy. By the time of the First World War, it had assumed in varying degrees the qualities and characteristics associated with the concept of modernity. In 1815 the basic processes of manufacture were still those of the skilled handicraftsman; by 1914 the techniques of large-scale rationalized production had become dominant, making mass consumption possible for the first time. In 1815 landholding was still largely in the grip of manorialism and even serfdom; by 1914 a system of individualized, mechanized, and scientific agriculture had forever ended the threat of famine. In 1815 the vast majority of Europeans still lived on the land; by 1914 urbanization had led to an internal migration from country to city that was transforming the habits and loyalties of the masses. In 1815 the established pattern of demographic development in Europe—a stable balance between natality and mortality—was just beginning to shift; by 1914 that stability had given way to exuberant growth, more than doubling the number of inhabitants.

These far-reaching changes in the way people lived and worked led to the emergence of a different relationship between the citizen and the community. The standard of living rose to a higher level than ever before, providing new wealth for the propertied and even modest comfort for many of the propertyless. Literacy started to increase, enabling the lower classes to overcome the ignorance and submissiveness that had kept them in subjugation throughout history. The spread of the franchise provided the masses with the opportunity, at least in theory, to participate in the political decisions affecting their lives. And this in turn meant that the functions of government began to alter, their emphasis shifting from the maintenance of security at home and abroad to the economic and social welfare of the individual. These changes seem so familiar now that it is

1. A. J. P. Taylor, *The Struggle for Mastery in Europe, 1848–1918* (Oxford, 1954), p. 255; Gerhard Masur, *Prophets of Yesterday: Studies in European Culture, 1890–1914* (London, 1963), p. 35.

easy to forget how recent they are. They all derive directly or indirectly from the process of economic rationalization, which created the material conditions for a society committed to the well-being of its citizens. The most significant result of the new methods of production, however, was not a higher level of affluence but a different set of beliefs, values, assumptions, and attitudes concerning man and the community. It is primarily in this sense that the nineteenth century can be considered a period of revolutionary change.

Out of affluence emerged a new concern for abused and oppressed minorities. Humaneness and liberality are a function of abundance and security. Despite a popular myth that the experience of suffering produces compassion for sufferers or that knowledge of oppression leads to sympathy with the oppressed, when men live in want, their dominant interest is self-preservation. It is when they are comfortable that they are most likely to consider the needs of others. That the governments of Europe began to be increasingly concerned for the welfare of the lower classes after 1815 is not surprising; they were motivated at least in part by fear of class conflict and revolution. Their decision to emancipate religious, ethnic, and racial minorities, on the other hand, reflects a new spirit of benevolence arising out of the material progress of the nineteenth century.

Take the case of the Jews in Europe. There had been defenders of the principle of toleration as early as the period of the religious wars between Protestants and Catholics. The philosophes of the Enlightenment, moreover, had opposed discrimination against dissenters, condemning it as a manifestation of the bigotry of organized religion. But princes and statesmen had been slow to respond to their arguments. When they did remove some of the disabilities imposed on nonconformists, it was generally because of expediency rather than principle. Until the nineteenth century, it was still taken for granted that those who did not share the religious convictions of the majority could not share its civic aspirations. Only after 1815 did Catholics in Protestant countries, Protestants in Catholic countries, and Jews in both begin to achieve legal equality. In France, to be sure, Jewish emancipation had been introduced as early as 1791, but elsewhere it came much later: 1814 in the Netherlands, 1830 in Belgium, 1845 in Norway, 1848 in Sweden, 1849 in Denmark, 1858 in England, 1864 in Portugal, 1867 in Austria and Hungary, 1868 in Spain, 1869 in the North German Confederation, 1870 in Italy, and 1874 in Switzerland. There were admittedly limits to the toleration accorded the Jews. Generally speaking, the intensity of anti-Semitism remained related to their proportion of the population: 0.2 percent in England around 1880, 0.2 in France, 1.2 in Germany, 3.3 in Russia, 4.0 in Rumania, and 7.2 in Austria. Yet in the light of the previous history of the Jews, the progress achieved during the nineteenth century seemed to presage the coming of an age free of all religious animosity.[2]

A new sympathy for scorned minorities appeared also in the suppression first of the slave trade and then of slaveholding. Before the French Revolution, when serfdom was still common in Europe, there had been general acceptance of slavery in the colonies. After all, why should the black man in Jamaica or Martinique have been treated better than the white man in Prussia or Russia? The nineteenth century made possible the abolition of slavery as an institution by reducing the economic need for a servile labor force. First came the prohibition of the slave trade, imposed by Denmark in 1792, England in 1807, Sweden in 1813, the Netherlands in 1814, France in 1818, Spain in 1820, and Portugal in 1830. The British took the lead in this movement, paying close to 2 million dollars to the Spaniards and 1.5 million to the Portuguese as compensation, patrolling the Atlantic to prevent smuggling, and freeing between 1815 and 1846 some 117,000 slaves who had been intercepted on the high seas.

The abolition of slavery itself proved to be a more difficult process. Despite a succession of measures and half measures adopted by France during the Revolution, the first effective emancipation was introduced in the British colonies in 1833, followed by the French colonies in 1848, the Portuguese colonies in 1858, India in the years after 1858, the Dutch East Indies between 1859 and 1869, the Dutch Antilles and Guiana in 1862, and the Spanish colonies, primarily Cuba, in 1870. The abolition of slavery thus came at about the same time as the abolition of serfdom, for essentially the same reasons.[3]

In the emancipation of religious minorities, the nineteenth century appears at its best, generous to those whose claim to freedom rested not on force but on justice. The optimism of the age led men to behave more

2. Georges Weill, *L'evéil des nationalités et le mouvement libéral (1815–1848)* (Paris, 1930), pp. 197–98; Carlton J. Hayes, *A Generation of Materialism, 1871–1900* (New York and London, 1941), p. 84; Émile Chénon, "L'église et les cultes de 1846 à 1870," in *Histoire générale de IVe siècle à nos jours*, ed. Ernest Lavisse and Alfred Rambaud, 12 vols. (Paris, 1893–1901), 11:994–95; idem, "L'église et les cultes de 1870 à nos jours," in ibid., 12:554; Pierre Benaerts, Henri Hauser, Fernand L'Huillier, and Jean Maurain, *Nationalité et nationalisme (1860–1878)*, new ed. (Paris, 1968), pp. 704–6; Erich Keyser, *Bevölkerungsgeschichte Deutschlands*, 2d ed. (Leipzig, 1941), p. 442; B. R. Mitchell, *European Historical Statistics, 1750–1970* (London and Basingstoke, 1975), pp. 19–20, 23, 26.

3. Parker Thomas Moon, *Imperialism and World Politics* (New York, 1926), pp. 78–79; Llewellyn Woodward, *The Age of Reform, 1815–1870*, 2d ed. (Oxford, 1962), p. 370; F. S. L. Lyons, *Internationalism in Europe, 1815–1914* (Leyden, 1963), pp. 291–92; Robert C. Binkley, *Realism and Nationalism, 1852–1871* (New York and London, 1935), p. 89; Albert Métin, "Les royaumes de Belgique et des Pays-Bas depuis 1870," in *Histoire générale*, ed. Lavisse and Rambaud, 12:420.

humanely toward those too weak to defend themselves, not only Jews and Negroes but the orphaned, the aged, the sick, the crippled, the insane, and the criminal. The dream of the thinkers of the Enlightenment seemed on the point of realization: a world free of oppression, exploitation, bigotry, and cruelty. The achievements of the nineteenth century must not be exaggerated, to be sure. It is clear in retrospect that the appearance of progress was greater than its reality. Behind the facade of fundamental reform, oligarchies old and new continued to exercise domination. Many of the traditional inequalities, oppressions, and injustices were only mitigated; some continued unabated. The transformation taking place was not as far-reaching as it appeared. But that is true of all political and social innovation; changes in the way people live and behave are never as drastic as those who experience them think. The point is that the illusion of rapid progress reflected the fact of gradual progress. This is the key to an understanding of the nineteenth century. Its reach exceeded its grasp, but it bettered the way of life in Europe to a greater extent than any previous age.

The mood of confidence and liberality that it bred came to an end with the First World War. This does not mean that the promise of the nineteenth century would have been fully realized if there had been no Sarajevo. There were signs long before 1914 that the era of Europe's domination of the world was drawing to a close. The rising political consciousness among colonial peoples, the increasing rigidity in the structure of the economy, the spreading social dissatisfaction of the lower classes, the rapid industrialization of overseas countries like America and Japan—all suggested that the heroic age of European civilization could not go on much longer. But if it had not been for the First World War, the process of decline would have been slow and gradual. The nations of the Continent might have had time to adjust to the loss of mastery; they might have been able to adapt to an era of diminishing opportunities. What the outbreak of hostilities did was to accelerate the tempo of a deterioration that was inevitable, but that under conditions of peace would have been endurable. As it turned out, the hopefulness fostered by a hundred years of uninterrupted progress was destroyed by a military conflict; out of it a different Europe emerged. What distinguished 1918 from 1914 was a new, desperate view of life.

The First World War was thus a boundary marker between two distinct ages, separating one category of historical experience from another. Yet its origins are still far from clear. The diplomatic documents, which have been studied with such meticulous care, tell what happened, but they do not tell whether it had to happen. Were the people who stumbled into war—statesmen, soldiers, intellectuals, businessmen, professionals, workers, peasants—merely caught up in a fortuitous combination of events that happened to lead to the outbreak of hostilities? Or were they responding in a dim, confused way to larger forces and ideas that they themselves did not fully grasp? The temptation to accept the latter interpretation is irresistible. For how could an effect of such vast magnitude have followed from such a minor cause as the Russian decision to order general rather than partial mobilization or the German inability to guess correctly what England would do in the event of an attack on France? We are forced to look for motivations greater than those revealed by the archives. There must have been a pattern of ideas, feelings, attitudes, and beliefs—what James Joll has called the "unspoken assumptions"—that led those responsible for diplomatic decisions to a world conflict. An examination of this pattern is indispensable for an understanding of the outbreak of the First World War.[4]

It is clear, to begin with, that many people of education and means had become disenchanted with mass civilization, with what they perceived as materialism stifling the nobler aspirations of man. In other words, even before the political and economic foundations of the nineteenth century crumbled, there was an intellectual rebellion against its ideals and purposes. Was this rebellion an expression of the malaise of a community experiencing sudden change in the relationship of interests and classes? Was it a reaction against the need to grapple with bewildering economic and social questions? Did it reflect the erosion of a sense of collective confidence? In any case, there is unmistakable evidence of a growing disillusionment with the goals and accomplishments of modern society.

In 1912, in his voluminous history of European thought, John Theodore Merz declared that "the creative forces of the human soul, such as manifest themselves in poetry, art, and religion . . . appear to have receded somewhat into the background, whilst, at the same time, much is expected of them." He added consolingly that "it would appear as if, at the end of the nineteenth century, philosophy was paving the way for a fuller and more original display" of the creativity of mind and spirit. "Wherever the vital forces in a society, or in an age, have not been absolutely exhausted—and I can find no sign of this in the present civilisation of Western Europe—such periods, where the higher creative and spiritual powers seem to be temporarily in abeyance, have always, sooner or later, been followed by periods of greater vigour and productiveness." In society as well as nature, all processes seem to exhaust themselves in the course of time; they call forth countermovements that gain force, as it were, through reaction and contrast. "This has, in modern times, been

4. James Joll, 1914: The Unspoken Assumptions (London, 1968), pp. 13–14.

abundantly evident in the rapidly succeeding phases of modern history."
Merz still groped for a reason to hope amid the gathering intellectual
gloom of the prewar years.

More pessimistic was the assessment by Stanley Leathes, which appeared at about the same time in the concluding volume of *The Cambridge Modern History*. "The age has been prosaic and unromantic," he
wrote. "The enthusiasm for the mechanical and scientific triumphs of the
early Victorian period has somewhat faded; the belief in constitutional
government and universal education as a remedy for all political and
social evils has been shaken; the blots on our economic and moral order
have been relentlessly drawn to light; self-complacency is no longer fashionable; it is more popular to decry than to praise the world in which we
live. The consolations of religion have for the moment lost their efficacy
in large sections of the European population." The zeal of the young and
ardent, he went on, is thrown into schemes of social regeneration, some
of them progressive and creative, others violent and destructive. All of
them alike, however, are materialistic in their aims. "Their kingdom is of
this world; they seek for no spiritual compensations, they admit no spiritual rapture; their professors represent all grades between the extreme of
self-devotion and the culmination of hate, envy, and greed." The age
simply lacked the saving grace of idealism.[5]

The way in which people reacted to what they perceived to be the
soullessness of their society varied. Some turned to literary or esthetic
movements that sought in private emotion a refuge from social complexity; they became symbolists, decadents, expressionists, or fauvists.
Others hoped to restore to man, corrupted by comfort and success, a
sense of collective purpose by some great program of reform—conservative, democratic, socialist, or anarchist. And then there were those who
saw in war a grand ennobling enterprise in which the individual was
forced to subordinate his selfish interests to the good of the whole. In a
national struggle for existence, the sickly intellectuality of a tired civilization would give way to an instinctive acceptance of life in the raw.
Combat demanded a single-minded commitment to survival that dissolved the petty preoccupations of peacetime. It was a purifying experience. The novelist, poet, and dramatist Filippo Tommaso Marinetti, for
example, voiced a yearning for the simple directness of armed force in his
"manifesto of futurism" in 1909: "We want to glorify war—the only
hygiene of the world—militarism, patriotism, the destructive action of
the anarchists, beautiful Ideas which kill, and contempt for woman."

5. John Theodore Merz, *A History of European Thought in the Nineteenth Century*, 4
vols. (Edinburgh and London, 1896–1914), 4:88–89; Stanley Leathes, "Modern Europe,"
in *The Cambridge Modern History*, ed. A. W. Ward, G. W. Prothero, and Stanley Leathes,
14 vols. (Cambridge and New York, 1902–12), 12:15.

This irrational aggressiveness challenged the harmonizing rationality of the nineteenth century.[6]

The intellectuals who saw in war an escape from materialism found support among the interpreters of natural science to whom the struggle for existence in the animal kingdom revealed how the fittest could survive in human society. They regarded military conflict as an ordeal out of which nations emerged hardened and vindicated. The mathematician and biologist Karl Pearson expressed this belief during the Boer War in a lecture implicitly justifying the struggle in Africa as the will of Providence: "History shows me one way, and one way only, in which a high state of civilization has been produced, namely, the struggle of race with race, and the survival of the physically and mentally fitter race. . . . This dependence of progress on the survival of the fitter race, terribly black as it may seem to some of you, gives the struggle for existence its redeeming features; it is the fiery crucible out of which comes the finer metal."

We may hope for a time when the sword shall be turned into the ploughshare, he continued, when American and German and English traders shall no longer compete in the markets of the world for their raw material and for their food supply, when the white man and the dark shall share the soil between them, and each till it as he pleases. "But, believe me, when that day comes, mankind will no longer progress." For the advance of humanity depends on the victory of the physically and mentally better organized. "The path of progress is strewn with the wreck of nations; traces are everywhere to be seen of the hecatombs of inferior races, and of victims who found not the narrow way to the greater perfection." These dead peoples are the stepping-stones on which mankind has risen to the higher intellectual and deeper emotional life of today.[7]

Ideas such as these had a profound influence in the years before 1914. They helped shape the popular attitude that a test of strength among nations was natural and perhaps desirable. This does not mean that the millions who greeted the coming of war with enthusiasm had studied the writings of the apologists of armed violence. But men who had never read Pearson or even heard of futurism had been exposed to a popularized version of their teachings in classrooms, newspapers, magazines, lectures, songs, and everyday conversations. The cult of force had won converts in all the countries of Europe. A French observer around the turn of the century commented on its wide acceptance in Great Britain, for example. "The divine mission, the special duties of a people, the right

6. Filippo Tommaso Marinetti, "Le Futurisme," Le Figaro (Paris), 20 February 1909, p. 1.

7. Karl Pearson, National Life from the Standpoint of Science: An Address Delivered at Newcastle, November 19, 1900 (London, 1901), pp. 19, 24, 61–62.

of the Deed and of Force—at first we are offended by such formulas," he wrote. "But when we discover how natural these points of view are in this country, by what influences of the system of education and of the environment also, no doubt, by what spontaneous development these ideas are formed and implanted in each person, are absorbed into the permanent substance of each mind so completely that it is no longer conscious of them, when we understand with what fervor everyone here considers them binding and justified by Religion, then we have to say to ourselves that we are indeed in the presence of a veritable moral code." This "spontaneous development," this "moral code" contributed significantly to the coming of the First World War.[8]

Diplomats could not remain immune to the widespread idea that force in international relations served the higher purposes of Providence. Of course, they had always recognized armed might as the ultimate arbiter of disputes among governments. The likelihood of its use increased in the opening years of the twentieth century, however, primarily as a result of tension between the opposing alliance systems but partly in response to the growing bellicosity of public opinion. In the spring of 1914, Gottlieb von Jagow, the German foreign minister, suggested to the French ambassador that Germany, France, and England agree on a program to partition central Africa without regard for the claims of other countries. "Everything indicates that the great nations will be the only ones capable of withstanding world competition," he explained, "and in the future the small ones must either disappear or become their satellites." This was not an uncommon view in the chancelleries of Europe. Lord Milner, politician, financial expert, and British proconsul in South Africa, left among his papers a "credo" stating that countries, like individuals, can advance only through struggle: "A Nationalist . . . believes that this is the law of human progress, that the competition between nations, each seeking its maximum development, is the Divine Order of the world, the law of Life and Progress." Men who expressed such views in their private utterances were bound to be influenced by them in their public actions.

Is it too much, then, to suggest that a belief in competitiveness as the law of life contributed to the rising tension among the Great Powers? The point is hard to prove because throughout history states have based their conduct toward one another on self-interest. But the rivalry between them, the distrust, pugnacity, and fear, grew sharply after the opening of the twentieth century. In 1904 Friedrich von Holstein, a highly influential official in the German foreign office, expressed this new belligerency in his memorandum concerning French designs in North Africa: "The tasks of a Great Power include not only the protection of its territorial boundaries, but also the protection of its just interests lying beyond those

8. André Chevrillon, *Études anglaises* (Paris, 1901), pp. 322–23.

boundaries. . . . Germany should object to the proposed annexation of Morocco by France not only for material reasons, but even more in order to maintain her prestige." As Europe lurched from crisis to crisis, from the clash over Morocco in 1905 to the clash over Bosnia-Herzegovina in 1908, from the new clash over Morocco in 1911 to the new clash over the Balkans in 1912, a basic assumption of the statesmen was that the security of one country could only be maintained through the insecurity of another, that in the international struggle for existence only the strong could prevail.[9]

To the generals the idea that the survival of the fittest is the dominant principle of relations among governments was even more self-evident. Taught that national greatness could be achieved only by armed might, they eagerly embraced the argument that the civilized world is like the primitive jungle, in a state of perpetual conflict, permanently involved in a war of all against all, devouring or being devoured. The teachings of Darwinism merely expressed more precisely what they had always assumed. In 1912 Friedrich von Bernhardi, a general in the German army, described military conflict as the highest manifestation of a universal vital force:

> Struggle is therefore a general law of nature, and the instinct of self-preservation which leads to struggle is altogether justified as a natural condition of all life. "To be a man is to be a fighter." To surrender, on the other hand, is a denial of life, whether in the existence of the individual or in the life of states, which are personifications of peoples. To assert one's own independent existence is the first and supreme law. Only by self-assertion is the state able to maintain for its citizens the conditions of life and insure for them the legal protection which each of them can justly demand of it. This duty of self-assertion, however, is by no means fulfilled by merely repelling hostile attacks. It includes the obligation to insure for the whole body of the people which the state embraces the possibility of life and development. . . . From this standpoint, we must also regard war, when it is waged for the highest and most precious values of a nation, as a moral necessity. In view of the nature of human existence, it is political idealism which calls for war, while materialism rejects it, at least in theory.[10]

9. *Documents diplomatiques français (1871–1914)*, 3d ser., 11 vols. (Paris, 1929–36), 10:168; *Times* (London), 27 July 1925, p. 13; *Die grosse Politik der europäischen Kabinette, 1871–1914: Sammlung der diplomatischen Akten des Auswärtigen Amtes*, ed. Johannes Lepsius, Albrecht Mendelssohn Bartholdy, and Friedrich Thimme, 40 vols. (Berlin, 1922–27), 20:208.

10. Friedrich von Bernhardi, *Deutschland und der nächste Krieg* (Stuttgart and Berlin, 1912), pp. 14, 19–20.

Not even the tragedy of the First World War could convince the generals that armed struggle was anything other than the expression of a fundamental law of nature. Franz Conrad von Hötzendorf, chief of staff of the Austro-Hungarian army in 1906–11 and 1912–17, maintains in his memoirs that the events that led to war were only manifestations of the struggle for existence, "the driving force in all things." Man does not stand outside nature; he too is subject to her laws and powerless against her rule. This rule, however, includes struggle, which nature inexorably imposes on him. Mankind will never become a congenial, peaceable flock. "Struggle is as old as humanity and will remain as old as humanity!" Philanthropic religions, moral teachings, and philosophic doctrines may now and then mitigate man's struggle for existence in its crudest form, but they will never succeed in eliminating it as the driving principle of his actions. "The catastrophe of the World War," Conrad concludes, "occurred inevitably and irresistibly in accordance with this great principle, as a result of the creative forces in the life of states and nations. It was like a thunderstorm which is driven by the constraint of nature to discharge its energy." As for the millions of casualties for which it was responsible, man must be ready to die in defense of his vital interests.

Since conflict among states was inevitable, the generals were always appealing for larger appropriations for national security. Each advance in military technology, each crisis in diplomatic relations, each shift in the political balance was followed by warnings of disaster unless there was an increase in armaments. Complaints could be heard even in Great Britain about the insatiable appetite of the military men for troops and supplies. "No lesson seems to be so deeply inculcated by the experience of life as that you never should trust experts," wrote Lord Salisbury. "If you believe the doctors, nothing is wholesome: if you believe the theologians, nothing is innocent: if you believe the soldiers, nothing is safe." This does not mean that the arms race was responsible for the outbreak of war in 1914. It was a symptom, not a cause. But its intensity is a measure of the insecurity and aggressiveness that characterized the diplomacy of the Great Powers. It reflected an underlying conviction that armed struggle was a law of nature, implacable yet providential, by which mankind was driven to higher achievement.[11]

Consider the sharp increase in expenditures for the military establishment on the eve of hostilities. The democratic states were as eager as the conservative ones to approve the requests of their generals for more manpower and money. In the spring of 1914, the Russian Duma, though re-

11. Franz Conrad von Hötzendorf, *Aus meiner Dienstzeit, 1906–1918*, 5 vols. (Vienna, Leipzig, and Munich, 1921–25), 4:128–29; Gwendolen Cecil, *Life of Robert, Marquis of Salisbury*, 4 vols. (London, 1921–32), 2:153.

luctant to use control over the budget to extend its own authority, voted enthusiastically for an army bill totaling 412 million dollars after a secret conversation between the prime minister and the parliamentary leaders. In 1913 the German Reichstag, dominated by the parties of the center and the left, approved a law enlarging the armed forces by close to 150,000 men. Indeed, the National Liberals inquired whether the general staff was really satisfied with the bill as presented by the war minister. They themselves thought that it did not go far enough. In France the militant republicans, who gained a majority in the Chamber of Deputies after the Dreyfus affair, supported the army with almost as much zeal as the conservative antirepublicans had displayed. Between 1905 and 1914 they appropriated a total of 325 million dollars for national defense, only 2 percent less than the war ministry had asked. And in 1913 they extended the term of military service from two to three years; as a result, 2.1 percent of the population was enlisted in the armed forces compared to 1.2 percent in Germany.

The intensity of the arms race can be measured by changes in the size and cost of the combined military establishments of the Great Powers of Europe: England, France, Germany, Italy, Austria-Hungary, and Russia. During the period 1870–80, Quincy Wright has estimated, the personnel of their armed forces grew by 59,000 men and their expenditures by 178 million dollars; in 1880–90, the increases were 184,000 men and 129 million dollars; in 1890–1900, 949,000 men and 242 million dollars; in 1900–1910, 349,000 men and 411 million dollars; and in 1910–14, 503,000 men and 559 million dollars. In these last four years, the rise in military appropriations exceeded that of any preceding decade. According to the calculations of the London *Economist*, the defense expenditures of all the states of Europe, large and small, increased 72 percent between 1858 and 1883, from 462 million to 793 million dollars; 83 percent between 1883 and 1908, from 793 million to 1,455 million dollars; and 63 percent between 1908 and 1913, from 1,455 million to 2,365 million dollars. Thus, in the last five years before the First World War, the rise in the cost of armaments was much larger absolutely and not much smaller relatively than during the two preceding periods of twenty-five years each. An expanding economy could still support this burden of military preparedness, but the growing costliness and sophistication of weapons meant that the hostilities of the future would be far more devastating than any that Europe had previously experienced.[12]

The destructiveness of mechanized warfare was intensified by strate-

---

12. Alfred Vagts, *A History of Militarism: Civilian and Military*, rev. ed. (New York, 1959), pp. 217, 333; Quincy Wright, *A Study of War*, 2 vols. (Chicago, 1942), 1:670–71; Taylor, *Struggle for Mastery*, pp. xxvii–xxviii; P. Jacobsen, "Armaments Expenditure of the World," *Economist*, 19 October 1929, Armaments Supplement, p. 3.

gies and tactics derived to a large extent from the experience of the preindustrial age. Although technological progress was multiplying the effectiveness of armaments, the generals were making their plans as if they were about to fight once again at Rossbach or Austerlitz. The lessons of the American Civil War or even the Crimean War were generally dismissed as applicable only to conditions unlikely to occur in the heartland of the Continent. On the vast plain extending from the English Channel to the Vistula, the military men assumed, an armed conflict would be decided, now as before, by the courage, determination, and self-sacrifice of the mass attack. A charge against the enemy's front remained the best way to confuse and demoralize him.

In his lectures at the École supérieure de guerre, Ferdinand Foch voiced the accepted view of the army leaders of Europe concerning military combat. Victory equals will power, he taught. Victory equals moral superiority on the part of the conqueror and moral dejection on the part of the conquered. Victory always goes to those who most deserve it. "*A battle won is a battle in which one will not concede that he is beaten.*" The will to conquer is therefore the first condition of victory, the first duty of every soldier; it is the "supreme resolve which those in command have to instill in the soldier's soul, when the occasion arises." The effect of such doctrines became abundantly clear to the hundreds of thousands of men who were mowed down by machine-gun and artillery fire in futile frontal attacks during August and September 1914.[13]

To many observers, however, even to those who recognized that the result would be a catastrophe, the outbreak of war was only a matter of time. The diplomatic objectives of the Great Powers seemed so irreconcilable, their economic rivalries so bitter, their military preparations so intense, their emotional hostilities so irrational that it was hard to believe that the statesmen could maintain the equilibrium of Europe much longer. Edward Mandell House, the friend and adviser of Woodrow Wilson, wrote to the president from Berlin on 29 May 1914 that the Old World was being driven to disaster by forces which it could not control: "The situation is extraordinary. It is jingoism run stark mad. Unless some one acting for you can bring about an understanding, there is some day to be an awful cataclysm. No one in Europe can do it. There is too much hatred, too many jealousies." Only the New World, with its unexhausted moral strength, might still prevent the coming of a devastating conflict. "It is an absorbing problem and one of tremendous consequence. I wish it might be solved and to the everlasting glory of your administration and

13. Ferdinand Foch, *Des principes de la guerre: Conférences faites a l'École supérieure de guerre* (Paris and Nancy, 1903), pp. 36–37; idem, *De la conduite de la guerre: La manoeuvre pour la bataille* (Paris and Nancy, 1904), p. 190.

our American civilization." Two months later, hostilities broke out and the nineteenth century came to an end. The "absorbing problem" remained unsolved.[14]

Still, it would be a mistake, though a tempting one, to assume that the coming of the war was a historic inevitability, the product of irresistible forces acting over a long period of time. In fact, it was the result not of a logical but of an illogical process; it arose not out of rational calculations but out of irrational emotions. The nations of Europe, despite their disputes over territory and status, had more to gain by cooperation than conflict. Their economic interests and social structures were to a large extent interconnected; their dominant classes and ruling elites were on the whole similar; their moral values and ethical standards were in all essential respects the same. Europe, in other words, was a homogeneous civilization in which a grave injury to any part was bound to have a serious effect on the whole. A recognition of this interdependence was thus a powerful force for peace.

The men responsible for the conduct of public affairs often revealed that they were aware of what effect a major war was likely to have. The same diplomats and politicians who at times described the struggle for existence as the law of life warned at other times against the disastrous consequences of a military conflict. What concerned them most was not the loss of life but the disruption of the economy and the spread of social unrest. They were haunted by the specter of revolution. The increasing militancy of labor—demonstrations, strikes, riots, and the growth of radicalism—convinced many of them that an armed struggle, particularly defeat in an armed struggle, could lead to mass uprisings. Was that not what happened in Russia after the war against Japan? And was that not likely to happen again on an even larger scale in the event of another war? It was a disturbing thought.

Fear of the social consequences of a military struggle appears repeatedly in the statements of political leaders on the eve of the war. In February 1914, for example, P. N. Durnovo, former minister of the interior, warned Czar Nicholas II that in the event of hostilities between Russia and Germany, a revolution would inevitably break out in the defeated country and spread to the country of the victor. The peasant dreams of obtaining a share of someone else's land, he wrote; the worker wants to seize the capital and the profit of the manufacturer. If Russia wins the next war, it will be possible to suppress the socialist movement. But if she loses, a revolution "in its most extreme form" is bound to occur because the government will be blamed for the disaster. Radical

14. *The Papers of Woodrow Wilson*, ed. Arthur S. Link, 35 vols. to date (Princeton, 1966–), 30:109.

slogans calling for a redistribution of the land and the division of all property will arouse the masses. The defeated army, having lost its most dependable men, having been infected by the desire of the rural population for a larger share of the land, will be too demoralized to defend law and order. "Russia will be flung into hopeless anarchy, the issue of which cannot be foreseen."

Even in England, where the political system was much more stable than in Russia, there was apprehension that the outbreak of hostilities might lead to a failure of the economy and the spread of social unrest. During the July crisis of 1914, Sir Edward Grey cautioned the Austrians that "a war would be accompanied or followed by a complete collapse of European credit and industry. In these days, in great industrial States, this would mean a state of things worse than that of 1848, and, irrespective of who were victors in the war, many things might be completely swept away." John Morley, his colleague in the cabinet and lord president of the council, said the same thing at the same time in almost the same words: "In the present temper of labour . . . this tremendous dislocation of industrial life must be fraught with public danger. The atmosphere of war cannot be friendly to order, in a democratic system that is verging on the humour of '48." As war approached, the thoughts of many statesmen turned uneasily to the great revolutionary uprising of the nineteenth century.[15]

In other words, a balance of fear helped maintain the peace of Europe, fear not only of the military and political results of a major conflict but of its economic and social effects. At the height of the second Moroccan crisis in the fall of 1911, Paul Cambon, the French ambassador in London, wrote that "for the most part, no one in Europe wants war, and they will look for any pretext in order to avoid it." The conclusion of a Franco-German agreement two months later bore out his prediction. King Edward VII of England, who could be surprisingly perceptive whenever he interrupted his pursuit of frivolity, summarized the situation aptly at the time of the diplomatic clash over the Austrian annexation of Bosnia-Herzegovina in 1908: "We are certainly living in critical times . . . but yet I hope that peace may be maintained—but only because Europe is *afraid* to go to war." Fear was in fact more effective than principle in preserving stability in international relations.[16]

15. *Documents of Russian History, 1914–1917*, ed. Frank Alfred Golder (New York and London, 1927), pp. 19–22; *British Documents on the Origins of the War, 1898–1914*, ed. G. P. Gooch and Harold Temperley, 11 vols. (London, 1926–38), 11:70; John Morley, *Memorandum on Resignation, August 1914* (London, 1928), pp. 5–6.

16. *Documents diplomatiques français (1871–1914)*, 2d ser., 14 vols. (Paris, 1930–55), 14:362; Philip Magnus, *King Edward the Seventh* (London, 1964), p. 417.

The businessmen of Europe were as apprehensive of war as the states-men. They too had contacts and connections that the outbreak of hostili-ties would disrupt. Some writers, before and after 1914, have argued that competition among the industrialists and financiers of the Great Powers was driving their governments to war. Yet it is clear that the economy was so integrated that the advantages of cooperation far outweighed those of conflict. For example, the two most bitter competitors in the export trade, England and Germany, were also among each other's best customers; any new markets gained by an armed struggle between them would be more than offset by the loss of old ones. Most businessmen therefore preferred to resolve economic differences by the peaceful de-limitation of territories and revenues.

Walther Rathenau, a leader of the German electrical industry, wrote in 1911 that it was difficult but by no means impossible to find ways of mitigating warlike tension by a process of "apportionment," thereby keeping it within tolerable bounds. "In this sense the concept of dis-armament is no empty utopia, but a modern and useful idea of decided importance." Even more illuminating is Morley's account of the report that David Lloyd George, at that time chancellor of the exchequer, pre-sented to the British cabinet on the eve of the war: "He had been con-sulting the Governor and Deputy Governor of the Bank of England, other men of light and leading in the City, also cotton men, and steel and coal men, etc., in the North of England, in Glasgow, etc., and they were all *aghast* at the bare idea of our plunging into the European conflict; how it would break down the whole system of credit with London as its centre, how it would cut up commerce and manufacture—they told him—how it would hit labour and wages and prices, and, when the winter came, would inevitably produce violence and tumult."

Far from encouraging their governments to use armed force, the busi-nessmen advocated restraint and accommodation. Herbert Feis, who had carefully studied the operations of the great banking houses of Europe in the prewar years, concluded that they sometimes provoked international hostility, but their interests generally disposed them toward peaceful ar-rangements. For them a war between the Great Powers was sure to sever important connections, harm many of their clients, decrease the value of some of the securities they had sold, and bring unpredictable dangers outweighing any immediate gains from domestic financing. Thus the leading firms were usually inclined to cooperate and settle whenever the situation demanded and public opinion sanctioned such a policy. "When the outcome of rivalry became obviously menacing as in the financing of Turkey, the Balkans, and China, important houses proved themselves capable of compromise. In times of crisis their weight was usually behind peaceful statesmanship. They could and sometimes did lift themselves above the clamor of national feeling." The historical evidence clearly supports this summary.[17]

Diplomats were even less willing than industrialists and financiers to risk war over economic differences. There had been times, to be sure, when they had intervened with armed force to collect unpaid debts or acquire lucrative markets, but they became progressively more reluctant to embark on foreign adventures for the sake of trade and investment. The business community, they came to feel, should learn to stand on its own two feet. Even England, which had in the past been so assiduous in promoting commerce and finance, began to favor a hands-off policy. Lord Salisbury in 1897 urged the members of the Association of Chambers of Commerce of the United Kingdom "to abandon this state of fear and to believe that which all past history teaches us—that, left alone, British industry, British enterprise, British resource is competent, and more than competent, to beat down every rivalry, under any circumstances, in any part of the globe, that might arise." His speech was greeted with cheers.

In 1914 Sir Edward Grey, speaking in Parliament, made it clearer still that the government intended to follow a course of nonintervention: "British financiers run their own business quite independent of politics, and, if we attempt to interfere, they naturally consider that we come under some obligation. If they do some particular thing, either in granting or withholding a loan, to oblige the Foreign Office, then, of course, we come under some obligation, and I do not think that is a desirable system." It is much better that the ministers should leave the banks to deal with questions of credit, he continued. There may be some cases in which loans have a political character and in which financiers come to the government to ask whether there is any objection to them. "But, generally speaking, . . . these are things in which the Foreign Office do not interfere." It was a significant departure from the policy of Peel or Palmerston.[18]

Opposition to force in international relations was increasing, moreover, among millions of people who held no position in government or business but who were convinced that a military struggle would destroy the standard of living that they had worked so hard to attain. Never had the peace movement been as strong as just before the First World War. In

17. Walther Rathenau, *Gesammelte Schriften*, 6 vols. (Berlin, 1925–29), 1:179; Morley, *Memorandum on Resignation*, p. 5; Herbert Feis, *Europe, the World's Banker, 1870–1914: An Account of European Foreign Investment and the Connection of World Finance with Diplomacy before the War* (New Haven, 1930), p. 468.

18. *Times* (London), 11 March 1897, p. 7; Great Britain, *Parliamentary Debates* (Commons), 5th ser. (1909–), 44:1448–49.

the past armed conflict had been accepted as a fact of life. Man was by nature an aggressive animal; rulers and statesmen were ambitious and pugnacious. That is how it had always been, how it would always be. In the course of the nineteenth century, however, the attitude toward war began to change. The belief emerged that hostility was not or at least did not have to be the natural condition of relations among states. Men could learn to live in harmony. Indeed, they must learn to do so if they hoped to go on enjoying the advantages that economic rationalization was making possible. Peace, not war, had become essential for survival. This view was propagated by many reformers, publicists, and organizations, which argued that the choice before society was cooperation or destruction.

The young British journalist Norman Angell, for example, whose book *The Great Illusion* was translated into all the major languages and read by countless thousands in every country, conceded that struggle is the law of survival, in human society as in the animal kingdom. But it is the struggle of man with the universe, not man with man. Dog does not eat dog. Even tigers do not live on one another; they live on their prey. The earth is man's prey. The struggle of man is the struggle of the organism, human society, in its adaptation to its environment, the world—not the struggle between different parts of the same organism. Will we, he asked, in blind obedience to primitive instincts and old prejudices, in submission to familiar catchwords and the indolence that makes a revision of familiar ideas unpleasant, continue to fight wars for political and economic reasons long after we have recognized how futile it is to fight them for religious reasons? Will we continue to struggle, as so many others had struggled during the first twelve hundred years of Christendom, spilling oceans of blood and wasting mountains of treasure, to achieve what is at bottom a logical absurdity, to accomplish something that can avail us nothing when accomplished and that, if it could avail us anything, would condemn the nations of the world to endless bloodshed and to the lasting defeat of all those aims that men, in their sober hours, know to be alone worthy of sustained endeavor? To ask the question was to answer it.[19]

The most vocal opposition to war, however, came not from middle-class reformers but from the spokesmen of organized labor. The socialists in particular maintained that a military conflict among nations would only serve the interests of the established order, increasing its wealth and power at the expense of the masses. They rejected with scorn the ideas and ideals that were used to justify armed struggle. As early as the *Communist Manifesto* of 1848, Marx and Engels had declared defiantly:

19. Norman Angell, *The Great Illusion: A Study of the Relation of Military Power in Nations to Their Economic and Social Advantage* (London, 1910), pp. 129–30, 304–5.

"The communists have been reproached for wanting to abolish fatherland and nationality. [But] the workers have no fatherland. One cannot
take from them what they do not have." Sixty years later, the fiery French
radical Gustave Hervé expressed the same uncompromising view: "The
proletarians have no fatherland. . . . The only war which is not a trick is
one at whose conclusion the proletarians, if they are victorious, can hope
through the expropriation of the capitalist class to put their hands on the
social wealth accumulated for generations by human labor and talent.
There is only one war which is worthy of intelligent men, and that is civil
war, the social Revolution."

The most authoritative statement of the socialist position came in
1907 at the congress of the Second International held in Stuttgart. It
adopted a resolution warning the established order of mass uprisings in
the event of a military conflict:

> If the outbreak of war threatens, it is the duty of the working classes
> and of their parliamentary representatives in the countries con-
> cerned, supported by the coordinating activity of the International
> [Socialist] Bureau, to exert every effort to prevent the outbreak of
> war by means which seem to them most effective, but which will
> naturally vary in accordance with the intensity of the class struggle
> and the intensity of the general political situation.
>
> Should war nevertheless break out, their duty is to intervene to
> bring it promptly to an end, and to strive with all their energies to
> use the economic and political crisis created by the war to arouse
> the people and thereby hasten the abolition of capitalistic class
> domination.[20]

The statement sounded bold and unequivocal.

Yet there were echoes and overtones in the debate on the war question
suggesting that on this issue, as on so many others, the socialists, without
fully realizing it, were drifting closer to the established order. The reformism nurtured by the rising standard of living of the working class
and its growing stake in the status quo was apparent in their attitude
toward armed conflict. August Bebel, the grand old man of the Social
Democratic party of Germany, who thirty-six years before had opposed
the establishment of the German Empire, now emphasized that nation-
hood embodied values worth defending: "What we are fighting is not the
fatherland as such, which belongs to the proletariat far more than to the
ruling classes, but the conditions which exist in that fatherland in the

20. Karl Marx and Friedrich Engels, *Werke*, 39 vols. (Berlin, 1960–69), 4:479; Gustave
Hervé, *Leur patrie* (Paris, 1905), pp. 152–53; *Internationaler Sozialisten-Kongress zu
Stuttgart, 18. bis 24. August 1907* (Berlin, 1907), pp. 66, 70.

interest of the ruling classes. . . . Hervé's idea that it makes no difference to the proletariat whether France belongs to Germany or Germany to France is absurd." And Jean Jaurès, though vehement in his antimilitarism, declared that "Hervéism . . . is in the process of retreating, of dying out. Hervé wants to destroy the fatherland. We want to socialize the fatherland for the benefit of the proletariat through the transformation of the means of production into the property of all. (Applause.) For the nation is a treasure house of human genius and progress, and it would not befit the proletariat to shatter these precious vessels of human culture." Here was a foreshadowing of the position that most socialists would take in the summer of 1914.

For the time being, however, it was easy to overlook the warning signs. What seemed to matter was that a strong antiwar movement had emerged. It extended from the left to the right, including diplomats, businessmen, intellectuals, and workers, and asserted by a variety of arguments that an armed conflict between states must not be allowed to occur.

Was it realistic, then, to believe that the forces for peace would prevail? There were certainly many observers, some of them quite perceptive, who thought so. Stanley Leathes wrote in 1910 that "peace also creates habits of peace; security breeds the love of security; we are never safe from the outbreak of some great national passion; but the desire of war for war's sake, the hunger for military glory, the national impulses and traditions which influenced the career and policy of the third Napoleon, seem for the time at any rate to have lost their operative power." In 1911 Émile Vandervelde, member of the Belgian parliament and chairman of the International Socialist Bureau, came to the same conclusion. A general war was highly unlikely, he maintained. "There are in Europe at this moment too many forces working for peace, starting with the Jewish capitalists, who are issuing financial warnings to certain governments, and ending with the socialists, who are firmly resolved either to prevent the mobilization of the lower classes or, in the event of defeat, to spring at the throat of those who govern." And in 1913 the Quakers of London declared at their annual meeting that the danger of a military struggle was subsiding: "With thankfulness we note an advance in the Peace Movement. We are probably nearer to a complete understanding with Germany than has been the case for many years. The forces that make for arbitration and international goodwill are gaining in strength and confidence." The opposition to war thus seemed to grow with every passing year.[21]

---

21. *Internationaler Sozialisten-Kongress 1907*, pp. 82, 89; Leathes, "Modern Europe," p. 8; Émile Vandervelde, "La guerre italo-turque et l'Internationale," *La revue socialiste,*

Why then did war come? Why did the statesmen plunge into a military conflict that they recognized was likely to destroy the stability their countries had enjoyed for almost a hundred years? A familiar explanation is that they were motivated by some great overriding purpose, by the ambition to make a major territorial acquisition or to gain a vital economic advantage. There was method in their madness. Yet this explanation, so popular in the embittered atmosphere of the immediate postwar era, has become progressively less persuasive. The archival materials now available reveal not reckless warmongers willfully inviting an armed struggle but frightened, bewildered men caught in a labyrinth from which they could find no escape. Even Fritz Fischer, who in 1961 in his *Grasp for World Power* made out a very damaging case against the leaders of Germany for their *Weltpolitik*, their pursuit of aggressive political and economic expansion, concedes that they did not want a general conflict. Their sin was—given the tenseness of the international situation in 1914, "a result in no small measure of Germany's world policy"—that they failed to realize that a limited war involving one of the Great Powers would bring with it the likelihood of an unlimited war involving all of them. By encouraging hostilities between Austria and Serbia and by risking hostilities with Russia and France, they must bear "a considerable share of the historical responsibility" for the war. Yet even they, once they recognized the danger of British intervention, tried to restrain Vienna, "to halt the march of destiny," though their efforts were half-hearted, belated, and promptly suspended. At bottom they were guilty not of arson but of playing with matches near an open powder keg.

An interesting variation on this theme appears in a provocative essay published in 1967 by Arno J. Mayer. He too maintains that the statesmen knowingly invited a major military conflict, but for reasons of domestic rather than foreign policy. The prewar years were a period of mounting internal tension for the nations of Europe. In the United Kingdom the danger of a civil war in Ireland and of a general strike in England eroded "the vital center" essential for compromise and accommodation. In France the struggle between right and left over the extension of military service and the progressive income tax led to cabinet instability and a growing emphasis on order at the expense of reform. In Italy the political and labor disturbances culminating in the explosive "red week" of June 1914 intensified middle-class hostility toward radicalism. In Germany the increasing strength of the parties favoring reform frightened the ruling classes, convincing them that they were approaching a revolutionary situation. In Austria-Hungary the power elites in

---

syndicaliste et coopérative 54 (1911):492; *Extracts from the Minutes and Proceedings of London Yearly Meeting of Friends Held in London* (London, 1913), p. 166.

both halves of the monarchy faced nationalistic unrest that was an expression of political, economic, and social dysfunction. Finally, in Russia the government confronted rising labor discontent, much of it politically and socially rather than economically motivated, as well as heightened restlessness among the peripheral national minorities. Thus all of the Great Powers were threatened by growing internal pressures and conflicts.

It would seem, Mayer concludes, that in this situation, as in other similar ones, the specter of revolution precipitated a counterrevolutionary response among vulnerable status groups—landed aristocrats, minor noblemen, petty bourgeois, marginal entrepreneurs, and declining artisans. There may in fact be a certain parallelism between the attitudes and actions of such crisis strata in domestic politics and the attitudes and actions of the makers of foreign policy who fear that their nation's power and prestige are declining. In both instances the threatened groups are especially prone to seek a preemptive showdown—armed repression at home or preventive war abroad—with the purpose of thereby arresting and reversing the course of history, which they feel is turning against them.[22]

His argument is so ingenious, so persuasive, that it should be true, even if it is not. It would explain so many obscure motives and puzzling actions in the summer of 1914. Its only weakness, but a serious one, is that there is little evidence to support it. No grand design, no fixed plan can be discerned in what the political leaders were doing during those feverish weeks and days before the outbreak of hostilities. If there were, it would surely have been revealed in some unguarded moment, in some secret diary, in some private conversation with an aide, a colleague, a friend, a wife. But there is none. What we find behind the mountains of documents is a small group of frightened, desperate men, afraid to go ahead, yet unwilling to draw back, heading for a catastrophe that they are unable to avert.

"Think of the responsibility you are advising me to assume!" agonized Nicholas II, pale and tense. "Think that this is a question of sending thousands and thousands of men to their death!" N. A. Maklakov, the Russian minister of the interior, was more philosophical. "In our country war cannot be popular in the innermost feelings of the masses of the people, and the ideas of revolution are more comprehensible to the people than a victory over the Germans," he conceded. Then he added in a mood of resignation: "We cannot escape our destiny," and crossed himself piously. Theobald von Bethmann Hollweg, the German chancellor,

22. Fritz Fischer, *Griff nach der Weltmacht: Die Kriegszielpolitik des kaiserlichen Deutschland 1914/18* (Düsseldorf, 1961), p. 97; Arno J. Mayer, "Domestic Causes of the First World War," in *The Responsibility of Power: Historical Essays in Honor of Hajo Holborn*, ed. Leonard Krieger and Fritz Stern (Garden City, N.Y., 1967), pp. 288–91.

thought that "a world war with its altogether incalculable consequences could vastly increase the power of the Social Democratic Party, because it preaches peace, and could overthrow many thrones." Friedrich von Pourtalès, the German ambassador, wept after presenting the declaration of war to the Russians. "I never could have believed that I should quit Petersburg under these conditions." Before departing, he embraced the Russian foreign minister. According to the Austrian ambassador in London, Sir Edward Grey feared that "if four large states—Austria-Hungary, Germany, Russia, and France—become involved in war, the result would be a situation amounting to the bankruptcy of Europe. No more credit would be obtainable and the industrial centers would be in revolt, so that in most countries, regardless of whether they were winners or losers, 'many an existing institution' would be 'swept away.'" In the House of Commons, the prominent Liberal politician Josiah Clement Wedgwood warned that the outbreak of hostilities would lead to hunger and unrest: "Starvation is coming in this country, and the people are not the docile serfs they were a hundred years ago. They are not going to put up with starvation in this country. When it comes, you will see something far more important than a European War—you will see a revolution." Does this sound like the language of men bent on national aggrandizement or social repression?[23]

It would be closer to the mark to say that the statesmen of 1914 faced an unprecedented danger of war with an outmoded system of diplomacy, with methods, attitudes, loyalties, and values derived from an earlier age when armed conflict between the Great Powers was frequent and relatively harmless. In the days of Chatham, Kaunitz, and Vergennes, it was common for the leaders of Europe to construct complex and interlocking alliances, which meant that the outbreak of hostilities in any part of the Continent would soon involve most of it. The level of military mobilization and technology, however, was such that even the losers suffered no lasting damage. After a few years, they would usually try to recoup their losses by a new war. But in the era of mass armies, airplanes, submarines, poison gas, and tanks, the political as well as economic consequences of

23. Maurice Paléologue, *La Russie des tsars pendant la Grande Guerre*, 3 vols. (Paris, 1921–22), 1:39; Sergei Dobrorolski, *Die Mobilmachung der russischen Armee 1914* (Berlin, 1922), p. 25; *Bayerische Dokumente zum Kriegsausbruch und zum Versailler Schuldspruch*, ed. Pius Dirr (Munich and Berlin, 1922), p. 113; M. F. Schilling, *How the War Began in 1914, Being the Diary of the Russian Foreign Office from the 3rd to the 20th (Old Style) of July, 1914* (London, 1925), pp. 77–78; *Österreich-Ungarns Aussenpolitik von der bosnischen Krise 1908 bis zum Kriegsausbruch 1914: Diplomatische Aktenstücke des Österreichisch-Ungarischen Ministeriums des Äussern*, ed. Ludwig Bittner and Hans Uebersberger, 9 vols. (Vienna and Leipzig, 1930), 8:603; Great Britain, *Parliamentary Debates* (Commons), 5th ser. (1909–), 65:1838.

combat could be disastrous. The training and experience of the men who had to deal with the crisis of 1914 were simply inappropriate to the circumstances of the twentieth century. Many of them recognized this, and yet they had nothing to fall back on, no method for averting the catastrophe. As they were drawn into the whirlpool, all they could do was hope or despair. David Lloyd George, who had been in a position to observe what was happening in the various capitals that summer, wrote almost twenty years later: "The picture which the events . . . present to me is that which you see in an estuary, when a river, which has been gliding steadily along towards the sea for a long distance without any consciousness of the final destiny which awaits it in the direction in which it flows, suddenly finds itself confronted with the immensity of the ocean and the terror of its waves." It may not be an original assessment, but it is a fair one.

Yet while the statesmen trembled at the prospect of a world war, the masses rejoiced. For them it was an exciting adventure, an escape from the drudgery of everyday life and the tedious routine of prosperity and progress. They were being summoned by something more elevating, more ennobling than the need to make a living. Leon Trotsky, a man without a country, eating the bitter bread of banishment in Vienna, tried to explain their elation:

> The patriotic enthusiasm of the masses in Austria-Hungary seemed especially surprising. What was it that drew to the square in front of the War Ministry the Viennese bootmaker's apprentice, Pospischil, half German, half Czech; or our greengrocer, Frau Maresch; or the cabman Frankl? What sort of an idea? The national idea? But Austria-Hungary was the very negation of any national idea. No, the moving force was something different.
>
> The people whose lives, day in and day out, pass in a monotony of hopelessness are many; they are the mainstay of modern society. The alarm of mobilization breaks into their lives like a promise; the familiar and long-hated is overthrown, and the new and unusual reign in its place. Changes still more incredible are in store for them in the future. For better or worse? For the better, of course—what can seem worse to Pospischil than "normal" conditions?
>
> I strode along the main streets of the familiar Vienna and watched a most amazing crowd fill the fashionable Ring, a crowd in which hopes had been awakened. But wasn't a small part of these hopes already being realized? Would it have been possible at any other time for porters, laundresses, shoemakers, apprentices and young-sters from the suburbs to feel themselves masters of the situation in the Ring? War affects everybody, and those who are oppressed and

deceived by life consequently feel that they are on an equal footing with the rich and powerful. It may seem a paradox, but in the moods of the Viennese crowd that was demonstrating the glory of the Hapsburg arms I detected something familiar to me from the October days of 1905, in St. Petersburg. No wonder that in history war has often been the mother of revolution.[24]

And as millions of men all over Europe marched toward their mortal rendezvous at Tannenberg or on the Marne, the nineteenth century, with its hopefulness and liberality, its confidence and stability, came to an end. Out of their bloody travail would emerge a sterner, crueler age.

24. *War Memoirs of David Lloyd George*, 6 vols. (Boston, 1933–37), 1:54; Leon Trotsky, *My Life: An Attempt at an Autobiography* (New York, 1930), pp. 233–34.

INDEX